Communications
in Computer and Information Science   1937

Rationale

The CCIS series is devoted to the publication of proceedings of computer science conferences. Its aim is to efficiently disseminate original research results in informatics in printed and electronic form. While the focus is on publication of peer-reviewed full papers presenting mature work, inclusion of reviewed short papers reporting on work in progress is welcome, too. Besides globally relevant meetings with internationally representative program committees guaranteeing a strict peer-reviewing and paper selection process, conferences run by societies or of high regional or national relevance are also considered for publication.

Topics

The topical scope of CCIS spans the entire spectrum of informatics ranging from foundational topics in the theory of computing to information and communications science and technology and a broad variety of interdisciplinary application fields.

Information for Volume Editors and Authors

Publication in CCIS is free of charge. No royalties are paid, however, we offer registered conference participants temporary free access to the online version of the conference proceedings on SpringerLink (http://link.springer.com) by means of an http referrer from the conference website and/or a number of complimentary printed copies, as specified in the official acceptance email of the event.

CCIS proceedings can be published in time for distribution at conferences or as postproceedings, and delivered in the form of printed books and/or electronically as USBs and/or e-content licenses for accessing proceedings at SpringerLink. Furthermore, CCIS proceedings are included in the CCIS electronic book series hosted in the SpringerLink digital library at http://link.springer.com/bookseries/7899. Conferences publishing in CCIS are allowed to use Online Conference Service (OCS) for managing the whole proceedings lifecycle (from submission and reviewing to preparing for publication) free of charge.

Publication process

The language of publication is exclusively English. Authors publishing in CCIS have to sign the Springer CCIS copyright transfer form, however, they are free to use their material published in CCIS for substantially changed, more elaborate subsequent publications elsewhere. For the preparation of the camera-ready papers/files, authors have to strictly adhere to the Springer CCIS Authors' Instructions and are strongly encouraged to use the CCIS LaTeX style files or templates.

Abstracting/Indexing

CCIS is abstracted/indexed in DBLP, Google Scholar, EI-Compendex, Mathematical Reviews, SCImago, Scopus. CCIS volumes are also submitted for the inclusion in ISI Proceedings.

How to start

To start the evaluation of your proposal for inclusion in the CCIS series, please send an e-mail to ccis@springer.com.

Teresa Guarda · Filipe Portela ·
Jose Maria Diaz-Nafria
Editors

Advanced Research in Technologies, Information, Innovation and Sustainability

Third International Conference, ARTIIS 2023
Madrid, Spain, October 18–20, 2023
Proceedings, Part III

 Springer

Editors
Teresa Guarda 🆔
Universidad Estatal Peninsula de Santa Elena
Campus Matriz
La Libertad, Ecuador

Filipe Portela 🆔
Algoritmi Research Centre
University of Minho
Guimarães, Portugal

Jose Maria Diaz-Nafria 🆔
Universidad a Distancia de Madrid
Madrid, Spain

ISSN 1865-0929 ISSN 1865-0937 (electronic)
Communications in Computer and Information Science
ISBN 978-3-031-48929-7 ISBN 978-3-031-48930-3 (eBook)
https://doi.org/10.1007/978-3-031-48930-3

This Springer imprint is published by the registered company Springer Nature Switzerland AG
The registered company address is: Gewerbestrasse 11, 6330 Cham, Switzerland

Paper in this product is recyclable.

Preface

The need for a greener and more digital world leads academia, governments, industry and citizens to look for emerging, sustainable, intelligent solutions and trends.

These new solutions and ideas must promote communication and ubiquitous computing between society agents, i.e., citizens, industry, organizations, net-worked machines and physical objects, and provide a promising vision of the future integrating the real world of knowledge agents and things with the virtual world of information. The emerging approaches in study or development can address several dimensions with a technological focus like Information, Innovation and Sustainability and topics: Computing Solutions, Data Intelligence, Ethics, Security, Privacy and Sustainability.

These topics are closely related to the field of Information Systems (IS) because all of them involve the use and management of technology and data to achieve specific purposes or goals. Computing Solutions are a crucial aspect of information systems as they provide the technical infrastructure and tools for organizations to manage and process data. Data Intelligence is also a key area of information systems as it involves the collection, analysis and interpretation of data to support decision-making and problem-solving. Sustainability is becoming an increasingly important aspect of information systems as organizations are recognizing the impact of technology on the environment and are looking for ways to reduce their carbon footprint. Ethics, Security and Privacy are also essential aspects of information systems as they involve the responsible and secure use of technology and data to protect individuals and organizations from potential harm.

The change observed in society modifies the landscape of human activity, particularly regarding knowledge acquisition and production, offering new possibilities and challenges that need to be explored, assessed and disseminated.

To expose and disseminate this, ARTIIS arose in 2021. ARTIIS is an international forum for researchers and practitioners to present and discuss the most recent innovations, trends, results, experiences and concerns from several perspectives of Technologies, Information, Innovation and Sustainability. This book is split into three volumes and contains a selection of 113 papers accepted for presentation and discussion at the International Conference on Advanced Research in Technologies, Information, Innovation and Sustainability (ARTIIS 2023) and its workshops. The third edition of ARTIIS, realized in 2023, received 297 contributions from 44 countries worldwide. The acceptance rate was 38.04%, 98 regular papers and 15 short papers.

The papers accepted to ARTIIS 2023 are published in the Communications in Computer and Information Science series (Springer CCIS). It is indexed in DBLP, Google Scholar, EI-Compendex, SCImago and Scopus. CCIS volumes are also submitted for inclusion in ISI Proceedings.

The conference proceedings are published in 3 CCIS volumes. The first 2 volumes (CCIS volumes 1935, 1936) consist of the peer-reviewed papers from the main conference track. In addition, 1 volume (CCIS 1937) contains the peer-reviewed papers of the 10 Special Sessions.

The first volume of the book contains all the papers on two topics: Computing Solutions and Data Intelligence:

- Computing Solutions addresses the development of applications and platforms involving computing and concerning some area of knowledge or society. It includes topics like Networks, Pervasive Computing, Gamification and Software Engineering.
- Data Intelligence focuses on data (e.g., text, images) acquisition and processing using smart techniques or tools. It includes topics like Computing Intelligence, Artificial Intelligence, Data Science and Computer Vision.

The second volume contains all the papers about Sustainability, and Ethics, Security and Privacy:

- Ethics, Security and Privacy shows a more strict and secure area of Information Systems where the end-user is the main concern. Vulnerabilities, Data Privacy and Cybersecurity are the main subjects of this topic.
- Sustainability explores a new type of computing: more green, connected, efficient and sustainable. Topics like Immersive Tech, Smart Cities and Sustainable Infrastructures are part of this topic.

The third volume contains the papers from the ten Special Sessions:

- Applications of Computational Mathematics to Simulation and Data Analysis (ACMaSDA 2023)
- Challenges and the Impact of Communication and Information Technologies on Education (CICITE 2023)
- Workshop on Gamification Application and Technologies (GAT 2023)
- Bridging Knowledge in a Fragmented World (glossaLAB 2023)
- Intelligent Systems for Health and Medical Care (ISHMC 2023)
- Intelligent Systems in Forensic Engineering (ISIFE 2023)
- International Symposium on Technological Innovations for Industry and Society (ISTIIS 2023)
- International Workshop on Electronic and Telecommunications (IWET 2023)
- Innovation in Educational Technology (JIUTE 2023)
- Smart Tourism and Information Systems (SMARTTIS 2023)

ARTIIS 2023 had the support of Universidad a Distancia de Madrid, Madrid, Spain; Universidad Estatal Península de Santa Elena, Ecuador; and the Algoritmi Research Center of Minho University, Portugal. It was realized in a hybrid format: face-to-face and virtual at Universidad a Distancia de Madrid – UDIMA, P.º del Gral. Martínez Campos, 5, 28010 Madrid, Spain – between the 18th and 20th of October 2023. Besides the main conference, ARTIIS 2023 also hosted ten special sessions.

The Program Committee was composed of a multidisciplinary group of more than 457 experts from 60 countries, with the responsibility for evaluating, in a double-blind review process, the submissions received for each of the main themes proposed for the conference and special sessions.

We acknowledge those who contributed to this book: authors, organizing chairs, steering committee, program committee, special sessions chairs, and editors. We sincerely appreciate their involvement and support, which were crucial for the success of the International Conference on Advanced Research in Technologies, Information, Innovation and Sustainability (ARTIIS 2023). We also wish to thank our publisher, Springer, for agreeing to publish the proceedings.

The success of this third edition gives us a lot of confidence to continue the work. So, we hope to see you in the fourth edition in 2024, which will be in Chile.

We cordially invite you to visit the ARTIIS website https://artiis.org.

September 2023

Teresa Guarda
Filipe Portela
Jose Maria Diaz-Nafria

Organization

General Chairs

Teresa Guarda   Universidad Estatal Península de Santa Elena, Ecuador/Universidad a Distancia de Madrid, Spain

Filipe Portela   Algoritmi Research Centre, UM, Portugal/Minho University, Portugal

Program Committee Chairs

Teresa Guarda   Universidad Estatal Península de Santa Elena, Ecuador

Filipe Portela   Minho University, Portugal

José María Díaz-Nafría   Universidad a Distancia de Madrid, Spain

Organizing Chairs

Isaac Seoane Pujol   Universidad a Distancia de Madrid, Spain

Jorge Morato Lara   Universidad Carlos III de Madrid, Spain

José María Díaz-Nafría   Universidad a Distancia de Madrid, Spain

Maria Fernanda Augusto   BITrum Research Group, Spain

Silvia Prieto Preboste   Universidad a Distancia de Madrid, Spain

Steering Committee

Andrei Tchernykh   CICESE Research Center, Mexico

Beatriz De La Iglesia   University of East Anglia, UK

Bruno Sousa   University of Coimbra, Portugal

Enrique Carrera   Universidad de las Fuerzas Armadas ESPE, Ecuador

Modestos Stavrakis   University of the Aegean, Greece

Ricardo Vardasca   ISLA Santarem, Portugal

Wolfgang Hofkirchner   Technische Universität Wien, Austria

Special Sessions Chairs

Abrar Ullah	Heriot-Watt University, Dubai
Teresa Guarda	Universidad Estatal Península de Santa Elena, Ecuador

ARTIIS Program Committee

A. Manuela Gonçalves	University of Minho, Portugal
Abbas Aljuboori	Al Zahra College for Women, Oman
Alberto Simões	Instituto Politécnico do Cávado e do Ave, Portugal
Alejandro Rodriguez	Universidad Politécnica de Madrid, Spain
Aleksandra Djordjevic	University of Belgrade, Serbia
Alfredo Cuzzocrea	University of Calabria, Italy
Alfredo Milani	University of Perugia, Italy
Ana Azevedo	Polytechnic Institute of Porto, Portugal
Ana Cláudia Campos	University of Algarve, Portugal
Ana Paula Teixeira	Universidade de Trás-os-Montes e Alto Douro, Portugal
Ana Pereira	Polytechnic Institute of Bragança, Portugal
Ana Ramires	Universidade Europeia, Portugal
Anacleto Correia	CINAV/Escola Naval, Portugal
Andreas Fricke	University of Potsdam, Germany
Andrei Tchernykh	CICESE Research Center, Mexico
Angel Dacal-Nieto	CTAG Centro Tecnológico de Automoción de Galicia, Spain
Anisha Kumari	National Institute of Technology Rourkela, India
Antonio Dourado	University of Coimbra, Portugal
António Fernandes	Instituto Politécnico de Bragança, Portugal
Antonio Jesús Muñoz-Montoro	Universidad de Málaga, Spain
Antonio Silva Sprock	Universidad Central de Venezuela, Venezuela
António Trigo	Instituto Politécnico de Coimbra, ISCAC, Portugal
Arnulfo Alanis Garza	Instituto Tecnológico de Tijuana, Mexico
Asma Patel	Staffordshire University, UK
Attila Körei	University of Miskolc, Hungary
Babar Shah	Zayed University, United Arab Emirates
Barna Iantovics	University of Medicine, Pharmacy, Science, and Technology of Târgu Mureş, Romania
Beatriz De La Iglesia	University of East Anglia, UK
Benedetto Barabino	Università degli Studi di Brescia, Italy

Bertil P. Marques	Instituto Superior de Engenharia do Porto, Portugal
Biswajeeban Mishra	University of Szeged, Hungary
Bruno Sousa	University of Coimbra, Portugal
Camille Salinesi	Université de Paris1 Panthéon-Sorbonne, France
Carina Pimentel	University of Aveiro, Portugal
Carina Silva	Escola Superior de Tecnologia da Saúde de Lisboa, Portugal
Carla Cavallo	University of Naples Federico II, Italy
Carlos Balsa	Instituto Politécnico de Bragança, Portugal
Carlos Costa	Universidade de Lisboa, Portugal
Carlos Fajardo	Fundación Universitaria Konrad Lorenz, Colombia
Carlos H. F. Alves	Federal Center of Technological Education, Brazil
Carlos Lopezosa	Universitat Pompeu Fabra Barcelona, Spain
Carlos R. Cunha	Instituto Politécnico de Bragança, Portugal
Carmen Guida	Università degli Studi di Napoli Federico II, Italy
Cecilia Avila	Fundación Universitaria Konrad Lorenz, Colombia
Cecilia Castro	Universidade do Minho, Portugal
Celia Ramos	University of the Algarve, Portugal
Chien-Sing Lee	Sunway University, Malaysia
Christian Grévisse	University of Luxembourg, Luxembourg
Christoph Schütz	Johannes Kepler University Linz, Austria
Christos Anagnostopoulos	University of Glasgow, UK
Clara Bento Vaz	Instituto Politécnico de Bragança, Portugal
Clarice Maraschin	Universidade Federal do Rio Grande do Sul, Brazil
Claudia Seabra	University of Coimbra, Portugal
Corrado Rindone	Università degli studi Mediterranea di Reggio Calabria, Italy
Daniele Granata	Università della Campania "Luigi Vanvitelli", Italy
Dasa Munkova	Constantine the Philosopher University in Nitra, Slovakia
Dimos Pantazis	Technological Education Institution of Athens, Greece
Elena Cantatore	Politecnico di Bari, Italy
Elena Cocuzza	University of Catania, Italy
Elisabetta Ronchieri	INFN CNAF, Italy
Elisete Mourão	Universidade de Trás-os-Montes e Alto Douro, Portugal
Emmanuel Okewu	University of Lagos, Nigeria

Enrique Carrera	Universidad de las Fuerzas Armadas, Ecuador
Erica Isa Mosca	Politecnico di Milano, Italy
Ester Scotto di Perta	University of Naples Federico II, Italy
Estrella Diaz	Castilla-La Mancha University, Spain
Eugen Rusu	Dunarea de Jos University of Galati, Romania
Fabio Alberto Schreiber	Politecnico di Milano, Italy
Fabio Rocha	Universidade Tiradentes, Brazil
Fabio Silveira	Federal University of São Paulo, Brazil
Fakhri Alam Khan	King Fahd University of Petroleum & Minerals, Saudi Arabia
Federica Gaglione	Università degli Studi del Sannio, Italy
Felipe S. Semaan	Fluminense Federal University, Brazil
Felix Härer	University of Fribourg, Switzerland
Fernanda A. Ferreira	Polytechnic Institute of Porto, Portugal
Fezile Ozdamli	Near East University, Turkey
Filipe Mota Pinto	Polytechnic Institute of Leiria, Portugal
Filipe Portela	University of Minho, Portugal
Flavia Marzano	Link Campus University, Italy
Flora Ferreira	University of Minho, Portugal
Florin Pop	University Politehnica of Bucharest, Romania
Francesco Mercaldo	University of Sannio, Italy
Francesco Palmieri	University of Salerno, Italy
Francesco Santini	Università di Perugia, Italy
Francisco Alvarez	Universidad Autónoma de Aguascalientes, Mexico
Frederico Branco	Universidade de Trás-os-Montes e Alto Douro, Portugal
Frederico Lopes	Universidade Federal do Rio Grande do Norte, Brazil
Gabriel Hornink	Federal University of Alfenas, Brazil
Geert Poels	Ghent University, Belgium
George Stalidis	Alexander Technological Educational Institute of Thessaloniki, Greece
Georgios Georgiadis	Aristotle University of Thessaloniki, Greece
Gerardo Carpentieri	University of Naples Federico II, Italy
Gianni D'Angelo	University of Salerno, Italy
Giovanni Paragliola	ICAR-CNR, Italy
Guillermo Rodriguez	ISISTAN-UNICEN, Argentina
Gustavo Gatica	Universidad Andrés Bello, Chile
Héctor Bedón	Universidad a Distancia de Madrid, Spain
Helia Guerra	University of Azores, Portugal
Henrique Vicente	Universidade de Évora, Portugal

Hugo Peixoto	University of Minho, Portugal
Humberto Rocha	Universidade de Coimbra, Portugal
Ilaria Matteucci	IIT-CNR, Italy
Inna Skarga-Bandurova	Oxford Brookes University, UK
Ioan Ciumasu	Université de Versailles Saint-Quentin, France
Ioannis Politis	Aristotle University of Thessaloniki, Greece
Ioannis Vrellis	University of Ioannina, Greece
Iqbal H. Sarker	Edith Cowan University, Australia
Isabel Lopes	Instituto Politécnico de Bragança, Portugal
J. Luis Luviano-Ortiz	University of Guanajuato, Mexico
Jakub Swacha	University of Szczecin, Poland
Joanna Kolodziej	NASK Warsaw and Cracow University of Technology, Poland
Jordi Vallverdú	Universitat Autònoma de Barcelona, Spain
Jorge Buele	Universidad Tecnológica Indoamerica, Ecuador
Jorge Herrera-Tapia	Universidad Laica Eloy Alfaro de Manabí, Ecuador
Jorge Luis Bacca Acosta	University of Girona, Spain
Jorge Oliveira e Sá	University of Minho, Portugal
José Carlos Paiva	University of Porto, Portugal
Jose Guillermo Guarnizo Marin	Santo Tomás University, Colombia
José Machado	University of Minho, Portugal
José María Díaz-Nafría	Madrid Open University, Spain
José Méndez Reboredo	University of Vigo, Spain
José Rufino	Polytechnic Institute of Bragança, Portugal
Juan-Ignacio Latorre-Biel	Public University of Navarre, Spain
Kalinka Kaloyanova	University of Sofia, Bulgaria
Kanchana Rajaram	SSN College of Engineering, India
Karine Ferreira	Instituto Nacional de Pesquisas Espaciais, Brazil
Kazuaki Tanaka	Kyushu Institute of Technology, Japan
Laura Verde	Università della Campania Luigi Vanvitelli, Italy
Lelio Campanile	Università degli Studi della Campania Luigi Vanvitelli, Italy
Leonardo Soto-Sumuano	Universidad de Guadalajara, Mexico
Leticia Vaca-Cardenas	Universidad Técnica de Manabí, Ecuador
L'ubomír Benko	Constantine the Philosopher University in Nitra, Slovakia
Luigi Piero Di Bonito	University of Campania Luigi Vanvitelli, Italy
Luis Gomes	Universidade dos Açores, Portugal
Luís Matos	Universidade do Minho, Portugal
Luiza de Macedo Mourelle	State University of Rio de Janeiro, Brazil
M. Filomena Teodoro	Portuguese Naval Academy, Portugal

Manuela Cañizares Espada	Universidad a Distancia de Madrid, Spain
Manuele Kirsch-Pinheiro	Université Paris 1 Panthéon-Sorbonne, France
Marcelo Fajardo-Pruna	Escuela Superior Politécnica del Litoral, Ecuador
Marcelo Leon	Universidad Tecnológica Empresarial de Guayaquil, Ecuador
Marcin Woźniak	Silesian University of Technology, Poland
Marco Gribaudo	Politecnico di Milano, Italy
Marco Zucca	University of Cagliari, Italy
Marco Cabezas González	Universidad de Salamanca, Spain
Margherita Lasorella	Polytechnic University of Bari, Italy
Maria Isabel Ribeiro	Instituto Politécnico Bragança, Portugal
Maria João Fernandes Polidoro	Politécnico do Porto, Portugal
Maria João Rodrigues	Universidade do Porto, Portugal
Maria José Abreu	Universidade do Minho, Portugal
Maria Macchiaroli	University of Salerno, Italy
Maria Sousa	CIEO Centre for Spatial and Organizational Dynamics, Portugal
Maria Stella de Biase	Università degli Studi della Campania Luigi Vanvitelli, Italy
Mariapia Raimondo	Università degli Studi della Campania Luigi Vanvitelli, Italy
Marílio Cardoso	Instituto Superior de Engenharia do Porto, Portugal
Marilisa Botte	University of Naples Federico II, Italy
Marina Alexandra Andrade	ISCTE Instituto Universitário de Lisboa, Portugal
Mario Pérez-Montoro	University of Barcelona, Spain
Mario Pinto	Politécnico do Porto, Portugal
Maritza Placencia	Universidad Nacional Mayor de San Marco, Peru
Martinha Piteira	Instituto Politécnico de Setúbal, Portugal
Mauro Iacono	Università degli Studi della Campania Luigi Vanvitelli, Italy
Michal Baczynski	University of Silesia in Katowice, Poland
Michal Munk	Constantine the Philosopher University in Nitra, Slovakia
Michel Soares	Universidade Federal de Sergipe, Brazil
Michele Mastroianni	University of Salerno, Italy
Milliam Maxime	Zekeng Ndadji University of Dschang, Cameroon
Mirka Mobilia	University of Salerno, Italy
Modestos Stavrakis	University of the Aegean, Greece
Mohamad Molaei Qelichi	University of Tehran, Iran
Mohammadsadegh Mohagheghi	Vali-e-Asr University of Rafsanjan, Iran
Mónica Pinto	Universidad de Málaga, Spain
Muhammad Younas	Oxford Brookes University, UK

Naveed Abbas	Islamia College, Peshawar, Malaysia
Naveenbalaji Gowthaman	University of KwaZulu-Natal, South Africa
Neelam Gohar	Shaheed Benazir Bhutto Women University, Pakistan
Nguyen D. Thanh	Banking University of Ho Chi Minh City, Vietnam
Nikolaos Matsatsinis	Technical University of Crete, Greece
Nishu Gupta	Norwegian University of Science and Technology in Gjøvik, Norway
Nuno C. Marques	Universidade Nova de Lisboa, Portugal
Nuno Pombo	University of Beira Interior, Portugal
Olivier Parisot	Luxembourg Institute of Science and Technology, Luxembourg
Omar Castellanos	Universidad Estatal Península de Santa Elena, Ecuador
Omid Fatahi Valilai	Constructor University, Germany
Oscar Dias	University of Minho, Portugal
Pankaj Mishra	G. B. Pant University of Agriculture and Technology, India
Paola Britos	Universidad Nacional de Río Negro - Sede Andina/Atlántica, Argentina
Paolino Di Felice	University of L'Aquila, Italy
Patricia Cano-Olivos	Universidad Popular Autónoma del Estado de Puebla, Mexico
Paula Amaral	Universidade Nova de Lisboa, Portugal
Paula Odete Fernandes	Instituto Politécnico de Bragança, Portugal
Paulo Piloto	Polytechnic Institute of Bragança, Portugal
Paulo Vasconcelos	University of Porto, Portugal
Pedro Gago	Polytechnic Institute of Leiria, Portugal
Piedade Carvalho	Instituto Superior de Engenharia do Porto, Portugal
Rafal Scherer	Częstochowa University of Technology, Poland
Raphael Gomes	Instituto Federal de Goiás, Brazil
Ricardo Cajo	Escuela Superior Politécnica del Litoral, Ecuador
Ricardo Correia	Instituto Politécnico de Bragança, Portugal
Ricardo Queirós	Politécnico do Porto, Portugal
Ricardo Vardasca	ISLA Santarem, Portugal
Robertas Damasevicius	Silesian University of Technology, Poland
Roberto Andrade	Escuela Politécnica Nacional, Ecuador
Roberto Nardone	University of Naples "Parthenope", Italy
Roman Chertovskih	University of Porto, Portugal
Ronan Guivarch	Université de Toulouse, France
Rosa Reis	Instituto Superior de Engenharia do Porto, Portugal

Rytis Maskeliunas, Kaunas	University of Technology, Lithuania
S. B. Kulkarni	SDMCET, India
Said Broumi	Hassan II University Mohammedia-Casablanca, Morocco
Samson Oruma	Østfold University College, Norway
Sanjay Misra	Østfold University, Norway
Sanket Mishra	BITS Pilani Hyderabad Campus, India
Sara Paiva	Instituto Politécnico de Viana do Castelo, Portugal
Sergio Cappucci	ENEA, Italy
Sergio Ilarri	University of Zaragoza, Spain
Shelly Sachdeva	National Institute of Technology Delhi, India
Sherali Zeadally	University of Kentucky, USA
Shuhei Kimura	Tottori University, Japan
Silvia Araújo	University of Minho, Portugal
Silvia Rossetti	Università degli Studi di Parma, Italy
Simone Belli	Universidad Complutense de Madrid, Spain
Simone Corrado	Università degli Studi della Basilicata, Italy
Smriti Agrawal	Chaitanya Bharathi Institute of Technology, India
Socrates Basbas	Aristotle University of Thessaloniki, Greece
Sofia Almeida	Universidade Europeia, Portugal
Sonia Casillas Martín	Universidad de Salamanca, Spain
Spyros Panagiotakis	Hellenic Mediterranean University, Greece
Stefania Regalbuto	Ca' Foscari University of Venice, Italy
Stefano Falcinelli	University of Perugia, Italy
Stephan Scheele	Fraunhofer IIS, Germany
Sumit Babu	Harcourt Butler Technical University, India
Syeda Sumbul Hossain	Daffodil International University, Bangladesh
Sylwia Krzysztofik	Lodz University of Technology, Poland
Tapiwa Gundu	Sol Plaatje University, South Africa
Telmo Pinto	University of Minho, Portugal
Tengku Adil Tengku Izhar	Universiti Teknologi MARA, Malaysia
Teresa Guarda	Universidad Estatal Península de Santa Elena, Ecuador
Tetiana Biloborodova	Volodymyr Dahl East Ukraine National University, Ukraine
Tiziana Campisi	Kore University of Enna, Italy
Ugo Fiore	Federico II University, Italy
Ulises Ruiz	Instituto Nacional de Astrofisica Óptica y Electrónica, Mexico
Vanda Lourenco	NOVA University of Lisbon, Portugal
Vasileios Gkioulos	Norwegian University of Science and Technology, Norway

Vicente Ferreira De Lucena Jr.	Federal University of Amazonas, Brazil
Victor Alves	University of Minho, Portugal
Victor Darriba	Universidade de Vigo, Spain
Virginie Felizardo	Universidade da Beira Interior, Portugal
Vitor Monteiro	University of Minho, Portugal
Vladimir Tcheverda	Institute of Petroleum Geology and Geophysics, Russia

Special Session Organizers

Applications of Computational Mathematics to Simulation and Data Analysis (ACMaSDA 2023)

Carlos Balsa	CEDRI-IPB, Portugal
Victoria Espinar	CITMaga - USC, Spain
Ronan Guivarch	IRIT-UFTMiP, France
Sílvio Gama	Universidade do Porto, Portugal

Challenges and the Impact of Communication and Information Technologies on Education (CICITE 2023)

| Teresa Guarda | Universidad Estatal Península de Santa Elena, Ecuador |
| Maria Fernanda Augusto | BITrum Research Group, Spain |

3rd Workshop on Gamification Application and Technologies (GAT 2023)

Ricardo Queirós	ESMAD, Portugal
Mário Pinto	ESMAD, Portugal
Filipe Portela	University of Minho, Portugal

Bridging Knowledge in a Fragmented World (glossaLAB 2023)

José María Díaz-Nafría	Universidad a Distancia de Madrid, Spain
Jorge Morato Lara	Universidad a Distancia de Madrid, Spain
Sonia Sánchez-Cuadrado	Universidad a Distancia de Madrid, Spain
Manuela Cañizares	Universidad a Distancia de Madrid, Spain
Héctor Bedón	Universidad a Distancia de Madrid, Spain
Isaac Seoane-Pujol	Universidad a Distancia de Madrid, Spain

Intelligent Systems for Health and Medical Care (ISHMC 2023)

Arnulfo Alanis	National Technological Institute of Mexico, Mexico
Bogart Yail Marquez	National Technological Institute of Mexico, Mexico
Rosario Baltazar	National Technological Institute of Mexico, Mexico

Intelligent Systems in Forensic Engineering (ISIFE 2023)

Alessia Amelio	University "G. d'Annunzio" Chieti-Pescara, Italy
Samuele Biondi	University "G. d'Annunzio" Chieti-Pescara, Italy
Regina Finocchiaro	University "G. d'Annunzio" Chieti-Pescara, Italy
Luciano Caroprese	University "G. d'Annunzio" Chieti-Pescara, Italy
Samantha Di Loreto	University "G. d'Annunzio" Chieti-Pescara, Italy
Sergio Montelpare	University "G. d'Annunzio" Chieti-Pescara, Italy

International Symposium on Technological Innovations for Industry and Society (ISTIIS 2023)

Filipe Portela	University of Minho, Portugal and IOTECH, Portugal
Rita Miranda	IOTECH, Portugal

International Workshop on Electronic and Telecommunications (IWET 2023)

Luis Chuquimarca	Universidad Estatal Península de Santa Elena, Ecuador
Carlos Peñafiel	Universidad Nacional del Chimborazo, Ecuador
Leticia Vaca	Universidad Técnica Manabí, Ecuador
Ricardo Cajo	Escuela Superior Politécnica del Litoral, Ecuador

Innovation in Educational Technology (JIUTE 2023)

Alba García Barrera	Universidad a Distancia de Madrid, Spain
Francisco David de la Peña Esteban	Universidad a Distancia de Madrid, Spain
Lucas Castro Martínez	Universidad a Distancia de Madrid, Spain
Verónica Nistal Anta	Universidad a Distancia de Madrid, Spain

Smart Tourism and Information Systems (SMARTTIS 2023)

Isabel Lopes	Instituto Politécnico de Bragança, Portugal
Isabel Ribeiro	Instituto Politécnico de Bragança, Portugal
Carlos Rompante Cunha	Instituto Politécnico de Bragança, Portugal

Special Sessions Program Committee

Adriano Mancini	Universitá Politecnica delle Marche, Italy
Ahmad Ali	Shenzhen University, China
Alba Garcia Barrera	Universidad a Distancia de Madrid, Spain
Ana Azevedo	CEOS.PP, ISCAP, Polytechnic of Porto, Portugal
Ana Dopico	Universidade de Vigo, Spain
Andres Muñoz	Universidad de Cádiz, Spain
Angel Recalde	Escuela Superior Politécnica del Litoral, Ecuador
Angel Torres Toukoumidis	Universidad Politécnica Salesiana, Ecuador
António Fernandes	Instituto Politécnico de Bragança, Portugal
Antonio Jesús Muñoz-Montoro	Universidad de Málaga, Spain
Antonio Mauricio Silva Sprock	Universidad Central de Venezuela, Venezuela
Antonio Moreira	Polytechnic Institute of Cávado and Ave, Portugal
Asma Patel	Aston University, UK
Barna Iantovics	UMFST, Romania
Benito Mendoza Trujillo	Universidada Nacional de Chimborazo, Ecuador
Bertil P. Marques	Polytechnic Institute of Porto, Portugal
Bogart Yail Marquez	Instituto Tecnológico Tijauna, Mexico
Bráulio Alturas	Instituto Universitário de Lisboa, Portugal
Carlos Balsa	Instituto Politécnico de Bragança, Portugal
Carlos Gordon	Universidad Técnica de Ambato, Ecuador
Carlos H. F. Alves	Federal Center of Technological Education, Brazil
Carlos Peñafiel	Universidad Nacional del Chimborazo, Ecuador
Carlos R. Cunha	Instituto Politécnico de Bragança, Portugal
Celia Ramos	University of the Algarve, Portugal
Chiara Braghin	Università degli Studi di Milano, Italy
Cristian Javier Rocha Jácome	Universidad de Sevilla, Spain
Daniel Santillán	UNACH, Ecuador
Datzania Villao	Universidad Estatal Península de Santa Elena, Ecuador
David Lizcano Casas	Madrid Open University, Spain
David Moreno	ESPOCH, Ecuador
Diego Paredes	UTN, Ecuador
Douglas Plaza	ESPOL, Ecuador

Eleni Christopoulou	Ionian University, Greece
Enrique-Javier Díez-Gutiérrez	Universidad de León, Spain
Estevan Gomez	Universidad de las Fuerzas Armadas, Ecuador
Fabrizio Messina	University of Catania, Italy
Fausto Calderón Pineda	Universidad Estatal Península de Santa Elena, Ecuador
Fernando Rodríguez Varela	Universidad Rey Juan Carlos, Spain
Filipe Pinto	Polytechnic Institute of Leiria, Portugal
Filipe Portela	University of Minho, Portugal
Francesco Cauteruccio	Polytechnic University of Marche, Italy
Franklin Eduardo Samaniego Riera	Universidad Nacional de Chimborazo, Ecuador
Frederico Branco	Universidade de Trás-Os-Montes e Alto Douro, Portugal
Frederico Lopes	UFRN, Brazil
Gerhard Chroust	Johannes Kepler University Linz, Austria
Giada Gasparini	University of Bologna, Italy
Giuseppe Festa	University of Salerno, Italy
Gunta Grinberga-Zalite	University of Life Sciences and Technologies, Latvia
Hector Bedon	Universidad a Distancia de Madrid, Spain
Hugo Moreno Aviles	Escuela Superior Politécnica de Chimborazo, Ecuador
Hugo Peixoto	University of Minho, Portugal
Ijaz Ahmad	Università Telematica "Leonardo Da Vinci", Italy
Ingars Eriņš	Riga Technical University, Latvia
Inna Skarga-Bandurova	Oxford Brookes University, UK
Ioan Ciumasu	UVSQ, France
Ioannis Vrellis	University of Ioannina, Greece
Isaac Seoane Pujol	Madrid Open University, Spain
Isabel Lopes	Instituto Politécnico de Bragança, Portugal
Isabel Pedrosa	Instituto Politécnico de Coimbra, Portugal
Jaciel Gustavo Kunz	FURG, Brazil
Jeniffer García Mendoza	Grupo Ananke, Ecuador
Jessica S. Ortiz	Universidad de las Fuerzas Armada, Ecuador
Jezreel Mejía Miranda	CIMAT, Mexico
Jhonattan Javier Barriga Andrade	IT Systems Security, Ecuador
João Cordeiro	University of Beira Interior, Portugal
Jorge Bernardino	Polytechnic Institute of Coimbra, Portugal
Jorge L. Hernandez-Ambato	Escuela Superior Politécnica de Chimborazo, Ecuador
Jorge Morato	Universidad Carlos III, Spain

Jorge Oliveira e Sá	University of Minho, Portugal
Jorge Oliveira	NOVA School of Science and Technology, Portugal
José Israel Hernández Vázquez	Instituto Tecnológico de León, Mexico
José María Díaz-Nafría	Madrid Open University, Spain
José Matos	University of Porto, Portugal
José Omar Hernández Vázquez	Instituto Tecnológico de León, Mexico
José Rufino	Polytechnic Institute of Bragança, Portugal
Jose Xavier Tomalá	Universidad Estatal Península de Santa Elena, Ecuador
Juan Pablo Ciafardini	UNLP, Argentina
Juan Rodriguez-Fernandez	Universidad de León, Spain
Juan V. Capella	Universitat Politècnica de València, Spain
Karolina Baras	University of Madeira, Portugal
Lasma Licite-Kurbe	Latvia University of Life Sciences and Technologies, Latvia
Leonardo Chancay-García	Universidad Técnica de Manabí, Ecuador
Leonardo Renteria	UNACH, Ecuador
Leticia Vaca-Cardenas	Universidad Técnica de Manabí, Ecuador
Lidice Haz	Universidad Estatal Península de Santa Elena, Ecuador
Linda Groma	Latvia University of Life Sciences and Technologies, Latvia
Lorena Molina Valdiviezo	Universidad Nacional de Chimborazo, Ecuador
Luis Alfonso Gaxiola	Universidad Autónoma de Baja California, Mexico
Luis Amaya	Universidad Estatal Península de Santa Elena, Ecuador
Luis Enrique Chuquimarca Jimenez	Universidad Estatal Península de Santa Elena, Ecuador
Luís Matos	Universidade do Minho, Portugal
Luis Mazon	BITrum Research Group, Ecuador
Manuel Montaño	Universidad Estatal Península de Santa Elena, Ecuador
Manuela Cañizares Espada	UDIMA, Spain
Manuele Kirsch Pinheiro	Paris 1 Panthéon-Sorbonne University, France
Marcela Palacios	Instituto Tecnológico Superior de Purísima del Rincón, Mexico
Marcelo Zambrano	Universidad Técnica del Norte, Ecuador
Marcia Marisol Bayas Sampedro	Universidad Estatal Península de Santa Elena, Ecuador
Marcos Cevallos	UCAB, Ecuador
Maria Covelo	UA, Portugal

María del Carmen Messina Scolaro	Universidad de la República, Uruguay
Maria Isabel Ribeiro	Instituto Politécnico Bragança, Portugal
Maria João Rodrigues	Universidade do Porto, Portugal
María Verdeja Muñiz	Universidad de Oviedo, Spain
Mario Pérez-Montoro	Universitat de Barcelona, Spain
Mario Pinto	ESMAD.IPP, Portugal
Mehran Pourvahab	University of Beira Interior, Portugal
Miguel Efraín Sangurima Pacheco	Universidad Nacional de Chimborazo, Ecuador
Mirna Muñoz Mata	Centro de Investigación en Matemáticas - Unidad Zacatecas, Mexico
Modestos Stavrakis	University of the Aegean, Greece
Nelia Gonzalez	Universidad Espíritu Santo, Ecuador
Nuno Pombo	University of Beira Interior, Portugal
Omar Castellanos	Universidad Estatal Península de Santa Elena, Ecuador
Panos Fitsilis	University of Thessaly, Greece
Paul Diaz	Universidad de las Fuerzas Armadas, Ecuador
Paula Odete Fernandes	Instituto Politécnico de Bragança, Portugal
Paulo Vasconcelos	University of Porto, Portugal
Pedro Aguado	Universidad de León, Spain
Pedro Gago	Polytechnic Institute of Leiria, Portugal
Pedro Oliveira	Instituto Politécnico de Bragança, Portugal
Piedade Carvalho	Instituto Superior de Engenharia do Porto, Portugal
Radmila Jankovic	Mathematical Institute of Serbian Academy of Sciences and Arts, Serbia
Rafael Angarita	Isep, Inria, France
Rainer E. Zimmermann	UAS for Technology and Economics Berlin (HTW), Germany
Regina Finocchiaro	"Gabriele d'Annunzio" Università di Chieti-Pescara, Italy
René Faruk Garzozi-Pincay	Universidad Estatal Península de Santa Elena, Ecuador
Ricardo Cajo	Escuela Superior Politécnica del Litoral, Ecuador
Ricardo Correia	Instituto Politécnico de Bragança, Portugal
Ricardo Godinho Bilro	ISCTE-Instituto Universitário de Lisboa, Portugal
Ricardo Queirós	Polytechnic Institute of Porto & CRACS - INESC TEC, Portugal
Roberth Abel Alcivar Cevallos	Universidad Técnica de Manabí, Ecuador
Roger Idrovo	Universidad de Navarra, Spain
Roman Chertovskih	University of Porto, Portugal
Ronan Guivarch	IRIT - Université de Toulouse, France

Rosa María Martínez	University of Almería, Spain
Rosa Reis	ISEP, Portugal
Rosario Baltazar Flores	Instituto Tecnológico de León, Mexico
Sang Guun Yoo	Escuela Politécnica Nacional, Ecuador
Sebastião Pais	University of Beira Interior, Portugal
Senka Borovac Zekan	University of Split, Croatia
Sergio Magdaleno	Instituto Tecnológico de Tijuana, Mexico
Silvia Prieto Preboste	Universidad a Distancia de Madrid, Spain
Sílvio Gama	Universidade do Porto, Portugal
Simone Belli	Universidad Complutense de Madrid, Spain
Siu Ming Yiu	University of Hong Kong, China
Surendrabikram Thapa	Virginia Tech, USA
Susana Burnes R.	Universidad Autónoma de Zacatecas, Mexico
Teresa Guarda	Universidad Estatal Península de Santa Elena, Ecuador
Tiago C. Pereira	University of Minho, Portugal
Ulises Ruiz	INAOE, Mexico
Verónica Crespo	Universidade da Coruña, Spain
Victor Huilcapi	Universidad Politécnica Salesiana, Ecuador
Victoria Otero-Espinar	University of Santiago de Compostela, Spain
Virginie Felizardo	Universidade da Beira Interior, Portugal
Wendoly Julieta Guadalupe Romero Rodriguez	Instituto Tecnológico Superior de Guanajuato, Mexico
Wolfgang Hofkirchner	Institute for a Global Sustainable Information Society, Austria

Sponsors

Universidad Estatal Península de Santa Elena, Ecuador
Universidade do Minho, Portugal
Universidad a Distancia de Madrid, Spain
Algoritmi Research Centre, Portugal
BITrum Research Group, Spain
The Institute for a Global Sustainable Information Society GSIS, Austria

Contents – Part III

xxviiiContents – Part III

Applications of Computational Mathematics to Simulation and Data Analysis (ACMaSDA 2023)

A Discussion on Variants
of an Anisotropic Model Applied
to Depth Completion

Vanel Lazcano[1]($\boxtimes$) and Felipe Calderero[2,3]

[1] Universidad Mayor, Avda. Manuel Montt 318, Providencia, Santiago, Chile
vanel.lazcano@umayor.cl
[2] Chief Product and Technology Officer at Ladorian, Madrid, Spain
[3] Nuclio Digital School, Madrid, Spain

Abstract. Depth data holds significant importance in numerous applications, ranging from video games to autonomous vehicles. Depth data can be acquired by sensors such as LiDAR sensors. Frequently, acquired depth map has holes or data that presents low confidence level. The task of depth data interpolation or completion stands as a fundamental requirement for such applications. Infinity Laplacian is an interpolator of data that can perform this task. The Infinity Laplacian represents the most straightforward interpolator, adhering to a set of appropriate axioms. In this study, we assessed three different variations of the infinity Laplacian for the purpose of completing sparse depth data. We sub-sampled the publicly available NUY_V2 dataset and evaluated the performance of these models by up-sampling depth data. In this paper, we compared the infinity Laplacian, unbalanced infinity Laplacian, balanced infinity Laplacian, and biased infinity Laplacian. Obtained results show that the balanced infinity Laplacian outperforms the other three models and also many contemporaneous models. The addition of a mechanism that balances between two eikonal operators gives the infinity the capability to reach better performance in the up-sampling task. Moving forward, our focus will be directed towards addressing the challenge of edge interpolation using the color reference image.

Keywords: depth completion · infinity Laplacian · reconfigurable model

1 Introduction

The acquisition of depth data can be accomplished using various sensors, including but not limited to Kinect, Time-of-Flight Camera, LiDAR sensor, or through the implementation of a stereo algorithm. Frequently, acquired or estimated depth maps present large areas without data, or the data present low confident values. The gaps in the depth data arise from sensor misinterpretations, occlusions among scene objects, reflections of objects, or misalignment between sensors.

© The Author(s), under exclusive license to Springer Nature Switzerland AG 2024
T. Guarda et al. (Eds.): ARTIIS 2023, CCIS 1937, pp. 3–16, 2024.
https://doi.org/10.1007/978-3-031-48930-3_1

Depth data plays a crucial role in various applications, including 3D cinema, unmanned vehicles, video games, and many other domains. In these applications is necessary to interpolate incomplete depth maps. Many models have been proposed to interpolate depth maps, from simple interpolation to complex models based on neural networks.

In this study, we introduce a hybrid pipeline that combines convolutional stages with an interpolator to effectively complete sparse depth maps. The central part of this pipeline is the interpolation stage, where we use the infinity Laplacian model [1,2]. The infinity interpolator, as introduced by Caselles in [4], stands as the most straightforward method that fulfills a suitable set of axioms. The contributions of this paper can be summarized in three main aspects:

i) Two new interpolation models are proposed: unbalanced infinity Laplacian, balanced infinity Laplacian, and the use of the biased infinity Laplacian.
ii) We evaluated the three models in i) and two models more, in the up-sampling task applied to a sub-sampled version of the public NYUV_2 dataset.
iii) Finally, we performed an ablation study.

1.1   Related Works

Numerous approaches have been proposed to address the challenge of depth map completion. Broadly, we can categorize them into two main approaches: those that leverage a reference color image of the scene and those that do not. Our focus lies in models that utilize the reference color image, and we will examine similar models to our approach.

In [11,12], authors propose the application of the infinity Laplacian to complete depth maps. The authors constructed a manifold based on the image domain and a specific metric. Within this manifold, they proceed to solve the infinity Laplacian. The author tested different metrics ($\mathcal{L}^1$, $\mathcal{L}^2$, and others) and different space colors ($sRGB$, XYZ, $CIE - L^*a^*b$, CMY) to get best performance in depth completion using a public available data set [15]. In [12] author proposes the use of $\mathcal{L}^p$, where exponent p is empirical estimated, they also use a metric that considers spatial term, photometric term, and an image gradient term. In [19] authors propose a model that segments the color reference image in superpixels, which correspond to regions with similar depth values. A cost map is used to gather super-pixel that correspond to the same object. In their experimental results, they present the influence of each component of their proposal in a final performance evaluation. In [7] the authors also use super-pixels to segment the reference image. Each super-pixel is represented by a plane. In case the plane does not represent properly the pixels, only inliers are considered to adjust a convex hull. The depth map interpolation is achieved using a pinhole camera model, which demonstrates superior performance compared to state-of-the-art models on a publicly available dataset [15]. In [20] the classical bilateral filter is proposed which has been used to complete holes in images, filter noise and attenuate artifacts, and many other applications. An extension of the bilateral filter to the gradient domain is presented in [9] applied to depth completion. The work in [17] uses a non-local structure regularization to keep fine details of the reconstructed depth map. The regularization combines a high-resolution color reference image with a weighting scheme that favors recovering details and structure. They use also edges of the reference color images preserving discontinuities and edges of the depth map. They evaluated their proposal in an up-sampling task in a public available data set [18]. The approach presented in [13] involves the application of a model that learns a joint filter using convolutional networks to complete depth maps, guided by a reference color image. Moreover, the proposal selectively transfers information on the salience of the color image to enhance the completion process. As a result, the model surpasses numerous state-of-the-art models with similar objectives.

The work in [14] proposes a model to learn affinities among pixels in the reference image with an attention base dynamic approach applied to depth completion. They propose a spatial propagation network that uses a non-linear propagation model. This concept involves decoupling the neighborhood of pixels into segments based on various distances. Subsequently, attention maps are generated recursively to refine these segments using adaptive affinity matrices. To facilitate rapid convergence, the approach incorporates diffusion suppression operations. They can reach similar results to other spatial propagation networks but in fewer iterations. Their approach exhibits superior performance compared to many state-of-the-art models in the up-sampling task on the dataset [18].

Additionally, Boscain et al. [3] presented a model to interpolate highly corrupted images. Their model can interpolate images with up to 80% of corrupted data. The authors used the model to inpaint gray-level images. Our proposal can recover depth data even with 95% of corrupted data. Finally, the work in [5] applied infinity Laplacian to image completion, segmentation, and clustering.

2 Proposed Model

2.1 Infinity Laplacian

The Infinity Laplacian, introduced in [4], represents the most straightforward interpolator that satisfies a set of interpolation axioms. Its expression is given by:

$$\Delta_{\infty,g} u = 0 \in \Omega, \tag{1}$$

where $\Delta_{\infty,g} u$ stands for the infinity Laplacian operator and g for the metric, and u for the depth map to complete. Given the domain of the images $\Omega \subset \mathbb{R}^2$ and a metric g, a manifold $\mathcal{M} = (\Omega, g)$ is constructed. Considering the manifold, the expression of the infinity Laplacian is given by,

$$\Delta_{\infty,g} u := D^2_{\mathcal{M}} u \left(\frac{\nabla u}{|\nabla u|}, \frac{\nabla u}{|\nabla u|} \right), \tag{2}$$

which is a degenerated second-order partial differential equation. Let us consider the depth map u as a function $u : \Omega \subset \mathbb{R}^2 \to \mathbb{R}$, and the known depth data is located in $\mathcal{O} \subset \Omega$, i.e. $u|_{\partial\mathcal{O}} = \theta$, which is the boundary condition for the infinity

Laplacian. Numerically, the infinity Laplacian is obtained as the average of two eikonal operators, specifically, between the positive and the negative eikonal operator,

$$\Delta_{\infty,g}u = \frac{1}{2}\left(\|\nabla u(\mathbf{x})\|_x^+ + \|\nabla u(\mathbf{x})\|_x^-\right) = 0, \tag{3}$$

where $\|\nabla u(\mathbf{x})\|_x^+$ and $\|\nabla u(\mathbf{x})\|_x^-$ are the positive eikonal operator and negative eikonal operator, respectively. Both operators will be described in detail in Sect. 3.

2.2 Unbalanced Infinity Laplacian

A slight modification of the infinity Laplacian in Eq. (3) is presented as follows:

$$\frac{1}{2}\left(c_1\|\nabla u(\mathbf{x})\|_x^+ + c_2\|\nabla u(\mathbf{x})\|_x^-\right) = 0. \tag{4}$$

where $c_1, c_2 \in \mathbb{R}$. If $c_1 = c_2$ we recover Eq. (3).

2.3 Balanced Infinity Laplacian

In our approach, we take into account a weight map $\alpha(\mathbf{x}) : \Omega \rightarrow [0,1]$ as we show in this expression,

$$\frac{1}{2}\left(\alpha(\mathbf{x})\|\nabla u(\mathbf{x})\|_x^+ + (1 - \alpha(\mathbf{x}))\|\nabla u(\mathbf{x})\|_x^-\right) = 0, \tag{5}$$

this weight map $\alpha(\mathbf{x})$ is a balance term between the positive eikonal operator and the negative eikonal operator. On one hand, if $\alpha(\mathbf{x}) = 1.0$, we obtain: $\frac{1}{2}(\|\nabla u\|_x^+) = 0$, which is an equation only for the positive eikonal operator. On the other hand, if $\alpha(\mathbf{x}) = 0.5$ we obtain $\frac{1}{2}\left(0.5\|\nabla u(\mathbf{x})\|_x^+ + 0.5\|\nabla u(\mathbf{x})\|_x^-\right) = 0$, recovering the infinity Laplacian Eq. (3). Finally, if $\alpha(\mathbf{x}) = 0.0$ we obtain $\frac{1}{2}(\|\nabla u(\mathbf{x})\|_x^-) = 0$, which represents the equation for the negative eikonal operator.

The balance map $\alpha(\mathbf{x})$ as in [8] varies between 0 and 1. The balance term is defined by the expression,

$$\alpha(\mathbf{x}) = \frac{1}{1 + e^{\beta_\alpha\left(|\|\nabla u(\mathbf{x})\|_x^+| - \tau_\alpha|\|\nabla u(\mathbf{x})\|_x^-|\right)}}, \tag{6}$$

Where β_α and τ_α in $\mathbb{R}$. On one hand, if $|\|\nabla u(\mathbf{x})\|_x^+| \gg \tau_\alpha|\|\nabla u(\mathbf{x})\|_x^-|$ the difference $\|\nabla u(\mathbf{x})\|_x^+| - \tau_\alpha|\|\nabla u(\mathbf{x})\|_x^-|$ will be positive, the exponential value $e^{\beta_\alpha(|\|\nabla u(\mathbf{x})\|_x^+| - \tau_\alpha|\|\nabla u(\mathbf{x})\|_x^-|)}$ will be large, and the value of the weight map in $\mathbf{x}$, $\alpha(\mathbf{x}) \approx 0$, in other words, the interpolation process exhibits higher confidence in the negative eikonal operator. In the other hand, if $|\|\nabla u(\mathbf{x})\|_x^+| \ll \tau_\alpha|\|\nabla u(\mathbf{x})\|_x^-|$ the difference $|\|\nabla u(\mathbf{x})\|_x^+| - \tau_\alpha|\|\nabla u(\mathbf{x})\|_x^-|$ should be negative, the exponential value $e^{\beta_\alpha(|\|\nabla u(\mathbf{x})\|_x^+| - \tau_\alpha|\|\nabla u(\mathbf{x})\|_x^+|)}$ should be small, and the value of the weight map $\alpha(\mathbf{x}) \approx 1$. This implies that the interpolation process has greater confidence in the positive eikonal operator.

2.4 Biased Infinity Laplacian

The biased infinity Laplacian, as mentioned in [4], was recognized for satisfying the same set of axioms as the regular infinity Laplacian. Its expression is given by:

$$\Delta_{\infty,g} u(\mathbf{x}) + \beta |\nabla u(\mathbf{x})|_\xi = 0, \tag{7}$$

where $\beta \in \mathbb{R}+$. If $\beta = 0$ we recover the infinity Laplacian.

3 Practical Model Implementation

Consider the discrete grid domain Ω. For a given point $\mathbf{x}$ in the grid, let $\mathcal{N}(\mathbf{x})$ denote its neighborhood. In [16], the positive eikonal operator is defined as follows:

$$\|\nabla u(\mathbf{x})\|_x^+ = \max_{\varsigma \in \mathcal{N}(\mathbf{x})} \frac{u(\varsigma) - u(\mathbf{x})}{d_{\mathbf{x}\varsigma}}. \tag{8}$$

In turn, the negative eikonal operator is defined as,

$$\|\nabla u(\mathbf{x})\|_x^- = \min_{\varsigma \in \mathcal{N}(\mathbf{x})} \frac{u(\varsigma) - u(\mathbf{x})}{d_{\mathbf{x}\varsigma}}. \tag{9}$$

Taking into account the aforementioned definitions, we proceed to compute the numerical implementation of the infinity Laplacian and its variations.

3.1 Numerical Implementation of the Infinity Laplacian

Let $\mathbf{y}$ and $\mathbf{z}$ represent the locations that maximize the positive eikonal and minimize the negative eikonal operator, respectively. With these definitions in mind, we can express the infinity Laplacian as follows:

$$\frac{1}{2} \left(\left(\frac{u(\mathbf{y}) - u(\mathbf{x})}{d_{\mathbf{xy}}} \right) + \left(\frac{u(\mathbf{z}) - u(\mathbf{x})}{d_{\mathbf{xz}}} \right) \right) = 0. \tag{10}$$

The solution of Eq. (10) is provided by:

$$u(\mathbf{x}) = \frac{d_{\mathbf{xz}} u(\mathbf{y}) + d_{\mathbf{xy}} u(\mathbf{z})}{d_{\mathbf{xz}} + d_{\mathbf{xy}}}. \tag{11}$$

The iterated version of the infinity Laplacian is expressed as follows:

$$u^{k+1}(\mathbf{x}) = \frac{d_{\mathbf{xz}} u^k(\mathbf{y}) + d_{\mathbf{xy}} u^k(\mathbf{z})}{d_{\mathbf{xz}} + d_{\mathbf{xy}}} \quad k = 1, 2, 3, \dots \tag{12}$$

3.2 Numerical Implementation for the Unbalanced Infinity Laplacian

Based on the aforementioned definition, we formulated the numerical implementation for the unbalanced infinity Laplacian,

$$\frac{1}{2}\left(c_1\left(\frac{u(\mathbf{y}) - u(\mathbf{x})}{d_{\mathbf{xy}}}\right) + c_2\left(\frac{u(\mathbf{z}) - u(\mathbf{x})}{d_{\mathbf{xz}}}\right)\right) = 0. \tag{13}$$

The solution for this equation is given by,

$$u(\mathbf{x}) = \frac{c_1 d_{\mathbf{xz}} u(\mathbf{y}) + c_2 d_{\mathbf{xy}} u(\mathbf{z})}{c_1 d_{\mathbf{xz}} + c_2 d_{\mathbf{xy}}}, \tag{14}$$

and its iterated version is given by,

$$u^{k+1}(\mathbf{x}) = \frac{c_1 d_{\mathbf{xz}} u^k(\mathbf{y}) + c_2 d_{\mathbf{xy}} u^k(\mathbf{z})}{c_1 d_{\mathbf{xz}} + c_2 d_{\mathbf{xy}}} \quad k = 1, 2, 3, ... \tag{15}$$

3.3 Numerical Implementation for the Balanced Infinity Laplacian

Similar to the unbalanced Laplacian we have the following numerical implementation for the balanced infinity Laplacian,

$$\frac{1}{2}\left(\alpha(\mathbf{x})\left(\frac{u(\mathbf{y}) - u(\mathbf{x})}{d_{\mathbf{xy}}}\right) + (1 - \alpha(\mathbf{x}))\left(\frac{u(\mathbf{z}) - u(\mathbf{x})}{d_{\mathbf{xz}}}\right)\right) = 0. \tag{16}$$

The solution of this equation is,

$$u(\mathbf{x}) = \frac{\alpha(\mathbf{x})d_{\mathbf{xz}} u(\mathbf{y}) + (1 - \alpha(\mathbf{x}))d_{\mathbf{xy}} u(\mathbf{z})}{\alpha(\mathbf{x})d_{\mathbf{xz}} + (1 - \alpha(\mathbf{x}))d_{\mathbf{xy}}}, \tag{17}$$

and its iterated version,

$$u^{k+1}(\mathbf{x}) = \frac{\alpha(\mathbf{x})d_{\mathbf{xz}} u^k(\mathbf{y}) + (1 - \alpha(\mathbf{x}))d_{\mathbf{xy}} u^k(\mathbf{z})}{\alpha(\mathbf{x})d_{\mathbf{xz}} + (1 - \alpha(\mathbf{x}))d_{\mathbf{xy}}} \quad k = 1, 2, 3, ... \tag{18}$$

3.4 Biased Infinity Laplacian

As in [11] biased infinity Laplacian is provided by the following equation,

$$\frac{1}{2}\left(\left(\frac{u(\mathbf{y}) - u(\mathbf{x})}{d_{\mathbf{xy}}}\right) + \left(\frac{u(\mathbf{z}) - u(\mathbf{x})}{d_{\mathbf{xz}}}\right)\right) + \beta\left|\frac{u(\mathbf{y}) - u(\mathbf{x})}{d_{\mathbf{xy}}}\right| = 0. \tag{19}$$

Its solution depends on the sign of $(u(\mathbf{y}) - u(\mathbf{x}))$. Particularly, if $(u(\mathbf{y}) - u(\mathbf{x})) \geq 0$ we have,

$$u(\mathbf{x}) = \frac{(1 + \beta)d_{\mathbf{xz}} u(\mathbf{y}) + d_{\mathbf{xy}} u(\mathbf{z})}{(1 + \beta)d_{\mathbf{xz}} + d_{\mathbf{xy}}}, \tag{20}$$

while if $(u(\mathbf{y}) - u(\mathbf{x})) < 0$ we have,

$$u(\mathbf{x}) = \frac{(1-\beta)d_{\mathbf{xz}}u(\mathbf{y}) + d_{\mathbf{xy}}u(\mathbf{z})}{(1-\beta)d_{\mathbf{xz}} + d_{\mathbf{xy}}}, \tag{21}$$

we can write both expression as,

$$u(\mathbf{x}) = \frac{(1 + \text{sign}\{u(\mathbf{y}) - u(\mathbf{x})\}\beta)d_{\mathbf{xz}}u(\mathbf{y}) + d_{\mathbf{xy}}u(\mathbf{z})}{(1 + \text{sign}\{u(\mathbf{y}) - u(\mathbf{x})\}\beta)d_{\mathbf{xz}} + d_{\mathbf{xy}}}. \tag{22}$$

Its iterated version,

$$u^{k+1}(\mathbf{x}) = \frac{(1 + \text{sign}\{u^k(\mathbf{y}) - u^k(\mathbf{x})\}\beta)d_{\mathbf{xz}}u^k(\mathbf{y}) + d_{\mathbf{xy}}u^k(\mathbf{z})}{(1 + \text{sign}\{u^k(\mathbf{y}) - u^k(\mathbf{x})\}\beta)d_{\mathbf{xz}} + d_{\mathbf{xy}}} \quad k = 1, 2, 3, \ldots \tag{23}$$

It is worth noting that all these iterative models are remarkably simple, involving only a weighted average, making them easy and fast to implement.

3.5 Metric Taken into Consideration

As we have seen in the above subsections the distance between two points in the manifold is fundamental to compute the eikonal operators. We considered the following distance between two points,

$$d_{\mathbf{xy}} = \left(\kappa_x \eta(\mathbf{x})\|\mathbf{x} - \mathbf{y}\|^p + \kappa_c(1 - \eta(\mathbf{x}))\|I(\mathbf{x}) - I(\mathbf{y})\|^q\right)^r, \tag{24}$$

where p, q, r are exponents in $\mathbb{R}^+$, $\eta(\mathbf{x})$ is a balance term analogous to those presented above, I is the color reference images of the scene defined as $I : \Omega \subset \mathbb{R}^2 \to \mathbb{R}^3$), and $\eta : \Omega \subset \mathbb{R}^2 \to [0, 1]$,

$$\eta(\mathbf{x}) = \frac{1}{1 + e^{\beta_\eta(\|\mathbf{x}-\mathbf{y}\| - \tau_\eta\|I(\mathbf{x})-I(\mathbf{y})\|)}} \tag{25}$$

where β_η and $\tau_\eta \in \mathbb{R}^+$. The Eq. 24 can be interpreted as a sum of two terms, one that compares spatial distance and a second that compares photometric distance. Given this balanced model depending on $\eta(\mathbf{x})$, if the $\|I(\mathbf{x}) - I(\mathbf{y})\| \gg \|\mathbf{x} - \mathbf{y}\|$ the distance is more confident in the spatial distance, and vice-versa if $\|\mathbf{x} - \mathbf{y}\| \gg \|I(\mathbf{x}) - I(\mathbf{y})\|$ the distance will be computed using mainly the photometric distance.

3.6 Metric Approximation

Given the manifold $\mathcal{M} = (\Omega, g)$, to compute the distance $d_{\mathbf{xy}}$ between two points, we must calculate the geodesic distance between point $\mathbf{x}$ and point $\mathbf{y}$, which is estimated as follows:

$$L_g(\mathbf{x}, \mathbf{y}) = \min\{\text{length}(L)\}, \tag{26}$$

being L the trajectory that connects $\mathbf{x}$ and $\mathbf{y}$. In practice, we have approximated the length of the geodesic path (L_g) by the distance $d_{\mathbf{xy}}$ defined in Eq. (24),

$$L_g(\mathbf{x}, \mathbf{y}) \approx d_{\mathbf{xy}}. \tag{27}$$

This approximation simplifies the computation of the distance between $\mathbf{x}$ and $\mathbf{y}$.

4   Adaptable Model

In Fig. 1, we present a block diagram illustrating the scheme of the adaptable Convolutional stage-infinity Laplacian model, as introduced in [10], which we employ in this study. In Fig. 1, the color reference image is depicted in the top left corner. The pipeline can follow the green path or the red-dotted path depending on the logic parameter "reversible". If the parameter is 1, we follow the green path. Otherwise, if the parameter is 0, we follow the red-dotted path. This parameter is estimated empirically in the training stage and will explain in the next section.

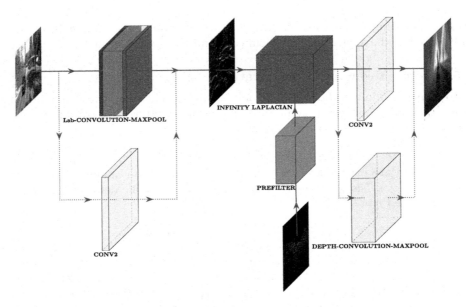

Fig. 1. Adaptable framework for the Convolutional Stage-Infinity Laplacian Model (Color figure online)

Following the green path, the model first processes each color component using Gabor filters, followed by max pooling of the data in each color component to reconstruct the color reference image (referred to as stage SC1). In the center of the figure, the model employs the infinity Laplacian or its variants, taking a color reference image and the sparse depth map as inputs for completion. The processed color image acts as a reference to guide the diffusion process. The infinity Laplacian Eq. (3) is solved using the proposed model (refer to Eq. (18)), and its output u is filtered and max-pooled using a final Convolution stage (SC2).

Additionally, following the red-dotted path, each color component of the reference-color-image is processed with average filters (SC2). The output of these filters is then max-pooled, and the processed color components are concatenated to construct a new color reference image. This new image, along with the sparse depth map, serves as the inputs for the infinity Laplacian. Once the depth completion is performed, the output is filtered using Gabor filters (SC1) and then max-pooled, resulting in the final filtered completed depth.

5   Training the Model, Dataset, and Experiments

The parameters of the model were estimated using the NYU_V2 dataset.

5.1   NYU_V2 Dataset

The NYU_V2 dataset comprises a publicly available collection of color images and depth maps of domestic scenes. It consists of 1449 images along with their corresponding depth maps, acquired using a Kinect sensor. Examples of the dataset, depicting the color reference images and their corresponding depth maps, are illustrated in Fig. 2. As depicted in Fig. 2, the images are of size 640 × 480 pixels. The depth map in (d), (e), and (f) is presented using the MATLAB colormap hot, where dark red indicates low depth values and bright yellow represents large depth values.

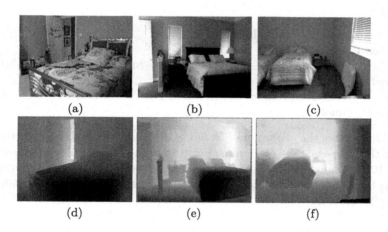

Fig. 2. Examples of images, and their corresponding depth maps, for the NYU_V2 dataset. Particularly, (a) and (d) correspond to color reference image 1002 and its depth map. In turn, (b) and (e) correspond to image 1025 and its depth map. (c) and (f)... (Color figure online)

5.2   Experiments and Protocols

We used the NYU_V2 data set to perform depth map up-sampling experiments. We down-sampled the depth data by a factor of 8, i.e. we have one sample of the depth map every other 8 × 8 square pixel. The remaining portion of the depth map is utilized as ground truth to evaluate the performance of the model. The standard protocol used to evaluate depth completion models in the sub-sampled NYU_V2 is:

i) Color images and their corresponding depth maps are used to train the model.
ii) Images 1001 to 1449, along with their corresponding depth ground truth, are utilized to evaluate the performance of the trained model.

We propose to assess four variations of the infinity Laplacian, including the original infinity Laplacian, in the up-sampling task using the NYU_V2 dataset.

5.3 Model Training

Parameters of our approach are estimated using the Particle Swarm Optimization (PSO) algorithm. Five color images (and corresponding depth maps) are considered to train the algorithm. We estimate 72 parameters that consider parameters of the metric such as p, q, r, s, κ_x, κ_c. Parameters of the infinity Laplacian such as: neighborhood size $\mathcal{N}(\mathbf{x})$, iteration number, c_1, c_2 or β_γ, τ_γ depending on the model. Parameters of the Gabor filters such σ_G, size of the filter, number of considered filters, and "reversible" parameter. The elements of the PSO:

i) We considered 100 individuals.
ii) 30 iterations.
iii) We minimize the $MSE + MAE$, (mean-square-error + mean-absolute-error).
iv) Each individual evolves as the iteration goes according to standard PSO dynamic equations.

Figure 3 illustrates the evolution of 50 out of 100 individuals during the training stage of the proposal. We observe in Fig. 3 that the convergence is fast and, in around 10 iterations most of the individuals converge to the best performance. In Table 1 we show the training performance obtained by the five models we consider in this study.

Table 1. Training performance of the five considered models.

Model number	Model name	$MSE + MAE$ [cm]
1	Infinity Laplacian	9.9727
2	Unbalanced infinity Laplacian	10.0208
3	Balanced infinity Laplacian	9.9220
4	Biased infinity Laplacian	9.9550

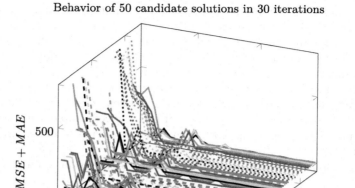

Fig. 3. Learning curve for candidate solutions μ_j ($j = 1, .., 50$) in 30 iterations.

6   Results

We have evaluated the four models in the up-sampling task using the test set of NYU_V2. We show the MSE, MAE, and the summation $MSE + MAE$ to compare in a better way the performance of the models. The obtained results of the four models evaluation are presented in Table 2. Additionally, we added a comparison with other contemporaneous models published in the literature.

Table 2. Results obtained from five proposed models

Model name	MSE	MAE	$MSE + MAE$
Infinity Laplacian	9.3509	2.8067	12.1576
Unbalanced infinity Laplacian	9.4013	2.8176	12.2189
Balanced infinity Laplacian	9.3166	2.7083	12.0249
Biased infinity Laplacian	9.3441	2.8064	12.1505
Bicubic interpolation	14.2200	–	–
High quality depth maps [17]	9.5600	–	–
Deep joint image filtering [13]	6.2000	–	–
Joint Static and Dynamic Guidance [6]	12.3100		

As we observe in Table 2 considering the four presented models, the best performance was obtained by the Balanced infinity Laplacian. The second performance was obtained by the Biased infinity Laplacian. Biased infinity Laplacian is more complex than the infinity Laplacian. The nonlinear component helps the biased infinity Laplacian to reach a better performance. Anyway, the inclusion of the balanced map $\gamma(\mathbf{x})$ to the infinity Laplacian, helps the infinity Laplacian to improve its performance, outperforming all the other variants.

Table 2 shows the results obtained by other models published in the literature. The balanced infinity Laplacian outperforms models presented in [17] and [6]. More complex models than our proposal such as Deep Joint Image Filtering [13], presents better performance. Our proposal is a low-cost implementation model that presents fast convergence and acceptable performance depending on the application.

Figure 4 displays examples of results obtained by the balanced infinity Laplacian.

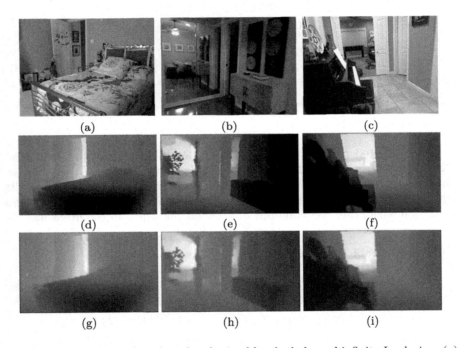

Fig. 4. Below are examples of results obtained by the balanced infinity Laplacian: (a), (b), and (c) - Color reference images; (d), (e), and (f) - Depth ground truth; (g), (h), and (i) - Results obtained by our proposal. (Color figure online)

Figure 4 showcases the results obtained by our proposal. The color reference images img_1002, img_1016, and img_1306 are displayed in (a), (b), and (c), respectively. The corresponding ground truth is shown in (d), (e), and (f). The obtained results by our model are presented in (g), (h), and (i). As we show in these figures the model presents acceptable performance in these three images. We observe in (g) that the model produce staircase artifact in the edge of the bed, also we observe the artifact in Figure (i) in the edge of the wall.

7 Conclusions

We have compared the performance of the infinity Laplacian and three variants. This comparison was performed in the up-sampling task in the NYU_V2 dataset. We empirically demonstrated that the inclusion of a mechanism that can balance locally between the two components of the infinity Laplacian improves its performance. The balanced infinity Laplacian outperforms the classical infinity Laplacian, the biased infinity Laplacian and many contemporaneous depth completion models. As future work, in order to tackle the staircase production problem we will combine our proposal with other interpolation models that are particularly robust to this kind of artifact, such as [9]. Additionally, alternative measures such as BIAS and SDE could be used to provide more information about the depth estimation error.

References

1. Aronsson, G.: Extension of functions satisfying Lipschitz conditions. Aktiv fuer Mathematik **6**(6), 551–561 (1967)
2. Aronsson, G.: On the partial differential equation $u_x^2 u_{,xx} + 2u_x u_y u_{xy} + u_y^2 u_{yy} = 0$. Aktiv fuer Matematik **7**(5), 395–425 (1968)
3. Boscain, U., Chertovskih, R., Gauthier, J.: Highly corrupted image inpainting through hypoelliptic diffusion. J. Math. Imaging Vis. **60**, 1231–1245 (2015)
4. Caselles, V., Igual, L., Sander, O.: An axiomatic approach to scalar data interpolation on surfaces. Numer. Math. **102**(3), 383–411 (2006)
5. Ennaji, H., Quéau, Y., Elmoataz, A.: Tug of war games and PDEs on graphs with applications in image and high dimensional data processing. Sci. Rep. **13**, 6045 (2023). https://doi.org/10.1038/s41598-023-32354-5
6. Ham, B., Cho, M., Ponce, J.: Robust image filtering using joint static and dynamic guidance. In: IEEE Conference on Computer Vision and Pattern Recognition. IEEE (2015)
7. Krauss, B., Schroeder, G., Gustke, M., Hussein, A.: Deterministic guided lidar depth map completion. In: IEEE Intelligent Vehicles Symposium (IV), pp. 824–831. IEEE (2021). https://doi.org/10.1109/IV48863.2021.9575867
8. Lazcano, V.: Some problems in depth enhanced video processing, Ph.D. thesis. Universitat Pompeu Fabra, Barcelona, Spain (2016). http://hdl.handle.net/10803/373917
9. Lazcano, V., Arias, P., Facciolo, G., Caselles, V.: A gradient based neighborhood filter for disparity interpolation. In: 2012 19th IEEE International Conference on Image Processing, pp. 873–876. IEEE (2012). https://doi.org/10.1109/ICIP.2012.6466999
10. Lazcano, V., Calderero, F.: Reconfigurable hybrid model convolutional stage infinity Laplacian applied to depth completion. In: AICCC 2021: 2021 4th Artificial Intelligence and Cloud Computing Conference, pp. 108–114, December 2021. ACM, Kyoto, Japan (2021)
11. Lazcano, V., Calderero, F., Ballester, C.: Depth image completion using anisotropic operators. In: Abraham, A., et al. (eds.) SoCPaR 2020. AISC, vol. 1383, pp. 593–604. Springer, Cham (2021). https://doi.org/10.1007/978-3-030-73689-7_57

12. Lazcano, V., Calderero, F., Ballester, C.: Biased-infinity Laplacian applied to depth completion using a balanced anisotropic metric. In: Liang, Q., Wang, W., Liu, X., Na, Z., Zhang, B. (eds.) CSPS 2021. LNEE, vol. 878, pp. 1048–1055. Springer, Singapore (2022). https://doi.org/10.1007/978-981-19-0390-8_132

13. Li, Y., Huang, J.-B., Ahuja, N., Yang, M.-H.: Deep joint image filtering. In: Leibe, B., Matas, J., Sebe, N., Welling, M. (eds.) ECCV 2016. LNCS, vol. 9908, pp. 154–169. Springer, Cham (2016). https://doi.org/10.1007/978-3-319-46493-0_10

14. Lin, Y., Cheng, T., Zhong, Q., Zhou, W., Yang, H.: Dynamic spatial propagation network for depth completion. In: AAAI 2022 Conference on Artificial Intelligence, AAAI (2022)

15. Liu, L., Liao, Y., Wang, Y., Geiger, A., Liu, Y.: Learning steering kernels for guided depth completion. IEEE Trans. Image Process. **30**, 2850–2861 (2021)

16. Manfredi, J., Oberman, A., Svirodov, A.: Nonlinear elliptic partial differential equations and p-harmonic functions on graphs. Differ. Integr. Eqn. **28**(12), 79–102 (2012)

17. Park, J., Kim, H., Yu-Wing, T., Brown, M., Kweon, I.: High quality depth map upsampling for 3D-TOF cameras. In: 2011 International Conference on Computer Vision, pp. 1623–1630. IEEE (2011). https://doi.org/10.1109/ICCV.2011.6126423

18. Silberman, N., Hoiem, D., Kohli, P., Fergus, R.: Indoor segmentation and support inference from RGBD images. In: Fitzgibbon, A., Lazebnik, S., Perona, P., Sato, Y., Schmid, C. (eds.) ECCV 2012. LNCS, vol. 7576, pp. 746–760. Springer, Heidelberg (2012). https://doi.org/10.1007/978-3-642-33715-4_54

19. Teutscher, D., Mangat, P., Wassermueller, O.: PDC: piecewise depth completion utilizing superpixels. In: IEEE International Intelligent Transportation Systems Conference (ITSC), pp. 2752–2758. IEEE, Indianapolis, USA (2021)

20. Tomasi, C., Manduchi, R.: Bilateral filter for gray and color images. In: Sixth International Conference on Computer Vision (IEEE Press), pp. 839–846. IEEE (1998)

Chaos Analysis and Machine Learning for Forecasting Climate Change in Some Countries of Latin America

Guido Tapia-Riera$^{(\boxtimes)}$ ⓘ, Saba Infante ⓘ, Isidro R. Amaro ⓘ,
and Francisco Hidrobo ⓘ

School of Mathematical and Computational Sciences, Yachay Tech University,
Urcuquí, Ecuador
{guido.tapia,sinfante,iamaro,fhidrobo}@yachaytech.edu.ec

Abstract. This manuscript aims to assess climate change in some Latin American countries via Chaos Analysis. Specifically, the False Nearest Neighbors method, Lyapunov Exponent, and BDS Test were implemented to study the chaos in a dataset consisting of three climate change-related variables: Primary energy consumption, Total greenhouse gas emissions, and Carbon Dioxide (CO_2) emissions. Throughout this study, we found that the process of climate change in the Latin American countries studied is chaotic, and forecasting values for the following years is a challenging task. However, by using the ARIMA and LSTM models and measuring their performance through MAPE and MSE, we observed that the approximations are not excessively large. In the analysis of these series it was shown that the ARIMA model yields better approximations than the LSTM model. It is important to note that when dealing with chaotic processes, making predictions becomes very challenging, and the errors tend to be high.

Keywords: Climate Change · Chaos Analysis · Machine Learning · Forecasting

1 Introduction

In the context of the Intergovernmental Panel on Climate Change (IPCC), climate change encompasses all variations in climate conditions over a period, regardless of whether they arise from natural fluctuations or are caused by human actions [1]. This environmental problem is one of the most important that arises in the life of living beings. The activities that contribute to these changes are those carried out by human society. Thus, anthropological activities have a great influence. In fact, among the factors that can be considered to study the causes of climate change are CO_2 emissions, primary energy consumption, and greenhouse gases. As contributing activities to this process we have that the combustion of fossil fuels and the destruction of forests constitute the main source (70%) of greenhouse gas emissions [2].

T. Guarda et al. (Eds.): ARTIIS 2023, CCIS 1937, pp. 17–30, 2024.
https://doi.org/10.1007/978-3-031-48930-3_2

Countries that belong to Latin America are taken into consideration because they are considered as vulnerable. The importance of studying climate change lies in the great impact it can have on life in general. In fact, factors such as those mentioned above can influence the geographical distribution of many infectious diseases [3]. For example, climate change could contribute to the development of some diseasesstas [4]. Then, the development of techniques that allow making inferences about this process is important for taking decisions.

Determining the behavior of phenomena that are modeled by a deterministic dynamical system is a complex task due to its irregular nature, nonlinear structure, high sensitivity to changes in the initial conditions and restriction of the dynamics in the immersion space. Additionally, using techniques of machine learning to make predictions is a hard task [5,6].

Studying time series is very useful. These allow finding or predicting different future data using data that are previously known. In this way, performing an analysis of the time series allows us to find answers to these natural phenomena. In particular, the areas of statistics and machine learning can help to predict some values that are necessary to make the interpretations of the presented data. Also, by modeling observations from different years as time series, future data can be predicted with respect to something specific; for example, possible temperature spectra can be determined from observations by analyzing a time series [7]. In this way, it is possible to analyze and understand the trend of these time series and thus reach conclusions of the additional temperature in a certain time range.

The present manuscript is organized as follows. Section 2.1 is dedicated to describe the data used, while Sects. 2.2, 2.3 and 2.4 are dedicated to describe Chaos Analysis tools, and in Sect. 2.5 we introduce briefly the LSTM model. Results and Discussion are exhibited in Sect. 3. Finally, the Conclusions are presented in Sect. 4.

1.1   Contribution and Related Work

The greatest contribution of this work is to know the impact of the different variables considered in Latin America[1]. This is due to the fact that countries other than those that are highly industrialized, such as the US or Canada, are being examined. Moreover, we use machine learning techniques for describing data and making predictions that enable future interpretations through the presented graphs in this work.

Another significant contribution lies in the analysis of the impact of the aforementioned variables on climate change. Since this can cause negative consequences in different areas, it can be approached from different perspectives. Several policies have been implemented in different countries and also the countries between them have signed several treaties in order to reduce the great

---

[1] In this work, for short we refer to Ecuador, Colombia, Peru, Brazil, Chile, Argentina, Bolivia, Honduras and El Salvador as Latin America. The rest of the Latin American countries were not considered because they do not present enough data during the period of time and/or in the variables studied.

impact that their different activities can have on this phenomenon. Thus, analyzing the policies adopted, for example the Kyoto Protocol or also the implementation of private or public organizations [8] can help stop and analyze the different negative effects in order to create solutions to the problem.

As it was mentioned above, data forecasting is important because it allows for action to be taken either in the short, medium, or long term. Machine learning techniques can be used for these types of predictions. In fact, the development of neural networks allows the creation of approximations of functions, making forecasts and exploratory graphs that combined with other methods such as dynamic systems, allow certain predictions of the phenomena studied [9]. Moreover, the combination between neural networks and dynamical systems as the chaotic can give good results to make predictions.

2   Materials and Methods

2.1   Dataset Description

The data set considered in this work was obtained from a GitHub public repository[2] maintained by Our World in Data [10]. Table 1 shows the selected variables for our study. Each of these corresponds to the sum of the values for the selected countries (which we refer as Latin America).

Table 1. Description of the selected variables.

Variable	Description
Primary energy consumption (V_1)	Primary energy consumption, measured in terawatt-hours
Total ghg (V_2)	Total greenhouse gas emissions including land-use change and forestry, measured in million tonnes of carbon dioxide-equivalents.
Per capita CO_2 emissions (V_3)	Carbon dioxide (CO_2) emissions from the burning of fossil fuels for energy and cement production

As we are working with time series, clearly, the variables must be measured in a time interval. Therefore, next we will describe the time period which these variables were observed. Table 2 shows the selected countries for our study and the period in which the variables were measured (we chose these periods because they are the longest available for each variable in the dataset used). Since we select all Latin America countries, we simple refer to them as Latin America (or LATAM).

---

[2] https://github.com/owid/energy-data/blob/master/owid-energy-codebook.csv and https://github.com/owid/co2-data/blob/master/owid-co2-codebook.csv.

Table 2. Description of the selected countries and periodicity of variables (which is annual).

Countries	Start	End
Latin America (V_1)	1980	2019
Latin America (V_2)	1990	2018
Latin America (V_3)	1950	2020

2.2   False Nearest Neighbors Method

Suppose we have a state space reconstruction of dimension d with data vectors using the delay time suggested by the mutual information function as given in the following equation

$$X(n) = [X(n), X(n+T), X(n+2\,T), \ldots, X(n+(d-1)T)]$$

where T is the delay time. If the nearest neighbor is examined in the state space of vector $X(n)$ at time n, it will be a vector

$$X^{NN}(n) = \left[x^{NN}(n), x^{NN}(n+T), x^{NN}(n+2\,T), \ldots, x^{NN}(n+(d-1)T)\right]$$

And its value at instant n will have a relationship with the value of vector $X(n)$ at this same instant. If the vector $X^{NN}(n)$ is close to $x(n)$, then it comes from a neighborhood of $x(n)$ at its dynamic origins. The vector is forward or backward by $x(n)$ on the orbit if the time steps along the orbit are sufficiently small, or it reaches the neighborhood of $x(n)$ by the evolution of 1 orbit along the attractor. Since the attractors of deterministic systems are compact, each point in the state space will have as many neighbors as the number of data points that make the state space well populated.

If $X^{NN}(n)$ is a false neighbor of $x(n)$ having reached its neighborhood by a projection of a higher dimension because the current dimension d does not display the attractor, then increasing the dimension to $d+1$ will move this false neighbor by $X(n)$. By inspecting all the data in the series and checking with which dimension all false neighbors are removed, the overlapping lower dimensional orbits will be removed sequentially. When no more false nearest neighbors are detected, the value d_θ at which the attractor is fully deployed will have been identified [11–13]

Through False Nearest Neighbors Method we deduce the best value of m (*i.e.*, embedding value for each case of study).

2.3   Lyapunov Exponent

In dynamical systems, Lyapunov exponents are quantities that can be calculated to define how the trajectories of a system evolve starting from certain initial conditions. Using these quantities, it can be determined whether the system will converge to a simple attractor or a strange one.

In general, deterministic dynamical systems have the same number of Lyapunov exponents as degrees of freedom of it, and their behavior is defined by the largest of these exponents. When the largest of the exponents is negative ($\lambda < 0$), meaning they are all negative), the trajectory of the dynamical system converges to a fixed point in phase space. When the largest Lyapunov exponent is zero ($\lambda = 0$), the trajectory converges to a periodic orbit. Finally, for the case where the largest Lyapunov exponent is greater than zero ($\lambda > 0$) two things can happen: i) if $\sum_i^n \lambda_i > 0$ the system is divergent; ii) in the case where $\sum_i^n \lambda_i < 0$ the system is bounded but does not stabilize in a periodic orbit or a fixed point. One of the uses of the Lyapunov exponents is the ability to quantify the speed with which two trajectories that start from a very close initial condition approach or move away with the evolution of time; that is, they measure the degree of sensitivity of the system to variations in the initial conditions [13,14].

Suppose that we start from two initial conditions x_0 and $x_0 + \epsilon_0$ for $t = 0$ and let the system evolve over time, obtaining two trajectories. If the difference between the trajectories is calculated, it evolves exponentially.

$$\epsilon_t \approx \epsilon_0 e^{\lambda t}$$

If the exponent $\lambda < 0$, the paths are combined into one, since $e^{\lambda t} \to 0$ when $t \to +\infty$; on the contrary, if the exponent $\lambda > 0$, the trajectories move exponentially away from each other. If the system is bounded, this exponential divergence is called sensitivity to conditions [14].

2.4   BDS Test

BDS test was originally proposed to determine whether observations in a time series are independent and identically distributed (iid), detecting all sorts of linear or non-linear dependencies. If $\{X_t\}$ is a time series composed of independent and identically distributed (*iid*) observations, the probability that a history of two observations is less than or equal to ε of each other, is given by

$$
\begin{aligned}
C_2(\varepsilon) &= P\left(|X_t - X_j| \le \varepsilon, |X_{t-1} - X_{j-1}| \le \varepsilon\right) \\
&= P\left(|X_t - X_j| \le \varepsilon\right) P\left(|X_{t-1} - X_{j-1}| \le \varepsilon\right) \\
&= P\left(|X_t - X_j| \le \varepsilon\right)^2 \\
&= [C_1(\varepsilon)]^2
\end{aligned}
\tag{1}
$$

Now, let's generalize (1) to a fase space of dimension m. We get

$$C_m(\varepsilon) = [C_{1\varepsilon}]^m \tag{2}$$

where (2) is a integral correlation such that estimator for a series with length n is given by

$$C_{mn}(\epsilon) = \frac{2}{(n-m+1)(n-m)} \sum_{s=1}^{n-m+1} \sum_{t=1}^{n-m+1} \prod_{s=1}^{m-1} H\left(\varepsilon - |X_{s+j} - X_{t+j}|\right)$$

where

$$H(R) = \begin{cases} 1 & \text{if } \varepsilon - |X_{s+j} - X_{t+j}| \geq 0 \\ 0 & \text{otherwise} \end{cases}$$

is the heaviside function that lists the number of m-dimensions that satisfy the proximity condition. Thus, the BDS statistic is defined as

$$W_m(\epsilon) = \sqrt{T} \frac{C_{mn}(\epsilon) - [C_1(\epsilon)]^m}{\widehat{\sigma}_m(\epsilon)}$$

where $\widehat{\sigma}_m(\epsilon)$ is the asymptotic estimator of the standard deviation of $C_{mn}(\epsilon) - [C_1(\epsilon)]$m. Under the null hypothesis of the *iid* data, the BDS test converges to a standard normal distribution. To test for nonlinear dependence, BDS is calculated on the residuals of a model that removes linear dependence from the data [6,11,15].

2.5 Long Short-Term Memory

The main idea of LSTM is to introduce an adaptive gating mechanism to determine what information to discard and what information to store. Long Short-Term Memory (LSTM) traditional recurrent neural networks (RNNs) contain cyclic connections that make them a powerful tool to learn complex temporal dynamics, and is capable of modeling longer term dependencies by having memory cells and gates that controls the information flow along with the memory cells. This method can be used for sequences, patterns recognition, and image processing applications. Long short-term memory (LSTM) and gated recurrent units (GRUs) address this issue. LSTMs, GRUs and their variants are a large part of RNN's recent success in natural language processing, speech recognition, and other real-world applications [16–19].

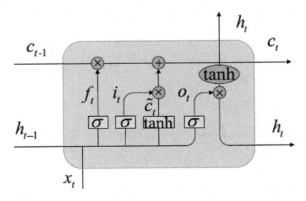

Fig. 1. LSTM structure diagram [19].

A standard LSTM block consists of four parts: i_t describes the input gate, f_t represents the forget gate, o_t represents the output gate, and c_t represents the memory unit. The LSTM framework is shown in Fig. 1. Let $x_{1:t} = (x_1, \ldots, x_t)$ be an input sequence and $y_{1:t} = (y_1, \ldots, y_t)$ represent an output sequence; an LSTM network computes a mapping iteratively between $x_{1:t} = (x_1, \ldots, x_t)$ and $y_{1:t} = (y_1, \ldots, y_t)$ using the following mathematical model:

$$f_t = \sigma \left[W_f \left(h_{t-1}, x_t \right) + b_f \right], \qquad Forget\,Gate$$
$$i_t = \sigma \left[W_i \left(h_{t-1}, x_t \right) + b_i \right], \qquad Input\,Gate$$
$$\tilde{c}_t = \tanh \left[W_c \left(h_{t-1}, x_t \right) + b_c \right], \qquad Cell\,Input$$
$$c_t = f_t \odot c_{t-1} + i_t \odot \tilde{c}_t, \qquad Cell\,State$$
$$o_t = \sigma \left[W_0 \left(h_{t-1}, x_t \right) + b_0 \right], \qquad Output\,Gate$$
$$h_t = o_t \odot \tanh \left(c_t \right), \qquad Cell\,Output$$

where the initial values $c_0 = 0$, $h_0 = 0$, refer to the number of input features and number of hidden units, respectively, the operator $\odot$ denotes the Hadamard product (element-wise product), and σ is the sigmoide function. The subscript t indexes the time steps. The description of the variables is:

- $x_t \in \mathbb{R}^d$: input vector to the LSTM unit;
- $f_t \in \mathbb{R}^h$: forget gate's activation vector;
- $i_t \in \mathbb{R}^h$: input/update gate's activation vector;
- $\tilde{c}_t \in \mathbb{R}^h$: cell input activation vector;
- $c_t \in \mathbb{R}^h$: cell state vector;
- $o_t \in \mathbb{R}^h$: output gate's activation vector;
- $h_t \in \mathbb{R}^h$: hidden state vector also known as output vector of the LSTM unit;
- $W \in \mathbb{R}^{h \times d}$, $U \in \mathbb{R}^{h \times h}$, $b \in \mathbb{R}^h$: weight matrices and bias vector parameters which need to be learned during training;
- σ: sigmoid activation function.

3   Results and Discussion

In this section, we will determine the non-linearity of the series in order to subsequently study the Lyapunov coefficients of each variable under analysis. Finally, we will use the ARIMA [20] and LSTM models to predict the values for the last 3 years of each series studied.

3.1   BDS Test

As we have mentioned, the BDS test allows us to verify the series' non-linearity, which is the first step to determining if the series is chaotic. Below we will show the results (Tables 3, 4, and 5) of applying the BDS test to each of our series.

Table 3. Standard deviation for different values of m and ϵ (Total energy consumption).

m	ϵ_1	ϵ_2	ϵ_3	ϵ_4
2	5.2177	5.7846	1.9020	-3.4504
3	-9.1998	5.0156	1.8899	-3.1554
4	-14.6471	7.6670	1.7973	-3.0420
5	-13.3166	10.6465	1.8387	-3.2723

Table 4. Standard deviation for different values of m and ϵ (Total green house emissions).

m	ϵ_1	ϵ_2	ϵ_3	ϵ_4
2	2.5339	-0.0224	-0.2343	-0.2343
3	2.1361	-0.1357	-0.3217	-0.3217
4	1.8237	-0.2303	-0.3928	-0.3928
5	1.3401	-0.3739	-0.4562	-0.4562

Table 5. Standard deviation for different values of m and ϵ (CO_2 emissions per capita).

m	ϵ_1	ϵ_2	ϵ_3	ϵ_4
2	1.4503	0.3624	-0.6923	0.7137
3	1.5806	0.5372	-0.4296	0.3728
4	1.3780	0.6742	-0.4729	-0.1365
5	2.0329	0.4897	-0.8033	-1.0301

Analyzing all p-values for the series considered in this work we reject the null hypothesis which means that the series is non-linear.

3.2 Deterministic Chaos

In this section, we identify the chaotic behavior of the time series studied in this manuscript throught computing the largest Lyapunov Exponent of the reconstructed phase space.

Total Energy Consumption

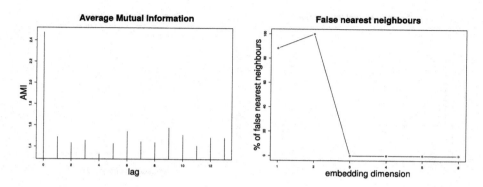

Fig. 2. (a) Average Mutual Information (b) False Nearest Neighbors.

Note that, through Fig. 2 we derive that theiler window[3] is 4, and the embedding dimension is 2.

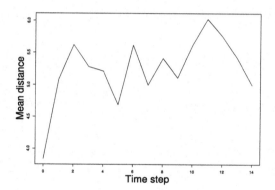

Fig. 3. Evolution of the logarithm of the mean distances among closet point.

The slope of the linear fit gives us an estimation of the maximum Lyapunov exponent which we denote with λ. In the case of total energy consumption $\lambda = 0.3$, which is greater than 0. Therefore, it is a chaotic process

---

[3] Also known as the time lag or temporal separation. It is used to remove the influence of short-term correlations and noise in a time series. See [5] for a formal definition.

Total Greenhouse Emissions

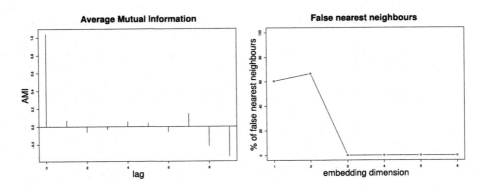

Fig. 4. (a) Average Mutual Information (b) False Nearest Neighbors

In Fig. 4 we derive that theiler window is 5, and the embedding dimension is 2.

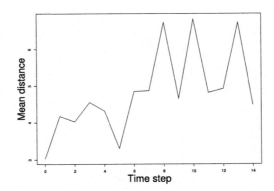

Fig. 5. Evolution of the logarithm of the mean distances among closet point

The total greenhouse emissions presents a value of λ of 0.3, which is greater than 0. Therefore, it is a chaotic process.

CO_2 Emissions per Capita

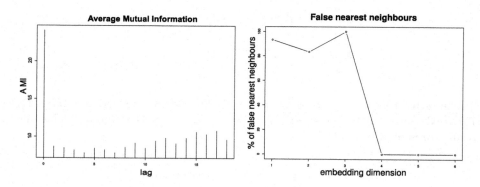

Fig. 6. (a) Average Mutual Information (b) False Nearest Neighbors

Analyzing Fig. 6, we determine that the theiler window has a size of 5, while the embedding dimension is found to be 2.

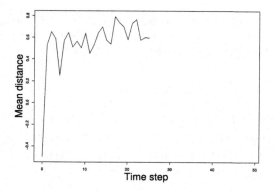

Fig. 7. Evolution of the logarithm of the mean distances among closet point

For $C0_2$ emissions per capita we got $\lambda = 0.16$. Then, this process also is a chaotic.

3.3   Forecasting

For the years 2018, 2019, and 2020, the predicted value using the ARIMA model was 32.256. Using the LSTM model, we obtained the following results which are shown in Table 6.

Table 6. Per capita CO2 emissions

Year	LSTM	MAPE	MSE	Real Value
2018	32.191	3.83	1.649	33.475
2019	31.822	1.676	0.294	32.364
2020	31.692	9.755	7.941	28.874

The ARIMA model forecasts for the years 2017, 2018, and 2019 are 6779.747, 7072.303, and 7169.884, respectively. Conversely, the LSTM model yields the results presented in Table 7.

Table 7. Primary energy consumption

Year	LSTM	MAPE	MSE	Real Value
2017	7229.494	96.600	85125.07	6937.732
2018	7245.178	5.320	133065.2	6880.397
2019	7304.822	7.75	276138.7	6779.333

ARIMA model's predictions for the years 2016, 2017, and 2018, yielding values of 3025.420, 3055.720, and 3054.922, respectively. On the other hand, the LSTM model produced the results displays in Table 8.

Table 8. Total ghg

Year	LSTM	MAPE	MSE	Real Value
2016	3089.259	2.187	4378.337	3023.09
2017	3114.481	2.984	8159.69	3024.15
2018	3142.873	5.490	26775.76	2979.24

4   Conclusions

False nearest neighbors and the mutual information criteria were utilized to determine the delay time (τ) and embedding dimension (m). These parameter estimations are crucial for accurately recreating the series attractor in the corresponding phase space. The dimension of the phase space was chosen as the smallest integer greater than the correlation dimension. Subsequently, the Lyapunov Exponent was calculated based on this dimension. The positive values of the Lyapunov Exponent obtained in this study indicate the chaotic nature of our series. Furthermore, through the BDS test, we confirmed the nonlinear characteristics of the series.

Since the series studied present a chaotic behavior, we proposed to conduct predictions through the ARIMA and LSTM models. Taking into account that our series are chaotic, we observe that the LSTM model provides good approximations, as the values of MAPE and MSE are not excessively large. On the other hand, the ARIMA model yields better approximations than the LSTM model. It is important to note that when dealing with chaotic processes, making predictions becomes very challenging, and the errors tend to be high. Finally, the results of this study pave the way for future research where a neural network with a different architecture can be adapted to enhance the accuracy.

Acknowledgment. This work was carried out under the project Statistical Methods for Modeling data generated by Complex Systems REGINV- MATH23-04, Yachay Tech University.

References

1. Inntergovernmental Panel on Climate Change (IPCC). G. Definitions of key terms - AR4 WGII Foreword, Preface, and Introduction – archive.ipcc.ch. 'archive.ipcc.ch/publications_and_data/ar4/wg2/en/frontmattersg.html'. Accessed 29 July 2023
2. Qin, D., et al.: Ipcc, 2007: Summary for policymakers (2007)
3. Kaffenberger, B.H., Shetlar, D., Norton, S.A., Rosenbach, M.: The effect of climate change on skin disease in north America. J. American Acad. Dermatol. **76**(1), 140–147 (2017)
4. Kilpatrick, A.M., Randolph, S.E.: Drivers, dynamics, and control of emerging vector-borne zoonotic diseases. The Lancet, **380**(9857), 1946–1955 (2012)
5. Kantz, H., Schreiber, T.: Nonlinear Time Series Analysis. Cambridge University Press, 2 edition, (2003)
6. Infante, S., Ortega, J., Cedeño, F.: Estimación de datos faltantes en estaciones meteorológicas de venezuela vía un modelo de redes neuronales. Revista de Climatología, **8**, 51–70 (2008)
7. Bloomfield, P., Douglas, N.: Climate spectra and detecting climate change. Clim. Change **21**(3), 275–287 (1992)
8. Green, J.F.: Order out of chaos: public and private rules for managing carbon. Global Environ. Politics **13**(2), 1–25 (2013)
9. Liu, Z., Peng, C., Xiang, W., Tian, D., Deng, X., Zhao, M.: Application of artificial neural networks in global climate change and ecological research: an overview. Chin. Sci. Bull. **55**(34), 3853–3863 (2010)
10. Ritchie, H., Roser, M., Rosado, P.: co_2 and greenhouse gas emissions. Our World in Data (2020). 'ourworldindata.org/co2-and-other-greenhouse-gas-emissions'
11. Sandubete Galán, J.E.: Quantifying chaos from time-series data through Lyapunov exponents: a computational data science approach. PhD thesis, Universidad Complitense de Madrid (2020)
12. Chatfield, C.: The Analysis of Time Series: An Introduction, Sixth Edition. Chapman & Hall/CRC Texts in Statistical Science. CRC Press (2016)
13. Diaz, A.F.: Dinámica caótica en economía : (teoría y aplicaciones). Mc Graw Hill (2000)
14. Huffaker, R., Bittelli, M., Rosa, R.: Nonlinear Time Series Analysis with R. OUP Oxford (2017)

15. Cedeño, N., Carillo, G., Ayala, M.J., Lalvay, S., Infante, S.: Analysis of chaos and predicting the price of crude oil in ecuador using deep learning models. In: Guarda, T., Portela, F., Santos, M.F. (eds.) Advanced Research in Technologies, Information, Innovation and Sustainability: First International Conference, ARTIIS 2021, La Libertad, Ecuador, November 25–27, 2021, Proceedings, pp. 318–332. Springer International Publishing, Cham (2021). https://doi.org/10.1007/978-3-030-90241-4_25
16. Choe, Y.J., Shin, J., Spencer, N.: Spencer. Probabilistic interpretations of recurrent neural networks, Probabilistic Graphical Models (2017)
17. Cho, K., et al.: Learning phrase representations using RNN encoder-decoder for statistical machine translation. In Proceedings of the 2014 Conference on Empirical Methods in Natural Language Processing (EMNLP), pp. 1724–1734, Doha, Qatar, October 2014. Association for Computational Linguistics (2014)
18. Memory, L.S.T.: Long Short-Term Memory. Neural Computation, **9**(8), 1735–1780, 11 (1997)
19. Liu, Y., Cheng, J., Zhang, H., Zou, H., Xiong, N.N.: Long short-term memory networks based on particle filter for object tracking. IEEE Access **8**, 216245–216258 (2020)
20. Brockwell, P.J., Davis, R.A.: Introduction to Time Series and Forecasting. Springer Texts in Statistics. Springer, New York (2006)

Climate Time Series Prediction by Convex Polygons and the Kalman Filter

Soto Jose[1,2]($\boxtimes$) (iD), Infante Saba[3] (iD), and Hernandez Aracelis[3] (iD)

[1] Universidad Tecnológica, San José, Uruguay
jose.soto@utec.edu.uy
[2] CENUR, Universidad de la República, Montevideo, Uruguay
[3] Yachay Tech University, Hacienda San José, Urcuquí 100119, Ecuador
{sinfante,ahernandez}@yachaytech.edu.ec

Abstract. The number of monitoring stations essential for a region is key for installation and maintenance cost purposes, but also for data correction in the event that stations fail and miss data. Estimates that incorporate the distance to secondary stations are generally used, but climate components are spatial and should take into account only one dimension. In this paper, we propose an algorithm for performing approximations of climate data, such as temperature and relative humidity based on neighboring stations, using the area of the largest convex polygon containing the point of interest to calculate the estimates, instead of the distance; In order to test this method, real data observations are used and compared using different indices, with the simulated values for a given station.

Keywords: Kalman Filter · Spatio-space models · Convex polygons

1 Introduction

The Kalman Filter (KF) was introduced in the literature by Kalman (Kalman) and Kalman-Bucy (Kalman-Bucy) publications in the 1960 s, where a solution to the problem of linear filtering of discrete data, using recursion, was presented. The Kalman derivation includes a large number of state-space models and due to advances in digital computation, its application became popular in different areas, ranging from assisted navigation to econometrics.

The state-space representation is a convenient notation for the estimation of stochastic models, where errors are assumed in the measurement of the system, allowing to include the handling of a wide range of time series models like the modeling of unobservable components and parameters that change over time.

The Kalman filter is based on a prediction and correction mechanism, i.e., the algorithm, starting from its previous estimate and adding a correction term proportional to the prediction error, predicts the new state.

The importance of studying the Kalman algorithm lies in the fact that it is the main procedure for estimating dynamical systems represented in the state-space form, which have many applications of interest.

T. Guarda et al. (Eds.): ARTIIS 2023, CCIS 1937, pp. 31–42, 2024.
https://doi.org/10.1007/978-3-031-48930-3_3

Sanchez et al. [9] proposes a methodology that combines time series with the models generated by a partial differential advection equation using mixtures of radial and diffusion basis functions, then implements the Ensemble Kalman Filter (FKEN) and the nonessential Kalman filter of ensembles (FKSEEN) to estimate and forecast rainfall states.

Ferreira et al. [4] using the Wold method, performs the estimation and prediction of spatio-temporal processes in the multivariate case. This approach allows to apply KF and obtain estimates in linear time processes, with short or medium scope.

Huang et al. [5] developed a space-time model, based on the Kalman Filter, and applied it to compare snow water and monthly precipitation. Bradley et al. [2] estimated the average monthly income in the United States, using a Bayesian methodology with spatio temporal multivariate systems. The authors, within each MCMC iteration, used Kalman filter smoothing and Kalman filtering.

In Soto and Infante [11], a method is proposed to estimate states and parameters, using the Kalman filter, in a mixed effects model defined by a stochastic differential equation.

The monitoring of climatic variables is fundamental in making forecasts in agricultural regions, which is why a constant measurement of changes is required. However, since weather stations are limited, it is necessary to infer and obtain approximate data of the conditions for the rest of the area.

The problem addressed in this work is the proposal of a method to obtain measurements in similar time, from observed stations available to the following stations.

The structure of the paper is organized as follows: Sect. 2 presents materials and methods, the source of the data used and the physical property relevant to the problem, the filtering technique used and the description of the state-space equations are referenced. Section 3 presents the results of the estimations performed with the proposed method, as well as the indices to determine the goodness-of-fit of the obtained estimations. Finally, Sect. 4 presents the discussions and conclusions of the paper.

2   Materials and Methods

2.1   Data Description

To test the proposed method, the authors extracted data corresponding to the year 2020 from a set of 26 weather stations belonging to the Agromet network (http://www.agromet.cl), whose network is formed by more than 100 weather stations in Chilean territory, generating data including temperature and relative humidity, with daily temperature data from the Maule region. This data set is updated by the Instituto de Investigaciones Agropecuarias (INIA) and is available on the website, an initiative between the Ministry of Agriculture, the Agricultural Research Institute (INIA), the Chilean Fruit Exporters Association (ASOEX), the Foundation for Fruit Development (FDF), the Cooperative Center for Wine Development (Centro Cooperativo para el Desarrollo Vitivinícola

S.A.) and the Chilean Wine Association (Asociación Vinos de Chile A.G.), to provide information related to climate and its effect on the different production processes. Figure 1 shows the location of 20 simulated stations, and using the data available from the stations (*red), the values of maximum and minimum daily temperature and maximum solar radiation were determined. In order to determine the prediction given by the model, we used the observations of the stations marked with the symbol(*), except for the data observed in station 11, and estimated the values of maximum temperature and solar radiation. Then, we compare, the values obtained between the simulated station 3(+blue) and the observed values of the real station 11(*red), to establish the similarity between the observed data and the simulated data.

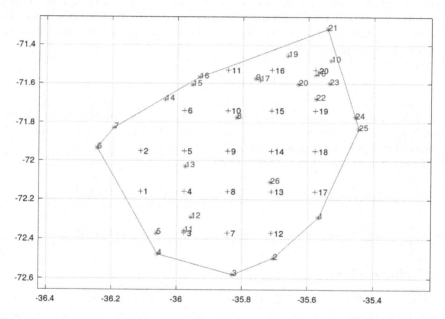

Fig. 1. Station locations with available data (red) and simulated stations (blue). (Color figure online)

2.2 Bayesian Inference Methods

We considered the state evolution density and the observation density

$$x_k = f(x_{k-1}) + u_k, \quad u_k \sim N(0, Q_k) \quad k = 1, \dots, t.$$
$$y_k = g(x_k) + v_k, \quad v_k \sim N(0, R_k)$$

where $x_k \in \mathbb{R}^n$ is the state of the system on the time step k, $y_k \in \mathbb{R}^m$ is the observation in the time step k, f is the nonlinear state dynamics function, g the observation function, $u_k \in \mathbb{R}^n$ represent the process noise vector and $v_k \in \mathbb{R}^m$ the noise vector of the observations.

The full probabilistic model is expressed by:

$$p\left(x_{1:t}, y_{1:t}\right) = f(x_1) \prod_{k=2}^{t} f\left(x_k|x_{k-1}\right) \prod_{k=1}^{t} g\left(y_k|x_k\right), \quad k = 1, \ldots, n$$

where $x_{1:n} = (x_1, \ldots, x_n)$, $y_{1:n} = (y_1, \ldots, y_n)$, $f(x_1)$ is the distribution of the initial state, $f\left(x_k|x_{k-1}\right)$ is the dynamic model which characterizes the dynamic behaviors of the system, $g\left(y_k|x_k\right)$ is the model for measurements, which describes how the measurements are distributed given the state.

In many state-space inference problems $p(x_t|y_{1:k})$ is the sequential estimation of the filtering distribution. Updating the filtering density can be done in principle using the standard filtering recursions. The Chapman-Kolmogorov equation describes the Bayesian prediction:

$$p\left(x_k|y_{1:k-1}\right) = \int p(x_k|x_{k-1})p(x_{k-1}|y_{1:k-1})dx_{k-1}$$

where $p(x_{k-1}|y_{1:k-1})$ denotes the prior and $p(x_k|y_{1:k-1})$ denotes the predictive density, $p(x_k|x_{k-1})$ denotes the one step state prediction and $y_{1:k-1}$ represents all measurements from beginning up to time $k-1$.

Filtered distribution for x_t is given by:

$$p\left(x_k|y_{1:k}\right) = \frac{p\left(x_k, y_k|y_{1:k-1}\right)}{p\left(y_k|y_{1:k-1}\right)} = \frac{g(y_k|x_k)p(x_k|y_{1:k-1})}{\int g(y_k|x_k)p(x_k|y_{1:k-1})dx_k}$$

where $p\left(x_k|y_{1:k}\right)$ is an posterior density and $g(y_k|x_k)$ is likelihood.

2.3   Kalman Filter

The Kalman filter is "the closed form solution to the Bayesian filtering equations for the filtering model, where the dynamic and measurement models are linear Gaussian" [10]. This algorithm estimates the new state from its previous estimate, adding a correction term proportional to the prediction error, by means of a prediction and correction mechanism.

Considering the state-space equation given by

$$\begin{cases} x_k = F_{k-1}x_{k-1} + q_{k-1}; \\ y_k = H_k x_k + r_k; \end{cases} \quad (1)$$

– The prediction step is

$$\begin{aligned} m_k^- &= F_{k-1}m_{k-1} \\ yk^- &= F_{k-1}P_{k-1}F_{k-1}^\top + Q_{k-1}: \end{aligned} \quad (2)$$

– The update step given by

$$v_k = y_k - H_k m_k^-$$
$$S_k = H_k P_k^- H_k^\top + R_k$$
$$K_k = P_k^- H_k^- H_k^\top S_k^{-1} \tag{3}$$
$$m_k = m_k^- + K_k v_k$$
$$P_k = P_k^- - K_k S_k K_k^\top$$

The recursion starts with m_0 as mean and P_0 as the covariance, the $x_k \in \mathbb{R}^n$ is the state, $y_k \in \mathbb{R}^m$ is the measure, q_{k-1} and r_k are the process noise of the state and observations with distribution $\mathcal{N}(0, Q_{k-1})$ and $\mathcal{N}(0, R_k)$ respectively, and the distribution of x_0 is the Gaussian $\mathcal{N}(m_0; P_0)$. The matrix F_{k-1} is the dynamic model transition matrix and H_k is the measurement model matrix.

2.4   Estimating the State-Space Equations

Given a set of stations $E = \{e_i\}$, located at coordinates (lat_i, lon_i), for i from 1 to n , and a data set

$$\{Y_j^T\}_{j=1}^k = \{(y_{1j}, y_{2j}, \ldots, y_{nj})^T\}_{j=1}^k,$$

where y_{ij} is the data for station e_i at time j.

Considering the convex envelope [1] of the stations as the set EC, and the a set $F = \{f_i\} \subset EC$ formed by k stations in the set EC, these stations can be distributed in the form of a rectangular grid, i.e. equally spaced or at random locations, denoted by x_{ij} the data of station f_i at time j, our objective is to find the values of x_{ij}, for $i = 1, \ldots, k$ and $j = 1, \ldots, T$.

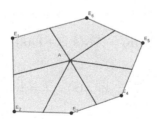

Fig. 2. Convex envelope for a single station.

For each station $f_i \in F$, we define a set of stations

$$\{es_{i1}, es_{i2}, \ldots, es_{ik_i}\} \subset E \cup F$$

which form the largest convex set that contains station es_i and has no other station of $E \cup F$ inside it, taking the polygon formed by the coordinates of the stations $\{es_{i1}, es_{i2}, \ldots, es_{ik_i}\}$ we associate $\{a_{ij}\}_{j=1}^{k_1}$ the proportional coefficients of the polygon area, where a_k is the proportional coefficient of the area of the polygon formed by the coordinates $\{es_i, es_{i_k}\}$ and the midpoints of $\{es_{i_k}, es_{i_{k-1}}\}$ and $\{es_{i_k}, es_{i_{k+1}}\}$. Thus we construct a matrix of coefficients a_i, of $m = k + n$ columns, where each row, between 1 and k, has sum equal to 1, for the rows between $k + 1$ and $k + n$ we define the diagonal equal to 1.

That is,

$$A_{m \times m} = \left(\begin{array}{ccc|c} a_{11} & a_{12} \ldots & a_{im} \\ a_{21} & a_{22} \ldots & a_{2m} \\ \vdots & \vdots & \vdots \\ a_{k1} & a_{k2} \ldots & a_{km} \\ \hline \mathbf{0}_{n \times k} & & \mathbf{I}_{n \times n} \end{array} \right) \tag{4}$$

and

$$H_{k \times m} = \left(\mathbf{I}_{n \times n} \; \mathbf{0}_{n \times k} \right) \tag{5}$$

Considering

$$X_t = x_{1t}, x_{2t}, \ldots, x_{kt}, y_{1t}, y_{2t}, \ldots, y_{kt})^T,$$

a vector of m coordinates, we can define our state-space system by

$$\begin{cases} X_{t+1} = AX_t + q_t \\ Y_t \;\; = HX_t + r_t \end{cases} \tag{6}$$

where the $X_k \in \mathbb{R}^n$ is the state, $Y_k \in \mathbb{R}^m$ is the measure, q_{k-1} and r_k are the process noise of the state and observations with distribution $\mathcal{N}(0, Q_{k-1})$ and $\mathcal{N}(0, R_k)$ respectively, and the distribution of x_0 is the Gaussian $\mathcal{N}(m_0; P_0)$.

2.5   Estimation of Covariance Functions

Consider a spatio-temporal process expressed as an infinite expansion of a moving average model [3],

$$\mathbf{Y}_t(\mathbf{s}) = \mathcal{M}_t(\mathbf{s})\boldsymbol{\beta} + \boldsymbol{\epsilon}_t(\mathbf{s}), \tag{7}$$

with

$$\epsilon_t(\mathbf{s}) = \sum_{j=1}^{\infty} \psi_j \eta_{t-j}(\mathbf{s}), \quad t = 1, \ldots, T$$

where $\left\{ \mathbf{Y}_t(\mathbf{s}) = \left(Y_t^{(1)}\mathbf{s}, \ldots, Y_t^{(L)}\mathbf{s} \right)^T \right\}$, is a space-time Gaussian process L - dimensional, s represents a location in a domain $\mathbf{D} = (x, y)^T \subset \mathbb{R}^2$, $\boldsymbol{\beta} = (\beta_1, \ldots, \beta_p)^T$ $\mathcal{M}_t(\mathbf{s}) = \left(M_t^{(1)}(\mathbf{s}), \ldots, M_t^{(p)}(\mathbf{s}) \right)$ is a vector of parameters, p-dimensional of known covariates, $\{\psi_j\}$ is a sequence of coefficients satisfying $\sum_{j=0}^{\infty} \psi_j^2 < \infty$, and $\{\epsilon_t(\mathbf{s})\}$ is a sequence of temporally independent and spatially stationary Gaussian processes (GP), with $\mathbb{E}(\eta_t(\mathbf{s})) = 0$ and the covariance function

$$C(\eta_t(\mathbf{s}), \eta_t(\tilde{\mathbf{s}})) = C^{\eta}(\|\mathbf{s} - \tilde{\mathbf{s}}\|; \theta), C^{\eta} : [0, \infty) \to \mathbb{R}, \mathbf{s}, \tilde{\mathbf{s}} \in \mathbf{D}$$

where $C^\eta \circ \|.\| : \mathbb{R}^2 \to \mathbb{R}$ is an isotropic covariance function, $\|.\|$ denotes the Euclidean distance, $\circ$ represents a composition, and θ is a parameter vector.

This representation is equivalent to the decomposition of a moving average process $MA(\infty)$ of the error sequence $\epsilon_t(\mathbf{s})$.

We say that a covariance function $C(\mathbf{s}, \tilde{\mathbf{s}})$ is stationary if it only depends on the displacement of $\mathbf{s}$, that is, if we can write $C(\mathbf{s}, \tilde{\mathbf{s}}) = C^0(h)$, for $h = \mathbf{s} - \tilde{\mathbf{s}}$. A covariance is isotropic if it only depends on the distance from $\mathbf{s}$, i.e., $C^d(\mathbf{s}, \tilde{\mathbf{s}}) = C^d(\mathbf{s}, d)$, where $d = \|\mathbf{s} - \tilde{\mathbf{s}}\|$.

A Gaussian process (GP) is a dependent process in which all finite - dimensional distributions are Gaussian and are defined by a function with mean $mu(.)$ and covariance function $C(\cdot, \cdot)$ and is denoted by:

$$\mathbf{Y}_t(\mathbf{s}) \sim GP(\mu(.), C(., .))$$

In the presence of a decomposition MA(∞) in a time-space process defined on (7), the covariance function is defined by:

$$C(\mathbf{s}, \tilde{\mathbf{s}}) = \mathbb{C}ov(\mathbf{Y}_t(\mathbf{s}), \mathbf{Y}_t(\tilde{\mathbf{s}})) = \sum_{i=0}^{\infty} \sum_{j=0}^{\infty} \psi_j \psi_i \mathbb{C}ov(\eta_{t-j}(\mathbf{s}), \eta_{t'-i}(\tilde{\mathbf{s}}))$$

$$= C^\eta(d) \sum_{j=0}^{\infty} \psi_j \psi_{j+|t-t'|}, \quad d = \|\mathbf{s} - \tilde{\mathbf{s}}\|$$

$$= C^\eta(d) K(\Delta t), \quad \Delta t = t - t'$$

where $K(\Delta t)$ is a time covariance function. That is, it can be of one of the following forms

Table 1. Covariance functions

Kernel	$K(x, y)$
Exponential	$\sigma^2 \exp\left(-\frac{|x-y|}{l}\right)$
Squared Exponential	$\sigma^2 \exp\left(-\frac{1}{2} \frac{|x-y|^2}{l^2}\right)$
Matérn	$\sigma^2 \frac{2^{1-\nu}}{\Gamma(\nu)} \left(\frac{|x-y|}{l}\right)^\nu \kappa_\nu \left(\frac{|x-y|}{l}\right)$
Brownian Motion	$\min(x, y)$

In summary, the algorithm can be described as follows:

Algorithm 1. Algorithm to approximate stations

Require: $Coor = \{(lat_i, lon_i)\}_{i=1}^{k}$ station coordinates,
   $\{Y_{ij}\}_{i,j}$ Data observed at the stations,
   $U_0 = (lat_0, long_0)$ Station coordinates to simulate , n stations.
Ensure: $\{Z_{0j}\}_j$ Simulated values for station 0.
   •Generate a set E, of n stations, in the set of convex envelope $Coor$.
   •Find the largest convex polygon containing each of the stations in the set $E \cup \{U_0\}$.
   •Estimate the coefficients of the state-space system, by the Eqs. (4) y (5).
   •Estimating $\{Z_{0j}\}_j$ by Kalman Filter with covariance functions of Table 1.

---

3   Results

In order to achieve this goal we proceeded as follows:

1. Using the coordinates of the 25 stations, excluding station 11(*red), we calculated the convex envelope using the algorithm proposed in [1].
2. We a set of simulated stations, located on the convex envelope, distributed as a regular grid. In the case under study, 20 stations were created, in Fig. 1, they are shown with the symbol (+blue).
3. We generated the coefficient matrix A, as described in Eq. 4.
4. Using the Kalman Filter, we estimated the values of the 20 stations (+blue).
5. Finally, we compared the observed values of the stations identified with 11 (*red) and 3 (+blue).

3.1   Space-Time Prediction

Our main goal is the spatio-temporal modeling of atmospheric indexes, so in order to determine the predictive ability we employ different indexes, in order to determine the performance of the proposed methodology, the following indicators were specifically tested using the differences between the simulated data and the observed data.

For a station i , let $\{x_j\}$ and $\{y_j\}$ be the observed and simulated data series, respectively, for j from 1 to T. Let us denote by $\bar{x}$ and $\bar{y}$, the values of the corresponding means, we consired:

The first of the indexes, the usual Root Mean Square Error (RMSE)

$$RMSE = \sqrt{\sum_{j=1}^{T} \frac{(x_j - y_j)^2}{T}}$$

and percent root mean square error, which we denote by RMSE2,

$$RMSE2 = \sqrt{\frac{1}{T} \sum_{j=1}^{T} \left(\frac{x_j - y_j}{x_j} \right)^2}$$

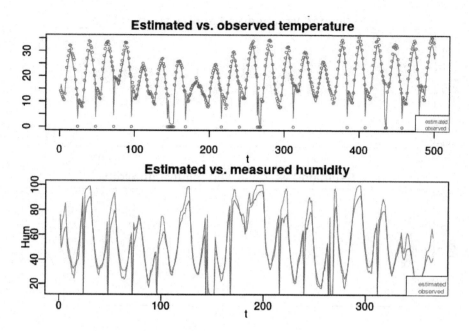

Fig. 3. Estimated vs. observed data for $n = 500$.

We also calculated the normalized mean bias factor (NMBF) [12]

$$NMBF = \begin{cases} \dfrac{\displaystyle\sum_{j=1}^{T} y_j}{\displaystyle\sum_{j=1}^{T} x_j} - 1 & \text{if } \overline{x} \geq \overline{y} \\[3em] 1 - \dfrac{\displaystyle\sum_{j=1}^{T} x_j}{\displaystyle\sum_{j=1}^{T} y_j} & \text{if } \overline{x} < \overline{y} \end{cases}$$

where $s_j = \dfrac{x_j}{\overline{x}}$ and $k_j = exp\left(-\ln\left|\dfrac{y_j}{\overline{y}}\right|\right)$.

Finally, the weighted and unweighted normalized root mean square error (WNNR and NNR) of the normalized coefficients [8] between the normalized ratios of the estimated and observed values.

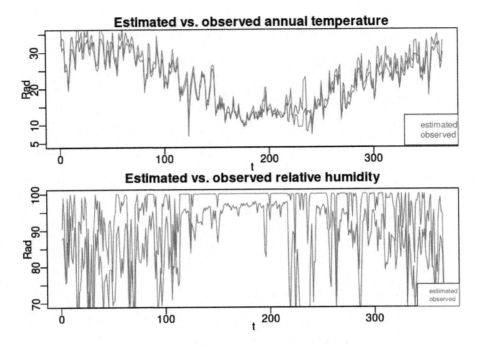

Fig. 4. Estimated vs. observed annual data.

$$WNNR = \frac{\displaystyle\sum_{j=1}^{T} s_j^2 (1 - k_j)^2}{\displaystyle\sum_t s_j k_j} \quad \text{and} \quad NNR = \frac{\displaystyle\sum_{t=1}^{T} (1 - k_j)^2}{\displaystyle\sum_{t=1}^{T} k_j}$$

The error rates obtained for the observations of station 11 (red color) and simulated station 3 (blue color) (see Fig. 3 and Fig. 4) in the estimations are shown in the Table 2.

Table 2. Summary of predictive indexes

	Daily n = 500		Annual n = 360	
	Temperature	Humidity	Temperature	Humidity
RMSE	0.0909	0.4252	0.1785	0.4324
RMSE2	0.0124	0.0150	0.0092	0.0051
WNNR	0.01002	0.0256	0.2735	0.4095
NNR	0.0697	0.0818	0.2529	0.3947
NMBF	0.0402	0.0602	−0.1178	−0.6047

In order to show the variability of the indices, presented in Table 2, 40 simulations were calculated and the results are summarized in Fig. 5.

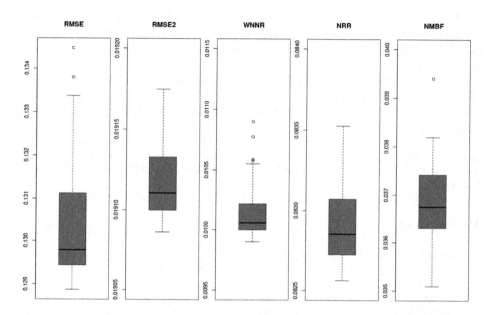

Fig. 5. Boxplot of the errors between observed and estimated temperature measurements.

4   Discussion and Conclusions

The data used and available in Agromet, were discriminated in hourly measurements, during the 365 d of the year 2020. Two time series were considered out of these: the first 500 observations of the year and the maximum daily values during the entire year 2020, of temperature and relative humidity, measured in (°C) and (%) respectively.

With the methodology presented, the values observed at station 11(+blue) were recovered from the values of the 25 stations(+blue), performing an estimation process using the Kalman Filter, with very small errors. In the case of hourly observations, the errors are in order of $5x10^{-2}$ in the case of temperature, and 5×10^{-2} in the case of relative humidity. For the daily maximum measurements, simulated during a year, the approximation order is close to 5×10^{-1}.

In the case of hourly observations, the errors are in the order of 5×10^{-2}, in the case of temperature and 5×10^{-2} in the case of relative humidity and for the daily maximum measurements, simulated during a year, the approximation order is close to 5×10^{-1}. Although the observations show a large variability, as seen in Figs. 3 and 4, they recovered quite well.

On the other hand, repeated simulations showed that the errors have low variability, as shown in Fig. 5, where it is shown that all error rates have variability close to 10^{-3}.

This shows that the simulation of station data, within the convex envelope, represents a very good alternative to the installation of new weather stations, due to the impact on maintenance costs and the approximations that it allows us to generate.

This offers many possibilities for future research to determine which other climatic variables maintain this behavior and can be recovered using the method and to establish conditions on the locations of the stations so that the approximations are acceptable.

Acknowledgement. This work was carried out under the project Statistical Methods for Modeling data generated by Complex Systems REGINV- MATH23-04, Yachay Tech University.

References

1. Berg, M., Ceong, O., Kreveld, M., Overmars, M.: Computational Geometry Algorithms and Applications, 3rd edn. Springer (2008). https://doi.org/10.1007/978-3-540-77974-2
2. Bradley, J.R., Holan, S.H., Wikle, C.K.: Multivariate spatio-temporal models for high-dimensional areal data with application to longitudinal employer-household dynamics. Ann. Appl. Stat. **9**(4), 1761–1791 (2015)
3. Ferreira, G., Mateu, J., Porcu, E.: Spatio-temporal analysis with short- and long-memory dependence: a state-space approach. TEST **27**(1), 221–245 (2017)
4. Ferreira, G., Mateu, J., Porcu, E.: Multivariate Kalman filtering for spatio-temporal processes. Stoch. Env. Res. Risk Assess. **36**, 4337–4354 (2022)
5. Huang, H.-C., Cressie, N.: Spatio-temporal prediction of snow water equivalent using the kalman filter. Computat. Stat. Data Anal. **22**(2), 159–175 (1996)
6. Kalman, R.: A new approach to linear filtering and prediction problems. Trans. ASME. J. Basic Eng. **82**, 35–94 (1960)
7. Kalman, R., Bucy, R.: New results in linear filtering and prediction theory. J. Basic Eng. **83**(1), 95–108 (1961). https://doi.org/10.1115/1.3658902
8. Poli, A., Cirillo, M.: On the use of the normalized mean square error in evaluating dispersion model performance. Atmos. Environ. **27**, 2427–2434 (1993)
9. Sánchez, L., Infante, S., Griffin, V., Rey, D.: Spatio-temporal dynamic model and parallelized ensemble Kalman filter for precipitation data. Brazilian J. Probability Stat. **30**(4), 653–675 (2016)
10. Särkkä, S.: Bayesian Filtering and Smoothing. Cambridge University Press (2013)
11. Soto, J., Infante, S.: Ensemble kalman filter and extended kalman filter for state-parameter dual estimation in mixed effects models defined by a stochastic differential equation. In: Basantes-Andrade, A., Naranjo-Toro, M., Zambrano Vizuete, M., Botto-Tobar, M. (eds.) TSIE 2019. AISC, vol. 1110, pp. 285–300. Springer, Cham (2020). https://doi.org/10.1007/978-3-030-37221-7_24
12. Yu, S., Eder, B., Dennis, R., Chu, S., Schwartz, S.: New unbiased symmetric metrics for evaluation of air quality models. Atmospheric Sci. Lett. **7**, 26–34 (2006)

Parametric Study of a Stochastic SEIR Model for a COVID-19 Post-Pandemic Scenario

Carlos Balsa[1]($\boxtimes$) (ID), Everaldo de Padua[2] (ID), Luan Pinto[2] (ID), and José Rufino[1] (ID)

[1] Research Centre in Digitalization and Intelligent Robotics (CeDRI), Laboratório para a Sustentabilidade e Tecnologia em Regiões de Montanha (SusTEC), Instituto Politécnico de Bragança, Campus de Santa Apolónia, 5300-253 Bragança, Portugal
{balsa,rufino}@ipb.pt
[2] Instituto Politécnico de Bragança, Bragança, Portugal
{a57328,a57329}@alunos.ipb.pt

Abstract. Despite the end of the COVID-19 pandemic was decreed by the WHO, this disease has not disappeared and continues to claim victims. Thus, it remains important to follow up, monitor, and project its evolution in the short term. To that end, mathematical models are a precious tool. Based on its results, it is possible to take preventive measures that minimize the spread of this contagious disease. This study focuses on the stochastic SEIR epidemic model adapted to a post-pandemic scenario. The main factors that influence the spread and containment of the disease are considered, namely, the rates of transmission, vaccination, and quarantine. The results obtained point to a probability of nearly 12% of the appearance of a major epidemic outbreak that could affect a large part of the population. Without vaccination, it is expected that an epidemic outbreak will infect 75% of the population. Therefore, the maintenance of adequate vaccination rates is an essential measure to overcome the loss of immunity from the vaccinated or recovered individuals.

Keywords: COVID-19 · post-pandemic scenario · parametric study · stochastic SEIR model

1 Introduction

The COVID-19 pandemic presented a serious threat to the human population in the years 2021 and 2022. Additionally, despite the fact that the epidemic has been mostly contained in many nations, occasional breakouts are still being reported, highlighting the need for continuous awareness and prudence.

It is well acknowledged that mathematical modeling and computational techniques have shown to be crucial in assisting public health authorities to design appropriate policies and make significant decisions intended to prevent the spread of the COVID-19 disease [5] in such a challenging situation. In this regard, a large number of academic and scientific investigations have been undertaken and published over the last years, with a special emphasis on the mathematical epidemic model Susceptible-Exposed-Infectious-Recovered (SEIR) [2,3,5,10].

T. Guarda et al. (Eds.): ARTIIS 2023, CCIS 1937, pp. 43–57, 2024.
https://doi.org/10.1007/978-3-031-48930-3_4

The SEIR model is a widely accepted framework for describing the spread of an infectious disease. It is based on the concept of compartmentalization, which separates a population into four distinct compartments, corresponding to one of the following states in relation to the disease:

– Susceptible (S): individuals that have not yet been infected with the disease and thus are at risk of contracting it;
– Exposed (E): individuals that have been infected but are not yet infectious;
– Infectious (I): individuals that have developed symptoms and are capable of transmitting the disease to others;
– Recovered (R): individuals that have recovered from the disease.

The model also incorporates a latency period, an important factor for contagious and spreading diseases such as COVID-19 [10]. The latency period is the time elapsed between infection and the onset of symptoms. This characteristic is particularly relevant for COVID-19, which has a latency period of several days.

The SEIR model enables to model the general dynamics of an infectious disease transmission and to estimate several important consequences of the epidemic, such as the number of infection cases in function of time, the peaks of infectious cases or the total proportion of the population that will be affected.

The SEIR model can also be enriched, by including additional compartments that have a significant impact on controlling the disease spread, corresponding to public health measures. In this study, new compartments, such as Vaccinated (V) and Quarantined (Q) individuals, were incorporated in the model. The corresponding control measures were of great importance in controlling the pandemic. Studies published when the appearance of the first vaccines for COVID-19 was outlined showed that an epidemiological outbreak could be prevented by combining a low vaccination rate with the quarantine of infected people [2,3].

In this work the SEIR model is also adapted to the specific context of COVID-19 spreading in a post-pandemic scenario, in which a huge part of the population is regularly vaccinated. Thus, this new epidemiological model considers not only the control measures represented by vaccination and quarantine, but also the loss of immunity by vaccinated or recovered individuals, making these individuals again susceptible to contracting the disease. The new model is based on previous compartmental models proposed in [1–3], adjusted to describe the current epidemiological situation. The resulting model is named SEIQRVD, for Susceptible, Exposed, Infected, Quarantined, Recovered, Vaccinated, and Deceased.

The success of mathematical modeling of epidemics depends greatly on adjusting the parameters of the model to reality. For this study, a thorough literature search was carried out on the values of all the parameters of the SEIQRVD model. For each of them, confidence intervals were collected that reflect their possible variations. Then, a parametric study was conducted in order to determine their impact on a given population and acquire insights on the factors that most influence the dynamics of the spread of the disease and on its prevention.

The parametric study was conducted on a stochastic version of SEIQRVD, also developed for this study. Stochastic models are based on a Monte Carlo process that consists on a large number of repetitions of the random behavior of the population. These models are considered more realistic than deterministic models, because the spread of an infectious disease is a random process that takes place locally through the close contact with infectious individuals [4].

The rest of the paper is organized as follows: in Sect. 2, the SEIQRVD model is introduced, along with the definition of its main parameters; Sect. 3 describes the algorithm in which the stochastic version of the model is based on; Sect. 4 elaborates on the parameter combinations tested; Sect. 5 is devoted to the presentation and discussion of the numerical results of the simulations conducted; Sect. 6 concludes the paper and lays out directions for future work.

2 Epidemiological SEIQRVD Model

The proposed SEIQRVD epidemiological model comprises seven distinct compartments, each one representing a different state relatively to the COVID-19 disease. A compartment contains a fraction of the population with N individuals. The complexity of the model arises from the interdependent relationships between the compartments and the transitions between them. The daily interactions between the different compartments, along with the corresponding rates of transition, are represented in Fig. 1.

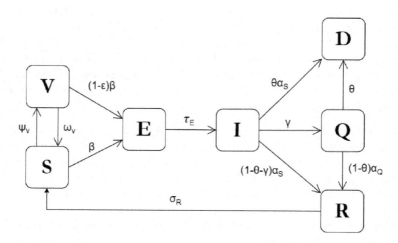

Fig. 1. SEIRDQV Compartment Transition Model.

The variables corresponding to each compartment, expressing the number of individuals of the population that are in a certain condition at day t, are:

- $S(t)$: individuals susceptible to contracting the disease;
- $E(t)$: individuals exposed to the disease but not yet infectious;
- $I(t)$: individuals who are infectious;
- $R(t)$: individuals who have recovered from the disease and are now immune;

– $V(t)$: individuals who have received a vaccine;
– $Q(t)$: individuals who are in quarantine;
– $D(t)$: individuals who have died from the disease.

From a deterministic perspective, the daily dynamic of the SEIQRVD model, illustrated in Fig. 1, is given by the system of ordinary differential equations:

$$
\begin{cases}
\frac{dS}{dt} = \omega_V V + \sigma_R R - \psi_V S - \frac{\beta I}{N} S \\[2mm]
\frac{dE}{dt} = \frac{\beta I}{N}(S + (1 - \varepsilon) V) - \tau_E E \\[2mm]
\frac{dI}{dt} = \tau_E E - \alpha_S (1 - \gamma) I - \gamma I \\[2mm]
\frac{dR}{dt} = \alpha_S (1 - \theta - \gamma) I + \alpha_Q (1 - \theta) Q - \sigma_R R \\[2mm]
\frac{dD}{dt} = \theta \alpha_S I + \theta \alpha_Q Q \\[2mm]
\frac{dV}{dt} = \psi_V S - \frac{\beta I}{N}(1 - \varepsilon) V - \omega_V V \\[2mm]
\frac{dQ}{dt} = \gamma I \alpha_Q Q
\end{cases}
\tag{1}
$$

with the initial conditions $S(0) = S_0, E(0) = E_0, I(0) = I_0, \ R(0) = R_0, D(0) = D_0, V(0) = V_0$ and $Q(0) = Q_0$.

The System (1) models the dynamic of a population with N individuals, in function of the time t (in days). Each equation describes the evolution of the amount of individuals that are in each state (compartment) of the infectious disease. The constants β, α_S, α_Q, γ, θ, ϵ, ψ_V, ω_V, τ_E and σ_R are the parameters of the model, and have the following meaning:

– ψ_V: vaccination rate, represented as the fraction of the population that receives the vaccine daily;
– ω_V: daily rate at which the vaccinated people lose immunity; it is expressed as the inverse of the number of days the vaccine remains effective;
– β: daily rate of transmission of the disease from an infected individual to a susceptible individual;
– ϵ: efficacy of the vaccine, representing the fraction of vaccinated individuals protected from the disease;
– τ_E: average latency period, representing the time between exposure to the disease and the onset of symptoms; it is expressed as the inverse of the latency period, in days;
– α_S: rate of transition from infected to recovered or deceased; it is expressed as the inverse of the infectious period, in days;
– α_Q: rate of transition from quarantined to recovered or deceased; it is expressed as the inverse of the quarantine period, in days;
– γ: fraction of individuals that are daily placed in quarantine;
– θ: fraction of infectious individuals who daily die due to the disease;

– σ_R: rate of loss of natural immunity, representing the fraction of recovered individuals who daily lose immunity.

The values of these parameters will determine the results given by the resolution of system (1). To obtain realistic results, these parameters must also be realistic, since they define how the events occur [6]. Most of the values used in this paper for these constants were collected from updated literature [1, 7]. A dataset of values [8] observed in all the world since the beginning of the epidemic was also used in order to obtain intervals that contain all the possible values that the parameters can currently take.

The method used in this study to define the values of the vaccination rate (ψ_V) and the death rate (θ) was a linear regression generated from the cumulative values available in the dataset [8]. The temporal range considered was the period from January 1 to March 24, 2023. The data are relative to Portugal and are the most up to date at the time of this work.

The quarantine parameters (γ and α_Q) were arbitrarily defined, since in the post-pandemic scenario the quarantine is no longer mandatory in many places.

The values of the transmission rate (β), a crucial parameter, are based on the basic reproduction number report elaborated by the portuguese health authorities [9]. The values of the vaccination protection rate (ω_V), vaccine effectiveness (ϵ), average latency duration (τ_E), recovered or deceased rate (α_S), and rate of loss of natural immunity (σ_R) were all obtained from the literature.

The values, or interval of values, for each parameter of the SEIQRVD model, are shown in Table 1, along with the bibliographic references from which they were collected.

Table 1. Values (or ranges) used for the parameters of the SEIRVQD model.

Parameter	Value(s)	Description	Reference
ψ_V	0.00018559	Vaccination rate	[8]
ω_V	1/180	Vaccine decline rate	[1]
β	0.1885	Transmission contact rate	[9]
ε	[0.903–0.976]	Vaccine efficiency	[1]
τ_E	1/5.2	Average latency period	[11]
α_S	0.0925069	Transition rate for recovered or deceased	[1]
γ	[0–0.5]	Quarantine rate	Arbitrary
θ	6.555×10^{-7}	Fraction of individuals who die from the disease	[8]
α_Q	0	Rate of quarantined who recovered or died	Arbitrary
σ_R	1/240	Natural immunity loss rate	[7]

3 Stochastic SEIQRVD Model

Stochastic models are mathematical representations aimed to capture the inherent unpredictability and uncertainty in diverse systems and processes. These models provide an effective framework for understanding and interpreting complex events influenced by probabilistic aspects.

In order to incorporate randomness factors that are inherent to the COVID-19 spread, a stochastic model was developed from the deterministic model represented by System (1). The stochastic model includes the same parameters of the deterministic model. However, their values are not fixed. Instead, they are randomly generated from distributions whose average values are those in Table 1.

On the other hand, contacts between people in the community occur randomly, between any member of the population, that is, the population is considered to be homogeneously mixed. Infectious individuals (I) have adequate contact to transmit the disease with other individuals randomly in time, according to a Poisson process with intensity β. Each contact is made with an individual randomly selected from the community. Any susceptible that receives such contact immediately becomes exposed (E) for a random period that follows an exponential distribution with mean $1/\sigma_E$. The infectious periods are also independent and exponentially distributed with a mean $1/\alpha_S$. The quarantine (γ) and death (θ) rates, as well as the quarantine period, are assumed to be constant.

The proposed stochastic SEIRVQD model is described by Algorithm 1 that outlines the main steps involved in simulating the spread of the disease and the various factors that influence the transmission dynamics. The population of N individuals is represented by a two-dimensional array of size N. The first dimension represents the individual state (S, E, I, R, Q, V or D), and the second dimension indicates the number of days in this state. Furthermore, as the model depicts a post-pandemic scenario, most of the population is initially immunized. But, even in a post-pandemic scenario, the initial presence of sick individuals, as well as susceptible and vaccinated persons, is required for the dynamics to occur. These states are randomly distributed within the population array.

Infectious individuals have contact, adequate to transmit the disease, with other individuals, randomly in time, according to a Poisson process with intensity β. When a contact occurs between an infected and a susceptible individual, this individual becomes exposed. However, when an infected and a vaccinated individuals interact, the vaccinated has a probability $1 - \epsilon$ of becoming exposed. This fact corresponds to the lack of efficiency that vaccination sometimes presents.

Similarly to the algorithm presented in [3], the stochastic SEIRVQD model features two methods for evolving states: i) interaction, which is defined by the Poisson distribution; and ii) the time of permanence in the exposed and infected states, which is defined by the exponential distribution with parameter given by one of the values shown in Table 1.

4   Parametric Evaluation

The impact of the main epidemic factors is studied through the corresponding stochastic model parameters: the rates of infection (β), vaccination (ψ_V), and quarantine (γ). These parameters are varied across a selected range of values and Algorithm 1 is executed for certain values combinations. Each run corresponds to a simulation of the spread of the disease in a population of N individuals.

Algorithm 1. Stochastic SEIRDVQ model

Require: N, I_0, V_0, max_{days}, ψ_V, ω_V, β, ϵ, τ_E, γ, θ, α_Q, σ_R
Ensure: res matrix, containing the number of individuals in a state by time in days
1: **for** $t \leftarrow 1...N_{rep}$ **do**
2:     choose V_0 random individuals and the relative vaccinated period
3:     choose I_0 random individuals and the corresponding infectious period
4:     **for** $t \leftarrow 1...max_{days}$ **do**
5:         **for** $n \leftarrow 1$ to N **do**
6:             $latency_n \leftarrow latency_n - 1$
7:             **if** $state_n$ = susceptible or vaccinated **then**
8:                 randomly choose β, in N, individuals to contact   ▷ excluding
quarantined and dead
9:                 **if** any contated people = infected **then**
10:                     **if** $state_n$ = susceptible or randval $> \epsilon$ **then**
11:                         $state_n \leftarrow$ exposed   ▷ with Poisson random τ_E days
12:                     **end if**
13:                 **else**
14:                     **if** $state_n$ = susceptible **and** randval $< \psi_v$ **then**
15:                         $state_n \leftarrow$ vaccinated
16:                     **else if** $latency_n = 0$ **then** $state_n \leftarrow$ susceptible
17:                     **end if**
18:                 **end if**
19:             **else if** $state_n$ = exposed **then**
20:                 **if** $latency_n = 0$ **then**
21:                     **if** randval $< \sigma_R$ **then**
22:                         $state_n \leftarrow$ infected   ▷ with exp. random τ_E days
23:                     **end if**
24:                 **end if**
25:             **else if** $state_n$ = infected **then**
26:                 **if** $latency_n = 0$ **then** $state_n \leftarrow$ recovered   ▷ with exp. random σ_R
days
27:                 **end if**
28:                 **if** rand $< \gamma$ **then** $state_n \leftarrow$ quarantine ▷ with exp. random α_Q days
29:                 **end if**
30:                 **if** rand $< \theta$ **then** $state_n \leftarrow$ died
31:                 **end if**
32:             **else if** $state_n$ = recovered **then**
33:                 **if** $latency_n = 0$ **then** $state_n \leftarrow$ susceptible
34:                 **end if**
35:             **else if** $state_n$ = quarantine **then**
36:                 **if** $latency_n = 0$ **then**
37:                     $state_n \leftarrow$ recovered   ▷ with exp. random σ_R days
38:                 **end if**
39:                 **if** rand $< \theta$ **then** $state_n \leftarrow$ died
40:             **end if**
41:         **end if**
42:     **end for**
43:     **end for**
44: **end for**

The motivation for the choice of those parameters is the intrinsic random-ness of the evolution of their values. Consider, for instance, the transmission rate (β), that can be estimated through the datasets made available by the portuguese health authorities, namely information on the basic reproduction number. This parameter has assumed different values over the pandemic period and still changes in the post-pandemic scenarios, as is reported monthly [9].

Regarding the vaccination rate (ψ_V), it is determined based on the new vac-cinations per day, and changes depending on the country or region, the vaccine availability, the health governmental system, as well as other factors.

With the end of the pandemic, the mandatory quarantine of the infected individuals disappeared. But self-isolation by the infected is a fact that is verified in some situations. Thus, the effect of the quarantine rate (γ) is also analysed.

The values of the parameters used in the simulations were those of Table 1, except for ψ_V, β, ε and γ. The values used for these are shown in Table 2.

Table 2. Values of ψ_V, β, ε and γ used in the simulations.

Parameter	Value(s)
ψ_V	{0, 0.00018559, 0.00151, 0.00301, 0.00451, 0.00621}
β	{0.1423, 0.1610, 0.1885, 0.3026, 0.4166}
ε	0.9395 (average of the extreme values of its range in Table 1)
γ	{0, 0.1, 0.2, 0.3, 0.4, 0.5} (range from Table 1 with a step of 0.1)

The first and last values for ψ_V are of 2023 (also in Table 1) and 2021, respec-tively [8]. The values in between were obtained via interpolation, corresponding to 25%, 50% and 75% of the difference between the values of 2021 and 2023.

The values for β include the current one, from Table 1 (0.1885), and others that surround it. These were either extracted or extrapolated from [9]: the first two values pertain to the years 2021 and 2022; the 5th is specific to 2020; the 4th value is an interpolation (average) of the current value and the one from 2020.

Considering the cardinality of the sets of values for ψ_V, β, and γ, a total of 17 different combinations (6+6+5) of these parameters were tested, by varying each parameter alone and fixing the other two parameters: thus, when varying γ, $\psi_V = 0.00018559$ (value from Table 1) and $\beta = 0.1885$ (value from Table 1); then, when varying ψ_V, $\gamma = 0$ (left value from its range in Table 1), and $\beta = 0.1885$; finally, when varying β, $\gamma = 0$ and $\psi_V = 0.00018559$.

A population of $N = 20000$ individuals was considered for the simulations. It was always assumed an initial number $I_0 = 80$ of infected individuals, an initial number $V_0 = 19600$ of vaccinated, and an initial number $S_0 = 320$ of susceptibles. These numbers were defined according to current data on Portugal, where 98% of the population is vaccinated [7]. Other initial conditions that were also kept the same were $E_0 = 0$, $R_0 = 0$, $D_0 = 0$, and $Q_0 = 0$. Each simulation considers the evolution of the population over one year (max$_{days}$ = 365), and was repeated $N_{rep} = 1000$ times (for each particular combination of model parameters).

It is worth mentioning that the overall number of combinations of β, $\gamma = 0$ and ψ_V, corresponding to $6 \times 6 \times 5 = 180$, is more than $10 \times$ the 17 combinations tested. But considering that each one takes $\approx 2\,\text{h}$ to be tested in the computational system used in this work (see Sect. 5), and so testing all 180 combinations would take 15 days of computational time, it was considered enough, for the exploratory goals of this research, to perform a limited parametric study, reserving thorough parametric tests and bigger populations for future work.

5   Simulations Results

This section presents the results obtained by the simulations conducted, based on an implementation of the Algorithm 1 in MATLAB. The computational environment used for this work was a virtual machine from the CeDRI cluster, assigned 32 virtual CPU-cores of a Intel Xeon W-3365 CPU and running Linux Ubuntu 20.04. Using this execution environment, each simulation (including its 1000 repetitions) of the spread of the disease in a population of 20000 individuals, during 365 days, takes an average of 118 min fully using the 32 CPU-cores.

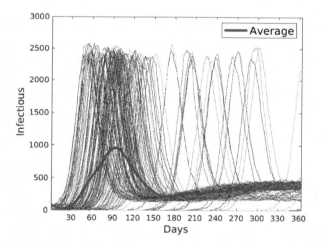

Fig. 2. Evolution of the number of infectious individuals in the 129 epidemic outbreaks that occur in 1000 repetitions of the simulation for $\psi_V = 0.00018559$, $\beta = 0.1885$, $\gamma = 0$.

Figure 2 shows selected results of 1000 repetitions of the stochastic simulation of the evolution of the population for the specific combination of parameters $\psi_V = 0.00018559$, $\beta = 0.1885$, $\gamma = 0$. Specifically, out of the 1000 repetitions of the simulation, only in 129 of them an epidemic outbreak has occurred. Thus, only the corresponding 129 curves relative to the infectious individuals are depicted in Fig. 2, along with the corresponding curve with the average values of the number of infected people on each day (thick red line). In the remaining 871 repetitions, the number of infected quickly decreases to zero. Therefore, the probability of the occurrence of an epidemic outbreak is 12.9%.

It can also be observed that the epidemic outbreak can occur at different times throughout the year. However, for a large number of simulation repetitions, the outbreak occurs around 100 days, where the curve of average values reaches its maximum. Moreover, all the peaks of the infected curves occur very close to 2500 individuals and, after reaching the peak, the number of infected people decreases and stabilizes below 500 individuals, with a slight upward trend.

Figure 3.a) shows the histograms of the total number of infected over the year, for all 1000 possible evolutions of the epidemic, and Fig. 3.b) contains the cases corresponding to a major outbreak. The number of repetitions that lead to a minor outbreak (the number of infectious individuals decreases to zero in a reduced number of days) have a frequency of 87.1%, indicating that this event is the one that has more probability to occur. In this case, the total number of infected does not exceed the initial one ($I_0 = 80$). In turn, the probability of a large outbreak occurring is 12.9%, and can affect between 5000 to 30000 individuals. The histogram for the major outbreak (Fig. 3.b)) shows that, in such case, the more probable number of infected individuals is near 25000.

a) Minor and major outbreak   a) Major outbreak

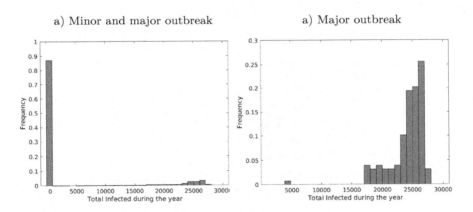

Fig. 3. Histograms of the total number of infected individuals along one year, for $\psi_V = 0.00018559$, $\beta = 0.1885$, $\gamma = 0$.

Figure 4 presents the evolution over a year of the average number of individuals in each compartment of the SEIQRVD model, for the same stochastic simulation previously described. A continuous decrease in the number of vaccinated individuals and consequent increase in susceptibles can be observed. From 60 days onwards, the number of susceptibles begins to decrease due to the increase in the number of infected people, which reaches its peak at around 100 days. From approximately 200 days onwards, there is a stabilization in the number of infected and recovered people. There is also a continuous increase in the number of susceptibles in proportion to the decrease in the number of vaccinated.

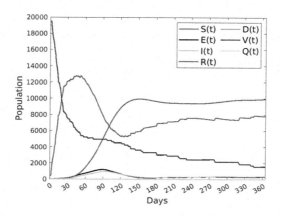

Fig. 4. Average number of individuals in each compartment, for $\psi_V = 0.00018559$, $\beta = 0.1885$, $\gamma = 0$.

The transmission contact rate (β) determines the transition from the susceptible to infected individuals. As such, it is one of the most important parameters in the epidemics dynamics. Its value determines the growth in the infected individuals. Figure 5 represents the results of simulations with the different values of the transmission rate (β) from Table 2, considering $\psi_V = 0.00018559$ and $\gamma = 0$.

Figure 5.a) depicts the evolution of the average number of infectious, and Fig. 5.b) shows the evolution of the average number of susceptibles. It can be observed a clear decrease in the infected peak with the decrease in β. When the infectious transmission rate assumes the maximum value $(\beta = 0.4166)$, there is a peak of infected people that reaches about 1700 individuals. When it takes its minimum value $(\beta = 0.1423)$, the peak of infected only reaches less than 600 individuals. In turn, the susceptibles increase in inverse proportion to the number of infected. The higher the β, the lower the number of susceptibles.

The effects of the vaccination rate (ψ_V) are depicted in Fig. 6. Figure 6.a) represents the evolution of the average number of infectious individuals in function of ψ_v. It turns out that the peak height of infected people directly depends on the vaccination rate. The higher the vaccination rate, the lower the peak. This is because there are fewer individuals susceptible to contract the infection, given that, as can be seen in the Fig. 6.b), the higher the vaccination rate, the lower the average number of susceptibles. Also, the higher the vaccination rate, the lower the level of stabilization of the number of susceptibles.

The probability of the total number of infected individuals over a year is depicted in the histograms of the Fig. 6.c) and 6.d). Figure 6.c) corresponds to $\psi_V = 0$ and Fig. 6.d) to $\psi_V = 6.21 \times 10^{-3}$. It is observed that increasing the vaccination rate reduces the probability of a large outbreak occurring. Without vaccination $(\psi_V = 0)$, there is almost a 30% probability that nearly 15000 people will be infected. But with a relatively small vaccination rate $(\psi_V = 6.21 \times 10^{-3})$,

a) Infectious   b) Susceptibles

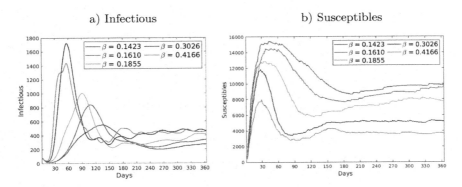

Fig. 5. Effects of the infectious transmission rate (β) on the average number of infectious and susceptibles individuals, considering $\psi_V = 0.00018559$ and $\gamma = 0$.

a) Infectious   b) Susceptibles

c) $\psi_V = 0$ d) $\psi_V = 6.21 \times 10^{-3}$

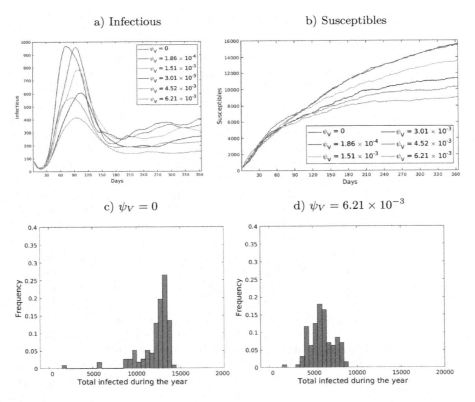

Fig. 6. Effects of the vaccination rate (ψ_V) on the average number of infectious and susceptibles individuals, and on the histograms of the total number of infected individuals, considering $\beta = 0.1885$ and $\gamma = 0$.

the total number with more probability to be infected (about 20%) is reduced to a value close to 5000. In the histogram of Fig. 3.a), it can also been observed that for $\psi_V = 0.00018559$ the total number of infected people is reduced to zero with a probability of about 88%.

Figure 7.a) shows the influence of the fraction of infectious individuals that are quarantined. It can be seen that this rate has a direct effect on the size of the epidemic outbreak. The increase in the quarantine rate leads to a reduction in the average size of the infectious peak and also to the lowering of the stabilization level of the number of infected people. On the other hand, as can be seen in Fig. 7.b), the increase in the rate of quarantine of infectious individuals leads to an increase in the average number of susceptibles due to the fact that there are fewer contagions.

a) Infectious   b) Susceptibles

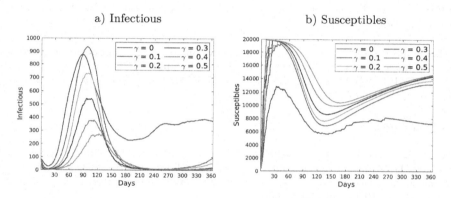

Fig. 7. Effects of the quarantine rate (γ) on the average number of infectious and susceptibles individuals, considering $\psi_V = 0.00018559$ and $\beta = 0.1885$.

6   Conclusion

This work presents a parametric study of the spread of the infectious disease COVID-19. A stochastic epidemiological model is proposed for modelling the spread of the disease in a given population with 20000 individuals. The model is adapted to the specificities of a post-pandemic scenario, by accounting for the effect of vaccination and loss of immunity. Furthermore, even though the model was created keeping in mind the COVID-19 pandemic, it can be easily adapted to the spread of other infectious diseases.

Starting from a population with a vaccination coverage of 98%, the risk of a major epidemic outbreak during the first year is about 12% if the actual vaccination rate is maintained. If there is no vaccination, an epidemic outbreak is expected that will infect about 15000 people. These results show that it is still important to monitor the evolution of the disease. The loss of immunity on the part of vaccinated and recovered individuals after a certain period makes it important to continue vaccinating to prevent the spread of the disease. To that end, the vaccination rate has to compensate for the rate of loss of immunity.

The results indicate that quarantine is still a good option to prevent the disease spread. However, as this preventive measure is not mandatory, being left to the individual decision of the infected person, in reality its implementation will be reduced.

Prevention measures must also take into account the transmission rates of contagion. This parameter is what most influences the spread of the disease in the population. In fact, this parameter will depend on the variant of the virus responsible for the infection.

In the future we intend to simulate the evolution of bigger populations with a large number of repetitions of the stochastic model proposed. Effectively, a high number of repetitions can better describe all possibles effects of the randomness of the pandemic dynamic.

Acknowledgements. The authors are grateful to the Foundation for Science and Technology (FCT, Portugal) for financial support through national funds FCT/MCTES (PIDDAC) CeDRI (UIDB/05757/2020 and UIDP/05757/2020) and SusTEC (LA/P/0007/2021).

References

1. Acuña-Zegarra, M.A., Díaz-Infante, S., Baca-Carrasco, D., Olmos-Liceaga, D.: COVID-19 optimal vaccination policies: a modeling study on efficacy, natural and vaccine-induced immunity responses. Math. Biosci. **337**, 108614 (2021). https://doi.org/10.1016/j.mbs.2021.108614
2. Balsa, C., Guarda, T., Lopes, I., Rufino, J.: Deterministic and stochastic simulation of the COVID-19 epidemic with the SEIR model. In: 2021 16th Iberian Conference on Information Systems and Technologies (CISTI). IEEE, June 2021. https://doi.org/10.23919/cisti52073.2021.9476595
3. Balsa, C., Lopes, I., Guarda, T., Rufino, J.: Computational simulation of the COVID-19 epidemic with the SEIR stochastic model. Comput. Math. Organ. Theor. (2021). https://doi.org/10.1007/s10588-021-09327-y
4. Britton, T.: Stochastic epidemic models: a survey. Math. Biosci. **225**(1), 24–35 (2010)
5. Deng, B., et al.: Mathematical models supporting control of COVID-19. China CDC Wkly. **4**(40), 895–901 (2022). https://doi.org/10.46234/ccdcw2022.186
6. Hethcote, H.W.: The mathematics of infectious diseases. SIAM Rev. **42**(4), 599–653 (2000)
7. Malato, J., et al.: Stability of hybrid versus vaccine immunity against BA.5 infection over 8 months. Lancet Infect. Dis. **23**(2), 148–150 (2023). https://doi.org/10.1016/s1473-3099(22)00833-7
8. Mathieu, E., et al.: Coronavirus pandemic (COVID-19). Our World in Data (2020). https://ourworldindata.org/coronavirus
9. Serviço Nacional de Saúde - Portuguese Ministry of Health.: Covid-19: curva epidémica e parâmetros de transmissibilidade, June 2023. https://www.insa.min-saude.pt/category/areas-de-atuacao/epidemiologia/covid-19-curva-epidemica-e-parametros-de-transmissibilidade/

10. Widyaningsih, P., Saputro, D.R.S., Nugroho, A.W.: Susceptible exposed infected recovery (SEIR) model with immigration: equilibria points and its application. In: AIP Conference Proceedings (2018). https://doi.org/10.1063/1.5054569
11. Xin, H., et al.: Estimating the latent period of coronavirus disease 2019 (COVID-19). Clin. Infect. Dis. **74**(9), 1678–1681 (2021). https://doi.org/10.1093/cid/ciab746

A Simple Mathematical Model to Steering Oceanic Debris to a Targeted Region

Carlos Balsa[1]([✉]) [iD], M. Victoria Otero-Espinar[2] [iD], and Sílvio Gama[3] [iD]

[1] Research Centre in Digitalization and Intelligent Robotics (CeDRI) and Laboratório para a Sustentabilidade e Tecnologia em Regiões de Montanha (SusTEC), Instituto Politécnico de Bragança, 5300-253 Bragança, Portugal
balsa@ipb.pt

[2] Departamento de Estatística, Análise Matemática e Optimización, Universidade de Santiago de Compostela and Galician Center for Mathematical Research and Technology (CITMAga), 15782 Santiago de Compostela, Spain
mvictoria.otero@usc.es

[3] Centro de Matemática da Universidade do Porto, Departamento de Matemática, Faculdade de Ciências, Universidade do Porto, Rua do Campo Alegre s/n, 4169-007 Porto, Portugal
smgama@fc.up.pt

Abstract. In this article, a simplified mathematical model is presented to depict the process of collecting ocean debris. The responsible autonomous vehicles for transporting the trash are represented as passive particles, while the ocean current is simulated by the movement of point vortices on a sphere. To ensure the autonomy of the vehicles, a system of piecewise constant controls is employed, using a limited number of predetermined switching points that determine their trajectories. Each control incurs an energy cost that is aimed to be minimized. This minimization is achieved by solving a nonlinear optimization problem on the spherical surface. The initial findings indicate the existence of multiple possible trajectories for autonomous vehicles.

Keywords: Ocean Pollution · Computation in Earth Sciences · Vortex Dynamics · Passive Tracer · Non-linear Optimization

1 Introduction

Plastic pollution of the oceans is a growing environmental crisis that requires immediate attention. According to estimates, approximately eight million tons of plastic waste are introduced into the oceans every year [11]. This excessive amount of plastic waste has devastating effects on marine life and ecosystems. Plastic pollution is also damaging fragile habitats such as coral reefs [13]. Initiatives such as the Ocean Cleanup Project aim to rid the oceans of plastic waste using innovative technologies [1]. The article [20] suggests that, the Ocean Cleanup's recommended method of utilizing 29 plastic collectors to track microplastic movement and density in the ocean, indicates that cleanup initiatives should emphasize addressing microplastic flow in coastal areas instead of focusing solely on regions where plastic waste gathers.

© The Author(s), under exclusive license to Springer Nature Switzerland AG 2024
T. Guarda et al. (Eds.): ARTIIS 2023, CCIS 1937, pp. 58–70, 2024.
https://doi.org/10.1007/978-3-031-48930-3_5

The absorption of ocean debris (for example, microplastics) by marine species has an influence on agriculture [10], and hence poses a risk to human health, according to [19]. Indeed, ocean pollution has an impact on agricultural techniques that rely on marine fertilizers (e.g., fish, seaweed, etc.).

In the work presented here, we will assume an idealized scenario where garbage collection is done by a set of autonomous vehicles that are initially located where the garbage has a higher density. Let's assume that the autonomous vehicles are relatively small, such that they can be treated as passive particles, meaning they do not alter the local structure of the velocity field of the flow.

Once the holds of these autonomous vehicles are full, they must travel to a specific area/location to deposit the collected material there. The movement of these vehicles use the ocean current as the main source of displacement, as well as have a system of piecewise constant controls, based on a small number of pre-defined switching points, whose sum of the squares of the amplitudes (objective function) is minimal. Here, the motion of point vortices on a sphere generates the ocean current.

The relevance of these point vortices stems from their ability to provide a simplified approximation of specific geophysical flows. These flows exhibit long-term persistence and are influenced by the Earth's curvature [21]. Vortex point models provide answers to numerous studies concerning the fundamental dynamics of atmospheric flows [18]. Point vortex conceptual models are utilized to identify and analyze physical phenomena that influence the structure and interactions of atmospheric and oceanic vortices [17].

Moreover, point vortices have recently been used in the modelling of pesticide dispersion in agricultural problems [12,22]. The presence of boundaries can also be addressed for path planning of an autonomous underwater vehicle like in [7] for steady flows, and in [8] for in a flow with tidal variations.

This work focuses on optimizing the displacement of a set of passive particle (autonomous vehicles) interacting with vortices on the surface of a sphere. More precisely, our focus lies in determining the ideal relocation of this group, specifically on the sphere, between two fixed regions, by minimizing the energy expended on moving each particle within a predetermined time frame required for the relocation.

Similar to previous studies [2,5], we tackle this problem by treating the displacement of the passive particle as an optimization problem. To accomplish this, we employ a direct numerical approach.

The provided time limit T for displacement is divided into n sub-intervals, where the controls remain constant during each sub-interval. To solve the ensuing nonlinear programming (NLP) problem, we employ numerical methods with the `fmincon` function from the Matlab Optimization Toolbox [16]. This function grants the flexibility to choose between the interior point method or the active set method for optimization [3,4].

The article is structured as follows: Sect. 2 introduces the equations that model the dynamics of a passive particle and the vortex points on a sphere. Section 3 presents the numerical method used to solve the optimal control problem involved in determining passive particle trajectories. Section 4 discusses the application of the mathematical model to the problem of ocean debris removal. The analysis includes cases where ocean currents are induced by one or two vortices. Finally, the article concludes with some final considerations in Sect. 5.

2   Point Vortices and Passive Particles on a Spherical Surface

The dynamics of N point vortices on a sphere, with their initial positions specified in spherical coordinates at $t = 0$, is described by the following system of ordinary differential equations ($i = 1, 2, \ldots, N$):

$$\dot{\theta}_i = -\frac{1}{4\pi R^2} \sum_{\substack{j=1 \\ j \neq i}}^{N} k_j \frac{\sin(\theta_j) \sin(\phi_i - \phi_j)}{1 - \cos(\gamma_{ij})}, \tag{1}$$

$$\dot{\phi}_i = \frac{1}{4\pi R^2} \sum_{\substack{j=1 \\ j \neq i}}^{N} k_j \frac{\sin(\theta_i) \cos(\theta_j) - \cos(\theta_i) \sin(\theta_j) \cos(\phi_i - \phi_j)}{\sin(\theta_i) \, (1 - \cos(\gamma_{ij}))}. \tag{2}$$

The present study is focused on a sphere with a constant radius indicated as R. The colatitude angle, denoted as θ, varies from 0 (at the North Pole) to π (at the South Pole) and corresponds to the angle formed between the radius passing through the North Pole, located at $(0, 0, R)$, and the radius passing through the vortex. The longitude angle ϕ lies within the interval $[0, 2\pi)$ and denotes the angular difference between the prime meridian and the meridian passing through the vortex position. Furthermore, γ_{ij} represents the central angle between the ith and jth vortex points and can be defined as follows:

$$\cos(\gamma_{ij}) = \cos(\theta_i) \cos(\theta_j) + \sin(\theta_i) \sin(\theta_j) \cos(\phi_i - \phi_j). \tag{3}$$

Equations (1) and (2) can be expressed more concisely using the Bogomolov notation [6] as follows:

$$\dot{\theta}_i = -\frac{1}{4\pi R^2} \sum_{\substack{j=1 \\ j \neq i}}^{N} k_j \frac{\alpha_{ij}}{1 - \cos(\gamma_{ij})}, \quad \dot{\phi}_i = \frac{1}{4\pi R^2} \sum_{\substack{j=1 \\ j \neq i}}^{N} k_j \frac{\beta_{ij}}{\sin(\theta_i) \, (1 - \cos(\gamma_{ij}))}, \tag{4}$$

with $\alpha_{ij} = \sin(\theta_j) \sin(\phi_i - \phi_j)$ and $\beta_{ij} = \sin(\theta_i) \cos(\theta_j) - \cos(\theta_i) \sin(\theta_j) \cos(\phi_i - \phi_j)$.

By definition, a point vortex with zero circulation is referred to as a passive particle. Hence, the motion of a system consisting of a single passive particle located at coordinates (θ_p, ϕ_p) and being advected by N point vortices, follows the equations Eqs. (1)–(2), with the additional equations that describe the behavior of the passive particle:

$$\dot{\theta}_p = -\frac{1}{4\pi R^2} \sum_{j=1}^{N} k_j \frac{\sin(\theta_j) \sin(\phi_p - \phi_j)}{1 - \cos(\gamma_{pj})}, \tag{5}$$

$$\dot{\phi}_p = \frac{1}{4\pi R^2} \sum_{j=1}^{N} k_j \frac{\cos(\theta_j) - \cot(\theta_p) \sin(\theta_j) \cos(\phi_p - \phi_j)}{1 - \cos(\gamma_{pj})}. \tag{6}$$

After applying appropriate initial conditions, we can introduce a time reparametrization $(\tau := t/R^2)$ in Eqs. (1)–(2) and (5)–(6). This allows us to set $R = 1$ throughout the subsequent analysis.

3   Numerical Solution of the Control Problem

The control problem at hand is derived from Eqs. (5)–(6), where we augment their right-hand sides with the angular controls u_θ and u_ϕ :

$$\dot{\theta}_p = -\frac{1}{4\pi} \sum_{j=1}^{N} k_j \, \frac{\sin(\theta_j)\sin(\phi_p - \phi_j)}{1 - \cos(\gamma_{pj})} + u_\theta, \tag{7}$$

$$\dot{\phi}_p = \frac{1}{4\pi} \sum_{j=1}^{N} k_j \, \frac{\cos(\theta_j) - \cot(\theta_p)\sin(\theta_j)\cos(\phi_p - \phi_j)}{1 - \cos(\gamma_{pj})} + u_\phi. \tag{8}$$

The function that we seek to minimize is

$$f(\mathbf{U}) = \int_0^T \|\mathbf{U}\|^2 \, dt, \tag{9}$$

where $\mathbf{U} = (u_\theta \; u_\phi)$, T is the time that the passive particle has to make the displacement from an initial point P_0 to the end point P_f. The displacement has to be done in exactly T units of time. The objective behind minimizing (9) is to find out the most effective strategy for guiding the particle from its initial point (P_0) to the final point (P_f) within the given time constraint T. This optimization for cost reduction has been studied in previous literature [3, 4, 14, 15].

The discretized problem is then solved using the Matlab function `fmincon` (as in [4]) with the objective function:

$$f_n = \Delta t \left(\|\mathbf{u}_0\|^2 + \|\mathbf{u}_1\|^2 + \ldots + \|\mathbf{u}_{n-1}\|^2 \right). \tag{10}$$

The method employed here is the discretization of the function (9) using the rule of rectangles. For constrained optimization, the solver offers multiple algorithms, including the interior point and active set methods, which are documented in [16]. Within each subinterval, the vortices' dynamics are integrated using the numerical scheme of fourth-order Runge-Kutta [9].

3.1   Transport Dynamics of a Passive Particle by a Single Vortex

For the scenario of the one vortex problem ($N = 1$), with the vortex positioned at the North Pole of the sphere and having a circulation of k, the motion of the passive particle is described by the following dynamics:

$$\begin{cases} \dot{\theta}_p = u_\theta, \\ \dot{\phi}_p = \frac{k}{4\pi} \frac{1}{1 - \cos(\theta_p)} + u_\phi, \end{cases} \tag{11}$$

given the initial condition $P_0 = (\theta_{p0}, , \phi_{p0})$. The variables u_θ and u_ϕ correspond to the angular controls exerted on the passive particle.

3.2 Transport Dynamics of a Passive Particle by Two Vortices

In the two vortices ($N = 2$) problem, the dynamics of the vortices positions $V_1(\tau) = (\theta_1, \phi_1)$ and $V_2(\tau) = (\theta_2, \phi_2)$ are given by

$$
\begin{cases}
\dot{\theta}_1 = -\frac{k_2}{4\pi} \frac{\sin(\theta_2)\sin(\phi_1-\phi_2)}{1-\cos(\gamma_{12})} \\[2mm]
\dot{\phi}_1 = -\frac{k_2}{4\pi} \frac{\cos(\theta_2)-\cot(\theta_1)\sin(\theta_2)\cos(\phi_1-\phi_2)}{\sin(\theta_1)(1-\cos(\gamma_{12}))} \\[2mm]
\dot{\theta}_2 = -\frac{k_1}{4\pi} \frac{\sin(\theta_1)\sin(\phi_2-\phi_1)}{1-\cos(\gamma_{21})} \\[2mm]
\dot{\phi}_2 = -\frac{k_1}{4\pi} \frac{\cos(\theta_1)-\cot(\theta_2)\sin(\theta_1)\cos(\phi_2-\phi_2)}{\sin(\theta_2)(1-\cos(\gamma_{21}))}
\end{cases}
\tag{12}
$$

with the given initial conditions $V_1(0) = (\theta_{10}, \phi_{10})$ and $V_2(0) = (\theta_{20}, \phi_{20})$. The value of $\cos(\gamma_{12})$ and $\cos(\gamma_{21})$ are computed in agreement with Eq. (3).

The interaction between the two vortices and the control significantly influences the dynamics of the passive particle, as depicted in

$$
\begin{cases}
\dot{\theta}_p = -\frac{1}{4\pi}\left(k_1 \frac{\sin(\theta_1)\sin(\phi_p-\phi_1)}{1-\cos(\gamma_{p1})} + k_2 \frac{\sin(\theta_2)\sin(\phi_p-\phi_2)}{1-\cos(\gamma_{p2})}\right) + u_\theta \\[2mm]
\dot{\phi}_p = \frac{1}{4\pi}\left(k_1 \frac{\cos(\theta_1)-\cot(\theta_p)\sin(\theta_1)\cos(\phi_p-\phi_1)}{1-\cos(\gamma_{p1})} + k_2 \frac{\cos(\theta_2)-\cot(\theta_p)\sin(\theta_2)\cos(\phi_p-\phi_2)}{1-\cos(\gamma_{p2})}\right) + u_\phi
\end{cases}
\tag{13}
$$

with the initial conditions $P_0 = (\theta_{p0}, \phi_{p0})$. As in the previous problem, the control applied to the passive particle is represented by the vector $\mathbf{U} = (u_\theta \ u_\phi)$.

4 Application Problem

As mentioned in the Introduction, the dynamics of passive particles induced by vortex points is used in this work to model the dynamics of a set of n_p trash collectors from a garbage patch located at a given point P_0 of the sphere. We consider all trash collectors with equal loads. These particles are transported one by one to a point P_f on the sphere for further processing (recycling, storage, etc.).

The initial location of the n_p trash particles is randomly generated in a square, centered on the point $C_0 = \left(\frac{2\pi}{3}, 0\right)$, with 0.15 units on a side.

The destination point of trash particles is $P_f = \left(\frac{\pi}{3}, \pi\right)$. The particle is considered to have reached the destination if its position $P(T)$ is at a distance from P_f less than 0.01, i.e.

$$
\|P(T) - P_f\| < 0.01.
$$

The trajectories were determined by the method described in Sect. 3 in which the dynamics of each particle are given by Eq. (11) or Eq. (13), and the controls are determined in order to minimize the objective function (10).

4.1 Motion Advected by a Single Vortex

In Fig. 4a, we can observe the optimal trajectory of $n_p = 25$ trash particles being advected by a single vortex with circulation $k = 2$, situated at the North Pole. The displacement of each trash particle is constrained by a time limit of $T = 10$. For each displacement a single constant control $\mathbf{u}_0 = (u_\theta, u_\phi)$ was used (n = 1). The average optimal control found was $\mathbf{u}_0 = (-0.105, 0.139)$ and the average objective function $f_1 = 1.16$.

Figure 1b illustrates the histogram of the single control $\mathbf{u}_0 = (u_\theta, u_\phi)$ responsible for the trajectories depicted in the preceding figure. The histogram demonstrates that u_θ values vary between -0.12 and -0.09, while the u_ϕ values range from 0.125 to 0.15.

In Fig. 2a, the optimal trajectory of $n_p = 25$ trash particles is depicted, being advected by a single vortex with circulation $k = 2$, situated at the North Pole. Each trash particle is allocated a time limit of $T = 10$ for its movement. The trajectories have been generated using four constant controls ($n = 4$) for each displacement. The average of the controls values are:
$\mathbf{u}_0 = (-1.06 \times 10^{-7}, 2.87 \times 10^{-8})$, $\mathbf{u}_1 = (-1.85 \times 10^{-8}, 1.66 \times 10^{-8})$,
$\mathbf{u}_2 = (-4.19 \times 10^{-1}, 5.52 \times 10^{-1})$, $\mathbf{u}_3 = (-7.37 \times 10^{-8}, 1.48 \times 10^{-7})$,
and the corresponding average objective function is $f_4 = 1.30 \times 10^{-6}$.

The histograms of the four controls, $\mathbf{u}_0, \mathbf{u}_1, \mathbf{u}_2$ and $\mathbf{u}_3$, responsible for the trajectories depicted in the Fig. 2a are presented in Fig. 2b. It is possible to observe in this histogram that the controls $\mathbf{u}_0, \mathbf{u}_1$ and $\mathbf{u}_3$ assume very small values in comparison with the values assumed by $\mathbf{u}_2$.

4.2 Motion Advected by Two Vortices

Figure 3a shows the optimal trajectory of $n_p = 25$ trash particles advected by two vortices initially located at $(\pi/10, \pi/4)$ and $(2\pi/3, \pi/3)$, both with circulation $k = 2$. The time limit for moving each trash particle is $T = 10$. For each displacement a single constant control ($n = 1$) have been used. The average of the control $\mathbf{u}_0$ and of the objective function f_1 are, respectively, $(0.0189, 0.0333)$ and 0.0257.

The histograms of the control $\mathbf{u}_0$ responsible for the trajectories shown in Fig. 3a are presented in Fig. 3b. In this histogram, it can be observed that the u_θ values vary between -0.04 and 0.08, while the u_ϕ values range from approximately 0.02 to 0.05.

Figure 4a shows the trajectory of $n_p = 25$ trash particles advected by two vortices initially located at $(\pi/10, \pi/4)$ and $(2\pi/3, \pi/3)$, both with circulation $k = 2$.

Each trash particle has an available time of $T = 10$. For each displacement four constant controls ($n = 4$) have been used. The average of the control values are:
$\mathbf{u}_0 = (0.0058, -0.0251)$, $\mathbf{u}_1 = (-0.0281, -0.0077)$,
$\mathbf{u}_2 = (0.0185, 0.0301)$, $\mathbf{u}_3 = (-0.0035, 0.0749)$,
and the corresponding average objective function is $f_4 = 0.3392$. When comparing the outcomes obtained using a single vortex, it is evident that both the control values and the objective function show higher values. Additionally, there are also some divergent trajectories observed among the majority of cases.

Figure 4b showcases the histograms of the four controls, namely $\mathbf{u}_0, \mathbf{u}_1, \mathbf{u}_2$ and $\mathbf{u}_3$ associated with the trajectories depicted in Fig. 4a. Upon analyzing this histogram,

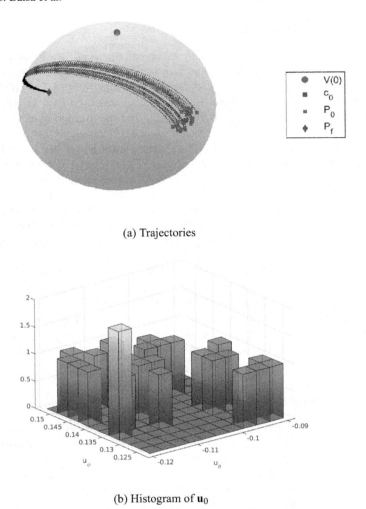

(a) Trajectories

(b) Histogram of $\mathbf{u}_0$

Fig. 1. Transport with $n = 1$ control of $n_p = 25$ trash particles advected by a single vortex ($N = 1$) located in the North Pole.

it becomes apparent that certain values significantly deviate from the most common values, which correspond to alternative trajectories that offer less direct connections between the starting and arrival points.

Figure 5 depicts the histograms illustrating the objective function values derived from the analysis of four specific scenarios: $N = 1$ with $n = 1$ and $n = 4$, and $N = 2$

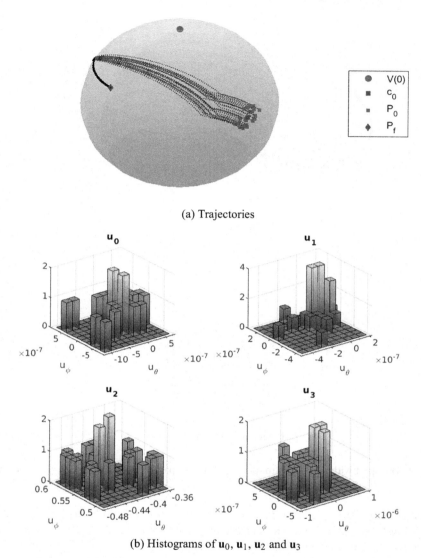

(a) Trajectories

(b) Histograms of $\mathbf{u}_0$, $\mathbf{u}_1$, $\mathbf{u}_2$ and $\mathbf{u}_3$

Fig. 2. Transport with $n = 4$ controls of $n_p = 25$ trash particles advected by $N = 1$ vortex located in the North Pole.

with $n = 1$ and $n = 4$. It is evident that there is no consistent pattern in the fluctuation of f_n concerning N or n. The minimum values occur when $N = 1$ and $n = 4$. Conversely, the maximum values are observed when $N = 2$ and $n = 4$. However, in

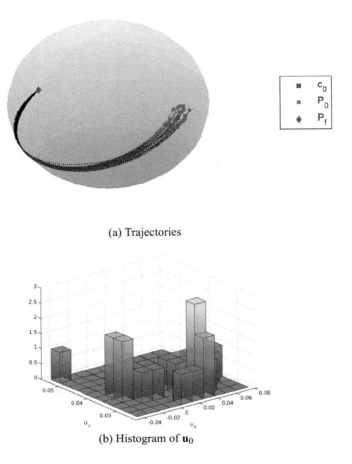

(a) Trajectories

(b) Histogram of $\mathbf{u}_0$

Fig. 3. Transport with $n = 1$ control of $n_p = 25$ trash particles advected by $N = 2$ vortices.

the latter case, the majority of f_n values are situated near 0, with only a small subset exceeding 6. These higher values correspond to alternative trajectories deviating from the direct trajectories depicted in Fig. 4a. Consequently, the findings highlight that the trajectories characterized by lower energy consumption (lower objective function values) are the ones that follow the most direct trajectories.

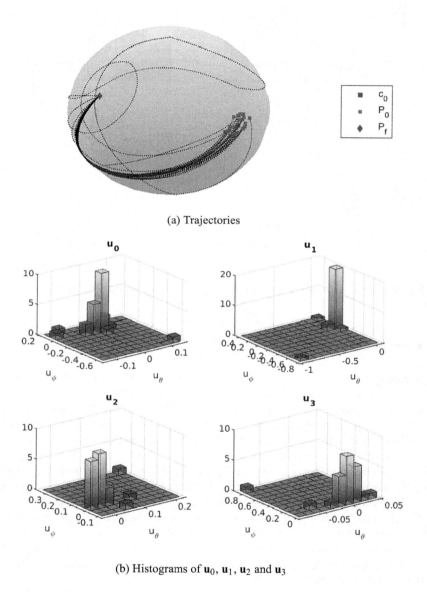

(a) Trajectories

(b) Histograms of $\mathbf{u}_0$, $\mathbf{u}_1$, $\mathbf{u}_2$ and $\mathbf{u}_3$

Fig. 4. Transport with $n = 4$ control of $n_p = 25$ trash particles advected by $N = 2$ vortices.

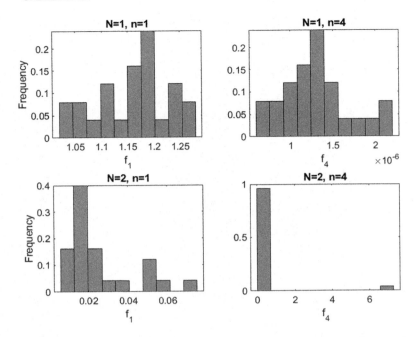

Fig. 5. Histogram of the objective function f_n resulting from the transport of $n_p = 25$ trash particles.

5   Conclusion

The cleaning of accumulated garbage in the oceans is a pressing problem. Waste, especially plastic, is affecting marine ecosystems and human food chains. In this work, a simple mathematical model for oceanic garbage collection is introduced. The autonomous vehicles responsible for the trash transport are modelled by passive particles and the ocean current is generated by the motion of point vortices on a sphere.

To achieve vehicle autonomy, a system of piecewise constant controls is employed, utilizing a limited number of pre-defined switching points that determine the vehicle's trajectory. Each control incurs an energy cost that is aimed to be minimized. This optimization is accomplished by solving a nonlinear problem on the spherical surface.

The preliminary findings focus on optimizing the displacement of a group of passive particles (representing autonomous vehicles) interacting with vortices on a sphere's surface. The results indicate the existence of multiple trajectories for transporting garbage particles. However, the energy costs are lower for the most direct trajectories between the starting point and the destination.

To progress further, it is crucial to refine the mathematical model to better align with the reality of autonomous vehicles. This entails incorporating specifications such as autonomy and degrees of freedom.

Acknowledgements. Carlos Balsa is grateful to the Foundation for Science and Technology (FCT, Portugal) for financial support through national funds FCT/MCTES (PIDDAC) to CeDRI (UIDB/05757/2020 and UIDP/05757/2020) and SusTEC (LA/P/0007/2021).

M. Victoria Otero-Espinar is partially supported by the Ministerio de Ciencia e Innovación, Agencia Estatal de Investigación (Spain), grant PID2020-115155GB-I00.

Sílvio Gama is partially supported by (i) CMUP, member of LASI, which is financed by national funds through FCT - Fundação para a Ciência e a Tecnologia, I.P., under the project with reference UIDB/00144/2020, and (ii) project SNAP NORTE-01-0145- FEDER-000085, co-financed by the European Regional Development Fund (ERDF) through the North Portugal Regional Operational Programme (NORTE2020) under Portugal 2020 Partnership Agreement.

References

1. The ocean cleanup. https://theoceancleanup.com/technology/
2. Balsa, C., Gama, S.: A control problem with passive particles driven by point vortices on the sphere. In: Guarda, T., Portela, F., Augusto, M.F. (eds.) Communications in Computer and Information Science, pp. 139–150. Springer, Cham (2022). https://doi.org/10.1007/978-3-031-20319-0_11
3. Balsa, C., Gama, S.: A numerical algorithm for optimal control problems with a viscous point vortex. In: Brito Palma, L., Neves-Silva, R., Gomes, L. (eds.) APCA International Conference on Automatic Control and Soft Computing, pp. 726–734. Springer, Heidelberg (2022). https://doi.org/10.1007/978-3-031-10047-5_64
4. Balsa, C., Gama, S.M.: The control of the displacement of a passive particle in a point vortex flow. J. Comput. Methods Sci. Eng. **21**(5), 1215–1229 (2021). https://doi.org/10.3233/jcm-204710
5. Balsa, C., Monville-Letu, R., Gama, S.: Optimization of vortex dynamics on a sphere. In: Garcia, M.V., Gordon-Gallegos, C. (eds.) CSEI: International Conference on Computer Science, Electronics and Industrial Engineering (CSEI), pp. 201–213. Springer, Cham (2023). https://doi.org/10.1007/978-3-031-30592-4_15
6. Bogomolov, V.A.: Dynamics of vorticity at a sphere. Fluid Dyn. **12**, 863–870 (1977)
7. Chertovskih, R., Karamzin, D., Khalil, N.T., Pereira, F.L.: An indirect numerical method for a time-optimal state-constrained control problem in a steady two-dimensional fluid flow. In: 2018 IEEE/OES Autonomous Underwater Vehicle Workshop (AUV). IEEE (2018). https://doi.org/10.1109/auv.2018.8729750
8. Chertovskih, R., Khalil, N.T., Pereira, F.L.: Time-optimal control problem with state constraints in a time-periodic flow field. In: Jaćimović, M., Khachay, M., Malkova, V., Posypkin, M. (eds.) OPTIMA 2019. CCIS, vol. 1145, pp. 340–354. Springer, Cham (2020). https://doi.org/10.1007/978-3-030-38603-0_25
9. Conte, S.D., De Boor, C.: Elementary numerical analysis: an algorithmic approach. SIAM (2017)
10. Derraik, J.G.: The pollution of the marine environment by plastic debris: a review. Mar. Pollut. Bull. **44**(9), 842–852 (2002)
11. Jambeck, J.R.: Plastic waste inputs from land into the ocean. Science **347**(6223), 768–771 (2015)
12. King, J., Xue, X., Yao, W., Jin, Z.: A fast analysis of pesticide spray dispersion by an agricultural aircraft very near the ground. Agriculture **12**(3) (2022). https://doi.org/10.3390/agriculture12030433. https://www.mdpi.com/2077-0472/12/3/433

13. Lamb, J.B., et al.: Plastic waste associated with disease on coral reefs. Science **359**(6374), 460–462 (2018)
14. Marques, G., Grilo, T., Gama, S., Pereira, F.L.: Optimal control of a passive particle advected by a point vortex. In: Guarda, T., Portela, F., Santos, M.F. (eds.) ARTIIS 2021. CCIS, vol. 1485, pp. 512–523. Springer, Cham (2021). https://doi.org/10.1007/978-3-030-90241-4_39
15. Marques, G., Gama, S., Pereira, F.L.: Optimal control of a passive particle advected by a Lamb-Oseen (viscous) vortex. Computation **10**(6), 87 (2022)
16. MathWorks: Matlab Optimization Toolbox: User's Guide (R2020a). The MathWorks Inc, Natick, Massachusetts, United State (2020)
17. Mokhov, I.I., Chefranov, S.G., Chefranov, A.G.: Point vortices dynamics on a rotating sphere and modeling of global atmospheric vortices interaction. Phys. Fluids **32**(10), 106605 (2020)
18. Polvani, L.M., Dritschel, D.G.: Wave and vortex dynamics on the surface of a sphere. J. Fluid Mech. **255**(1), 35 (1993). https://doi.org/10.1017/s0022112093002381
19. Rochman, C.M.: The complex mixture, fate and toxicity of chemicals associated with plastic debris in the marine environment. In: Marine Anthropogenic Litter, pp. 117–140 (2015)
20. Rochman, C.M.: Strategies for reducing ocean plastic debris should be diverse and guided by science. Environ. Res. Lett. **11**(4), 041001 (2016)
21. Vankerschaver, J., Leok, M.: A novel formulation of point vortex dynamics on the sphere: geometrical and numerical aspects. J. Nonlinear Sci. **24**(1), 1–37 (2013). https://doi.org/10.1007/s00332-013-9182-5
22. Zhang, B., Tang, Q., Chen, L.P., Xu, M.: Numerical simulation of wake vortices of crop spraying aircraft close to the ground. Biosyst. Eng. **145**, 52–64 (2016). https://doi.org/10.1016/j.biosystemseng.2016.02.014. https://www.sciencedirect.com/science/article/abs/pii/S1537511015302993

Challenges and the Impact of Communication and Information Technologies on Education (CICITE 2023)

Software Solution to Automatize Evaluation and Accreditation Process in Higher Education

Hristina Kostadinova[1]([✉]), George Totkov[2], and Stoyan Atanasov[2]

[1] New Bulgarian University, Sofia, Bulgaria
hkostadinova@gmail.com
[2] University of Plovdiv "Paisii Hilendarski", Plovdiv, Bulgaria

Abstract. How to measure the quality of education is one of the challenges when trying to provide competitive teaching and learning service. Educational institutions, evaluation and accreditation agencies, and experts in different professional fields are involved in this process. The widespread approach is for the providers of educational services to try to improve their performance by keeping the recommendations of the formalized group of standards, known as Standards and guidelines for quality assurance in the European Higher Education Area. Because of the complexity of the activities done and resources processed, there is an obvious need for automated assistance during the accreditation is provided. The focus of this work is the workflow of the accreditation procedures and the implementation of a software solution that utilizes this process. Detailed descriptions of the key components, such as criteria systems which include qualitative and quantitative indicators and automated raw data normalization and calibration are part of the research. The architecture of a software prototype used to maintain the accreditation procedure is discussed.

Keywords: Evaluation · Accreditation · Quality Assurance · Higher Education Institutions · European Standards and Guidelines · ESG

1 Introduction

Quality assurance in education can be achieved by dynamic measurement of the strengths and weaknesses of the higher education institutions (HEIs) that pretend to be evaluated. The process of HEIs accreditation consists of several different stages and in most cases involves experts in different fields. There is a variety of accreditation procedure types, which have to be processed by the authorized evaluation agencies. A common approach in the process of evaluating the quality of educational services is to use Standards and guidelines for quality assurance in the European Higher Education Area (ESG) [1]. This set of standards consists of key points and instructions about the most important requirements of the qualitative educational service. These ten standards are used to focus on the significant circumstances needed to provide efficient teaching and learning. They also set a frame that leads all the involved experts, when the accreditation procedure has to be conducted. Because of the subjective nature of the quality measurement, it

T. Guarda et al. (Eds.): ARTIIS 2023, CCIS 1937, pp. 73–86, 2024.
https://doi.org/10.1007/978-3-031-48930-3_6

is extremely hard to make the process of evaluation more transparent and easy to go through its steps. Different approaches for automatized quality assurance measurement are presented in [2–6]. They can be applied both in higher and secondary education and formalize the models used to obey the requirements for quality in education.

2   Quality Assurance in Education – Key Points

The main focus of most of the accreditation institutions, while trying to find a way to measure the quality of education is on the **student-centric approach** and **comparative analysis** or the so-called **benchmarking** [7–10]. These two pillars of the evaluation procedure conduction carry out the need for automatized means to make this approach possible to apply. They also lead to significant changes in the process of providing accreditation procedures, based on accredited periods and the organization of the whole process. The requirement of implementing the benchmarking approach forces all the HEIs to be evaluated at the same time and to try to collect appropriate data about this current period. Another important point in the process of accreditation is to make the data collected by the HEIs to be appropriate to be used for comparative analysis, even if HEIs are of different sizes, have programs in different professional fields, etc. To keep track of the focused points described in the standards (ESG), more detailed information about the measured indicators has to be given. This is the reason, why most of the evaluation institutions work with criteria systems, which include indicators, grouped by standards [7, 11]. Research in the explored area shows that there are significant difficulties to fit the main goal to assure student-centric learning and to populate and affirm good practices with the currently used criteria systems [12–14].

The key pillars that form the backbone of the accreditation process and impact the main type of the provided activities are set to achieve the most efficient management of the large context of quality assurance.

Accreditation procedures vary by **type** and this types are included in different categories. There are institutional and program type of procedures. Program accreditation can be about **majors from the regulated professions, doctoral programs** or **professional fields. Evaluation of projects** and **distant learning programs** can be also provided. Another important fact about the types of procedures is that the procedure can be for a starting education in a program, or creating educational institution or to evaluate an existing ones. The **post accreditation control process** is part of the continuous quality assurance.

Detailed research and analysis shows that the most appropriate approach that can be applied to manage this variety of procedure types is to use an appropriate **criteria system**, that consists of two types of **indicators (qualitative and quantitative)** and is based on the standards main objectives. Different criteria systems can be used in each procedure type, although there are some common indicators and some specific ones.

Significant role on the final evaluation result is the **information provided by the HEI** to prove its achievements in the accredited area. This information is a large **raw data set**, which is hard to collect and make appropriate to be compared with others HEIs data. Important problems in this area are the **missing data** and **inconsistency** and the **difference in accreditation periods** for the concrete HEI. Another key feature of the raw data collection is that some information is **stored by the HEIs locally**, some is **stored globally** in repositories, maintained by the Ministry of Education and other legal institutions. This fact makes the process of collection hard to provide.

At the end of each evaluation process the result is summarized in an evaluation report which ends up with a set of grades per standard, final grade and list of recommendations. There is always a bit of subjectivity in grading which has to be overcome. The last but not least is the necessity of giving recommendations of the HEI how to improve the quality in the current accredited area. The main problem here is to provide meaningful, efficient and easy to evaluate and check the level of complying with the recommendations.

Summarizing the situation of the evaluation and accreditation process there is an obvious need of **automatization** of most of the activities in this field. The main objective of this work is to present a software prototype that serves to maintain the process of evaluation and accreditation, basically trying to formalize the rules of the evaluation procedures. It will include easy-to-use services, exposed in a web context to automatize the main activities done manually up to this moment.

The key points in the proposed prototype are: using an appropriate criteria system and automatically creating a comparative report based on the quantitative indicators in the criteria system. The evaluation and accreditation process and the architecture of the digital platform are presented in this study.

3 Software Solutions that Support Accreditation Process

Because of specific needs of an accreditation process, including different kind of information related to both educational and administrative service provided by the HEIs, there is a great variety of software systems, used to help the stakeholders involved in it. Some of these systems are mainly constructed to maintain the full set of subsystems in a HEI [15–17]. Such systems are often divided into a bunch of modules, each one responsible to work with a concrete flow of activities. Examples of that kind of flows are: Course Management, Administration, Stuff Management, Communication Service, Financial Management and many others. All these modules provide means to store in a common database, the information need for the quality measurement. Another important type of software solutions focusing the same purpose is based on the usage of a predefined framework that serves as main entry point and gives the rules for stressing on the important aspects of the educational services and the conditions provided to enhance these services [18]. This framework is the core component of the solution and change in its nature, leads to a change in the related workflows. Besides the centralized approach used in such systems, there are examples of platforms that focus on the steps of automatizing the activities while going from one stage of the accreditation procedure to another [19, 20]. There are also additional modules in the existing solutions that serve to collect and process data, based on machine learning, big data processing and natural language processing [17].

The conclusion made by the result of exploring different types of accreditation software applications is that most of the do not focus on the main pillar in quality assurance: the standards and related to them criteria sets which are the backbone of considering the comparative data to make file evaluation. Important fact that has to be mentioned is the lack of flexibility of the software architectures described in the related work, including monolithic architecture and centralized data base. The objectives of this work is to present a flexible software solution, that focuses on easily updatable criteria systems.

4 Evaluation and Accreditation Process

The process of evaluation and accreditation consists of several phases, closely connected to each other. The main purpose of this work is to create a software solution that provides means to automatize these phases and the operations that they include.

Evaluation and accreditation stages are:

Stage 0. Modeling – Preparation and Configuration Activities;
Stage 1. Starting the Accreditation Procedure;
Stage 2. Self-evaluation;
Stage 3. Raw Data Processing;
Stage 4. Evaluation;
Stage 5. Evaluation Procedure Results Analysis.

The relationships between the stages and the activities which are managed by the system are shown in Fig. 1. The detailed description about the listed stages follows in this section.

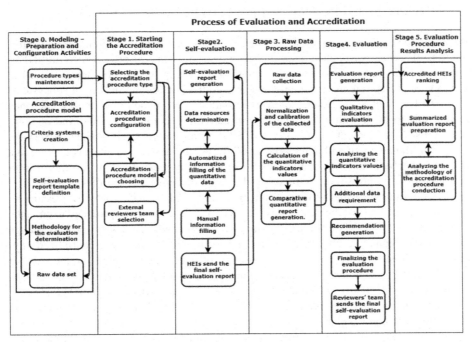

Fig. 1. Evaluation and accreditation process. Stages and activities workflow.

4.1 Stage 0. Modeling – Preparation and Configuration Activities

The process of providing an accreditation procedure needs the preparation of the necessary data, models, and rules that will be used during the evaluation.

1. **Procedure types maintenance**: accreditation procedures of different types, such as Institutional Accreditation, Accrediting Professional Field, Accreditation of Doctoral programs, etc., have to be provided.
2. **Accreditation procedure model**: the complete model of the accreditation procedure includes four important activities:
   - 2.1.1. **Criteria systems creation**. This is one of the most important parts of the process. In the end of it, a set of qualitative and quantitative indicators will serve to make the comparative analysis of the accredited field. The criteria systems keep the structure given by the ESG and represent a set of qualitative and quantitative indicators grouped by standards. Part of the criteria system is the information about the weights of each standard, group of indicators, and given indicators, according to the evaluation strategy. Sample indicators in a sample criteria system are shown in [15, 16].
   - 2.1.2. **Self-evaluation report template definition**. A set of template reports, according to the type of the procedure are provided and one of the appropriate is chosen for the current evaluation.
   - 2.1.3. **Methodology for the evaluation determination.** There is a variety of approaches for the evaluation and grading, that can be applied. Some of the various techniques are based on a dynamic change in the relationship between the qualitative and quantitative indicators and the impact of each of the two groups. The currently used approach has to be preliminary fixed.
   - 2.1.4. **Raw data set.** A large amount of information about the situation in the concrete professional field and/or the HEIs has to be collected and calibrated, to use for a comparative report. A data set of registered external reviewers, along with their professional profiles is supported.

4.2 Stage 1. Starting the Accreditation Procedure

The first activities when the accreditation procedure starts, set the main configuration of the procedure, applied for all the evaluated institutions, and the concrete requirements that have to be performed. The list below shows the most important phases of this stage:

1. **Selecting the accreditation procedure type.** The procedure type has to be chosen of the preliminary set of types, given according to the legal regulation.
2. **Accreditation procedure configuration.** Setting the rules, according to the accreditation procedure: the professional field selection, if this fit to the accreditation procedure type, date periods, accredited HEIs and professional fields, etc.
3. **Accreditation procedure model choosing:** criteria system selection, self-evaluation report template, methodology of evaluation.
4. **External reviewers team selection.** The process of selection depends on the type of procedure and the evaluated HEIs. In a case of a professional field accreditation type, the reviewers have to be experts in the concrete field, in the case of institutional accreditation there is no such requirement.

4.3   Stage 2. Self-evaluation

In this stage are included the most time-consuming activities that the teams in the accredited HEIs have to do. The collection of data and its summarization in a self-evaluation report, accompanied by proofs for all the declared achievements need extreme assistance from the digital platform. The steps that have to be passed are:

1. **Self-evaluation report generation.** According to the procedure type, the criteria system was chosen, and the accredited HEIs, a frame of self-evaluation reports for each HEI is generated automatically.
2. **Data resources determination.** To fill in part of the needed data about the achievements of the HEI, these sources where the data is stored have to be provided. Some part of these sources are stored in centralized repositories, but others are placed on a HEI's local repos and need to be given by each HEI.
3. **Automatized information filling of the quantitative data.** Based on the resources given in the previous step the system provides automatic means to fill the quantitative data into the self-evaluation report.
4. **Manual information filling.** The qualitative data and the missing quantitative data have to be manually filled in by the accreditation HEI's team. The attachments of the proofs of the HEIs' achievements have to be provided at this stage.
5. **HEIs send the final self-evaluation report.**

4.4   Stage 3. Raw Data Processing

The third stage includes the activities that are needed to create a comparative report about the evaluated field, that serves the external reviewers' team to make objective, reasoned decisions. The set of raw data includes information about the programs, courses, students, lecturers and their publications, etc. Sample raw data is shown in Table 2. The results of this stage are used to complete the whole process of evaluation by minimizing the opinion-based evaluation. The phases included in this stage are:

1. **Raw data collection.** The data provided by the HEIs and central, national repositories, supported by the Ministry of Education and other related institutions are collected to be manipulated by the software system.
2. **Normalization and calibration of the collected data.** There is a bunch of problems that have to be solved to make the data appropriate to form the comparative report. Detailed information about these problems and efficient solutions are given in [21, 22].
3. **Calculation of the quantitative indicators values.** Using the criteria system, which includes a set of quantitative indicators and the normalized, calibrated data, the result is obtaining the final values of the quantitative indicators values. This step includes an additional categorization of the indicators and the necessary formulas used, accompanied by a relationship between the indicators and the collected raw data. A description of the approaches applied to cope with the challenges in this stage can be found in [21, 22].
4. **Comparative quantitative report generation.** The information about HEIs' strengths and weaknesses is summarized according to the frame of the criteria system

and the quantitative indicators included in it. The external reviewers' team can use this report to determine more accurately the evaluation results (Table 1).

Table 1. Qualitative and Quantitative Indicators in a Sample Criteria System.

	Indicator
	Qualitative
Standard 3	3.1. There are forms for development and stimulation of students with achievements in the respective major / doctoral program.
	3.2. HEI formulates policies to improve assessment methods and introduces good assessment practices
	Quantitative
	3.1. Average annual relative share of courses (compared to their total number), in whose curricula there are activities that stimulate the creative activity of students.
	3.2. Average annual relative share of students (in percentages) in relation to their total number, respectively. year, participated in surveys assessing the quality of teaching.

Table 2. Raw Data Related to Quantitative Indicators - Sample.

Quantitative Indicator	Raw Data
3.1	Number of required courses in the forms of education
3.1	Number of required courses, which activities stimulate the creative activity of students (projects, films, coursework, etc.)
3.2	Number of students
3.2	Number of students, participated in surveys assessing the quality of teaching

4.5 Stage 4. Evaluation

The stage of evaluation includes processing about recording the results of the self-evaluation report examination and site visit impressions. The external reviewers' team has checked if the pretended of HEIs' achievements are proven and compared the strengths and the weaknesses of each HEI to the others. The key point is the comparison of the good practices applied in the process of education. The main phases that are implemented by the software application are:

1. **Evaluation report generation.** The evaluation report is generated according to the procedure type, the evaluation report template, and each HEI, which is accredited. The data that is saved in the self-evaluation report is automatically loaded into the evaluation report.

2. **Qualitative indicators evaluation.** The external reviewers have to give their grades to each HEI about the qualitative indicators, included in the criteria system.
3. **Analyzing the quantitative indicators values.** The information of the comparative report, based on the quantitative indicators can serve to normalize the evaluation of the qualitative indicators and the opposite. Steps 2 and 3 have to be executed simultaneously, to achieve optimal results.
4. **Additional data requirements.** The reviewers' team can claim additional information if there are not enough proofs of the included in the self-evaluation report data.
5. **Recommendation generation.** One of the final steps in the process of accreditation is the formulation of the recommendations for each HEI, and how to improve the educational service. The team of reviewers can be assisted by the software module, that automatically generates recommendations, based on the most significant weaknesses of the HEI, according to the other HEIs' strengths and weaknesses. Different approaches in this direction are given in [23].
6. **Finalizing the evaluation procedure.** This is the last step in the evaluation procedure when the final version of the evaluation report is sent to the involved institutions.
7. **The Reviewers' team sends the final self-evaluation report.**

4.6   Stage 5. Evaluation Procedure Results Analysis

The final stage of the evaluation process aims to give summarized information about the situation of the accredited area (professional field). This stage can be used to improve the process of accreditation too. Its phases are:

1. **Accredited HEIs ranking.** The ordered list of accredited HEIs, based on the final grades and filtered by each standard grade will give opportunities to make conclusions about improving the whole scientific and educational area.
2. **Summarized evaluation report preparation.** The information about all the accredited HEIs has to be summarized and the reasons for the situation, explored locally and globally have to be given. Possible methods to increase the quality of education about each HEI and for all involved institutions have to be provided.
3. **Analyzing the methodology of the accreditation procedure conduction.** The last important point is to determine the gaps in the process of evaluation and possible ways to make it better.

Summarizing the above-described stages with their activities and the relationship between all of them are illustrated in Fig. 1.

5   Evaluation and Accreditation Software Platform

A prototype of a software platform that serves the processes described in the previous sections is created. It is implemented as a web-based application and includes a set of modules that are responsible to give the required functionalities to efficiently work with the accreditation procedure context.

5.1   Software Solution Architecture and Implementation

The architecture of the system, including its modules is the focus in this section. There are two main parts serve the basic flow: **User Management** and **Accreditation and Evaluation Context** (Fig. 2).

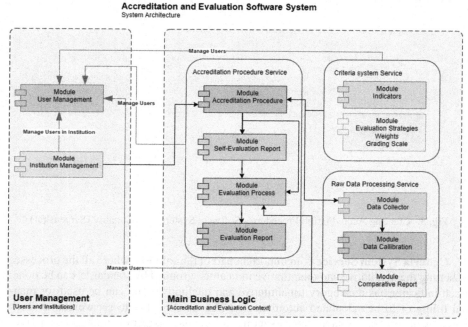

Fig. 2. Accreditation and evaluation software system architecture.

The **user management** part is responsible for the institutions, including HEIs, evaluation and accreditation agencies, and their authorized users, who can execute different tasks, according to their role privileges.

The **evaluation and accreditation part** of the system is divided into several services, which makes the system easy to maintain, scalable, and easily extensible.

Accreditation Procedure Service is used to provide the functionalities of the process of configuration, self-evaluation, and evaluation. It executes the algorithms that assure the correct flow during the stages and a combination of the user management part of the system and the other two services in this context makes it possible to lead the user from the start to the end of the procedure. Part of the functionalities of the accreditation procedure service include some specific steps, based on the concrete procedure type. Figure 3 illustrates the first part of the procedure creation. This example is about a Program Accreditation – Professional Field type of procedure. The next step is to choose the professional field that will be evaluated. Based on the professional field, all the HEIs that provide education in this field are loaded in the list of possible accredited HEIs. After the selection of the procedure type, the criteria system has to be chosen, based on previously loaded list of created criteria systems. The set of the qualitative and quantitative indicators are included in the criteria system. The last part of the procedure creation is to choose the accreditation period of time.

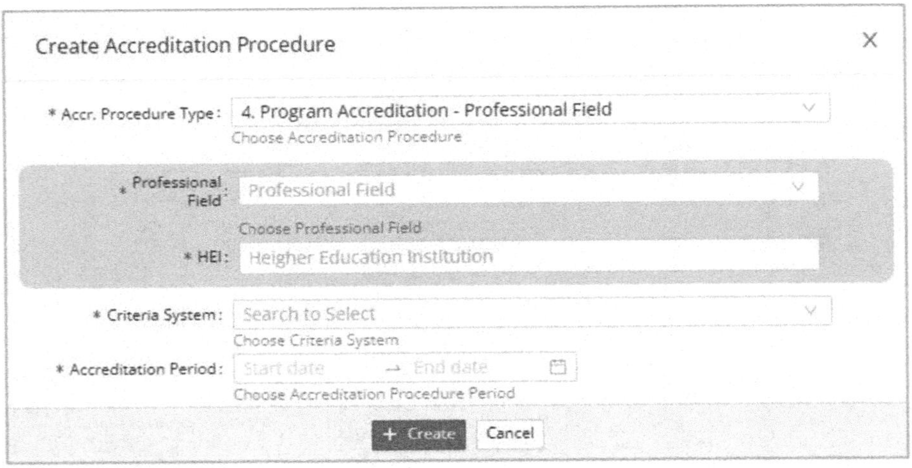

Fig. 3. Creating Accreditation Procedure - Software System Functionality (Screenshot)

Criteria System Service is an important part of the solution, where all the processes of setting the qualitative and quantitative indicators, grouped by standards, can be done. Each indicator has a category (quantitative and qualitative) and can be used for manual filling or to be calculated automatically. The functionality to set weights to each component of the criteria system, including standards, categories, indicators provides flexibility in the grading model. Indicators management functionality is show in Fig. 4.

Criteria systems are represented in a form of a tree and can be copied, edited and reused in different procedure types and concrete accreditation process. Natural relationship between the criteria system and the raw data, collected to create a comparative report is assured by both services: criteria system service and raw data processing service. Illustration of part of a sample criteria system used in a Program Accreditation – Professional Field procedure type is show in Fig. 5

Raw Data Processing Service is separated from the other described services and is used to collect, normalize and calibrate the information needed to automatically fill the data into the self-evaluation report. It includes means to create the comparative report, based on the data about all the accredited HEIs. The types of the raw data need to be determined before the relationship to the quantitative indicators is established. Part of the functionalities that concern the raw data processing is show in Fig. 6.

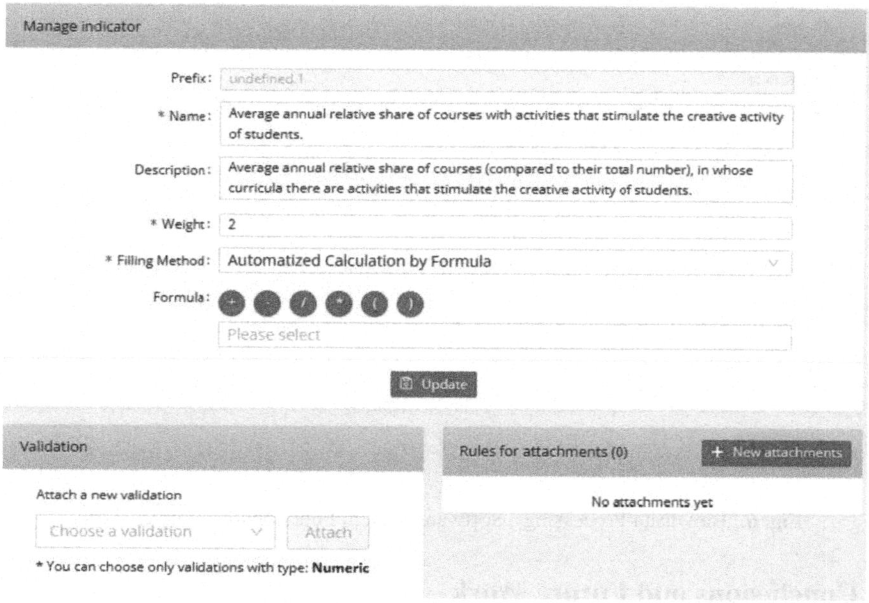

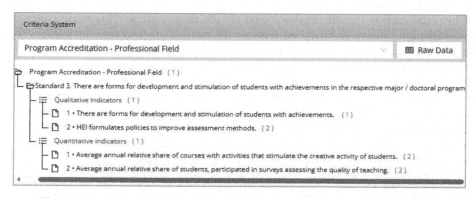

Fig. 4. Indicators Management Software System Functionality (Screenshot)

Fig. 5. Criteria System Management - Software System Functionality (Screenshot)

The system prototype is created along with the NEAA and its functionalities cover the main flow, needed to perform: **raw data management**, **criteria system manipulation**, **automatized generation of the self-evaluation and evaluation report**, and **accreditation procedures conduction**, including the **institutions and user management**.

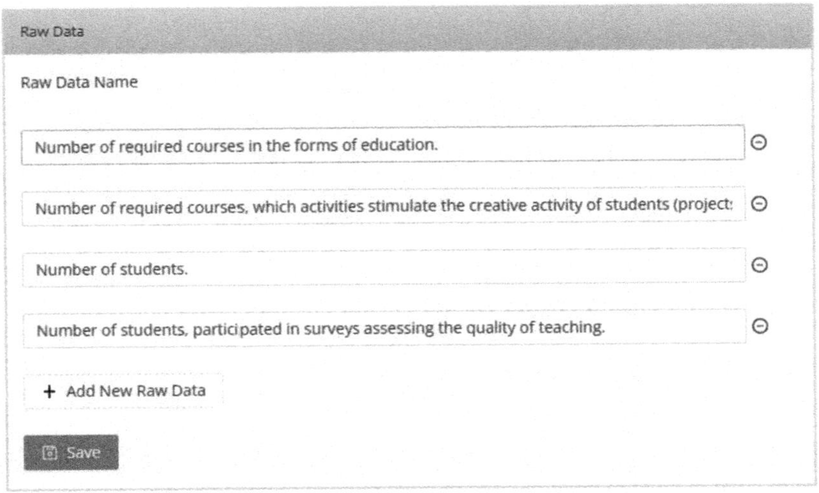

Fig. 6. Raw Data Processing - Software System Functionality (Screenshot)

6 Conclusions and Future Work

The process of quality assurance in education includes a variety of activities formalized in an accreditation procedure. The complexity of the procedures and the large group of involved experts lead the obvious need for digital assistance. This work explores the evaluation process in detail and presents the main stages and their subroutines to achieve the basic purpose: to implement a software solution that utilizes the steps in quality assurance in education. The key points of the presented work are summarized in the sections of the paper, stressing the relationship between the required activities and the architecture of the platform. As a result, a working web-based digital system for providing means to automatize the accreditation procedures is created. The solution is developed to mainly serve the needs of the NEAA in Bulgaria, the context is directed to the higher education, but the same approach can be applied both in the secondary school and in every environment where the quality has to be measured.

The next steps of the quality assurance process automation include:

- Establish the connection to the central and local sources to automatize the process of raw data collection and maintenance;
- Implement a relation to additional modules, based on machine learning mechanisms to improve the recommendations generation;
- Provide experiments with accreditation procedures of different types., which are set to be provided to different periods of time;
- Improve the approach about criteria system generation, by reusing the common indicators and add specific, where needed.

Acknowledgements. The research is partially supported by the grant No. BG05M2OP001-1.002-0002-C02 "Digitization of the economy in an environment of Big data".

References

1. European Standards and Guidelines. ENQA (2015). https://www.enqa.eu/esg-standards-and-guidelines-for-quality-assurance-in-the-european-higher-education-area/. Accessed 30 May 2023
2. Gaftandzhieva, S.: Model and System for Dynamic Quality Evaluation in Higher Education, (Plovdiv: University of Plovdiv "Paisii Hilendarski", PhD thesis) (2017)
3. Gaftandzhieva, S., Doneva, R., Totkov, G.: Dynamic quality evaluation in higher education. TEM J. **7**, 3 (2018)
4. Docheva, M., Totkov, G., Gaftandzhieva, S., Doneva, R.: Hybrid model for quality evaluation in secondary education. IOP Conf. Ser.: Mater. Sci. Eng. 1031 012068 (2021)
5. Docheva, M., Gaftandzhieva, S., Doneva, R., Totkov, G.: Model for quality evaluation in secondary education Edulearn20 Proceedings, pp. 3745–3755 (2020)
6. Gaftandzhieva, S., Totkov, G., Doneva, R.: E-Learning Quality Evaluation (University Good Practices). University Publisher, Paisii Hilendarski (2020)
7. Bulgarian National Evaluation and Accreditation Agency. https://www.neaa.government. bg/en. Accessed 30 May 2023
8. Accreditation Organisation of the Netherlands and Flanders (NVAO). https://www.nvao.net/. Accessed 30 May 2023
9. The UK's quality body for higher education (QAA). https://www.qaa.ac.uk/. Accessed 30 May 2023
10. The Finnish Education Evaluation Centre (FINEEC). https://auditoinnit.karvi.fi/. Accessed 30 May 2023
11. Tavares, O., Sin, C.: Institutional Accreditation Across Europe: Do Assessment Criteria Mirror Higher Education's Missions?, EDULEARN22 (14th annual International Conference on Education and New Learning Technologies), 4th–6th of July (2022)
12. Nestares, M.T.: Analysis of the Evaluation System for The Renewal of Accreditation in University Master's Degrees in the Educational Field in Andalusia, EDULEARN22 (14th annual International Conference on Education and New Learning Technologies), 4th–6th of July (2022)
13. Mursidi, A., et al.: Development of internal quality assurance model in higher education institution. In: 10th International Conference on E-Education, E-Business, E-Management and E-Learning (2019)
14. Cao, Y.X., Li, X.F.: Quality and quality assurance in Chinese private higher education a multi-dimensional analysis and a proposed framework, Quality Assurance in Education, ISSN: 0968–4883 (2014)
15. Elhosenyl, M., Metawa, N., Ella Hassanien, A.: An automated information system to ensure quality in higher education institutions. In: Proceedings of the 12th International Computer Engineering Conference (ICENCO) (2016)
16. Javed, Y., Alenezi, M.A.: Case study on sustainable quality, assurance in higher education. Sustainability **15**, 8136 (2023). https://doi.org/10.3390/su15108136
17. Okebukola, P., Uvalic-Trumbic, S.: Quality Assurance in Higher Education Across the World (2023)
18. Sorour, A., Atkins, C., Stanier, F., Alharbi, F.: Comparative frameworks for monitoring quality assurance in higher education institutions using business intelligence. In: International Conference on Computing and Information Technology, Kingdom of Saudi Arabia, vol. 01, issue: ICCIT- 144, pp. 20–24 (2020)
19. Elhoseny, M., Metawa, N., Darwish, A., Ella Hassanien, A.: Intelligent information system to ensure quality in higher education institutions, towards an automated e-university. Int. J. Comput. Intell. Stud. (2017)

20. Kommey, B., Gyimah, F., Kponyo, J.J., Andam-Akorful, S.A.: A web based system for easy and secured managing process of university accreditation information. Indon. J. Comput. Eng. Design **4**(1), 17 (2022). https://doi.org/10.35806/ijoced.v4i1.240

21. Kostadinova, H.R., Totkov, G.: Complex Assessment of Similar Objects in the European Higher Education Area, EDULEARN22 (14th annual International Conference on Education and New Learning Technologies), 4th–6th of July (2022)

22. Kostadinova, H.R., Totkov, G.: Automatized Congruence of Reviewers' Assessments and Raw Data for Educational Objects in Comparative Quality Evaluation, EDULEARN23 (15th annual International Conference on Education and New Learning Technologies), 3th–5th of July (2023)

23. Kostadinova, H.R., Totkov, G., Atanasov, St.: Automatized SWOT Analysis of the Quality Level in Higher Education Institutions. In: Proceedings of the 15th International Conference Education and Research in the Information Society, pp. 50–58. Plovdiv, Bulgaria, October 13–14, 2022

Using Educational Robotics to Explore and Teach Trochoidal Curves

Attila Körei[1]([✉])(iD) and Szilvia Szilágyi[2](iD)

[1] Institute of Mathematics, Department of Applied Mathematics,
University of Miskolc, Miskolc, Hungary
`attila.korei@uni-miskolc.hu`
[2] Institute of Mathematics, Department of Analysis, University of Miskolc,
Miskolc, Hungary
`szilvia.szilagyi@uni-miskolc.hu`
`http://www.uni-miskolc.hu/~matka`, `http://www.uni-miskolc.hu/~matszisz`

Abstract. We give a new way of representing two large families of trochoidal curves, the epi- and hypotrochoids, in a classroom environment. The drawing of curves with educational robots is embedded in a complex learning process, making the use of dynamic geometry software an integral part of the STEAM-based methodology. In our paper, we provide a detailed description of the working principle of the robots developed for the methodology, with a full elaboration of the mathematical background. This active learning methodology was tested on university computer science students. The quantitative analysis of the questionnaire responses confirms the method's success.

Keywords: Parametric equations for plane curves · Epitrochoid · Hypotrochoid · Dynamic geometry software · STEAM-based learning

1 Introduction

Creative problem-solving skills and innovative solutions are increasingly important in 21st century education [5]. Developments over the past decades have led to the availability of a wide range of robotic learning tools, all with the common goal of innovation and motivating learners in the learning process. As robots become more and more prevalent in our world, it is important and obvious to integrate them into education [1]. Seymour Papert is credited with the constructionism learning theory, which is the basis of the STEM and STEAM methodology. His approach to experiential and project-based education has the advantage of being experimental and exploratory, integrating different knowledge groups, and making theoretical knowledge tangible through learning-by-making. Teamwork, collaboration, and sharing skills are important in the STEAM methodology [2].

Prepared in the "National Laboratory for Social Innovation" project (RRF-2.3.1-21-2022-00013), within the framework of Hungary's Recovery and Resilience Plan, with the support of the Recovery and Resilience Facility of the European Union.

T. Guarda et al. (Eds.): ARTIIS 2023, CCIS 1937, pp. 87–101, 2024.
https://doi.org/10.1007/978-3-031-48930-3_7

Of all the different types of educational robots, LEGO robots are the focus of our attention. Using the STEAM-based methodology, we developed a complex project-based learning programme where participants learn about trochoidal curves and their properties. In this paper, we summarise the results of this teaching program. After the introductory section, a brief overview of the tools for drawing parametric curves is given, emphasizing drawing epi- and hypotrochoid curves. This is followed by a section on parametric equations of trochoids and some of their important properties. The fourth section presents the objectives and the methodology developed. The educational robot constructs for drawing trochoidal curves are described in the next section. The implementation of the experiment and the results are presented in the sixth section. Some concluding remarks are made at the end of the paper.

2   State of the Art - Drawing Devices for Parametric Curves

Few subjects are in Calculus of such many practical applications and visually pleasing results as parametric curves. Most of these curves have their innate mathematical beauty (Fig. 1). The parametric curve is simply the idea that a point moving in the two-dimensional plane follows a path. Trochoidal curves have been at the center of study by several artists and scientists [12] and are the main topic of our work. This family of parametric curves includes cycloids, ellipses and circles, epitrochoids, hypotrochoids, as well as cardioids, astroids, limaçons, and all roses [4].

(a) Pattern with 5 trochoidal curves.   (b) Pattern with 4 trochoidal curves.

Fig. 1. Beautiful trochoids.

If two tangent circles have their centers on the same side of the common tangent line, and one circle remains fixed while the other is rolled around it without slipping, a *hypotrochoid* is traced by any point on a diameter or extended diameter of the rolling circle. If two tangent circles have their centers on opposite sides of the common tangent line, and one circle remains fixed while the other is rolled around it without slipping, an *epitrochoid* is traced by any point on a diameter or extended diameter of the rolling circle. The term *trochoid* is used to refer to either a hypotrochoid or an epitrochoid [4]. The German artist of the sixteenth century Albrecht Dürer is credited to be the first to have incorporated trochoids, specifically hypotrochoidal curves in his art [10]. He introduced the hypocycloid curve and the more general family of trochoid curves in his 1525 four-volume geometry treatise *The Art of Measurement with Compass and Straightedge* [10].

(a) An old Spirograph kit from 1967.   (b) Drawing a hypotrochoid with the toy.

(c) Hoot-Nanny toy.   (d) Mini LEGO Technic "Spirograph".

Fig. 2. Drawing tools.

Drawing toys based on gears have been around since at least 1908. The instrument called spirograph was invented by the Polish mathematician Bruno Abdank-Abakanowicz between 1881 and 1900 for drawing spirals [3]. The well-known toy version was developed by the British engineer Denys Fisher (Fig. 2a and Fig. 2b) and was first sold in 1965 [12]. The spirograph produces graphs of trochoids using toothed disks and rings to prevent slipping, but because none of the holes for the pen reach the circumference of the disks, the spirograph cannot be used to draw all types of epi- and hypotrochoids [4]. Although many other mechanical drawing tools preceded and followed it (Hoot-Nanny, harmonograph, cycloid drawing machine), this modest set of gears has become a favourite toy of a generation. It remains one of the most well-remembered today [9]. This game is enduringly successful, with many versions of the original spirograph game still available for purchase.

Last year we presented a game-based learning experiment called Parametric Graph Project (PGP). In the first part of the project, we used the spirograph mechanism to draw several notable parametric curves using LEGO gears and then wrote parametric equations for the curves based on measured and calculated data from the characteristics of the LEGO parts [7]. During the PGP, the idea came up to build educational robots for drawing. In studying the available literature, it became clear that there are many drawing robots capable of creating beautiful patterns, but we could not find any educational robots where the drawing structure was designed according to the mathematical definition used to produce curves. Note that most so-called spirograph robots are not based on the principle of the original spirograph but on the mechanism of the Hoot-Nanny game (Fig. 2c and Fig. 2d).

3   Parametric Equations for Trochoids

The most common way to give a position of a moving point is to define the parametric equations of its orbit. In this case, the coordinates of the point are given by different functions depending on the same variable. In the plane, this means that the coordinates of the moving point are $(x(t), y(t))$ for some real parameter t, where x and y are continuous functions of t.

This paper focuses on the members of a general curve family called trochoids. To define a trochoid, we need two circles: one is fixed, and the other is rolling inside or outside along it without slipping. The trochoid is the curve traced by a point, often called the pole, which is kept fixed with respect to the moving circle. For determining the parametric equations of the trochoids, suppose that the center of the fixed circle is at the origin and has radius R, denote the radius of the moving circle by r, and let d be the distance between the pole and the centre of the moving circle. The values R, r, and d are called the parametric constants of the curve. Considering the trochoids' geometric interpretation, we assume that the parametric constants R and r are positive real numbers and d is a non-negative real number.

First, assume that the moving circle rolls outside the fixed one. In this case, the curve traced by the pole is called an epitrochoid, and its parametric equations are

$$x(t) = (R + r) \cos t - d \cos \left(\frac{R + r}{r} t \right),$$

$$y(t) = (R + r) \sin t - d \sin \left(\frac{R + r}{r} t \right). \tag{1}$$

If the moving circle rolls inside the fixed one, the obtained curve is a hypotrochoid, with the parametric equations

$$x(t) = (R - r) \cos t + d \cos \left(\frac{R - r}{r} t \right),$$

$$y(t) = (R - r) \sin t - d \sin \left(\frac{R - r}{r} t \right). \tag{2}$$

In both cases parameter $t \in \mathbb{R}$ denotes the angle between a line through the center of the circles and the x-axis [8].

Depending on the relation between d and r, we distinguish three main types of trochoids. If $d < r$, we obtain a curtate trochoid; if $d > r$, we have a prolate trochoid. In particular, if $d = r$, then the obtained special trochoids are called epicycloid and hypocycloid. In addition to this grouping, further special curves are obtained by a particular choice of parametric constants. Some examples are listed in Table 1.

Table 1. Special trochoids

Epitrochoids		Hypotrochoids	
$d = 0$	circle	$d = 0, r \neq R$	circle
$r = R$	limaçon	$2r = R, r \neq d$	ellipse
$d = r = R$	cardioid	$d = r = \frac{R}{4}$	astroid
$d = r = \frac{R}{2}$	nephroid	$d = R - r$	rhodonea or rose

The ratio of the radius of the moving circle to the radius of the fixed circle is also an important feature of trochoidal curves. Suppose that r/R is a rational number and $r/R = p/q$, where p and q are relatively prime natural numbers. Then the period of the trochoid is $2p\pi$, which means that the moving circle will return to its initial position after p revolutions while the parameter t has traversed the interval $[0, 2p\pi]$. A cusp of an epicycloid or a hypocycloid is defined as a point where the curve meets the fixed circle. If r/R is a rational number and can be reduced to p/q where p and q are prime numbers, then the curve has q cusps. For example, the cardioid is a 1-cusped, and the nephroid is a 2-cusped epicycloid (Table 1). For further examples, see the curves in Fig. 3. In Fig. 3a, an epicycloid is presented with parametric constants $r = d = 2.4$ and $R = 5.6$. Since $\frac{2.4}{5.6} = \frac{3}{7}$, the period of the curve is 6π and it has 7 cusps. In Fig 3b, a hypocycloid is shown with $r = d = 3.2$ and $R = 11.2$. In this case $\frac{3.2}{11.2} = \frac{2}{7}$, so the period is 4π and the curve has also 7 cusps. The fixed circles are also depicted in both figures to identify the cusps easily.

Finally, if r/R is not rational, the moving circle will never return to its original position, and the curve will keep having new cusps as the circle keeps rolling around the fixed circle.

(a) A 7-cusped epicycloid.   (b) A 7-cusped hypocycloid.

Fig. 3. Trochoids with cusps.

4   Goals and Methodology

Although the topic of parametric graphs is an extremely varied and aesthetically pleasing subject, it presents many difficulties from a student's point of view. It is problematic to draw trochoidal curves accurately by hand except for the circle. Engineering drawings are multi-step tasks requiring several hours of drawing for these curves, which require high accuracy, where only a ruler and a compass are allowed. On the other hand, the writing and derivation of parametric equations is a complex process in the case of trochoidal curves, building strongly on the knowledge acquired previously. One reason for the problems is working with the four variable quantities: t, d, r, R. Experience shows that students find it difficult to distinguish the concepts of *parametric constants* (d, r, R) and *changing parameter* (t) [7].

Our aim was to develop a methodology to visualise the difference between these two concepts. We wanted to create a STEAM-based pilot framework because educational robots provide a good opportunity to attract and maintain attention until the engaging geometry of trochoidal curves takes over to sustain interest. The kernel of the developed methodology consists of two components. We rely on the easy re-buildability of LEGO robots, complemented by the use of Desmos dynamic geometry software for targeted builds. The BDSP methodology is modelled on the Deming cycle (PDCA) [11]. Here, the four-cycle steps are building, drawing, studying, and planning, so the BDSP methodology consists of four successive steps, which are repeated cyclically (Fig. 4). The Build-draw-study-plan procedure is the following:

1. *Build*: Building or rebuilding the LEGO robot and coding.
2. *Draw*: Testing the robot, drawing trochoidal curves.
3. *Study*: Identifying the drawn shapes using dynamic geometry software. Examining the period of the drawn curve by manipulating the changing parameter.
4. *Plan*: Design a new pattern using dynamic geometric software by manipulating the values of the variables (d, r, R, t). Plan the robot redesign to draw the new pattern. Re-run the cycle.

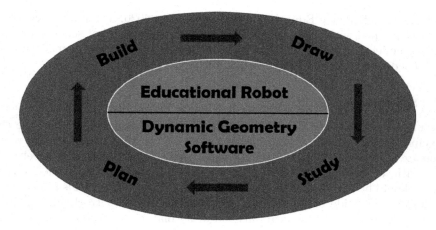

Fig. 4. Build-draw-study-plan cycle.

A building guide is needed to start the cycle, and students can follow the steps to build the basic drawing robot. The program code for drawing the first trochoidal curve is given in the building guide. In the experiment, participants first drew a cardioid with the robot model shown in Fig. 6b. Immediately after the BDSP experiment, they were asked to complete an online questionnaire using Google Forms. In the questionnaire, participants responded to the questions asked on a 5-point Likert scale, indicating a value between strongly agree (5) and strongly disagree (1). The questionnaire explored students' perspectives and measured their attitudes, confidence, and anxiety during STEAM-based learning supported by dynamic geometry software in the BDSP experiment. The research questions are the following:

(1) What are the students' attitudes towards dynamic geometry software-aided STEAM-based learning?
(2) Does the experiment help university students better understand the difference between the parametric constant and the changing parameter?

The first step on the road to the implementation of the experiment was developing drawing robots and creating building guides using Studio 2.0 design software. In the second step, we created Desmos animations for the different robot constructs that model the robot's behaviour. The three parametric constants (d, r, R) can be manipulated with a slider. The interval of the changing parameter (t) is given by writing down the starting and ending points.

The next section presents the robots we developed and used in the BDSP methodological experiment.

5 LEGO Robots Drawing Trochoidal Curves

LEGO educational robotic kits can be used to design and build a wide variety of constructions suitable for drawing epi- and hypotrochoids. For this purpose, we used the SPIKE Prime Educational kit, released in 2020, as our robotics lab is mainly equipped with such sets. Of course, other types of robot sets can also be used to model the process of creating trochoidal curves, but one or more motors are needed to achieve rotating movements.

5.1 Spirograph-Like Robots

The most obvious solution for building a trochoid drawing robot is to use the principle of spirographs. Spirograph is a drawing toy that uses cogs and racks to create circular patterns. Spirograph sets usually consist of plastic wheels and rings with toothed edges. The wheels have variously placed holes in the interior. A pen should be placed through one of the holes, and as the wheel is rolled along the inside or outside of the ring or along another wheel, a trochoidal curve is drawn (Fig. 2b). As we use gears instead of normal wheels, the non-slip rolling of circles is ensured. Unfortunately, only curtate trochoids can be drawn with this device because the pen can not be fixed on the circumference of the moving gear or outside it.

In spirograph-like robot models, gears are used to model the circles that generate the trochoids. When drawing an epitrochoid, one gear is fixed, and the other is rotated by a motor around the fixed one. A writing instrument is attached to the moving circle to model the pole, which draws the path traversed by the pole on a sheet of paper. The hypotrochoid is more difficult to draw because the moving circle must roll inside the fixed circle. A ring with teeth inside is needed to model a fixed circle, but such an element is not included in the core set. However, the SPIKE Prime Extension kit contains circle gear racks (banana gears) which can be used to assemble a ring with a diameter of 14 cm. Rotating another gear inside this ring, a hypotrochoid curve can be generated.

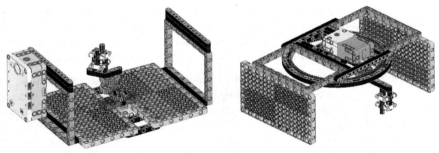

(a) An epitrochoid drawing model (upside-down).

(b) A hypotrochoid drawing model.

Fig. 5. Spirograph-like drawing robots.

We have already determined the parametric constants r and R in the trochoid equations by mounting a pair of gears in the model. This implies that the types of curves that can be drawn with spirograph-like robots are limited, depending on the available LEGO gear sizes. So, for example, we cannot draw an ellipse as a special hypotrochoid since, in that case, a circle with a radius of 3.5 cm would have to be rolled within the available ring with a radius of 7 cm, but there is no LEGO gear of this size. We have more freedom in setting the value of d since the writing device can be fixed at any distance from the center of the moving circle, as long as it does not compromise the stable operation. Staying with the hypotrochoid example, if we choose a gear with a radius of 3 cm as the moving circle, then by setting the distance d to 4 cm, our robot will be able to draw a rose since then the relationship $d = R - r$ is fulfilled.

In Fig. 5, two prototypes of spirograph-like robots are shown. The model in Fig. 5b was introduced in [6].

5.2 SCARA-Style Robots

The SCARA robot is one of the common types of industrial robots first developed in the 1980's in Japan. The SCARA name stands for Selective Compliance Articulated Robot Arm. The main feature of the SCARA robot is that it has a jointed 2-link arm driven by two independent motors (Fig. 6a).

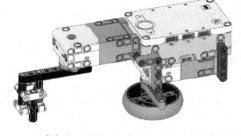

(a) A typical SCARA robot.   (b) A trochoid drawing model.

Fig. 6. A SCARA robot and a SCARA-style drawing robot.

The SCARA-style drawing robot also has two motors; one rotates the whole structure while the other rotates an arm to which the drawing head with the pen is attached (Fig. 6b). The idea for the construction was inspired by the observation that trochoidal curves can be produced by a combination of two circular motions. Indeed, for example, in the case of an epitrochoid, the centre C of the moving circle moves on a circle of radius $R + r$, while the pole follows a circular path of radius d centred on C. By rotating the whole structure, we ensure that the circle of radius $R + r$ is traversed while the other motor is used to rotate the drawing head, ensuring the pole's rotation movement.

We then check the parametric equations of the hypotrochoid curves drawn by the SCARA-like robot (the epitrochoid case can be derived in a similar way).

We call the motor that rotates the drawing head the arm motor and the other motor that rotates the whole structure the main motor. Assume that the speed of the arm motor is c times that of the main motor, i.e., while the main motor makes one revolution, the arm motor makes c revolutions. When drawing a hypotrochoid, the two motors must rotate in opposite directions. This means that the actual angular rotation of the drawing head is the difference between the angular rotation of the two motors. In Fig. 7, the distance between the rotation axles of the two motors is denoted by b, and d is the radius of the circle traversed by the drawing head. The centre of this circle is denoted by C, while the point around which the robot rotates is the origin and is denoted by O. P denotes the actual position of the pole, which is at the centre of the drawing head.

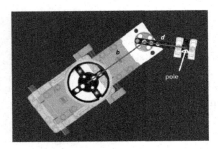

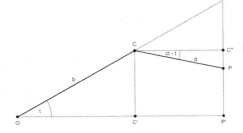

(a) The robot from bottom view.   (b) Determining the coordinates of the pole.

Fig. 7. Hypotrochoid drawing robot at the position after the main motor has turned at angle t.

While the main motor makes t turns, the robot arm holding the drawing head closes an angle $ct - t$ compared to its original position. Denote by $(x(t), y(t))$ the coordinates of the pole P after rotating the main motor by t. Then

$$
\begin{aligned}
x(t) = OC' + C'P' &= b\cos t + d\cos(ct - t) \\
y(t) = P'C'' - PC'' &= b\sin t - d\sin(ct - t),
\end{aligned}
\tag{3}
$$

where $t \in \mathbf{R}$. By comparing equations (3) and the hypotrochoid equations (2), we can observe that these equations are identical with $b = R - r$ and $c = \frac{R}{r}$. For epitrochoids, c has the same meaning; the distance b is the sum of the radii $(b = R + r)$, and P is on the other side of C when starting the motion. So, the parametric equations of an epitrochoid with the notations used in Fig. 7b are

$$
\begin{aligned}
x(t) &= b\cos t - d\cos(ct + t) \\
y(t) &= b\sin t - d\sin(ct + t),
\end{aligned}
\tag{4}
$$

where $t \in \mathbf{R}$.

The value of the parametric constant b is given by the construction of the robot and cannot be changed after assembly. For example, $b = 8$ cm in the model shown in Fig. 6b. For both equation variants, d denotes the pole distance, which can be varied as the drawing head can be fixed at different distances from the arm motor axle. If the drawing head is held by a standard LEGO beam, the head can be fixed at every 8 mm since the LEGO beam has holes at this distance. The drawing head can be fixed at any distance if it is mounted in a sliding manner to allow step-less adjustment. In this case, however, the exact value of the distance d can only be set by measurement.

The biggest advantage of a SCARA-style robot over the spirograph-like ones is that by specifying the speed of the motors relative to each other, we can display many more curves; moreover, both types of trochoid can be drawn with the same robot. In a spirograph-like robot, the size of the built-in gears and the adjustment of the pole distance clearly define the trochoid to be drawn. In this case, only the motor speed and the number of its rotations can be specified in the program, which has no effect on the nature of the curve. In contrast, in the case of SCARA-style robots, we can achieve the desired curve by changing the program code accordingly. Suppose that we want to draw a trochoid with parametric constants R, r, d. Note that only one of the radii can be chosen relatively freely because the other is determined by the relation $b = R \pm r$. First, the pole distance d must be set manually on the robot by fixing the drawing head at a distance d from the arm motor axle. Then calculate the missing radius from the relation $b = R \pm r$, depending on which type of trochoid should be drawn. Determine the parametric constant c by $c = \frac{R}{r}$. In the program, the speed of the arm motor must be set to c times that of the main motor. Divide the period of the curve by 2π; this p value gives how many revolutions are required for the main motor to close the curve (if the period is finite). Set the number of revolutions to p for the main motor and cp for the arm motor to complete the movement at the same time. Finally, start both motors in the same direction if the curve is epitrochoid; otherwise, the motors must rotate in opposite directions.

Table 2. Settings for drawing trochoids. m_{speed}, m_{rot} denotes the speed and the number of rotations of the main motor, and a_{speed}, a_{rot} are the values for the arm motor.

curve	type	b	c	d	R	r	period	m_{speed}	a_{speed}	m_{rot}	a_{rot}	direction
cardioid	epitrochoid	8	1	4	4	4	2π	10	10	1	1	identical
Figure 3a	epitrochoid	8	$\frac{7}{3}$	2.4	5.6	2.4	6π	10	$\frac{70}{3}$	3	7	identical
ellipse	hypotrochoid	8	2	1.6	16	8	2π	10	20	1	2	opposite
Figure 3b	hypotrochoid	8	3.5	3.2	11.2	3.2	4π	10	35	2	7	opposite

As an illustration, Table 2 contains some recommended settings for drawing trochoids with a SCARA-style robot, where b is assumed to be 8 cm. Two of the examples are special trochoids, mentioned in Table 1; the others are shown in Fig. 3. The last five columns provide the program's settings, while the values in the other columns help identify the curve in Desmos using the corresponding equations. In all cases, the speed of the main motor is equal to a moderate 10, so that the speed of the arm motor can be easily calculated.

6   The Experiment and Its Results

In this section, we describe the experiment and the questionnaire design used for the quantitative measurement and then analyse the results.

6.1   Description of the Experiment

The experiment involved a total of 26 students (18–20 years old) in three groups. The computer science students worked with the robots in extra seminars for the Calculus course. The students worked in pairs or alone. In our experience, university computer science students generally don't like working in pairs with robots anymore. They prefer not to have to share the work but can build, code and test on their own. We gained this experience in the Building and Programming Race Robots course, allowing pair and individual work in the experiment. Students could choose the way they worked (Fig. 8).

(a) Building.   (b) Drawing.

Fig. 8. Working with robots.

The experiment lasted 90 min. Before the first robot was built, the students were briefly introduced to the task, the building instructions, and the code to draw the first curve. Building the robots took 20–25 min, including writing the code. Two teachers supervising the work, who they could ask for help if needed. The Trochoidal Curves Designer created with the Desmos app was presented before the robot was built so that after the first drawing was done, the students could check that the robot drew the same curve as the planner. Afterward, we gave them the opportunity to realise their own ideas, following the steps of the BDSP methodology. A surprisingly large variety of trochoidal curves were produced during the experiment. Participants managed to draw four-six different curves with the robot. In the lectures and exercises of the Calculus course, they had already been introduced to parametric equations of plane curves, so finding the exact equations for the curve they had drawn by the robot was part of the task also.

6.2   The Questionnaire

The online questionnaire contained six questions. The first three questions collected information on participants' learning enjoyment. The other three questions gathered information about participants' learning experiences. The questions were the following.

(1) How interesting do you find the experiment with the drawing robot to generate curves?
(2) Did you enjoy the opportunity to design and build a new construction of your imagination in this STEAM project?
(3) Did working with the robot increase your interest in plane curves?
(4) How useful do you find drawing parametric curves with an educational robot?
(5) To what extent has the STEAM-based methodology helped understand the parametric constant and the changing parameter concept?
(6) How much did drawing with a robot help you learn about the mathematics of trochoidal curves?

6.3   Data Analysis

To answer the research questions, we asked students 3-3 online questions. When analysing the data, we split the responses into two groups accordingly.

The mean of the answers to the first question is 4.04. The mode is 5, and the standard deviation is 1.04. The mean of the answers to the second question is the highest, 4.23. The mode of the second question is 5. The mean of the answers to the third question is only 3.73, with a standard deviation of 1.22. The mode is 4. 76.92% of participants gave at least 10 points of a maximum of 15 points for the first set of questions. The quantitative results for the first three questions show that university students were keen to work with robots and interested in STEAM-based negotiation of trochoidal curves. The methodology effectively attracted their attention to exploring the diverse world of plane curves. We found that the students in the experiment showed a strong positive attitude towards STEAM-based learning supported by dynamic geometry software, which answers our first research question. This answer confirms that there is a place for educational robotics in higher education learning techniques.

The mean of the answers to the fourth question is 4.23. The mode is 5, and the standard deviation is 1.03. The mean of the answers to the fifth question is extremely highest, 4.42. The mode of the second question is 5 as well. 88.46% of the respondents gave a rating of 4 or higher for the fifth question, so the methodology helped students better understand the difference between the parametric constant and the changing parameter. The mean of the answers to the last question is 4.31, with a standard deviation of 0,97. The first three questions of the questionnaire received very high scores, and the second three were better than the previous three. The average for all three questions is above 4.2. The most frequent sample value is 5 for the second three questions (Fig. 9). We also received a positive response to our second research question: the methodology used was not only liked by the students but was also considered effective in understanding, distinguishing, and practically using the basic concepts needed to deal with trochoidal curves.

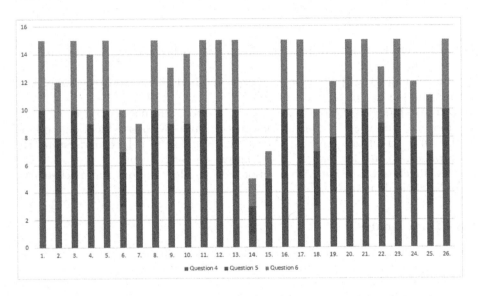

Fig. 9. The university student's self-reported learning rating

7   Conclusion

Teaching the topic of parametric curves opens up the possibility of using a wide range of STEAM tools. The diverse world of trochoidal curves is worth exploring using dynamic geometry software. In order to give students a physical experience of these curves, we have developed several drawing robot constructions based on different principles. The spirograph-like robots draw only the curve defined by the built-in gears; here, only the pole distance can be varied by changing the position of the drawing head. In the case of the SCARA-style robot, it is possible to vary the parameters in the code so that a much wider spectre of trochoids can be drawn with the same construction.

The success of the BDSP experiment encourages us to explore new fields of Calculus course for first-year students where the results of educational robotics can be effectively used.

References

1. Danahy, E., Wang, E., Brockman, J., Carberry, A., Shapiro, B., Rogers, C.: LEGO-based robotics in higher education: 15 years of student creativity. Int. J. Adv. Rob. Syst. **11**(2), 1–15 (2014). https://doi.org/10.5772/58249
2. Eteokleous, N., Nisiforou, E.: Designing, constructing, and programming robots for learning. IGI Global (2022). https://doi.org/10.4018/978-1-7998-7443-0
3. Goldstein, C., Ritter, J., Gray, J.: L'Europe mathématiques: histoires, mythes, identités. Maison des Sciences de l'Homme (1996)
4. Hall, L.M.: Trochoids, roses, and thorns-beyond the spirograph. Coll. Math. J. **23**(1), 20–35 (1992)
5. Henriksen, D., Mishra, P., Fisser, P.: Infusing creativity and technology in 21st century education: a systemic view for change. Educ. Technol. Soc. **19**, 27–37 (2016)
6. Körei, A., Szilágyi, S.: Displaying parametric curves with virtual and physical tools. Teach. Math. **XXV**(2), 61–73 (2022). https://doi.org/10.57016/TM-EHGC7743
7. Körei, A., Szilágyi, S.: Parametric graph project - using LEGO gears for drawing curves. In: Advanced Research in Technologies, Information, Innovation and Sustainability, pp. 101–114 (2022). https://doi.org/10.1007/978-3-031-20319-0_8
8. Lockwood, H.: A Book of Curves. Cambridge U.P, Cambridge (1967)
9. Roussel, R., Cani, M.P., Léon, J.C., Mitra, N.J.: Exploratory design of mechanical devices with motion constraints. Comput. Graph. **74**, 244–256 (2018). https://doi.org/10.1016/j.cag.2018.05.023
10. Simoson, A.J.: Albrecht Dürer's trochoidal woodcuts. Primus **18**(6), 489–499 (2008). https://doi.org/10.1080/10511970701625068
11. Swamidass, P.M. (ed.): Deming cycle (PDCA), pp. 155–155. Springer, US, Boston, MA (2000). https://doi.org/10.1007/1-4020-0612-8_229
12. Tsiotras, P., Reyes Castro, L.I.: The artistic geometry of consensus protocols. In: LaViers, A., Egerstedt, M. (eds.) Controls and Art, pp. 129–153. Springer, Cham (2014). https://doi.org/10.1007/978-3-319-03904-6_6

Impact of Mobile Technology on Learning and Library Policies

Irena Peteva⑩, Stoyan Denchev⑩, and Elisaveta Tsvetkova$^{(\boxtimes)}$ ⑩

University of Library Studies and Information Technologies, Sofia, Bulgaria
{i.peteva,s.denchev,e.cvetkova}@unibit.bg

Abstract. This paper presents interim results of a study conducted in 2021 and being currently continued. The study aims to analyse the up-to-date demands of information and knowledge users in regard to library and information services. Its main task is to determine to what degree information users use mobile devices to read, learn and access information resources. A considerable part of the survey is dedicated to the analysis of the implementation of mobile digital services and learning in library service as well as to the users' awareness and support of international policies for mobile access to learning and library services and resources.

The study has been conducted as part of a research project entitled "Information portal for mobile learning and mobile access to library services and resources", won in the Competition for financial support for projects of junior basic researchers and postdocs – 2019, organized by the National Science Fund at the Ministry of Education and Science of the Republic of Bulgaria, Contract №KP-06-M35/2 from 18.12.2019, led by Chief Assist. Prof. Elisaveta Dimitrova Tsvetkova, PhD.

The main goal of the project is through a systematic study of the issues related to mobile learning and mobile access to library services and resources to achieve new scientific knowledge, combined and presented in a common information Internet portal, to reveal and summarise the positive changes that modern mobile technologies provide as opportunities for access to training and information.

Keywords: Mobile digital libraries · Mobile learning · Digital libraries · Education · Mobile technologies · Research project

1 Introduction

The introduction of new information and communication technologies to both personal and social life radically modifies people's thinking, attitudes and demands. The contemporary cultural and educational environment creates active users who are unrestricted in their quests and who aspire to solve problems and permanently develop their skills. There is a need for constant unlimited access to all the knowledge and information accumulated worldwide, a need for transformation of the means to acquire and apply this knowledge. Modern users clearly realise that one of their universal human rights is the right to access to information and education and look for the most convenient opportunities for unobstructed achievement of the limitless information exchange's potential [2].

T. Guarda et al. (Eds.): ARTIIS 2023, CCIS 1937, pp. 102–115, 2024.
https://doi.org/10.1007/978-3-031-48930-3_8

Contemporary users of information and educational services require numerous changes in the approaches to provision of access to information resources. The impact of the globalisation process and modern information technologies results in a need for innovative approaches to provide knowledge and information, such as mobile digital libraries and mobile learning.

The change in users' expectations and current technological advances lead to the creation of e-learning and mobile learning, of digital and mobile digital libraries. These new forms aim to optimise the collection, systematisation, exchange and use of information and knowledge in order to satisfy as effectively as possible modern society's demands.

2 "A Mobile Population" and IFLA Trend Report 2021 Update

The International Federation of Library Associations and Institutions (IFLA) highlights the strong influence of mobile technologies on present-day society by calling it "a mobile population" [3]. In January 2022 IFLA released the IFLA Trend Report 2021 Update, based on the ideas submitted by emerging library leaders ahead of the World Library and Information Congress.

IFLA's Trend Report series - launched in 2013, and updated in 2016, 2017, 2018 and 2019 - is there to support sustainability as a key part of individual and organisational development. "The Update shares 20 different suggested trends - some complementary, some contradictory – expected to mark the information field. For each one, a short section highlights key questions and aspects, as well as potential responses for the library field." [3].

All the reported trends concern significant aspects of modern information environment and three of them are closely related to the work of a research team at the University of Library Studies and Information Technologies, who run a research project entitled "Information portal for mobile learning and mobile access to library services and resources", whose main goal is to achieve new scientific knowledge, organised and presented in a common information Internet portal, to reveal and summarise the positive changes that modern mobile technologies provide as opportunities for access to training and information.

The three trends emphasised by IFLA and proving the relevance and importance of the research subjects of the above-mentioned project are:

- **Virtual is here to stay** - people continue to prefer to access library services remotely, putting into question the value of spaces and physical offerings;
- **A mobile population** - with people ever more nomadic, the concept of a 'local' library becomes less relevant, and the need to provide joined-up services across borders rises;
- **A single, global collection** - with digitisation of resources and possibilities to work across institutions, it is no longer so relevant to talk about local collections, but rather access to universal resources [3].

The fact that similar trends in the development of the information environment have been observed worldwide underlines the crucial role that the implementation of mobile technologies in information and educational provision plays in order to allow contemporary library institutions to satisfy the emerging needs that readers have and to answer adequately the changes in modern learning information environment.

3 Literature Review of Information Sources in the Field of Mobile Digital Libraries and Mobile Learning

Although mobile learning is one of the latest trends in education policies, it already has many advocates around the world [6]. Its potential is assessed by both students and scientists, teachers, representatives of technology companies and several international organizations.

The most serious attention and support mobile learning undoubtedly receives from the United Nations Educational, Scientific and Cultural Organization (UNESCO). UNESCO experts explain the reason for this: "Today there are over six billion mobile phone subscriptions worldwide, and for everyone person who accesses the internet from a computer two do so from a mobile device." [8].

A relatively new phenomenon in the information world, mobile library services and resources, are increasingly used in library practice. Several large international organizations are working to support the modern development of libraries and the inclusion of mobile and digital technologies in their activities. Several scientists and practitioners describe in their works the benefits of the inclusion of mobile technologies in the provision of information services to users, the ways and opportunities for their implementation and finally the satisfaction of readers with the new library opportunities [6].

The largest contribution in terms of digital and mobile digital libraries have 3 major international organizations – Electronic Information for Libraries (EIFL), International Federation of Library Associations and Institutions (IFLA) and American Library Association (ALA).

Details concerning information sources in the field of mobile digital libraries and mobile learning are provided in 2021 in a paper presented at the 13-th International Conference on Education and New Learning Technologies, 5th-6th July 2021, Palma, Mallorca, Spain [5].

4 A Survey on "Mobile Digital Libraries and Mobile Learning"

The contemporary information environment and changing users' attitudes are central to the survey on "Mobile digital libraries and mobile learning" conducted among information users in June – July 2021. The study has been realised as part of the project "Information portal for mobile learning and mobile access to library services and resources" [1, 4, 7]. It has a permanent character, thus a place and an impact even in the present social environment. The relevance of such a study is determined by the key role libraries play in global information society by answering users' demands with new, up-to-date solutions for access to information, such as providing mobile access to information and learning services.

4.1 Main Goal of the Study

The main goal of the survey on "Mobile digital libraries and mobile learning" is to analyse the needs and requirements that knowledge and information users have in regard to library and learning services, to assess to what extent mobile devices are used for reading, learning and information processing, to determine whether the introduction of mobile digital services and learning in library services is supported, to clarify whether users are aware of international policies for mobile access to learning and library services and resources and whether they support them.

4.2 Research Tasks

The goal of the empirical study is achieved by the solution of the following research tasks:

- To determine to what extent mobile devices are used on a daily basis and specifically for reading and search of information;
- To determine and analyse information users' level of awareness concerning mobile digital libraries as well as their attitude towards the subject;
- To determine information users' level of awareness and attitude towards mobile learning and lifelong learning;
- To analyse information users' level of awareness and attitude towards existing practices for mobile learning in the European information and learning environment;
- To summarise users' opinion on library institutions' participation and role in providing access to information and lifelong learning for all, including via the creation of mobile digital libraries and mobile forms of continuous learning.

4.3 Methodology of the Study

In order to achieve the goal set and fulfill the research tasks of the empirical study a questionnaire with three sections has been devised: PART 1. Mobile devices, applications and mobile digital libraries; PART 2. Mobile learning and lifelong learning; PART 3. Policies for mobile information provision and mobile learning.

The questionnaire includes close-ended, multiple choice (applying the Likert-type scale) and open-ended questions.

Participants in the study are university students as they are active users of information resources and digital services.

The survey has been realised via an online structured-type questionnaire form and the Google Forms application. Thus, in June – July 2021, 136 answers have been collected from students at the University of Library Studies and Information Technologies, Sofia, with varied professional and socio-demographic profiles:

- gender - men (n = 52, 38.2%) and women (n = 84, 61.8%);
- age - 18–25 years (n = 58, 42.6%), 26 – 29 years (n = 11, 8.1%), 30–39 years (n = 36, 26.5%), 40–50 years (n = 29, 21.3%) and over 50 years (n = 2, 1.5%);
- education – secondary (n = 53, 39%), professional secondary (n = 42, 30,9%) and higher education (n = 41, 30.1%);

- residency - Sofia (n = 107, 78.7%), cities (n = 15, 11%), towns (n = 9, 6.6%) and villages (n = 5, 3.7%);
- educational qualification – studying for a bachelor's degree (n = 120, 88.2%), a master's degree (n = 8, 5.9%) and a doctor's degree (n = 8, 5.9%).

The questionnaire had been forwarded to 1943 respondents from two of the university's faculties – Faculty of library studies and cultucral heritage – n = 71, 52.2% and Faculty of information sciences – n = 65, 47.8%. The empirical data has been entered and processed with the statistics software IBM SPSS Statistics 21.

5   Research Analisys Data

5.1   PART 1. Mobile Devices, Applications and Mobile Digital Libraries

The first part of the questionnaire concerns mobile digital libraries and mobile services offered to readers. The questions aim to determine users' level of awareness and attitude towards mobile and digital libraries in Bulgaria and worldwide. Another task fulfilled in this part of the study is to determine and analyse to what extent users employ mobile devices in their day-to-day life and specifically for reading and information searching.

The survey shows that on a daily basis young people mostly use the following mobile devices: a smartphone – 91.2% and a laptop (notebook) – 80.9%, then an iPhone – 19.9%, a tablet – 18.4%, an e-reader – 13.2% and an iPad – 2.2%, the question allowing respondents to choose more than one answer (Table 1). The data indicates that users have an extremely high level of mobile coverage in line with contemporary information trends.

Table 1. Distribution of answers to the question "What mobile devices do you use on a daily basis?".

		Responses		Percent of Cases
		N	Percent	
	Smart Phone	124	40,4%	91,2%
	Notebook	110	35,8%	80,9%
	Tablet	25	8,1%	18,4%
	iPad	3	1,0%	2,2%
	iPhone	27	8,8%	19,9%
	e-Reader	18	5,9%	13,2%
Total		307	100,0%	225,7%

It should be noted that 77,9% of the respondents answer positively the question „Do you use any mobile device (smartphone, tablet, iPad, iPhone, e-reader) to read fiction?" (Fig. 1).

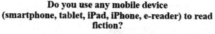

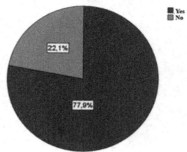

Fig. 1. Distribution of answers to the question „Do you use any mobile device (smartphone, tablet, iPad, iPhone, e-reader) to read fiction?"

Table 2. Use of library services available via mobile devices

Mobile library services	Responses		Percent of Cases
	N	Percent	
Search in electronic databases and access to the full text of documents	76	25.1%	56.3%
Search in a library's bibliographic database	75	24.8%	55.6%
Mobile access to the full text of library documents	50	16.5%	37%
Mobile instructions for use of resources and services	35	11.6%	25.9%
Mobile tour of the library	33	10.9%	24.4%
SMS-service	10	3.3%	7.4%
I have not used any mobile library services	24	7.9%	17.8%
Total	303	100%	224.4%

What library services available via mobile devices are mostly used is another question allowing respondents to select more than one answer. The results are shown in Table 2.

As it can be seen in Table 2, the prevailing students are those who are active users of mobile services concerning searches in electronic databases and access to the full text of documents – 56.3%, searches in a library's bibliographic database – 55.6%, mobile access to the full text of library documents – 37%, etc.

It is thus not a coincidence that almost all respondents approve of the creation of mobile digital libraries – 87.5%, partial approval has been expressed by 8.8% and only 3.7% disapprove (Fig. 2).

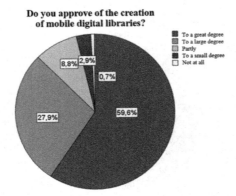

Fig. 2. Attitude of the respondents towards the creation of mobile digital libraries

Nevertheless, the respondents say that Bulgarian libraries' mobile services are not sufficiently well-known and accessible for users – 61.8%, that the opportunities provided by contemporary digital technologies are not fully exploited by Bulgarian libraries in their activities– 60.3% and that an enhancement of mobile and information services offered by Bulgarian library institutions is needed – 88.2% (Fig. 3).

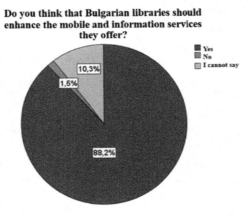

Fig. 3. Distribution of answers to the question „Do you think that Bulgarian libraries should enhance the mobile and information services they offer?"

Table 3 makes clear the degree of users' satisfaction with the quality and opportunities of mobile services offered by Bulgarian libraries.

Table 3 shows that more than half of the students surveyed give neutral responses – 53.7% (neither satisfied, nor dissatisfied), which reveals a need for enhancement of the mobile library services that new "digital generations" actively look for, especially during the global COVID-19 pandemic. This need is also confirmed by the respondents' strong conviction that mobile learning and mobile access to library services and resources

Table 3. Degree of satisfaction with the quality of mobile services offered by Bulgarian libraries

Degree of satisfaction	N	Percent	Cumulative Percent
Highly satisfied	9	6.6%	6.6%
Mostly satisfied	38	27.9%	34.6%
Neither satisfied, nor dissatisfied	73	53.7%	88.2%
Mostly dissatisfied	15	11%	99.3%
Highly dissatisfied	1	0.7%	100%
Total	136	100%	

encourage reading, information literacy and digital competence among young generations – 75%; that new information technologies provide libraries with more opportunities
to initiate various up-to-date courses of development thus acquiring high social status
and prestige in the contemporary information environment – 83.1% (Fig. 4); that mobile
learning and mobile access to library services and resources allow library institutions
to actively participate in the conservation and promotion of national and global cultural
and historical heritage – 77.9%; that the application of modern information and communication technologies (ICT) is the adequate response to present information demands
and challenges and confirms the library's key role as a cultural, educational and moral
institution – 68.4%, that mobile educational and library services are an effective way to
access resources and information in times of crisis such as COVID-19 – 89%.

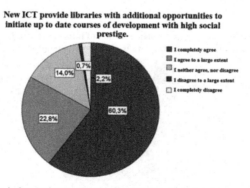

New ICT provide libraries with additional opportunities to
initiate up to date courses of development with high social
prestige.

- I completely agree
- I agree to a large extent
- I neither agree, nor disagree
- I disagree to a large extent
- I completely disagree

Fig. 4. The role of new information technologies in libraries' development in the contemporary
information society

5.2 PART 2. Mobile Learning and Lifelong Learning

The second part of the study concerns mobile learning and lifelong learning. It aims to
determine information users' level of awareness and attitude towards these two subjects.

It should be noted that respondents are, to a large degree, aware of the concept of mobile learning – 52.2%, partly aware – 35.3% or to a small degree/not at all aware of the opportunities provided by mobile learning for personal lifelong development – 12.5% (Fig. 5).

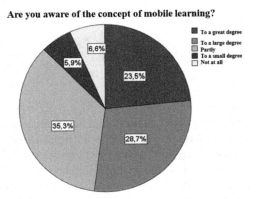

Fig. 5. Respondents' awareness of the concept of mobile learning

Young generations fully approve of the implementation of ICT in the educational process – 84.6%, partly approve – 10.3% and an insignificant part of the respondents approve to a small degree or not at all of the use of ICT in pedagogical practices – 5.1% (Fig. 6).

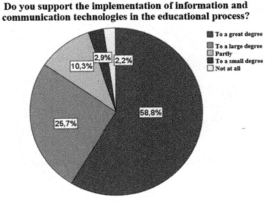

Fig. 6. Distribution of answers to the question „Do you support the implementation of information and communication technologies in the educational process?"

The students surveyed show similar strong support for the implementation of mobile devices as an effective didactic means in formal education – 67.6%, 22.1% partly support and 10.3% are rather reluctant. In regard to informal education 65.4% express complete support, 26.5% – partial support and only 8.1% have a negative attitude (Tables 4 and 5).

Table 4. Respondents' approval of the use of mobile devices in formal education

	Number	Percent	Valid percent	Cumulative percent
To a great degree	47	34,6	34,6	34,6
To a large degree	45	33,1	33,1	67,6
Partly	30	22,1	22,1	89,7
To a small degree	10	7,4	7,4	97,1
Not at all	4	2,9	2,9	100,0
Total	136	100,0	100,0	

Table 5. Respondents' approval of the use of mobile devices in informal education

	Number	Percent	Valid percent	Cumulative percent
To a great degree	47	34,6	34,6	34,6
To a large degree	42	30,9	30,9	65,4
Partly	36	26,5	26,5	91,9
To a small degree	6	4,4	4,4	96,3
Not at all	5	3,7	3,7	100,0
Total	136	100,0	100,0	

The data collected proves that users' awareness of policies for mobile learning should be raised, but it is worth noting that respondents have a positive attitude towards the employment in learning processes of the limitless opportunities offered by ICT and especially by mobile devices.

5.3 PART 3. Policies for Mobile Information Provision and Mobile Learning

The third part of the study concerns policies for mobile learning both on national and European scale as well as libraries' role in them. The survey aims to clarify information users' level of awareness and their attitude towards these subjects.

The analysis of the data collected shows that a considerable part of the students are not informed – 54.5%, 27.9% are partially informed and only 17.6% are mostly informed about national strategic documents and policies encouraging the development of digital libraries, mobile digital libraries and mobile learning (Fig. 7).

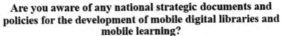

**Are you aware of any national strategic documents and
policies for the development of mobile digital libraries and
mobile learning?**

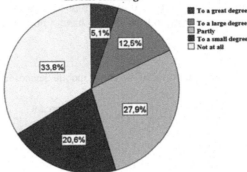

Fig. 7. Respondents' awareness of national strategic documents and policies encouraging the development of digital libraries, mobile digital libraries and mobile learning

Similar trends can be outlined concerning young people's awareness of international initiatives such as the UNESCO Mobile Learning Week: 59.6% are not informed, 28.7% are partially informed and only 11.7% are well-informed about the goals and activities of this forum (Fig. 8).

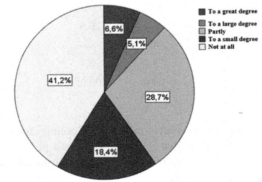

Are you aware of the UNESCO Mobile Learning Week?

Fig. 8. Respondents' awareness of the UNESCO Mobile Learning Week

As to library institutions' participation in the provision of access to learning and information for all during the whole life including through mobile digital libraries and mobile forms of continuous learning the students surveyed are unanimous – 82.4% fully support, 16.2% partially support and 1.4% do not support such activities (Fig. 9).

Most of the respondents reckon that the creation of an information portal for mobile forms of learning and information provision among library and education communities

Do you support the participation of library institutions in efforts to achieve access to lifelong education and information for all?

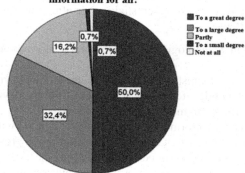

Fig. 9. Respondents' support for library institutions' participation in the provision of access to learning and information for all during the whole life

will facilitate the access to information and resources for users – 81.7%, and only 14.7% are partially not at all of this opinion – 3.6% (Fig. 10).

Will the creation of an information portal for mobile forms of learning and information provision facilitate the access to information and resources?

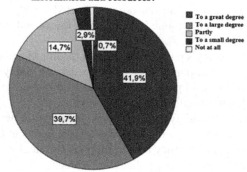

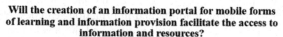

Fig. 10. Distribution of answers to the question „Will the creation of an information portal for mobile forms of learning and information provision facilitate the access to information and resources?"

The content analysis of the open-ended questions reveals that some of the key functional and content features that an information portal for mobile library services needs to adequately satisfy users are: a user-friendly interface, clear instructions for navigation, large volumes of information and documents, proper maintenance and free access to libraries' applications.

6 Results and Discussion

The main conclusions of the research study made after a thorough analysis of the data collected are as follows:

- The use of mobile technologies by contemporary information users is prevalent and highly active;
- A remarkable part – almost 80% - of readers use mobile devices to read fiction;
- The provision of mobile information, learning and library services is the much-needed and adequate response to modern users' demands;
- Library users need an information environment compliant with European and global tendencies and including digital and mobile information provision;
- Information users value the opportunities and perspectives offered by mobile and digital forms of knowledge and information provision and support their realisation and development, but are, nevertheless, not sufficiently informed about the subject and aware of the global trends related to it;
- A need for a common information Internet portal which unites existing resources on the above-mentioned subjects and promotes them to anyone interested has been identified.

The summary of the analysis of the survey's results proves that modern information users use very actively mobile devices, especially mobile phones, both in their day-to-day life as well as for reading, learning and information searches. Nonetheless, the possibility for mobile library service is still limited and the level of awareness of this subject needs to be raised. The responses collected clearly show a positive attitude towards the introduction of mobile information services and the creation of digital and mobile digital libraries.

Furthermore, the study's results indicate that the introduction of mobile information technologies in the contemporary educational system is widely welcomed by users and can satisfy their demands in present-day global learning and information environment respecting every learner's individual requirements.

In order to properly satisfy modern users' information needs and to allow library institutions to function in line with up-to-date global trends in the information environment a responsible national policy and development strategies for mobile technologies' integration in learning and library policies are needed.

The promotion of mobile forms of learning and information provision among the library and the educational communities as well as, not less importantly, the political and business elite will catalyse the broader application of the latest advancements of information technologies in scientific research, educational and information fields [4]. Mobile access to cultural institutions' digital collections will be recognised as a modern approach to socialisation of cultural heritage documents, stimulation of scientific research and conservation of societies' cultural identities.

7 Conclusion

This paper and the study presented aim to highlight the key role of mobile technologies in contemporary information and learning approaches and to contribute to the promotion of their possibilities and impact on modern information environment among the research community, library and information experts and information users.

Being portable and widely spread mobile technologies and devices have the potential to positively change teaching, learning and the provision of information resources and services and to accelerate the overcoming of numerous challenges related to literacy, equality and access to education worldwide. New mobile technologies transform on a daily basis modern information users, contemporary institutions, the whole society. Their impact on learning and library policies is thus inevitable. At present successful libraries are both traditional and digital, accessible via new mobile technologies.

References

1. Garvanova, M., Tsvetkova, E.: The vision of library specialists regarding mobile digital libraries and mobile learning. In: Chova, L.G., Martínez, A.L., Torres, I.C. (eds.), ICERI2021 Proceedings. 14th Annual International Conference of Education, Research and Innovation, Seville, Spain, 2021, pp. 1848–1853. IATED Academy, Spain (2021)
2. Denchev, S., Peteva, I.: Culture de transparence. Société, information, bibliothèques. Préface de Robert Estivals. L'Harmattan, Paris (2010)
3. IFLA Trend Report 2021 Update. https://repository.ifla.org/bitstream/123456789/1830/1/IFLA%20TREND%20REPORT%202021%20UPDATE.pdf. Accessed 29 May 2023
4. Information Portal for Mobile Learning and Mobile Access to Library Services and Resources. Homepage. https://www.mobilib.unibit.bg. Accessed 21 May 2023
5. Tsvetkova, E.: A bibliographical overview of information sources in the field of mobile learning and mobile digital libraries. In: Chova, L.G., Martínez, A.L., Torres, I.C. (eds.), EDULEARN21 Proceedings. 13-th International Conference on Education and New Learning Technologies, Palma, Mallorca, Spain, pp. 5002–5011. IATED Academy, Spain (2021)
6. Tsvetkova, E., Garvanova, M.: Attitude of library specialists and information users to mobile digital libraries – comparative analysis. In: Chova, L.G., Martínez, A.L., Torres, I.C. (eds.), INTED2022 Proceedings. 16th Annual International Technology, Education and Development Conference – INTED2022, 7–8 March 2022, Valencia, Spain, Virtual Confer-ence, pp. 5811–5818. IATED Academy, Spain (2022)
7. UNESCO. Publications on mobile learning". https://en.unesco.org/themes/ict-education/mobile-learning/publications. Accessed 31 March 2023

Use of Simulators as a Digital Resource for Knowledge Transference

Teresa Guarda[1,2]([✉]) [iD] and José María Díaz-Nafría[1] [iD]

[1] Madrid Open University, Madrid, Spain
tguarda@gmail.com
[2] Universidad Estatal Península de Santa Elena, La Libertad, Ecuador

Abstract. In recent years, simulators have emerged as powerful knowledge transfer tools in medicine, aviation, engineering, and many other industries. Simulators provide an immersive and interactive learning environment, and it allows users to gain practical experience and gain critical skills without requiring real-world resources or exposure to potential risk The use of simulators as digital proxies provide new learning opportunities characterized by applications, benefits, limitations and challenges which are discussed. On these bases, the future potential of simulators in transforming educational and training approaches is also considered.

Keywords: Simulator · Knowledge Transference · Application Fields · Challenges

1 Introduction

Knowledge switch is a fundamental manner in education and training, permitting people to gather new skills, extend their knowledge, and expand abilities in numerous fields. Traditionally, expertise switch has relied on traditional coaching methods, together with lectures, textbooks, and palms-on schooling. However, those processes often have barriers in phrases of accessibility, price, and protection.

Simulators emerged as a device considered very effective for transferring experience and integrating knowledge, revolutionizing the way they can practice and learn in a realistic way. Simulators use knowledge environments that replicate real, national or international scenarios in an immersive and interactive environment. In this context, users can carry out simulated studies, without the need for physical resources, and without any exposure to risks [1, 2].

Simulators encompass a wide variety of computer-based systems that mimic complex processes and environments [3]. Users can practice their skills and knowledge with the simulators. They can make decisions and experience the realistic consequences of their actions [4]. Currently simulators are used in many areas, from medicine to military training, among many other areas (Table 1). As a result of using simulators, their users can improve strategies and/or methodologies and improve their learning outcomes and motivations [3, 5].

T. Guarda et al. (Eds.): ARTIIS 2023, CCIS 1937, pp. 116–127, 2024.
https://doi.org/10.1007/978-3-031-48930-3_9

The aim of this work is to explore the use of simulators as digital resources in knowledge transference, clarify the advantages, applications and challenges associated with simulators. Furthermore, it examines the future potential of simulators in transforming education and training.

Simulators allows users, students, educators and instructors to face challenges, streamline the process of knowledge transfer, improve skill acquisition, and also create safe and engaging learning environments for students in various domains [5, 6].

Table 1. Simulators application areas.

Area	Description
Healthcare	Medical simulators are employed for training healthcare professionals, such as surgeons, anesthesiologists, and emergency responders. They provide a safe environment to practice surgical procedures, diagnose diseases, and train in emergency situations
Aviation	Flight simulators are extensively used for pilot training, aircraft design, and testing. These simulators provide realistic environments to train pilots in different scenarios and emergency situations
Automotive	Driving simulators help in testing and evaluating vehicle performance, driver behavior, and road safety. They are used for driver training, vehicle design, and testing of advanced driver-assistance systems (ADAS) and autonomous vehicles
Military	Military simulators are used for training soldiers in tactical operations, combat scenarios, and weapon systems. They help simulate battlefield conditions, improve decision-making skills, and enhance situational awareness
Energy and Power Systems	Simulators are employed in the energy sector to simulate and optimize the performance of power plants, electrical grids, and renewable energy systems. They aid in training operators, analyzing system behavior, and planning for contingencies
Space Exploration	Space mission simulators are used to train astronauts, simulate space missions, and test spacecraft designs. They provide realistic experiences of space travel, extravehicular activities (EVAs), and spacecraft operations
Construction and Engineering	Construction simulators assist in training operators of heavy machinery, such as cranes, excavators, and bulldozers. They are also used for planning and optimizing construction processes, simulating the behavior of structures, and testing new engineering designs

(*continued*)

Table 1. (*continued*)

Area	Description
Disaster Management	Simulators are employed in disaster management and emergency response training. They simulate natural disasters, such as earthquakes and floods, to train responders in handling emergency situations and testing evacuation plans
Education and Training	Simulators are increasingly utilized in educational institutions to provide hands-on training in various disciplines, including engineering, medicine, and aviation. They offer practical experience and enhance learning outcomes
Gaming and Entertainment	Simulators are widely used in the gaming industry to create realistic and immersive experiences. They simulate various activities such as driving, flying, sports, and even virtual reality simulations

2 Simulators and Knowledge Transfer

Simulators have emerged as indispensable tools for knowledge transfer, offering a unique and effective approach to learning and skill acquisition. Simulators offer users with immersive and interactive digital environments [1]. These environments are a replica of reality, which are supposed to allow users to practice and gain experience, that will allow them to gather and expand important abilities in a secure and controlled environment [7].

A simulator is a machine that reproduces the behavior of a system under certain conditions, which allows people who need to work with that system to practice [8]. The similarity between the virtual and the real systems varies from a very simplified version to an indistinguishable digital counterpart, in the case of *digital twins* [9]. Simulators often combine mechanical or electronic parts and virtual parts that help simulate reality, that is, real-world processes, environments or situations [10]. Simulators can use emerging technologies such as Artificial Intelligence (AI) and within all areas that include AI such as virtual reality, machine learning, machine learning, among others [11]; to create highly realistic scenarios, and interactive simulations [12].

Simulators, therefore, can be used professionally or as a tool for leisure and entertainment. In the first case, these devices are indispensable for the training of people who will have a great responsibility in their charge, since their eventual mistakes would endanger the lives of third parties. Thanks to the simulator, these individuals can train until they acquire the necessary experience and skills to perform professionally [13].

The ability to repeat scenarios and analyze performance allows for continuous improvement and mastery of skills [14]. And if users make mistakes in a simulator, nobody is in risk [1, 7].

Furthermore, simulators offer flexibility in terms of accessibility and scalability. They can be accessed remotely, allowing learners to engage in training from different locations. This aspect is particularly beneficial for individuals in remote areas or those unable to access physical training facilities. Simulators also facilitate scalability by accommodating a large number of users simultaneously, making them suitable for both individual and group training scenarios. In case of digital twins, the role of simulators extends into the professional practice itself to test solutions before they are applied to the real world, offering a seamless integration of learning and practice.

3 Applications of Simulators

Simulators have revolutionized training methodologies and knowledge transfer in numerous fields, offering realistic and immersive learning experiences. This section explores the diverse applications of simulators across different domains, highlighting their contributions to skill acquisition, competency development, and enhanced training outcomes.

Simulators play a crucial role in medical education and training. Surgical simulators allow medical students, residents, and experienced surgeons to practice procedures and refine their surgical skills [12, 15, 26]. Virtual reality-based simulators provide a realistic environment for practicing minimally invasive surgeries, endoscopic procedures, and complex interventions [16]. Simulation training enhances surgical proficiency, improves patient safety, and reduces the learning curve for new techniques [17, 18].

In addition to surgical simulators, patient simulators or mannequins are extensively used to train healthcare in various clinical scenarios. These simulators accurately replicate physiological responses and allow learners to practice clinical skills, emergency management, and critical decision-making [16, 19]. Simulated scenarios include cardiac arrest, trauma situations, obstetric emergencies [20, 21], and more, enabling healthcare providers to develop their skills in a controlled environment before encountering real-life emergencies [7, 22].

Flight simulators are integral to pilot training programs in the aviation industry. They provide realistic flight experiences, allowing pilots to practice takeoffs, landings, instrument procedures, and emergency situations. Flight simulators replicate cockpit environments, flight controls, and visual displays to create highly immersive training scenarios. These simulators contribute to improved pilot performance, enhanced situational awareness, and better response to critical incidents [23].

Aerospace engineering also benefits from simulators in design, testing, and training [24].

Simulators are widely used in engineering to simulate and test various systems and processes. For example, automotive manufacturers utilize simulators to design and optimize vehicle performance, assess crash safety, and simulate driving scenarios [25]; in civil engineering, to model and simulate structural behavior, analyze the impact of loads, and optimize infrastructure designs [27–29]; in aerospace engineering, to design and test prototypes, analyze structural performance, model behaviors in extreme environmental conditions [24].

In manufacturing industries, simulators aid in training operators and technicians. Process simulators allow individuals to practice operating complex machinery and equipment without the risk of damage or accidents [25]. By providing a virtual environment to learn and refine their skills, simulators contribute to increased productivity, reduced downtime, and improved product quality.

Simulators find applications in numerous other fields as well. For example, driving simulators are used in driver education and training programs to enhance road safety and assess driver skills. Simulators are employed in the energy sector for training operators in power plant operations, maintenance, and emergency protocols. They are also utilized in the maritime industry to simulate ship handling, navigation, and port operations.

These applications across different fields demonstrate the versatility and effectiveness of simulators in facilitating knowledge transfer. Simulators provide learners with realistic and practical experiences, allowing them to develop skills, refine techniques, and make informed decisions [6].

In the field of education simulators can be utilized in classroom settings to supplement theoretical learning with practical applications. For instance, in physics education, simulators can enable students to visualize and interact with complex physical phenomena, fostering a deeper understanding of fundamental concepts [28, 29]. For example, in electrician training, simulators can simulate electrical systems, wiring diagrams, and troubleshooting scenarios, enabling learners to gain practical experience in a safe and controlled environment. This approach can significantly reduce training costs and minimize the risk of accidents during the learning process.

Furthermore, simulators have the potential to revolutionize the field of virtual apprenticeships [30]. By connecting learners with experts remotely, simulators can facilitate collaborative learning and mentorship across geographical boundaries. Learners can engage in simulated tasks and receive real-time feedback and guidance from experienced professionals, accelerating their learning curve and fostering a sense of mentorship and community.

As simulators continue to advance, incorporating artificial intelligence (AI) and machine learning algorithms, they can adapt and personalize learning experiences based on individual learners' needs and performance [31]. Intelligent simulators can analyze learner interactions, identify areas for improvement, and provide targeted feedback and guidance, tailoring the learning process to each learner's unique requirements [32, 33]. This personalized approach has the potential to enhance knowledge transfer and improve learning outcomes significantly.

However, along with the advancements in simulator technology, it is crucial to address the ethical considerations and challenges associated with their use [16, 33]. These include ensuring the validity and accuracy of simulations, promoting diversity and inclusion in simulator design, addressing potential biases, and maintaining data privacy and security.

4   Benefits of Simulators in Knowledge Transfer

Simulators offer a wide range of benefits in facilitating knowledge transfer, revolutionizing traditional learning methodologies. This section explores the key advantages of using simulators as digital resources for knowledge acquisition and skill development [6, 8, 28, 29, 34, 35] (Table 2).

Table 2. Benefits of Simulators in knowledge transfer process.

Benefits	Description
Realistic and Immersive Experiences	Simulators provide learners with realistic and immersive experiences, replicating real-world scenarios in a controlled environment. By simulating complex processes, environments, or situations, simulators enable learners to engage with practical applications of theoretical concepts. This realism enhances engagement and deepens understanding, resulting in more effective knowledge transfer
Safe Learning Environment	Simulators offer a safe and controlled learning environment, particularly in high-risk fields such as medicine, aviation, and military training. Learners can practice skills and make decisions without the risk of physical harm to themselves or others. By removing the potential for accidents or adverse consequences, simulators create a space where learners can explore and learn from their mistakes, promoting a risk-free learning experience
Repetition and Practice	Simulators allow learners to repeat scenarios and practice skills as many times as needed. This repetitive practice contributes to skill mastery and proficiency development. Learners can refine their techniques, experiment with different approaches, and analyze the outcomes of their actions. The ability to repeat and review simulations enhances learning retention and ensures continuous improvement
Enhanced Transfer of Complex Concepts	Simulators are particularly effective in facilitating the transfer of complex concepts that are challenging to visualize or experience in real-world settings. For example, simulators can depict microscopic processes in biology, complex mathematical models, or intricate engineering simulations. By providing visual representations and interactive experiences, simulators simplify the understanding and application of complex concepts

(*continued*)

Table 2. (*continued*)

Benefits	Description
Understanding Complex Systems	Simulators facilitate the modeling of complex system whose relations might be simple, but the aggregate behavior becomes complex. The modeling of the simple parts eases the approach to the system dynamics complexity
Transferability to Real-World Contexts	Simulators aim to closely replicate real-world situations, making the skills and knowledge acquired in simulated environments highly transferable. Learners can apply what they have learned directly to real-world contexts, minimizing the gap between theory and practice. This transferability enhances the practicality and applicability of the acquired knowledge and skills

In conclusion, simulators offer a multitude of benefits in knowledge transfer. From providing realistic and immersive experiences to ensuring a safe learning environment, simulators enhance engagement, enable repetitive practice, and foster interactivity. They also offer time and cost efficiencies, scalability, objective performance measurement, and facilitate the transfer of complex concepts.

5   Challenges and Considerations

While simulators offer numerous benefits in facilitating knowledge transfer, their implementation and usage also present various challenges and considerations. These challenges must be acknowledged and addressed to ensure the effective utilization of simulators in educational settings [36]. This section explores some of the key challenges and considerations associated with the use of simulators in knowledge transfer.

Simulators often rely on advanced technologies, and their successful operation requires a robust technical infrastructure. However, though some professional application might require highly sophisticated solutions as required in the realistic modeling of urban environments, spacecrafts or nanotechnology, the learning performance is not necessarily aligned to the fidelity of the simulation as regards cognitive gains [37].

The effectiveness of simulators in knowledge transfer heavily relies on their ability to provide realistic and valid learning experiences [8]. Simulators must accurately replicate real-world scenarios, behaviors, and responses to ensure learners can effectively apply acquired knowledge and skills. But this often requires rather a functional alignment than physical fidelity or resemblance [33].

Achieving high levels of realism and validity can be challenging, especially in complex domains where subtle nuances and dynamic interactions are critical. Thus, striking a balance between realism and educational objectives is crucial to avoid overly simplified or overly complex simulations [12, 37]. Indeed, it has been found that sophisticated simulations might increase learning motivation but, at the same time, reduce learning outcomes due to learner's overload and distraction [38].

In addition, the learning outcomes underpinned by simulation requires awareness on model discrepancy in order to boost critical and autonomous learning capacity and scientific attitudes [39].

Ensuring consistent quality across different simulators and training programs poses another challenge. There is a need for standardized guidelines and protocols for simulator development, implementation, and assessment. Establishing quality assurance processes, accreditation standards, and peer-reviewed validation studies are essential to maintain the credibility and reliability of simulators as educational tools [6, 33, 40].

The successful integration of simulators into educational settings requires adequately trained instructors who can effectively guide learners and facilitate meaningful learning experiences. Instructors must possess the necessary skills to navigate simulators, provide constructive feedback, and help learners transfer knowledge gained from simulations to real-world applications [18, 22, 40]. Training programs and ongoing support for instructors are crucial to maximize the potential of simulators in knowledge transfer.

The use of simulators raises ethical considerations, particularly in fields such as healthcare and emergency services. Simulations involving sensitive scenarios or patient interactions require careful consideration of ethical guidelines, privacy, confidentiality, and the potential psychological impact on learners. Balancing the educational benefits of simulation with ethical considerations is paramount to ensure learner well-being and maintain professional standards [41].

Bridging this transfer gap requires careful instructional design, feedback mechanisms, and deliberate practice opportunities that facilitate the transfer and generalization of skills beyond the simulator environment [7].

Simulators developed in one cultural or contextual setting may not fully capture the nuances or specificities of other settings. It is crucial to consider cultural and contextual factors to ensure simulators align with learners' backgrounds, local practices, and specific learning objectives. Customization and adaptation of simulators to different cultural and contextual contexts can enhance their effectiveness and relevance.

6   Future Perspectives and Conclusions

The use of simulators as digital resources for knowledge transfer has demonstrated immense potential across various fields. As technology continues to advance and our understanding of learning processes evolves, there are several exciting future perspectives for the utilization of simulators in enhancing knowledge transfer.

Simulators have the potential to offer personalized and adaptive learning experiences. By capturing data on learners' performance, simulators can adapt the difficulty level, scenarios, and feedback to individual learners' needs. Artificial intelligence and machine learning algorithms can analyze learner data, identify areas of improvement, and dynamically adjust the simulation parameters, creating tailored learning experiences that optimize knowledge transfer.

The integration of gamification elements and serious games in simulators can enhance engagement, motivation, and knowledge retention. Game-based approaches can provide learners with immersive and interactive experiences, making the learning process enjoyable and stimulating. Future simulators may incorporate game mechanics, such as scoring systems, challenges, and rewards, to create engaging and dynamic learning environments.

Advancements in connectivity and communication technologies open up possibilities for remote and collaborative learning using simulators. Learners can engage in realistic simulations, collaborate with peers or experts located in different geographical locations, and benefit from diverse perspectives and experiences. Remote and collaborative learning through simulators can facilitate knowledge transfer in a global and interconnected world.

These future perspectives highlight the exciting potential of simulators in knowledge transfer. As technology evolves and our understanding of learning processes deepens, simulators will continue to evolve, providing increasingly immersive, personalized, and effective learning experiences. Collaboration among researchers, practitioners, and technology developers will be essential to explore and realize these future perspectives, ultimately leveraging the way knowledge is transferred and acquired through simulators.

Simulators have emerged as valuable digital resources for knowledge transfer across various fields and have revolutionized training methodologies and knowledge transfer in numerous fields, offering realistic and immersive learning experiences. The ability to provide immediate feedback, assess performance, and facilitate deliberate practice contributes to accelerated learning and improved competency.

The benefits of simulators in knowledge transfer are numerous. They promote active engagement, enhance knowledge retention, and foster the development of critical thinking and problem-solving skills. Simulators also support collaboration and teamwork, enabling learners to work together in realistic scenarios. Furthermore, simulators have the potential to personalize learning experiences, adapt to individual learner needs, and provide tailored feedback, thereby maximizing the effectiveness of knowledge transfer.

However, the use of simulators in knowledge transfer is not without its challenges and considerations. Technical issues, ensuring realism and validity, standardization and quality assurance, instructor training and support, proper adaptation to learning objectives, ethical considerations, transferability to real-world settings, and cultural and contextual adaptation are all factors that require careful attention. Overcoming these challenges and addressing these considerations is crucial to fully harness the potential of simulators and optimize their effectiveness in knowledge transfer.

Looking ahead, the future of simulators in knowledge transfer appears promising. Advancements in virtual reality and augmented reality technologies will enhance the immersive and interactive nature of simulators, which nevertheless needs to be balanced with the learning objectives to avoid overload and distraction. Personalized and adaptive learning experiences, gamification and serious games, remote and collaborative learning, real-time feedback and analytics, and lifelong learning and professional development are among the future perspectives that hold great potential for simulators.

To fully realize the future potential of simulators, collaborative efforts among educators, researchers, developers, and policymakers are essential.

In conclusion, simulators serve as valuable digital resources for knowledge transfer, offering immersive and practical learning experiences. Their applications span various fields, and they provide learners with opportunities to develop skills, refine techniques, and make informed decisions. As technology advances and we continue to explore new avenues in education and training, simulators will play an increasingly vital role in shaping the future of knowledge transfer, enabling learners to acquire expertise and thrive in their respective domains, though the attentive design of the learning process will always be a key of success.

References

1. Aarno, D., Engblom, J.: Software and System Development Using Virtual Platforms: Full-System Simulation with Wind River Simics. Morgan Kaufmann (2014)
2. Abedini, M., Zhang, C.: Performance assessment of concrete and steel material models in ls-dyna for enhanced numerical simulation, a state of the art review. Arch. Comput. Meth. Eng. **28**, 2921–2942 (2021). https://doi.org/10.1007/s11831-020-09483-5
3. Abramov, N.B., Goman, M.G., Khrabrov, A.N., Soemarwoto, B.I.: Aerodynamic modeling for poststall flight simulation of a transport airplane. J. Aircr. **56**(4), 1427–1440 (2019). https://doi.org/10.2514/1.C034790
4. Alam, A.: Should robots replace teachers? Mobilisation of AI and learning analytics in education. En IEEE (Ed.), International Conference on Advances in Computing, Communication, and Control (ICAC3), pp. 1–12 (2021). https://doi.org/10.1109/ICAC353642.2021.9697300
5. Angelini, M.L., García-Carbonell, A.: Developing English speaking skills through simulation-based instruction. Teach. English Technol. **19**(2), 3–20 (2019). https://cejsh.icm.edu.pl/cejsh/element/bwmeta1.element.desklight-5975cf37-b4e4-499c-aff4-1e9556abc130/c/ARTICLE1.pdf
6. Armstrong, P., Peckler, B., Pilkinton-Ching, J., McQuade, D., Rogan, A.: Effect of simulation training on nurse leadership in a shared leadership model for cardiopulmonary resuscitation in the emergency department. (2021). Emerg. Med. Austral. **33**(2), 255–261 (2021). https://doi.org/10.1111/1742-6723.13605
7. Aronsson, S., Artman, H., Brynielsson, J., Lindquist, S., Ramberg, R.: Design of simulator training: a comparative study of Swedish dynamic decision-making training facilities. Cogn. Technol. Work **23**, 117–130 (2021). https://doi.org/10.1007/s10111-019-00605-z
8. Asad, M.M., Naz, A., Churi, P., Tahanzadeh, M.M.: Virtual reality as pedagogical tool to enhance experiential learning: a systematic literature review. Educ. Res. Int. **2021**, 1–17 (2021). https://doi.org/10.1155/2021/7061623
9. Brynjarsdóttir, J.: Learning about physical parameters: the importance of model discrepancy. Inverse Probl. **30**(11) (2014). https://doi.org/10.1088/0266-5611/30/11/114007
10. Chernikova, O., Heitzmann, N., Stadler, M., Holzberger, D., Seidel, T., Fischer, F.: Simulation-based learning in higher education: a meta-analysis. Rev. Educ. Res. **90**(4), 499–541 (2020). https://doi.org/10.3102/0034654320933544
11. Council, N.R.: Learning Science Through Computer Games and Simulations. National Academies Press (2011)
12. Dinnar, S.M., Dede, C.J., Straub, C., Korjus, K.: Artificial intelligence and technology in teaching negotiation. Negot. J. **37**(1), 65–82 (2021). https://doi.org/10.1111/nejo.12351
13. Farashahi, M.: Effectiveness of teaching methods in business education: a comparison study on the learning outcomes of lectures, case studies and simulations. Int. J. Manage. Educ. **16**(1), 131–142 (2018). https://doi.org/10.1016/j.ijme.2018.01.003
14. Hamstra, S.J.: Reconsidering fidelity in simulation-based training. Acad. Med. **89**(3), 387–392 (2014). https://doi.org/10.1097/ACM.0000000000000130

15. Issenberg, S.B.: Features and uses of high-fidelity medical simulations that lead to effective learning: a BEME systematic review. Med. Teach. **27**(1), 10–28 (2005). https://doi.org/10.1080/01421590500046924
16. Jones, K.: Simulations: A Handbook for Teachers and Trainers. Routledge, London (2013)
17. Kaddoura, M.A.: New graduate nurses' perceptions of the effects of clinical simulation on their critical thinking, learning, and confidence. J. Contin. Educ. Nurs. **41**(11), 506–516 (2010). https://doi.org/10.3928/01484834-20090916-07
18. Lamb, R.L.: A meta-analysis with examination of moderators of student cognition, affect, and learning outcomes while using serious educational games, serious games, and simulations. Comput. Hum. Behav. **80**, 158–167 (2018). https://doi.org/10.1016/j.chb.2017.10.040
19. Lasater, K.: High-fidelity simulation and the development of clinical judgment: students' experiences. J. Nurs. Educ. **46**(6), 269–276 (2007). https://doi.org/10.3928/01484834-20070601-06
20. Lawson, W.S.: Ochsner obstetrics and gynecology simulation program: a review of the literature and description of a multidisciplinary simulation program targeting management of obstetric emergencies. Ochsner J. **20**(4), 39 (2020). https://doi.org/10.31486/toj.20.0014
21. Lee, J., Kim, H., Kim, K.H., Jung, D., Jowsey, T., Webster, C.S.: Effective virtual patient simulators for medical communication training: a systematic review. Med. Educ. **54**(9), 786–795 (2020). https://doi.org/10.1111/medu.14152
22. Li, H.C.: Strategy for improving the football teaching quality by AI and metaverse-empowered in mobile internet environment. Wireless Netw. (2022). https://doi.org/10.1007/s11276-022-03000-1
23. Ludwig, S., Rausch, A.: The relationship between problem-solving behaviour and performance–Analysing tool use and information retrieval in a computer-based office simulation. J. Comput. Assist. Learn. **39**(2), 617–643 (2023). https://doi.org/10.1111/jcal.12770
24. Lungu, A.J., Swinkels, W., Claesen, L., Tu, P., Egger, J., Chen, X.: A review on the applications of virtual reality, augmented reality and mixed reality in surgical simulation: an extension to different kinds of surgery. Expert Rev. Med. Devices **18**(1), 47–62 (2021). https://doi.org/10.1080/17434440.2021.1860750
25. Makransky, G.T.: Adding immersive virtual reality to a science lab simulation causes more presence but less learning. Learn. Instr. **60**, 225–236 (2019). https://doi.org/10.1016/j.learninstruc.2017.12.007
26. McDougall, E.M.: Validation of surgical simulators. J. Endourol. **21**(3), 244–247 (2007). https://doi.org/10.1089/end.2007.9985
27. Mourtzis, D.: Simulation in the design and operation of manufacturing systems: state of the art and new trends. Int. J. Product. Res. **58**(7), 1927–194 (2020)
28. Norman, G.D.: The minimal relationship between simulation fidelity and transfer of learning. Med. Educ. **46**(7), 636–647 (2012). https://doi.org/10.1111/j.1365-2923.2012.04243.x
29. Plotzky, C., Lindwedel, U.S., Loessl, B., König, P., Kunze, C., Meng, M.: Virtual reality simulations in nurse education: a systematic mapping review. Nurse Educ. Today **101**, 104868 (2011). https://doi.org/10.1016/j.nedt.2021.104868
30. Pottle, J.: Virtual reality and the transformation of medical education. Future Healthcare J. **6**(3) (2019). 10.7861%2Ffhj.2019–0036
31. Qi, D.R.-N.: Virtual reality operating room with AI guidance: design and validation of a fire scenario. Surg. Endosc. **35**(2), 779–786 (2021). https://doi.org/10.1007/s00464-020-07447-1
32. Rasheed, A.S.: Digital twin: values, challenges and enablers from a modeling perspective. IEEE Access **8**, 21980–22012 (2020). https://doi.org/10.1109/ACCESS.2020.2970143
33. Sharafat, A., Khan, S.M., Latif, K., Seo, J.: BIM-based tunnel information modeling framework for visualization, management, and simulation of drill-and-blast tunneling projects. J. Comput. Civil Eng. 35(2), 1–25 (2021). https://doi.org/10.1061/(ASCE)CP.1943-5487.0000955

34. Sokolowski, J., Durak, U., Mustafee, N., Tolk, A.: 50 Years of Seminal Computer Simulation Research. Springer Nature Switzerland AG (2019). https://doi.org/10.1007/978-3-030-171 64-3

35. Soutis, C.: Aerospace engineering requirements in building with composites. (W. Publishing., Ed.) Polymer composites in the aerospace industry, pp. 3–22 (2020). https://doi.org/10.1016/ B978-0-08-102679-3.00001-0

36. Steadman, R.H.: Simulation-based training is superior to problem-based learning for the acquisition of critical assessment and management skills. Crit. Care Med. **34**(1), 151–157 (2006). https://doi.org/10.1097/01.CCM.0000190619.42013.94

37. Sterman, J.D.: Learning in and about complex systems. Syst. Dyn. Rev. **20**(2–3), 291–330 (1994). https://doi.org/10.1002/sdr.4260100214

38. Weller, J.M.: Simulation in clinical teaching and learning. Med. J. Aust. **196**(9), 1–5 (2012). https://doi.org/10.5694/mja10.11474

39. Wu, T.C., Ho, C.T.: A scoping review of metaverse in emergency medicine. Austral. Emerg. Care **26**(2023), 74–83 (2022). https://doi.org/10.1016/j.auec.2022.08.002

40. Xie, C.S.: Learning and teaching engineering design through modeling and simulation on a CAD platform. Comput. Appl. Eng. Educ. **26**(4), 824–840 (2018). https://doi.org/10.1002/ cae.21920

41. Yeo, D., Kim, G., Kim, S.: Toward immersive self-driving simulations: Reports from a user study across six platforms. In: 2020 CHI Conference on Human Factors in Computing Systems, pp. 1–12 (2020). https://doi.org/10.1145/3313831.3376787

Workshop on Gamification Application and Technologies (GAT 2023)

The Foggy Frontier: Exploring the Fog and Edge Computing for Online Games

João Paulo Sousa[1] ⓘ, Rogério Tavares[1(✉)] ⓘ, and Jesús M. Torres[2] ⓘ

[1] Research Centre in Digitalization and Intelligent Robotics (CeDRI), Instituto Politécnico de Bragança, Bragança, Portugal
{jpaulo,rogerio.tavares}@ipb.pt
[2] Universidad de La Laguna, Laguna, Spain
jmtorres@ull.es

Abstract. Currently, online games are based on Cloud Computing, where data is transferred from Gaming Devices to be saved or processed in the Cloud. This type of scenario has associated several problems, volume of external data among them, latency, geographic restriction of contents, matchmaking of players in multiplayer games. This article aims to present a review of the main features of Fog Computing, where they are exposed, their main components and ways of use, as well as real-life case studies. It is then discussed how Fog and Edge computing can be a powerful ally for video game studios in different contexts.

Keywords: video games · fog computing · edge computing · cloud gaming

1 Introduction

Fog computing was first introduced by Cisco in 2012 [1] and is described as "a highly virtualized platform that provides computational services between end devices and traditional Cloud Computing (CC) data centers usually, but not exclusively, located in the edge of the network" [2]. In its origins is the concept of CDN (Content Distributed Networks), created in the late 1990s, in which the Akamai network was a pioneer [3]: "Originally, CDNs improved website performance by caching static site content at the edge of the Internet, close to end users". Over time these networks have become host applications on Edge Servers. Therefore, Fog and Edge computing come with the need for distributed computing architectures to support the growing number of connected devices, sensors and other Internet of Things (IoT) devices. These architectures allow data processing, storage and communication to take place at the edge of the network, closer to where data is generated and consumed [4–6].

In recent years, we have seen the adoption of Cloud Computing by the gaming industry, offering a range of benefits for players, developers, and game companies in general. This has happened because CC has been able to provide solutions for a set of increasingly complex gaming challenges. Starting with more basic aspects, it allows for the availability of an infrastructure that supports a large portion of your game's needs overnight, without worrying about installation, maintenance, and management.

T. Guarda et al. (Eds.): ARTIIS 2023, CCIS 1937, pp. 131–139, 2024.
https://doi.org/10.1007/978-3-031-48930-3_10

The ability of CC to provide unlimited resources enables the gaming industry to address scalability issues as their game grows in terms of users and new content. The availability of new resources and functionalities allows game studios and developers to create games with more features, respond more quickly and efficiently to player needs, and find new ways to monetize their games. Some game development software companies already have integrated service platforms that offer features such as real-time player performance monitoring, push content delivery, streaming ads, videogame diagnostics, multiplayer support infrastructure, and more [7, 8]. This infrastructure-as-a-service and platform-as-a-service paradigm has allowed the gaming industry to focus on its business, while developers can do what they love most, which is creating fantastic new games using the new resources that CC can provide. Several studies point to the strong adoption and advantages of Cloud Computing in the gaming industry [9, 10]. However, CC does have some limitations, primarily in terms of response time to requests, as there is a centralized single point that must manage all the information, and connectivity, where CC requires a reliable and stable connection that may not always be possible in mobile scenarios with limited or unstable connectivity. It is within this scenario that this study emerges, aiming to delve into the role that Fog and Edge computing can play in the gaming industry by analyzing their characteristics, advantages, disadvantages, and scenarios where their use can bring a real contribution to the gaming industry.

2   Literature Review

As opposed to traditional cloud computing, fog computing emphasizes decentralization of the computer structure, located between the devices that produce the data and the cloud. Using fog computing, the cloud computation capability is lowered to the edge of the network so that users can access faster communication and software services.

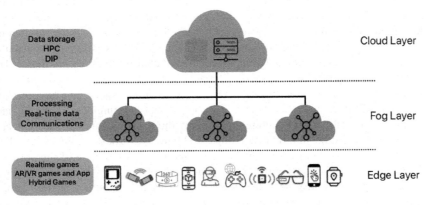

Fig. 1. Fog Computing architecture.

Figure 1 shows that the most typical fog computing architecture is composed of three basic layers (Ni et al., 2018): cloud, fog, and edge.

- Cloud layer: This layer represents the foundation of this three-tiered architecture. It provides robust computational resources and massive storage capabilities that are accessible over the internet. The cloud layer functions as the primary location for big data storage and large-scale computation, with resources being shared across multiple users and locations. It follows a multi-tenant model, where infrastructure, platforms, and software are provided as services over the internet. This layer is characterized by its virtually unlimited storage, high reliability, high scalability, and the ability to support diverse applications.

- Fog layer: It serves as an intermediate between the cloud layer and the edge layer. It primarily provides localized computation and storage resources, facilitating lower latency and reducing the bandwidth needed for communication with the cloud. The fog layer often integrates with various edge devices to provide real-time data processing and analytics. In essence, the fog layer helps to improve efficiency, response time, and network congestion, by distributing resources and services spatially across the network, closer to the end-users.

- Edge Layer. It is closest to the data source and serves as the point of origin for data in this architecture. This layer is primarily characterized by edge devices, such as IoT sensors, smartphones, and embedded devices, which produce and process data. The edge layer can process data locally in real-time without needing to interact with the cloud layer, enhancing the performance of applications that require immediate feedback. It also increases security and privacy, as data can be processed locally without the need for transmission over the network. This reduces latency and conserves bandwidth, enabling the potential for offline functionality.

2.1 Games as Challenges of Fog Computing

Due to the distributed nature of the Fog Computing architecture, computing can take place on edge devices, on Fog nodes or in the Cloud. This is depending on the needs of the moment and available resources. A discussion on this topic is presented in [11] and identifies six challenges in relation to resource management: application placement, resource scheduling, task offloading, load balancing, resource allocation, and resource provisioning. Another study [12] identifies several challenges that fog computing faces, such as: being a distributed framework with different network resources and a wide variety of devices; Decentralization also brings several challenges to distributed mobile computing in which connection interruptions and the probability of failure are more frequent. The challenge of managing an infrastructure in a decentralized way, with thousands of devices that are sometimes connected or disconnected and their heterogeneity in terms of firmware, software configuration, different protocols and individual requirements. Some of the characteristics that make this technology attractive (decentralization, geographic distribution, heterogeneity), also prone to numerous security and privacy threats related to data and services. In which, several studies identify types of attacks and issues related to privacy in the exchange of data and information between the various actors of this architecture [4, 13].

3 Gaming

While it is noticeable that we can see how fog computing makes it possible to extend the physical location of computations and storage away from the centrality of cloud servers [14], in the case of games this needs to be further detailed.

Unlike other media, some digital games, such as shooters or real time strategy, require a lot of speed. In general, not all cloud gaming methods can provide this, which leads to the need for other implementations or variations. Without this speed, like high frame rates, the time difference between the player seeing his enemy, and not being able to respond in time, leads to defeat, and to the loss of ranking, or money, in the case of professional eSports. The latency is one of the biggest enemies of video games, it has the potential to quickly deteriorate your enjoyment of playing. The mere presence of a small delay can make a multiplayer game virtually unplayable. Imagine a scenario where there is a noticeable 200 ms delay between your inputs and the corresponding display response – you might feel an overwhelming urge to throw your computer out the window. The most popular cloud gaming methods [15] are identified in Fig. 2.

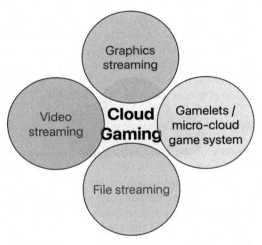

Fig. 2. Cloud gaming methods.

- Video streaming (or pixel streaming): the game runs on the cloud server and the rendered output is streamed as video to the client. Success stories: Onlive, Nvidia Geforce Now, and Playstation Now. Since everything happens on the server and in the game, the client can be very simple, and cheating is impossible since the client has no data from the games. Due to the high usage of the servers, delays (lag), high bandwidth consumption and latency can occur.
- File streaming: in this method, the client downloads a minimal set of files from the cloud server and runs the game locally. The client starts with a minimal set and progressively downloads the rest as needed. This minimizes the problems of video streaming, but the player must have a strong enough device to be able to run the game, which ultimately leaves out Smart TVs, smartphones, tablets and basic computers.

- Graphics streaming: here a mixed approach happens, in which the game runs on the server, but the graphic libraries are transmitted to the client, so that it can render locally. Some of these libraries, such as Direct3D, are hardware dependent, which makes rendering difficult on some devices, but others, such as OpenGL are not, which allows the use of a wider variety of equipment.
- Gamelets or micro-cloud game system: these are Edge Nodes that also have a hybrid approach between video and file streaming, however, the intensive processing is delegated to a gamelet node, which is closer to the client. In this way, bandwidth and processing are equivalent to a traditional Cloud system, but benefit from the proximity of a micro-cloud, decreasing latency. These systems, due to this characteristic, end up also benefiting mobile devices, such as smartphones, tablets and mobile consoles [15, 16]

Although the use of games in Fog and Edge still seems to be in its infancy, this article aims to advocate for its possibilities and concrete examples.

An important case is the game for competitions Valorant, from Riot Games. This company is well known for its Real Time Strategy game, League of Legends, which is widely used in e-sports competitions. Valorant, on the other hand, is a Team Based Tactical First-Person Shooter, comparable to the pioneer Counter Strike in a futuristic environment, i.e., a competition game also used in e-sports championships. Games used in this type of competition, such as League of Legends and Valorant, are not just fast, they must be very fast. In the case of Valorant, which was promised to be played at a minimum of 30 FPS, even on simpler machines with integrated graphics, and thus form a community with more players, several precautions were taken. On the code side of the game, the Unreal Engine was used in its mobile device mode, Unreal Engine's mobile rendering path, and not of a desktop computer [17], and also in the infrastructure of the servers [18] as a speed of 128 ticks, very high even for competitive game servers [19]. Riot Games runs its services, from games to the website, almost exclusively on Amazon AWS. Game servers cannot be too fragmented as players would struggle to find other players, who are scattered on other servers, making matchmaking difficult to create teams and start matches. Amazon AWS, in 2023, offers 31 global cloud regions and 32 local zones, which are smaller cloud regions. If neither of these two solutions provides the latency needed, Amazon can still use AWS Outposts, hardware that can be installed in a data center closer to customers, thus using Fog computing on game servers [18].

In another case, now from a strict infrastructure perspective, the Google Stadia service, active from 2019 to 2023, "To help reduce latency and insure a premium gaming experience, Google's approach includes about 7,500 edge nodes" [10] in order to bring streaming data closer to customers, so that it could achieve the promised 8k resolution at a frame rate of 120 FPS, very impressive features even for dedicated gaming consoles like Sony PlayStation and Microsoft Xbox.

In the mobile games approach, when the telecommunications provider brings the workloads closer to the client, it is a type of mobile architecture called MEC (Mobile Edge Computing, or Multi-Access Edge Computing). In this way, the workload is computed in the cellular tower or in some closer location, through a microserver, instead of traveling to the ISP (Internet Service Provider), co-locating edge devices with the mobile network infrastructure [20].

4 Discussion and Final Remarks

The gaming industry has experienced outstanding growth over the years, driven by the evolution of technology and internet access. However, one aspect that seems to have been not effectively used is the potential of Fog and Edge Computing in this sector. While this potential has already been recognized in areas such as IoT, autonomous vehicles, industry automation, and healthcare [1, 21, 22], there isn't much attention from the gaming industry towards these technologies. This section aims to advocate for their advantages and potential use, while also indicating where some of the major challenges may lie.

4.1 Advantages of Using Fog and Edge Computing in Digital Games

There can be several advantages of developing digital games based on a Fog Computing architecture. Some of the most obvious are:

- Scalability: game servers can scale dynamically to handle real-time player traffic. This means computing and storage resources can be automatically adjusted to meet the demands of the game.
- Low latency: Fog computing allows game servers to be deployed closer to players, reducing latency and improving the gaming experience. With processing closer to players, responses to game commands are faster, improving gameplay and reducing interruptions and delays.
- Reduced network traffic: With edge computing, game data can be processed closer to the source, rather than centralizing all traffic in the cloud. Reducing the load on central traffic points translates into reduced bandwidth costs and improved network stability.
- Improved security: Distributing data processing and storage across multiple local points rather than centralizing it in the cloud can help minimize exposure to cyberattacks and the possibility of security breaches at a single central point.
- Greater data privacy: reducing the amount of information that needs to be sent to the cloud can help protect confidential player information and minimize the risk of data privacy breaches.
- Cost reduction: the improvement of some of the previous points could translate into the reduction of the operating and support costs of the entire infrastructure. Also, when you choose to host your backend on a cloud service that you don't have direct control over, it can lead to your game servers being dispersed across various locations within the country or even internationally. This geographical distribution of resources can result in expensive connectivity issues due to long-distance connections.
- Improved player experience: with the improvement of some of the technical aspects above, players will have a more fluid and enjoyable experience during the game.

– Minimize geographical barriers: Consider an online multiplayer game that relies on high latency to ensure fair and engaging gameplay. With Fog Computing architecture, you can create servers in multiple geographic locations, allowing players from different parts of the world to play together without significant latency. This increases the possibility of finding players for the game, improving the user experience and making the game more popular. Additionally, players can connect to servers in their region, reducing the possibility of latency inequalities that may give one player or another an advantage.

– Customization of game content: there are mobile games where players need to explore locations to find objects and accomplish missions, like Pokemon Go or some augmented reality games. Based on sensors that are connected to Fog computing, it is possible to know that the user is inside a museum with an exhibition of the Palaeolithic period, and it is possible to load into a game scenario and new players who are in space to between them explore the space and fulfill the challenges of the mission launched in the meantime.

4.2 Case Studies

The decentralized architecture of Fog computing can be a great ally for game studios, regarding the imposition of restrictions on content and mechanics that games can offer in certain countries. The case of PUBG Mobile, a well-known battle royale game, which underwent content changes by national authorities [23]. In this case, content restriction policies and mechanics could be injected into Fog Nodes that together with a kind of gateway could reconvert interaction between players with different access policies can play in a shared session. The increasing concern about personal data privacy, digital footprint and data retention will cause countries to implement their own policies and there is tighter enforcement making it difficult to do business model on a centralised cloud architecture. Fog computing's distributed architecture can help overcome these problems by offering a computing and data storage infrastructure that is more flexible to each country's legislation. Also by having our game infrastructure based on cloud computing where there is no control over where the content and game logic may be, there might be a need for you to engage in legislative or legal procedures with entities that can prove to be difficult to collaborate with. This is necessary to ensure that the location of your data complies with local industry regulations, including privacy laws, which can be a challenging and time-consuming process.

Large-scale eSports competitions can also benefit from decreased latency through the proximity of the nodes. As we saw, one of the solutions is to add regional Fog nodes between cloud datacenters and the end user, reducing the latency between user interactions in that region. However, a balance point has to be found, since by placing a Fog node in each region (e.g. city), there is the risk of the service becoming extremely segmented, limiting players to interact with players from other regions. On the other hand, players generally prefer to play with familiar opponents who are usually geographically close. They are also often interested in knowing their ranking in relation to these players. By conducting matchmaking on a nearby server, matchmaking among potential players can be accelerated, even considering lists of players with whom a player frequently interacts. Also, Edge nodes can store information about player preferences to optimize matchups.

To realize benefits across multiplayer games in general, investment in interconnected edge data centers is necessary, ensuring that users are always connected to their nearest node in these edge data centers. These nodes must then interconnect with high-quality links, independent of the user's Internet Service Provider (ISP). There are some cloud providers that offer this, such as Hathora and EdgeGap [20].

To summarize, we discuss here the advantages for the use of fog computing for games, as well as concrete cases, and show how games currently use mainly the cloud, not using the advantages fog and edge computing could add. We do not investigate the reasons that lead to this underutilization, whether economic, political, or technical structures, but we advocate that the proper implementation of these technologies can greatly advance the performance of games, compared to what is currently presented.

Acknowledgements. The authors are grateful to the Foundation for Science and Technology (FCT, Portugal) for financial support through national funds FCT/MCTES (PIDDAC) to CeDRI (UIDB/05757/2020 and UIDP/05757/2020) and SusTEC (LA/P/0007/2021).

References

1. Bonomi, F., Milito, R., Zhu, J., Addepalli, S.: Fog computing and its role in the internet of things. In: Proceedings of the First Edition of the MCC Workshop Mobile Cloud Computing, pp. 13–16. Association for Computing Machinery, New York, NY, USA (2012). https://doi.org/10.1145/2342509.2342513
2. Saini, K., Raj, P.: Chapter Eight - Edge platforms, frameworks and applications. In: Raj, P., Saini, K., Surianarayanan, C. (eds.), Advances in Computers, pp. 237–258. Elsevier (2022). https://doi.org/10.1016/bs.adcom.2022.02.005
3. Nygren, E., Sitaraman, R.K., Sun, J.: The Akamai network: a platform for high-performance internet applications. ACM SIGOPS Oper. Syst. Rev. **44**, 2–19 (2010). https://doi.org/10.1145/1842733.1842736
4. Alwakeel, A.M.: An overview of fog computing and edge computing security and privacy issues. Sensors. **21**, 8226 (2021). https://doi.org/10.3390/s21248226
5. De Donno, M., Tange, K., Dragoni, N.: Foundations and evolution of modern computing paradigms: cloud, IoT, edge, and fog, IEEE. Access **7**, 150936–150948 (2019). https://doi.org/10.1109/ACCESS.2019.2947652
6. Muniswamaiah, M., Agerwala, T., Tappert, C.C.: Fog Computing and the Internet of Things (IoT): a review. In: 2021 8th IEEE International Conference on Cyber Security and Cloud Computing. CSCloud2021 7th IEEE International Conference on Fog and Edge Computing, pp. 10–12. Scalable Cloud EdgeCom (2021). https://doi.org/10.1109/CSCloud-EdgeCom52276.2021.00012
7. Epic, Epic Online Services | Services, Epic Online Service (2023). https://dev.epicgames.com/en-US/services. Accessed 26 June 2023
8. Unity, Unity Gaming Services (2023). https://unity.com/pt/solutions/gaming-services. Accessed 26 June 2023
9. Cai, W., et al.: A survey on cloud gaming: future of computer games. IEEE Access **4**, 7605–7620 (2016). https://doi.org/10.1109/ACCESS.2016.2590500
10. Weckel, A.: Google Stadia - Next Gen Gaming Utilizing Cloud Compute; Another Important Workload Moves Towards the Cloud Pushing for Higher Speed Networking, Credo (2019). https://credosemi.com/google-stadia-next-gen-gaming-utilizing-cloud-compute-another-important-workload-moves-towards-the-cloud-pushing-for-higher-speed-networking/. Accessed 3 June 2023

11. Ghobaei-Arani, M., Souri, A., Rahmanian, A.A.: Resource management approaches in fog computing: a comprehensive review. J. Grid Comput. **18**, 1–42 (2020). https://doi.org/10. 1007/s10723-019-09491-1

12. Sabireen, H., Neelanarayanan, V.: A review on fog computing: architecture, fog with IoT, algorithms and research challenges. ICT Express **7**(2), 162–176 (2021). https://doi.org/10. 1016/j.icte.2021.05.004

13. Mukherjee, M., et al.: Security and privacy in fog computing: challenges. IEEE Access **5**, 19293–19304 (2017). https://doi.org/10.1109/ACCESS.2017.2749422

14. Assila, B., Kobbane, A., El Koutbi, M.: A many-to-one matching game approach to achieve low-latency exploiting fogs and caching. In: 2018 9th IFIP International Conference on New Technologies, Mobility and Security, pp. 1–2. NTMS (2018). https://doi.org/10.1109/NTMS. 2018.8328671

15. Anand, B., Wenren, P.: CloudHide: towards latency hiding techniques for thin-client cloud gaming. In: Proceedings of the Thematic Workshops of ACM Multimedia, pp. 144–152. ACM, Mountain View California USA (2017). https://doi.org/10.1145/3126686.3126777

16. Anand, B., Hao Edwin, A.J.: Gamelets—multiplayer mobile games with distributed micro-clouds. In: 2014 Seventh International Conference on Mobile Computing and Ubiquitous Networking, pp. 14–20. ICMU (2014). https://doi.org/10.1109/ICMU.2014.6799051

17. VALORANT's foundation is Unreal Engine, Unreal Engine (2020). https://www.unrealeng ine.com/en-US/tech-blog/valorant-s-foundation-is-unreal-engine. Accessed 2 June 2023

18. Butler, G.: Riot Games' 'valorant' use of Edge computing (2023). https://www.datacenterdy namics.com/en/analysis/riot-games-valorant-use-of-edge-computing/. Accessed 2 June 2023

19. Davison, E.: Valorant's super-fast servers are attracting streamers and pros in droves. Here's why., Wash. Post. (2020). https://www.washingtonpost.com/video-games/esports/2020/04/ 14/valorant-tick-rate-servers-pros-streamers/. Accessed 2 June 2023

20. Cozens, B.: What can video games teach us about edge computing? (2022). https://www.red hat.com/en/blog/what-can-video-games-teach-us-about-edge-computing. Accessed 3 June 2023

21. Atieh, A.T.: The next generation cloud technologies: a review on distributed cloud. Fog Edge Comput Opportun. Challen. **1**, 1–15 (2021)

22. Yousefpour, A., et al.: All One Needs to Know about Fog Computing and Related Edge Computing Paradigms: A Complete Survey (2018)

23. Kain, E.: Tencent Replaced "PUBG" In China With "Game For Peace" Which Is Hilarious And Terrifying All At Once, Forbes (2019). https://www.forbes.com/sites/erikkain/2019/05/ 08/tencent-replaced-pubg-in-china-with-game-for-peace-which-is-hilarious-and-terrifying-all-at-once/. Accessed 7 June 2023

GERF - Gamified Educational Virtual Escape Room Framework for Innovative Micro-Learning and Adaptive Learning Experiences

Ricardo Queirós[(✉)] [iD]

School of Media Arts and Design, Polytechnic of Porto and CRACS - INESC TEC,
Porto, Portugal
ricardoqueiros@esmad.ipp.pt

Abstract. This paper introduces GERF, a Gamified Educational Virtual Escape Room Framework designed to enhance micro-learning and adaptive learning experiences in educational settings. The framework incorporates a user taxonomy based on the user type hexad, addressing the preferences and motivations of different learners profiles. GERF focuses on two key facets: interoperability and analytics. To ensure seamless integration of Escape Room (ER) platforms with Learning Management Systems (LMS), the Learning Tools Interoperability (LTI) specification is used. This enables smooth and efficient communication between ERs and LMS platforms. Additionally, GERF uses the xAPI specification to capture and transmit experiential data in the form of xAPI statements, which are then sent to a Learning Record Store (LRS). By leveraging these learning analytics, educators gain valuable insights into students' interactions within the ER, facilitating the adaptation of learning content based on individual learning needs. Ultimately, GERF empowers educators to create personalized learning experiences within the ER environment, fostering student engagement and learning outcomes.

Keywords: Gamification · Interoperability · Learning Analytics

1 Introduction

In the fast-paced landscape of education, innovative approaches to engage learners are constantly changing. Gamification, a concept that applies game mechanics and elements to non-game contexts, has emerged as a promising solution to captivate students' attention and drive meaningful learning experiences. One particularly captivating application of gamification in education is the creation of educational virtual escape rooms, where learners navigate through challenging puzzles and scenarios to achieve specific learning objectives in a time-limit frame.

© The Author(s), under exclusive license to Springer Nature Switzerland AG 2024
T. Guarda et al. (Eds.): ARTIIS 2023, CCIS 1937, pp. 140–148, 2024.
https://doi.org/10.1007/978-3-031-48930-3_11

This paper presents the Gamified Educational Virtual Escape Room Framework (GERF), a platform designed to foster micro-learning and adaptive learning experiences within the educational domain. At its core, GERF is centered around a comprehensive user taxonomy, known as the user type hexad, which takes into account the diverse learning preferences, motivations, and behaviors of individuals. By catering to different user types, GERF seeks to create immersive learning environments that resonate with learners on a personal level, fostering higher levels of engagement and knowledge retention.

One of the primary challenges in deploying gamified educational escape rooms is the seamless integration of such platforms with existing Learning Management Systems (LMS). To address this concern, GERF leverages the Learning Tools Interoperability (LTI) specification[1] from IMS Global Learning Consortium, enabling ER platforms to seamlessly interface with LMS systems. This interoperability ensures that educators can easily incorporate escape rooms into their curricula without the need for extensive technical knowledge or modifications to their existing learning environments.

GERF further enhances its efficacy by harnessing the power of learning analytics through the Experience API (xAPI) specification[2]. Within the escape room experience, every action and decision made by learners are transformed into xAPI statements, encapsulating valuable experiential data. These xAPI statements are then transmitted to a centralized Learning Record Store (LRS), enabling educators to access comprehensive insights into student interactions and learning patterns. By using these learning analytics, teachers can gain a deeper understanding of individual learning behaviors, strengths, and weaknesses, empowering them to adapt instructional strategies and content to better suit each student's unique needs.

The fusion of gamification, user taxonomy, interoperability, and learning analytics in GERF offers a transformative educational approach. This paper provides a comprehensive exploration of the framework's architecture, design principles, and functionalities, while also illustrating its potential impact on educational settings.

In the following sections, we will delve into the technical intricacies of GERF, examining its implementation, practicality, and empirical results. We aim to shed light on the numerous benefits GERF brings to the table, demonstrating how this gamified escape room framework has the potential to shape the future of education by enhancing both the process and outcomes of learning.

2   Related Work

Over the past few years, the concept of gamifying escape room experiences has gained significant traction in the field of education. Several gamification frameworks have been proposed to enhance the learning potential of escape rooms and

---

[1] https://www.imsglobal.org/spec/lti/v1p3.
[2] https://xapi.com/specification/.

cater to diverse learner needs. This section presents a review of existing gamification frameworks for escape rooms and highlights their approaches, strengths, and limitations.

- Escape EDU: focuses on integrating educational content seamlessly into escape room scenarios. It employs narrative-driven puzzles that align with specific learning objectives. Participants are presented with challenges related to the educational content they are studying, encouraging them to apply theoretical knowledge to solve real-world problems. Although Escape EDU offers a captivating learning experience, its limited personalization and adaptive learning elements restrict its potential for addressing individual learner preferences and motivations.
- escapED [2]: intends to provide educationalists and other interested parties a guideline to help develop and deliver educational escape rooms and other interactive GBL experiences of similar designs.
- Room2Educ8 [4]: a learner-centred framework for EER design that follows Design Thinking principles. It provides detailed heuristics for empathising with learners, defining learning objectives and constraints, adding narrative, designing puzzles, briefing and debriefing participants, prototyping and playtesting, documenting the whole process, and evaluating the EER experience.
- Breakout EDU: developed by GameLearn, incorporates a wide range of gamification elements, such as gamified badges, time-based challenges, and leaderboards. It focuses on fostering healthy competition among learners, encouraging them to strive for better performance. The framework's rich set of gamification features boosts engagement and motivation. However, the emphasis on competition might not suit all learners, potentially excluding those who thrive in cooperative learning environments.

Below is a comparative table comparing four gamification escape room frameworks: Escape EDU, escapED, Room2Educ8, and BreakoutEDU (Table 1).

Table 1. Gamification frameworks comparision.

Framework	Target	DT	Learning Objectives	Levels	Customization
Escape EDU	K-12	Limited	Aligned to Curriculum	Multiple	Limited
escapED	HE	Extensive	Open-Ended	Customizable	High
Room2Educ8	K-12, HE	Moderate	Subject-Focused	Multiple	Moderate
BreakoutEDU	K-12, HE	Limited	Problem-Solving	Multiple	Limited

The criteria used for comparison are listed in the columns. The criteria used was:

1. Framework: This column lists the names of the four gamification escape room frameworks being compared, namely Escape EDU, escapED, Room2Educ8, and BreakoutEDU.

2. Target Audience: This column indicates the intended audience for each framework. "K-12" refers to primary and secondary education levels, while "Higher Education" (HE) refers to colleges and universities.
3. Design Thinking (DT) Integration: This column assesses the extent to which design thinking principles are integrated into the framework's design. Design thinking is a problem-solving approach that involves understanding users' needs and preferences.
4. Learning Objectives: This column identifies the learning objectives or educational goals addressed by each escape room framework. Some frameworks may be designed to align with specific curriculum standards or learning outcomes.
5. Difficulty Levels: This column indicates the range of difficulty levels offered by the frameworks. Multiple difficulty levels may cater to different skill levels of participants.
6. Customization Options: This column assesses the level of customization allowed within each framework. High customization options provide users with greater flexibility in designing their escape room experiences.

3   GERF

The Gamified Educational Virtual Escape Room Framework (GERF) is designed to provide enhanced micro-learning and adaptive learning experiences. Central to the framework's design is the incorporation of a user taxonomy, which caters to the diverse preferences and motivations of different learner profiles.

In fact, GERF aims to bridge the gap between adaptive learning, learning interoperability, and comprehensive learning analytics. By combining the user taxonomy approach, learning analytics through xAPI, and LTI specification for interoperability, GERF offers a holistic and personalized educational virtual escape room experience that caters to individual learners' preferences while providing educators with valuable insights for targeted instructional adjustments.

The GERF architecture is presented in Fig. 1.

Identifying the target audience, integrating the Escape Room with educational systems using IMS LTI, and harvesting actions through xAPI and LRS are crucial steps in creating an effective and impactful gamified learning experience. These approaches not only engage students but also provide valuable data and insights that empower educators to optimize the learning process and achieve better learning outcomes. These three processes are detailed in the following subsections.

3.1   Identification of Target Audience and Gamification Elements

In this section, discuss the importance of understanding the target audience who will use the Escape Room (ER). Explain how gamification can be tailored to meet the specific needs of students, teachers, or interest groups.

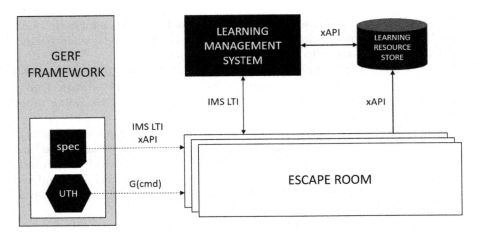

Fig. 1. GERF architecture.

Gamifying an Escape Room requires a deep understanding of the target audience to create an engaging and motivating experience. There are several User types taxonomies as frameworks that classify users based on their psychological profiles and behavioral tendencies. These frameworks have been widely used in various fields, including human-computer interaction and marketing, to help designers understand their target audience and create more engaging and effective products [7].

The User Type Hexad model [6] provides valuable insights into the different player types, each with unique motivations and preferences. It classifies users into six different types (Socialisers, Free Spirits, Achievers, Disruptors, Players, and Philanthropists):

- Socialisers: These players are driven by social interactions and collaboration. In the Escape Room, they may thrive in group puzzles that require teamwork and communication.
- Free Spirits: Free Spirits seek exploration and discovery. Including hidden clues, non-linear puzzles, and interactive elements can cater to their adventurous nature.
- Achievers: Achievers are goal-oriented and enjoy challenges. Incorporating complex puzzles, time pressure, and rewarding achievements can keep them engaged.
- Disruptors: Disruptors enjoy bending or breaking the rules of the game. Providing opportunities for creative problem-solving and unconventional solutions will appeal to them.
- Players: Players are competitive and strive for high scores or rankings. Including a leaderboard or time-based challenges can ignite their competitive spirit.
- Philanthropists: Philanthropists are motivated by contributing to a greater cause. Introducing educational elements or tying the Escape Room to real-world issues can resonate with them.

By identifying the dominant player types within the target audience, the gamification elements can be customized to create a balanced and inclusive experience that caters to different motivations and preferences.

Other popular user type taxonomies include the Bartle Taxonomy of Player Types [1], the Self-Determination Theory of Motivation [3], and the Big Five Personality Traits [5]. These frameworks provide valuable insights into how users interact with software applications and can enrich the design process to create more personalized experiences.

The injection of the gamification elements should be based on a previous survey in the target audience in order to identify the dominant user type(s). For each identified user profile, the most suitable gamification components should be used according the following the expression.

$$\sum_{i=1}^{length(UTH)} G(components_i) + G(mechanics_i) + G(dynamics_i)$$

Gamification components are represented by three layers as defined in the Pyramid of Elements of Gamification – a model developed by Kevin Werbach and Dan Hunter in their book "For the Win: How Game Thinking Can Revolutionize Your Business" [8]. In this model, the authors outline the key elements or building blocks of gamification, which is the use of game design principles and mechanics in non-game contexts to engage and motivate people. The pyramid is used to represent the hierarchy and relationships between these elements. The model includes three main layers:

- Dynamics: At the base of the pyramid are the dynamics, which are the core motivational drivers in gamification. These dynamics include elements such as rewards, status, achievements, competition, and cooperation.
- Mechanics: The next layer consists of mechanics, which are the specific actions or features that enable the dynamics to function. Examples of mechanics are points, badges, levels, leaderboards, challenges, and quests.
- Components: Above mechanics are components, which are the actual tools or components used in a gamified system. For instance, virtual goods, avatars, challenges, and progress bars are considered components.

3.2   Integration with Educational Systems

In this section, address the significance of integrating the ER with existing educational systems, such as Learning Management Systems (LMS). One of the most popular specification is the IMS LTI specification (IMS Learning Tools Interoperability) which establishes a standard set of messages and protocols for communication between a Learning Management System (LMS) and external tools or applications. This standardization ensures that various tools and applications can seamlessly work with different LMS platforms, making it easier for educators to use a variety of tools to enhance the learning experience.

In version 1.3 of the specification, the LTI Advantage is integrated as an extension to offer additional services that aim to improve the interoperability, security, and user experience of the LTI platform. The primary services provided by LTI Advantage are as follows:

- Deep Linking: This feature allows educators to create direct links to specific content items in an external tool, like a particular quiz or assignment. This way, users can access specific content without navigating through the external tool's interface.
- Assignment and Grade Services: This service enables the exchange of assignment and grade data between the LMS and external tools. Educators can create and grade assignments directly within the LMS while using external tools to provide additional functionality or content.
- Names and Role Provisioning Services: This service facilitates the exchange of user and role data between the LMS and external tools. As a result, external tools can customize the user experience based on the user's role or other user-related information.

Integrating the Escape Room with Learning Management Systems (LMS) using the IMS LTI specification offers several benefits for both educators and students:

- Seamless Access to Educational Content: By integrating the ER with LMS, educators can seamlessly provide relevant learning materials, resources, and supplementary content to enhance the educational aspect of the experience.
- Single Sign-On (SSO) and User Management: IMS LTI enables Single Sign-On, allowing students to access the Escape Room using their LMS credentials. This simplifies the login process and eliminates the need for multiple accounts, streamlining user management for educators.
- Activity Tracking and Grading: The integration allows tracking of student interactions within the Escape Room, enabling educators to monitor their progress, participation, and performance. It also facilitates automated grading for activities completed in the ER.
- Learning Analytics: Integrating ER data with LMS analytics provides a comprehensive view of student engagement and performance, helping educators identify strengths and areas for improvement in their teaching methods.
- Mobile Accessibility: With IMS LTI support, the Escape Room can be accessed across various devices, ensuring flexibility and convenience for students who prefer different learning environments.

3.3 Harvesting Actions and Visualizing Insights

In this section, discuss the importance of collecting data on student interactions within the ER.

One of the most promising specification for analytics is the xAPI specification, a newer specification that allows for more flexible tracking and reporting of learning activities, beyond what is possible with SCORM. xAPI enables the collection and analysis of data about a wide range of learning experiences, including informal and social learning. Adopting the Experience API (xAPI) and utilizing a Learning Record Store (LRS) enables the collection and analysis of detailed data on student interactions within the Escape Room:

- Granular Data Collection: xAPI allows tracking a wide range of actions, such as interactions with objects, puzzle-solving approaches, decision-making, and communication with other participants. This level of granularity provides valuable insights into individual and group behaviors.
- Rich Learning Analytics: By storing this data in an LRS, educators gain access to rich learning analytics. They can visualize students' progress, patterns, and areas of strength or struggle, facilitating data-driven decision-making in the teaching process.
- Personalized Learning: Analyzing individual actions and learning behaviors allows educators to personalize the learning experience for each student. By understanding their strengths and weaknesses, tailored interventions and resources can be provided.
- Assessment and Feedback: xAPI enables the collection of formative assessment data during the Escape Room experience. Educators can provide timely feedback and support based on students' interactions, promoting a continuous learning process.
- Learning Path Adaptation: The insights gathered from xAPI data can inform the adaptation of learning paths within the Escape Room. Educators can optimize the sequence of challenges or adjust the difficulty level based on observed student performance.

4 Conclusions

In conclusion, the introduction of GERF, our Gamified Educational Virtual Escape Room Framework, represents a significant step forward in enhancing micro-learning and adaptive learning experiences within educational settings. By incorporating a user taxonomy based on the user type hexad, we acknowledge and address the diverse preferences and motivations of different learner profiles, catering to individual needs.

GERF focuses on two critical facets: interoperability and analytics. Through the implementation of the Learning Tools Interoperability (LTI) specification, we ensure a seamless integration of Escape Room (ER) platforms with Learning Management Systems (LMS). This seamless communication between ERs and LMS platforms streamlines the learning experience for both educators and students, maximizing efficiency and effectiveness.

Furthermore, GERF leverages the xAPI specification to capture and transmit experiential data in the form of xAPI statements, which are then stored in a Learning Record Store (LRS). These learning analytics provides educators with valuable insights into students' interactions within the ER. Armed with this data, educators can make informed decisions and adapt learning content to suit individual learning needs, nurturing personalized learning experiences.

As a future work, there are several potential directions to further enhance and expand the GERF (Gamified Educational Virtual Escape Room Framework) and its impact on educational settings. Some potential areas of future work include:

- Adaptive learning strategies: Incorporating more sophisticated adaptive learning strategies can provide a more personalized and tailored learning experience for each student. By leveraging data from learning analytics, GERF can dynamically adjust the difficulty level, content, and pacing of challenges to suit individual learners' strengths and weaknesses.
- Inclusive design: Conducting research and development to ensure GERF's inclusivity for diverse learners, including those with disabilities or learning differences, is crucial. Making the framework accessible and accommodating to all students can foster a more inclusive and equitable learning environment.
- Collaborative learning: Exploring ways to integrate collaborative learning elements within the virtual escape room experience can promote teamwork, communication, and problem-solving skills. Group challenges or multi-player scenarios could provide unique learning opportunities.
- Integration of new technologies: Keeping abreast of emerging technologies and their potential integration with GERF can lead to exciting possibilities. For instance, incorporating virtual reality or augmented reality elements could further immerse students in the learning environment.
- Integration with curricula: Aligning GERF with various educational curricula and subjects can expand its applicability across different disciplines and grade levels. Ensuring a smooth integration with existing educational materials can increase its adoption by educators.

References

1. Bartle, R.A.: Hearts, clubs, diamonds, spades: players who suit muds. J. MUD Res. **1**(1), 19 (1996)
2. Clarke, S., Peel, D., Arnab, S., Morini, L., Keegan, H., Wood, O.: Escaped: a framework for creating educational escape rooms and interactive games to for higher/further education. Int. J. Ser. Games **4** (2017). https://doi.org/10.17083/ijsg.v4i3.180
3. Deci, E.L., Ryan, R.M.: Self-determination theory: a macrotheory of human motivation, development, and health. Can. Psychol. **49**(3), 182–185 (2008)
4. Fotaris, P., Mastoras, T.: Room2educ8: a framework for creating educational escape rooms based on design thinking principles. Educ. Sci. **12**, 768 (2022). https://doi.org/10.3390/educsci12110768
5. Goldberg, L.R.: The structure of phenotypic personality traits. Am. Psychol. **48**(1), 26–34 (1993)
6. Marczewski, A.: User Types, 1st edn, pp. 65–80. CreateSpace Independent Publishing Platform (2015)
7. McCarthy, J.D., McCarthy, K., Smyth, B.: User type taxonomies for personalised interactive systems. In: Proceedings of the 2022 CHI Conference on Human Factors in Computing Systems. ACM (2022). https://doi.org/10.1145/3450439.3480504
8. Werbach, K., Hunter, D.: For the Win: How Game Thinking Can Revolutionize Your Business. Wharton Digital Press (2012)

Bridging Knowledge in a Fragmented World (glossaLAB 2023)

Factors Affecting the Reliability of Information: The Case of ChatGPT

Jorge Morato[1] , Jose María Diaz-Nafria[2]([✉]) , and Sonia Sanchez-Cuadrado[3]

[1] Universidad Carlos III de Madrid, Av. Universidad 30, 28911 Leganes, Spain
`jmorato@inf.uc3m.es`
[2] Universidad a Distancia de Madrid, Pº General Martinez Campos 5, 28010 Madrid, Spain
`josemaria.diaz.n@udima.es`
[3] Universidad Complutense, C/ Santisima Trinidad, 37, 28010 Madrid, Spain
`sscuadrado@ucm.es`

Abstract. The abundance of current information makes it necessary to select the highest quality documents. For this purpose, it is necessary to deepen the knowledge of information quality systems. The different dimensions of quality are analyzed, and different problems related to these dimensions are discussed. The paper groups these issues into different facets: primary information, its manipulation and interpretation, and the publication and dissemination of information. The impact of these interdependent facets on the production of untruthful information is discussed. Finally, ChatGPT is analyzed as a use case. It is shown how these problems and facets have an impact on the quality of the system and the mentions made by experts are analyzed. Different challenges that artificial intelligence systems face are concluded.

Keywords: Information quality · Information accuracy · trustworthiness · ChatGPT

1 Introduction: Information Quality

The current overabundance of information has made it critical to select the highest quality sources of information. Information quality refers to the degree to which information meets specific criteria or standards, ensuring, amongst others, its accuracy, reliability, relevance, completeness, timeliness, and accessibility. In this work, we consider information quality and data quality as interchangeable concepts, according to a relatively broad understanding in the literature, although the difference is also often argued, in which case, data is considered as an underlying supporter of information [1–4]. The reason to consider this correspondence—though not its equivalence—has been thoroughly discussed by one of the current authors with the purpose to address information and meaning in a very wide sense, based on cross-disciplinary foundations [5–7]. Nevertheless, we will narrow here our focus to propositional semantic information, in a sense of semantics which is environmentally and pragmatically situated (op.cit.).

T. Guarda et al. (Eds.): ARTIIS 2023, CCIS 1937, pp. 151–164, 2024.
https://doi.org/10.1007/978-3-031-48930-3_12

The academic literature provides various definitions and dimensions of *information quality*, highlighting its multifaceted nature. Redman states that the quality of information is the degree to which the data and the corresponding information accurately represent reality [8]. In a similar way, Pipino et al. say that Information quality is the degree to which data correctly and consistently represents the real-world constructs it purports to represent [9]. These senses are aligned to the classical theories of truth as both correspondence and coherence [10], and can be conveniently formalised in terms of Floridi's Correctness Theory of Truth [3, 11]. In this view, information as true-beared provides a proxy to a reality the informee has no direct access to by means of a model the informee needs to reconstruct in base of a shared semantics, queries and answers. Whenever the proxy access offers a true distal access to the target reality, the information can be qualified as true-bearer, which for Floridi equates with semantic information itself [3].

In a more analytical sense, to evaluate the quality of the information some characteristics have been defined, also called dimensions [12, 13]:

- *Accuracy*: It is factual awareness. The information should not be erroneous, representing reality as accurately as possible.
- *Consistency*: The information must be internally consistent, with no contradictions or discrepancies. This information must also be externally consistent, aligned with corroborated and accepted external sources and data.
- *Completeness*: The information must be complete, without omitting critical elements that could affect its understanding or applicability.
- *Objectivity*: Refers to the quality of being impartial, and free of prejudices, avoiding subjective viewpoints.
- *Accessibility*: Information must be easily accessible to users. This implies implementing an organization and structure that facilitates its location and retrieval.
- *Reliability*: Information should be obtained from reliable sources or credible data. In this sense, traceability of information is a desirable feature.

These dimensions are focused on the information, without taking into account the user. However, the usefulness of the information—or effectiveness in terms of Floridi's model of information, referred to above, as proxy access to the target reality—depends mainly on the users, on their ability to relate it to their information needs, their previous knowledge, their current interests and, in general, to the reality around them.

Besides, there are other definitions of information quality that emphasize the reliability of the information. This is the case of the definition given by Wang and Strong [14], where *information quality* is defined as its fitness for use, or its ability to meet users' needs in a given context. This definition refers to the characteristics and attributes of information that determine the information's relevance to user needs and intentions, which ensure that information is valuable for decision-making and other purposes [15]. In a similar vein, Wang et al. define information quality as the potential of a dataset to achieve a specific (scientific or practical) goal using a given empirical analysis method [16]. These definitions emphasize users' usefulness, for decision-making or problem-solving, versus reliability.

These considerations of utility and intention do not imply stepping out of semantics since it can be endorsed from a wide sense of semantics in which pragmatics are strongly entangled, as thoroughly discussed in [5–7]. Indeed, we can look at them through the glasses of the pragmatic theory of truth [10], which in Floridi's formal model can be expressed by exchanging pure true-bearing by distal successful interaction as the support of correctness [3, 11]. On these grounds the aforementioned dimensions are to be completed by additional ones, such as:

- *Relevance*: Information should be aligned with the specific needs and requirements of the user, providing valuable insights or answers to their questions.
- *Clarity*: Information should be presented in a clear, concise, and understandable manner, facilitating easy comprehension by the intended audience.
- *Timeliness*: Information should be up-to-date and provided in a timely manner, enabling users to make informed decisions or take appropriate actions without significant delays.

All these dimensions must be taken into account in order to know which are the possible problems that can affect the effectiveness of the information processes, from the reliability of the sources to appropriateness of the subsequent actions until the information is delivered to the informee. The objective of this paper is to clarify the interdependence between these variables within the information life cycle.

The remainder of this paper is organized as follows: The next section presents a proposed classification of problems associated with the reliability of information, discussing the primary factors that influence it and their interrelationships. Subsequently, it is discussed the impact of information unreliability. Furthermore, an illustrative example highlighting the challenges encountered by chatbots, like GPT, is provided in the following section. Finally, the paper concludes with a summary of key findings and implications.

2 Exploring Information Reliability

In the past, the scarcity of information in digital format was a problem for information systems, but this is no longer the case, on the contrary, it has evolved to the opposite extreme, towards the overabundance of digital documentation. In the era of universal access to the web and digital documents, the selection of reliable sources has become a crucial task. This fact has made critical the need to establish criteria to know which information has a higher degree of being considered true or reliable [17, 18], which can be put—adopting a stance aligned with Floridi's strong semantic account of information—in terms of identifying genuine information and separating it from what can be considered junk information since it fails to be true-bearer or to cause a successful interaction, as discussed above.

Since the acquisition of information is the starting point for data ingestion in artificial intelligence systems, inferential models or knowledge bases, the characterization of the problems that may hinder the results of these applications is crucial for their correct operation. In this section, we will examine the interdependence of the factors that affect its reliability and credibility. The various issues that arise in this regard can be classified into three different, albeit interdependent, aspects:

1. *Reliability of Primary Information* [13, 17–24]: This facet represents those aspects more related to the information in its purest state, without alterations of any kind for its diffusion. Although the quality of information is usually described from this perspective, in our opinion it is also necessary to consider how it is presented and distributed. One of the causes of poor accuracy is errors caused by mishandling of data. A well-known example is the problems caused by the Excel record limit in the coronavirus outbreak [25].

2. *Information interpretation and manipulation* [12, 19, 20]: Learning follows an incremental process, where elementary knowledge is connected with different information pieces creating more complex and coherent knowledge structures. As human beings, we create belief systems that tend to accept or reject new information. Moreover, as social beings, communication is essential for social interaction, and it provides the means to convince the rest of the group. There are different motives to do this, from financial motives (e.g., advertising for selling more) to other motivations such as gaining leadership (e.g., politics). The biased interpretation of reality can be reinforced by the internal mechanisms of each person (e.g., selecting only those facts consistent with our own beliefs) or by external agents (e.g., a person trying to convince others of a certain point of view by exaggerating some characteristics of products).

3. *Publication and dissemination* [23, 26–28]: Information needs to be published in order to be transmitted effectively to the target informee. In this transition from the production of the data to its publication in the media, problems may arise that hinder understanding and access to the information.

In [23] the facets of Manipulation and Publication and Dissemination are grouped under the name *Representation Dimension*. Different researchers have described lifecycles for data and information [23, 29]. Figure 1 shows that in the data lifecycle the described facets impact in different phases in the realization processes in Data LifeCycle (DLC) proposed by El Arass & Souissi [29].

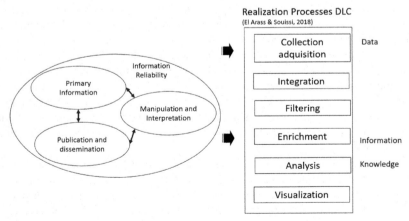

Fig. 1. Reliability facets with the realization process in Data LifeCycle (DLC).

Table 1 shows some well-known issues that affect information reliability. All the issues are classified by their facet and the dimension of quality that affects them. In order to clarify concepts a brief description has been added in the last column. Some of these problems have the consequence of hindering the application of the scientific method, e.g.,

Table 1. Reliability facets and their related issues, along with an indication of the quality dimensions affected.

Facet	Issue	Dimension	Clarifications and notes
Primary Information	Information gaps	Completeness	Lack of completeness
	Volatility/ Obsolescence	Timeliness Completeness	The truthfulness and the completeness of a statement may vary with the course of time
	Misinformation	Accuracy	False or inaccurate information that is shared without intent to mislead. It includes misunderstandings, lack of knowledge of the informant and all kinds of mistakes in the information transmission chain
	Source reliability	Objectivity	The reliability of the media in which the information is published
Manipulation and interpretation	Bias	Completeness Objectivity Accuracy	Sources that show a unique vision of reality, avoiding alternative explanations. The bias may be political, ideological, commercial, or personal
	Contradictory facts	Consistency	This issue arises when the information is inconsistent with other data or our previous knowledge
	Cherry picking	Completeness Objectivity Accuracy	It is a way to manipulate reality by selecting only the data that support a particular point of view, and omitting any information that might contradict it

(*continued*)

Table 1. (*continued*)

Facet	Issue	Dimension	Clarifications and notes
	Disinformation	Accuracy	It is the deliberate spread of false or misleading information with the intention to deceive, manipulate, or mislead others
	Echo chamber	Completeness Objectivity Accuracy	It occurs when the receiver selects sources of information that avoid alternative viewpoints or contradictory information. The result is confirmation bias, i.e., beliefs or ideas are confirmed by avoiding alternative viewpoints
	Exaggeration	Objectivity	Disproportionately increasing the weight of one factor or the repeated mention of other factors can distort reality
Publication and dissemination	Low readability	Clarity	It is the ease with which a text can be understood. Long sentences, ambiguity, jargon, slang, or technical terms can make the text difficult to understand
	Lack of accessibility	Accessibility	It is the lack of assurance that information is available and usable by all persons
	Lack of prior knowledge	Relevance	The individual's level of education and prior knowledge of the subject matter may limit their understanding and interpretation of the facts
	Semantic issues	Clarity	Synonyms, polysemic words, or metaphors can hinder some tasks such as data integration and enrichment

biased information and cherry-picking can lead to a non-falsifiable scenario. As can be noted some dimensions have more weight, like accuracy, completeness, and objectivity. Others less mentioned have in practice a high impact like timeliness, source reliability, or consistency.

These facets are interdependent; for instance, poor readability affects the understanding of the text. In turn, these misunderstandings can increase the misinformation of a piece of information. Another example can be illustrated when analyzing the need to select only some sources for their veracity, which can indirectly cause a bias in the information. A last example can be shown with poor accessibility, which by limiting access to the information it may lead to information gaps.

2.1 The Impact of Inaccurate Information

The impact of unreliable information results in lower performance of artificial intelligence algorithms and in Big Data projects. According to Gartner's analysis of poor data quality, it produces losses of at least $9.7 million per year [30]. This fact was the reason why the V of *Veracity* was added to the 3Vs of Big Data [31]. Estimating the credibility or veracity of data has also been a priority in the context of the web [24, 32].

The generation of this false information and its propagation does not always imply that those involved have bad intentions. In order to exemplify this fact, two examples can be provided. On the one hand, in social sciences the mere information of how a metric is computed produces inaccurate results, producing misinformation. This is the case exemplified with the Index H [33], or the drop in performance with the Google Flu Tool [34]. On the other hand, regarding the spread of the information, Vosoughi et al. demonstrated that fake tweets are retweeted much more than verified stories [35].

In order to detect consistency problems, cross-checking and fact-checking are usually used. Although similar, these systems compare contradictory sources, in the first case, or facts, in the second case.

2.2 The Case of ChatGPT

It is a common misconception that thanks to the current large volume of data, erroneous information in some datasets can be ignored. Different reported cases have created growing concern about the impact of poor data quality in big data projects [36].

ChatGPT is a product of OpenAI that was launched on November 30, 2022. The acronym GPT stands for the phrase Generative Pretrained Transformer. This chatbot tries to answer users' questions with a high degree of accuracy, which thanks to user feedback is constantly improving. The development of ChatGPT is linked to several advances in Natural Language Processing and Artificial Intelligence in recent years. Its success is based on the highly satisfactory results achieved with the large volume of data processed. The texts produced are built from scratch, which means that they cannot be found elsewhere. The neural network contains a cloud of patterns that share common features. The concept cloud is actually an n-dimensional space, in which spatial closeness implies a similarity of meanings (Fig. 2). To estimate this similarity, the tokens are described by hundreds of semantic features. They apply multi-sense embedding with thousand parameters, and with vectors longer than a word. The training was performed with Wikipedia, Common Crawl, Webtext2 (with Reddit posts), ebooks, GitHub, etc. For this purpose, it stores the information in a simplified format. Thanks to storing several senses of each word it can handle homonymy in an effective way [37]. It also determines the main terms in context by means of the attention layer [38]. All data processing is done by an unsupervised system without human surveillance. However, a supervised layer was added, with adjustment of the outputs with a manually generated and classified chat corpus. In addition, an RLFHF (Reinforcement Learning from Human Feedback) process was included, in which the different alternative answers given by ChatGPT are scored.

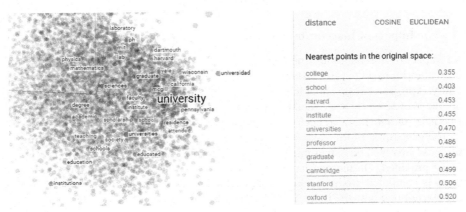

Fig. 2. Neural network of close concepts to the term "University" (source: www.projector.tensor flow.org)

Different approaches have been proposed to apply similar AI services to major search engines. One example is Bard. In a demonstration Bard gave a wrong answer to the question "What new discoveries from the James Webb Space Telescope can I tell my 9-year-old about?" [39]. In this question, the timeline is critical, but it is difficult to know what the real problem was, since Bard doesn't provide the sources employed for giving the answer. This is not the case with the competence product, the chatbot of Bing, that gave a correct answer, but it shows a limited set of sources to obtain the answer.

There is some concern about the responses ChatGPT may give to health-related queries. Although the work of Ayers et al. showed that most of the responses about additions were correct and evidence-based (2 incorrect out of 23) [40]. On the other hand, there was no mention of resources to help the population and the questions were not based on real scenarios.

In 2023, 43 experts from different universities and companies made an analysis indicating the potential applications and risks of ChatGPT [20]. In the opinion of these experts, misinformation and rumors, which can spread ChatGPT, is one of the biggest problems faced by this application to be used in fields such as education or healthcare. The risk of malicious use and propaganda, which this system tends to amplify, was also detected.

An analysis of the article by Dwivedi et al. [20] was carried out to find out which dimensions and issues—referred to in Table 1—are most frequently mentioned in these

43 interviews. The results can be seen in Figs. 3 and 4. An interesting point of both graphs are the aspects that have not been identified by experts as problems. For example, despite the error in the Bard program, there is no mention of information volatility.

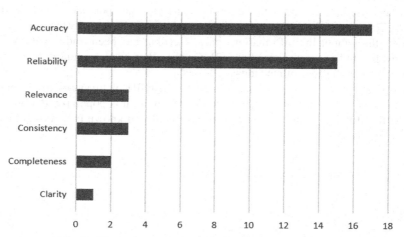

Fig. 3. Dimensions mentioned in expert interviews in [20].

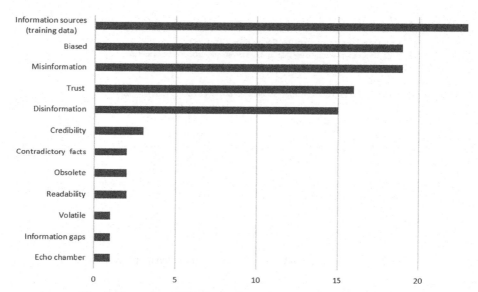

Fig. 4. Issues from Table 1 mentioned in expert interviews in [20].

In the cycle shown in Fig. 1, the effect that ChatGPT can cause can be particularly detrimental since the ease of generating texts that are difficult to identify as automatically created can contribute to information's bias and exaggeration. In this sense, it is foreseeable that there will be an increase in disinformation on the Internet as ChatGPT massively generates credible texts from, for example, inaccurate or outright erroneous sources. It would be necessary to at least acknowledge the main sources that agree with the opinion expressed in the response.

The problem is that often, the automatic determination of which statement is true tends to be based on the one with the most occurrences, i.e., popularity is equated with veracity. This approach may overstimate sources that have the capacity to reproduce their messages throughout the information space, fact that has been traditionally criticize in the media studies for decades [41, 42]. On the other hand, popularity has obvious disadvantages in the case of new ideas.

A similar approach is applied in systems like ChatGPT by means of voting systems. Since the appropriateness of an answer can be voted on, it is popularity that is used to estimate truthfulness, while we know well that an alleged known fact does not have to be true (Fig. 5).

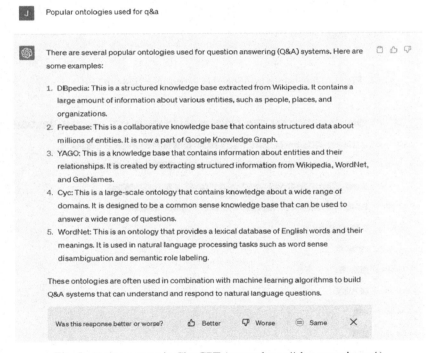

Fig. 5. Voting system in ChatGPT (source:https://chat.openai.com/).

In addition, Fig. 6 shows those aspects not mentioned in Table 1 but whose importance has been considered very relevant in the article by Dwivedi et al. [20]. Specifically, Fig. 6 emphasizes the legal recognition and copyright aspects. This is a consequence of the reference absence to the sources of the information generated. The lack of authorship has repercussions on its quality, since there is no responsibility for the information generated. ChatGPT owes part of its results to a large number of anonymous authors who have generated a large number of contributions. Lack of recognition may cause that those sectors where recognition is critical, such as academia, to stop making their research available. One way to achieve this could be for academic journals to veto their inclusion in the chatbot database, harming the quantity and quality of available information.

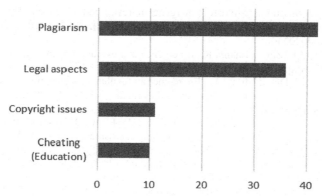

Fig. 6. Other issues mentioned by Dwivedi et al. [20].

3 Conclusions

The current overabundance of information makes it necessary to go deeper into systems to determine which information is more reliable and of higher quality. Otherwise, we are taking for information what cannot be qualified as such, but rather information and disinformation. In extreme—but nevertheless frequent—situations the whole purpose of the information processes fails, from both the semantic and the pragmatic dimensions.

This paper has shown a new classification of the problems that can affect the unreliability of information. These problems are directly related to those mentioned in the literature on information quality, and represent diverse failures in the general model of information processes. As argued in the paper, the different problems are often presented in groups. This is because some problems in one facet can lead to problems in others. In this way, perverse cycles can be generated, in which erroneous information can be amplified in a marked way with the passage of time and the interrelationships between the different facets.

As an example, in the case of ChatGPT, despite its obvious virtues, there are good reasons to believe that it can become a powerful disinformation and misinformation system. It also presents obvious problems in relation to the lack of recognition of works.

References

1. Sequoiah-Grayson, S., Floridi, L.: Semantic conceptions of information. In: Zalta, E.N., (ed.). The Stanford Encyclopedia of Philosophy (Spring 2022 Edition). https://plato.stanford.edu/archives/spr2022/entries/information-semantic/

2. CIHI: CIHI's Information Quality Framework. Canadian Institute for Health Information (CIHI). Ottawa, Canada (2017)
3. Floridi, L.: The Philosophy of Information. Oxford University Press, Oxford, UK (2011)
4. Díaz-Nafría, J.M., Salto-Alemany, F., Pérez-Montoro, M. (coord.): glossariumBITri: Interdisciplinary Elucidation of Concepts, Metaphors, Theories and Problems Concerning Information. UPSE-BITrum, Santa Elena, Ecuador (2016)
5. Díaz-Nafría, J.M., Zimmermann, R.: Emergence and evolution of meaning. The GDI revisiting programme. Part 2: regressive perspective. Information 4(2), 240–261 (2013). https://doi.org/10.3390/info4020240
6. Díaz-Nafría, J.M., Zimmermann, R.: Emergence and evolution of meaning. Triple C 11(1), 13–35 (2013). https://doi.org/10.31269/triplec.v11i1.334
7. Zimmermann, R., Díaz-Nafría, J.M.: Emergence and evolution of meaning. The GDI revisiting programme. Part 1: progressive perspective. Informationb 3(3), 472–503 (2012). https://doi.org/10.3390/info3030472
8. Redman, T.C.: Data quality: a view from the field. DM Rev. 11, 38–41 (2001)
9. Pipino, L.L., Lee, Y.W., Wang, R.Y.: Data quality assessment. Commun. ACM 45, 211–218 (2002). https://doi.org/10.1145/505248.505271
10. Glanzberg, M.: Truth. In: Zalta, E.N. (ed.) The Stanford Encyclopedia of Philosophy (2021). https://plato.stanford.edu/archives/sum2021/entries/truth/ (2021)
11. Floridi, L.: Outline of a theory of truth as correctness for semantic information. tripleC 7(2), 142–157 (2009). https://doi.org/10.31269/triplec.v7i2.131
12. Arazy, O., Kopak, R., Hadar, I.: Heuristic principles and differential judgments in the assessment of information quality. JAIS 18, 403–432 (2017). https://doi.org/10.17705/1jais.00458
13. Lee, Y.W., Strong, D.M., Kahn, B.K., Wang, R.Y.: AIMQ: a methodology for information quality assessment. Inform. Manage. 40, 133–146 (2002). https://doi.org/10.1016/S0378-7206(02)00043-5
14. Wang, R.Y., Strong, D.M.: Beyond accuracy: what data quality means to data consumers. J. Manag. Inf. Syst. 12, 5–33 (1996). https://doi.org/10.1080/07421222.1996.11518099
15. Strong, D.M., Lee, Y.W., Wang, R.Y.: Data quality in context. Commun. ACM 40, 103–110 (1997). https://doi.org/10.1145/253769.253804
16. Wang, R.Y., Strong, D.M., Liew, C.-W.: Information quality research: its past, present and future. In: Proceedings of the 33rd Annual Hawaii International Conference on System Sciences, pp. 213–222. IEEE (2002)
17. Pérez, A., et al.: Fostering teenagers' assessment of information reliability: effects of a classroom intervention focused on critical source dimensions. Learn. Instr. 58, 53–64 (2018). https://doi.org/10.1016/j.learninstruc.2018.04.006
18. Tabibian, B., Valera, I., Farajtabar, M., Song, L., Schölkopf, B., Gomez-Rodriguez, M.: Distilling information reliability and source trustworthiness from digital traces. In: Proceedings of the 26th International Conference on World Wide Web. pp. 847–855. International World Wide Web Conferences Steering Committee, Perth Australia (2017)
19. Diaz Ruiz, C., Nilsson, T.: Disinformation and echo chambers: how disinformation circulates on social media through identity-driven controversies. J. Public Policy Mark. 42, 18–35 (2023). https://doi.org/10.1177/07439156221103852
20. Dwivedi, Y.K., Kshetri, N., Hughes, L., Slade, E.L., et al.: Opinion Paper: "So what if ChatGPT wrote it?" Multidisciplinary perspectives on opportunities, challenges and implications of generative conversational AI for research, practice and policy. Int. J. Inform. Manage. 71, 102642 (2023). https://doi.org/10.1016/j.ijinfomgt.2023.102642
21. Phuong, J., et al.: Information needs and priority use cases of population health researchers to improve preparedness for future hurricanes and floods. J. Am. Med. Inform. Assoc. 28, 249–260 (2021). https://doi.org/10.1093/jamia/ocaa195

22. Stvilia, B., Gasser, L., Twidale, M.B., Smith, L.C.: A framework for information quality assessment. J. Am. Soc. Inf. Sci. **58**, 1720–1733 (2007). https://doi.org/10.1002/asi.20652
23. Taleb, I., Serhani, M.A., Bouhaddioui, C., Dssouli, R.: Big data quality framework: a holistic approach to continuous quality management. J. Big Data. **8**, 76 (2021). https://doi.org/10.1186/s40537-021-00468-0
24. Shah, A.A., Ravana, S.D., Hamid, S., Maizatul Akmar, I.: Web credibility assessment: affecting factors and assessment techniques, Inform. Res. **20**(1), 655 (2015) http://informationr.net/ir/20-1/paper663.html#.YJp4YLX7SUk
25. Hern, A.: Covid: how Excel may have caused loss of 16,000 test results in England | Health policy | The Guardian (2020). https://www.theguardian.com/politics/2020/oct/05/how-excel-may-have-caused-loss-of-16000-covid-tests-in-england
26. Foley, O., Helfert, M.: Information quality and accessibility. In: Sobh, T. (ed.) Innovations and Advances in Computer Sciences and Engineering, pp. 477–481. Springer, Netherlands, Dordrecht (2010)
27. Morato, J., Iglesias, A., Campillo, A., Sanchez-Cuadrado, S.: Automated readability assessment for spanish e-government information. J Inform Systems Eng. **6**, em0137 (2021). https://doi.org/10.29333/jisem/9620
28. Crawford-Manning, F., et al.: Evaluation of quality and readability of online patient information on osteoporosis and osteoporosis drug treatment and recommendations for improvement. Osteoporos Int. **32**, 1567–1584 (2021). https://doi.org/10.1007/s00198-020-05800-7
29. El Arass, M., Souissi, N.: Data lifecycle: from big data to SmartData. In: 2018 IEEE 5th International Congress on Information Science and Technology (CiSt), pp. 80–87. IEEE, Marrakech (2018)
30. Molinari, A., Nollo, G.: The quality concerns in health care Big Data. In: 2020 IEEE 20th Mediterranean Electrotechnical Conference (MELECON), pp. 302–305. IEEE, Palermo, Italy (2020)
31. Ghasemaghaei, M.: Understanding the impact of big data on firm performance: the necessity of conceptually differentiating among big data characteristics. Int. J. Inf. Manage. **57**, 102055 (2021). https://doi.org/10.1016/j.ijinfomgt.2019.102055
32. Pendyala, V.: Veracity of web information. In: Veracity of Big Data, pp. 17–33. Apress, Berkeley, CA (2018)
33. Koltun, V., Hafner, D.: The h-index is no longer an effective correlate of scientific reputation. PLoS ONE **16**, e0253397 (2021). https://doi.org/10.1371/journal.pone.0253397
34. Lazer, D., Kennedy, R., King, G., Vespignani, A.: The parable of google flu: traps in big data analysis. Science **343**, 1203–1205 (2014). https://doi.org/10.1126/science.1248506
35. Vosoughi, S., Roy, D., Aral, S.: The spread of true and false news online. Science **359**, 1146–1151 (2018). https://doi.org/10.1126/science.aap9559
36. Hardford, T.: Big data: a big mistake? Significance, pp. 14–19 (2014). https://doi.org/10.1111/j.1740-9713.2014.00778.x
37. Ruas, T., Grosky, W., Aizawa, A.: Multi-sense embeddings through a word sense disambiguation process. Expert Syst. Appl. **136**, 288–303 (2019). https://doi.org/10.1016/j.eswa.2019.06.026
38. Vaswani, A., et al.: Attention is all you need. In: Proceedings of the 31st International Conference on Neural Information Processing Systems. pp. 6000–6010. Curran Associates Inc., Red Hook, NY, USA (2017)
39. Vicent, J.: Google's AI chatbot Bard makes factual error in first demo. The Verge, Feb, 8 (2023). https://www.theverge.com/2023/2/8/23590864/google-ai-chatbot-bard-mistake-error-exoplanet-demo
40. Ayers, J.W., et al.: Evaluating artificial intelligence responses to public health questions. JAMA Netw. Open **6**, e2317517 (2023). https://doi.org/10.1001/jamanetworkopen.2023.17517

41. Christensen, C.: A decade of WikiLeaks: So what? Int. J. Media Cultural Politics **10**(3), 273–284 (2014). https://doi.org/10.1386/macp.10.3.273_1
42. Ramonet, I.: La tyrannie de la communication. Gallimard, Paris (2001)

QuinuaSmartApp: A Real-Time Agriculture Precision IoT Cloud Platform to Crops Monitoring

Héctor Bedón[1]([✉])(iD), Miguel Chicchon[2](iD), Billy Grados[3](iD), Daniel Paz[3](iD), and Jose Maria Díaz-Nafría[1](iD)

[1] Universidad a Distancia de Madrid-UDIMA, Escuela de Ciencias Tecnicas e Ingenieria, Collado Villalba, Spain
{hectormanuel.bedon,josemaria.diaz.n}@udima.es
[2] Escuela de Posgrado, Pontificia Universidad Católica del Perú Lima, Lima, Peru
mchicchon@pucp.edu.pe
[3] Grupo de Tecnologias Exponenciales(GITX-ULIMA), Universidad de Lima, Lima, Peru
{bgrados,dpazz}@ulima.edu.pe

Abstract. IoT networks, cloud-based applications and the use of artificial intelligence models in precision agriculture present an important opportunity to increase production and optimize the use of water resources, which will allow the development of sustainable and responsible agriculture in the face of global food security. In order to provide real-time remote monitoring of quinoa crops, this article proposes and implements an integrated architecture based on sensor networks, drones with multispectral and Lidar cameras and cloud computing-based applications. The system has hardware and software applications that enable Quinoa crop monitoring during the different stages of its growth. Additionally, it comprises weather stations providing real-time data which permits actualising the predictive models that can be used for local climate change projections. The monitoring of the level of humidity in the crop field through soil stations feeds the training database based on machine learning that allows generating the projection of water demand, which allows more efficient and better-planned use of crop water. Additionally, it implements a service of warning messages, attended by experts who are connected to the system in order to provide technical recommendations to help deal with this issue in order to lessen the impact of pests and diseases in the field.

Keywords: IoT · Sensor Networks · Machine learning · Cloud Computing · Precision Agriculture

---

Supported by Programa Nacional de Innovación Agraria (PNIA).

1   Introduction

Precision Agriculture (PA) [1], designed to improve profitability and/or minimize environmental impact in the medium and long term [2], provides a localized management of crops and the means to study soil characteristics, crop behavior, phytosanitary, among others, of each portion of the fields.

Awareness of soil and crop variability started in the 1970 s and 1980 s, when companies such as CENEX, FARMERS Central Union Exchange Inc. and Control Data Corporation, of Minnesota-USA, established the first concept of soil and plant variability and its benefits by management for zones instead of the entire planted area.

Agricultural engineering refers to the use of sensors and Global Positioning System (GPS) in agricultural machines for mapping and application of inputs with varied doses. Massey Ferguson, 1982, was the first to produce a commercial result with a grain productivity mapping system. In the 1990 s, John Deere, Case, AGCO and New Holland developed PA, which is now widely used in vineyards in Chile [3]. In 1982, the performance monitor was developed. 1984 marks the positioning system. In 1985/96 the variable dose technology appears. In 1991 the first performance monitoring system was sold in Europe. In 1996 performance monitoring models are in the market e.g. Field Star, Green Star, among others. EIP-AGRI [4], European Union, proposes seven points to be resolved to incorporate PA in Europe.

In 2009, in Latin America, Argentina [2] achieved that 30% of producers use PA in wheat, corn, sugarcane and tobacco. Mexico [5], currently uses PA for greater efficiency and yield of large-scale crops.

Europe and the USA investigated how to increase production performance in the scope of projects FIspace [6], SmartAgrifood [7], Finish [8], Fractals [9], Speedupeurope [10], based on ICTs through of the Internet of Things (IoT). There are commercial architectures such as IBM Cloud, Microsoft Azure, Google Cloud Platform, Libelium and open source-based architectures such as Kaa [11], OpenAG Initiative [12] that allow rapid deployment of IoT solutions. Currently, there are many IoT implementations in agriculture as described in [13] that propose a cloud-based IoT solution, also in [14] they show that Big Data and the concept of decentralized cloud operation will help farmers operate more efficiently and more securely and finally [15] explore the use of ultra-low power microcontroller as sensor hardware. Actually, there is a great interest in using artificial intelligence technologies applied to agriculture [16] combining recent advances in Deep Learning (DL) and Internet of Things (IoT) [17] in the direction that has been worked in this research. Hence, our objective is to design, develop and integrate into a single system called QuinuasmartApp with some features already identified for IoT-based solutions, cloud computing applications and artificial intelligence models developed until now. Section 2 describes the QuinuaSmartApp project. Section 3 shows the sensor network implemented. Section 4 raises the cloud infrastructure used and finally in Sect. 5 we show the conclusions of this article.

2   QuinuaSmartApp

QuinuaSmartApp (see Fig. 1) proposes to automate crop management in an intelligent, remote and real-time way, to obtain information on known and not yet known factors determining the productivity of organic quinoa implemented in the peasant community of San Lorenzo, Jauja, Peru. An IoT network of wireless sensors is deployed in the field of quinoa cultivation to collect information on the soil and the environment through monitoring stations on different parameters such as temperature, conductivity and soil moisture and meteorological information such as temperature, radiation , wind speed, pressure, etc. These stations connect to the Internet through a gateway that uses the mobile network. Drones equipped with Lidar, Multispectral and visible spectrum cameras are also used, which allow knowing parameters such as crop growth, planting density and NDVI of the crop field. The collected data is sent to a database located in the Google GCP Internet cloud. Two applications have been developed, a Web application and a mobile application for accessing data both at the management level and at the technical and/or scientific level. At the management level, the system allows the registration and notification of alerts and messages from the farmer to the engineer responsible for the crop field, facilitating preventive and/or corrective actions in time to prevent or reduce the harmful manifestation of pests, phytopathogens and external abiotic factors. The system also makes it possible to have a unique historical record of the crop field similar to the one a person has in their clinical history where data such as the type of crop that has been carried out, on what date, what types of pesticides have been used, what type of incidents have occurred, etc. The data recorded and/or obtained by the sensor devices have made it possible to model the water demand of the quinoa crop, which allows an optimal use of the water resource. At the climate projection level, the system allows viewing the 50-year climate prediction of the region where the crop field is located so that the farmer can carry out adequate planting planning. Finally, the system implements a marketplace functionality, where the farmer offers his products for sale from the moment they are planted and a company can register its purchase requirements. The system allows real-time historical statistics and visual projection reports that facilitate decision making in the field of cultivation. At a scientific level, the data recorded in the system have allowed feeding models such as Aquacrop [18], which allows forecasting the yield of the quinoa crop to achieve a natural and sustainable organic crop over time.

Quinuasmartapp articulates the information flow of the different types of information, both management and operational information, whether technical and/or scientific, using the cyber-subsidiarity model [19] in order to achieve a sustainable system.

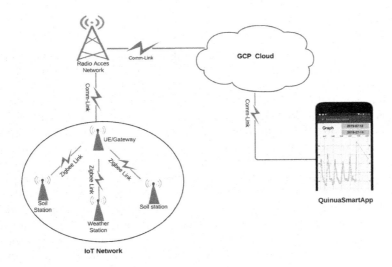

Fig. 1. QuinuaSmartApp system overview.

3   IoT Network

It's constructed a low-power wide-area network (LPWAN) to monitor quinoa cultivation in real-time. This network is comprised of three types of IoT stations, as detailed below: a soil station, a weather station, and a gateway station.

3.1   Soil Station

The soil station (Fig. 2) is built up using two different kinds of Decagon devices, the GS1 and GS3 devices [20], which will be detailed below.

GS1 Devices. It contains a single sensor that determines volumetric water content (VWC) by measuring the dielectric constant of the medium using capacitance and frequency domain technology. The 70 MHz frequency minimizes salinity and textural effects, making the GS1 accurate in almost any soil or soilless medium. It arrives with generic calibrations for mineral soils and soilless media included in its operator manual. This sensor obtains its measurement in analog mode. Therefore, we use the conversion equation included in the datasheet:

$$\theta = 4.94 \cdot 10^{-4} \text{mV} - 0.554 \tag{1}$$

where θ represents the volumetric water content and mV represents the sensor's output when it is excited between 3 and 15.

Fig. 2. Soil station.

GS3 Devices. The Decagon GS3 sensor is an accurate tool for monitoring electrical conductivity, volumetric water content, and temperature in soil and soilless substrates. The GS3 determines volumetric water content (VWC) by measuring the dielectric constant ϵ of the medium using capacitance/frequency-domain technology. Decagon digital sensors have a 1-wire serial interface for communicating sensor measurements. The sensor supports two different protocols: SDI-12 and DDI-Serial. Both interfaces are documented in their datasheet. Each protocol has advantages and implementation challenges. There are differences in voltage levels, logic levels, and signal timing for each protocol. The SDI-12 protocol is used in this project and it is a standard protocol for interfacing sensors to data loggers and data acquisition equipment. Multiple sensors with unique addresses can share a common 3-wire bus (power, ground, and data). Two-way communication between the sensor and logger is possible by sharing the data line for transmit and receive as defined by the standard sensor measurements triggered by protocol command. Figure 3 depicts the data flux captured by the GS1/GS3 devices in the soil station.

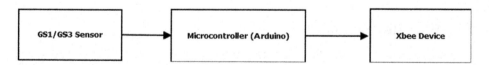

Fig. 3. The stream of data from the GS1/GS3 devices in the Soil station.

3.2 Gateway Station

Using the Zegbee protocol, this station (Fig. 4) acts as a gateway for the soil and weather stations. A USB cable and a SparkFun XBee Explorer USB are used to connect the Raspberry Pi Zero W to the XBee coordinator module. It also contains a 4G modem that functions as user equipment (UE) for mobile network connectivity. The gateway is based on a low-power single-board computer Raspberry Pi Model Zero W with a 1 GHz ARM processor on the CPU motherboard. Additionally, it has one USB port, one HDMI port, 512 MB RAM, one micro SD storage socket, and forty GPIO interface ports. It is compatible with Raspbian, the Debian-based Linux distribution used in this project. The Raspberry Pi connects to a 4G modem through Wi-Fi (802.11n) to access the Google Cloud Platform (GCP). MQTT is the message protocol used to connect to GCP. Finally, we put an SQLite database in the Raspberry with the purpose of duplicating the data acquired from soil and weather stations while limiting Raspberry's memory space in the event of an internet outage.

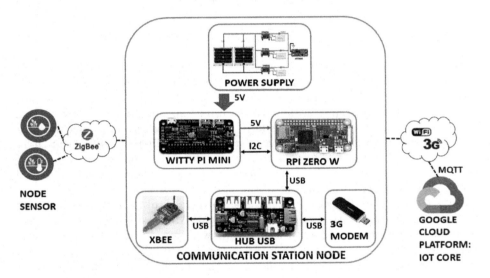

Fig. 4. Gateway communication station components

3.3   Wheather Station

This node (Fig. 5) collects data from the climate sensors connected to an Arduino Mega 2560 pro mini. This data is sent to a Raspberry Pi Zero W through a serial connection and then processed by the gateway program similar to the communications station node (Fig. 6). The sensors used in the station are:

Weather Meters. These sensors of ARGENT Data Systems allow the measurement of climatic variables such as wind speed, wind direction and rainfall. The wind vane reports wind direction as a voltage which is produced by the combination of eight resistors inside the sensor. The vane's magnet may close two switches at once, allowing up to sixteen possible positions to be indicated. The cup-type anemometer measures wind speed by simply closing a switch in each rotation. A wind speed of 2.4011 KPH produces one switch closure per second. Finally, the rain gauge is a self-emptying bucket-type rain gauge which activates a momentary button closure for each 0.2794 mm of rain that is collected.

Fig. 5. Weather station

Wattmeter. This sensor is a module that measures the voltage, current and power of an embedded system with a high-resolution, high-precision and maximum relative error of $\pm0.2\%$. It is used for power consumption and battery life evaluation.

BME280. This sensor is an environmental sensor of high precision and small size that integrates an onboard temperature sensor, humidity sensor and barometer. Environmental Sensor has based on BoSCH MEMS sensor (Micro-Electro-Mechanical System) and provides both SPI and I2C interfaces. The temperature measuring range is $-40°C$ to $+85\,°C$, resolution of $0.1\,°C$ and deviation of $\pm0.5\,°C$. The humidity measuring range is 0 to 100% RH, resolution of 0.1% RH and deviation of $\pm2\%$ RH. The pressure measuring range is 300 to 1100 hPa.

Davis 6450. The Solar Radiation Sensor, or solar pyranometer, measures global radiation, the sum at the point of measurement of both the direct and diffuse components of solar irradiance. Detects solar radiation at wavelengths of 300 to 1100 nm. The resolution is $1\,W/m2$ and the range is from 0 to $1800\,W/m2$.

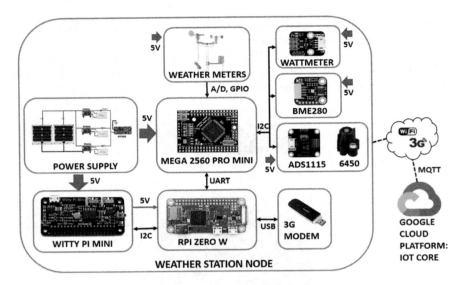

Fig. 6. Weather station components

3.4   Drone Cameras Integration

The drones allow the acquisition of multispectral images, which in turn enables the determination of the NDVI index of the cultivation field. In addition, LIDAR images facilitate the identification of crops' growth, as well as high-resolution images that allow the estimation of sowing density.

LIDAR Camera Integration. Integration of a LiDAR VLP16 Puck Lite sensor was achieved in the Matrice 600 PRO drone from the DJI brand. The integration process consists of the stage of acquisition of position/orientation data from the drone and the point cloud of the LiDAR sensor in real-time. For this purpose, an ODROID minicomputer was used to execute a program in Robot Operating System (ROS) that communicates with said elements using the DJI And Velodyne SDK. For the mechanical integration of the electronic components in the drone, a structure was designed and printed using 3D printing technology. Finally, the data processing stage obtained after scanning the fields is carried out using a program written in Python language. The 3D information from the field allows specialists to track the size of the crop throughout the growing stage. The results obtained are evaluated based on a comparison with a point cloud generated from images obtained from a DJI Phantom 4 drone with an RGB camera. The georeferenced point cloud generation process can be seen in Fig. 7.

Multispectral Camera Integration. Integration of a multispectral camera model ADCmicro of the Tetracam brand was achieved in the drone model Matrice 600 PRO of the DJI brand. The integration process consists of the

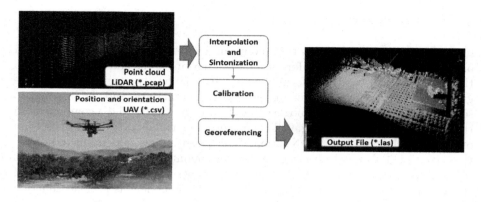

Fig. 7. Georeferenced point cloud generation process

stage of acquisition of position data from a Tetracam GPS and the multispectral camera in real-time powered by an 11.1V battery. For the mechanical integration of the electronic components in the drone, a structure was designed and printed using 3D printing technology. Finally, the data processing stage obtained was carried out after capturing the images of the crop fields using the PixelWrech2 program to process each image and then generating the mosaic with the Pix4DMapper program. The information of the NDVI index enables the analysis and location of places in the field with little vigor of the crop that requires some action by the specialist. In addition, the images obtained by a DJI Phantom 4 drone were used as support for the analysis of the results. The georeferenced orthomosaic generation process can be seen in Fig. 8. The images obtained by the multispectral camera are processed using an algorithm based on deep learning to perform crop and weed segmentation [21].

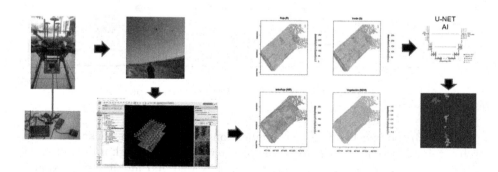

Fig. 8. NDVI orthomosaic generation process

4   Cloud-Based Applications

QuinuaSmartApp implements IoT, mobile and web applications and modules in order to support the flow of information from sensors to the end-user application through the cloud-based platform. The IoT module has two components on the ground (the program for retrieving the environmental data, and the program to send the information to the Google Cloud Platform - GCP), and a component on the cloud, as illustrated in Fig. 9. The first program collaborates with the second one sending the data in a JSON format. This program has credentials to publish the data to IoT Core which is the service for communication with small devices like the stations, and it sends the telemetry events through the publishing and subscribing service (Cloud Pub/Sub). The last component is a cloud function that is automatically triggered when a new event arrives and stores the sensor data to a NoSQL database called Cloud Datastore.

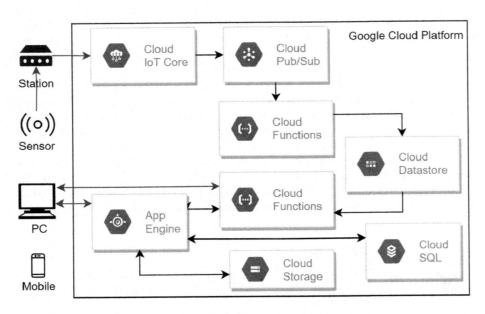

Fig. 9. GCP architecture of QuinuasmartApp

The web module has two web applications (frontend and backend) and a web service. The end-user accesses the server web apps through a browser that retrieves the client web app as depicted in the "web and mobile applications" figure. This client web app gets the data from the backend server web app and the web service in GCP. The backend and frontend use an app engine service for each one and the web service uses a cloud function. Both GCP services obtain the data from Datastore, Cloud SQL and Cloud Storage. Datastore saves sensor data, Cloud SQL stores master and configuration data like the name for a station, sensors, etc., and Cloud Storage hosts images for icons, logos, etc. The farmer and the researcher use web applications through the frontend client web app. The admin uses the backend server web app through the browser that renders the HTML contents and necessary related elements. These web and mobile applications are represented in Fig. 10.

The web module has two web applications (frontend and backend) and a web service. The frontend is used by the researcher who monitors the sensor data. There are 4 main options: issues, activity history, monitoring (Fig. 10a), and predictions.

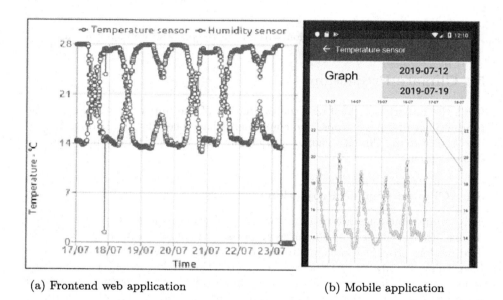

(a) Frontend web application   (b) Mobile application

Fig. 10. Monitoring screens

The backend is used by the admin in order to set the configuration data like sensor and station names, etc. Admin panel has the following main options: access, IoT and agriculture. In the access option, the admin user configures users, roles, and groups. In IoT: magnitude, stations, sensors (Fig. 11), and gateways. In agriculture, access is provided for external consultants to: plant species, plant varieties, plant afflictions; while administrators can manage fields, crops, intentions of crops, crop issues, crop activity history, and crop reports.

The mobile module is used by the farmer who is responsible for working in the field and uses the mobile application on a handheld device with internet connectivity. As a farmer, he registers its fields, crops, issues and farming activities. He can monitor the current condition of the soil through the sensors through the data displayed in graphical reports (Fig. 10b).

Fig. 11. Sensor configuration screen from the backend web application

5   Climate Projection

With the intention to facilitate the evaluation of the impact of weather on the productivity of quinoa crops, two components have been devised and integrated into the system: Climate change projection and Water demand projection of quinoa crops.

5.1   Climate Change Projection

This component estimate climate change projection simulated by the climatic models used in phase 5 by the intercomparison of coupled models (CMP5) [22]. The models provide local climate projections for this area, generating a first future climate database for the region, as a decision-making tool for farmers and other users of the basin (Fig. 12). The climatic projections show a significant warming from 2,0° of temperature for the RCP2.6 scenario to 3,5° of temperature for the RCP8.5 scenario expected in the entire evaluated area of the Jauja valley for the next fifty years, together with a decrease in precipitation.

5.2   Water Demand Projection

This component focuses on the utilization of water resources in agricultural activities related to Quinoa production in Peru's central region (Jauja - Junn). The goal is to optimize production processes and crops to maximize quinoa production using machine learning, specifically the development of an artificial neural network model that allows to establish approximate predictions of reference evapo-transpiration, to estimate the water footprint or water resource required for quinua crops, in order to promote responsible and optimal use of this resource, which is likely to be scarce in the future. This goal is primarily realized by the selection of input variables important to the neural network model, which were gathered from various data sources resulting from the construction of the IoT network in the cultivation area. The relationship between

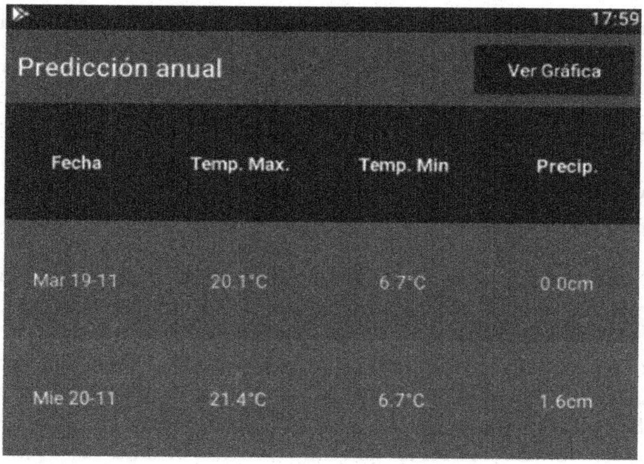

Fig. 12. Climate change projection shown for the mobile application

the predictor variables and their respective variable responses was statistically analyzed using the methodology of minimum partial squares (PLS), and thus the model's prescindible variables were selected, so that the artificial neuronal network model could be trained. Finally, after ongoing optimization of the artificial neural network model, the final structure is formed, as well as the model accuracy measurement, using statistical error and adjustment measures that allow to predict the water requirement of the investigated field of production.

6   Conclusions

In this article, we show how the QuinuasmartApp system has been designed and implemented to monitor in real time the cultivation of quinoa in the peasant community of San Lorenzo, Jauja, Junin in the Peruvian Andes. At the hardware level, a wireless IoT network of environmental monitoring stations, soil moisture monitoring stations and gateway communication stations that connect to the mobile network have been implemented and integrated. The crop field monitoring system is complemented by data obtained by drones equipped with multispectral, visible and Lidar cameras. At the software level, a web application and a software application in the Internet cloud have been implemented that allow the recording and visualization of the data acquired in the system in real time. A marketplace module has been implemented that allows farmers to offer their products as well as allows companies to publish the demand for agricultural products. Finally, with the data obtained, we create and integrate automatic learning methods into the platform to analyze the water demand of the quinoa crop that allow optimizing the use of water. Climate change forecast models have also been implemented as useful tools for farmers in planning their crops. A cyber-subsidiarity model has been followed in order to achieve a sustainable system.

Acknowledgment. QuinuasmartApp was partially financed by the National Agrarian Innovation Program (PNIA) of Peru.

References

1. Khanna, A., Kaur, S.: Evolution of Internet of Things (IoT) and its significant impact in the field of precision agriculture. Comput. Electron. Agric. **157**, 218–231 (2019)
2. Swinton, S., Lowenberg-deboer, J.: Global adoption of precision agriculture technologies: who, when and why. Third European Conference On Precision Agriculture, pp. 557–562 (2001)
3. Mulla, D.: Twenty five years of remote sensing in precision agriculture: key advances and remaining knowledge gaps. Biosyst. Eng.. **114**, 358–371 (2013), Special Issue: Sensing Technologies for Sustainable Agriculture
4. Baudry, J., Others: EIP-AGRI focus group benefits of landscape features for arable crop production (2016). https://hal.inrae.fr/hal-02800942
5. Negrete, J.: Precision Agriculture in Mexico. Current Status and Perspectives, International Journal Of Horticulture (2017)
6. Beulens, A., Verdouw, C., Wolfert, J.: FIspace: future internet business collaboration networks in agri-food, transport and logistics. In: 8th Igls-Forum onSystem Dynamics and Innovation in Food Networks (2014). Igls/Innsbruck, Austria; Conference date: 17–02-2014 Through 21–02-2014
7. Verdouw, C., Kruize, J.: Digital twins in farm management: illustrations from the FIWARE accelerators SmartAgriFood and Fractals (2017)
8. Sundmaeker, H., Verdouw: Dynamic business collaboration in supply chains with future internet technologies: acceleration of SME-driven app development (2014)
9. Verdouw, C., Kruize, J., Wolfert, J.: Accelerating internet-based innovation in agriculture and food: opportunities of the future internet accelerator programme - WUR. Poster (scientific) (2015). https://www.wur.nl/en/Publication-details.htm?publicationId=publication-way-353037343433
10. Laarman, S.: Speed Up or Slow Down: a case study into perceived bureaucracy in public-private accelerator programs (2016,1)
11. KaaIoT Technologies. https://www.kaaproject.org/agriculture. Accessed 23 May 2023
12. Openag initiative website. https://www.media.mit.edu/groups/open-agriculture-openag/. Accessed 23 May 2023
13. Dholu, M., Ghodinde, K.: Internet of Things (IoT) for precision agriculture application. In: 2018 2nd International Conference On Trends In Electronics And Informatics (ICOEI), pp. 339–342 (2018)
14. Suciu, G., Istrate, C., Ditu, M.: Secure smart agriculture monitoring technique through isolation. In: 2019 Global IoT Summit (GIoTS), pp. 1–5 (2019)
15. Kjellby, R., Cenkeramaddi, L., Frøytlog, A., Lozano, B., Soumya, J., Bhange, M.: Long-range Self-powered IoT devices for agriculture aquaponics based on multi-hop topology. In: 2019 IEEE 5th World Forum On Internet of Things (WF-IoT), pp. 545–549 (2019)
16. Saranya, T., Deisy, C., Sridevi, S., Anbananthen, K.: A comparative study of deep learning and Internet of Things for precision agriculture. Eng. Appl. Artif. Intell. **122**, 106034 (2023)
17. Oliveira, R., Silva, R.: Artificial intelligence in agriculture: benefits, challenges, and trends. Appl. Sci. **13**, 7405 (2023)

18. Aquacrop website. https://www.fao.org/aquacrop/es/. Accessed 22 May 2023
19. Dıaz-Nafrıa, J., Cañizares-Espada, M., Seoane-Pujol, I., Montaño-Gómez, J., Guarda, T.: Enabling sustainable management through Kalman filtering in glossaLAB: a case study on cyber-subsidiarity. Dev. Adv. Defense Secur.: Proc. MICRADS **2021**, 47–60 (2021)
20. Meter group Inc., https://www.metergroup.com/. Accessed 22 May 2023
21. Apaza, M., Monzón, H., Garrido, R.: Semantic segmentation of weeds and crops in multispectral images by using a convolutional neural networks based on U-Net (2020)
22. García López, Y., Bedón Monzón, H., Durán Gómez, M.: Proyección climática para el periodo 2006–2075 para el valle de Jauja, simulada por la intercomparación de modelos acoplados CSIRO Mk 3.0, MIROC-ESM y CNRM de fase 5 (CMIP5). Ingeniería Industrial, pp. 297–330 (2022)

Digital Platforms, Digitization of Community Businesses in the Province of Santa Elena - Ecuador

L. A. Núñez[1]([⊠]) [ID], R. A. Castro[2], and J. R. Rodrigues[3] [ID]

[1] Universidad Estatal Península de Santa Elena, Santa Elena, Santa Elena EC240204, Ecuador
lnunez_ing@hotmail.com
[2] Escuela Superior Politécnica del Litoral, Guayaquil, Guayas EC090112, Ecuador
ronacast@espol.edu.ec
[3] Universidade da Coruña, AC15001 Coruña, Spain
jakson.soares@udc.es

Abstract. The work collects the needs of community enterprises in a sector of Ecuador aimed at sustainability from social commitment and economic stability. The theoretical framework examines theories, trends, structures of digital platforms, as well as ventures from their own contexts and realities. The research methodology is descriptive, visualizing characteristics, conditions, situations, and other details that project tourist activity in the communes of Libertador Bolívar and Olón. The incorporation of a technological platform designed with some benefits for owners and tourists is proposed. Primary and secondary information was considered using survey, interview, and observation techniques. The discussion of results allowed a clear vision of the shortcomings of community ventures with respect to digital platforms and to express viable solutions in a timely manner. Among the conclusions, scientific references, benefits of digitization and its adaptation in enterprises were emphasized.

Keywords: digital platforms · community ventures · technologies · digital economy

1 Introduction

The digital transformation marks milestones since 1960, where its performance was characterized by individual activities and the incorporation of technological tools that facilitated the work of business functions; With the appearance of the Internet in 1980, communication between companies and the inputs they provide flowed. Technology currently integrates visible products and services not only in the modernity of articles but in increasingly efficient goods known as the internet of things. By virtue of this, large or small businesses require prospective structures that mark the horizon for their expansion into local, national, or international markets and ventures have greater complexity to visualize their expectations, probably because their actions are aimed at immediate solutions and to the extent of their possibilities.

T. Guarda et al. (Eds.): ARTIIS 2023, CCIS 1937, pp. 180–194, 2024.
https://doi.org/10.1007/978-3-031-48930-3_14

Today there are administrative and technological tools that facilitate real and concrete planning to establish a desired future, they are digital platforms that; beyond setting a trend, streamline and simplify business work, moving from a traditional business to a digital world demanded by users voluntarily or involuntarily, much more since we experienced the pandemic under forcibly changing personal and working conditions. In the field of digitalization, the so-called traditional players lost space and must be creative to stay in the market, probably be on par with tech entrepreneurs or so-called "tech giants".

With these narratives highlighting the changes in the way in which companies have provided services, figures are also reflected below, for example, from Electronic Commerce Camera (March 2020), it states that from the purchase report from Mercado Libre in its platform demonstrated 1.7 million new shoppers, a significantly higher customer conversion rate, and double-digit growth in the consumer goods and food category [1]. With these results, it is reasonable that many potential customers resistant to adopting remote media build habits and loyalty in these channels and remain regular customers once the pandemic crisis is over.

According to the Ecuadorian Chamber of Electronic Commerce (2020, p.15), since the appearance of Covid-19, investments have been made in advertising and product promotion, mainly aimed at social media (61%), messaging (36%), e-mail (25%), web page (29%) to boost sales through Streaming, Facebook, Shopify, Mercado Libre, Woocommerce, among others; however, sales are declining by 56%, have completely stopped at 32% and have only grown by 12%. [1]. Precisely, thanks to these services, it has been possible to offer the products or goods in a different way since it cannot be done in person. As an example of this, you can find the gyms that offered virtual classes, virtual concerts, visits to museums and other experiences such as artists who are also encouraging others to get involved in art through telematic means. The various ways in which individuals meet needs are too numerous to list completely, but through digitalization it has been possible to meet these needs in the lockdown period [2].

According to the United Nations Organization - UN, during the pandemic era, different sectors remained standing thanks to the internet, such as education, but tourism was the most affected by the pandemic, due to the fact that travel agencies closed their doors, others remained thanks to the different promotions that were agreed for the coming years but at low costs until the economy is reactivated again, due to this social change and with regard to the advancement in tourism and new information technologies. Information and communication, the term Tourism 3.0 appears where tourists have at their fingertips, 24 h a day, all the necessary and recurring information to travel, such as information on destinations, opinions, and experiences of other users [3].

In Ecuador, the situation was also complex in the tourism sector, its economy was paralyzed without exploiting its natural and cultural wealth. By the year 2022 the tourism industry has grown with a contribution of 1.8% in relation to 2021 of 1.5%, being ranked 15 out of 18 industries nationwide. Tourism currently contributes 2.2% of the gross domestic product of the national economy directly [4]. In this sense, the tourism sector is fundamental in the development of the country since there are many attractions for national and international tourists, particularly from community enterprises, opportunities for outdoor recreation, harmony and coexistence with inhabitants and nature, empowerment of assets of each area and improve the economies of the territories.

For Santa Elena, an eminently tourist province in Ecuador, after the crisis the economic reactivation knocks on the door, according to the Chamber of Tourism of the same town, it estimates that 200,000 tourists have arrived, 25% more than on the end of the year holiday 2021. Carlos Abad, president of the Chamber of Tourism of the province of Santa Elena affirms that a new phase begins for those of us who have investments in the country's spas, he said that tourist activity will once again be sustainable as it was before the pandemic. We are still a long way from going beyond the red balance we have [5].

Indeed, the present work focuses on the province of Santa Elena, Libertador Bolívar and Olón communes to analyze the current situation of community enterprises, to know their strengths and weaknesses; Based on the diagnosis, establish the best alternatives to promote this type of business led by vulnerable social groups with limited economic resources who have been able to overcome the pandemic but who need new ways of reaching tourists, posing the question, is the incorporation of digital platforms influences the promotion of community ventures?

Indeed, this paper focuses on the province of Santa Elena, communes Libertador Bolívar and Olón analyzing the current situation of the community enterprises, know their strengths and weaknesses and from the diagnosis establish improvements that incorporate new ways of reaching tourists. The study is defined within a descriptive level investigation with a qualitative -quantitative approach, using surveys, interviews, and observation sheets; the question arises: does the incorporation of digital platforms influence the promotion of community enterprises?

2 Theoretical Framework

2.1 Digital Platforms: Definitions, Application, and Impact On Tourism

This segment includes aspects on definitions of digital platforms, ecosystem of digital platforms, types of platforms, and applicability to tourist services:

Rock Content Blog (2019) defines the digital platform as "Internet spaces that allow the running various applications or programs in one place to meet different needs. Each one has different functions that help users solve different types of problems in an automated way, using fewer resources" [6].

Freire V. Melanie, (2018), points out that "A virtual platform is a system that allows the execution of various applications under the same environment, giving users the possibility of accessing them through the Internet" [7].

Marshall W. Van Alstyne, in his article The New Rules of Strategy in the Digital Economy, indicates that "Technology dramatically simplifies the development and scaling of platforms, allows participation with almost no disagreements, which reinforces network effects and improves the ability to collect, analyze and exchange large amounts of data that increase the value of the platform for everyone (…) [8]. Although platforms come in many forms, they all have an ecosystem with the same basic structure and four types of actors. Platform owners control intellectual property and governance. Providers interface with users".

Digital platforms have benefits and risks, Daniel & Natalia state that "The phenomenon of software liberalization compared to licensed software has generated the development of open-source platforms that allow modifications from a copyleft license compared to closed platforms owned by a manufacturer." On the other hand, Marshall W. Van Alstyne [9] highlights the difference between opting for an open or closed platform, given that sometimes they are the ones that receive the most interactions regarding user requirements.

The evolution of the internet, according to Castro Rojas [10], in his text Digital networks and communication, he emphasizes that he has been very involved in the respective updates given to this type of system, he indicates that: "it is the network as a platform, which covers all connected devices; Web 2.0 applications are the ones that best take advantage of the potentialities of that platform: software as a service that is constantly updated and improves as it is used, consuming and mixing data from multiple sources, including individual users, who contribute their own data and services in such a way that they allow reuse by others, thus creating network effects through a participatory architecture.

Currently, for the Orange Institution [11] several options of digital tools have emerged that apply as added value for any activity that is required and even more so in tourist services, highlighting four divisions of new or improved technological developments: The cloud has allowed the creation of technological platforms that offer new disintermediation services, favoring and promoting the appearance of new transformative agents in the tourism sector. Mobile, the entire ecosystem made up of mobile devices with an Internet connection, as well as all the platforms, services and applications associated with them. Internet of Things, a set of devices and objects connected to the Internet with special attention to its application in home automation and sensorization. Social (Social networks and collaborative economy), digital platforms through which users participate, collaborate, share, and exchange content, goods, and services.

In the selected sector of tourism, Accenture [12] shows that the industry without a chimney as it is called is still at the forefront in the use of technology. Thinking that a traveler had to approach the airlines for example to carry out their transactions and that of course it was not for everyone, today we can buy our ticket online, check-in through sensors leaving aside contact with the customer service at the airport, the printed ticket is no longer required, but simply go through a scanner on our cell phone. It is also mentioned that the trip is no longer just the trip as such, now, many services are connected, platforms that make a visit the best experience, there is a relationship between flight, accommodation, tours, assistance, etc.

Identifying the benefits of digitalization and its applicability in tourism, the concept of "travel experiences" increases expectations; the security and peace of mind of the costumer for the management of their information and data is another element that favors the use of technologies. In this context, in Fig. 1, as an example, the participation of the so-called "technological players" with the transformation stages that the communities of the province of Santa Elena access, classifying them within the "traditional competitors" due to its realities of nature, resources and social conditions; however, they need to go through a reinvention so as not to disappear from the market.

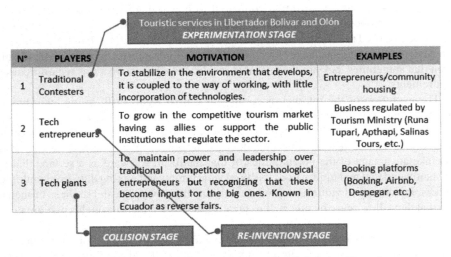

Fig. 1. Technological players and the stages of digital transformation

2.2 Entrepreneurship, a Look from Reality Latin America

Recognizing the impact that entrepreneurship marks worldwide lead to the strengthening of the entrepreneurial culture in countries whose economies generate stability from their income. In Latin American countries: Mexico, Costa Rica, Venezuela, Colombia, Ecuador, and others, their economies find full justification to stimulate the entrepreneurial spirit due to the evident inability of the economic and social system to generate employment in quantity and quality required that overcome exclusion, marginality, and backwardness of broad sectors of the population [13].

Vives, Corral & Isusi (2005) [14], point out some realities of the Latin American context and even with the passing of the years they continue to be the same experiences:

- Need to find solutions to poverty and exclusion based on the creation of economic opportunities for groups that supply goods and services. These sensitive groups are supported and aspects such as supply from nearby places, improvement of the quality of products and services are improved.
- There are companies in countries like Brazil and Colombia that contribute to sustainable development focusing on environmental conservation and biodiversity, use natural products, buying part of their inputs under fair trade conditions and organic origin.
- The incentive to be more responsible in SMEs often comes through the value chain to which they belong; Generally, the pressure is exerted by their clients, who, in many cases, are the largest companies.

- In terms of markets, most SMEs tend to serve local markets and are not exposed to international pressures or incentives. Civil society does not care about them and prefers to use their resources in large companies where they have greatest impact.
- By their nature they tend to be local, dependent on customers and employees who live close to the company, they get involved in community activities, and their responsible practices include concerns for addressing social and environmental problems.

Zamora (2017) [15], points out that "The entrepreneurial capacity of society, education, market opening, social and cultural norms, among other aspects, make it possible to generate productive activities in the country, while regulations in the market of work, bureaucracy and corruption are elements that hinder the dynamism of the productive sector".

Particularly in Ecuador, the study on entrepreneurship is led by the Business School of the University [16] ESPOL, GEM (2019–2020), reflecting that the country for the year 2019 has a stagnant economy with a close GDP variation. At 0%; however, the unemployment rate has remained stable, clarifying that a large part of the labor force moves towards underemployment made up of adequate and inadequate employment. It also shows the framework conditions for Ecuador, among the strengths: physical infrastructure, social and cultural norms, post-secondary entrepreneurship education; among the weaknesses: government policies related to taxes and bureaucracy, financing for entrepreneurs and the transfer of research and development.

For Núñez Guale (2012) [17] "Entrepreneurship becomes an imperative need for many families, professionals and people in general, as it allows undertaking productive projects, generating own resources, improving the quality of life and contributing to the progress of society" (p. 8).

According to data from the Ministry of Tourism - MITUR of 2018, the arrival of foreigners to the country maintains a sustained growth, between January and May of this year, the increase was 57% with the arrival of 952,488 people, compared to the same period in 2017. On the part of this State portfolio, it is admitted that the receptive tourism growth is due to the new promotion strategy that they have implemented as of August 2017, with the entry into the system of Online International Travel Agencies-OTA (by its definition in English). This system provides travelers from various countries in the world where the promotion campaign is being developed, the possibility of knowing immediately the various services that the country has in terms of tourism. [18].

The province of Santa Elena offers beautiful beaches, gastronomy, welcoming nature, accommodation, recreational spaces, etc. It has a population of 308,693 inhabitants INEC, (2010) [19]. It has climatic, environmental, and social conditions that give way to small enterprises, its visitors use technologies more frequently to know in advance the sites to visit; however, it is not so easy for these activities to adapt to the new demands because it implies the incorporation of resources and trained human capital to respond to modernity.

3 Methodology

The study was conducted in Ecuador in 2 communes of the province of Santa Elena: Libertador Bolívar with an area of 1,476 hectares located at km 50 north of the province with a population of approximately 4,000 inhabitants. It is located 131 km. From Guayaquil. It has a dimension of 3,100 m. beach length, has flora and fauna [20]. Olón Commune, 11 km from Libertador Bolívar, has an area of 5,780 ha. 195 km from Guayaquil, with a population of approximately 2,200 inhabitants. It has four kilometers of beach, a community also dedicated to tourism, above all sustainable, fishing, agriculture, and crafts. In recent years it has experienced growth and tourism development, implementing various types of accommodation (lodge, inns, cabins) and international and gourmet restaurants [21].

Maintaining the link of the problem raised through the question: does the incorporation of digital platforms influence the promotion of community enterprises? and taking into account that this type of ventures work from the perspective of sustainability, the research instruments were aligned with the indicators of Corporate Social Responsibility - CSR but at the level of SMEs, which is the closest to the ventures, therefore they are adjusted to their realities and include parameters regarding digital platforms. The methodology was organized as follows:

Preliminary phase: Contextualization, exploratory bibliographic study to know the realities of the communities subject to study with the intervention of representatives of the sector or enterprises, facilitating to know the trajectory of the population and its tourist growth.

Qualitative phase: a) Interview with experts, its design was supported by CSR indicators and categories and choice of variables for the quantitative method were generated from these results. From the sustained dialogue with the leaders of the sector, the potential of its inhabitants was known, but also some limitations in their activities, governance with the authorities of the moment does not always flow in favor of the communities, the intervention of enterprises external becomes a stimulus for the inhabitants and the central theme of technology is relatively growing. Below are the participants (Table 1):

Table 1. Experts and social agents - Interview

Name	Entity/Company	Job Title
Paulina León Castro, Eng	Ministry of Tourism/Prefecture	Tourism Management and Promotion Specialist
Jefferson Tigrero, Eng	EmoTourism	Manager
Otto Vera Palacios, Eng	Municipality of the canton Santa Elena	Mayor
Jacinto Ángel	Commune Libertador Bolívar	Commune President
José Reyes	Olón Commune	Commune President

Qualitative phase: b) Observation, the researchers have their residences close to the populations studied, which facilitates information and transfer. The observation sheet collected inputs in the various visits that were completed and are reflected in the SWOT Strategic Matrix in the Results section.

Quantitative phase: Survey of entrepreneurs from studied communes, maintaining the link with the sustainability of community ventures, the survey instrument was also guided by CSR indicators but designed by eight sections to gradually address their realities. A series of visits was planned for field work since this type of tourist activity does not always have technology or connectivity facilities. The population distribution is as follows (Table 2):

Table 2. Distribution of population under study - Survey

Parameter	Value
Study population	Community tourism ventures in communes Libertador Bolívar, Olón - Santa Elena – Ecuador
Universe (sampling frame)	643 business (business demographic data taken from the commune council)
Sampling procedure	Application of surveys in the field
Information collection	Survey form
Sample size	250 surveys
Sample characteristics	Lodgings, restaurants, craft shops, clothing sales, costume jewelry and typical food sales
Survey date	April 2023

The instruments allowed to know the realities of the enterprises but also how they are venturing into the sustainability of their territories and activities, creating and innovating conditions to increase the acceptance of tourists, looking for mechanisms to modernize their businesses, generating alliances with the tourism ecosystem to take advantage of/exchange resources, strengthening knowledge to incorporate new trends, among other details. The eleven CSR indicators at the enterprise level are: Respect for the environment, Development of human potential, Commitments to the community, Social innovation, Quality of administration, Ecological product/service, Responsibility with internal/external clients, Policies and prevention behaviors, Measurement of customer satisfaction, Measurement of supplier perception; and Creativity.

4 Results or Findings

a) Interview applied to experts from the tourism sector in populations of Ecuador, contrasting and synthesizing the results were the following:

– The experts and professionals interviewed have not only been part of public functions in the province, but some of them are also active members of the tourist activity, gaining extensive experience.

- Despite the potential of its inhabitants to develop community tourism, they present some limitations such as: the will of each community member, constant change of authorities, political rivalry of rulers, little associative work, little knowledge in forms of organization and dissemination of products. For the strengths we can mention adventure tourism, natural attractions, several residents with their own initiatives, improvement of internal road connection and with other provinces.
- Governance with the authorities on duty is a fundamental aspect to achieve the development of tourism in the province. Even though the rulers recognize the sustainability of tourism as an important source of income, a good commonwealth is not always achieved and political or territorial rivalries arise, planning priorities, preferences to work or not with leaders, etc.
- For the sector of the province of Santa Elena, the development of technology, the internet and digital platforms barely reaches 38% adding the criteria of the participants, this becomes a limitation in the tourist activity since the economic recovery is based on digitization of services and products.

b) **Surveys applied to entrepreneurs,** from the 8 sections that the survey instrument has, the results are presented in a summarized and relevant way (Table 3):

Table 3. Survey Application Results

Section	Results
Economic activity of the business	Businesses are 93% family. The economic sustenance is medium in low seasons but high in good periods. The resources for the business are always obtained in the community. The concentration of tourist activity is divided into **32% accommodation, 44% restaurants**, 12% handicrafts, 7% recreation and 5% other activities
Community Features	The communities surveyed have a beach, culture, accommodation, gastronomy, handicrafts, crops, hiking, sports, etc. There is always job opportunity among community activities. The most frequent means of communication are word of mouth at 37%, personalized 25%, **social networks 22.5%, web pages 15.5%**. The visit of tourists to these communities is about 19% local, 28% national and 53% international, of which the majority come from the US and South America
Characteristics of your business	**89% exceed 10 years of business validity**. Mostly the businesses have up to 6 people working permanently and with remuneration between $300.oo and $400.oo. 96% of the businesses are owned and 4% rented. Among the strengths of the venture, the location stands out

(continued)

Table 3. (*continued*)

Section	Results
Support for ventures	Businesses are established from **own capital with 32%, bank credit 40%**, 21% family contribution and loans to third parties with 7%. Among the public sector organizations that provide support in education/training and credits/microcredits are 73% municipalities, 20% Prefecture and 7% Community Board
Relationship of the business with its community	The residents have an apathetic attitude towards collective progress in 78%. They almost always collaborate in environmental care. Entrepreneurs almost always have sufficient preparation to attend to businesses. Jobs are always filled with personnel from the same community
Possibility of improvement	The businesses are equipped with guide service 4.5%, transport 19%, translation 5.5%, **internet 29.5%, digital communication 15%**, basic services 26.5%. The access roads to the community are considered mostly regular. To increase the tourist influx there are aspects that must be improved such as customer service in 32%, community services in 8%, internationalization 11%, training 39%, alliances 10%
Trainings	Trainings have been provided by the municipality, prefecture, and ministries preferably, very little by universities. Training is considered necessary in areas such as customer service 38%, foreign language 31%, financial and administrative 24%, preparation of tourist services 7%
Strengthening of enterprises	The growth achieved by each business is very good. We fully agree that it is important to have experience from other environments in addition to always being willing

c) Observation sheet – situational diagnosis

d) Consolidation of research instruments with the variable "Digital Platforms", to maintain the link of the problem raised, relevant information from the applied research instruments was contrasted, synthesizing (Table 4):

Interview Instrument: The expressed criterion of the interviewees falls on some elements that highlight the lack of digital platforms in the promotion of community enterprises: Little knowledge of entrepreneurs for the dissemination and promotion of products, Lack of priorities in planning from the governance of authorities leaving the

Table 4. SWOT Strategic Matrix

	Strengths	Weakness
	F1 Communes with natural resources attractive to foreign tourists. **F2** Sufficient natural resources that allow adapting ecological environments. **F3** Inhabitants willing to improve their services. **F4** Managers with clear projections for development.	**D1** Natives without knowledge of the English language. **D2** Natives with limitations in technological tools. **D3** Little knowledge of the setting of places.
Opportunities **O1** High mobility of foreign tourists to the country and communes throughout the year. **O2** Favorable climate throughout the year. **O3** State institutions promoting tourism development. **O4** Adequate road access **O5** Alliances/agreements with national and international institutions	**F1, O1, O4:** Offer a tourism portfolio based on the benefits of the communes studied. **F1, F2, O1, O4:** Design and implementation of resources to improve hotel services and generate loyalty. **F3, O3:** Manage approaches with municipal institutions to optimize actions for the benefit of the commune. **F1, O1, O2:** Offer a package of diverse products according to alliances.	**D1, D3, O3:** Search for allies and advice to counteract deficiencies in the community. **D2, O3, O5:** Implementation of a technological platform and procedures to join the promotion campaign for tourist destinations maintained by MINTUR. **D2, O5:** training programs in technological tools with partner universities.
Threats **A1** Competence of the environment with experience managers. **A2** Business owners of foreign nationality with economic resources and knowledge of other environments	**F2, A1, A2:** Manage professional training to improve tourist services. **F3, F4, A1:** Active participation of community members in programs that are carried out with a focus on sustainability.	**D3, A1, A2:** Training of community entrepreneurs for the optimization of resources.

opportunities of having digital platforms in the background, Settlement of foreign businesses not used for the dissemination of tourist activities and Limited development of technologies and connectivity in the province of Santa Elena that stops tourism growth.

Survey Instrument: From the 8 sections of the survey 6 stand out: Economic activity of the business, Characteristics of the community, Characteristics of the business, Support ventures, Possibility of improvement and Training; where information concerning the incorporation of digital platforms in community ventures is captured, synthesizing:

- Lodgings and Restaurants are the most outstanding tourist activities, adding up to 76%, and these are the ones that should be better systematized to reach the client.

- Personalized means of communication are the most used, leaving only 38% of social networks and web pages, noting the need to seek mechanisms to increase the promotion of community ventures.
- It is highlighted that the businesses have more than 10 years of validity; however, in relation to the previous literal these have not been able to become references from the promotion in digital networks.
- Incorporating own capital and bank credit, the enterprises reach 72% for their financing, which leads us to reflect that the economic possibilities would allow the implementation of communication and digitization systems for the promotion of activities.
- Regarding the equipment of tourist services, digital communication reaches 15% while the internet 29.5%. It is necessary to improve these invaluable tools when promoting community enterprises.

Observation Instrument: From the SWOT strategic matrix, some solutions were proposed for the promotion of community enterprises, the most notable being the implementation of technological platforms and campaigns to promote tourist destinations, training programs in technological tools; as well as the design of tourist portfolios or product packages offering the benefits of the communities.

5 Discussion

With the study and analysis of the two variables in this research work: Digital Platforms and Community Enterprises; And, in accordance with the statement of the problem, does the incorporation of digital platforms influence the promotion of community enterprises? is weighted:

From the context of the theoretical framework, digital platforms open the doors of any business towards a globalized world, an economic activity does not grow and is not competent only in the region where it is created, it is forced to expand to other markets. The members of the business ecosystem increasingly demand new possibilities or coverage of needs; In this sense, even the simplest undertakings must be at the level of these demands so as not to disappear from the competitive market. This invisible network of owners, suppliers, producers, and consumers makes each agent meet their requirements, but that same solution is an input from another agent that is not necessarily framed in the same line of service or product. Digital platforms help simplify customer needs regardless of time, cost, or distance.

Every large or small business, SME or entrepreneurship is obliged to conduct its activities not only in a traditional way, but it is imperative to adapt to technologies and expand its market to service networks. For the study in the communities of Libertador Bolívar and Olón, community enterprises must improve their services and infrastructure and become benchmarks from the incorporation of international tourist routes. The results indicate that the highest percentage of visitors are from other locations in the country and foreigners, therefore easy communication is necessary for its promotion and dissemination, defining some actions:

- Implementation of digital platforms whose design allows easy handling for owners and tourists with necessary and updated information.

– Incorporation or improvement of Facebook pages of businesses and communities.
– Implementation of technological applications with all the benefits of the site
– Incorporation of permanent assistance with foreign language proficiency
– Adaptation and ecological improvement in all tourist services provided by the communes.

Based on the results of the 2 variables, where it is reflected that digital platforms have not been optimally exploited for the promotion of community enterprises, the "Business Route Map" tool to identify improvement actions in the two communes studied; the relevant aspects are summarized below:

– From the client's point of view, their basic needs are relaxed, rest, vacation, meet. Consult with friends, social networks, digital advertisements, newspapers, magazines, travel costs, mobility, language, stay, security, food, lodging, weather, type of monetary exchanges, forms of payment and others. As for the experiences, it allows her to be a satisfied customer, share her experiences on social networks, motivated to take new services, value the stay.
– From the point of view of the enterprise, its basic needs will be search for artisans in the community to improve their lodging environments, alliance with other entertainment venues inside and outside the communes, alliances with private transport and drivers, creation of a web page, Implementation of a tourist application. Their experiences will be: Become known for compliance with services, development and maintenance of tourist activity, satisfied customer and loyalty, positive publicity based on user comments, development of the online service.

With the need to incorporate digital platforms to promote community ventures, a web page and an App were designed, appropriate technological tools for communication with tourists; it offers modernity, security, tranquility, and permanent contact with your tourist service company. The web development will be based on an informative platform and would consist of the following options: *Start*, shows the initial section of the website with featured images in a carousel of photos referring to the Libertador Bolívar and Olón communes, going from their landscapes to the sports that can be practiced. *Gallery* consists of videos and images that promote the different activities that the communes have: paragliding, horseback riding, mountain biking, among others. *Menu*, containing a review of the activities of the communes as well as of other partner communities in the implementation of strategies. *Location*, the location of the communes is found via Google Maps, it will help first-time tourists in Ecuadorian lands. Blog, this section contains relevant news from the communes and its surroundings; In this way, the tourist will be able to have knowledge of the different events about them and nearby sectors that are part of the product portfolio. *Comments*, section for foreign and local visitors; positive points that will boost the website and rank within the first search results of Google or Bing.

6 Conclusions

The research made it possible to identify the context of the two variables more clearly: Digital Platforms and Community Entrepreneurships, to know the itinerary marked from their emergence to the present moment and how they interfere in social and economic results. In the case of Ecuador and specifically the Libertador Bolívar and Olón communes, rural sectors of the country, community businesses gain preferences from foreign tourists in relation to other nearby sectors and it is here where digital platforms through their benefits and applicability play an important role to promote tourist attractions, from the same space or connected through networks of the entrepreneurial ecosystem, achieving in an automated way, solving problems that would traditionally imply greater times and costs.

With the incorporation of digital platforms, community ventures in the towns of Libertador Bolívar and Olón can improve the results reflected in this study. The very nature of this type of business aligned with sustainability means that its activities are frequently carried out in a traditional way; but as we have already experienced and argued in statistical data, the pandemic has pushed all people, users or providers, to digitize services; In addition, the characteristics of the new generations is to always be connected to technological benefits. Consequently, it is pertinent that owners and collaborators gradually specialize and dominate the digital world to give tourist activities considerable momentum internationally.

For the collection of information, it was mentioned that the instruments were framed in CSR indicators but at the level of enterprises, justifying their uses since many of these parameters deal directly or indirectly with technologies. With the results obtained, an inference is that digital platforms manage to promote the promotion of community enterprises but pigeonholed in improvement processes. Consequently, the benefits of digitalization can be applied in the communes studied, since the results on economic resources allow it; In addition, all the actors in the tourism sector seek a common goal and would be interested in participating either as platform owners, interface providers, producers of tourism offers or as service consumers.

After observing the need to incorporate some technological tool to promote community ventures, a website and later an app were designed. With the support of the sectional governments to incorporate into current platforms the benefits offered by the communes studied would be part of the tourist network that Ecuador implements. As traditional competitors, the ventures would leave their experimentation stage if the proposed technology were mastered, but it is also important to have the "technological giants" of the tourism sector because they have accumulated experience on user behavior and have known how to readapt. For the purposes of the pandemic, among the suggestions that are left in the study is the opportunity to take advantage of the alliances that have platforms such as Airbnb, Trivago, Booking, among others.

References

1. Cámara de Comercio Electrónico, "Situation of Companies during COVID-19 Ecuador" Universidad Espíritu Santo UEES. https://cece.ec/wp-content/uploads/2020/06/Situacion-de-las-empresas-durante-el-Covid19-en-Ecuador.pdf. Accessed 6 2023
2. Haeffele, S., Hobson, A., Storr, V.H.: Coming back from covid-19: lessons is entrepreneurship from disaster recovery research. SSRN Electronic J. (2020). https://doi.org/10.2139/ssrn.3592966
3. CEPAL. Digital Technologies for a new future. Santiago: United Nations (2022)

4. Ministerio de Turismo. Rendición de cuentas Ministerio de Turismo 2021. Quito: Gobierno del Encuentro (2022). https://www.turismo.gob.ec/wp-content/uploads/2022/03/Informe-Rendicio%CC%81n-de-Cuentas-2021-Textual.pdf
5. Diario Expreso. https://www.expreso.ec/actualidad/reactivacion-economica-toca-puerta-turismo-santa-elena-122602.html. Accessed 28 Feb 2023
6. Rock Content. https://rockcontent.com/es/blog/plataformas-digitales/. Aaccessed 14 Feb 2019
7. Freire, M., Rojas, M..: Preparation of a digital platforms for the commercial development of SMEs producing honey from Ecuador to promote its consumption. (Unpublished degree thesis) University of Santiago de Guayaquil, Ecuador (2018)
8. Marshall, V., Geoffrey P., Sangeet P.: The new rules of strategy in the digital economy. In Harvard Business Review. https://es.scribd.com/document/378645326/HBRs-Must-Reads-2017-Las-nuevas-reglas-de-la-estrategia-en-la-economia-digital-Harvard-Business-Review-in-Spanish-3-pdf (2017)
9. Arias, D., Jaría, N.: Mobile device platforms and servitization: Towards an Integrative model. Dyna-Management, vol. 2, num. 1, Universitat de Barcelona (2014). http://hdl.handle.net/2445/63126
10. Castro, S.: Digital networks and communication, history of platforms and new social links, UNR Editora, pp. 11. Universidad Nacional del Rosario (2013)
11. Foundation, O.: Digital Transformation in the Tourism Sector. Orange Foundation, Spain (2016)
12. Accenture, Digital transformation Initiative (2017) http://reports.weforum.org/digital-transformation
13. Arce Castro, B.: Characteristics that distinguish Small and Medium Enterprises. Pearson, Mexico (2010)
14. Vives, A., Corral, A., Isusi, I.: Corporate Social Responsibility in SMEs in Latin America, 1st edn. ikei Research & Consultancy, Washington DC, United States (2005)
15. Zamora Boza, C.: The importance of entrepreneurship in the economy: the case of Ecuador. Spaces 39(07), 15–27 (2017). https://www.revistaespacios.com/a18v39n07/in183907.html
16. ESPAE: Global Entrepreneurship Monitor Ecuador 2019 - 2020, 1–59. ISSN 1390 – 3047 (2020). https://www.espae.espol.edu.ec/wp-content/uploads/documentos/GEM_Ecuador_2019.pdf
17. Núñez Guale, L.: The Entrepreneurship Unit and the strengthening of the Entrepreneurial Culture, in the students at the School of Commercial Engineering, of the Peninsula State University of Santa Elena, in the year 2010, (Unpublished postgraduate thesis) State University of Bolivar, Guaranda, Ecuador (2012)
18. El Comercio. https://www.elcomercio.com/viajar/cerca-millon-extranjeros-arribaron-ecuador.html. Accessed 13 June 2023
19. National Institute of Statistics and Census – INEC (2010)
20. Diario El Telégrafo. https://www.eltelegrafo.com.ec/noticias/guayas/1/el-turismo-familiar-motiva-a-comuna-libertador-bolivar. Accessed 10 July 2023
21. Tourist environment. https://www.entornoturistico.com/olon-un-espacio-de-naturaleza-y-confort-en-la-costa-del-ecuador/. Accessed 6 july 2023

Intelligent Systems for Health and Medical Care (ISHMC 2023)

Analysis of Marketing Campaigns Results Through Unsupervised Learning with Apriori Association Modeling

Ramón Loaiza Chávez[✉] and Bogart Yail Márquez Lobato

Maestría en Tecnologías de Información, Instituto Tecnológico de Tijuana, TecNM, Tijuana, B.C, México
{m22210059,bogart}@tectijuana.edu.mx

Abstract. One of the most popular data mining methods for extracting association rules from huge data sets is the apriori algorithm, which can be databases or databanks. One of the entities that have benefited the most from it have been supermarket chains in the area of marketing and advertising campaigns, thanks to the discovery of combinations of products that customers usually buy together, or relationships between items and merchants, and having the knowledge of these combinations allows companies to better plan their marketing campaigns. The article shows the results of an exercise with a databank of marketing campaigns in order to generate association rules, interpret the results, and detect which factors are common to customers who tend to accept marketing offers.

Keywords: Marketing · Data Mining · Association Rules · Apriori

1 Introduction

The use of traditional statistics to transform data into knowledge has its foundations in manual interpretation and analysis. This type of manual probing of data collection is time-consuming, expensive, and very subjective for any application. In fact, even with the use of computer programs, this form of human data analysis is becoming utterly unfeasible in many sectors as data quantities expand substantially [1]. Traditional statistics differ from data mining in that formal statistical reasoning depends on hypotheses and their testing against data. In contrast, data mining is based on discovery, i.e., the automatic extraction of patterns from data. In simpler terms, while statistics is driven by people's theories, data mining is driven by facts [2]. The process of generating association rules from a transaction dataset and finding common itemsets is one of the most widely used data mining techniques. Due to their combinatorial explosion, it is challenging to find frequent itemsets (sets with a frequency greater than or equal to a user-specified required support). The generation of association rules with confidence more than or equal to the user-specified minimal confidence is simple after frequent itemsets have been gathered, and as the amount of common itemsets rises, so does the number of presented rules [3, 4].

T. Guarda et al. (Eds.): ARTIIS 2023, CCIS 1937, pp. 197–209, 2024.
https://doi.org/10.1007/978-3-031-48930-3_15

2 Traditional Marketing Approach

Due to the fact that implementation is viewed as an action that results from strategy preparation, traditional models for marketing implementation are basically sequential. The drawback is that the study of consumer needs in order to generate a marketing strategy has been fraught with issues recognizing and comprehending the customer, along with the surrounding situational conditions, which hampers an organization's ability to implement an effective marketing campaign across a specific market [5, 6]. Dynamics of buyer-seller power are impacted by changes in consumer information access and marketers' data collection and utilization. Technology that makes easy comparison shopping and more options for where to buy products has given individual consumers and business customers more leverage [7]. Due to the cyclical nature of marketing, which involves interactions between consumers, marketers, and society, offerings are continuously updated and improved to satisfy shifting consumer demands [8].

3 Knowledge Discovery in Databases (KDD)

Without explicit programming, machine learning is the process of teaching a machine to think like a human being to carry out a specific activity. The mix of statistics, mathematics, computer programming, sophisticated problem solving, data collecting, and working with data to clean, prepare, and employ it constitutes data science. Once prepared, the data gathered through the data science process can be fed into a machine to produce knowledge [9]. Knowledge Discovery in Databases (KDD), a discipline concerned with the application of algorithms to provide meaning to data, is a method for acquiring knowledge [1].

The KDD process consists of transforming large volumes of data that are often difficult to understand into forms that are easier to interpret in order to generate statistics or predictive models. Data analysis and discovery algorithms belong to one of the phases of the KDD process, with the objective of developing a specific list of patterns (or models) on the data. [1]. Also includes the steps performed before data mining, such as data transformation, preprocessing, sanitizing and selection. When the goal of data mining is to find connections or links between specific values of categorical variables in huge data sets, association rule techniques are applied. [10]. The KDD process generally follows the following characteristics: the size of the database or knowledge base must be significantly large; valid rules must be sought for a significant amount of data, but not necessarily for all data; for the rules discovered to be stable and reliable, a significant amount of data must be gathered during a long length of time. It may be inferred from the aforementioned traits that data handling methods play a role in the effectiveness of data mining, knowing how to manage a considerable number of rules, maintaining the rules and verifying their veracity over a significantly long period of time. Therefore, a couple of essential problems must be solved to make data mining viable: design of algorithms oriented to association rules or patterns, and design of efficient algorithms to update and manage the discovered rules [11].

4 Association Rules

Discovering associations or correlations between a group of items is known as association. They are typically defined as rules that list the attribute-value combinations that frequently occur in conjunction in a particular collection of data. [2]. An example of how restrictions and metrics of interest can be used to guarantee data mining completion is association rules [12]. One of the most significant issues in knowledge discovery alongside data mining is identifying common itemsets. Due to this problem, in databases with very huge volumes, numerous algorithms have been created to extract common itemsets [2]. Association rules are constantly used by retailers to show relationships between data elements as an aid to activities such as marketing and advertising, product distribution strategies and inventory analysis [13]. Another way to define it would be a set of consequences that happen in a transactional database when specific conditions are satisfied set by the user that provide knowledge, because it effectively synthesizes the data, which facilitates the discovery of "hidden relationships" that exist in the data [14].

Typically, an association rule mining algorithm has two steps to operate. In the initial, within a collection of elements, all itemsets that satisfy specific requirements are located. From itemsets, the second phase generates rules that fulfill the required confidence criteria. The primary benefit of association rule mining is its ability to quickly find any association that is present in the collected information. One way to visualize this is to consider a set of tuples as an association rule, where each tuple contains a set of elements. With the help of these linkages, the underlying regularities in the domain are fully portrayed and unlike functional dependencies, the resulting relationships are not inherent in the data, and do not represent any kind of causation or correlation [15, 16].

5 Apriori Algorithm

The most well-known and significant method for frequent item set mining is called Apriori, and it was developed by R. Agrawal and R. Srikant in 1994 for the frequently set mining of boolean association rules. The algorithm's name derives from the statement that it makes use of prior knowledge of common features [12, 17]. Apriori is a popular method that is used to extract frequent item sets, it was proposed to find all frequent items and build all association rules related to these sets by a quick algorithm. Association rules typically govern the sequence of the data and aid in highlighting features of the material that they share [2, 4].

6 Materials

6.1 Databank

The databank was obtained from the Kaggle website, a platform that makes code and data available to its users for data science related work. The databank's primary goal is to develop a predictive model that will enable a business to get the most out of its upcoming marketing campaign [18]. The content of the database is described below (Table 1):

Table 1. Description of the databank fields [18].

Field	Description
AcceptedCmp1	1 if the customer accepted the offer in the 1st campaign, 0 else way
AcceptedCmp2	1 if the customer accepted the offer in the 2nd campaign, 0 else way
AcceptedCmp3	1 if the customer accepted the offer in the 3rd campaign, 0 else way
AcceptedCmp4	1 if the customer accepted the offer in the 4th campaign, 0 else way
AcceptedCmp5	1 if the customer accepted the offer in the 5th campaign, else way
Response	1 if the customer accepted the offer in the last campaign, 0 else way
Complain	1 if the customer filed a claim within the last 2 years
DtCliente	Date of registration of the client in the company
Education	Client's educational level
Marital	Client's marital status
Kidhome	Number of young children in the client's household
Teenhome	Number of adolescents in the client's household
Income	Annual income of the client's household
MntFishProducts	Value spent on fishery products in the last 2 years
MntMeatProducts	Value spent on meat products in the last 2 years
MntFruits	Value spent on fruit products in the last 2 years
MntSweetProducts	Value spent on sweet products in the last 2 years
MntWines	Value spent on wine products in the last 2 years
MntGoldProds	Value spent on gold products in the last 2 years
NumDealsPurchases	Number of purchases made at a discount
NumCatalogPurchases	Number of purchases made using catalogue
NumStorePurchases	Number of purchases made directly in stores
NumWebPurchases	Number of purchases made through the company's website
NumWebVisitsMonth	Number of visits to the company's website in the last month
Recency	Number of days elapsed since last purchase

6.2 Model Fields

For the exercise, it is planned to use the apriori algorithm, a data mining algorithm that allows finding links between fields to create (generate) association rules. With an unsupervised algorithm will be used, in order to make the modeling more efficient, only dichotomous data from the selected databank will be used. The following is a list of the selected fields from the databank that meet the criteria of being dichotomous, and therefore will be used in the exercise (Fig. 1).

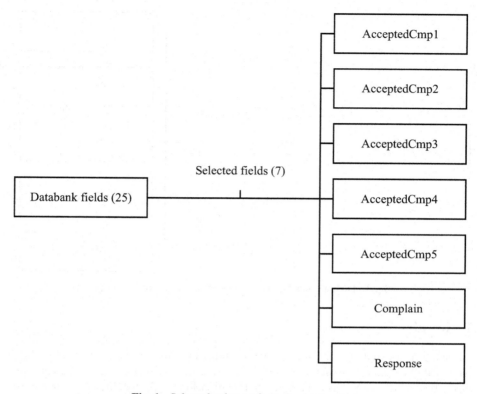

Fig. 1. Selected columns from the databank.

In addition to the fields listed above, the fields that determine the customer's level of education and marital status were used, because these data may have some relationship with the customer's purchase, therefore, these two fields were separated into several to have more dichotomous data for the exercise, as a result, the extra fields generated are listed below (Figs. 2 and 3).

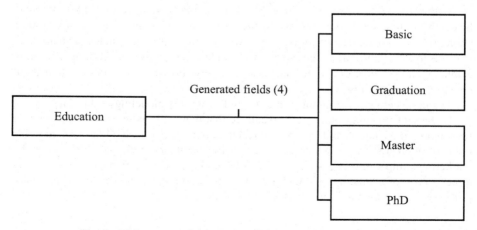

Fig. 2. Dichotomous fields generated from the education column.

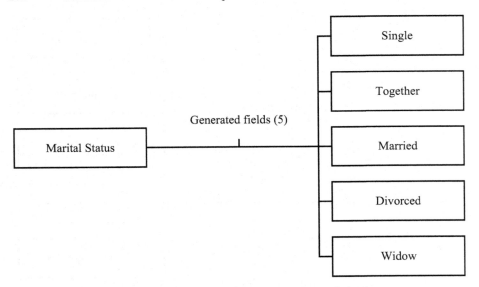

Fig. 3. Dichotomous fields generated from the marital column.

7   Results

To obtain results with the unsupervised algorithm, a minimum rule confidence of 50% was used in the apriori association modeling. In the case of increasing this percentage, this is because the model is not able to find relationships with such high confidence. At the same time, the model only takes into account the true values, because the positive values are the ones, we are interested in evaluating and analyzing, aiming to know if a customer will be likely to accept a marketing campaign offer. The tool to be used to generate the model and the graphs is an IBM program, SPSS Modeler, which is a solution with a set of data mining tools that allows to generate in a simple way model with the use of own data or data generated by another SPSS solution. Then, the result of the modeling is displayed in a mesh graph, which visualizes all the links, where the strongest links appear with thicker lines. (Fig. 4)

Within the graph, a set of 3 links is shown: strong links, medium links and weak links. In the first set, which belongs to the strong links, it can be seen that it finds a strong relationship on the type of education with the marital status. On the primary goal, which is to determine if a consumer would accept the offer from the upcoming marketing campaign, it finds no correlation. The mesh plot below provides more information about the strong linkages (Fig. 5).

The table below corresponds to the strong links of the modeling (Table 2).

In the set of medium links, it is visualized that they still maintain several lines corresponding to education and marital status, but at the same time, the lines related to the fields of interest increase, which are whether the customers in the past had accepted a marketing campaign offer, where the model found a strong relationship with the customer's level of education, and with less thick lines, marital status. Below is the mesh plot showing the medium links in detail (Fig. 6).

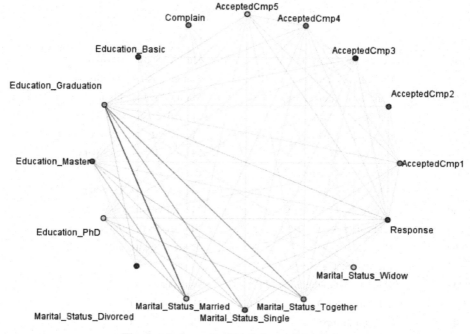

Fig. 4. Mesh graph with all the resulting links.

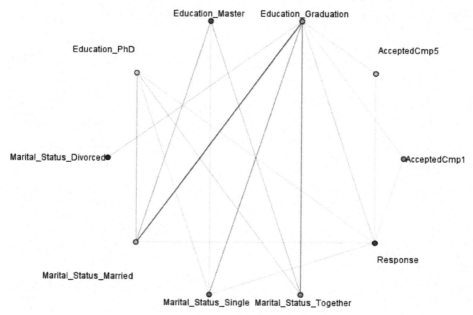

Fig. 5. Mesh graph of strong links.

Table 2. Summary of strong links.

Links	Field 1	Field 2
186	Education_Graduation = "1"	Marital_Status_Married = "1"
119	Education_Graduation = "1"	Marital_Status_Together = "1"
115	Education_Graduation = "1"	Marital_Status_Single = "1"
93	Education_Master = "1"	Marital_Status_Married = "1"
82	Education_PhD = "1"	Marital_Status_Married = "1"
73	Education_Master = "1"	Marital_Status_Together = "1"
62	Education_Graduation = "1"	Response = "1"
62	Education_PhD = "1"	Marital_Status_Together = "1"
60	Education_Graduation = "1"	Marital_Status_Divorced = "1"
55	Education_Master = "1"	Marital_Status_Single = "1"
50	Education_PhD = "1"	Marital_Status_Single = "1"
49	Marital_Status_Single = "1"	Response = "1"
43	Education_Graduation = "1"	AcceptedCmp5 = "1"
41	Education_PhD = "1"	Response = "1"
40	AcceptedCmp5 = "1"	Response = "1"
39	Marital_Status_Married = "1"	Response = "1"
38	AcceptedCmp1 = "1"	Response = "1"
38	Education_Graduation = "1"	AcceptedCmp1 = "1"

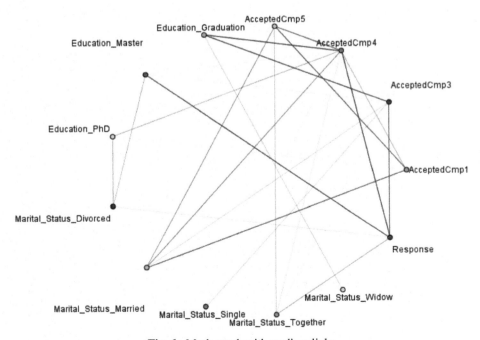

Fig. 6. Mesh graph with medium links.

The table below shows the relationships of the modeled medium links (Table 3).

Table 3. Summary of medium links.

Links	Field 1	Field 2
35	Education_Graduation = "1"	AcceptedCmp4 = "1"
34	Education_Master = "1"	Response = "1"
34	Education_Graduation = "1"	AcceptedCmp3 = "1"
34	AcceptedCmp4 = "1"	Response = "1"
32	AcceptedCmp1 = "1"	AcceptedCmp5 = "1"
32	Marital_Status_Married = "1"	AcceptedCmp1 = "1"
32	AcceptedCmp3 = "1"	Response = "1"
32	AcceptedCmp4 = "1"	AcceptedCmp5 = "1"
28	Marital_Status_Married = "1"	AcceptedCmp4 = "1"
27	Marital_Status_Married = "1"	AcceptedCmp5 = "1"
26	Education_PhD = "1"	Marital_Status_Divorced = "1"
25	Marital_Status_Together = "1"	Response = "1"
25	Education_PhD = "1"	AcceptedCmp4 = "1"
25	AcceptedCmp1 = "1"	AcceptedCmp4 = "1"
24	Education_Master = "1"	Marital_Status_Divorced = "1"
22	Education_Graduation = "1"	Marital_Status_Widow = "1"
22	Marital_Status_Together = "1"	AcceptedCmp5 = "1"
21	Marital_Status_Single = "1"	AcceptedCmp3 = "1"
21	Marital_Status_Married = "1"	AcceptedCmp3 = "1"
19	Marital_Status_Together = "1"	AcceptedCmp4 = "1"
19	Marital_Status_Divorced = "1"	Response = "1"
17	Education_Master = "1"	AcceptedCmp3 = "1"
16	Marital_Status_Together = "1"	AcceptedCmp3 = "1"
15	Education_PhD = "1"	AcceptedCmp1 = "1"
15	Education_PhD = "1"	AcceptedCmp5 = "1"
15	Education_Master = "1"	AcceptedCmp4 = "1"
15	Marital_Status_Single = "1"	AcceptedCmp4 = "1"

In the last group, which belongs to the weak links, the number of fields is extended, where it can be seen that all the fields of interest are taken into account, which are whether the customer has accepted one of the five marketing campaigns registered in the database, and whether the customer accepted the last marketing offer. Within the graph that is generated in this group, thick lines are marked that relate the level of education of the customer, in turn, the five parameters used to determine if a client has agreed to a marketing campaign offer are linked together frequently, indicating that they have done so in the past, it is most likely that it is likely to accept a second offer of another campaign. Lines are also generated above the field indicating whether the customer has ever had a purchase complication. Below is the mesh graph showing the weak links in detail (Fig. 7).

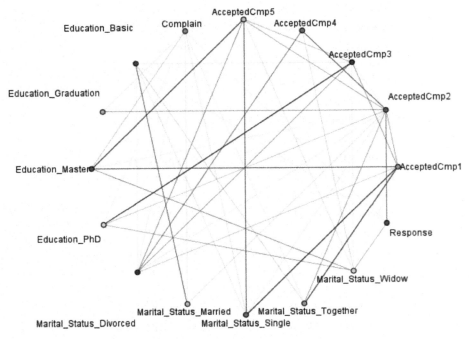

Fig. 7. Mesh graph with weak links.

The table below shows the weak link relationships of the modeling (Table 4).

Table 4. Summary of weak links.

Links	Field 1	Field 2
14	Education_PhD = "1"	AcceptedCmp3 = "1"
14	Marital_Status_Single = "1"	AcceptedCmp1 = "1"
13	Education_Master = "1"	AcceptedCmp5 = "1"
13	Marital_Status_Together = "1"	AcceptedCmp1 = "1"

(continued)

Table 4. (*continued*)

Links	Field 1	Field 2
12	Education_Master = "1"	AcceptedCmp1 = "1"
11	Marital_Status_Single = "1"	AcceptedCmp5 = "1"
11	AcceptedCmp2 = "1"	AcceptedCmp4 = "1"
10	Education_Basic = "1"	Marital_Status_Married = "1"
9	Marital_Status_Divorced = "1"	AcceptedCmp4 = "1"
9	AcceptedCmp2 = "1"	Response = "1"
8	Marital_Status_Divorced = "1"	AcceptedCmp3 = "1"
8	AcceptedCmp1 = "1"	AcceptedCmp3 = "1"
8	Education_Master = "1"	Marital_Status_Widow = "1"
8	Marital_Status_Divorced = "1"	AcceptedCmp5 = "1"
8	Education_Graduation = "1"	AcceptedCmp2 = "1"
8	AcceptedCmp1 = "1"	AcceptedCmp2 = "1"
7	Education_PhD = "1"	Marital_Status_Widow = "1"
7	AcceptedCmp2 = "1"	AcceptedCmp5 = "1"
7	Marital_Status_Divorced = "1"	AcceptedCmp2 = "1"
6	Marital_Status_Widow = "1"	Response = "1"
6	AcceptedCmp3 = "1"	AcceptedCmp5 = "1"
5	Marital_Status_Divorced = "1"	AcceptedCmp1 = "1"
5	Education_Master = "1"	Complain = "1"
5	Education_PhD = "1"	AcceptedCmp2 = "1"
4	Marital_Status_Widow = "1"	AcceptedCmp4 = "1"
4	Education_Basic = "1"	Marital_Status_Together = "1"
3	Marital_Status_Single = "1"	Complain = "1"
3	Marital_Status_Married = "1"	AcceptedCmp2 = "1"
3	Marital_Status_Widow = "1"	AcceptedCmp5 = "1"
3	Education_Basic = "1"	Marital_Status_Single = "1"
2	Marital_Status_Together = "1"	Complain = "1"
2	Education_Graduation = "1"	Complain = "1"
2	Education_Basic = "1"	AcceptedCmp3 = "1"
2	Marital_Status_Divorced = "1"	AcceptedCmp2 = "1"
2	Marital_Status_Married = "1"	Complain = "1"
2	Marital_Status_Single = "1"	AcceptedCmp2 = "1"
2	AcceptedCmp2 = "1"	AcceptedCmp3 = "1"
1	Education_Basic = "1"	Marital_Status_Divorced = "1"
1	Marital_Status_Divorced = "1"	Complain = "1"
1	Education_Master = "1"	AcceptedCmp2 = "1"
1	Education_Basic = "1"	Response = "1"
1	Marital_Status_Widow = "1"	AcceptedCmp1 = "1"
1	Marital_Status_Widow = "1"	AcceptedCmp3 = "1"
1	Education_PhD = "1"	Complain = "1"
1	Complain = "1"	Response = "1"

8   Conclusion

With the marketing knowledge base used, it was possible to apply the association rules and interpret the results generated by the apriori algorithm. From the beginning, only the results considered "true" or "positive" were used to focus the analysis on customers who have already accepted a marketing offer in the past and to see what this group of people have. Among the most interesting results of the model, is that all those who have already accepted an offer one or more times, have in common that they have not made a complaint, and also that the more customers accept more marketing offers, the stronger the relationship with the next marketing campaign, or, to put it another way, the more probable it is that they will take up the proposal of the upcoming marketing campaign.

References

1. Fayyad, U., Piatetsky-Shapiro, G., Smyth, P.: From data mining to knowledge discovery in databases. AI Mag. **17**(3), 37–54 (1996). https://doi.org/10.1609/AIMAG.V17I3.1230
2. Zhang, C., Zhang, S.: Association rule mining. In: Lecture Notes in Computer Science, vol. 2307. Springer, Berlin Heidelberg (2002). https://doi.org/10.1007/3-540-46027-6
3. Wu, X., et al.: Top 10 algorithms in data mining. Knowl. Inf. Syst. **14**(1), 1–37 (2008). https://doi.org/10.1007/s10115-007-0114-2
4. Li, G., Hamilton, H.J.: Basic association rules. In: Proceedings of the 2004 SIAM International Conference on Data Mining, pp. 166–177. Society for Industrial and Applied Mathematics, Philadelphia, PA (2004). https://doi.org/10.1137/1.9781611972740.16
5. Piercy, N.F.: Marketing implementation: the implications of marketing paradigm weakness for the strategy execution process. J. Acad. Mark. Sci. **26**(3), 222–236 (1998). https://doi.org/10.1177/0092070398263004/METRICS
6. McDonald, M., Christopher, M., Bass, M.: Marketing. Macmillan Education UK, London (2003). https://doi.org/10.1007/978-1-4039-3741-4
7. Ferrell, O.C.. Hartline, M.D., Hochstein, B.: Marketing strategy: text and cases (2021)
8. Dann, S., Dann, S.J.: E-marketing: Theory and Application. Palgrave Macmillan (2011)
9. Silaparasetty, N.: Machine Learning Concepts with Python and the Jupyter Notebook Environment: Using Tensorflow 2.0. Apress, Berkeley, CA (2020). https://doi.org/10.1007/978-1-4842-5967-2
10. Nasereddin, H.H.O.: Stream data mining. Int. J. Web Appl. **3**(2), 90–97 (2011). Accessed 17 Apr 2023. https://www.researchgate.net/publication/220500800_Stream_Data_Mining
11. Cheung, D.W., Han, J., Ng, V.T., Wong, C.Y.: Maintenance of discovered association rules in large databases: an incremental updating technique. In: Proceedings of the Twelfth International Conference on Data Engineering, IEEE Computing Social Press, pp. 106–114 (1996). https://doi.org/10.1109/ICDE.1996.492094
12. Ha, J., Kambe, M., Pe, J.: Data Mining. Elsevier (2012). https://doi.org/10.1016/C2009-0-61819-5
13. Knowledge Discovery in Databases, pp. 11–44. Springer, Berlin, Heidelberg (1999).https://doi.org/10.1007/3-540-48316-0_2
14. Gkoulalas-Divanis, A., Verykios, V.S.: Association rule hiding for data mining. In: Advances in Database Systems, vol. 41. Springer US, Boston, MA (2010). https://doi.org/10.1007/978-1-4419-6569-1
15. Liu, B., Hsu, W., Ma, Y.: Pruning and summarizing the discovered associations. In: Proceedings of the Fifth ACM SIGKDD International Conference on Knowledge Discovery and Data Mining. ACM, New York, NY, USA (1999). https://doi.org/10.1145/312129.312216

16. Dunhan, M.H.: Data Mining: Introductory and Advanced Topics. Prentice Hall. Prentice Hall/Pearson Education (2003). https://books.google.com/books/about/Data_Mining_Introductory_and_Advanced_To.html?hl=es&id=30LBQgAACAAJ. Accessed 16 May 2023
17. Rao, S., Gupta, P.: Implementing improved algorithm over APRIORI data mining association rule algorithm. Int. J. Comput. Sci. Technol. 3(1), 489–493 (2012). https://www.researchgate.net/publication/284602613_Implementing_improved_algorithm_over_APRIORI_data_mining_association_rule_algorithm. Accessed 17 Apr 2023
18. Saldanha, R.: Marketing Campaign | Kaggle (2020). https://www.kaggle.com/datasets/rodsaldanha/arketing-campaign. Accessed 25 Apr 2023

Mobile Application to Identify Non-perishable Products Using Machine Learning Techniques

Javier Sotelo[1]($\boxtimes$) , Arnulfo Alanis[2] , and Bogart Yail[2]

[1] Master's Degree in Information Technologies, Department of Systems and Computing, National Technology of Mexico, Campus Tijuana, Calzada del Tecnológico S/N, Fraccionamiento Tomas Aquino. Tijuana, Baja California. C.P. 22414, Tijuana, B.C., Mexico
javier.sotelo@tectijuana.edu.mx
[2] Systems and Computer Department, National Technology of Mexico, Campus Tijuana, Calzada del Tecnológico S/N, Fraccionamiento Tomas Aquino. Tijuana, Baja California. C.P., 22414, Tijuana, B.C., Mexico
alanis@tectijuana.edu.mx, bogart@tectiuana.edu.mx

Abstract. A properly trained object detection system may be able to automate a large number of tasks that are performed on a daily basis. Among these activities we find the recognition of household products, such as food, which currently has not taken advantage of the benefits that machine learning can offer. Detecting inputs such as fruit can expand the knowledge we have of the pantry of our home, having such information at the right time and place can save the need to carry long lists of errands and worries of acquiring a duplicate product or forgetting it completely. This article presents a mobile application that handles a learning model trained by machine learning techniques so that the device is able to recognize the object that is focusing the device camera and check that it corresponds to one of the inputs given as input variables at the time of training.

Keywords: Deep Learning · Machine Learning · Artificial Intelligence · Internet of Things · E-Commerce

1 Introduction

Artificial intelligence has been evolving in recent years, allowing us to see how the technology that surrounds us has managed to implement some type of this intelligence, usually deep learning, to predict user behavior or suggest preferences in the content you are looking for. There are applications and services that, using machine learning techniques, offer us the possibility of recognizing people and objects in images, very frequent in camera applications for mobile devices, however, the potential of object recognition has yet to be fully exploited [1]. It is enough just to recognize a range of objects such as those in the home to bring improvements to the accuracy of recommender systems and to implement new technologies. Taking this to a practical example, if we have a device capable of recognizing the inputs present in a house, by collecting that information it could automatically generate an errand list according to the products that the user has already consumed or is used to buying. It could even do the shopping for the user. Today's technological devices strive to make their users consume less time in their daily activities and use it for other purposes, automating tasks that previously required interaction with rudimentary and impractical systems. For example in the area of home automation, a device called uControl from its touch screen can turn on the fan, lamps, television and other appliances, replacing the previous physical interaction with a digital one that takes less effort and can serve for people with locomotor problems or for the comfort of healthy people [2]. This type of products can be found in the market, currently working with voice commands, replacing the digital interaction by an even easier to handle, the speech. Thanks to technological advances, many of the activities that we used to perform are already being done by certain devices on their own, and the things we do every day will be done by the devices of the future. Taking into account this automation trend and knowing that people's time is very valuable, this article aims to create a system that can be able to detect inputs through the camera of a mobile device, in order to automate the registration of product information in the application. This process requires user interaction, with the new implementation will not be necessary to auto-complete the product registration forms.

2 State of Art

2.1 Object Detection

Object detection consists of finding in an image the location of an object labeled with a category. During this process, frames that delimit the objects, known as bounding boxes, or sets of pixels within the image are located and classified [3, 4]. Usually, the bounding box is a square or rectangular figure, which can cause difficulties when detecting objects with certain diagonal angles, since pixels within the figure that do not match the object detector training data are considered as noise. Rotated bounding boxes can be used to improve detection accuracy [5]. The category can be given by the user (supervised) or by the detector system itself (unsupervised). Depending on the detector system, it may be able to detect one object or multiple objects at once in a single image. As examples of object detection we can find face detectors, vehicle detectors, animal detectors, recipes detectors, etc. [3, 4, 6].

2.2 Feature Learning

Feature learning, also known as representation learning, are a set of machine learning techniques that consist of automatically discovering representations or qualities in data in order to be analyzed, classified, or effective for a desired task. It is commonly seen in training deep network models so that they can carry out a subsequent activity. Some of the feature learning techniques include principal component analysis (PCA) and the Empirical Cumulative Distribution Function (ECDF) [4, 7].

2.3 Machine Learning

Machine learning allows a system, software or application to be able to learn from the data it receives as input or parameter instead of learning explicitly through programming. If a traditional application seeks to add a new feature, the programmer has to change its source code so that the program "acquires" that feature which can be, for example in a search app, recommending users to visit a website based on the content they consume in the application, as a form of advertising. Modifications to the code are required for each type of content that is possible to be consumed by the user. The machine learning can receive these searches as its input data and by means of learning algorithms can train a predictive model capable of recommending users to visit websites in a similar way as it would be done in code. These recommendations are called data outputs, which are refined as more searches are performed. It is considered a branch of artificial intelligence (AI) and others such as deep learning or neural networks derive from it [8].

2.4 TensorFlow

TensorFlow is a set of numerical computation software libraries, written in the Python language and created by Google Brain Team, initially with the aim of facilitating the research of machine learning and deep learning projects. Currently it can be used in other areas of artificial intelligence [9]. It has four environments of use, the first is for desktop environments such as Windows, Linux, etc., the second is the web environment, where the JavaScript language is handled; the third is the environment of mobile devices that is called TensorFlow Lite and the last is for production environments. It can use the GPU of the devices to perform better operations although it also supports the use of CPU. Teachable machine trains the model without the need to get into this topic, offering the option to export it in the environment needed.

2.5 Teachable Machine

Teachable Machine is a web-based tool that allows creating machine learning models in a fast, simple and accessible way for everyone [10]. This tool is used because it is not required to know how to use the TensorFlow Python code libraries, also the web page does the logical work from the cloud, therefore a high performance computer is not required.

2.6 EInt

The EInt smart appliance mobile application (Fig. 1) is an application intended to run on a smart device that is embedded in the refrigerator [11]. Currently its scope is limited to devices with the Android operating system such as phones and tablets. It was developed with the Android Studio IDE [12] for devices running version 5.0 or higher of the Android operating system.

Fig. 1. User interface of the main menu of the EInt mobile application, still under development.

3 Proposal

It is proposed to make a modification to the EInt mobile application and implement an interface for the registration of inputs using only the camera, in order to eliminate the need for manual data entry through forms. The use of an existing mobile application instead of developing a new one is due to the fact that the application has elements such as a database and views to see its records, which serves as a basis for testing the new object detection functionality, in addition to the fact that it can be used for future work.

For its development, a modification was made to the Java code of the example offered by Teachable Machine through GitHub [13]. The number of products that the application can recognize is limited to the samples given to the previously trained learning model. For this demonstration, 45 image samples are used for each product. It is important to note that this sample number is for testing purposes, in production environments it is recommended to use a massive amount of data, because the larger the sample number, the higher the image recognition accuracy.

3.1 Model Training

Before implementing the object detection functionality in the mobile application, a learning model was trained and some tests of its performance were made on the Teachable Machine website. There is a sample of 6 classes where each class corresponds to a different fruit and for each fruit 45 images are assigned. The tool takes 85% of the sample to teach it to classify the images, the remaining 15% is used to test its performance. When it finishes processing all the images, an epoch is considered to have been performed. In total 100 epochs are performed. At the end of the epochs, the web tool allows to check the performance of the model with the webcam of the device (a Windows computer in this case). Figure 2 shows the demonstration of the model, it can be seen that the learning model is trained where a banana is detected. Once the training is completed and since the project is a mobile application, the model is exported for use with TensorFlow Lite.

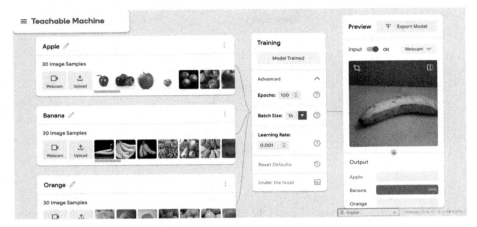

Fig. 2. Teachable Machine development environment.

The input data of the model are the images of the products to be identified by the application (images uploaded to Teachable Machine), the output data are displayed by means of a label containing the product identifier, the product name and the percentage of certainty about it. Figure 3 shows that the camera is focusing on a banana and the application recognizes it by displaying a label with a percentage of 100% that the product in question is the input recognized by the learning model. This percentage is a prediction and may fail depending on the model.

When the model is fully trained the tool shows details about the training of the model. Table 1 shows the accuracy for each product class where all the inputs, except for banana, show a perfect accuracy of 1 for each of the seven samples. In the case of banana it shows an accuracy of 0.86 or 86%.

Similar to the previous table but in greater detail, there is a confusion matrix of the model, shown in Fig. 4, where the Y axis corresponds to each of the products, the X axis corresponds to what the model predicts after training and the number indicates the number of times that the product on the Y axis is predicted with respect to the one on the X axis. For example, in the case of avocado, it is predicted in all 7 samples as an avocado and 0 times as the rest of the inputs. In the case of the banana, it is confused 1 time with the avocado, it is predicted 6 times as banana and for the rest of inputs it is predicted 0.The higher the number of the matrix, the higher the accuracy of the object. The banana has an accuracy of 86%, this is due to the fact that one of the samples taken (photographs) the model confuses it with an avocado. The confusion occurs because the image has more resemblance to those found within the avocado group, than to those found within the banana group. These inputs have no resemblance to each other, neither

Fig. 3. Application interface for adding product using the camera.

Table 1. Detection accuracy for each product class.

Class	Accuracy	Number of samples
Avocado	1.00	7
Apple	1.00	7
Orange	1.00	7
Potato	1.00	7
Banana	0.86	7
Tomato	1.00	7

in shape nor in color. This type of confusion usually occurs when there is "noise" in the sample. Such noise can be the background of the image, what is behind the fruit when the camera captures the image.

Finally, the accuracy of the model is shown. It is the percentage of correct classifications during learning. It consists of a division of classified samples by the total number of samples. In the graph shown in Fig. 5, we can see the correctly classified samples as the lower line shown very close to 1.0 (0.98 approximately), and the total of samples positioned in the 1.0, for this sample 100 epochs are handled. The accuracy is not perfect due to the confusion in detecting the banana input as 86% which is reflected in this graph. However, the system only fails 1 out of 7 banana samples out of a total of 45 per input class. The division of the correctly classified samples by the total of 270 yields a result very close to 1.0.

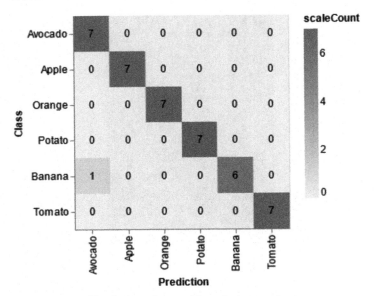

Fig. 4. Learning model confusion matrix.

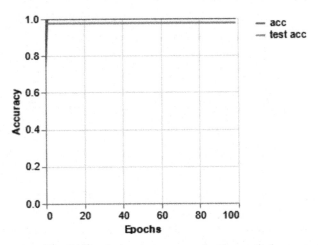

Fig. 5. Graph showing accuracy by time period.

3.2 Interaction with the Application

The user interaction with the application is given by means of components found in all types of mobile applications, for example, buttons that when selected perform a certain function, icons that when touched perform an action related to their drawing, such as the camera icon that opens the camera. In the case of the interface to add product, the camera of the device is used where the user receives the name of the product that is being focused, presenting a situation in which both the person and the device recognize the same object. For the latter, the input being observed must be within its learning range, otherwise the application will not detect it. Figure 6 shows that the application focuses on an empty cup where there is a 68% certainty that it is an apple. The program will always try to relate the image with the objects it can recognize.

Fig. 6. Application interface where the camera focuses on an empty cup.

The detection of inputs with the camera of the devices is considered ubiquitous computing because by registering the product in the system without the user having to interact with registration forms, the old user interface and interaction is replaced by a mobile system that does it automatically, and by being able to detect food, the person achieves greater integration with the device.

4 Results

The Teachable Machine API is used instead of the TensorFlow API because it makes model development and deployment faster and easier to understand, although it has disadvantages such as not having enough customization of model training but it works for the purpose of showing its operation in this research work. With the learning model implemented in the EInt application, a product will be registered using object detection. The step-by-step process is shown below. First, in the main menu, select the option 'My pantry', to see the interface where the registered inputs are located as shown in Fig. 7.

In the pantry interface there are some products registered in the traditional way (with a form). To add a new product, select the floating ball, this will load the interface to register a product shown in Fig. 8.

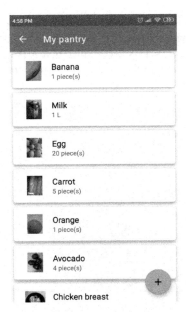

Fig. 7. User interface of an order list.

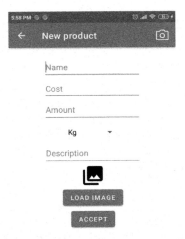

Fig. 8. Interface to add an input in the application.

This interface presents a form where a product can be registered. After filling in the fields and uploading an image from the device storage a new product is registered. This can be done automatically by selecting the camera icon (located in the upper left corner of the screen). In this example the new image recognition technology is handled, therefore, the camera icon is selected to go to the input registration interface using machine learning as shown in Fig. 9. The program shows a 100% prediction that the focused object is an apple. This percentage may drop if the object is not focused well or if there is not enough illumination.

Fig. 9. Application camera interface where an apple is in focus.

When the camera is correctly focused on the input and the application recognizes the object, the icon shown in the top bar of the application is selected to start its registration. It is not necessary to select it when it is at 100%, it is sufficient that the product label matches the image. Once this is done, the application will take a picture of the input, register the product and display the registered inputs in the screen that was shown in previous Fig. 7. Taking into consideration the user's input list, it is possible to select the new product that was added to display the details. Selecting the new "Apple" card displays the product detail interface as shown in Fig. 10.

When registering products with the camera, only some information fields are auto-completed: the name, a product unit (corresponds to one piece), and the product image, however the description and price remain empty. There is the option of selecting the floating sphere with a pencil icon to fill in the missing data. It is necessary to select the floating sphere again for the changes to be saved. The product can be edited again at any time the user needs it. It is planned in the future to increase the scope of the auto-completion by displaying a brief description of the product and an approximation of its price. Figure 11 shows as a second result an example where focusing on two objects and one of them not being identified by the application, causes the detection accuracy to decrease.

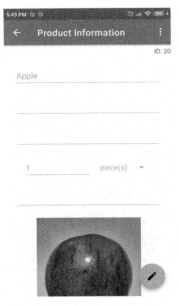

Fig. 10. Product detail interface.

Fig. 11. Camera interface focusing on an orange and a salt shaker.

Any object that obstructs the input that you want to register by the application will cause conflict at the moment of detecting the image. The same may occur if two different fruits are used. A certain degree of user discipline is required to give the application a chance to register inputs. In this case, even with the low accuracy, the fruit is detected and therefore there would be no problem for the user to register it. The model is capable of detecting multiple inputs at the same time but due to programming limitations, the application is not specified what to do in case of multiple inputs. It is therefore necessary to register each product separately.

5 Conclusions

We can see that machine learning and image recognition can help reduce the interaction time with the computer by auto-completing forms that normally require us to fill them out with the keyboard or search the device's storage for the requested file as was the case with the product image. Computer interaction was not eliminated, but replaced by another form of interaction that requires us to spend less time.

Beyond autofill forms, other possible uses for this technology is to generate errand lists, if the camera is focused on each of the products in the refrigerator, the application could recognize which products are needed to complete the errand.

The research showed a way to record fruit and vegetables using camera and image recognition techniques. There are plans to improve the prediction model so that it can detect other types of inputs as well as the state they are in, for example, if they are ripe, unripe, rotten, etc. In addition, we are looking to expand the type of products to be detected, not only to fruits but also to beverages, canned food, among other types of food. When this happens, there will be a new limitation, the user's storage space. The application currently has an approximate weight of 70 megabytes, before implementing the learning model its weight was around 20 mb. The artificial intelligence feature made the application increase its storage requirement by more than double, however much of this weight corresponds to the image recognition code and the camera and tensorflow libraries. With 6 inputs as the product recognition limit, the model weighs only 775 kilobytes. Even with this light file, if it is contemplated to expand it using massive data, it will be necessary to look for solutions in the cloud to perform the storage and image processing work, because the larger the model, the greater the CPU and GPU resource required. Future work is planned to make the application useful in areas of E-Commerce, as currently businesses and food distribution markets do not handle recognition technologies to verify the integrity or storage of their products.

In addition, it is planned in the future to work with other computing techniques such as neural networks, extreme learning, pattern recognition, etc. The EInt project originally seeks to develop an intelligent device that can be embedded in a refrigerator and through a connection to temperature sensors, cameras, etc. allow to keep track of household supplies. The camera that will be linked to this device will perform the same function presented in the results, with the difference that this camera will be inside the refrigerator and the registration of the product will be automatic, without any interaction with the user.

References

1. Shapovalov, V., Shapovalov, Y., Bilyk, Z., Megalinska, A., Muzyka, I.: The Google Lens analyzing quality: an analysis of the possibility to use in the educational process (2019)
2. López, C., Espinoza, M., Padilla, A.B.: Implementación de una solución de domótica basado en las mejores soluciones y prácticas del mercado actual. Sinergia e Innovación **3**(1), 88 (2015). https://doi.org/10.19083/sinergia.2015.409
3. Fujiyoshi, H., Hirakawa, T., Yamashita, T.: Deep learning-based image recognition for autonomous driving. IATSS Res. **43**(4), 244–252 (2019)
4. Xiao, T., Reed, C. J., Wang, X., Keutzer, K., Darrell, T.: Region similarity representation learning. In: Proceedings of the IEEE/CVF International Conference on Computer Vision, pp. 10539–10548 (2021)
5. Xie, X., Cheng, G., Wang, J., Yao, X., Han, J.: Oriented R-CNN for object detection. In: Proceedings of the IEEE/CVF International Conference on Computer Vision, pp. 3520–3529 (2021)
6. Ann, E.T.L., Hao, N.S., Wei, G.W., Hee, K.C.: Feast in: a machine learning image recognition model of recipe and lifestyle applications. In MATEC Web of Conferences, vol. 335, pp. 04006. EDP Sciences (2021)
7. Plötz, T., Hammerla, N.Y., Olivier, P.L.: Feature learning for activity recognition in ubiquitous computing. In: Twenty-Second International Joint Conference on Artificial Intelligence (2011)
8. Hurwitz, J., Kirsch, D., Jeong, D.H., Song, C.G., Chang. R., Hodges, L.: Machine Learning For Dummies. John Wiley & Sons, Inc. 2018. 3-4
9. Zaccone, G., Karim, M.R., Menshawy, A.: Deep Learning with TensorFlow, pp. 29–30. Packt Publishing Ltd. (2017)
10. Teachable Machine. Version 2.4.5. Google (2022)
11. Camacho, C.A.C., Alanis, A., Sotelo, J., Romero, K., Jimenez, S.: Multiagent system for home appliances on Internet of Things (MAS-HAIoT). In: Jezic, G., Chen-Burger, J., Kusek, M., Sperka, R., Howlett, R.J., Jain, Lakhmi C. (eds.) Agents and Multi-Agent Systems: Technologies and Applications 2021: Proceedings of 15th KES International Conference, KES-AMSTA 2021, June 2021, pp. 349–360. Springer Singapore, Singapore (2021). https://doi.org/10.1007/978-981-16-2994-5_29
12. Android Studio. Version 2021.3.1. Google (2022)
13. TensorFlow Lite Image Classification Demo. Version commit ee26f25be4c4215a01e3d3e9f268a8bf95dcdd07. TensorFlow (2020)

Efficient Spike Detection with Singular Spectrum Analysis Filter

Ousmane Khouma[1(✉)], Mamadou L. Ndiaye[2], and Idy Diop[2]

[1] Université Amadou Mahtar MBOW, Diamniadio, Senegal
ousmane.khouma@uam.edu.sn
[2] Ecole Supérieure Polytechnique, Université Cheikh Anta DIOP, Dakar, Senegal
{mamadoulamine.ndiaye,idy.diop}@esp.sn
https://www.uam.sn/

Abstract. Several technological tools have been developed to aid neurologists in accurately diagnosing epilepsy, which is among the diseases commonly addressed in neurological clinics. In real-life conditions, the recording of surface or depth electroencephalogram (EEG) is always disrupted by artifacts, making it difficult to analyze critical and interictal paroxysmal events (IPE) or spikes of short durations. Artifact synchronizations are commonly observed, which can lead to medical interpretation errors. Often, data analysis is limited to visual inspection of EEG tracings, which does not always enable the identification of certain epilepsy events. Therefore, it is necessary to reduce or even eliminate noise for better data processing. Given the structure of EEG signals, we will study filters that allow us to highlight transient events. In this paper, We suggest utilizing the Singular Spectrum Analysis (SSA) filter for improved detection of spikes within EEG signals. Before choosing the SSA filter, a comparison with other filters such as high-pass, and Kalman filters was conducted. SSA filter is paired with the fractal dimension (FD) detector for automated spike detection. FD is based spike detection method using adaptive threshold.

Keywords: Epilepsy · EEG · Singular Spectrum Analysis · Filter · Spike detection

1 Introduction

Epilepsy is defined by the abnormal and excessive firing of neuronal populations, ranging in significance [1]. Electroencephalogram (EEG) allows doctors to better diagnose diseases. During EEG data acquisition, various noises of different origins can be added to the signal. The goal of this study is to identify a filter that is well-suited for processing EEG signals. There is a wide range of filters available. By evaluating the input and output signal-to-noise ratio, we assess the filters' performance to select the most suitable option for processing EEG signals. The SSA filter has shown the best performance. It relies mainly on the

T. Guarda et al. (Eds.): ARTIIS 2023, CCIS 1937, pp. 223–236, 2024.
https://doi.org/10.1007/978-3-031-48930-3_17

singular value decomposition of the input data. The versatility of the SSA filter has been well-established as an effective approach for data analysis [2,3].

Within this manuscript, we put forth the utilization of the SSA filter to assist detection methods in better identifying spikes that are challenging to spot through simple visual inspection of electroencephalographic data. To illustrate the performance of the SSA filter, we have chosen the FD method to detect spikes.

After the introduction, Sect. 2 studies the SSA filter. In Sect. 3, we present the spike detection based on fractal dimension. The Sect. 4 focuses on comparing the performance of different filters applied to EEG signals. Section 5 examines and analyzes the results obtained from real data recorded from patients diagnosed with drug-resistant epilepsy in the temporal lobe. The final section provides the conclusion of the paper.

2   Study of the SSA Filter

2.1   Singular Value Decomposition

The Singular Value Decomposition (SVD) encompasses several scientific fields. It fills the gaps of the Eigenvalue Decomposition, which only applies to certain square matrices [4].

As a result, the Singular Value Decomposition applies to all matrices without restriction. It also allows for generalization of diagonalization in the case of rectangular matrices.

For a matrix A of size m x n, there exist two square orthogonal matrices U and V of respective sizes m x m and n x n such that:

$$A = U \sum V^T \qquad (1)$$

where $\sum$ is a diagonal matrix of size m x n with real and positive coefficients and V^T represents transposed matrix [5].

This matrix contains the elements $\sigma_1, \sigma_2, \dots, \sigma_k$ called singular values of A, such that : $\sigma_1 \geq \sigma_2 \geq, \dots, \geq \sigma_k \geq 0$ where $k = minimum\{m,n\}$.

Furthermore, the right and left singular vectors of matrix A are respectively the first k columns of $U = (u_1, u_2, ..., u_m)$ and $V = (v_1, v_2, ..., v_n)$.

The matrix $\sum$ (Eq. 1) can have different structures.

Case 1: $k = m$ $(m < n)$, **we obtain the following structure:**

$$\sum = (\sum{}_k, 0) \qquad (2)$$

where $\sum_k$ represents a diagonal matrix comprising the singular values [4]. Indeed, we can simplify the expression of the decomposition of matrix A (Eq. 1) as follows:

$$A = U(\sum{}_k, 0) \begin{pmatrix} V_1^T \\ V_2^T \end{pmatrix} \qquad (3)$$

The block V_2^T is multiplied by 0, which allows us to obtain the following relation:

$$A = U \sum_k V_1^T \tag{4}$$

where U and $\sum_k$ are square matrices of size m x m. The size of the matrix V_1^T is equal to m x n.

Case 2: $k = n$ $(n < m)$, **we have the following structure:**

$$\sum = \begin{pmatrix} \sum_k \\ 0 \end{pmatrix} \tag{5}$$

For this case, we also obtain a simplified expression of A.

$$A = (U_1, U_2) \begin{pmatrix} \sum_k \\ 0 \end{pmatrix} V^T \tag{6}$$

For this expression, the block U_2 is also multiplied by 0, resulting in the reduced expression of matrix A.

$$A = U_1 \sum_k V^T \tag{7}$$

where $\sum_k$ and V are square matrices of size n x n. The size of the matrix U_1 is equal to m x n.

The Eqs. (4) and (7) are called the reduced singular value decomposition of matrix A. This reduced form is highly important in practice. It is also interesting to transform these reduced equations into a sum of rank-1 matrices. The Eqs. (4) and (7) then become [4]:

$$A = \sum_{i=1}^{k} \sigma_i u_i v_i^T \tag{8}$$

Case 3: The matrix A is square $(m = n)$, **and all the other matrices in the decomposition are also square.**

Furthermore, the theoretical determination of singular values and associated singular vectors seems to be very difficult. Therefore, we resort to solving eigenvalue and eigenvector problems of the matrices AA^T and $A^T A$.

Let A be a matrix of size m × n with $m > n$. By multiplying both sides of Eq. (1) by A^T, we obtain the following equation:

$$AA^T = V \sum^T U^T U \sum V^T \tag{9}$$

Since the matrix U is orthogonal, $U^T U = I$ (I being the identity matrix). We then obtain the following equation:

$$AA^T = V \sum^2 V^T \tag{10}$$

The matrix A^T A is a square matrix of size n x n. Therefore, it is diagonalizable in an orthonormal basis of eigenvectors. Its eigenvalue decomposition is:

$$AA^T = V \prod V^T \tag{11}$$

where $\sum^2 = \prod$

Thus, the singular values of matrix A represent the square root of the eigen-values λ_i ($\sigma_i = \sqrt{\lambda_i}$). Finally, the pair ($\prod, V$) represents the eigenvalue decomposition of the matrix $A^T A$.

Similarly, the pair ($\prod, U$) represents the eigenvalue decomposition of the matrix AA^T.

Therefore, we can note that the diagonalizations of $A^T A$ and AA^T determine the singular vectors V and U, respectively.

Moreover, the Singular Spectrum Analysis (SSA) filter is primarily delineated through two sequential steps, each accompanied by its respective mathematical equations. In the initial step, the data undergoes decomposition, followed by the subsequent step of reconstructing the original data. The reconstituted segment (devoid of noise) is then employed for forecasting new data points within the signal.

2.2 Decomposition Step of the SSA Filter

This stage encompasses two fundamental components: embedding and singular value decomposition. In the embedding step, the time series s representing the EEG signal is mapped into k delayed vectors of size l [6].

$$X_i = \big[\, Z_{i-1}, Z_i, \ldots, Z_{i+l-2} \,\big]^T \tag{12}$$

$1 \leq i \leq k$ with $k = r - l + 1$, l represents the window width ($1 \leq l \leq r$). The suitable window size is contingent upon the specific application and the existing understanding of the signals being analyzed. The trajectory matrix of the series s is constructed by inserting each X_i into the ith column of an l x k matrix.

$$X = \big[x_1, x_2, \ldots, x_k\big] = \begin{bmatrix} Z_0 & Z_1 & Z_2 & \cdots & Z_{k-1} \\ Z_1 & Z_2 & Z_3 & \cdots & Z_k \\ Z_2 & Z_3 & Z_4 & \cdots & Z_{k+1} \\ \vdots & \vdots & \vdots & \ddots & \vdots \\ Z_{l-1} & Z_l & Z_{l+1} & \cdots & Z_{r-1} \end{bmatrix} \tag{13}$$

It should be noted that the trajectory matrix takes the form of a Hankel matrix, implying that the elements along its diagonals adhere to a specific pattern $i+j = constant$.

Certainly, the Singular Value Decomposition (SVD) of the trajectory matrix is calculated and expressed as the summation of elementary bi-orthogonal rank - 1 matrices. Considering the eigenvalues and corresponding eigenvectors of $Z = XX^T$ as $\lambda_1, \lambda_2, \ldots, \lambda_l$ and $e_1, e_2, \ldots, e_l$ respectively.

If $V_i = X^T e_i / \sqrt{\lambda_i}$, then the SVD of the trajectory matrix can be written as:

$$X = X_1 + X_2 + \ldots + X_d \tag{14}$$

where $d = argmax_i(\lambda_i > 0)$ and $X_i = \sqrt{\lambda_i} e_i V_i^T$. The ith triplet of the SVD decomposition consists of V_i, e_i, and λ_i. The projection of the time series onto the direction of each vector gives the corresponding temporal principal component.

2.3   Reconstruction Step of the SSA Filter

This part consists of two steps: grouping and diagonal averaging.

- **Mean Grouping**: This step divides the set of indices $\{1, 2, ..., d\}$ into m disjoint sets $I_1, I_2, \ldots, I_m$. For each group $I_j = \{i_{j1}, i_{j2}, \ldots, i_{jp}\}$, we have $X_{Ij} = \{X_{j_1}, X_{j_2}, ..., X_{j_p}\}$. The grouping of triplets with the expansion of all matrices X_{Ij} is determined by the following relation:

$$X = X_{I1} + X_{I2} + \ldots + X_{Id} \tag{15}$$

  There exists no universal guideline for grouping. The grouping criterion is contingent upon the unique nature of the problem and the relative influence of signals and noise within each specific application.
- **Diagonal Averaging**: In the final step of the analysis, each group is transformed into a series of length r. For a matrix Y of size l x k, the $q^t h$ element of the time series g_q is calculated by taking the average of the elements of the matrix above the diagonal $i + j = q + 2$, where i and j are the row and column indices of Y, respectively [7].

3   Spike Detection Based on Fractal Dimension

We employ the Katz algorithm to compute the fractal dimension in this research paper [8].

3.1   Katz Algorithm

The algorithm proposed by Katz [9] for calculating the fractal dimension is somewhat slower in computation compared to other methods. However, it presents the benefit of being directly derived from the waveform, thereby obviating the need for a preliminary binary sequence generation in the preprocessing stage. The fractal dimension (FD) of the curve can be formulated using the subsequent equation:

$$D = \frac{\log_{10}(L)}{\log_{10}(d)} \tag{16}$$

Let **L** stand for the overall curve length or the cumulative sum of distances between consecutive points. The symbol **d** represents the estimated diameter, which corresponds to the distance between the initial point in the time series and the point with the greatest separation. The formula for calculating **d** is given by:

$$d = max(distance(1, i)) \tag{17}$$

In Katz's method, the determination of the fractal dimension (FD) relies on evaluating the distances between each individual point within the sequence and the initial point. The point "i" is chosen such that it maximizes its distance from the initial point. However, the FD can be affected by the choice of units of measurement. If different units are used, the resulting fractal dimension may vary.

To address this issue, the Katz method introduces a common unit of measure called the average level or distance between consecutive points, denoted as "a". This allows for distance normalization. The expression for distance normalization in the Katz method is as follows:

$$D = \frac{\log_{10}(L/a)}{\log_{10}(d/a)} \tag{18}$$

By defining n as size of the steps in the time series or the number of the stages of the curve, then $n = L/a$, we obtain:

$$D = \frac{\log_{10}(n)}{\log_{10}(d/L) + \log_{10}(n)} \tag{19}$$

where, Eq. (19) gives us the Katz approach to calculate fractal dimension.

3.2 Flexible Spike Detection Utilizing Fractal Dimension

Within this spike detection technique, a pair of sliding windows is employed to scrutinize the signal. For each of these windows, the Fractal Dimension (FD) is computed utilizing the Katz algorithm, facilitating the identification of significant signal points.

The variations of the FD are calculated by:

$$G_t = |FD_{t+1} - FD_t| \tag{20}$$

With $t = 1, 2, \ldots, L - 1$. In this case, the adaptive threshold is characterized as the median value within the distribution. Instances where the peak values of parameter G surpass this threshold are designated as the localization points for spikes within the EEG signal. Figure 1 presents the stages of adaptive spike detection. For the sake of simplicity, a parametric approach is embraced. As

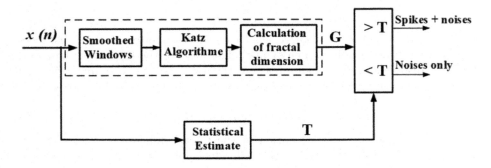

Fig. 1. Blocks of adaptive spikes detection using fractal dimension

noise follows a stochastic process, the output of the diagram similarly adheres to a random process (Fig 1), characterized by a median value of μ and a standard deviation of σ. Hence, the threshold can be approximated using the subsequent equation:

$$T = \mu + p\sigma \tag{21}$$

where T represents the adaptive detection threshold for identifying spike presence, and the multiplier p is contingent upon P_{fa} (probability of false alarm) [10].

4   Experimental Comparison of Filters

In this section, we showcase the real-world outcomes of the filters.

To achieve this, we manipulate the signal-to-noise ratio by introducing additive white Gaussian noise (AWGN). To emulate the impact of amplifier noise in EEG signals, we assess the filters' efficacy in a quantitative manner by computing the signal-to-noise ratio at the filters' output. This computation is accomplished using the following formula:

$$SNR_{Output}(dB) = \frac{\sum_i (x(i))^2}{\sum_i (x_d(i) - x(i))^2} \tag{22}$$

where x and x_d represent, respectively, the original (unnoisy) signal and the denoised signal (the output of the filter).

The SSA filter, like many filters, plays a crucial role in the processing of non-stationary signals (**such as EEG signals**). Numerous parameters necessitate meticulous adjustment through an extensive array of trials. The filtering procedure for a specific signal is particularly responsive to the careful selection of these parameters. When the window length (K) and the embedding component (J) are chosen to be too large, some important information from the original signal is eliminated by the filter. On the other hand, if K and J are too small, the filter may not sufficiently attenuate the interfering noise. Therefore, we should strive to find a compromise between these two limits. The quantity of chosen eigenvectors is contingent upon the intricacy of the intended component. For simulating this filter, the following configurations were employed: $K = 20$ and $J = 2$.

We also vary the signal-to-noise ratio (SNR) at the input of the filter. This allows us to plot the output SNR curve as a function of the input SNR.

The signal obtained at the output of the SSA filter in Fig. 2 shows that the spikes are visible after filtering. This demonstrates that the events (IPE) to be detected are preserved after filtering. Therefore, the filter has the ability to eliminate noise without altering the useful information (IPE).

We have plotted (see Fig. 3) the curve of the output SNR (dB) to evaluate the applicability of the studied filters for highly noisy EEG signals.

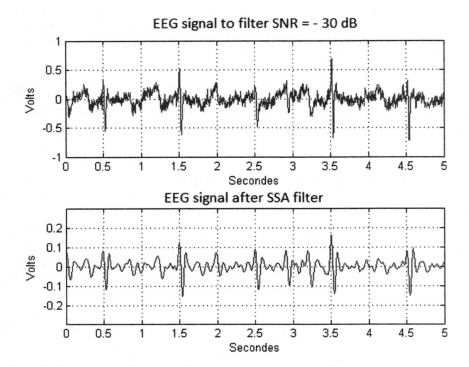

Fig. 2. SSA Filter with $SNR = -30dB$

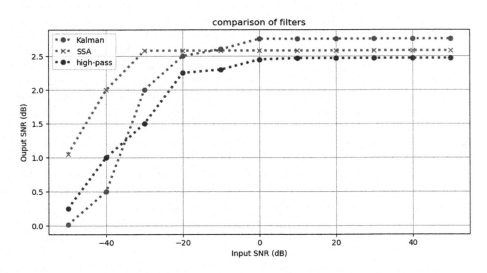

Fig. 3. Comparing SNR of High Pass, Kalman, and SSA filters

The cutoff frequency used for the high-pass filter is 5 Hz. This value was chosen based on the frequency content of the rhythms present in the EEG [11]. The model function used is Chebyshev. Figure 4 (see Fig. 3) demonstrates instability in the system for negative values of the input Signal-to-Noise Ratio (SNR). This indicates that the high-pass filter is ineffective in handling heavily noisy EEG signals.

For the Kalman filter, Fig. 3 (see Fig. 3) demonstrates that the output Signal-to-Noise Ratio (SNR) values gradually and significantly increase based on the input SNR values within the range of $[-50dB, -10dB]$. From **-10 dB** onwards, the output SNR values remain constant. Therefore, the Kalman filter preserves the morphology of the spikes for SNR ≥ -10 dB.

For the range $[-50dB, -30dB]$, the output Signal-to-Noise Ratio (SNR) values of the SSA filter progressively increase. This filter exhibits variation within this range as it modifies the EPICs of the EEG signal. From the $-30dB$ value onwards, the curve shows that the output SNR becomes constant. Moreover, SSA is a versatile and data-responsive technique that can be tailored to accommodate the characteristics of the data. This demonstrates the robustness of this filter against noisy signals. Therefore, the filter will be applied before using the proposed detection method.

5   Effective Detection of Spikes

Figure 4 depicts the simulation blocks for the detection of spikes within an EEG signal. We apply the SSA filter prior to using the fractal dimension detector. In this part, the tests are performed on multiple signals of different morphologies. These signals are extracted from the recording of EEG signals from two patients (P1 and P2) suffering from pharmacoresistant temporal lobe epilepsy [12].

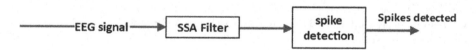

Fig. 4. Block for spikes detection with SSA filter

To evaluate the performance of this detector, we use several indices. By definition, false alarms or false negative (FN) indicate the portions detected as spikes when they are not actual epileptic events. As for true positve (TP) detections, they inform us about the correctly detected spikes. Finally, missed detections (MD) represent the spikes that were not found by the detector.

– The false alarm rate (FA) is calculated as follows [13]:

$$Rate_{FN} = \frac{FA}{TP + FN} \qquad (23)$$

- Sensitivity, also known as the true positive rate, measures the detector's capability to identify and detect spikes accurately.

$$Rate_{TP} = \frac{TP}{TP + MD} \tag{24}$$

- Selectivity quantifies the detector's capacity to discriminate and reject false alarms.

$$Selectivity = \frac{TP}{TP + FN} = 1 - Rate_{FN} \tag{25}$$

Likewise, a detection algorithm necessitates an additional metric known as the detection delay (DD). It represents the temporal difference between the actual onset of the spike in terms of electrical activity (in the EEG, not at the clinical level) and the moment at which it is detected.

$$DD = |t_{spike} - t_{algo}| \tag{26}$$

With t_{pointe} representing the actual onset time of the spike and t_{algo} representing the time provided by the detection algorithm, this performance indicator is calculated for each spike and evaluates the algorithm's ability to rapidly detect a spike.

Taking into account these performance indicators, we will plot Receiver Operating Characteristic (ROC) curves.

Figure 5 portrays a depiction of identified spikes (shown in blue and green, representing the EEG signal and the instances of spike detection, respectively) utilizing the FD method in conjunction with the SSA filter.

The FD method with the SSA filter applied to both databases demonstrates good sensitivity and yields a lower false alarm rate.

Based on the test results with the SSA and Kalman filters, we plotted the performance indicators of the detector as points in the ROC space (see Fig. 6 and Fig. 7). We observed that there are points that are close to the ideal point. We also noticed that the FD method with the SSA filter yields good results for sensitivity and selectivity.

Table 1. Average performance of detection (FD) with SSA filter (P1 data)

Parameters	−30 dB	−10 dB	0 dB	20 dB	40 dB	60 dB
sensitivity (%)	90	97	99	100	100	100
FA (%)	2	5	7	23	11	8
selectivity (%)	98	95	93	77	89	92

In Tables 1, 2, 3 and 4, we depict the average performance indicators of the FD method using SSA and Kalman filters. The indicators are computed for various signal-to-noise ratio (SNR) values.

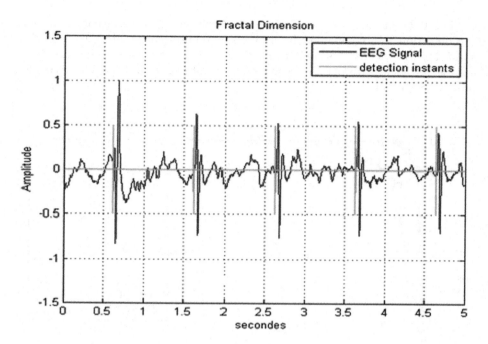

Fig. 5. IPE detected using adaptive FD (Color figure online)

Table 2. Average performance of detection (FD) with Kalman filter (P1 data).

Parameters	−30 dB	−10 dB	0 dB	20 dB	40 dB	60 dB
sensitivity (%)	85	92	96	100	100	100
FA (%)	7	11	17	43	28	23
selectivity (%)	93	89	83	57	72	77

Table 3. Average performance of detection (FD) with SSA filter (P2 data)

Parameters	−30 dB	−10 dB	0 dB	20 dB	40 dB	60 dB
sensitivity (%)	94	99	100	100	100	100
FA (%)	1	4	22	15	11	6
selectivity (%)	99	96	78	85	89	94

Table 4. Average performance of detection (FD) with Kalman filter (P2 data).

Parameters	−30 dB	−10 dB	0 dB	20 dB	40 dB	60 dB
sensitivity (%)	89	97	100	100	100	100
FA (%)	4	11	56	37	21	17
selectivity (%)	96	89	44	63	79	83

The FD method with the Kalman filter exhibits good sensitivity; however, the detection is accompanied by a significant false alarm rate. On the other hand, FD with SSA yields similar sensitivities but a lower false alarm rate. Both approaches yield satisfactory results in terms of sensitivity and selectivity for positive SNR values.

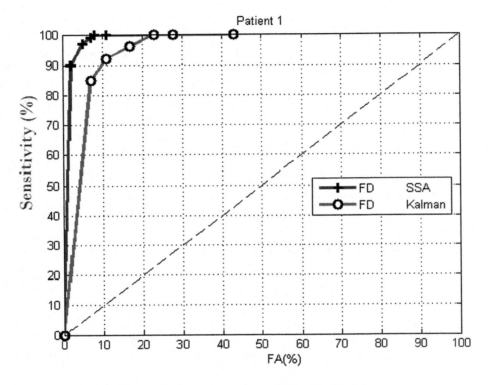

Fig. 6. Performance curves of FD with P1 data

Consequently, in Database P2, the pinnacle achievement is demonstrated with a sensitivity of 100% and selectivity of 98%. When considering all databases, the median values for sensitivity and selectivity stand at 99% and 90%, respectively, according to the conducted evaluations. Furthermore, the processing time for one-hour signal durations is approximately 6 s, showcasing impressive efficiency as it facilitates the detection of numerous spikes within this time frame.

Therefore, the performance curves indicate that the proposed detectors yield favorable outcomes in sensitivity and selectivity, regardless of the noise level present in the signal.

All simulations were carried out on a DELL Intel(R) Core(TM) i5-6300U CPU @ 2.40 GHz 2.50 GHz with 8 GB of RAM. Additionally, all suggested solutions were implemented within the Matlab and Python environments.

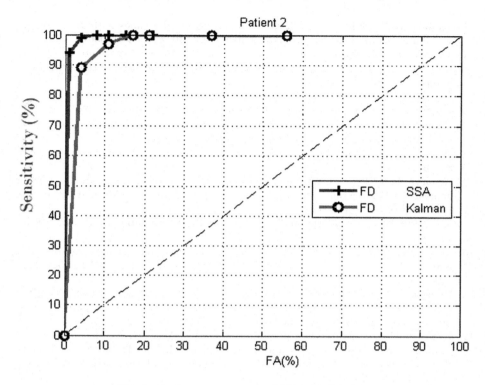

Fig. 7. Performance curves of FD with P2 data

6   Conclusion

To avoid misinterpretation of spikes, it is necessary to apply filtering methods to reduce or eliminate artifacts present in EEG signals during their acquisition. The tests on the filters in relation to the Signal-to-Noise Ratio (SNR) have shown that the SSA filter alters the useful information in EEG signals to a lesser extent. The high-pass filter exhibits weaknesses for highly noisy signals. It is unable to separate the noise from the event (spike) without distorting the signal. This filter modifies the morphology of the spikes by removing artifacts for highly noisy signals. The Kalman and SSA filters were chosen to be combined with the proposed detector. The results have shown that the FD detector with the SSA filter provides the best performance in terms of sensitivity, selectivity, and execution time.

References

1. Löscher, W., Schmidt, D.: Modern antiepileptic drug development has failed to deliver: ways out of the current dilemma. Epilepsia **52**(4), 657–78 (2011)

2. Jemwa, G.T., Aldrich, C.: Classification of process dynamics with Monte Carlo singular spectrum analysis. Comput. Chem. Eng. **30**, 816–831 (2006)
3. Tzagkarakis, G., Papadopouli, M., Panagiotis, T.: Singular spectrum analysis of traffic workload in a large-scale wireless lan. In: Proceedings of the 10th ACM Symposium, pp. 99–108 (2007)
4. Fresnel, J.: Algèbre des matrices, Hermann (2013)
5. Trefethen, L., Bau, D.: Numerical linear algebra ≫, vol. 50. Siam (1997)
6. Hamed, A., Saeid, S.: Spike detection approaches for noisy neuronal data: assessment and comparison. Neurocomputing **133**, 491–506 (2014)
7. Hassani, H.: Singular spectrum analysis: methodology and comparison. J. Data Sci. **5**(2), 239–257 (2007)
8. Acharya, U.R., Faust, O., Kannathal, N., Chua, T., Laxminarayan, S.: Non-linear analysis of EEG signals at various sleep stages, Computer. Methods Programs Biomed. **80**, 37–45 (2005)
9. Katz, M.: Fractals and the analysis of waveforms, Computer. Biol. Med. **18**(3), 145–156 (1988)
10. Mukhopadhyay, S., Ray, G.C.: A new interpretation of nonlinear energy operator and its efficiency in spike detection. IEEE Trans. Biomed Eng. **49**(12), 1526–1533 (2002)
11. Rebeca, R.V.: Contribution á la détection et á l'analyse des signaux EEG épileptiques: débruitage et séparation de sources. Institut national polytechnique de Lorraine, Université de Nancy, France, Ph D (2010)
12. LTSI Homepage. http://www.ltsi.univ-rennes1.fr/. Accessed 18 June 2023
13. Fukumori, K., Yoshida, N., Sugano, H., Nakajima, M., Tanaka, T.: Epileptic spike detection using neural networks with linear-phase convolutions. IEEE J. Biomed. Health Inform. **26**, 1045–1056 (2021)

MangoFruitDDS: A Standard Mango Fruit Diseases Dataset Made in Africa

Demba Faye[1]([✉]) [iD], Idy Diop[1] [iD], Nalla Mbaye[2], Doudou Dione[1],
and Marius Mintu Diedhiou[2]

[1] Polytechnic School of Dakar, Cheikh Anta DIOP University, Dakar, Senegal
demba.faye@esp.sn
[2] Plant Protection and Phytochemistry Laboratory, Department of Plant Biology,
Cheikh Anta DIOP University, Dakar, Senegal

Abstract. Mango is a lucrative fruit produced in tropical and sub-tropical areas. It is the third most traded tropical fruit after pineapple and avocado in the international market. In Senegal, the average production of mango fruits between the 2015–2016 and 2021–2022 seasons is 126,551 tons. Mango fruit is also leading the fruit exportation of the country. For example, in the 2017–2018 season, the quantity of mangoes exported was estimated at 17.5% of the country's fruit production, ahead of melon (13.4%) and watermelon (11.6%). There are, therefore several pests and diseases that reduce both the quantity and quality of mango production in the country. Several solutions based on Convolutional Neural Networks (CNNs) are proposed by researchers during the last years to automatically diagnose these pests and diseases. But the main limitation of these solutions is the lack of data since CNNs are data-intensive. Due to climatic variations from one geographical area to another, these solutions can only be adapted to certain areas. We propose in this work a mango fruit diseases dataset of 862 images collected from an orchard located in Senegal. Two combinations of data augmentation techniques, namely "Flip_Contrast_AffineTransformation" and "Flip_Zoom_AffineTransformation" are used to generate respectively two datasets: Dataset1 and Dataset2 of 37,432 images each one. Eight CNNs, including seven well-known ones and a proposed light weight Convolutional Neural Network (LCNN), are applied to both datasets to detect and identify the treated diseases. Results show that on Dataset1, DenseNet121 and ResNet50 give the best accuracy and F1_score both equal to 98.20%, on Dataset2, InceptionV3 and MobileNetV2 achieve both the best accuracy and F1_score of 98.20%. The proposed LCNN also achieved excellent results (accuracy: 95.25% and F1_score: 95.20%) on dataset1. Due to its light weight, it is therefore deployed in an offline Android mobile application to help users detect mango diseases from captured images.

Keywords: mango · diseases · CNN · Deep Learning · data augmentation · classification

T. Guarda et al. (Eds.): ARTIIS 2023, CCIS 1937, pp. 237–250, 2024.
https://doi.org/10.1007/978-3-031-48930-3_18

1 Introduction

Mango, known by its scientific name Magnifera Indica L., is a tropical and subtropical tree. The regions where it is most cultivated are the following: Asia, Latin America, and Africa. In terms of quantity exported in the international market, after pineapple and avocado, mango was the third most traded fruit [1]. In Senegal, mango production represents a significant part of fruit production. For example, in 2022, it accounted for 43.80% of fruit production valued at 277,400 tons. Between the 2015–2016 and 2021–2022 seasons, mango production in Senegal has seen a rollercoaster ride with an average of 126,551 tons with an annual variation of −1.1% [2]. Fruit exports of Senegal are also mainly dominated by mango. During the 2017–2018 season, for example, the quantity of mango exported was estimated at 21,297 tons, or 17.5% of the country's fruit production. After mango, come melon (13.4%) and watermelon (11.6%) [3].

However, mango production suffers from huge losses due to pests and diseases. These problems reduce not only the quantity but also the quality of mango production. In Africa, these issues are exacerbated by poverty and the lack of infrastructure, especially in the most remote areas. Therefore, identification of these diseases is relatively costly for farmers and time consuming.

In the last decade, thanks to the advances noted in the field of Artificial Intelligence (AI), especially in Deep Learning (DL), several solutions have been proposed by researchers for the automatic diagnosis of mango diseases.

However, the principal limit of these proposed solutions is the lack of data. DL algorithms are very data-intensive and it is the quantity and quality of the data, and not the mathematical modulization, that mostly influences the performance of DL models [1, 4]. One of the keys to the successful use of DL is having a good dataset to begin with. It is important, however, to note that, regarding crop diseases, characteristics may vary from one geographical area to another due to climatic variations. Therefore, the already proposed solutions are only suitable for certain geographical areas.

We propose in this paper, to the best of our knowledge, the first ready-to-use, standard, and publicly available dataset of mango fruits from Africa. Images are collected from a mango orchard located in Senegal, one of the top mango producers in west Africa. The dataset contains 862 images of four mango diseases namely Alternaria, Anthracnose, Aspergillus and Lasiodiplodia. An additional category in the dataset is healthy fruits.

The specific contributions of this paper include:

- Applying the top two combinations of data augmentation techniques such as "Flip_Contrast_AffineTransformation" and "Flip_Zoom_AffineTransformation" proposed in our paper [1] to generate two augmented datasets.
- A comparative analysis of eight convolutional neural networks (CNNs), namely VGG16, DenseNet121, MobileNetV2, NASMobileNet, ResNet50, InceptionV3, EfficientNetV2B1 and a proposed LCNN, based on their performances on disease classification.
- Developing an offline mobile application that can detect mango diseases using captured images.

The remainder of the paper is organized as follows: Sect. 2 deals with related works, Sect. 3 deals with data acquisition, combinations of data augmentation techniques used and implementation details of the CNNs used, Sect. 4 presents and discusses the results of the CNN models. The final section concludes the paper and announces the future work of authors.

2 Related Works

This section is divided into two subsections. The first deals with proposed solutions based on mango leaf image datasets and the second is related to solutions based on mango fruit image datasets.

2.1 DL Solutions Based on Mango Leaf Image Dataset

During the last five years, researchers have proposed several solutions based on DL, especially CNNs to identify mango leaf diseases.

For example, Gulavnai and al. [5] used a mango leaf dataset of 8853 images and a ResNet-CNNs (ResNet18, ResNet34 and ResNet50) and the Transfer Learning technique for an automatic detection and identification of four mango leaf diseases named, powdery mildew, anthracnose, golmich and red rust Results show that ResNet50 gives best accuracy (91.50%). Authors of [6] proposed a multilayer convolutional neural network (MCNN) to classify mango healthy leafs and affected ones by anthracnose disease. They used a datatset of 2200 images including 1070 images captured in the real-time environment in India and 1130 images taken from the PlantVillage dataset. In [7], Pham et al. developped a self-collected dataset of 450 mango leaf images and a Feed-Forward Neural Network (FFNN) with Hybrid Metaheuristic Feature Selection (HMFS) to classifier three mango diseases named Gall Midge, Anthracnose and Powdery Mildew. Their model achieved an accuracy of 89,41% more than comparative CNN such as AlexNet (78.64%), VGG1 (79.92%) and ResNet (84.88%). Saleem and al. in [8], used a self-collected dataset containing at first 2220 diseased mango leaves and 8880 images at end, after performing data augmentation techniques such as rotation, flipping and transformation. This dataset is used with a Fully-convolutional-network (FrCNnet) model for the segmentation of the diseased part of the mango leaf. Diseases treated are Blossom Blight, Anthracnose, and Apical Necrosis. The segmentation accuracy of their model is 99.2% with a false negative rate (FNR) of 0.8%. Authors in [9] developed a lightweight convolutional neural network (LCNN) and applied it on a dataset of mango leaf images to classify diseased leaves. The proposed LCNN achieves an accuracy of 98%. In [10], authors proposed a system based on Optimized Recurrent Neural Network (WO-RNN) and a dataset of mango leaf images gathered from standard resources. The proposed model achieves 96% accuracy and 93% F1-score in the mango leaf diseases classification. In [4] Ahmed et al. proposed a standard and publicly available mango leaf dataset named MangoLeafBD and including seven diseases (Anthracnose, Cutting Weevil, Die Back, Powdery Mildew, Gall Midge, Bacterial Canker, and Sooty Mould). They add a final category namely Heathy to their datatset. Leaf images are captured using mobile phone camera. After rotation and zooming operations, the dataset contains finally 4000 images including 500 per category.

2.2   DL Solutions Based on Mango Fruit Image Dataset

There are few DL solutions based on fruit images reported in the literature. Recently, three solutions have been proposed. For example, in [11], authors developed a dataset of 438 mango fruit images divided into 2 classes namely Anthracnose and Healthy. They applied AlexNet CNN model on this dataset for the detection of mangoes infected with anthracnose. The proposed system can isolate diseased mangoes with an accuracy more than 70%. Kusrini1et al. in [12] compared the performances of five CNNs namely VGG16, ResNet50, InceptionResNet-V2, Inception-V3, and DenseNet on a self-collected mango fruits dataset including 635 images divided into five pest classes and a disease class. The goal is to identify pests and diseases on mango fruit. VGG16 model achieves the best performance with validation and testing accuracies of 89% and 90%, respectively. Authors of [13] constructed a dataset of 20 classes including 31804 leaf and fruit images. 11 classes of the dataset include images of infected mango leaves, 7 classes have photographs of infected mango fruit, 1 class of healthy leaf images and 1 class of healthy fruit images. The dataset is gathered from several Internet sites like Mendeley, Krishi Batayon, Flickr, Plantix, Google, etc. They tested several CNNs (AlexNet, InceptionV3, Desnet169, VGG16 and MobileNetV2,) on their dataset and finaly, DenseNet169 gives the best performance with accuracy, precision, recall, and F1-scores of 97.81%, 97%, 96%, and 96%, respectively. This model is then deployed in a mobile application to aid in the identification of mango diseases and the recommendation of pesticides. Table 1 summarizes all the proposed solutions based on the paper title, year of publication, data sources, data type, number of images in the dataset, CNNs used, and performance obtained in the classification.

Table 1. Summary of proposed solutions using mango leaf or fruit images dataset

Paper	Year	Sources	Diseases	Data Type	No of Images	CNNs	Results
[5]	2019	Real-time environment	Powdery Mildew, Anthracnose, Galmich and Red Rust	Leaf images	8 853	ResNet18, ResNet34 and ResNet50	Best accuracy of 91.50% with ResNet50
[6]	2019	Real-time environment and PlantVillage Dataset	Anthracnose	Leaf images	2 200	MCNN	Accuracy of 97.13%
[7]	2020	Real-time environment	Gall Midge, Anthracnose and Powdery Mildew	Leaf Images	450	FFNN with HMFS	Accuracy of 89,41%
[8]	2021	Real-time environment	Blossom Blight, Anthracnose, and Apical Necrosis	Leaf Images	2 220	FrCNnet	Accuracy of 99.2% with a false negativerate (FNR) of 0.8%

(continued)

Table 1. (*continued*)

Paper	Year	Sources	Diseases	Data Type	No of Images	CNNs	Results
[9]	2023	*	*	Leaf Images	*	LCNN	Accuracy of 98%
[10]	2023	Standard resources (Internet, Pubic Datasets)	*	Leaf Images	*	WO-RNN	Accuracy of 96% and F1-score of 93%
[4]	2023	Real-time environment	Anthracnose, Cutting Weevil, Die Back, Powdery Mildew, Gall Midge, Bacterial Canker, and Sooty Mould	Leaf Images	1 800	ResNet50, CNN and CNN-SVM	Best Precision, Recall and F1_score are 91%, 90% and 90% respectively with CNN-SVM model
[11]	2021	Real-time environment	Anthracnose	Fruit Images	4 388	AlexNet	Accuracy of 70%
[12]	2022	Real-time environment	Capnodium_mangiferae, cynopterus_titthaecheilus, deanolis_albizonalis, pseudaulacaspis_cockerelli and pseudococcus_longispinus	Fruit Images	635	GG16, ResNet50, InceptionResNet-V2, Inception-V3, and DenseNet	Best accuracy of 89% with VGG16
[13]	2023	Internet sites like Mendeley, Krishi Batayon, Flickr, Plantix, Google, etc	Anthracnose, Bacterial Canke, Black Ro, Fruit Borer, Gall Midge, Giant Mealybug, Coating Mite Cutting Weevil Mealybug, Mysterious Cracking, Powdery Mildew, Red Rust, Scab and Sooty Mold	Leaf and Fruit images	31 804	AlexNet, InceptionV3, Desnet169, VGG16 and MobileNetV2	Bests accuracy, precision, recall, and F1-scores of 97.81%, 97%, 96%, and 96%, respectively with DenseNet169

3   Materials and Methods

3.1   Data Acquisition

MangoFruitDDS is a dataset gathered from an orchard located in Senegal, one of the top mango producers in west African. This orchard (latitude = 14.7851140, longitude = −17.0702470) is located more precisely in the Niayes area which is one of the largest mango producing areas in the country. Fruit images are captured using mobile phone camera with an initial size of 4160*3120. Images are then pre-processed by cropping, resizing and background removing techniques. The final size of images is 224*224 in

JPG format. Diseased mango fruit images captured are labelled by human experts. The following images on the Fig. 1 illustrates the composition of the dataset.

The dataset contains 862 mango fruit images including 170 images for Alternaria, 132 for Anthracnose, 186 for Aspergillus, 166 for Lasidiplodia and 208 for Healthy onces. All the steps realised in this work are represented in the Fig. 2. The dataset is available on the Mendeley Data platform under the name "SenMangFruitDDS" [14].

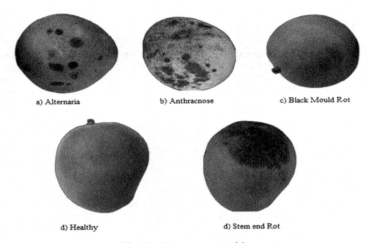

a) Alternaria   b) Anthracnose   c) Black Mould Rot

d) Healthy   d) Stem end Rot

Fig. 1. Dataset composition

3.2 Data Augmentation

In this paper, from the original dataset, we generated two augmented datasets using the two best combinations of data augmentation techniques obtained in our paper [1]. They allowed us to achieve very good performance in the classification of four mango leaf diseases using a small initial dataset. These combinations are **Flip_Contrast_AffineTransformation** and **Flip_Zoom_AffineTransformation**. Fig. 3 depicts their workflow.

Parameters used are following :

- Flip: images are horizontally and vertically flipped using flip parameter, respectively 1 and 0.
- Contrast-Brightness: for each image, two new images are generated using the combination of contrast and brightness parameters {1.5; 3} and {2.5; 5}.
- Zoom: each image is zoomed in from the center two times using zoom parameters 1.5 and 3.
- Affine Transformation: it is performed using an input matrix (In_m) and an output matrix (Out_m) of the same size 2×3. Input matrix is In_m = [(0, 0);(223, 0);(0, 223)]. For each image, based on this input matrix, five images are generated using output matrix:

Out_m1: [(0, 0); (150, 0); (89, 223)]
Out_m2: [(0, 0); (67, 0); (89, 223)]
Out_m3: [(0, 0); (133, 0); (89, 223)]
Out_m4: [(0, 0); (133, 0); (198, 223)]
Out_m5: [(0, 0); (90, 0); (0, 200)]

Figure 4 shows an example where both combinations have been applied. They are performed in python using the Open Source Computer Vision Library (OpenCV). Two augmented datasets of 37.432 images are generated after applying these two combinations. In the following sections, we call Datastet1 the one obtained by the Flip_Contrast_AffTrans combination and Dataset2 the second obtained by Flip_Zoom_AffTrans.

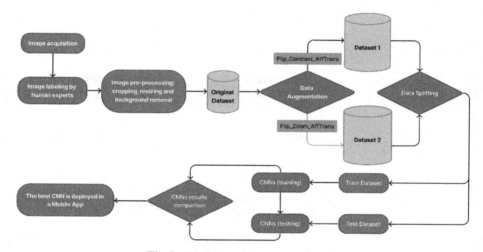

Fig. 2. Workflow of the proposed work

3.3 Convolutional Neural Networks (CNNs)

A CNN is a Deep Learning model built up on essentially three types of layers: Convolutional layers, Pooling layers and Fully-connected or Dense layers. They have been booming since the success of AlexNet in 2012 during the (ILSVRC) competition [15]. In the last five years, in the field of crop disease classification, researchers have proposed several solutions based mainly on CNNs. The latest generation of CNNs has achieved impressive results in image classification area and is considered as the leading method for object classification in computer vision. CNNs differ by their depth (number of layers), number of units in layers, activation function, loss function and others adjustable parameters like dropout rate, learning rat, batch size, number of epochs, etc.

In this paper, seven well-known CNNs namely VGG16, ResNet50, DensNet121, EfficientNetV2B1, MobileNetV2, NASMobileNet, InceptionV3 and a proposed LCNN are applied to the datasets to know how well these models can leverage its.

The LCNN is based on VGG16 and composed of nine convolutional layers each followed by a Rectified Linear Unit (ReLU), three maximum pooling layers each followed by a Dropout. The Flatten layer is used to convert the features obtained from the previous layers into a 1D array. It is followed by three Dense layers, the last of which acts as an output layer with softmax activation. The Fig. 5 shows the implementation details of the proposed LCNN.

All CNNs are implemented using the Tensorflow framework and its popular Keras library. The models are trained on a server with 32 GB of RAM and NVIDIA GPU.

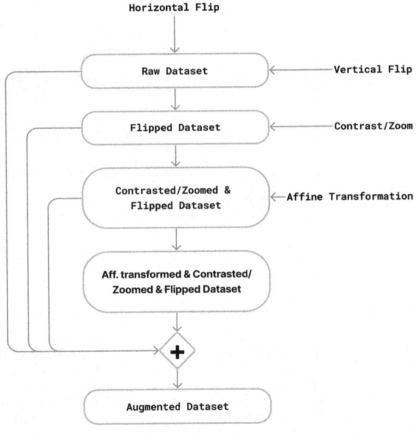

Fig. 3. Data augmentation workflow

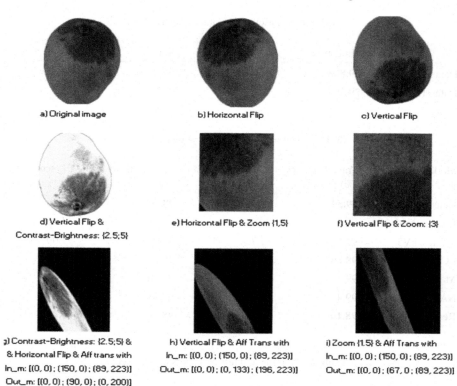

a) Original image

b) Horizontal Flip

c) Vertical Flip

d) Vertical Flip &
Contrast-Brightness: {2.5;5}

e) Horizontal Flip & Zoom {1,5}

f) Vertical Flip & Zoom: {3}

g) Contrast-Brightness: {2.5;5} &
& Horizontal Flip & Aff trans with
In_m: [(0, 0) ; (150, 0) ; (89, 223)]
Out_m: [(0, 0) ; (90, 0) ; (0, 200)]

h) Vertical Flip & Aff Trans with
In_m: [(0, 0) ; (150, 0) ; (89, 223)]
Out_m: [(0, 0) ; (0, 133) ; (196, 223)]

i) Zoom {1.5} & Aff Trans with
In_m: [(0, 0) ; (150, 0) ; (89, 223)]
Out_m: [(0, 0) ; (67, 0 ; (89, 223)]

Fig. 4. Example of application of the two data augmentation techniques combinations on an image

4   Results and Discussions

The initial dataset of 862 images is splitted as following: 80% (690 images) for training and validation data and 20% for testing data (172 images). Augmentation techniques are only applied on the training and validation data. Test data remains equal to 172 images. Table 2 shows the distribution of Dataset1 and Dataset2 for training, validation and test data. Training and testing the eight CNNs on both datasets produced very satisfactory results in terms of accuracy and f1_score, as shown in Tables 3 and 4.

Table 2. Dataset1 and Dataset2 distribution

	Validation	Test	Total	Training
Dataset1	29 808	7 452	172	37 432
Dataset2	29 808	7 452	172	37 432

Table 3. Training and testing results on Dataset1

Model	Train Accuracy (%)	Val Accuracy (%)	Test Accuracy (%)	F1_score (%)
DenseNet121	**99.54**	**99.44**	**98.20**	**98.20**
EfficientNetV2B1	99.54	99.08	93.41	93.42
InceptionV3	99.44	97.76	97.00	97.00
LCNN	98.86	97.11	95.25	95.20
MobileNetV2	99.3	99.06	97.60	97.60
NASMobileNet	99.47	95.21	93.41	93.41
ResNet50	**98.10**	**98.00**	**98.20**	**98.20**

Table 4. Training and testing results on Dataset2

Model	Train Accuracy (%)	Val Accuracy (%)	Test Accuracy (%)	F1_score (%)
DenseNet121	97.29	94.53	92.81	92.81
EfficientNetV2B1	99.46	99.24	88.62	88.54
InceptionV3	**99.34**	**99.12**	**98.20**	**98.20**
LCNN	96.03	93.25	89.35	89.35
MobileNetV2	**99.22**	**97.82**	**98.20**	**98.20**
NASMobileNet	99.43	96.04	94.01	94.01
ResNet50	97.84	98.38	88.62	88.62

Results show that on Dataset1, DenseNet121 and ResNet50 give the best accuracy and F1_score equal each to 98.20%. On Dataset2, InceptionV3 and MobileNetV2 achieve the best accuracy and F1_score of 98.20% each. But overall, CNNs perform better on Dataset1. Figure 6 shows the training results of these CNNs on Dataset1 and Dataset2 (Table 5).

Table 5. Size comparison of CNNs

Model	Train Accuracy (%)
DenseNet121	433
ResNet50	178
InceptionV3	314
MobileNetV2	159
ResNet50	178

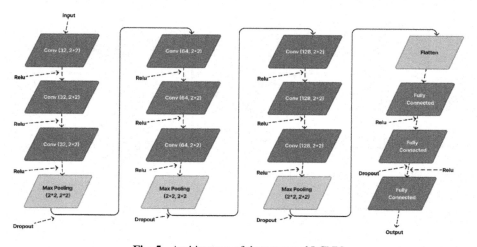

Fig. 5. Architecture of the proposed LCNN

The proposed LCNN did not perform as well as the well-known CNNSs, but achieved very good results on both datasets. The best results were obtained on Dataset1 (accuracy: 95.25% and F1_score: 95.20%). What's more, since it's lighter than the best-performing CNNs, i.e. it's made up of 12 layers, unlike, for example, ResNet50, which is made up of 50 layers, and denseNet121, which is made up of 121 layers. This LCNN is deployed in a mobile applicaton we developped. The main function (see Fig. 7) of the mobile application is to enable mango growers to automatically diagnose a disease without the help of an expert. The mobile application allows users to diagnose a disease on an image captured directly by the phone's camera or saved in the gallery. The application is in french langage and works without internet, so it can be used even in the most remote areas or those without internet coverage.

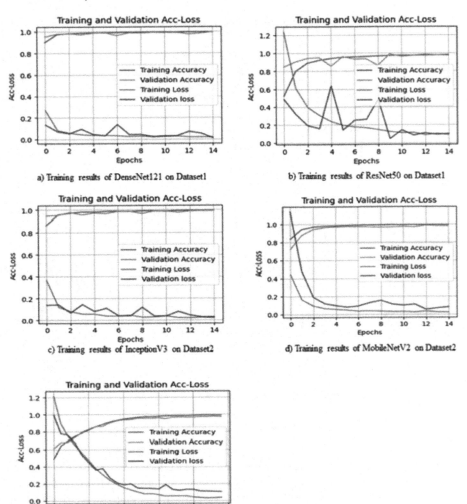

a) Training results of DenseNet121 on Dataset1

b) Training results of ResNet50 on Dataset1

c) Training results of InceptionV3 on Dataset2

d) Training results of MobileNetV2 on Dataset2

e) Training results of the LCNN on Dataset1

Fig. 6. Training results of CNNs on Datset1 and Dataset2

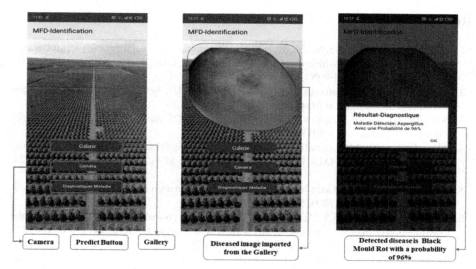

Fig. 7. Mobile application screenshots

5 Conclusion and Future Works

An available and ready-to-use mango fruit diseases dataset made in Africa is presented in this paper. Two combinations of data augmentation techniques are applied to the proposed dataset to obtain two generated datasets named Dataset1 and Dataset2. Eight CNNs, including seven well-known ones and a proposed LCNN, are applied to both datasets to detect and identify the four treated diseases. Results show that on Dataset1, DenseNet121 and ResNet50 give the best accuracy and F1_score both equal to 98.20%, on Dataset2, InceptionV3 and MobileNetV2 achieve the best accuracy and F1_score of 98.20% each. The proposed LCNN also achieved excellent results (accuracy: 95.25% and F1_score: 95.20%) on the Dataset1. It is therefore deployed in an Android offline mobile application to help users detecting mango diseases using captured images.

Our future work will involve extending our dataset by adding mango fruit images affected by others diseases or pests, such as fruit flies. We will improve the mobile application by adding other useful functions for mango growers.

Acknowledgments. Authors would like to thank IRD (Institut de Recherche pour le Développement) SENEGAL for access to their server which was used in this study.

Conflict of Interest. Authors declare that they have no conflict of interest.

Ethical Approval. This article does not contain any studies with animals performed by any of the authors.

Informed Consent. Informed consent was obtained from all individual participants included in the study.

References

1. Faye, D., Diop, I., Mbaye, N., Dione, D.: A combination of data augmentation techniques for mango leaf diseases classification. Glob. J. Comput. Sci. Technol. (2023). https://doi.org/10.34257/GJCSTGVOL23IS1PG1
2. National Agency of Statistics and Demography (ANSD), Senegal. Bulletin mensuel des statistiues économiques et financières de février (2023)
3. National Agency of Statistics and Demography (ANSD), Senegal. Economic and Social situation of Senegal (SES 2017–2018)
4. Ahmed, S., et al.: MangoLeafBD: a comprehensive image dataset to classify diseased and healthy mango leaves. Data Brief **47**, 108941 (2023). https://doi.org/10.1016/j.dib.2023.108941
5. Gulavnai, S., Patil, R.: Deep learning for image based mango leaf disease detection. Int. J. Recent Technol. Eng. **8**(3S3), 54–56 (2019)
6. Singh, U.P., Chouhan, S.S., Jain, S., Jain, S.: Multilayer convolution neural network for the classification of mango leaves infected by anthracnose disease. IEEE Access **7**, 43721–43729 (2019). https://doi.org/10.1109/ACCESS.2019.2907383
7. Pham, T.N., Tran, L.V., Dao, S.V.T.: Early disease classification of mango leaves using feed-forward neural network and hybrid metaheuristic feature selection. IEEE Access **8**, 189960–189973 (2020)
8. Saleem, R., Hussain Shah, J., Sharif, M., Jillani Ansari, G.: Mango leaf disease identification using fully resolution convolutional network. Comput. Mater. Continua **69**(3), 3581–3601 (2021)
9. Mahbub, N.I., Naznin, F., Hasan, M.I., Shifat, S.M.R., Hossain, M.A., Islam, M.Z.: Detect Bangladeshi mango leaf diseases using lightweight convolutional neural network. In: 2023 International Conference on Electrical, Computer and Communication Engineering (ECCE), Chittagong, Bangladesh, pp. 1–6 (2023). https://doi.org/10.1109/ECCE57851.2023.10101648
10. Selvakumar, A., Balasundaram, A.: Automated mango leaf infection classification using weighted and deep features with optimized recurrent neural network concept. Imaging Sci. J. (2023). https://doi.org/10.1080/13682199.2023.2204036
11. Wongsila, S., Chantrasri, P., Sureephong, P.: Machine learning algorithm development for detection of mango infected by anthracnose disease. In: 2021 Joint International Conference on Digital Arts, Media and Technology with ECTI Northern Section Conference on Electrical, Electronics, Computer and Telecommunication Engineering, Cha-am, Thailand, pp. 249–252 (2021). https://doi.org/10.1109/ECTIDAMTNCON51128.2021.9425737
12. Kusrini, K., Suputa, S., Setyanto, A., Agastya, I.M.A., Priantoro, H., Pariyasto, S.: A comparative study of mango fruit pest and disease recognition. TELKOMNIKA (Telecommun/ Compu. Electron. Control) **20**(6), 1264 (2022). https://doi.org/10.12928/telkomnika.v20i6.21783
13. Rahaman, M.N., et al.: A deep learning based smartphone application for detecting mango diseases and pesticide suggestions. Int. J. Comput. Dig. Syst. **13**(1), 1273–1286 (2023). https://doi.org/10.12785/ijcds/1301104
14. Faye, D., Diop, I., Mbaye, N., Diedhiou, M.M.: SenMangoFruitDDS. Mendeley Data, V1 (2023). https://doi.org/10.17632/jvszp9cbpw.1
15. Faye, D., Diop, I.: Survey on crop disease detection and identification based on deep learning. In: Mambo, A.D., Gueye, A., Bassioni, G. (eds.) Innovations and Interdisciplinary Solutions for Underserved Areas: 5th EAI International Conference, InterSol 2022, Abuja, Nigeria, March 23-24, 2022, Proceedings, pp. 210–222. Springer Nature Switzerland, Cham (2022). https://doi.org/10.1007/978-3-031-23116-2_18

Management System for Pregnancy Evolution Tracking

Jonathan Sánchez Luna[1]([✉]) [iD], Arnulfo Alanis[2] [iD], Efrain Patiño[3] [iD],
and Bogart Yail[2] [iD]

[1] Master's Degree in Information Technologies, Department of Systems and Computing,
National Technological of México, Campus Tijuana, Calzada del Tecnológico S/N,
Fraccionamiento Tomas Aquino, C.P. 22414 Tijuana, Baja California, Mexico
m2221006@tectijuana.edu.mx

[2] Systems and Computer Department, National Technological of México, Campus Tijuana,
Calzada del Tecnológico S/N, Fraccionamiento Tomas Aquino, C.P. 22414 Tijuana,
Baja California, Mexico
alanis@tectijuana.edu.mx, bogart@tectiuana.edu.mx

[3] Interships and Social Service Coordination, Ceux Tijuana School of Medicine, Rampa
Yumalinda 4850, Chapultepec Alamar, C.P. 22110 Tijuana, Baja California, Mexico
epatino@correo.xochicalco.edu.mx

Abstract. In the field of obstetric ultrasound, technological advances have taken
leaps and bounds since the beginning of the practice in the late 50's. This discipline
requires academic development and sometimes even certifications, not only for
the correct use of the equipment, devices or artifacts by means of how these
ultrasound scans are performed, but also to be able to provide accurate results by
reading parameters to evaluate possible risk factors during the gestation process
of a patient. It is for this reason, and for the increasingly common integration of
Information Technologies in different branches of the medical sector, that we can
see a lack of implementation of efficient management systems to keep track of
the background and evolution of pregnancy on patients, and the respective fetus
health.

Keywords: Information Technologies · Management System · Gynecology ·
Obstetrics · Pregnancy · Fetus Health

1 Introduction

Pregnancy is one of the most significant events when we refer to human life, since it is
in this period that the conditions and integrity of the next human being to be given birth
are defined. Fortunately, at present there are tools and specialized equipment to carry
out continuous monitoring regarding the evolution of the fetus, during the 3 trimesters
of the gestation period.

Sonography, better known as ultrasound, is the image representation of the rebound
of high-frequency sound waves, which allow visualization of the interior of the human
body, which allows a timely diagnosis of different types of diseases in various vital

T. Guarda et al. (Eds.): ARTIIS 2023, CCIS 1937, pp. 251–264, 2024.
https://doi.org/10.1007/978-3-031-48930-3_19

organs, as well as the study of pregnant women, which allow us to carry out timely monitoring of the development of the fetus, throughout the entire gestation period.

The specialized equipment for performing ultrasounds also plays a very important role, since the integrity of the results obtained from the evaluation of ultrasound images is directly proportional to the quality of those images, which is defined taking into account the technical specifications and characteristics of the equipment in use, as well as the skill and experience of the sonographer who operates it.

Another important aspect is the health of the pregnant woman, as well as the medical background in terms of clinical history, since during the gestation period, there are medical conditions that could put the development of the fetus at risk, even causing its death.

With the correct integration of information technologies resources, and organized techniques, it is possible to enhance the results by means of ultrasound images and patient medical history, having an organized and structured storage of all the data in a management system, in order to optimize diagnosis times, since the software is in charge of collecting information in an organized form, based on parameters already established by the major medical organizations, in terms of Gynecology and Obstetrics.

By adding each evaluation of the pregnant patient and fetus health, and the respective clinical history, we can build the necessary infrastructure to apply Artificial Intelligence processes to obtain medical indicators of care and even predictions, taking into account all the acquired data in terms of sonographic images which then can be processed using deep learning techniques, and concurrent dataset information corresponding to other patients with similar medical background conditions using data mining techniques.

2 Ultrasound History in Gynecology and Obtetrics

In the mid-50's, the idea of using ultrasound in the field of Gynecology was introduced at the hands of Obstetrician Ian Donald during his military service, who in collaboration with engineer Tom Brown, and the incorporation of recently graduated industrial designer, Dugald Cameron, took this idea of production for the elaboration of physical prototypes, at the beginning of the 60's, that would allow the visualization of the fetus in pregnant women, during their early gestation period, mainly applying pelvic ultrasounds using Full Bladder Technique [1].

During the 60's, the first ultrasound equipment was manufactured, which they called "Diasonograph" (see Fig. 1), which was quite large and weighed around 1 ton in its first versions [1].

Soon the development of the new models was in the hands of the engineers who were graduating at that time, from schools in different parts of the world, in parallel with the emergence of new companies dedicated to the commercialization of ultrasound equipment, and whose designs were each ever more ergonomic and versatile. It was in this decade that different studies that could be performed were discovered, as well as parameters and measurements that were available, using existing ultrasound technologies and techniques [2].

It was not until 1975, when the first real-time ultrasound equipment was produced, presented as a handle that could be easily manipulated, but which consisted of an invasive technique, since the exploration route was intravaginal. The advantage that this equipment offered was the good image quality that was obtained, that taken into account the epoch, it represented a significant advance [2].

During the following decades, in addition to progress in terms of ergonomics and technical capabilities of ultrasound equipment, multiple contributions were made to the development of techniques and applications that are currently used, which at the time were presented as seminal papers, which ranged from fetal biometry, fetal anomalies, fetal chromosome abnormalities, invasive procedures, ultrasound-guided therapeutic procedures, doppler ultrasound, fetal activity, gynecological scanning, and reproductive medicine [2].

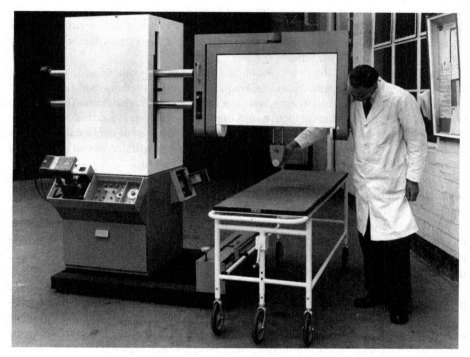

Fig. 1. The first Diasonograph (1960) [1].

Thanks to the technological advances that occur every day, the technical quality of the researchers, the effort of the experts in the field of gynecology and obstetrics, and the interdisciplinary collaboration with information technologies, we currently have specialized equipment capable of acquiring 2D ultrasound images in real time, and through advanced image processing techniques, projecting a 3D vision of the ROI (Region Of Interest), although it is important to consider that this type of image requires greater computational power, which tends to sacrifice the speed of real-time image acquisition. As of today, researchers are still working on techniques and products to achieve 3D imaging in real time, or as close as possible [3].

3 Importance of Ultrasounds in Gynecology and Obstetrics

Within the medical sector, the specialties of Gynecology and Obstetrics play a very important role in the existence of the human being, since it is through these disciplines that various studies are carried out regarding the diagnosis of diseases, reproductive health and adverse conditions, as well as the monitoring and evaluation of pregnancy, through the use of ultrasound equipment, essential technology to the point of not being able to conceive the practice of both disciplines without it [4].

The practice of Ultrasounds, thanks to the ability to provide the specialist with sonographic images using high-frequency sound waves, has become the preferred method for the study and evaluation of fetal development in pregnant women, throughout the gestation period. [5]. This period comprises 3 trimesters, between which, periodic reviews must be carried out to assess different parameters and detect risk factors that may endanger the integrity of the fetus.

Since the creation of the first ultrasound equipment for visualizing fetuses inside a woman's uterus, new methods and techniques have been implemented that offer us increasingly better ultrasound images, and even visual representations in real time, for the study and evaluation of different focus points that are of great importance to determine the state in which the product is, and that allows the early detection of abnormal conditions for monitoring and timely treatment, even having the opportunity to correct some of them thanks to recent advances in the area of fetal surgery [6].

Unlike the first ultrasound equipment used in gynecological/obstetric examinations, where only flat black and white images were obtained [1], and with the constant development by engineers who have been involved in the progress of this technology, new methods and techniques have been emerging in the use of sound waves, which improve the visual extraction capacity, from the static to the dynamic, and which in turn have allowed their application for the study and examination of different points of reference in the fetus, for the identification and evaluation of its correct development [4].

Among the main aspects that define the importance of ultrasound practice for the evaluation of the development of the fetus in pregnant women, are anoxia, prematurity and congenital defects, since they correspond to the major causes of perinatal and infant mortality, as well as such as growth retardation during the end of pregnancy, this being the reason why the care protocol during pregnancy includes performing at least 3 ultrasound explorations, one for each trimester of pregnancy, in addition to establishing that all fetuses should be explored as if it were high risk [7].

4 Pregnancy Main Diagnosis Parameters For Fetuses Via Ultrasound Practice, As Well As For The Patient Via Medical History

As previously mentioned, the protocol establishes the application of at least 3 ultrasounds during the entire gestation period, which corresponds to one exploration in each of the trimesters. The periods for performing these ultrasounds are established below [7]:

- First Quarter Exploration: Week 11 – 13.6 (Preferably Week 12)

- Second Quarter Exploration: Week 20 – 22 (Preferably Week 21)
- Third Quarter Exploration: Week 37 + 1 for low risk pregnancies and Week 28 + 1, 32 + 1 and 37 + 1 serially for Growth Retardation high risk cases

Each of those explorations require the diagnosis and interpretation of parameters that indicate the health of the patient, as well as the fetus health [7, 8].

4.1 First Quarter Exploration Parameters

Fetus parameters that can be evaluated, to obtain the first quarter ultrasound basic image set (see Fig. 2):

- Fetal Gestational Age (GA)
- Trisomy 21 (Down Syndrome)
- Transversus of the skull with the ossified fetal calotte and identification of the midline, choroid plexus and measurement of the Biparietal Diameter (BPD)
- Mid-sagittal including the fetus in neutral position with the measurement of the Crown Rump Length (CRL)
- Measurement of Nuchal Translucency (NT) in a mid-sagittal section that includes the head and upper part of the fetal thorax, following the guidelines of the Fetal Medicine Foundation
- Transverse of the belly at the level of the cord insertion
- Front-tangential of the face with the correct identification of the orbits
- Sections showing the long bones of the upper and lower extremities, feet and hands
- Determination of the ductus venosus flow velocity waveform, calculation of the pulsatility index and end-diastolic velocity
- Determination of the average pulsatility index of the uterine arteries
- If the fetal situation, the gestational age and the scanning allow it, images or clips will be captured that allow the evaluation of other anatomical structures: kidneys, diaphragms, heart
- Risk of aneuploidies (chromosomal abnormalities)
- Alteration of the nasal bone of the fetus

Patient parameters that can be evaluated:

- Background of preeclampsia
- Background of diabetes
- Background of chronic hypertension
- Preterm labor symptoms or backgrounds
- Background of chronic kidney disease
- Cervix length restriction
- Background of autoimmune disorders
- Background of multiple gestation

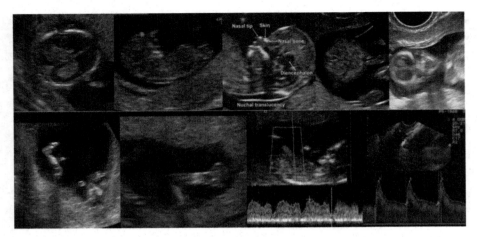

Fig. 2. Example of First Quarter Ultrasound Image set [7].

4.2   Second Quarter Exploration Parameters (Morphologic Evaluation)

The second quarter ultrasound basic image set is divided into 2 important parts, and corresponds to the most comprehensive sonographic diagnosis session (see Fig. 3).

Fetus parameters corresponding to Fetal Biometrics:

- Biparietal Diameter (BPD)
- Head Circumference (HC)
- Abdominal Circumference (AC)
- Femur Length (FL)

Fetus parameters corresponding to Fetal Anatomy:

- Head transthalamic view, which includes frontal horns of lateral ventricles, thalamus, and hippocampal gyrus
- Head transventricular view, which includes frontal horns, the cavum of the septum pellucidum and the posterior horns of the ventricle with the choroid plexuses inside
- Head transcerebellar view, which includes cavum of the septum pellucidum, the anterior horns of the VL, the thalami, the cerebellum and the cisterna magna with a correct visualization of the occipital bone
- Axial including the fetal thorax with identification of a single rib, lungs, and heart
- Heart 4-chamber plane with open and closed atrioventricular valves
- Heart 5-chamber plane
- Heart plane of 3 vessels-trachea
- Heart ventricular filling with color Doppler
- Heart aortic outlet with color Doppler
- Transverse abdominis showing a single rib and including stomach and portal process
- Transverse at the renal level, evaluation of the renal pelvis
- Transverse at the bladder level with color Doppler application to identify the umbilical arteries
- Plane including the fetal insertion of the umbilical cord

- Sagittal in which the lung parenchyma, diaphragm and right kidney are identified
- Sagittal in which the lung parenchyma, diaphragm, stomach and left kidney are identified
- Mid-sagittal showing the lumbosacral, thoracic, and cervical spine, surrounded by amniotic fluid
- Coronal showing the vertebral processes of the lumbosacral, thoracic, and cervical spine
- Transverse face plane at orbital level
- Front-tangential identifying nose, upper and lower lip and chin
- Median sagittal (Fetal profile assessment)
- Planes that allow the identification of the long bones of the 4 extremities, the 5 fingers of both hands and the orientation of the feet
- Position of the placenta
- Amount of amniotic fluid

Patient parameters that can be evaluated:

- Risk of preeclampsia
- Risk of preterm labor

Fig. 3. Example of Second Quarter Ultrasound Image set (Morphologic) [7].

4.3 Third Quarter Exploration Parameters

Following a strict quality criterion, in this particular quarter, we acquire the corresponding imageset to confirm the correct evolution of the following parameters:

- Biparietal Diameter (BPD)

- Head Circumference (HC)
- Abdominal Circumference (AC)
- Femur Length (FL)
- Estimated Fetal Weight (starting on week 24), using Hadlock curves [11]
- Percentile according to Gestational Age (GA) and fetal sex

4.4 High Risk Pregnancy Parameters

In those cases, in which there are signs of a risky pregnancy during the first two quarters, it is necessary to perform additional control ultrasounds to observe the correct development of the pregnancy, specifically fetal growth. On the next 2 tables, we can observe the risk factors that justify these additional control ultrasounds, divided in mayor risk factors and minor risk factors, respectively, indicating the MCA/UA-PI (Middle Cerebral/Umbilical Artery Pilsatility Index) ratios [7, 9] (Tables 1 and 2).

Table 1. Mayor risk factors (One or more risk factors).

Risk factor	Odds Ratio
Maternal age > 40 years	3.2
Smoker > 10 cigars/day	2.2
Daily intense physical exercise	3.3
Toxic consumption during pregnancy	3.3
Antecedent of death	6.4
Previous preeclampsia < 34 weeks	5
Pathological uterine veins in first quarter	5
Risk of preeclampsia (> 1/75)	4
Chronic hypertension	2.5
Pregestational diabetes	6
Nephropathy	5.3
Autoimmune disease	6.2
Refractive intestine in second quarter	2.1
Metrorrhagia In A Similar Quantity Superior To A Rule	2.6
Multiple gestation	4
Body mass index > 35	Difficult to control due to uterine height
Myomatous uterus	Difficult to control due to uterine height

Table 2. Minor risk factors (Three or more risk factors).

Risk factor	Odds Ratio
Maternal age > 35 years	1.4
Assisted reproductive technique	1.6
Nulliparity	1.9
Body mass index < 20	1.2
Body mass index 25–35	1.2
Smoker (1 to 10 cigars daily)	1.5
Preeclampsia background > 34 weeks	1.8
Birth interval < 6 months	1.3

4.5 Main Risk Factors During All the Gestational Period

The Main risk factors, that are described by all mayor health organizations as well as the International Society of Ultrasound in Obstetrics and Gynecology, including but not limited to those that can be identified by signs and symptoms that are considered obstetric emergency, are:

- Arterial Hypertension
- Loss of Consciousness
- Obstetric Seizures
- Gestational Diabetes
- Preeclampsia
- Obstetric Hemorrhage
- Background of Preterm Labor
- Background of chronic kidney disease
- Cervix length restriction
- Background of autoimmune disorders
- Specific Sexually Transmitted Diseases

5   Current Situation for OB/GYN Practices

Currently in the health sector, and more specifically in the field of gynecology and obstetrics, the demand for ultrasound services for pregnant women is abundant, since according to data from the National Institute of Statistics and Geography (INEGI), in 2021, 1,912,178 pregnancies were registered among all age groups, only in Mexico [12]. This offers us a perspective regarding the need for continuous improvement, in terms of the hardware and software that existing ultrasound equipment have, for a better extraction of images, since the quality and sharpness of those ultrasounds tend to be a problem when evaluating possible risk factors in the fetus, whether it's genetically, morphologic or structurally.

Although it is true, science is advancing by leaps and bounds and image processing devices are increasingly capable, the evaluation of ultrasound scans, the reading of parameters, the interpretation of the values corresponding to the risk factors and the analysis of the fetal heart rate, are tasks that a specialist, in this case a sonographer, must perform manually, and tend to be tasks that consume considerable time, depending on several factors, such as the current gestation period, fetal activity, the image quality produced by the equipment in use, visual interference, among others [1].

Specifically, the results obtained in an ultrasound depend entirely on the correct interpretation of the sonographer, who, as in all disciplines where the human intervenes, there is the possibility of error or omission [7], further complicating the correct diagnosis if we add the parameters and values of the Mother's clinical history, which by the way, does not have a standardized structure or organization of data that should be used by the different clinics in the country, much less throughout the entire world, despite the fact that there are efforts by the main world health organizations, which encourage the use of protocols and checklists, as a standardized guideline in all disciplines of the health sector [13].

Another critical problem is that, some medical institutions or clinics surrogate the ultrasound explorations, hence making those image sets unavailable to retrieve a complete record on each exploration in real time. Most of these surrogate services don't offer the acquisition of the image sets in form of image files, instead, they offer the preview of the whole image set via an API (Application Programing Interface) that has to be queried every time you need a specific set of images or image by itself, making it extremely difficult to maintain a complete database to which we can apply Artificial Intelligence techniques.

6 Proposal

Taking into account that institutions and medical offices seek to improve their patient care processes, using standardized guidelines promoted by different health organizations, and the various studies that show that the correct use of protocols and checklists reduces the mortality rate [14], it is necessary to take these practices to a more advanced level with the application of Information Technologies, for the acquisition, storage, classification, processing and data analysis, to optimize decision-making, and more assertive diagnosis using Artificial Intelligence techniques.

The objective of this paper is to explore the benefits that can be obtained with the use of a standardized protocol to capture, store and share relevant consutation, diagnosis results, as well as personal information using a single data structure, building a big data ecosystem along all health sector clinics, that allow computer experts to build and deploy frameworks capable of applying Artificial Intelligence techniques along the majority of pregnancy cases in all the health service providers around a region or even the entire country, with the goal of being able to obtain optimized diagnosis with the help of Deep Learning techniques on ultrasounds Image Sets, and Data Mining techniques on patients medical history records, and enhancing the current guidelines described in the Oficial Mexican Standard NOM-024-SSA3-2012, which indicates as essential, the registration, exchange and consolidation of information between all health service providers that belongs to the National Health System, whether if they are private, social or public [15].

The methodology for this proposal, is difficult by nature because of the need of constant requests of practices and technical considerations integration into official norms, as well as laws that apply to all the National Health System (Including public, social or private health service providers) [10]:

– Propose the integration of this standardized protocol into the corresponding Mexican Official Standard, for the acquisition of database records of patients
– Propose the integration of universal API-based ultrasounds image sets manager
– Execute both proposals long enough to obtain the necessary information and build a Big Data Ecosystem, in database records as well as image sets
– Build a documented solution and request approval of the Secretary of Health to encourage developers to design solutions using the generated big data ecosystem
– Promote the results that can be obtained using AI solutions within the generated big data ecosystem (Data and Image Sets)

There are 2 main data inputs in terms of Information Technologies applied to Obstetrics and Gynecology, specifically pregnancy and fetus development, that corresponds to a minimal of 3 records along the 3 quarters of a regular gestation period, or additional records in the case of high-risk pregnancies (control consultation):

• Fetus ultrasound explorations image sets
• Pregnant patient's medical history and parameters results on each consultation record set

6.1 Fetus Ultrasounds Image Set Structure

In the first instance, it is necessary to apply protocols and guidelines so that the images resulting from ultrasounds performed on pregnant women throughout their gestation period are available on-demand, so that an organized image set can be obtained. These image sets should be stored as any high-quality image format file (PNG, JPEG, TIFF, etc.) and organized as follows:

• One parent folder for each patient, named as the ID or Membership Number followed by the patient's name
• A child folder for each pregnancy instance, named as the ID of pregnancy case used on the clinical history
• A grandson folder for each ultrasound exploration of each pregnancy instance, named as the ID of exploration session used on the clinical history, followed by the week number of that particular pregnancy case
• A high-quality format image file for each parameter described in the section "Pregnancy Main Diagnosis Parameters For Fetuses Via Ultrasound Practice, As Well As For The Patient Via Medical History" of this article, named by the parameter codename or abbreviation.

6.2 Pregnant Patient's Medical History and Parameters Result on Each Consultation Record Set

The use of checklists and standardized protocols is fundamental nowadays to improve the patients care process [14], and encourage medical institutions to acquire historical and immediate information about the health status of a patient, but there is still a lack in terms of data processing and analysis. Having the information on physical papers is no longer viable in the era of Information Technologies, but keeping the information on word documents in a form of a report indicating the results of every parameter diagnosed on an ultrasound session, is not that useful neither, in terms of applying Data Mining processes for example.

The proposed data structure, to obtain the ability of data processing, includes the use of software applications that use the same fields, formats and constraints, using a NO-SQL database, due to the variety of parameters that has to be reviewed on every ultrasound exploration, whether if it's a regular pregnancy case or a high-risk pregnancy case, and needs to be stored as follows:

- A main record set containing all personal data of the patient, with unique patient ID, including but not limited to:

  - Gender
  - Age
  - Chronical medical conditions
  - Known deceases
  - Special medications or treatments
  - Number of pregnancies (including whether they were successful or not)
  - Ethnic group
  - Relatives medical background
  - Blood type
  - As well as any other relevant data that has to be taking in mind on a pregnancy case

- A secondary record for each pregnancy case of the patient, with unique pregnancy ID, including but not limited to:

  - Date of last menstruation
  - Initial symptoms
  - Biometrics test results
  - Blood pressure
  - And relevant parameters that the gynecologist considers relevant

- Subsequent child records of a particular ultrasound exploration inside each pregnancy record of the patient, linked through the pregnancy ID, that contains all the individual parameters diagnosed on that particular exploration. Especially main risk factors during all the pregnancy, described in Subsect. 4.5 of this document.

6.3   Scopes on the Use of the Proposed Image and Data Structure

Having a large set of images following the structure proposed in the previous subsections, we can obtain a general sampling of the whole image database of ultrasounds performed at each medical institution, as well as a whole record database of the clinical history of patients who have gone through the gestation cycle. After all data has been acquired, Deep Learning techniques can be used to detect risk factors, which can be detected throughout the gestational period, mainly in the first 2 trimesters of fetal development in a pregnancy, among which are: the detection of limbs, nuchal translucency (NT: Nuchal Translucency), crown-rump length (Crown-Rump length), abdominal circumference (AC: Abdominal Cicumference), head circumference (HC; Head Circumference), heart rate, among others [5].

The techniques in terms of Information Technology that are intended to be used for the correct development of the project include the application of Deep Learning methodologies for the selection, segmentation, analysis, classification and evaluation of image samples, as well as Data Mining techniques. For the identification of criteria for and even the prediction of medical care conditions, taking as input the data of the patient's medical history.

It is for this reason, and for the increasingly common integration of Information Technologies in different branches of the medical sector, that in recent years interdisciplinary studies and projects have been carried out for the integration of Artificial Intelligence in Obstetric activities, in order to develop tools and applications that support the specialist sonographer, for the selection, analysis and evaluation of ultrasound images by means of pattern recognition using Deep Learning techniques [5].

The long-term objective is to provide the necessary bases for the application of Artificial Intelligence, in the detection of risk factors, in a scalable way, during the entire gestation period in pregnancy, and to carry out a complementary preliminary evaluation, taking into account the patient's medical history, in order to detect risk factors that may occur in the future and even predict possible future medical conditions, and thus be able to provide better monitoring of fetal development, and lower mortality ratio.

7 Conclusions

Despite all the protocols exposed within the health sector, specifically gynecology and obstetrics, to record medical conditions, there is a great need for a comprehensive management system that contains all parameters individually, stored in a structured way in a database that is available on-demand, and that also contains in a linked way, the image set of the ultrasounds performed during the patient's gestational period, whether current or historical.

The integration of techniques and methods within the technological field of Artificial Intelligence will represent significant support within this specific discipline on medical institutions, as it will enhance the study of fetal development in a precise and efficient manner, automatically. This, in turn, will reduce study and exploration times, since with a correct ultrasound session where different angles of the fetus and its contours are taken, the intelligent system will collect the necessary information in terms of measurements, movements, frequencies and pattern detection, in order to carry out an exhaustive processing of parameters, which will be compared with the knowledge base, the clinical history of patients and logical maps within the intelligent system, in order to determine anomalies or discrepancies, comparing the readings obtained with the established ranges within the normal and abnormal spectra.

References

1. Macdonald, A.S.: From first concepts to Diasonograph: the role of product design in the first medical obstetric ultrasound machines in 1960s Glasgow. Ultrasound **28**(3), 187 (2020)
2. Campbell, S.: OBGYN.net Conference CoverageFIGO 2000 International Federation of Gynecology & Obstetrics. https://www.contemporaryobgyn.net/view/history-ultrasound-obstetrics-and-gynecology (2006)
3. Huang, Q., Zeng, Z.: A review on real-time 3D ultrasound imaging technology. BioMed Res. Int. **2017**, 1–20 (2017). https://doi.org/10.1155/2017/6027029
4. Abramowicz, J.S.: Obstetric ultrasound: where are we and where are we going? Ultrasonography **40**(1), 57–74 (2021). https://doi.org/10.14366/usg.20088
5. Whitworth, M., Bricker, L., Mullan, C.: Ultrasound for fetal assessment in early pregnancy. Cochrane Database Syste. Rev. **2015**(7), CD007058 (2015)
6. Leiva, B.J., Muñoz, H., Rencoret, G., Pons, A.: Cirugía Fetal. Rev. Med. Clin. Condes **25**(6), 972–978 (2014)
7. Bennasar, M., Borobio, V., Puerto, B.: Protocolo: Screening Ecográfico. Last updated 18 Oct 2016
8. Secretaría de Salud: Instituto Nacional de Perinatología, Normas y Procedimientos de Obstetricia (2021). https://inper.mx/descargas-2019/pdf/ManualObstetriciaCAP02_01.pdf
9. International Society of Ultrasound in Obstetrics and Gynecology: ISUOG practice guidelines: diagnosis and management of small-for-gestational-age fetus and fetal growth restriction. Ultrasound Obstet. Gynecol. **56**, 298–312 (2020). https://doi.org/10.1002/uog.22134
10. CCNN (Comité Consultivo Nacional de Normalización), Norma Oficial Mexicana NOM-007-SSA2–2016: Para la atención de la mujer durante el embarazo, parto y puerperio, y de la persona recién nacida
11. Hadlock, F.P., et al.: Sonographic estimation of fetal weight. The value of femur length in addition to head and abdomen measurements. Radiology **150**(2), 535–540 (1984)
12. INEGI homepage, Natalidad y Fecundidad, Nacimientos (2021). https://www.inegi.org.mx/temas/natalidad/#Informacion_general
13. Gawande, A.: The checklist manifesto: how to get things right. Metropolitan Books (2009)
14. Mussalli, G.M.: Does standardization of care through clinical guidelines improve outcomes and reduce medical liability? Obstet. Gynecol. **117**(3), 732–733 (2011)
15. CCNN (Comité Consultivo Nacional de Normalización), Norma Oficial Mexicana NOM-024-SSA3-2012: Sistemas de información de registro electrónico para la salud. Intercambio de información en salud

Intelligent Emotion Prediction System for Help in Telemedicine Therapies of Children with ASD

Denisse Herrera[1]([✉]) [ID], Arnulfo Alanis[2] [ID], Rosario Baltazar[3] [ID],
and Daniel Velazquez[4] [ID]

[1] Information Technology, Systems and Computing Department, Tecnologico Nacional de
México-Campus Tijuana, Tijuana, B.C., Mexico
m22210043@tecttijuana.edu.mx
[2] Systems and Computing Department, Tecnológico Nacional de México-Campus Tijuana,
Tijuana, B.C., Mexico
alanis@tectijuana.edu.mx
[3] Division of Postgraduate Studies Research, Tecnológico Nacional de México-Campus Leon,
Leon, Gto., Mexico
rosario.baltazar@leon.tecnm.mx
[4] Pro Autismo, Tijuana, B.C., Mexico

Abstract. This paper proposes the creation of an intelligent system capable of differentiating between basic emotions as a result of identifying micro expressions in children with Autism Spectrum Disorder (ASD). This system will be developed with the aim of serving as a tool for therapists and caregivers of children with ASD; so that, when the child expresses an emotion that can't be readily identified, the system can recognize it and allow the therapist or caregiver to give the child the necessary tools to help them understand their emotional state. This way they can process the emotion, regulate it, and if necessary, express it in a better way. All with the goal of improving the emotional intelligence of the child. The model was trained with Google's Teachable Machine software using a dataset that contains images of micro-expressions referencing six basic emotions provided by the Chinese Academy of Sciences Micro-expression (CASME) Databases.

Keywords: Facial recognition · ASD · Emotional Intelligence · Micro-expressions · Telemedicine · Teachable Machine

1 Introduction

Teletherapy has been of great help in these recent unpredictable times. During the COVID-19 pandemic, the use of tele-assessment for ASD diagnostic evaluations went from 6% pre-pandemic to 78% in late 2021 [1] Thanks to this many caregivers where allowed to participate in their children's therapy sessions un-like before in traditional in-person therapy. When survey about these changes, most enjoyed taking an active role in these assessments, along with the fact that it improved access for some families who previously faced multiple barriers to participating in in-person assessments——like lack of

T. Guarda et al. (Eds.): ARTIIS 2023, CCIS 1937, pp. 265–278, 2024.
https://doi.org/10.1007/978-3-031-48930-3_20

transportation, living in rural areas, or having difficulties taking time off work. Not only did caretakers benefited from these changes, providers reported that assessing children in their home setting provided valuable clinical information, improved child comfort, and in terms of logistics, increased their flexibility with scheduling and increased efficiency due to children not having to adjust to new environments [2]. Due to all of these factors, teletherapy has remained as a viable resource even after a return to normalcy.

However, despite these benefits for therapists and caregivers, children with Autism Spectrum Disorder (ASD)—who have differences in social interaction, communication, and sensory perception—have these differences made more stark when communicating through video calls [3]. The inability to analyse non-verbal cues can result in a lower ability of transferring information between patient and therapist due to the fact that it creates a certain level of uncertainty and discomfort for the child [4] They can also experience more stress, often have less capacity to interpret verbal and non-verbal cues, and feel less empowered to participate [5]. Communicating through a screen also limits the ability to recognize facial emotions, which is crucial for social competence [6], and a skill that's already limited in children with ASD. As these children become adolescents and young adults, they may have some struggles in forming and maintaining friendships, communicating with people of the same age and adults, or comprehending what behaviors are expected of them at school or work [7]. These discrepancies in communication and interpersonal relationships—which are the main factors that contribute to an ASD diagnosis—lead to low levels of emotional intelligence in these individuals [8]. And it is this incapacity of emotional intelligence which appears to be a causal factor in the development of "abnormal"—as perceived by others—social behaviors [9].

One way to minimize these social limitations is to support these children from an early age with therapies focused on emotional intelligence. To help with these aspects, we suggest the creation of an intelligent system that is capable of recognizing emotions which could then be implemented during teletherapy sessions. It would have the main goal of telling both therapist and patient what emotion is currently being expressed, thus allowing the therapist to coach the patient by talking to them about their current emotional state. In so, giving them tools to better manage and understand their emotions; therefore, enhancing their emotional intelligence.

The rest of the paper is organized as follows: Sect. 2 provides details on the related works found—those that focus on recognizing emotions in children with ASD—-Sect. 3 describes the proposed system created, the database and the platform that was used to create the model, followed by a discussion of the results of three different models created in Sect. 4. A brief conclusion and analysis of future works is talked about in Sect. 5.

2 Related Works

The few works currently available that focus on recognizing expressions in children with ASD were created using databases that contain macro expressions—which have higher intensity and longer duration compared to micro-expressions [10]. Such as CaptureMyEmotion [11] an application designed for children with ASD that allows them to take a photo of an object that elicits an emotion in them and a photo of their face is captured at the same time. Thus accurately showing a representation of the facial expression that the child is displaying while viewing the object. Their model then measures that facial expression and compares it with their training data giving as a result the emotion that comes closest in similarity measurements. Their main goal is that the caregiver can see these pictures and use them as a way to talk to the child about emotions and collect insight into what makes them respond that way. While similar in nature to our proposal, there are several studies that show facial expressions in children with ASD are "notably distinct from those in typically developing children" [12]. Along with the fact that the datasets used to train the models in these applications are usually obtained from neurotypical people.

2.1 Facial Recognition in ASD Individuals

The mechanisms that produce facial expressions in autism revolve around understanding the overall dynamics of the entire face, localized movements in specific facial regions, along with the dynamic relationships between movements in different areas of the face [12]. These individuals also display more neutral expressions which can be seen as ambiguous compared to their neurotypical counterparts [13]. Moreover, there have been a large number of studies that established that facial expressions of children with ASD are often perceived as "atypical, awkward or less engaging" by other neurotypical observers [13, 14].

2.2 Micro-expressions

Keeping this in mind, we decided to utilize micro-expressions to train this model given that they are involuntary and made unconsciously. Neuropsychological research has found that voluntary(macro) and involuntary(micro) expressions are controlled by two different pathways in the brain [15]. Micro-expressions may be produced due to willingly trying to inhibit an emotion, which would then cause a macro-expresion [15]. It is in this inhibition that these micro-expressions appear, a battle between involuntarily wanting to react to a stimuli but also not wanting to show it. They are brief, local and subtle, with a very short duration of less than 500 ms. Due to their involuntary nature, these expressions can be useful in revealing one's true feelings and intentions [16]. There is a lack of micro-expression data, which poses a challenge to micro-expression recognition. In order to train deep learning models, there is a need for a good amount of training data to help produce a better working model. This lack of data hinders applications of these models in fields where limited data is available, as it is in this case. Current commonly used micro-expression databases include: Chinese Academy of Sciences Micro-expression (CASME) Databases [17], CASME II [18], CAS(ME)2 [19], CAS(ME)3 [20], Spontaneous Micro-expression Database (SMIC) [21], Spon-taneous Micro-Facial Movement Dataset (SAMM) [22] and Micro-and-Macro Expression Warehouse (MMEW) [23]. There is a limited number of samples in most of these databases, which limits the development of deep learning in micro-expression analysis. The newest one that happened to contain the most amount of data—1,109 manually tagged micro-expressions—was CAS(ME)3 [20], and therefore was the dataset that was used to train the model.

3 Proposed System

To achieve the development of this predictive model, it was necessary to obtain access to a dataset of micro-expressions vast enough to create training and test data. Once the data was cleaned and all the images were collected they were classified by one of six emotions. These sets were separated as classes and passed through Google's Teachable Machine [24] platform, which was used to train and create several predictive models—Sect. 4 of this paper will focus on three of the models generated. The advantage of using the Teachable Machine platform is that it has a low barrier to entry, user-friendly interface and gives us the ability to export the model to TensorFlow format in case we need more specificity to train the model. Its limitations are that the only factors that we're able to modify are the number epochs, the size of the batch and the learning rate. The model would be considered fully usable once it's capable of correctly differentiating between the six emotions it's trained with.

3.1 CAS(ME)3

The database with which we worked was CAS(ME)3 [20]. Belonging to the Chinese Academy of Sciences Micro-expression, it offers about 80 h of video with more than 8,000,000 frames, including 1,109 manually tagged micro-expressions and 3,490 macro-expressions. It is composed of 3 parts—Part A, Part B and Part C—with a male/female ratio of 112/135 and an average age of 22.74 years. Part A contains a relatively large number of labeled images of micro and macro expressions. Part B comprises of unlabeled emotions due to serious frame drop during the recording process which impeded manual micro-expression labeling. Part C contains videos recorded during a mock trial, to test the claim that people are more likely to produce more expressions in social situations than in solitary ones. However these videos were focused on identifying expressions that signified the participant was lying, which did not pertain to our investigation. For this research we worked with Part A, since this is the one that contained the micro-expressions already labeled with the emotion they express. This part contains 100 participants, and each of them was asked to watch 13 emotional stimuli and keep their faces expressionless. A total of 1,300 video clips, 943 micro-expressions and 3,143 macro-expressions were recorded, which were tagged by professional coders. Each clip belongs to a basic type of emotion, be it disgust, fear, sadness, anger, or happiness. The length of the videos ranges from 34 to 144 s. To obtain these clips each participant entered a laboratory set up and was asked to sit in front of a monitor where they would be presented with videos of emotional stimulation. She was then instructed to be aware of when an expression was about to express itself while watching the videos, as they should try to suppress it immediately and keep a neutral face. He was also asked to keep his body and head still while watching the videos.

Each tagged micro-expression is equivalent to 15 to 45 frames of images, which last from 0.5 to 1.5 s considering that the capture of these was in 30 frames per second.

3.2 Teachable Machine

Google's Teachable Machine (teachablemachine.withgoogle.com) is a web-based program to help you train and create custom machine learning classification models without much technical knowledge [24]. Using machine learning allows systems to learn by analyzing data without being explicitly programmed. This platform doesn't require coding and works by using a webcam, images, or sound. By using transfer learning, it finds patterns in images or sound samples and rapidly creates an intuitive classification model. With transfer learning, users can train a model using their own data over a previously trained base model that was trained from a large dataset in a specific domain. It is possible to download that trained model locally, using Tensorflow.js. This allows for a greater sense of privacy and ownership than systems that send and process data to a remote machine, and a more flexible and less permanent structure to play and experiment with machine learning, without needing to worry about storing and saving large files, datasets, or models to the cloud. An example of the platform's interface is shown in Fig. 1.

3.3 Model Training

The data analysis was started with only two emotions to see what kind of results Teachable Machine gave. This platform allows you to divide your data in classes, which were used to differentiate emotions. Within each class you can either upload your files or use a webcam to capture images in real time. In this first instance approximately 200 representative images of the emotion of disgust and happiness each were uploaded. Initially, the default options offered by the platform were left for the training: 50 epochs, a batch size of 32, and a learning range of 0.001. To test the model, images were used that showed a subject performing a micro-expression at its peak, according to the labeling provided by the coders. These images were of subjects the model had not seen during its training to prevent bias. As a result, the model presented high favoritism to the emotion of disgust. Every image that was fed to the model was classified as such with an alleged

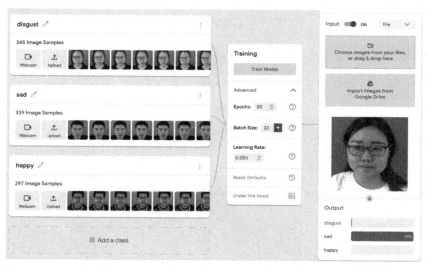

Fig. 1. Screenshot of Google's Teachable Machine interface after training a model with 3 classes: disgust, happy and sad.

99% to 100% accuracy. When reviewing the graphs provided by the "Under the hood" option of the platform–which contains a graph of the accuracy and loss per epoch along with an accuracy per class and a confusion matrix—it showed a level of certainty of 0.999 starting on the sixth epoch. Initially it was hypothesized that this favoritism was due to the small quantity of images provided and the high degree of epochs chosen to train with. In subsequent analyses, these factors were modified to find the point that gave greater accuracy without risking overtraining.

4 Results and Discussion

To check if increasing the number of training images improved the accuracy of the model, it was decided to use all available images after cleaning up the dataset. The number of epochs, batch number and learning rate was left the same and the model was retrained now testing six emotions. The model continued to overestimate its low level of loss (0.00078), reaching a peak accuracy (0.99) after the fourth or fifth epoch. Looking at the confusion matrix, it assessed that all the images shown to the model during the test period (which is determined by the platform to be 15% of the images used) were predicted correctly. However, when we tested new images the predictions were no better than chance, either confidently guessing incorrectly or guessing equally between all emotions–i.e. −99% the wrong emotion or roughly guessing 15% of each emotion. In order to ascertain what was the cause of this overconfidence, it was decided to first test two emotions until a better outcome was reached. Since the model had the most difficulty distinguishing between sadness and disgust, these were the first emotions tested.

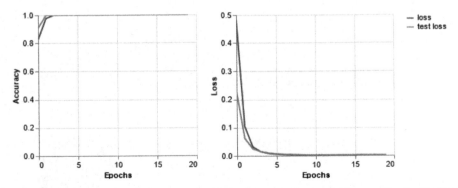

Fig. 2. Graph showing level of accuracy and loss of two emotion model.Orange line for the level of the model and blue line for the level when tested (Color figure online)

4.1 Sadness vs Disgust

This model was trained using 345 images of micro-expression showing disgust and 339 images displaying sadness. It had a batch size of 16, a learning rate of 0.001 and it

CLASS	ACCURACY	# SAMPLES
Sad	0.99	290
Disgust	1.00	290

Confusion Matrix

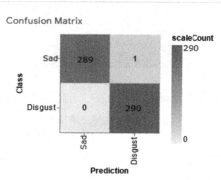

Fig. 3. Confusion matrix generated for this model, showing that only one image was incorrectly identified for the emotion of sadness

trained for 20 epochs. These parameters were chosen since the initial testing had shown that the accuracy levels either remained the same, or started to decrease once a model was trained for more than 20 epochs. A batch size of 32 was also tested previous to this model, but the model showed a higher accuracy using a batch size of 16. Once trained, it gave the favorable results of a high level of accuracy (0.99 for the model and 0.78 during the test) and a low level of loss (0.00054 for the model and 0.00079 when tested by the platform) as shown in Fig. 2. It correctly identified all but one images, as shown in the confusion matrix generated in Fig. 3.

In order to conduct testing of our own, images where chosen from the dataset which displayed the emotion at its apex—where it's allegedly easiest to identify and differentiate from the others. These images were of subjects the model hadn't seen before. Ten images of each emotion were chosen. For the emotion of disgust all tested images were guessed correctly. For the emotion of sadness all but one were correct. An example of this model being tested with an apex image of disgust is shown in Fig. 4.

With these promising results we decided to add another emotion to the model.

4.2 Sadness vs Disgust vs Happiness

Using the same parameters as before (batch size of 16, learning rate of 0.001 and 20 epochs) in this model we included the emotion of happiness—labeled as "happy"— adding 297 images displaying this emotion. Since this emotion is considered the polar opposite of the emotions tested before, it was hypothesized that the model would have no problem distinguishing this emotion from the others. Once trained it showed a similar level of accuracy and loss than the model before as shown in Fig. 5.

Fig. 4. Example of image being correctly identified as the emotion disgust

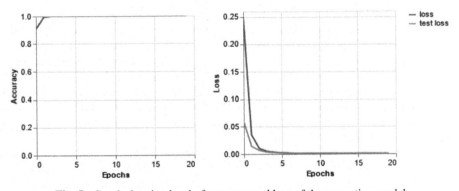

Fig. 5. Graph showing level of accuracy and loss of three emotion model

This model was similarly tested, it was fed ten images of each emotion but the results given were drastically different. Although the level of accuracy was high, just like the first model had shown, once tested with our own images the model was confidently incorrect. These numbers were given in the confusion matrix generated, shown in Fig. 6. For whichever emotion it guessed, it did so with 99% certainty, even though the emotion it predicted wasn't right half of the time. For the emotion of disgust—the one that did the best–it guessed 7 correctly and for the remaining guessed sadness. For sadness it guessed 6 correctly, 3 for disgust and 1 happy. Finally, the emotion the model had most trouble with was happiness, it only guessed correctly twice, 3 times choosing sadness and 5 times choosing disgust.

4.3 Testing Two Emotions with Only Apex Images

Since the model was having trouble when being tested with more than two emotions, it was decided to try and train a model using only images displaying the apex of each micro-expression, instead of the entire clip which consisted of 15 to 30 frames each. This with the idea of only showing the model the peak expression of each emotion and hopefully avoiding confusion with gestures made before or after the peak that could be similar to other emotions. However, doing so would limit the number of images to 49 per emotion, saving the 10 needed to conduct tests, instead of the few hundreds that were being tested before.

The emotions chosen to train this model were happiness and disgust, given that the model was having trouble when happiness was introduced in the previous iteration. The idea was that these images may be easier to identify and would allow the model to learn the emotion of happiness better.

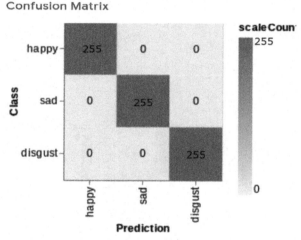

Fig. 6. Confusion matrix generated for three emotion model, showing that all images were guessed correctly, even though our testing showed otherwise.

The model was first trained using the same parameters of the previous models, but results were not good. In this case a batch size of 32 worked better. As far as epochs, we tested two options—50 and 20. We started with 50, but the accuracy levels were not as high as previous models, as shown in Fig. 7. In order to get this level of accuracy, the model had to be trained several times—most results could only get up to a 0.8 accuracy, as shown in Fig. 8.

The model generated that exhibited the most accuracy got to a peak level of 0.988 and it remained constant after 20 epochs. Therefore it was decided to train again with a lower number of epochs. As with the model tested with 50 epochs, this time it also took several attempts before successfully training a model that showed good accuracy and loss levels. The loss and accuracy levels for the final model generated are shown in Fig. 9.

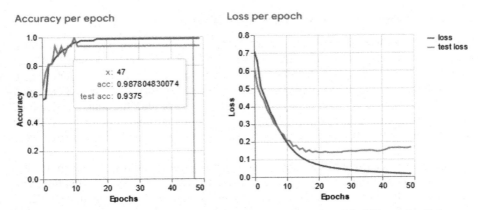

Fig. 7. Graph showing level of accuracy and loss of apex image model of 50 epochs. It shows a continuous increase in loss after epoch 20

CLASS	ACCURACY	# SAMPLES
Happy	0.88	8
Disgust	1.00	8

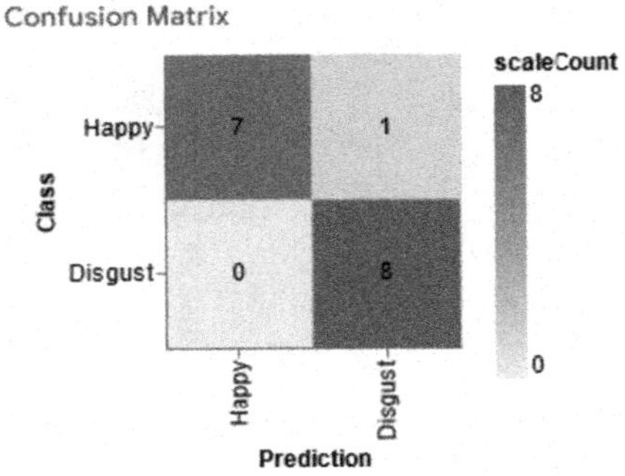

Confusion Matrix

Fig. 8. Confusion matrix of the apex model tested with 50 epochs.

Once acquired, it was tested with the 10 images saved before. For the emotion of disgust, all but one were guessed correctly. However, for happiness only 7 were correctly identified. When looking at the test images, it was noticed that the images that were misclassified were of female presenting faces. This prompted us to check the training data and it was noticed that most images for the disgust class where of female faces, compared to the emotion of happiness which were mainly male.

It was hypothesized that this could have been a factor that was giving the model this bias, guessing all female faces as disgust and male faces as happiness. Examples of these incorrect guesses are shown in Figs. 10 and 11. The low number of images is also likely a great contributing factor for this low level of accuracy when testing.

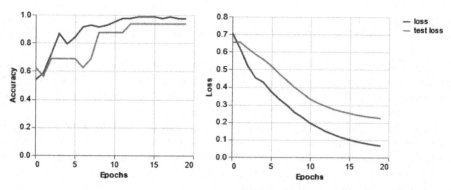

Fig. 9. Graph showing level of accuracy and loss of apex image model of 20 epochs

5 Conclusion and Future Work

Our research has revealed that the limitations in the available data remain the primary obstacle hindering our progress. However, we have identified potential avenues for improvement in our future investigations. Additional training on various platforms and the exploration of alternative strategies, such as manual coding or exporting the model to TensorFlow, hold promise for achieving better results in our study.

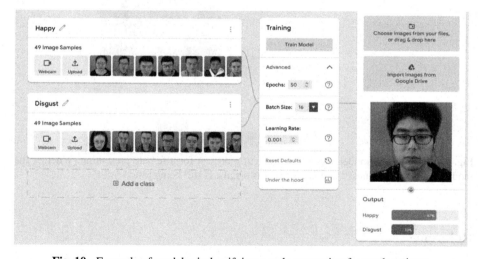

Fig. 10. Example of model misclassifying a male presenting face as happiness

The next phase of our research will involve implementing these improvements to further enhance the model's performance. Additionally, we recognize the importance of testing the model's accuracy in distinguishing micro-expressions in children with Autism Spectrum Disorder (ASD). To achieve this, we aim to work with the Asociaci´on Pro Autismo A.C. (Pro Autism Association) [25], a private charitable institution approved by the Government of the State of Baja California, which operates the Interdisciplinary Center for Autism Care (CINAA) and provides services to children, youth, and adults with ASD.

One of our future goals is to collaborate with the school to create an original dataset tailored specifically to the unique expressions and mannerisms of children with ASD. This undertaking will not only contribute valuable data to our research but also address the lack of publicly available datasets for this particular context.

In summary, while our current findings are limited by the available data, we are optimistic about the potential improvements that lie ahead. Through our continued efforts and collaboration with Asociaci´on Pro Autismo A.C., we aim to advance our understanding of micro-expression recognition in children with ASD and make significant contributions to the field of autism research.

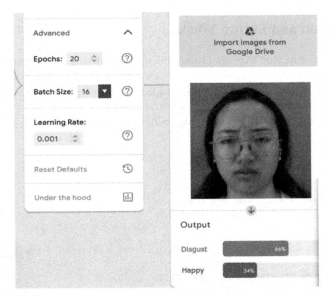

Fig. 11. Example of model accurately predicting disgust for a female presenting. Whether the model has a bias for guessing females faces as disgust is still being tested

References

1. Wagner, L., et al.: Transitioning to telemedicine during COVID-19: impact on perceptions and use of telemedicine procedures for the diagnosis of autism in toddlers. J. Autism Dev. Disord. **52**(5), 2247–2257 (2021)
2. Alfuraydan, M., Croxall, J., Hurt, L., Kerr, M., Brophy, S.: Use of telehealth for facilitating the diagnostic assessment of Autism Spectrum Disorder (ASD): a scoping review. PLOS ONE **15**(7), e0236415 (2020)
3. Doherty, M., Neilson, S., O'Sullivan, J., et al.: Barriers to healthcare and self-reported adverse outcomes for autistic adults: a cross-sectional study. BMJ Open **12**(2), e056904 (2022)

4. Shaw, S.C., Davis, L.J., Doherty, M.: Considering autistic patients in the era of telemedicine: the need for an adaptable, equitable, and compassionate approach. BJGP Open **6**(1), 1–4 (2022)
5. Zolyomi, A., Begel, A., Waldern, J., et al.: Managing stress: the needs of autistic adults in video calling. Proc. ACM Hum. Comput. Interact. **3**, 1–29 (2019)
6. Izard, C., Fine, S., Schultz, D., Mostow, A., Ackerman, B., Youngstrom, E.: Emotion knowledge as a predictor of social behavior and academic competence in children at risk. Psychol. Sci. **12**(1), 18–23 (2001)
7. Rodriguez, P.: El trastorno del espectro autista. Una intriga que dura 80 a ños. Canarias Pediatrica **45**(1), 6–7 (2021)
8. Petrides, K., Hudry, C., Michalaria, G., Swami, V., Sevdalis, N.: Comparison of the trait emotional intelligence profiles of individuals with and without Asperger syndrome. Autism **15**, 671–682 (2011)
9. Kaypaklı, G.Y., Tamam, L.: Emotional intelligence in attention deficit hyper-activity disorder. Psikiyatride Güncel Yakla˛sımlar **11**(1), 112–119 (2019)
10. Xia, B., Wang, W., Wang, S., Chen, E.: Learning from macro-expression: a micro-expression recognition framework. In: Proceedings of the 28th ACM International Conference on Multimedia (MM'20), pp. 2936–2944 (2020)
11. Gay, V., Leijdekkers, P., Agcanas, J., Wong, F., Wu, Q.: CaptureMyEmotion: Helping Autistic Children Understand their Emotions Using Facial Expression Recognition and Mobile Technologies (2013)
12. Guha, T., Yang, Z., Grossman, R., Narayanan, S.: A computational study of expressive facial dynamics in children with autism. IEEE Trans. Affect. Comput. **9**(1), 14–20 (2018)
13. Yirmiya, N., Kasari, C., Sigman, M., Mundy, P.: Facial expressions of affect in autistic mentally retarded and normal children. J. Child Psychol. Psychiatry **30**(5), 725–735 (1989)
14. Grossman, R.: Judgments of social awkwardness from brief exposure to children with and without high-functioning autism. Autism **19**(5), 580–587 (2015)
15. Rinn, W.: The neuropsychology of facial expression: A review of the neurological and psychological mechanisms for producing facial expressions. Psychol. Bull. **95**, 52–77 (1984)
16. Ekman, P.: Lie catching and microexpressions. In: The Philosophy of Deception, pp. 118–133. Oxford Univ Press, London, U.K. (2009)
17. Yan, W.-J., Wu, Q., Liu, Y.-J., Wang, S.-J., Fu, X.: CASME database: a dataset of spontaneous micro-expressions collected from neutralized faces. In: Proceedings of the IEEE 10th International Conference Workshops Automation Face Gesture Recognition, pp. 1–7 (2013)
18. Yan, W.-J., et al.: CASME II: an improved spontaneous micro-expression database and the baseline evaluation. PLoS ONE **9**(1), e86041 (2014). https://doi.org/10.1371/journal.pone.0086041
19. Qu, F., Wang, S.-J., Yan, W.-J., Li, H., Wu, S., Fu, X.: CAS(ME): a database for spontaneous macro-expression and micro-expression spotting and recognition. IEEE Trans. Affecti. Comput. **9**(4), 424–436 (2018)
20. Li, J., et al.: CAS(ME)3: a third generation facial spontaneous micro-expression database with depth information and high ecological validity. IEEE Trans. Pattern Anal. Mach. Intell. **45**(3), 2782–2800 (2023)
21. Li, X., Pfister, T., Huang, X., Zhao, G., Pietikäinen, M.: A spontaneous micro-expression database: Inducement collection and baseline. In: Proceedings of the IEEE 10th International Conference on Workshops Automation Face Gesture Recognition, pp. 1–6 (2013)
22. Davison, A.K., Lansley, C., Costen, N., Tan, K., Yap, M.H.: SAMM: a spontaneous micro-facial movement dataset. IEEE Trans. Affective Comput **9**(1), 116–129 (2018)
23. Ben, X., et al.: Video-based facial micro-expression analysis: a survey of datasets features and algorithms. IEEE Trans. Pattern Anal. Mach. Intell. **44**, 5826–5846 (2021)

24. Carney, M., Webster, B., Alvarado, I., Phillips, K., et al.: Teachable machine: approachable web-based tool for exploring machine learning classification. In: Extended Abstracts of the 2020 CHI Conference on Human Factors in Computing Systems (2020)
25. Pro Autismo A.C. (n.d.). https://www.proautismo.com/

Intelligent Systems in Forensic Engineering (ISIFE 2023)

Social Media Intelligence as a Tool for Conducting Intelligence Activities

Antonio Teti[✉]

University "G. d'Annunzio" Chieti-Pescara, 66100 Chieti, Italy
antonio.teti@unich.it

Abstract. The information security of an organization must be based on the ability to guarantee the confidentiality and integrity of information relating to intellectual property, production processes, technological processes, business plans and in particular the data held regarding potential threats. In such a context, the massive and indiscriminate use of social media by company employees represents a huge vulnerability for information security. Accordingly, social espionage can be defined as an attempt to gain a competitive advantage by acquiring all publicly and semi-publicly available information in social media. In this regard, Social Media Intelligence activities, which are essentially based on the use of platforms capable of searching, collecting, filtering and assembling a considerable amount of useful information from social media, have taken on a decisive role. In this paper, we aim to analyze the phenomenon of social espionage and focus on two relevant ways of conducting it in the context of social media intelligence, briefly reviewing the main characteristics of both of them. The first one is the use of Social Media Intelligence (SOCMINT) platforms to capture social data streams that can be employed to learn useful information, for example, about the company where someone is employed. The second one is related to fake social profiles suitably constructed to capture the information held in different social conversations.

Keywords: Social Media Intelligence · SOCMINT · Web Intelligence

1 Introduction

An organization's information can be divided into auditable information released by the company and non-auditable information that can be acquired online, regardless of the company's wishes. This information may be collected directly by making search queries, creating alerts and filters, and interacting with competitors and customer communities (e.g., following Twitter profiles, subscribing to a forum, liking a competitor's Facebook page), or indirectly through various social media aggregation.

In this regard, the information security of an organization must be based on the ability to guarantee the confidentiality and integrity of information relating to intellectual property, production processes, technological processes, business plans and in particular the data held regarding potential threats competitive. Consequently, in this particular scenario, the protection of trade secrets assumes the connotation of the vital element

© The Author(s), under exclusive license to Springer Nature Switzerland AG 2024
T. Guarda et al. (Eds.): ARTIIS 2023, CCIS 1937, pp. 281–291, 2024.
https://doi.org/10.1007/978-3-031-48930-3_21

on which to build the future of the company. The ability to access the most valuable information of a company or organization, as we have been able to understand, represents a fundamental objective for anyone who wants to understand what are the vulnerabilities, needs, trends, set objectives and expectations of their competitors.

When the productive activities of a company insist on several geographically dislocated locations even in different countries, the risk of conducting internal espionage activities increases considerably. Even the assignment to external companies (outsourcing) of some company services (e.g. IT services, cybersecurity, training, etc.) can represent a serious problem for the confidentiality of company data. The massive and indiscriminate use of social media by company employees represents a huge vulnerability for information security. The ignorance of the population on the correct use of social media also plays a role. Every day and incessantly, information of all kinds is entered on the Internet, and in particular on social media, from the more private personal ones to those relating to the work that takes place within one's workplace, without excluding those relating to one's friends and co-workers. Conversations conducted on Facebook, Twitter, Instagram, including those apparently restricted to a WhatsApp group, remain private only if a user decides not to spread them.

In such a context, social espionage can be defined as an attempt to gain a competitive advantage by acquiring all publicly and semi-publicly available information in social media. It should be noted that social espionage is one of the methodologies that can be used to conduct IT espionage activities, which are based on the use of security hackers and malicious software (Trojan horse, Spyware, Rootkit and Backdoor) that allow, often through the use of social engineering methodologies, to intercept the vulnerabilities of a computer system to access it and obtain the desired information [1]. It should be noted that social espionage does not assume the connotation of theft of information, given that it is publicly available (or semi-publicly) on social media.

In Fig. 1, it is possible to deduce the trends that tend to promote social espionage.

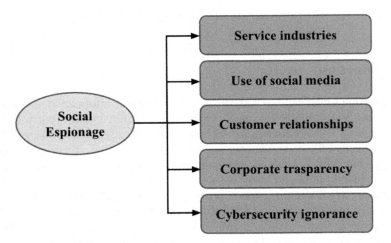

Fig. 1. Trends promoting shift to social espionage.

Social espionage emerges from the three meeting points of enterprises (suppliers, competitors, customers) as actors, social media (technology platform) as an asset, and competitive intelligence as an activity that connects actors and resources together in a harmonious way [2–4]. The lack of training courses for personnel working in the organization represents a further element of risk for the dissemination of company information. It is known that most of the espionage activities are conducted on the basis of the users' superficiality in the use of information technologies and on the lack of adoption of cyber security procedures in the workplace [1].

Social Media Intelligence (SOCMINT) is the process of capturing, collecting and analyzing data from social media platforms to obtain data and information of specific interest useful for satisfying the information needs of the top decision-makers of an organization. This can require the adoption of a multiform data collection process from multiple social media platforms such as, for example, Facebook, Twitter, Instagram, LinkedIn, to monitor the trends of the masses, identify communication patterns, propaganda and psychological conditioning and to obtain information, for example, on the behavior of its customers, on the reputation of the brand or the service offered or on the "sentiment" referred to the reference market. SOCMINT is essential for any organization (public, private, institutional) that intends to constantly evaluate the presence of information within the social digital ecosystem of Cyberspace. It can involve using advanced analytics tools and techniques for data mining, such as natural language processing and machine learning, to process the vast masses of data constantly produced by social media. It should be noted that SOCMINT finds its most natural application for the enhancement of Competitive Intelligence (CI). CI focuses on obtaining information about strategic capabilities, intellectual properties, product formulations, technological processes, business plans, and potential competitive threats [5]. According to [6], CI includes the search for information on competitors and target markets, as well as data relating to competitors in relation to business opportunities and possible weaknesses of competitors. Based on this evidence, the protection of trade secrets assumes strategic importance for the company and for its very survival.

It should be emphasized that running a SOCMINT activity requires different skills that can guarantee an accurate selection of the information to be acquired, a deep and detailed analysis of the selected information and a correct assembly of the selected data that can translate into a "product of intelligence" useful for the top decision-makers of the organization. Typically, among the techniques adopted, the following are highlighted: (i) Social Network Analysis, used to analyze the relationships and interactions between individuals and groups on social media platforms. It allows you to identify the leading influencers, the connections between individuals or groups and behavioral patterns; (ii) Natural Language Processing, allowing you to analyze the sentiment, tone and context of social media posts, comments and conversations. They allow you to identify underlying themes, opinions, and emotions related to specific topics or issues; (iii) Geolocation, to identify the physical location of social media users/groups based on their posts or the profile information that produced them. It allows you to identify the geographical context in which specific events or incidents are taking place and to trace the movement of individuals or groups.

The techniques and methodologies used can be different and must be identified and personalized on the basis of the reference target. In the literature, at the moment, being a particularly innovative technique and above all modelable on the basis of the cognitive needs of the "customer", detailed examples of platforms of this type are not available. However, it is possible to cite two examples of real application of SOCMINT, both referable to the current ongoing Russian-Ukrainian conflict. The first can be traced back to an activity conducted by Radio Free Europe/Radio Liberty (RFE/RL) in collaboration with the Conflict Intelligence Team (CIT), which made it possible to highlight the deployment of troops by the Russian army a few weeks before the 2022 invasion of Ukraine[1]; the second refers to the use of a SOCMINT model which made it possible, through the analysis of images, posts and other information taken from social media, to identify the perpetrators of a massacre carried out in Ukraine by Russian soldiers[2].

In this paper, we aim to analyze the phenomenon of social espionage and focus on two relevant ways of conducting it in the context of social media intelligence, briefly reviewing the main characteristics of both of them. The first one is the use of Social Media Intelligence (SOCMINT) platforms to capture social data streams that can be employed to learn useful information, for example, about the company where someone is employed. The second one is related to fake social profiles suitably constructed to capture the information held in different social conversations. In this case, it would be the victim of a human intelligence methodology, better known as Virtual Human Intelligence VHUMINT [7].

To the best of our knowledge, it is the first work where social espionage is studied and analyzed in the context of social media intelligence.

The paper is organized as follows. Section 2 presents the main characteristics of a typical SOCMINT platform and describes a state-of-the-art SOCMINT architecture. Section 3 introduces the concept of persuasive communication in social media which is connected to the VHUMINT. Finally, Sect. 4 draws conclusions about the previously described concepts and outlines future work directions.

2 Social Media Intelligence Platforms

Let's assume we want to acquire from the most common social media information attributable to the activities conducted by a company and the level of exposure to the dangers of an espionage activity. The first step is to create a platform that allows to analyze the data present in the three most used social media: Facebook, Twitter, Instagram. The next step is to choose an optimized platform for retrieving posts from the three social channels based on specific tracking criteria. Among the numerous real-time tracker platforms available on the market, i.e. capable of tracking hashtags, accounts, keywords and Uniform Resource Locator in real time (URL) contained in the messages, we find: Metricool, Hashtracking, Tweetreach, Keyhole, AgoraPulse, Hashtagify, Socialert. These

---

[1] https://www.svoboda.org/a/na-ukrainu-edut-rodnye-voennyh-O-perebroske-vojsk/31661739. html.

[2] https://www.ilsole24ore.com/art/da-foto-responsabile-ecco-come-L-ai-individua-criminali-gue-AEk4qpuB?refresh_ce=1.

platforms constantly analyze all the information entered into social networks according to keywords.

At this point it is advisable to proceed with the creation of a system based on criteria for tracking the posts published in the previously selected social channels (Facebook, Twitter and Instagram) which allows for the extrapolation of such contents by means of an online monitoring platform. We then proceed with the creation of a special storage system for storing the data collected in specific databases which will be indexed together with the Key Performance Indicators (KPI) provided by the online monitoring platform. We will then proceed with the creation of an Application Programming Interface (API) to extract the raw data in json format and to allow the analyzes that will subsequently be used by means of an Analytics dashboard or tool, in order to allow the visualization of the data (see Fig. 2).

To understand the evolution of the phenomenon over time, it is essential to analyze the following elements:

- **Reach**: measures the diffusion of the message that spreads in social media, in terms of the potential number of people who have viewed it. In the case of a communication campaign aimed at increasing awareness, it indicates the possible number of potential consumers who have been subjected to the message, and consequently who have become aware of the brand. It is an important measure but it must be combined with other metrics that integrate the information with the number of people who have actually interacted or with other users who spread the message (Influencers, People Involved);
- **Sentiment**: sentiment refers to the feeling/mood expressed by a subject through his message, and is measured in terms of intensity, i.e. whether it is positive, negative or neutral. The measure refers to individual results (mention), or more generally to a topic of discussion, in aggregate form. The Net Promoter Score (NPS), on the other hand, is an index derived from sentiment, and represents the difference between the number of promoters of the discussion topic, people who speak well of it, and the number of detractors. Also in this case, it is useful to consider the variation of these two metrics over time to evaluate their impact and the effect it has on the community;
- **Influencers**: they are the web and social media users who manage with their opinions to influence the respective opinions and decisions of a more or less consistent pool of other users, as they have built a certain credibility and a reputation as experts regarding one or more themes;
- **Engagement**: it is the metric that groups all the interactions that people have with the "discussion" or with other users, or on a message. In particular, it represents the sum of likes, comments and shares of a post. To obtain higher quality data, it is also advisable to measure the relationship between the total engagement of posts in a certain period, and the number of views of these posts, or the number of fans/followers in that given period, to understand how many active people within their community;
- **Number and variation of people involved**: they represent those people who take an action against the "discussion", who interact with likes, comments or shares. It is important to analyze these data, as well as their reciprocal variation over time (e.g. fans remain unchanged but people involved increase following a company campaign, or vice versa, etc.).

- **Total impressions**: the number of times a page featuring content is loaded during the campaign period. Impressions alone, however, are not significant because they usually represent a huge number, in the order of millions, which however does not correspond to an equal number of people who have actually viewed the video;
- **Multimedia contents in the texts**: repeatability of the same multimedia contents in the posts of a topic (e.g. 100 posts 25 with the same images).

On the basis of the analysis of the information elements indicated above, and according to their enhancement by an intelligence analyst, it will be possible to achieve specific vertical knowledge on a specific target.

A system for tracking and analyzing social media which adheres to this general architecture and concepts has been proposed in [8]. The system, called SocMINT, gives users the option to gather information from various social networking sites, and it offers an interactive dashboard that supports multidimensional analysis and uses a deep learning-based approach to forecast social sentiment in relation to both textual and visual data. A method is also put out for determining the overall sentiment of a photograph based on both visual and textual information, and it is implemented into the analytics system. A two-stage deep learning classifier is used in the model. The image is stage one, and the text inside the image is step two. By doing this, content from social media platforms like MEMEs can be incorporated into the study.

The visual feature extractor is trained by fine-tuning the basic model pre-trained on ImageNet and is based on the VGG16 network architecture. The textual feature extractor first finds and recognizes text in images before performing sentiment analysis, whereas the visual feature extractor applies to the entire image. The textual sentiment classifier uses transfer learning of the classifier utilizing a BERT layer as its foundation.

More specifically, the system workflow is characterized by the following steps:

- Data collection,
- Data storage,
- Social KPIs,
- Sentiment analysis,
- SocMINT.

In the data collection step, data is gathered from Instagram, Facebook and Twitter. Data collection process is performed through queries on hashtags and keywords from a list of selected social media accounts. Data is preprocessed to include various information, such as the text of the post, publication date, author, list of hashtags and user mentions found in the post as well as links to media in the post, number of likes or reactions, number of reposts and geolocalisation if available. The different posts are collected in a relational table, together with metadata and the included media.

For data storage, MongoDB is used as a Database Management System (DBMS) to collect the data from social networks. The structure of the database is composed of three main fields: user, storing the information regarding the user, rawposts, which is a raw collection of the posts from the social networks and posts, which is a collection of data that will be adopted for the visualization in SocMINT.

The social KPIs employed by the system to evaluate the performances of social media posts and users can be classified as trend and multimedia KPIs.

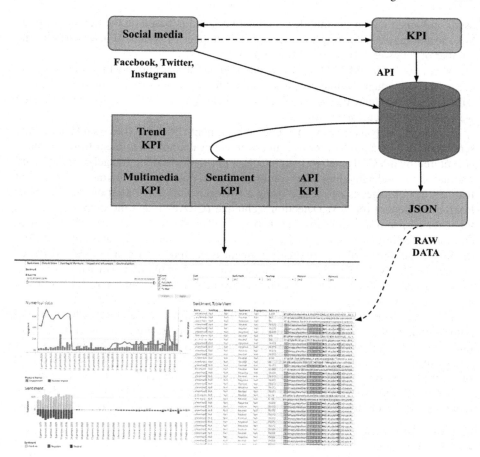

Fig. 2. SOCMINT online monitoring platform.

The trend KPIs are adopted to monitor the trends that emerge through time and characterize a phenomenon in social media. They are: (i) engagement, (ii) quantity of posts published, (iii) degree centrality, (iv) closeness centrality, and (v) entropy. Engagement is a typical metric that reflects the interest users have shown in a piece of content by engaging directly with it. The quantity of posts published is the number of published posts containing a set of keywords or hashtags. In the context of social media, a user's degree centrality can be determined by counting their friends on Facebook, followers and following on Twitter, and following on Instagram, while the degree centrality of a community group or page, both open and private, can be determined by counting subscribers and users who have subscribed, indicating interest in the contents of the page. Closeness centrality can be used to measure the influence of users within a community. This is because it offers an efficient measurement of the dissemination of information within a network, operating under the premise that the better a node's positioning within a social network, the higher its closeness centrality value. Finally, entropy evaluates the users' influence within the mobile social network and is based on the number of node links in the graph, by taking into account the number of friends (Facebook) and the number of followers (Twitter and Instagram).

About the multimedia KPIs, the combination, or more accurately the weighted average, of the individual sentiment values acquired for the text and image linked to the post will be used to evaluate the post's overall sentiment. The user will choose the associated weights to enable customization.

Sentiment analysis is performed by two sentiment classifiers (i.e. visual and textual sentiment) and by a module for overall sentiment evaluation. Sentiment from an image is captured by a VGG16 network architecture pre-trained on the ImageNet dataset and fine-tuned for understanding what can or cannot be positive. The extraction of textual features from images is performed using a two-step workflow based on the Character Region Awareness for Text Detection technique (CRAFT), and the output is used as input for a spatial attention residual network (STAR-Net). Finally, overall sentiment analysis is performed as a weighted average of the single sentiment that is obtained from the image and text analysis. Textual sentiment is computed from a pre-trained BERT layer embedded in the neural network model, which is then fine-tuned on a portion of the domain dataset in order to perform sentiment prediction. At the end, an overall sentiment score is generated as the combination of visual and textual sentiment scores.

For each aforementioned model, fine-tuning consisted in training the basic model with a training set and validating it with a validation set for avoiding the overfitting. Fine-tuning was stopped when validation error started increasing while training error was decreasing. On a total of 20,000 posts for the validation and training set, the consumed time for fine-tuning the BERT and VGG16 models was 40 and 27 min, respectively.

The SocMINT visualization and analysis dashboard is populated from a dynamic input that can be modified at any moment by the user and is made up of the following:

- A list of keywords;
- A list of hashtags;
- A list of social platforms accounts/handles.

SocMINT includes five main views: (i) sentiment, (ii) multimedia, (iii) hashtag, (iv) influencers and (v) map of location data.

3 Human Intelligence Methodology

A second relevant aspect of SOCMINT is the human intelligence methodology (VHUMINT), which is also connected to the creation of fake social profiles suitably constructed to capture the information held in different social conversations.

The key aspect underlying this phenomenon is persuasive communication, which is the set of persuasion strategies and methods useful for carrying out activities of influence and psychological persuasion, aimed at trying to influence the decisions of others. Persuasive communication in social media, so that it can produce effective and profitable results, cannot disregard the adoption of a profile analysis scheme with which one intends to interact. The profile analysis, especially in intelligence activities, represents the starting point of VHUMINT activities. For example, suppose you conduct an information search on a Facebook profile. The attention will have to focus on the analysis of the fields Education, Places where he lived, Contact and basic information, Relationship, Family members, Places visited, Sport, Movies, TV programs, Books, Application and games, Like, Events, Reviews, Group, Followers, etc. On the basis of the information taken from these fields it will be possible to proceed with the creation of a frame of knowledge which allows to outline the characteristics of the profile. One of the most common theories that emerges in the literature on virtual relationships is that of Social Penetration Theory (SPT). Conceived by psychologists Irwin Altman and Dalmas Taylor [9], SPT argues that relationships form and develop as information is gradually exchanged between two or more people. The individuals involved in the relationship exchange information according to the cost-benefit analysis of the relationship. When the perceived benefits outweigh the risk of disclosing information, a relationship will form the "Lives a Followers Friends" links on Facebook can provide us with a precise indication of the social, cultural and economic environment in which you live, including interests and tastes. The "Stories" link, enriched by stories, comments, hashtags and emoticons, allows us to learn which emotional states the user experiences or has experienced and consequently what the suggestions, considerations and welcome topics may be.

"Likes too_" present in the posts can say a lot, such as the degree of appreciation (or disgust) of a particular statement, an event, an image or a comment posted on the social network by another profile. Another important clue, capable of providing valuable information, is represented by the photos published on the profile. If they portray the person in various poses, more or less captivating, they denote the evident desire to satisfy one's ego, but they may contain subliminal messages referring, for example, to sexual aspects (photos in skimpy or very veiled clothes), cultural (the person has himself immortalized against the background of a bookstore, in front of a training institute, at the entrance to a university, etc.), professional (photo in one's office or studio, image of the company in which he works, brand of the institution or company, etc.), sportsmen (in gymnastic gear or while playing a sport). The photos of cities, landscapes, famous places, means of transport, denote the desire to convey a message referable to personal depth: a person who travels, in the collective imagination, exercises a prestigious, important and highly profitable profession. The irrepressible desire to appear important and interesting assumes, for the individual, the connotation of the primary objective to be achieved, to be accepted, esteemed, loved but above all to assume a higher level of visibility than others. This irrepressible ambition manifests itself in a non-place like the virtual world, made up mostly of people we don't know. The image society is based on a culture made up of icons generated by the world of politics, sport, fashion, entertainment and television, which permanently provide indications on behaviors, lines of thought, habits and customs to adopt to ensure a continuous and higher level of interest and importance. Emblematic is the video made by director Shaun Hington, titled "What's on your mind?" (available on YouTube), which suggests a completely different interpretation of the contents of posts published on social networks: often behind the carefully chosen images and words, there are completely different realities, made up of loneliness, boredom, failures and pain. The images published on social networks become an absolute priority which often leads to oversharing, i.e. sharing every single detail of one's private life online, if not even of every single day lived. Two psychologists from Harvard University, Diana Tamir and Jason Mitchell, have conducted research which has shown that 30–40% of communications between individuals concern topics of a personal nature, a percentage that rises to 80% within social networks. The desire to communicate one's thoughts, emotions and reflections to others is strongly connected to the activation of brain areas designated for the perception of the sense of gratification and pleasure. The research shows the existence of a form of satisfaction that arises from the impulse to talk about oneself to others, comparable to a primary need such as food and sex. Another element that emerged from the research is that relating to the role played by social media as tools capable of inducing the individual to play a role that does not correspond to reality in an attempt to hide the negative aspects of one's personality from him, enhancing the positive aspects, most of the time not even possessed. If self-centeredness and megalomania can assume a predominant role in social networks, it is also true that the need to expose oneself and show off is alive and widespread, and this produces an increase in the number of personal information entered in one's profile. Once the limits of understanding the vulnerability of personal privacy have been overcome, the user runs the risk of overcoming even those of intimacy, slipping down a tunnel that leads to the loss of a sense of reality. If such a condition can produce disastrous effects for the user, for a VHUMINT Collector, it represents the ideal scenario for conducting information acquisition activities thanks to the use of a fake profile built according to the characteristics of the identified target (see Fig. 3).

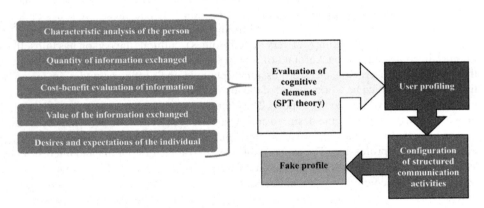

Fig. 3. Stages of the evaluation of the SPT profile.

4   Conclusion

Social Media Intelligence can allow you to search, extract and assemble data and information that can take on the connotation of an "intelligence product" that can be used in different sectors, such as defense, economic, industrial, social, political.

In this work, we provided an overview of SOCMINT under the social espionage perspective, which can be defined as an attempt to gain a competitive advantage by acquiring all publicly and semi-publicly available information in social media. Accordingly, we analyzed two different forms of social espionage, the first one referring to SOCMINT platforms and architectures, the second one which is connected to the creation of fake social profiles suitably constructed to capture the information held in different social conversations.

Artificial intelligence platforms, in this regard, can represent a suitable tool for the automatic processing of information, allowing to quickly produce that knowledge useful to the top decision-makers of the organization to identify the best decisions to take. Depending on the unstoppable exponential increase in data present on the Internet, and in particular on social media, the use of artificial intelligence platforms equipped with special algorithms built to conduct research and data extraction activities that are actually useful for the creation of an "intelligence product" in different sectors, such as the economic, industrial, political, social and defense sectors, represents the "highway" on which to concentrate investments for the coming years.

References

1. Teti, A.: Cyber Espionage and Cyber Counterintelligence. Cyber espionage and counter espionage. Rubbettino, 221 p. (2018). ISBN-13:978-8849852660
2. Håkansson, H., Snehota, I.: No business is an island: the network concept of business strategy. Scand. J. Manag. **5**(3), 187–200 (1989)
3. Easton, G.: Case research as a methodology for industrial networks: a realist apology. In: Naude, P., Turnbull, P.W. (eds.) Network Dynamics in International Marketing, pp. 73–87. Elsevier Science, Oxford (1998)
4. Håkansson, H., Ford, D.: How should companies interact in business networks. J. Bus. Res. **55**, 133–139 (2002)
5. Fitzpatrick, W.: Uncovering trade secrets: the legal and ethical conundrum of creative competitive intelligence. SAM Adv. Manag. J. **68**(3) (2003)
6. Miller, S.H.: Competitive Intelligence-An Overview. Competitive Intelligence Magazine. http://www.ipo.org/AM/Template.cfm?Section=Home&Template=/CM/ContentDisplay. cfm&ContentID=15904 (2005). Retrieved 14 May 2011
7. Teti, A.: Virtual Humint. The new frontier of Intelligence, 165 p. Rubbettino (2020). ISBN-13:978-8849860078
8. Mameli, M., Paolanti, M., Morbidoni, C., et al.: Social media analytics system for action inspection on social networks. Soc. Netw. Anal. Min. **12**, 33 (2022)
9. Altman, I., Taylor, D.A.: Social Penetration: The Development of Interpersonal Relationships, 459. Holt, Rinehart, & Winston, New York (1973)

Geometrical Acoustics in Cultural Heritage Conservation and Promotion: Digitalization of the Acoustic Characteristics

Sergio Montelpare[1], Mariano Pierantozzi[1], Samantha Di Loreto[1],
Alessandro Ricciutelli[1(✉)], and Marta ferrara[2]

[1] University "G. d'Annunzio" of Chieti-Pescara, Engineering and Geology
Department (INGEO), Viale Pindaro 42, 65127 Pescara, Italy
`alessandro.ricciutelli@unich.it`
[2] University of Teramo Campus "Aurelio Saliceti", Political Science Department,
Via R. Balzarini 1, 64100 Teramo, Italy

Abstract. In 2003, UNESCO, with the Convention for the Safeguarding of Intangible Cultural Heritage (ICH), recognized the acoustic characteristics of a cultural heritage building as qualities to be safeguarded. After this milestone, multiple researchers have investigated methods and tools to evaluate, understand, characterize and store the acoustic intangible information. This paper illustrates an experimental and numerical approach useful to accurately measure the acoustic fingerprint of a cultural heritage building; the unique identification of this fingerprint opens the way to a legal protection of the intangible heritage of the sound response of the building. The proposed approach allows to define a forensic process to legally preserve the uniqueness of the acoustic fingerprint of a building. The proposed procedure involves acoustic software that use ray tracing algorithms to simulate the sound propagation; in order to calibrate the numerical models with respect to the experimental measurements, they were used genetics algorithms that allowed to precisely calibrate the absorption coefficients of the building's materials. This paper aims to investigates the pros and cons of using such techniques and algorithms in intangible cultural heritage acoustic's preservation and digitization by analyzing its applications and results on case studies.

Keywords: cultural heritage · digitization · room acoustics · acoustic fingerprint

1 Introduction

The rapid pace of globalization, coupled with ongoing shifts such as natural disasters and global pandemics, has heightened the vulnerabilities faced by intangible cultural heritage. These invaluable treasures are increasingly at risk. It is

T. Guarda et al. (Eds.): ARTIIS 2023, CCIS 1937, pp. 292–303, 2024.
https://doi.org/10.1007/978-3-031-48930-3_22

crucial to take immediate action, particularly in safeguarding the living cultures of vulnerable communities, in order to ensure their continuity and preservation.

Architectural acoustics is a field of scientific inquiry that focuses on the study of sound environments within architectural structures. Traditionally, research in this area has primarily centered around concert halls, opera houses, and theaters. Nevertheless, the pursuit of favorable indoor acoustic environments extends beyond these performance spaces alone [10].

In recent times, there has been a growing recognition of the significance of architectural acoustics in historic buildings. In particular, the conservation of cultural heritage is nowadays a very important aspect of our lives. Thanks to such legacy we gain knowledge about our ancestors, methods of production and ways of their life.

In [27] it examined the some aspects as: the widespread adoption of 3D digital technologies in the field of Intangible Cultural Heritage (ICH); the specific technologies employed in the research and the types of research being conducted.

Particular attention has been paid in literature on the optimal location of acoustic materials for sound treatments [8, 11, 19].

Recent studies into cultural computing, otherwise known as the interdisciplinary field of "digital humanities", have triggered a growing number of algorithmic advancements to facilitate ICH data usage, which deserves a systemic collation [6, 14, 18, 20].

Firat et all. [1] explores the rationale behind classifying sensory objects of cultural significance as tangible heritage assets, with a focus on heritage, sensory semiotics, and acoustics. It also delves into the methods of digitalization used to preserve and reconstruct acoustic heritage, emphasizing their quantifiable and computable characteristics.

Sound heritage as a legal concept with a collective and cultural relevance represents a quite recent goal achieved in the Supranational legal framework.

International Law considers sound and acoustic as a part of the intangible or immaterial heritage, according to the ICH, (2003) about the oral traditions and expressions (Art. 2, §2, lett. a)), while European Law (art. 167 TFEU) implicitly suggests that acoustic can be considered in the cultural heritage of EU significance adopting an extensive approach [21].

The sound-legal theory shows more regulatory criticalities at the National legal level that can be summarized in:

- the lack of an autonomous conceptualization of the sound heritage, with a preference for the sound intangible protection according to International Law;
- the lack of an interdisciplinary perspective to the topic, considering that acoustic as a constitutive landscape or site item resulting from the interaction between sound and the environment;
- finally, a trend toward a sectoriality legal design to issues linked to the sound heritage (i.e. the environment penal protection).

The idea that heritage sound might be fully guaranteed through the immaterial protection appears too reductive and inadequate [15] to safeguard the sound uniqueness characterizing a cultural monument or a destroyed site.

Moreover, sometimes National regulation considers the sound under its material profile as a sound res or a musical res but doesn't provide an autonomous conceptualization of the sound heritage. For instance, music is materially protected in the form of the musical score and, consequentially, as a part of the library cultural heritage (see art. 10, c. 4, lett. d) [4], It. Cultural Code) but it doesn't have a specific legal statute.

1.1 Contribution of This Work

The transfer of acoustic information in the digital domain in addition to allowing (potentially) greater resistance to wear and tear of time, allows a more effective search of content, based on melodies whistled by the user (query by humming) or sound examples from other audio files (query by example).

To ensure data retention, it is advisable that acoustic information is restored by working on (digital) copies obtained from those perfectly matching the original. This way of proceeding allows you to decide on a case by case basis what type of restoration approach to take.

All calculation methods presented in this paper are those currently applied in the ODEON room acoustic software.

The ODEON software uses ray tracing algorithms to simulate sound propagation and shows that careful postprocessing of the measured data can lead to high agreement with advanced room acoustics measurments.

ODEON room acoustic software has been applied to obtain accurate room acoustics predictions. In the simulation process the first step is to import a 3D model of the room, previously drawn in a modelling software. In the simulations, all the receivers have been located at the same positions used in the measurement and later the model was calibrated according to the classical procedure described in ISO 3382-1 [16].

To calibrate the numerical models with respect to the experimental measurements, genetic algorithms were used that allowed the absorption coefficients of the building materials to be precisely calibrated.

The paper is organized as follows: Sect. 2 presents room acoustic model, illustrated in detail the numerical simulation and the storage of the acoustic information in forensic science. Finally, Sect. 3 summarizes the conclusion of the work and comments on possible future extensions.

2   Material and Methods

This section explains the procedures used to objectively evaluate the acoustic quality of the San Biagio's Temple through experimental measurements and simulation techniques. During this analysis, various typical positions for natural sound sources and different audience areas are considered, which determine the adopted methodology.

The San Biagio's Temple, one of the most important works of Antonio Cordini (known as Antonio Da Sangallo - the elder), is in Montepulciano, a town in

Siena's province that played a significant role in Tuscany's architecture Renaissance [25].

Figure 1 shows the St. Biagio temple and its plan.

Fig. 1. St. Biagio Temple and its plan.

2.1 Room Acoustic Measurements and Model Calibration

Prior to numerical modeling, experimental acoustic measurements were carried out for the case study.

These acoustical parameters suitable for measurements should preferably meet the principles in ISO 3382-1 [12], which implies a sound source that is omnidirectional and parameters derived from the impulse response in the octave band from 125 Hz to 4000 Hz.

The main acoustic parameters were calculated using the impulse response technique [7, 24]: reverberation parameters (such as T30, T20, EDT), energy parameters (C80, D50, Ts) all in the $125 [Hz]$–$4000 [Hz]$ frequency range.

Table 1 reports the average values of the measured acoustic characteristics in the temple, together with the standard deviation of the results across the different microphone locations.

These are needed as references for the calibration of the numerical model.

Usually, the process employed in geometrical acoustics of cultural heritage assets is parallel but not identical to industrial architectural acoustics. Calibrating a numerical model of these assets is more complex given their nature. This technique uses a geometric model to which the absorption coefficients of the respective materials are then applied in order to simulate the acoustic phenomenon with a ray tracing algorithm and obtain the desired data.

Table 1. Results of measurement in the Temple of St. Biagio (in parenthesis, the standard deviation among all the measured values in the different positions is reported.

Frequency (Hz)	125	250	500	1000	2000	4000
T30 [s]	5,71 (0,22)	5,50 (0,20)	5,01 (0,08)	4,07 (0,07)	3,26 (0,04)	2,50 (0,04)
Ts [ms]	388,72 (40,67)	423,14 (36,59)	371,43 (52,37)	287,21 (38,24)	240,08 (29,63)	180,38 (25,67)
EDT	5,45 (0,54)	5,55 (0,28)	4,93 (0,18)	4,03 (0,15)	3,28 (0,14)	2,53 (0,13)
D50	0,19 (0,06)	0,11 (0,05)	0,13 (0,10)	0,20 (0,09)	0,20 (0,09)	0,26 (0,09)
C80	5,20 (1,46)	7,91 (1,60)	7,53 (3,02)	4,95 (2,11)	4,45 (1,75)	2,79 (1,60)

The geometric model was made on the basis of the data obtained from a laser scanner survey, using 3D software.

The construction of a three-dimensional simplified geometrical model of the cathedrals provides the starting point towards reliable computer-aided acoustical simulations [26].

Subsequently, this 3-D model was imported within Odeon Acoustics, where the exact conditions present during the experimental acoustic survey (position of sources and receivers, temperature, and relative humidity) were recreated.

Figure 2 shows the numerical model of the St. Biagio temple.

At this point, the only remaining step to be able to obtain a calibrated model for a true representation of the acoustic phenomenon is to calibrate the absorption coefficients of the materials of which the church is composed. One of the factors that determine the complexity mentioned earlier lies in being able to obtain absorption coefficients that best reflect those of the materials that make up the cultural asset.

The starting values to be used for the material absorption coefficients are taken from standards. To calibrate them, one of the techniques used is to manually alter the values until results from the simulations are as close as possible (i.e., within JND limits) to those obtained in the experimental survey.

This process is usually repeated, which in addition to being inaccurate also makes it time-consuming, both from the point of view of limits imposed by computation time and from the point of view of time spent manually.

Instead, the work presented, as previously said, involves the use of a system of genetic algorithms that do this work autonomously following the directions we impose on them.

2.2 Genetic Material Optimizer

A genetic algorithm (GA) is a metaheuristic solution finding system inspired by natural evolution.

Simulating the process of mutation, recombination, and genetic selection, this type of algorithm is often used to solve problems and optimize solutions under conditions denoted by parameters and variables.

In the specific case, underlying its operation is a genetic representation of the domain of solutions and a "fitness" function to evaluate that domain.

The working flow of a genetic algorithm is shown in Fig. 3 below [17].

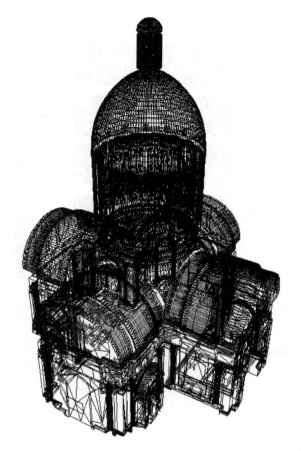

Fig. 2. Numerical model of the St. Biagio temple.

The way it operates can be described in five main steps:

– **Initialisation:** it starts from an initial population of individuals. The population size and the representation of individuals depend on the specific problem being solved;
– **Fitness Function:** the GA performs a process of selection and recombination through a fitness function to produce a second population;
– **Selection:** individuals are selected from the current population to become parents for the next generation based on their fitness. Individuals with higher physical fitness are more likely to be selected, but some form of stochastic selection is also used to maintain diversity in the population;
– **Crossover:** the crossover involves exchanging genetic information between two or more parents to create new solutions. The choice of crossover technique depends on the problem and representation used;

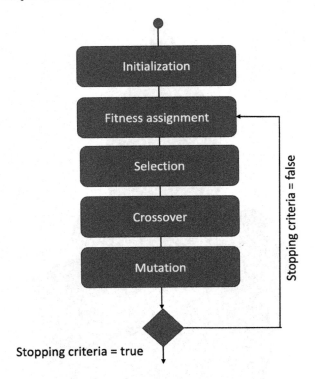

Fig. 3. Working flow of a genetic algorithm.

– **Mutation:** a mutation operator shall be applied to the offspring generated in the crossover phase. The mutation introduces small random changes to the genetic information of the offspring, helping to explore new areas of the research space.

Fitness value gets evaluated on a set of generations, and this can be an expensive process for a certain number of problems using Genetic Algorithms. If a Genetic algorithm is not put to use in the best manner, it may not converge to an optimal solution.

In Odeon's material optimization system, eight GAs work simultaneously and independently, one for each band octave.

The algorithm starts from a random step [23] where all individuals in the populations are generated with an absorption coefficient that varies randomly over a range specific set by the user, creating a starting zero generation. Subsequently, the evolutionary process begins filtering the best individuals by selecting them as parents, which produces individuals "offspring" who inherit some of the advantages previously generated [22].

This process is repeated no until the solutions converge on the basis of the criteria set. The calculation continues until it reaches a solution that minimizes the errors. This solution may not be perfect and unambiguous, but it aims to reduce the error to a minimum.

As already mentioned in the general denotation, this algorithm needs a function called "fitness function," which, in the specific case of Odeon, generates a number that leads the GA to evaluate which are the best candidates, controlling for genetic evolution. In principle, this function could evaluate how much better the simulated pulse responds than those detected and subsequently imported into the program.

However, this would not make the calculation accurate, since neither of the two datasets would have suitable evaluation parameters. The developers, therefore, decided to set acoustic indices as comparison values, setting as minimization criteria for the fitness function the respective subjective limen (ISO 3382 minimums) of the JNDs [5].

As for the specific case of the Temple of St. Blaise, they were initially selected materials from literature. Then, analyzing the results of the first simulations, the respective absorption coefficients were manually modulated, and then calibration by the genetic algorithm was started.

The simulations in the case study use a tuning process, based on an adjustment of the values of the absorption coefficients of the temple structure, so that the simulated average reverberation times differ, on average, by no more than 1 JND (5%) from those measured on-site for each frequency of the octave band.

The following Table 2 reports the main values of the absorption coefficients used in the simulations after the correction described above.

Table 2. Calibrated material's absorption coefficient's list.

	63	125	250	500	1000	2000	4000	8000
Carrara's Marble	0.01	0.01	0.01	0.02	0.03	0.03	0.04	0.05
Wood	0.11	0.11	0.12	0.12	0.12	0.1	0.1	0.1
Travertine	0.05	0.05	0.05	0.05	0.05	0.05	0.03	0.03
North facing door	0.11	0.11	0.12	0.12	0.12	0.1	0.1	0.1
East facing door	1	1	1	1	1	1	1	1
Plaster	0.02	0.03	0.04	0.04	0.06	0.07	0.07	0.09
Pavement	0.018	0.021	0.025	0.028	0.03	0.03	0.036	0.045
Statues	0.01	0.01	0.01	0.02	0.03	0.03	0.04	0.05
Glass	0.42	0.35	0.25	0.18	0.12	0.07	0.04	0.03
Organ	0.24	0.13	0.07	0.03	0.02	0.01	0	0
Plasterboard	0.28	0.28	0.22	0.17	0.09	0.1	0.11	0.11

It is verified that the difference between the value of the simulated and the measured indexes did not exceed the "Just-noticeable differences" limen provided by Bork [2] and Bradley [9].

2.3   Result and Discussion

The results obtained by the software are then compared with the measured data for all source-receiver positions and frequency bands. The relative mean errors to the just noticeable difference (JND) are also computed.

Figure 4 shows a comparison of the spectral behaviour in octave bands of spatially averaged values for the R1, R7, R10, R13, R16 and R24 source posi-

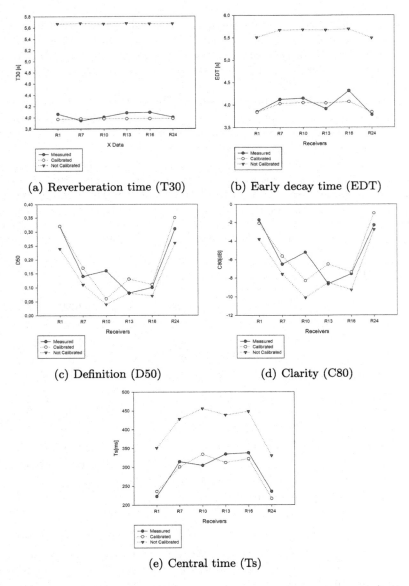

(a) Reverberation time (T30)   (b) Early decay time (EDT)

(c) Definition (D50)   (d) Clarity (C80)

(e) Central time (Ts)

Fig. 4. Simulated and experimental values of the acoustical parameters as functions of the frequency.

tions, of acoustic parameters: measured, calibrated with GA algorithm and not calibrated.

These results indicate that the computational model reliably represents the sound field of the environment, evaluating both the spatial average of each parameter in the different octave bands and the spectral average value calculated at each reception point.

2.4 Legal Protection

Currently, heritage regulatory models suffer from a partial approach to the sound that neglects the multisensory issues related to heritage landscapes and cultural sites or monuments (Art. 2(1 a), Faro Convention, 2005) [13] and the dizzying technological supply on heritage goods enriching the cultural proposals and services.

Assuming the best legal protection for the heritage sound related to sites or landscapes as an objective of Supranational and National Law in the digital era, the protection of the intangible good's digital model could represent an accessible and challenging legislative option.

In this way, the tangible format of the heritage sound could move from the valorization of the digital acoustic representation as cultural good to safeguard because of its strict connection to a specifical monument or architecture.

However, the heritage acoustic tangible format will have to provide some minimum legal standards that are: sound authenticity, integrity, replicability and measurability, in compliance with European General Data Protection Regulation (UE) reg. no. 2016/679) [3].

3 Conclusion

This paper aims to investigate the pros and cons of using such techniques and algorithms in intangible cultural heritage acoustic's preservation and digitization by analyzing its applications and results on case studies. The proposed approach allows to define a forensic process to legally preserve the uniqueness of the acoustic fingerprint of cultural heritage.

Similar to how a fingerprint is unique to an individual, the acoustic fingerprint of a cultural heritage site is distinct and can provide valuable insights into its identity, history, and cultural context.

By examining the acoustic fingerprint of the St. Biagio Temple, the researchers have gained a deeper understanding of the acoustic behaviour associated with the heritage.

The process of capturing the acoustic fingerprint involves using specialized equipment and techniques to measure and record various acoustic parameters such as reverberation time, frequency response, impulse response, and sound transmission characteristics. These measurements help in documenting and preserving the acoustic signature of a heritage site or object.

In order to calibrate numerical models with respect to the experimental measurements, they were used genetics algorithms that allowed to precisely calibrate the absorption coefficients of the building's materials.

The results of the case study, indicate that the computational model reliably represents the sound field of the environment, evaluating both the spatial average of each parameter in the different octave bands and the spectral average value calculated at each reception point.

Acoustic fingerprinting techniques can be employed in a variety of applications related to cultural heritage.

Furthermore, the acoustic fingerprint can contribute to the digitization and virtual representation of cultural heritage.

By accurately capturing and reproducing the acoustic properties of a site or object, virtual environments can provide a more comprehensive and authentic experience for users, enhancing the understanding and appreciation of cultural heritage.

Overall, the study and analysis of the acoustic fingerprint of a cultural heritage site offer valuable insights into its history, and cultural significance, and contribute to its preservation and dissemination in the digital age.

References

1. Acoustics as tangible heritage: Re-embodying the sensory heritage in the boundless reign of sight https://doi.org/10.1515/pdtc-2020-0028
2. Bork, I.: A comparison of room simulation software - the 2nd round robin on room acoustical computer simulation. Acta Acust. United Acust. **86**(6), 943–956 (2000)
3. Regulation 2016/679 - protection of natural persons with regard to the processing of personal data and on the free movement of such data, and repealing directive 95/46/ec (general data protection regulation) (2016). https://www.eumonitor.eu/9353000/1/j4nvk6yhcbpeywk_j9vvik7m1c3gyxp/vk3t7p3lbczq#:~:text=Regulation%20(EU)%202016%2F679%20of%20the%20European%20Parliament%20and,2016%2C%20pp
4. Misure urgenti per la semplificazione e l'innovazione digitale (20g00096) (2020). https://www.normattiva.it/uri-res/N2Ls?urn:nir:stato:decreto.legge:2020-07-16;76~art10-com4
5. A/S, O.: https://odeon.dk/ (DTU Science Park, Diplomvej Bldg 381 DK-2800 Kgs Lyngby, Denmark). https://odeon.dk/downloads/user-manual/
6. Barbuti, N.: From digital cultural heritage to digital culture: evolution in digital humanities. In: Proceedings of the 1st International Conference on Digital Tools & Uses Congress. DTUC 2018, Association for Computing Machinery, New York, NY, USA (2018). https://doi.org/10.1145/3240117.3240142
7. Beranek, L.L.: Acoustics. Society of America through the American Institute of Physics, New York (1993)
8. Bessey, R., Gully, T., Harper, P.: Room acoustics model calibration: a case study with measurements. Can. Acoust. **45**(3), 46–47 (2017). https://jcaa.caa-aca.ca/index.php/jcaa/article/view/3073
9. Bradley, J.S.: Predictors of speech intelligibility in rooms. J. Acoust. Soc. Am. **80**(3), 837–845 (1986). https://doi.org/10.1121/1.393907
10. Brezina, P.: Acoustics of historic spaces as a form of intangible cultural heritage. Antiquity **87**(336), 574–580 (2013). https://doi.org/10.1017/S0003598X00049139
11. Christensen, C.L.: Investigating room acoustics by simulations and measurements. Noise Vib. Worldwide **44**(8), 21–27 (2013). https://doi.org/10.1260/0957-4565.44.8.21

12. Ente Italiano di Normazione: Uni en iso 3382-1:2009 acustica - misurazione dei parametri acustici degli ambienti - parte 1: Sale da spettacolo. Standard, Ente Italiano di Normazione (2009). https://store.uni.com/p/UNINI338201/uni-en-iso-3382-1-2009/UNINI338201

13. Council of Europe Treaty Series: Council of Europe framework convention on the value of cultural heritage for society (2005). https://rm.coe.int/1680083746

14. Foni, A.E., Papagiannakis, G., Magnenat-Thalmann, N.: A taxonomy of visualization strategies for cultural heritage applications. J. Comput. Cult. Herit. **3**(1), 1–21 (2010). https://doi.org/10.1145/1805961.1805962

15. Fırat, H.B.: Acoustics as tangible heritage: re-embodying the sensory heritage in the boundless reign of sight. Preserv. Digit. Technol. Cult. **50**(1), 3–14 (2021). https://doi.org/10.1515/pdtc-2020-0028

16. International standard ISO: Acoustics - measurement of room acoustic parameters - part 2: Reverberation time in ordinary rooms. Standard ISO 3382-2:2008, International Organization for Standardization (2008). https://www.iso.org/standard/36201.html

17. Jain, S.: Introduction to genetic algorithm & their application in data science (Published On July 31, 2017 and Last Modified On June 7th, 2020). https://www.analyticsvidhya.com/blog/2017/07/introduction-to-genetic-algorithm/

18. Koller, D., Frischer, B., Humphreys, G.: Research challenges for digital archives of 3d cultural heritage models. J. Comput. Cult. Herit. **2**(3), 1–7 (2010). https://doi.org/10.1145/1658346.1658347

19. Labia, L., Shtrepi, L., Astolfi, A.: Improved room acoustics quality in meeting rooms: investigation on the optimal configurations of sound-absorptive and sound-diffusive panels. Acoustics **2**(3), 451–473 (2020). https://doi.org/10.3390/acoustics2030025

20. Lenzerini, F.: Intangible cultural heritage: the living culture of peoples. Eur. J. Int. Law **22**(1), 101–120 (2011). https://doi.org/10.1093/ejil/chr006

21. Foirillo, M.: Verso il patrimonio culturale dell'Europa Unita. Rivista AIC **4**, 1–14 (2011). http://www.rivistaaaic.it

22. Marseguerra, M., Zio, E.: Optimizing maintenance and repair policies via a combination of genetic algorithms and monte carlo simulation. Reliab. Eng. Syst. Saf. **68**(1), 69–83 (2000) https://doi.org/10.1016/S0951-8320(00)00007-7, https://www.sciencedirect.com/science/article/pii/S0951832000000077

23. Metropolis, N., Ulam, S.: The Monte Carlo method. J. Am. Stat. Assoc. **44**(247), 335–341 (1949)

24. Spagnolo, R.: Manuale di Acustica Applicata. CittàStudiEdizioni (2008)

25. Ricciutelli, A., Lori, V., Lops, C., Serpilli, F., Montelpare, S.: Churches acoustics as intangible cultural heritage: experimental and numerical characterization of the temple of San Biaggio. Int. J. Architect. Herit. 1–14 (2023). https://doi.org/10.1080/15583058.2023.2214510

26. Savioja, L., Svensson, U.P.: Overview of geometrical room acoustic modeling techniques. J. Acoust. Soc. Am. **138**(2), 708–730 (2015). https://doi.org/10.1121/1.4926438

27. Skublewska-Paszkowska, M., Milosz, M., Powroznik, P., Lukasik, E.: 3d technologies for intangible cultural heritage preservation-literature review for selected databases. Herit. Sci. **10**(1), 3 (2022). https://doi.org/10.1186/s40494-021-00633-x

The Language of the Forensic Structural Engineering

Regina Finocchiaro[1], Samuele Biondi[1(✉)] (iD), and Franco Bontempi[2]

[1] Engineering and Geology Department, "Gabriele d'Annunzio" Università Di Chieti-Pescara,
Viale Pindaro 42, 65127 Pescara, Italy
samuele.biondi@unich.it

[2] Structural and Geotechnical Engineering Department, "Sapienza" Università Di Roma,
Piazzale Aldo Moro 5, 00185 Roma, Italy

Abstract. If a structural problem has to be evaluated, it certainly appears necessary for an Engineer to consider the building, of whatever type, as a hierarchical and organized system. However, in a Legal context, the purely technical description of state of facts, associated with the meticulous application of the theory and the different Codes, does not always help to outline a clear boundary between right and wrong, between safety and failure. This paper will illustrate a part of the legal procedure that substantiates the evaluations of Forensic Engineering, focusing on the relationship between Legal and Court Actors in the common difficulties of the context. Finally, the scope is to introduce the "situational awareness" approach. Analyzing the representation techniques of the real context will allow creating of consolidated lines of communication between different actors. These communication lines, through conceptual diagrams and maps, aim to illustrate a logic that is as universally shareable as possible. It is important to offer to the Court keys to access the Engineer's approach, to transform Engineering Report into a perfectly integrated cog in the Justice machine. When the Engineering technicalities, languages or approaches meet the horizons of social sensitivity and a common vision of the facts is expanded, a union point arises from which logical scheme lines depart in order to obtain correct understanding and right solutions. However, as discussed in a case study, we have to take into account that may not be always possible to obtain this goal.

Keywords: Situational Awareness · Structural Forensic Engineering · Back Analysis · Forward Analysis

1 Introduction

The Technical Consultancy tool is used by the Jurisdiction to understand the technical-scientific contents of a Forensic Engineering event and therefore to permit to the Court be able to express a complete and coherent judgment.

At the basis of any Technical Advice there is an Engineer study which ranges from purely scientific notions to Code frameworks and which allows to frame in a technically and scientifically correct way the causes and effects that the analyzed fact contain; causes

T. Guarda et al. (Eds.): ARTIIS 2023, CCIS 1937, pp. 304–314, 2024.
https://doi.org/10.1007/978-3-031-48930-3_23

and effects are generally the results of a project that led to the realization of a certain structure or infrastructure.

But having a deep and correct knowledge and understanding of project hypotheses is not trivial; above all the problem becomes even more complicated when the full knowledge of design becomes part of a performance analysis process.

The original project, together with the negative event that puts it in the spotlight, becomes the protagonist in a judicial scene with its Actors, a protagonist in the form of a legal evidence. It is important to underline how the legal evidence remains the same in the different legal contexts and how complex it is to manage it for the Engineer, called to "anatomize" and explain conditions subject to a high degree of ambiguity and uncertainty.

We will deal, in Sect. 2, with the topic of Situational Awareness as an instrument that concerns Judges and Engineers figures as decision-makers in complex and dynamic areas on the understanding of a critical situation.

Section 3 shows the normal and conceptual approach to a Structural Design while Sect. 4 explains procedures and roles in the Forensic Case.

Finally Sect. 5 discusses an interesting Structural Forensic Case Study while Sect. 6 concludes the paper showing how a lack of knowledge can compromise the Judicial effort in order to obtain an equilibrate decision.

2 Situational Awareness

It is necessary to lead the Engineer to a "Situational Awareness", i.e. to the perception of the elements within a time and space volume, the understanding of their meaning and to the projection of their state.

Situational awareness is a key principle in managing and understanding events; it is essential to become aware of figures, objects and actions that interact with each other, contextualizing them in terms of place and time.

Let us venture a similarity between the Forensic Engineer's role in an assigned case and a battlefield approach.

It is well known [1] that the United States Army Field Manual defines "Situational Awareness" as "… *knowledge and understanding of the current situation which promotes timely, relevant and accurate assessment of friendly, enemy and other operations within the battlespace in order to facilitate decision making …*" (Fig. 1).

This definition focuses on the operations carried out by any party involved; we can deduce how the measure of a situational awareness, together with the ability of one's knowledge and one's work, is fundamental to best practice the profession, that of the Forensic Expert Engineer in relation to the Judge, in this case.

According to [5] reporting, Situational Awareness refers to a state of understanding in which we intend to predict how it will change with time.

The Homeland Security Act of 2002 [3] on the other hand, defined the Situational Awareness as "… *information gathered from a variety of sources that, when communicated to emergency managers and decision makers, can form the basis for incident management decision-making …*".

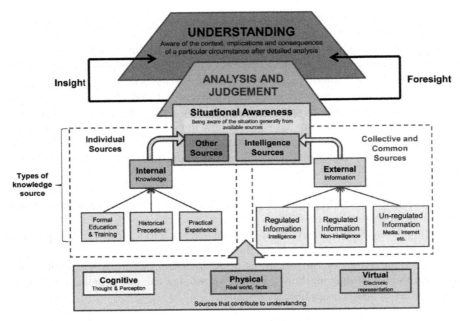

Fig. 1. Overall Situational Awareness Scheme

In this manner it underlined importance of information collecting and final purpose for which it is used, that is to communicate it to "... *decision makers* ...": in case of Forensic Engineering to the Judge, and consequently to the other Parties.

As reported [4], for a GIS software house, Situational Awareness is a "... *human mental process that can be enhanced using technology to access, analyze, and present information to have a greater understanding of existing conditions and how they will change over time* ...". All of this is intended to be carry out [4] in order to integrate a myriad of technologies to provide users with access to information based on their circumstances.

Analyzing these definitions or those discussed both previously in [2] and successively in [6–9], we deduce how Situational Awareness becomes an initial and essential condition for the decision-making process, as shown in Fig. 1.

In a Forensic Engineering context, the notions, intuition and experience of the Engineer are at the service of the Judge.

The scheme shown in Fig. 1 describes as a whole the global composition of Situational Awareness, given by the sum of the various situational awareness, which leads to understanding and finally to analysis and judgment which must be weighted and unambiguous.

Situational Awareness is the full understanding of a given context and, through the knowledge of all the elements and variables that compose and define it (such as actors, data, information) with respect to time or space, the robust insight of changing effects.

Considering the multidisciplinary nature of a Forensic Engineering Case, such as for example the media influence, the Situational Awareness becomes increasingly relevant.

Data and information exchange is a prerequisite for understanding every aspect of the Process. In fact, different actors not only assume different roles but they have different cultural background. The sum of Situational Awareness deriving from different scientific and humanistic studies respectively for Engineers and Judges, leads to an integrated understanding of the contest. It is decisive both for the decision-making and provisional process.

3   The Approach to Structural Design

Temporarily neglecting the external influencing factors, in order to create an initial domain for a case study it is first necessary to determine how a structure has to be described and discussed [14].

These concepts, and their use, have been studied during the professional graduating and training and have been applied during professional activity. But it is essential to establish and to assign them an approach order.

In a survey, having a pen and a block-note, you have to check the various aspects of a structure in an orderly manner. Structure description certainly first considers detailing aspects such as geometric arrangement of various sections, element thicknesses, the global inertia, etc.

In a higher level it is necessary, for example, to indicate how the beam axis is arranged, to indicate structure axis position, to detect the presence or not of unexpected curvatures as well as the presence of defects in substructures (for example braces): i.e., you have to look for more detailed geometric aspects. The detail of all used materials falls within the two levels described above regarding initial decomposition too.

However the most important and relevant aspect, from a logical point of view, is the third i.e. to define a structure is the detection how various components are connected to each other: this allows you to define the real load paths, i.e. you can detect how the load from the application point flows the foundations and, contemporary, stresses structural components.

All of this is particularly sensitive in an existing structure that has suffered a collapse or damage: often connections are only inferable and not yet verifiable.

A coherent and correct scheme and classification of these three levels is the basis of the analysis of an existing structure, as well as any new design of the structure itself. Schematically, the three levels can be defined as follows (Fig. 2).

There is a first Micro-level, which concerns the sizing of the single sections; then we have a slightly more articulated Meso-level, which concerns the optimization in design phase and shape definition of the structure and finally a Macro-level, that concerns part connections in topological terms.

The Fig. 2 depicts just this conceptual hierarchy, which is above the conceptual level and has been managed in this manner by the Engineer.

In the back of a structure, the idea that it is made up of elements organized in a hierarchical form is fundamental. A structure, in general, is understood as a system that needs to be decomposed in order to define its elementary parts.

If this decomposition approach is assumed as fundamental and the concept of hierarchy is considered absolute, it is true that, in certain situations, the collapse of a "small" element, in a "delicate" position, can propagate its effect and cause the overall collapse, especially when the static scheme is not redundant.

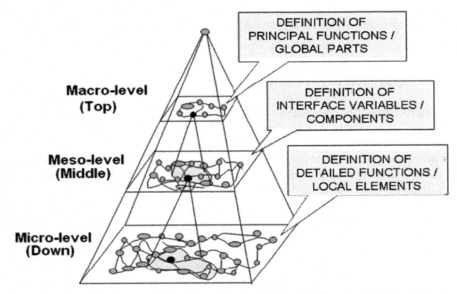

Fig. 2. Structural system: theoretical system decomposition at different analysis levels (macro-meso-micro)

Clearly the collapse of a steel structure due to the failure of a single weald bead is a limiting case not a general case, but it can occur: it is also true that there are particular situations in which small parts of the structure, even secondary or undersigned ones, can significantly affect the structural integrity.

Therefore, it is essential, when analyzing a structure in order to evaluate its safety margins or when designing a new structure, to have clear understanding of the various parts that make up the whole and to manage the decomposition conceptually.

It is necessary to have a perfectly clear understanding of the geometrical position, structural function and the possibility of "failure" for each element, as well as their consequences on the overall structure.

4   Procedures and Roles in Forensic Case

In case of Forensic Engineering, we must not pause on Forward Analysis concepts, which concern pure engineering design, but we have to pay attention to one of Forensic Engineering key procedures: Back Analysis or Reverse Analysis and its time-functional connection, as discussed in [15] and shown in Fig. 3.

Forward Analysis is used to assess if a structure is performing safely as it was intended to, while Back Analysis is carried out to determine the condition that caused the detected failure.

Through Back Analysis or Reverse Analysis, the Engineer searches, with a backwards elaboration, for the criticalities of the failed structure, until he goes back to the design phase, in order to reconstruct the causes of the failure event.

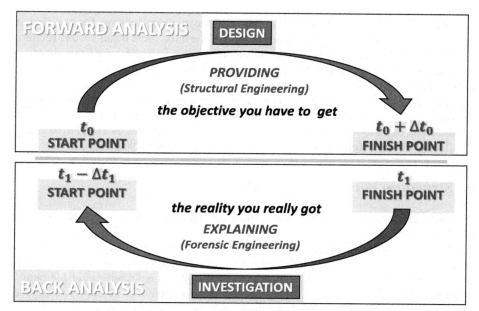

Fig. 3. Time-functional connection of Structural Engineering (Design) and Forensic Engineering (Investigation)

The Engineer thus passes from the usual role of designer, who uses a provisional process for the purpose of a work creation, to the role of investigator, who through the back analysis procedure studies the built object under investigation.

The Back Analysis process, [10, 11], contains both deterministic and probabilistic contents in order of a correct understanding of a failure. It is Engineer choice to select sampling method and type of probabilistic analysis to be used in Analysis. It is deterministic to select mechanical and geometrical model, it is deterministic to select global model input parameters; it is probabilistic to define them as random variables by assigning them with statistical distributions this aim.

It is a mix of deterministic and probabilistic approach to compute: normally a regular deterministic analysis is run at first followed by probabilistic analysis in order to evaluate the fitness of each solution.

Therefore, an initial set of parameters is integrated by different new set of parameters in order to compute the fitness of each solution and to memorize the best solution.

This best solution depends on maximum cycle approach and it permits to define the "real" original set of parameters and, according to failure level and evolution, to define the actual set of parameters of structure under discussion. This set can be used in a

Forward Analysis in order to define both actual Safety Level and repairing strategies in the case of a non-complete structural collapse.

If the Back Analysis is consistent, it is possible that the process of failure is correctly reconstructed by identifying the causal triggers and presenting it in terms of liability to the Judge.

Investigating the failure triggering cause alone without looking for the design intrinsic defects can lead to a misrepresentation of the etiological nexus reconstruction.

The risk is that the investigation itself may turn into a failure for the Court.

This procedure appears to be consolidated and robust, especially in the case of a failure that results in a dramatic collapse.

In the present paper, a reference is made to an apparently simple real case in which the Back Analysis is also a Forward Analysis in the aim to define the initial, un-failed, conditions in order to recreate them. In this context, if the Court needs a legal agreement, a real short circuit is formed which makes the situation unsolvable.

5   Structural Forensic Case Study

A Structural System is a complex system made up of a series of aspects that characterize its identity and nature.

The mandatory effort required to deal with these systems, either singularly or as a sum of parts, not only makes structural design and numerical analysis extremely elaborate, but also, given the increasing difficulty due to the high degree of ambiguity and uncertainty, it could be possible that the knowledge of the Engineer may not be sufficient for the reconstruction process of the initial situations leading to a failure, as discussed in [16–18].

In this regard, this paper discusses a real case that the Authors encountered within the context of a judicial procedure.

Let's imagine we are dealing with a building, simple and built for normal residential use. This building was designed, according to an old Code, disregarding seismic actions. We assume as "initial" t_0 the actual design time, without seismic provisions as at original design and construction time. Now the building site is assumed to be a seismic prone one and, according to local actual Code, building must be seismically adequate since its theoretical capacity, $C(t_0)$, is clearly lower than the theoretical demand, $D(t_0)$.

Practically, both at the Damage Limit State and at Life Safety Limit State, we now have to assume:

$$C(t_0) \ll D(t_0) \tag{1}$$

For these reasons, an assignment for seismic retrofitting was determined by Property and an Engineer was selected. The Engineer carried out the design phase referred to in (2), i.e. starting from a structural situation in no longer acceptable operating and safety conditions, t_0, a complex retrofitting project was carried out which it must lead, in a subsequent time, $t_0+\Delta t_0$, to obtaining an adequate building for new functions and new required safety levels.

$$t_0 \text{ design} \Rightarrow t_0+\Delta t_0 \tag{2}$$

To do this, the Design Engineer performs, as typically required by current Code, the material qualification in actual state, in retrofitting design "initial" state t_0, but obviously, due normally to unrequested design effort and experimental cost, he does not analyze the real response of the structure at this initial state, he does not study experimentally its capacity but defines a theoretical value, $C(t_0)$, because he believes that this must be exceeded by a target capacity $C(t_0+\Delta t_0)^*$ which is the real target of the project.

$$C(t_0+\Delta t_0)^* \geq D(t_0) \gg C(t_0) \tag{3}$$

So it can be imagined that the Design Engineer has an initial limited knowledge level (here named LC according to current Italian Code) of the structure $LC(t_0) = F(LC_m(t_0)) \neq F(LC_m(t_0); LC_s(t_0))$ which is a function of the knowledge of the materials, $LC_m(t_0)$, but which is not a function of the knowledge of the structure itself, $LC_s(t_0)$.

The design process then continues in a well-defined and standardized context: project external validation, public works contract, retrofitting execution by means of partial demolitions and structural elements improvements. But once the works have been partially carried out, a dispute is started between the Contracting Authority and the Contractor Firm: a legal dispute after a work stop ordered by the Contracting Authority. A process has to be carried out at Civil Court in order to quantify the contractual damage. This quantification is not trivial but it is conceptually very difficult to operate from a structural forensic point of view.

At current time, t_1, after contract interruption, the Contracting Authority states that works were carried out inadequately and, above all, with a damage to original structure: structure therefore shows a different, lower, capacity, $C(t_1)$, compared to the initial one, $C(t_0)$, which was also insufficient.

$$C(t_1) \neq C(t_0)$$
$$C(t_1) < C(t_0) < C(t_0+\Delta t_0)^* \geq D(t_0) \gg C(t_0) \tag{4}$$

At this point, a Court-Appointed Engineer is normally selected [12]: he is the Official Technical Consultant (OTC) figure.

The question could appear simple: to evaluate the Contracting Authority economic damage to be charged to Contractor Firm or to define a Judicial Settlement. This appearance could be misleading.

In fact, in the latter case the OTC has, for example, to assess whether the simple removal of incorrect works can really restore the structural asset to its initial condition, without damages, and therefore can close the dispute between the Parties.

The OTC can make an accurate survey of the state of the places, Fig. 4, and he can develop an adequate experimental investigation on the quality of the materials used for the structural improvement. Taking in mind the seismic response at the basis of (1) and (2), he can hypothesize to carry out an adequate investigation on the building through monitoring frequency domain response of the structure.

It can appears as decisive approach to resolve the OTC Court-Appointment.

The frequency domain response of the structure can define the real Capacity in the current state, $C_R(t_1)$, after the poorly performed works.

The real Capacity, $C_R(t_1)$, has to be taken into account in (4) it confirms the hypothesis of the Contracting Authority: $C_R(t_1) < C(t_0+\Delta t_0)^* \geq D(t_0) \gg C(t_0)$.

This confirmation is not the judicial solution. In fact in order to decide on the damage for the Contracting Authority, to impose the right sanction to Contractor Firm or to define Judicial Settlement conditions the real conditions of the structure at the start of the works, $C_R(t_0)$, could be known.

This knowledge is fundamental to propose a procedure for real conditions, $C_R(t_0)$, reconstitution considering fortunately that we are talking about damage and not collapse.

Fig. 4. Laser-scanner image of a building subject to a complex seismic improvement intervention

Shortly, the Judge can ask to the OTC for the activity (5) in terms of knowledge. Above all, he can ask to the OTC to carry out a design which, by removing the works built in an inadequate way (6), can allow the achievement of a new target capacity, considering the damage caused by the works, $C(t_1+\Delta t_1)^*$, which could be equivalent to the one the building had, $C_R(t_0)$, at public works contract subscription.

This new target capacity not necessarily coincides with the theoretical one of the ante-operam state, $C(t_0)$, but has to coincide with the real one of the ante-operam state, $C_R(t_0)$, in order to obtain a correct Judicial Settlement.

$$t_1 \text{ investigation} \Rightarrow t_1 - \Delta t_1 = t_0 + \Delta t_0 \tag{5}$$

$$t_1 \text{ design} \Rightarrow t_1 + \Delta t_1 \tag{6}$$

$$C(t_1+\Delta t_1)^* < C(t_0+\Delta t_0)^* \geq D(t_0) \gg C(t_0)$$
$$\Downarrow \tag{7}$$
$$C(t_1+\Delta t_1)^* = C_R(t_0) \neq C(t_0)$$

In practice, the Judge can imagine conferring the assignment (6) to achieve the objective (7). The goal, $C(t_0)$, could appear smart and simple to be reached.

But due to the above discussed incomplete initial level of knowledge of the structure, $LC(t_0) = F(LC_m(t_0)) \neq F(LC_m(t_0); LC_s(t_0))$, the Judge can obtain at maximum that condition (8) is reached, in which the maximum result is a reasonable approximation of $C(t_1+\Delta t_1)^* \cong C_R(t_0)$.

$$\left\{ \begin{array}{l} C(t_1+\Delta t_1)^* < C(t_0+\Delta t_0)^* \geq D(t_0) \gg C(t_0) \\ LC(t_0) = F(LC_m(t_0)) \neq F(LC_m(t_0); LC_s(t_0)) \end{array} \right\}$$

$$\therefore$$

$$C(t_1+\Delta t_1)^* \cong C_R(t_0) \neq C(t_0)$$

(8)

Can the Judge be satisfied with this outcome; can the Court validate, for example, a Judicial Settlement between the Parties?

Above all the question is: can the Artificial Intelligence solve this problem?

In the Authors opinion, the answer is negative: this judgment is devoted to Forensic Engineer sensitivity, to his experience, to the Therefore Operator, $\therefore$, not to the Certainty.

6 Conclusions

According to a simple case study, it can be seen that in certain, current, circumstances the Situational Awareness, in order to be correctly approached discussed in [13], must accept the unattainability of some requests. The Judge has to accept a complete level of clarity unattainable, regardless of the contribution of the Forensic Engineer.

In fact, in the case study above discussed, there is a difficulty in understanding the project phases but above all, there is possible to detect the unawareness of the impossibility of bringing a case back to its initial conditions.

This unawareness is for the person, the Judge, who has to take the decision. This because, legitimately and according to state-of-practice, the actual initial conditions have not been defined preliminarily.

The Judge's request becomes what lawyers identify with the Latin expression "probatio diabolica" (i.e. "devil's proof" or "diabolical proof"). It is a legal requirement to achieve an impossible proof, understood as the impossibility of demonstrating that Devil exists.

Although, therefore, the request to know the real situation, and not the theoretical one, at zero time is extremely legitimate, it could be impossible to reach.

If a system is managed, if a reality is changed, if an incomplete knowledge is at disposal, we have to state the impossibility of reproducing the initial conditions: this also in the apparently less complex case of a damaged and non-collapsed structure.

Acknowledgements. Eng. Regina Finocchiaro thanks both Law Department (Prof. F. Auletta) of University "Federico II" of Naples (Lead Partner) and Legal and Social Sciences Department (Prof. R. Martino) of University "G. d'Annunzio" of Chieti-Pescara (Consortium headquarters) for the support in "Organizational Models and Digital Innovation: the New Office for the System Efficiency Process – Justice (MOD-UPP)". This Project – PON Governance and Institutional Capacity 2014- 2020 (Axis I, Specific Objective 1.4, Action 1.4.1) – deals with the "Unitary project on the diffusion of the Process Office and for the implementation of innovative operating models in the judicial offices for the disposal of the backlog".

References

1. Flashpoint Homepage: https://flashpoint.io/. Last accessed 28 June 2023
2. Mica, R.E., Daniel, J. G. (ed.) Situation Awareness Analysis and Measurement, 1th edn. CRC Press (2000). ISBN 9780805821345
3. United States Congress: Homeland Security Act of 2002. 107th Congress. Section 515 (6 U.S.C. 321d(b)(1)) (2002). http://www.dhs.gov/xlibrary/assets/hr_5005_enr.pdf
4. ESRI: Public Safety and Homeland Security Situational Awareness. ESRI. February 2008: http://www.esri.com/library/whitepapers/pdfs/situational-awareness.pdf (2008)
5. Virtual Social Media Working Group and DHS First Responder Group: Using Social Media for Enhanced Situational Awareness and Decision Support. Department of Homeland Security, United States Government. https://www.dhs.gov/publications (2014)
6. Lovering, T.: Odin's ravens from situational awareness to understanding, The Three Swords Mag. **27**, 50–52 (2014). https://www.jwc.nato.int/images/stories/threeswords/6525_JWC_Magazine_November_2014_ORIG_singles.pdf
7. Appling, S., et al.: Social media for situational awareness: joint-interagency field experimentation. Procedia Eng. **107**, 319–324 (2015)
8. Snyder, L.S., Karimzadeh, M., Stober, C., Ebert, D.S.: Situational awareness enhanced through social media analytics: a survey of first responders. In: 2019 IEEE International Symposium on Technologies for Homeland Security (HST), pp. 1–8 (2019). Woburn, MA, USA. https://doi.org/10.1109/HST47167.2019.9033003
9. Department of Army, Headquarters: TC 3-22.69 Advanced Situational Awareness: April 2021 (2021). https://armypubs.army.mil/epubs/DR_pubs/DR_a/ARN34875-TC_3-22.69-000-WEB-1.pdf
10. Zhu, C., Zhao, H., Zhao, M.: Back analysis of geomechanical parameters in underground engineering using artificial bee colony. Sci. World J. **2014**, 1–13 (2014). https://doi.org/10.1155/2014/693812
11. Mandal, J., Narwal, S., Gupte, S.S.: Back analysis of failed slopes – a case study. Int. J. Eng. Res. Technol. **6**(05), 1070–1078 (2017)
12. Office of the Executive Secretary, Supreme Court of Virginia Homepage. https://www.vacourts.gov/. Last accessed 28 June 2023
13. Stella, F.: Leggi scientifiche e spiegazione causale nel diritto penale. Giuffrè Editore (2000). in Italian
14. Bontempi, F.: Ingegneria forense strutturale. Basi del progetto e ricostruzione dei collassi. IF CRASC'15, III Convegno di Ingegneria Forense, IV Convegno su crolli, Affidabilità strutturale, Consolidamento, Sapienza Università di Roma, 14–16 Maggio (2015). In Italian
15. Bontempi, F.: Ingegneria forense in campo strutturale. Concetti, metodi, strumenti. Dario Flaccovio Editore (2017). in Italian
16. Mistretta, P. S.: Ingegneria Forense: procedure, metodi e guida pratica per l'espletamento dei più frequenti incarichi in ambito civile e penale. Dario Flaccovio Editore (2020). in Italian
17. Augenti, N.: Ingegneria Forense: Indagini sui crolli e grandi dissesti. Hoepli (2021). in Italian
18. D'Orazio, M., Zampini, G., Maracchini, G.: Ingegneria forense per le costruzioni. Maggioli Editore (2022). in Italian

International Symposium
on Technological Innovations
for Industry and Society (ISTIIS 2023)

Coffee Silverskin: Unveiling a Versatile Agri-Food By-Product for Ethical Textile Coatings

Agata Nolasco[1]($\boxtimes$) ⓘ, Francesco Esposito[2], Teresa Cirillo[1], Augusta Silva[3]($\boxtimes$) ⓘ, and Carla Silva[3]($\boxtimes$) ⓘ

[1] Department of Agricultural Sciences, University of Naples "Federico II", Via Università 100, 80055 Portici, Naples, Italy
agata.nolasco@unina.it
[2] Department of Public Health, University of Naples "Federico II", Via Sergio Pansini, 5, 80131 Naples, Italy
[3] CITEVE, Centro Tecnológico das Indústrias Têxtil E Do Vestuário, R. Fernando Mesquita 2785, 4760-034 Vila Nova de Famalicão, Portugal
{asilva,cjsilva}@citeve.pt

Abstract. In response to the growing focus on sustainability and ethical practices, there is an increasing interest in developing sustainable coated textiles with agri-food by-products as alternatives to traditional animal leather. This transition not only addresses ethical concerns but also contributes to waste reduction within the agri-food industry, fostering a more circular and sustainable approach. The coffee silverskin (CS), a by-product of the coffee processing industry, is gaining significant attention for its potential in sustainable resource optimization and value creation. This study explores the versatility of coffee silverskin as a sustainable coating material for textiles. The innovative exploration of CS as a bio-based coating material involves different residue treatment procedures and formulations to assess its suitability for coatings. The use of planetary ball milling as a pretreatment method has resulted in a homogeneous deconstruction of the integument, yielding a uniform and soft coating. In conclusion, this study represents a significant step towards sustainable coated textiles as an ethical alternative to animal leather. By harnessing the potential of coffee silverskin, the textile industry can contribute to a more sustainable and responsible future.

Keywords: Coffee Silverskin · Sustainable textiles · Bio-based coatings · Circular economy · Alternative Leather

1 Introduction

In recent years, the growing focus on sustainability and ethical practices has led to an increased interest in (re)utilizing nature residues and developing sustainable coated textiles with food by-products as viable alternatives to the use of animal skin. This shift reflects a collective commitment to reducing environmental impact and promoting responsible sourcing within the textile industry.

T. Guarda et al. (Eds.): ARTIIS 2023, CCIS 1937, pp. 317–327, 2024.
https://doi.org/10.1007/978-3-031-48930-3_24

The leather industry holds a long-standing history as a traditional manufacturing sector, and its products rank among the most globally traded commodities [1]. Leather is considered a bio-based and biodegradable material since its production relies on utilizing by-products of the food industry, specifically derived from meat processing [2]. However, it is important to note that certain leather varieties are sourced from more exotic animals such as alligators, snakes, and sharks, known for their unique patterns, naturally occurring marks, and distinctive structures [3, 4]. For this reason, the leather industry has given rise to significant ethical concerns surrounding animal rights and welfare, as well as posing challenges in terms of environmental pollution. The production of leather entails the intricate processing of raw animal skin and hides through a tanning process, necessitating the use of diverse chemicals, such as sodium chloride, ammonium chloride, sulphate, and chromium [5]. Unfortunately, this tanning procedure generates solid, liquid, and gaseous waste, along with the emission of toxic chemicals, leading to significant environmental repercussions [6]. Moreover, these processes expose workers in tanneries to potential health risks associated with carcinogenic compounds [5].

As the industry continues to evolve, there is an increasing focus on sustainable and ethical alternatives to conventional leather. The utilization of agri-industry residues and food by-products presents a promising solution to address these challenges. These valuable by-products can be effectively repurposed, either as natural dyes [7] or transformed into bio-based materials suitable for the textile industry [8]. By embracing bio-based coatings as alternatives to traditional leather, which are cruelty-free and animal-friendly, the textile industry can proactively address ethical concerns and provide consumers with more ethical choices. Additionally, this transition contributes to the reduction of waste generated in the agri-food industry, fostering a more sustainable and circular approach [9]. Each year, within the European Union (EU), the food and forestry-based industries collectively produce approximately 900 million tonnes of waste [10]. Instead of discarding these residues as waste, they can be repurposed to create added value across various applications [11, 12]. In specific, the utilization of bio-based coatings fosters innovation and versatility in the textile industry. These coatings offer flexibility in terms of application methods, customization, and the incorporation of functional properties [13]. This versatility allows for the development of diverse textile products with improved performance characteristics, unique aesthetics, and enhanced functionality [8].

The agri-food by-products derived from the coffee production chain are currently gathering significant attention and success. This can be attributed to the prominence of coffee as one of the most crucial and commercially valuable chains globally [14]. The valorization of these by-products exemplify a prime opportunity within the agri-food industry for sustainable resource optimization and value creation. The coffee production generates significant by-products, involves different countries and includes several process steps before obtaining the final well-known beverage. Two major categories of coffee by-products can be distinguished. The pre-roasting by-products, such as skin, pulp, husks, mucilage and parchment, generated in producing countries and the post-roasting by-products, coffee silverskin and spent coffee grounds, which have a broader distribution [15, 16]. However, through the process of valorization, these by-products can be transformed into valuable commodities, presenting a range of potential applications and benefits [17, 18]. This study, aligned with the circular economy principles, is focused on the exploration of the versability of the coffee silverskin (CS) as a sustainable material for coating textiles. This by-product is the integument, a thin protective layer, that covers the two hemispheres of the green coffee beans and is detached from them due to the high temperature of the roasting process.

2 Materials and Methods

This study aimed to explore the versatility of coffee silverskin as a sustainable material for developing coated textiles, providing eco-friendly alternatives to natural leather. Different approaches were adopted for each case, and the methodologies used are described below.

2.1 Sample and Materials

The coffee silverskin (CS) utilized in this study was generously supplied by two coffee industries located in the Campania region of Italy. It was obtained through a blending process involving roasted green beans of *Coffea arabica* and *Coffea robusta* (in unspecified ratio). It is common practice for coffee companies to blend different varieties during the roasting process to obtain different aromas and the resulting CS is collected through suction cyclones [19]. Different coating pastes were prepared mixing the CS residue with commercial products Impranil ECO DLS and Imprafix 2794 from Covestro (Germany), Rolflex Bio OP 90 from Lamberti (Italy) and Tubicoat Verdicker LP from CHT (Germany), that were generously supplied.

2.2 Residue Pre-treatments

Prior to processing, the coffee silverskin sample was initially ground to a particle size of 0.2 mm using the Retsch SM 300 cutting mill (Retsch GmbH, Haan, Germany). Following this phase, the ground coffee silverskin (CS) underwent two different routes. One path involved its immediate use for the coating formulation (1), as described below. Meanwhile, the other path involved an additional pre-treatment phase utilizing ball milling to further reduce its particle size. To facilitate understanding the various steps, from the treatment of the CS residue to the final evaluations of the obtained coatings, these have been outlined in Fig. 1.

Coating Formulation (1). The coating paste was formulated by mixing 8% of the ground CS with Impranil ECO DLS as the polymer base, and Imprafix 2794 as the crosslinker. Tubicoat Verdicker LP was gradually added until a good viscosity of the paste was achieved (~8 Pa.s).

Ball Milling Treatment. The CS sample, previously ground with the cutting mill equipment, was subjected to a further processing using a Retsch PM100 planetary ball milling (BM) system (Retsch GmbH, Haan, Germany) under wet conditions. The milling process was performed using a 125 mL zirconia milling cup and 5 mm zirconia spheres. The BM treatment lasted for 2 h at 400 rpm. A mixture of ground coffee silverskin and distilled water was used in a ratio of 1:7. After the BM treatment, a sludge-like consistency was obtained as a result. Utilizing this residue, the coating formulations (2) and (3) were developed.

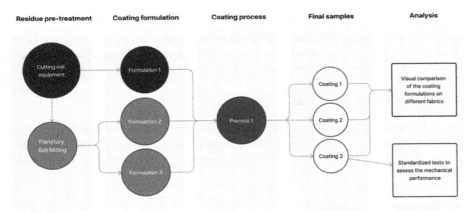

Fig. 1. Flow diagram of the steps carried out for the realization of the coatings with coffee silverskin.

Coating Formulation (2). The coating paste was formulated by mixing an amount of 60% of the sludge-CS (8% CS solid content) obtained after the BM treatment with Impranil ECO DLS and Imprafix 2794. Tubicoat Verdicker LP was incrementally incorporated to achieve an optimal texture and workability of the paste.

Coating Formulation (3). Another coating paste was formulated by mixing 60% of the sludge-CS with Impranil ECO DLS and Imprafix 2794.

Coating Process. The coating formulations eq. (1), (2), and (3) were applied following the specified process. Cotton and elastane (97:3) fabrics were used as textile substrates for the coatings. The textile substrate was coated using a knife coating process, with the application of three layers of the coating formulations. The first layer had a thickness of < 0.01 mm, while the next two layers had a thickness of 0.1 mm. Each layer was dried at 100 °C for 5 min. Following the application of all layers, the substrate was subjected to thermofixation at 150 °C for 5 min. In some coating samples, a thin layer (<0.01 mm) of Rolflex Bio OP 90 topcoat was applied. This inclusion aimed to enhance the mechanical properties of the coating while also evaluating its influence on the final aesthetic appearance of the coated substrate.

2.3 Visual Comparison of Different Coffee Silverskin Coatings

The different coatings obtained were intended for a visual evaluation of their final aesthetic appearance. The primary objective of this experimental phase was to examine how different residue pre-treatment and coating paste formulations could impact the colour and overall aesthetic appeal of the resulting coatings. By conducting this test, valuable insights were obtained concerning the visual characteristics and overall attractiveness of the coated substrates.

2.4 Evaluation of Coated Substrates

The coatings derived from formulation eq. (3) underwent a comprehensive characterization to evaluate their appropriateness for the intended final application. Prior to the assessment, these coatings were subjected to a calendering process at a temperature of 140 °C and a pressure of 5 bar for 30 s. This treatment aimed to further enhance their properties and ensure their suitability for practical usage. To assess the performance of the developed solutions, a series of standardized tests were conducted. These included colour fastness to artificial light: Xenon arc fading lamp test (ISO 105-B02:2014), Martindale Abrasion Resistance (ISO 5470-2:2003), determination of resistance to damage by flexing (De Mattia method and Crumple/Flex) (ISO 7854:1995), colour fastness to water (ISO 105-E01:2013), and colour fastness to rubbing in dry and wet conditions (ISO 105-X12:2016).

3 Results

3.1 Visual Comparison of Different Coffee Silverskin Coatings

Multiple coatings utilizing coffee silverskin were prepared using various residue treatments and formulations. The primary objective of these coatings was to assess their final visual appearance, as it plays a crucial role in influencing customer perception and preferences.

The outcome of the coatings varied significantly depending on the pre-treatment of the residue and the formulation used for the coating paste, as showed in the Figs. 2, 3 and 4. The coating shown in Fig. 2, was obtained with the residue without the initial pre-treatment with the Ball milling, following the application of formulation eq. (1). Traces of aggregate granules are visibly present on the surface, which not only impacts the visual appearance of the coating but also affects its texture and feel. The addition of the Rolflex Bio OP 90 topcoat layer has enhanced the texture by providing a slightly matte finish, although it still retains a rough feel. The coating was applied to a cotton and elastane textile substrate (97:3) but considering its particular texture, the coating may be less suitable for garments due to its rough surface.

To address the issue of granules on the coating surface, an additional pre-treatment step was introduced, involving the use of planetary ball milling in wet conditions. The ball milling provides a highly efficient and effective method for size reduction of materials, resulting in the production of smaller particles [20]. One of the key advantages of this process lies in the tumbling motion of the balls inside the milling equipment, which promotes efficient mixing of materials. This dynamic mixing action ensures enhanced homogeneity and uniform distribution of components within the final product. Furthermore, the choice of wet treatment conditions utilizing water as a solvent exerts a significant impact on the morphological and structural modifications achieved through ball milling [21]. Formulations eq. (2) and (3) of the coating paste were prepared using CS-sludge obtained from the treatment with the planetary ball milling. To maintain an equivalent effective CS solid content as formulation (1), which contained 8% silverskin, 60% CS-sludge was utilized. This CS-sludge proportion allowed to a significant decrease in the total amount of other polymer additives required.

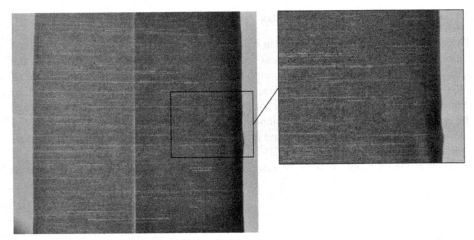

Fig. 2. Coating made with coffee silverskin, following the application of formulation 1 on a cotton and elastane (97:3) textile substrate. A zoomed-in view has been provided. In half of the coating sample (left side) a layer of a topcoat was applied.

Based on these results, two distinct formulations were developed. The application of the paste obtained from the formulation eq. (2) resulted in an excellent coating with a soft and pleasant texture, showcasing a vivid and uniform dark brown colour with a homogenous layer (Fig. 3). Furthermore, the addition of the topcoat enhanced the coating's texture, giving it a velvety and slightly opaque appearance. The coating exhibited remarkable effectiveness, establishing its potential as a compelling alternative to animal skin, particularly owing to its intense colour.

Fig. 3. Coating made with coffee silverskin, following the application of formulation 2 on a cotton and elastane (97:3) textile substrate. A zoomed-in view has been provided. In half of the coating sample (left side) a layer of topcoat was applied.

The primary goal of the third formulation eq. (3) was to maximize the economic and environmental sustainability of the coating by reducing the number of polymers used. This formulation exclusively utilized water-based polymers. The resulting coating (Fig. 4) demonstrated outstanding outcomes in terms of texture and visual appeal. The colour of the coating appeared as a lighter brown, reminiscent of the natural appearance of animal skin, offering a visually appealing alternative. The coating exhibits a consistent and soft texture to the touch, while visually displaying unique variations due to the inherent natural colour of the coffee silverskin, rendering each coating distinct and unique. It is evident from this outcome that the polymers incorporated in formulation eq. (2) enhance the colours, imparting vividness and brilliance to the coatings. Similarly, the application of the topcoat layer on the coating surface resulted in a smoother finish, further enhancing its soft and velvety touch.

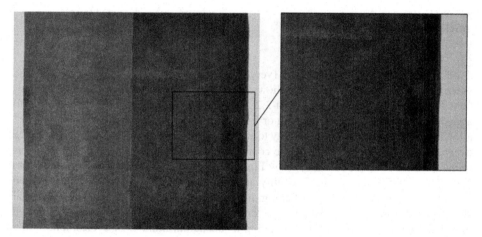

Fig. 4. Coating made with coffee silverskin, following the application of formulation eq. 3 on a cotton and elastane (97:3) textile substrate. A zoomed-in view has been provided. In half of the coating sample (left side) a layer of topcoat was applied

3.2 Evaluation of Coated Substrates

In light of the remarkable outcomes achieved by this latter sustainable formulation, a comprehensive series of standardized tests (Sect. 2.4 of Materials and Methods) was performed. By conducting these standardized tests, the mechanical properties, durability, and colourfastness of the coated substrates can be evaluated, providing valuable information to ensure their suitability for practical applications. The corresponding results are presented in Table 1.

The Colour Fastness to Artificial Light (ISO 105-B02:2014) evaluates the resistance of the coating to fading or discoloration when exposed to simulated sunlight using a Xenon arc fading lamp. It helps determine the coatings' colour stability and durability under prolonged exposure to light. The European scale consists of 8 strips of blue

Table 1. Results of standardized tests on coffee silverskin coating (formulation 3)

Standardized Tests		Values
Colour Fastness to Artificial Light (ISO 105-B02:2014)		1–2 – Low fastness
Martindale Abrasion Resistance (ISO 5470–2:2003)		3 – Moderate alteration
Determination of Resistance to Damage by Flexing (ISO 7854:1995)	De Mattia method	0 - No alteration
	Crumple/Flex method	1 – Slight alteration
Colour Fastness to Rubbing (ISO 105-X12:2016)	Dry conditions	4–5 – High fastness
	Wet conditions	2–3 - Moderate alteration
Colour Fastness to Water (ISO 105-E01:2013)		4 – Good fastness

dyed wool fabric, numbered from 1 (very low fastness) to 8 (very high fastness). The values obtained from this analysis show a low fastness to artificial light. The Martindale Abrasion Resistance (ISO 5470-2:2003) assesses the resistance of the coating to abrasion and wear caused by rubbing or friction. It simulates everyday usage scenarios, allowing to gauge the coatings' ability to withstand wear and maintain their appearance over time. The result obtained on the coating showed moderate alterations. The determination of Resistance to Damage by Flexing (De Mattia method and Crumple/Flex) (ISO 7854:1995) evaluate the flexibility and resistance of the coating to damage when subjected to repeated bending or flexing. It helps assess its ability to endure mechanical stress without cracking or losing integrity. In both methods, the tested coating exhibited minimal alterations, even after undergoing a substantial number of cycles, amounting to 150,000 and 9,000 for the De Mattia and Crumble/Flex method, respectively. These results indicate significant flexural strength. Colour Fastness to Rubbing in Dry and Wet Conditions (ISO 105-X12:2016) test evaluate the colour fastness of the coating when rubbed against different materials. The test was assessed in dry and wet conditions. It helps assess how the coatings hold up against friction, which is essential for maintaining their appearance and performance during everyday use. The strength ratings, based on the Grey Scale for staining, vary from 1 (poor rating) to 5 (better rating). Results from this test demonstrate that the coating exhibits excellent colour fastness under dry conditions, with ratings of 4–5. However, when the sample is exposed to wet conditions, more noticeable changes in colour are observed. The Colour Fastness to Water (ISO 105-E01:2013) measures the ability of the coating to resist colour change or bleeding when exposed to water. A multifibre fabric is used to assess colour transfer and the change in colour of the coating is assessed using the Grey Scale. From the test conducted, the coating exhibits a good fastness to water.

These results are essential for manufacturers and designers to ensure that the textiles meet the specific performance requirements. Additionally, the test results can be used to compare different textile materials and make informed decisions during the product development process. It is important to highlight that the subsequent analyses were conducted on the coating without the topcoat layer. Incorporating an additional protective layer could significantly enhance the coating's performance, particularly in terms of resistance to abrasion and colour fastness to rubbing. This improvement would provide added durability and stability to the coating, making it more suitable for demanding applications.

4 Discussion

Coffee silverskin has gathered significant attention due to its promising potential for reuse in various sectors. Its nutritional and chemical composition has piqued the interest of the food and nutraceutical industries [22, 23]. Furthermore, the morphological and structural characteristics of the integument have demonstrated promising potential in developing innovative packaging solutions [24]. From a technological perspective, coffee silverskin has emerged as one of the most promising by-products within the coffee industry [16]. This is primarily attributed to its exceptionally low moisture content (~7–10%) and a relatively high protein content (~18–20%), which can serve as plasticizers or offer opportunities for enhanced interfacial adhesion with polar polymer matrices due to the presence of functional groups [16, 25]. In a preliminary study on the characterization of coffee silverskin [26], Scanning Electron Microscopy (SEM) analysis revealed a compact and wrinkled surface, indicating that the fibrous structure of cellulose is surrounded by a matrix of less structured components like hemicellulose/lignin. At higher magnification, near-spherical particles ranging from approximately 0.5 to 5 μm were observed on the integument's surface, potentially attributed to the lignin and/or protein fraction. By utilizing planetary ball milling, the coffee silverskin's structural integrity was effectively altered, promoting a more uniform and consistent coating. Furthermore, the mechanical treatment may have introduced modifications to the integument's composition, enhancing its ability to form strong bonds with polar polymer matrices due to the presence of functional groups within its protein content [27]. This unique combination of uniformity and enhanced adhesion potential opens exciting possibilities for its application in sustainable and innovative coated textile solutions. Furthermore, the conducted standardized tests revealed interesting results concerning the coating's resistance to bending, breakage, and colour stability under diverse stress conditions. These results indicate the potential of the coating to withstand various mechanical and environmental challenges, making it a promising candidate for practical applications.

5 Conclusion

Developing sustainable coated textiles with food by-products aligns with the principles of environmental conservation and resource efficiency. By minimizing the use of animal skin and opting for bio-based coatings, the industry can reduce its reliance on resource-intensive processes associated with traditional leather production. While a complete replacement of leather with bio-based coatings may not be feasible for all applications or preferences, their utilization represents a significant stride towards a more sustainable, ethical, and environmentally conscious textile industry. This study focuses its investigation on the coffee roasting by-product, aiming to assess its viability as a coating material, its mechanical properties, and its resistance against various stress conditions through standardized tests. The novelty of this research lies in exploring an untested waste material within the textile industry. Additionally, the utilization of ball milling as a pre-treatment step emerges as a valuable tool to achieve a more uniform coating, allowing the formulation of a coating paste with a smaller amount of polymers. The results conducted on the coffee silverskin coating indicate suitable mechanical durability but limited colour fastness when subjected to light exposure. Further studies will be undertaken to enhance the coating's potential, while preserving its visual appearance and tactile qualities. This study paves the way for interesting research into the reuse of unexplored waste materials from the food chain and the promotion of innovative and sustainable approaches to textile production.

Acknowledgement. The authors acknowledge the financial support from integrated project be@t – Textile Bioeconomy (TC-C12-i01, Sustainable Bioeconomy No. 02/C12-i01/202), promoted by the Recovery and Resilience Plan (RRP), Next Generation EU, for the period 2021–2026.

References

1. Meyer, M., Dietrich, S., Schulz, H., Mondschein, A.: Comparison of the technical performance of leather, artificial leather, and trendy alternatives. Coatings **11**(2), 226 (2021)
2. Ozgunay, H., Colak, S., Mutlu, M.M., Akyuz, F.: Characterization of leather industry wastes. Polish J. Env. Stud. **16**(6), 867–873 (2007)
3. Demeroukas, M., Ritchie, F.: Skin and leather. Basic Condition Reporting: A Handbook, 111. 4rt edn. Rowman & Littlefield (2015)
4. Wainaina, P.N., Ongarora, B., Tanui, P.: Manufacture of exotic leather and small leather goods from ovine stomach. Skin **30**, 6 (2022)
5. Hashmi, G.J., Dastageer, G., Sajid, M.S., Ali, Z., Malik, M.F., Liaqat, I.: Leather industry and environment: Pakistan scenario. Int. J. Appl. Biol. Forensics **1**(2), 20–25 (2017)
6. Sivaram, N.M., Barik, D.: Toxic waste from leather industries. In: Energy from toxic organic waste for heat and power generation, pp. 55–67. Woodhead Publishing (2019)
7. İşmal, Ö.E.: Greener natural dyeing pathway using a by-product of olive oil; prina and biomordants. Fibers Polym. **18**(4), 773–785 (2017)
8. Zhang, C., et al.: From plant phenols to novel bio-based polymers. Prog. Polym. Sci. **125**, 101473 (2022)
9. Gavahian, M., Mathad, G.N., Pandiselvam, R., Lin, J., Sun, D.W.: Emerging technologies to obtain pectin from food processing by-products: a strategy for enhancing resource efficiency. Trends Food Sci. Technol. **115**, 42–54 (2021)
10. Coelho, L., et al.: Innovation of textiles through natural by-products and wastes. Waste Text. Leather Sect. (2020)
11. Alexandri, M., Maina, S., Tsouko, E., Papapostolou, H., Koutinas, A., Kourmentza, K.: Valorization of fruit processing by-product streams into integrated biorefinery concepts: extraction of value-added compounds and bioconversion to chemicals. In: Valorization of Agri-Food Wastes and By-Products, pp. 927–945. Elsevier (2021)

12. Difonzo, G., Grassi, S., Paciulli, M.: Upcycling of agro-food chain by-products to obtain high-value-added foods. Foods **11**(14), 2043 (2022)
13. Silva, A., Vilaça, H., Antunes, J., Rocha, A., Silva, C.: Textile bio-based and bioactive coatings using vegetal waste and by-products. Base Diseño e Innovación **7**(7), 57–70 (2022)
14. Barreto Peixoto, J.A., Silva, J.F., Oliveira, M.B.P., Alves, R.C.: Sustainability issues along the coffee chain: from the field to the cup. Comp. Rev. Food Sci. Food Safe. **22**(1), 287–332 (2023)
15. Castillo, M., Fernández-Gómez, B., Martínez Sáez, N., Iriondo-DeHond, A., Mesa, M.D.: Coffee by-products (2019)
16. Hejna, A.: Potential applications of by-products from the coffee industry in polymer technology–Current state and perspectives. Waste Manage. **121**, 296–330 (2021)
17. Hoseini, M., Cocco, S., Casucci, C., Cardelli, V., Corti, G.: Coffee by-products derived resources. A review. Biomass Bioenergy **148**, 106009 (2021)
18. Durán-Aranguren, D.D., Robledo, S., Gomez-Restrepo, E., Arboleda Valencia, J.W., Tarazona, N.A.: Scientometric overview of coffee by-products and their applications. Molecules **26**(24), 7605 (2021)
19. Lachenmeier, D.W., et al.: Coffee by products as sustainable novel foods: report of the 2nd international electronic conference on foods—"future foods and food technologies for a sustainable world". Foods **11**, 3 (2022)
20. Zhang, J., Bai, Y., Dong, H., Wu, Q., Ye, X.: Influence of ball size distribution on grinding effect in horizontal planetary ball mill. Adv. Powder Technol. **25**(3), 983–990 (2014)
21. Avolio, R., Bonadies, I., Capitani, D., Errico, M.E., Gentile, G., Avella, M.A.: Multitechnique approach to assess the effect of ball milling on cellulose. Carbohyd. Polym. **87**(1), 265–273 (2012)
22. Nzekoue, F.K., et al.: Coffee silverskin: characterization of B-vitamins, macronutrients, minerals and phytosterols. Food Chem. **372**, 131188 (2022)
23. Machado, M., et al.: Bioactive potential and chemical composition of coffee by-products: from pulp to silverskin. Foods **12**(12), 2354 (2023)
24. Garcia, C.V., Kim, Y.T.: Spent coffee grounds and coffee silverskin as potential materials for packaging: a review. J. Polym. Environ. **29**, 2372–2384 (2021)
25. Toschi, T.G., Cardenia, V., Bonaga, G., Mandrioli, M., Rodriguez-Estrada, M.T.: Coffee silverskin: characterization, possible uses, and safety aspects. J. Agric. Food Chem. **62**(44), 10836–10844 (2014)
26. Nolasco, A., et al.: Valorization of coffee industry wastes: Comprehensive physicochemical characterization of coffee silverskin and multipurpose recycling applications. J. Cleaner Product. **370**, 133520 (2022)
27. Hejna, A., Barczewski, M., Kosmela, P., Mysiukiewicz, O., Kuzmin, A.: Coffee silverskin as a multifunctional waste filler for high-density polyethylene green composites. J. Compos. Sci. **5**(2), 44 (2021)

Towards a Modular IOT Simulation System for Industry

Tiago Coelho[1], Ricardo Rodrigues[2], Rita Miranda[2], and Filipe Portela[1,2(✉)]

[1] University of Minho, Guimarães, Portugal
cfp@dsi.uminho.pt
[2] IOTECH – Innovation on Technology, Trofa, Portugal

Abstract. In this article, there is approached the simulation of Industry 4.0 environments, being used as an example, the textile industry. There will be explained the concept of simulating Industry 4.0 factory floors, approaching many topics such as the benefits of this solution, how it can be used in every industry sector, and most importantly the work and research that has been done around the subject area. The textile industry will be used as an example and, therefore, there will be explained later in the document more specific details regarding the appliance of the solution to the industry sector that is being approached. This explanation will include the required materials for the development of a prototype, as well as the used methods and expected results. In terms of results, this study created a scalable architecture and three data models that can config and store the simulation data.

Keywords: Internet of Things · Cyber-physical systems · Industry 4.0 · Textile Industry · Cloud Computing

1 Introduction

Nowadays, more and more industrial businesses have been joining the Industry 4.0 paradigm and therefore, the way that work is done is being transformed. With this transformation, comes the necessity of making industrial activities as efficient as possible to be able to take full advantage of Industry 4.0 characteristics [1].

One of the main barriers to adopting Industry 4.0 technologies corresponds to the lack of knowledge about the paradigm which stops industrial businesses from reaching their maximum potential [2]. Due to this factor, a solution that would demonstrate how the concept works would be pertinent. These factors led to the following research question: "How can an Industry 4.0 factory floor be simulated?".

The process of modeling and developing an industrial business is quite a complex process that involves a lot of careful planning and high costs. Due to this factor, a solution that allows to model a factory floor and observe its behavior until the desired result is obtained would be seamless. This solution would consist of the simulation of a factory floor activity. With it, people could observe how an Industry 4.0 industrial business works and be able to make the best choices leading to cost reduction and total efficiency when the business is actually implemented.

© The Author(s), under exclusive license to Springer Nature Switzerland AG 2024
T. Guarda et al. (Eds.): ARTIIS 2023, CCIS 1937, pp. 328–342, 2024.
https://doi.org/10.1007/978-3-031-48930-3_25

Before reaching the final result there was made a research on existing solutions regarding the simulation of Industry 4.0 environments, being able to conclude that there are not many. After, there were discussed modular architectures for the system as well as the respective data models. The implementation of the system started to be thought in a Raspberry Pi environment, along with the choosing of all the components required to build the prototype such as sensors of different natures.

This solution consists of a prototype that is a small-scale factory model with implemented hardware components. Some of these components retrieve data that is vital for the business and can then be transformed to create useful information and display it in real-time for the users to observe it.

In a fast-developing scene such as Industry 4.0, it is crucial to have something that reduces the risk of failure and increases the possibility of building a successful business, understanding first how it will work and being able to change some aspects or characteristics of the system to achieve top standards.

The present study intends to address the challenge of making people understand the Industry 4.0 concept as well as making it possible to model factories that are to be integrated into this paradigm. Thus, this article provides a set of technologies and how they can be used to create a simulation in which it is possible to observe a small factory working and data that is generated through the activity.

Regarding the document structure, there will be a section relative to the literature review, in which there will be exposed the most important concepts for Industry 4.0 and the project that is being approached. Then, used methods for reaching the final solution will be explained, as well as the required material to develop it. Next, the results are exposed along with a possible architecture of the system that is also explained. Finally, the last section of the document corresponds to the conclusions that were taken from the development of this project.

2 Background

To obtain knowledge regarding the theme that is being approached, a literature review was made with the purpose of studying what other authors created and what is their perspective on the involved subjects. This task required the use of some indexing tools, being them the following: Google Scholar, Scopus, and World of Science. The used documents in the research were obtained with the use of the following queries: "the internet of things"; "industry 4.0"; "cyber-physical systems"; "simulation"; "cloud computing". All the documents were carefully analyzed to make sure that the information that they contained was accurate and assertive.

2.1 Industry 4.0 and its Main Concepts

Until the present day, there have been four industrial revolutions. The first is known by the introduction of mechanization to the industrial processes. In the second industrial revolution, electrical energy started to be heavily used. The third one is characterized by the digitalization of industrial processes. Lastly, the fourth industrial revolution emerged, in which were combined internet technologies with smart objects [3]. This resulted in the digitalization of manufacturing processes, which reduces manual and human intervention [4] and adds more flexibility, mass customization with better quality products, and increased productivity [5]. There are some key technologies that without, Industry 4.0 would not exist. As per Hermann et al., (2016), these key technologies are Cyber-Physical Systems, The Internet of Things, and Smart Factories. The main characteristic of these technologies is the constant communication that is maintained between them as well as the information exchange.

Luigi Atzori, Antionio lera, and Giacomo Morabito [7] present the Internet of Things as being the pervasive presence of objects that maintain a certain level of interaction between them to achieve a common goal. To fulfill the common purpose between these objects, which consist of machines and smart devices, there are some essential technologies such as radio-frequency identification or wireless sensor networks [8]. The Internet of Things concept was first introduced in 1999, being the only associated technology, the RFID (radio-frequency identification). This technology allowed the existence of objects that interacted between them and that were uniquely identifiable and operable. As an example of RFID use, there is the existence of an RFID reader and an RFID tag. This led to the possibility of identifying, tracing, and tracking products and, therefore, this technology started to be widely used in every sector that involved logistics [9]. Besides the Internet of Things, it is also important to mention cyber-physical systems. It consists of a system that integrates both cyber and physical components that communicate between them through communication technologies like the Internet. These systems' main purpose is to control and monitor the physical part using the cyber part [10]. Regarding these systems' activity, the changes that happen in the physical part are monitored so that the system can adapt to these changes through intelligent decisions that are applied to the physical components, ending, therefore, by impacting the physical environment autonomously [11].

It is yet important to mention that the Internet of Things is crucial for the good functioning of these systems offering the necessary technologies that allow communication between their components and, therefore, affecting their overall performance [12].

Over the years, Industry 4.0 has been suffering many changes with the emergence of new technologies and concepts such as artificial intelligence, new generations of wireless cellular technology (5G/6G), and quantum computing. The constant pressure that is put on the different industries to keep up with the evolving pace is what makes them adopt these technologies and consequently develop more and more the Industry 4.0 concept and eventually create a new paradigm such as Industry 5.0 which is already starting to be approached [13]. It is also important to have into consideration some of the limitations of Industry 4.0. Since it requires the use of many electronics, one of the issues with this factor corresponds to electronic waste. Then, there are the security concerns related not only to the systems but also to the data that is generated and is highly valuable [14].

2.2 Cloud Computing and its Variants in Industry 4.0

With the emergence of the Internet of Things, a new way of producing data appeared with the communication between smart devices that is made possible using a network. Due to the large quantity of data produced, it is natural to have the necessity of storing and treating it properly to preserve its integrity and then be presented efficiently [15].

This technology has the main objective of providing computing services or data storage over the Internet which allows its users to have access to third-party software and hardware components. Due to these characteristics, the storage capabilities and computing resources make cloud computing an essential technology for IoT success [16]. Among the software and hardware resources, cloud computing offers various options such as servers, apps, or data storage. The services that cloud computing provides can be classified into different categories, being these the following: Infrastructure as a service (IaaS), Platform as a service (PaaS), and Software as a service (SaaS) [17]. As mentioned before, cloud computing is extremely important for IoT success, having, however, some integration challenges must be addressed. The Internet of Things includes various devices that support different applications and have different interfaces. This existing heterogeneity implies that specialized services must be developed for each application. In what comes to privacy and security many IoT systems have been attacked over the years. Therefore, it is essential to highlight the importance of secure and private systems since, in this case, they deal with loads of sensitive data [17]. Related to cloud computing, there are other important technologies such as edge computing and fog computing. Following Shi et al., (2016), edge computing is a paradigm that is based on enabling technologies to compute processes at the edge of a network which allows data to be processed closer to its source and consequently reducing the processing times. It is important to mention that data processing is executed not only by data consumers but also by data producers.

Besides edge computing, there is fog computing which is more focused on the infrastructure part. CISCO presented the following definition for fog computing: "highly virtualized platform that provides compute, storage, and networking services between end devices. And traditional Cloud computing Data Centers, typically, but not exclusively located at the edge of network" [19].

Fog computing uses its own infrastructure to potentiate the edge and cloud resources and coordinate the use of geographically distributed edge devices which surpasses edge computing limitations [20].

2.3 Control and Data Acquisition Systems in Industry 4.0

There are some systems that focus on controlling and monitoring industrial processes for example SCADA systems which stands for Supervisory Control and Data Acquisition [21]. These systems are composed of hardware and software elements corresponding the hardware to Remote Control Units (RTU), Master Terminal Unit (MTU), actuators and sensors, whereas the software components correspond to Human Machine Interface (HMI) and a database.

The RTUs are responsible for collecting real-time provided by sensors and forwarding it to the MTU. The MTU is responsible for sending the data received from the RTUs to the HMI and controls the RTUs. The HMI is responsible for presenting the gathered data to the operators and allows them to control the system through commands sent to the MTU [22].

3   Material and Methods

In the present section, there will be exposed the used methods, all the steps that were done during the development of this project, and the required material. It will also include a scheme for the disposal of the components, an image of a possible system architecture, and the due explanation.

3.1   The Methodology Used in the Study

The present research follows the case study methodology, in which the objective is to understand how people can easily understand the functioning of Industry 4.0 and model and plan their business as they wish, being then able to simulate it and verify if it corresponds to the desired result. Following the case study methodology, this research had to be divided into different stages [23]:

a) Problem definition – The first step is to find what is the problem that is intended to be approached. After observing the difficulties that many people must understand Industry 4.0, its potential, and how it works, it was concluded that the lack of knowledge represented a problem. This results in business owners not knowing how to improve and people who want to build a business not making the best possible choices leading sometimes to unpleasant occurrences such as excessive costs or poor performance.

b) Solution proposition and requirements – Facing the previously mentioned problem, it was thought that having a way to simulate an Industry 4.0 factory floor would be ideal. Then, it was also thought it would be ideal to have something that could be brought to fairs and conferences for people to be able to observe it. Therefore, the solution has to be universal so that it can be applied to all industrial sectors and, has also to be easily portable to be possible to transport it easily to different places.

c) After all, it was decided that the development of a prototype would be essential, and it would contain different components that together simulate an industrial environment in Industry 4.0, being yet possible to access and visualize important data relative to the simulation.

d) Solution characteristics and architecture – The next step was to think about what the solution idea was, and what were the requirements and try to come to a conclusion regarding the prototype structure. Next, there has to be thought about how the components will interact between themselves, and what materials will be used considering both hardware and software. Finally, after knowing what components would be used it is required to define an architecture for the system which was done by drawing different schemes and discussing which one suits best the purpose of the project.

e) Collecting and analyzing data – This document approaches the testing stage of this prototype and, consequently, there is no collected and analyzed data. What has been done corresponds only to a proposal, having the solution not been developed. In the future, it is intended to develop it and test its characteristics such as modularity and scalability through the tuning of different parameters of the system. Therefore, when this is done, it will also be developed a technical report that will contain important data which is essential to make a good choice in what comes to the best approach.

3.2   Used Tools in the Study

For the development of this project, there is a wide set of materials of different natures that are required. To be able to have small-scale manufacturing machines it can be used a 3D printer and the appropriate software to design the components.

Regarding the hardware components, there will be used several sensors (e.g., ESP8266, Raspberry Pi Pico), servo motors, an Arduino a Raspberry Pi, and all the necessary cables. Regarding the software part, there will be used MySQL to create the database, Grafana to create and access the analytics, NodeJS to establish the communication between client and server, and Docker that will have all these containers. There will also be used some simulation algorithms such as "Discrete Event Simulation", "Monte Carlo Simulation" and "Agent-Based Modeling".

4   Case Study

Now that all the process behind getting to the final solution proposition, there must be a more detailed explanation approaching all the project elements and how they will work to fulfill their purpose through different steps.

1. Having portability as an important requirement, there were discussed different ways of creating a structure that would contain all the elements, concluding that a case with a handle would be the more adequate one. Due to all the components that the prototype contains, there is quite some complexity in managing all the elements and, due to this factor, the case is divided into two halves. The most superficial one is where it is possible to observe the simulation occurring. The bottom part serves the purpose of cable, device, and other components management. (Fig. 1) shows how the components can be organized in the superficial half. The M1...M6 represent the machines that will be simulated, and the control unit represents the device that will allow control of the number of products to be produced. The gray area represents the platform in which the product will move from stage to stage and, the arrows on top of it represent the flow of the platform and consequently of the product.

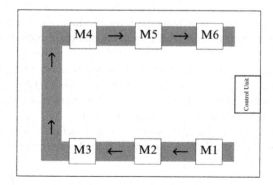

Fig. 1. Elements organization model

2. Now that the portability requirement is satisfied, there is also the modularity one. To respect this requirement, it was thought that with the use of magnets, it would be possible to move the printed manufacturing machines to different places and even change the number of machines that are in the system. Through custom software, the machines can have different tasks assigned to them, which allows the system to be able not only to represent different products within the same industrial sector but also different industries.

3. Part of the simulation corresponds to the progression of the product, transitioning from one manufacturing stage to another, and so on. To do so, there will be used servo motors that will be programmed to make a platform move and, consequently, make the product progress in the production process.

4. As the product moves, it will pass from machine to machine and, to represent the activity state of each one, the 3D-printed components will have integrated LEDs that will light up when the product is in them.

5. Since it is pretended to simulate Industry 4.0 factory floor, a big part of this project sits on the data generated using smart objects. Therefore, along the production course, several sensors will produce data that will then be transformed into important information and displayed in a dashboard, such as Grafana, which corresponds to a web application that provides analytics and interactive visualization.

6. Last, but not least, the users will be able to control some system parameters such as the number of products to be produced using an integrated display connected to a control unit like a Raspberry Pi. Then, it communicates with an Arduino that will be responsible for controlling all the hardware that composes the system.

4.1 Architecture

In Fig. 2, it is possible to observe a possible architecture for such a solution that is divided into four different layers that include different components and technologies that can be used to develop the system. The layers are the Interface, Data Processing, Data Acquisition and API.

Now that the architecture has been presented, it is important to explain what each layer contains.

- **Interface**: The "Interface" represents both the Grafana, in which the analytics will be accessed and the application where the users can choose the number of products to be produced.
- **Data Processing**: The "Raspberry Pi" will serve as a local server where the data will be processed, and it will have docker installed in it so that it is possible to have different containers that are required to make the system function. These containers are Grafana, NodeJS, MosquitoMQTT, and MySQL.
- **Data Acquisition**: Regarding the manufacturing machines, they will be simulated using different microcontrollers as it is possible to observe on the right side. The M1,

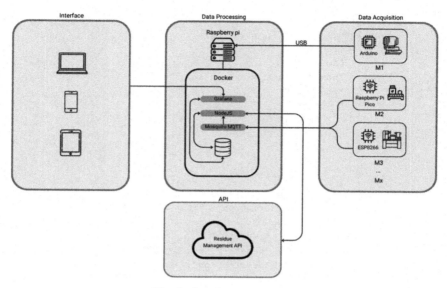

Fig. 2. Solution Architecture

M2, M3, and so on, represent possible simulated machines and it is possible to see that there are used different devices. M2 and M3 are connected to the MosquitoMQTT, which corresponds to an MQTT Broker, to make it possible to establish communication between the wireless microcontrollers and the local server. The M1 is using an Arduino that communicates with the Raspberry Pi through the USB/Serial protocol. All these machines will produce data relative to the simulation.

- **API**: Finally, there is a "Residue Management API" that is used for trading information regarding the created residues during the production process.

4.2 Data Model

As mentioned before, one of the main characteristics of this system is data generation. To be able to manage the solution, there were created three data models that were developed having into consideration the nature of the project and the industry in which the project is inserted, corresponding to the textile industry. One corresponds to the configuration of the factory and the other two correspond to the input and output of each simulation. The following code corresponds to the data model regarding the factory representation.

```
configModel = {
    "machines": [
        {
            "id": 1,
            "name": "Machine 1",
            "position": {
                "x": 10,
                "y": 10
            },
            "tasks": [
                {
                    "id": 1,
                    "name": "Task 1",
                    "description": "Task 1 description",
                    "input": {
                        "id": 1,
                        "name": "Input 1",
                        "description": "Input 1 description",
                        "quantity": 10,
                        "unit": "kg",
                    },
                    "output": {
                        "id": 1,
                        "name": "Output 1",
                        "description": "Output 1 description",
                        "time": 10,
                        "consumption": {
                            "electric": 10,
                            "gas": 10,
                            "water": 10,
                            "air": 10
                        },
                        "pollution": {
                            "CO2": 10,
                            "CO": 10,
                            "NOx": 10,
```

```
        "SOx": 10
    },
    "waste": [{
        "id": 1,
        "name": "Waste 1",
        "description": "Waste 1 description",
        "quantity": 10,
        "type": "solid",
        "unit": "kg",
    },
    ]
                }
            }
        ]
    }
]
}
```

The configuration data model was designed to contain data about all the elements that integrate the system and how their disposal is made.

The system contains several machines, each with a unique ID, name, and position in the system. Each machine can perform certain tasks, being also specified. For each task, there is an input and an output. The input corresponds to the material that is set to be transformed by the machine and by a certain task. The output contains information not only about what has been transformed but also about other parameters, such as resource consumption, pollution, and waste that has been made.

Next, there is the data model that corresponds to the input of each production process.

```
inputModel = {
    "po": 1,
    "machines": [
        {
            "id": 1,
            "tasks": [
                {
                    "id": 1,
                    "quantity": 10,
                }
            ]
        }
    ]
}
```

As it is possible to observe in the code above, the input for the production order contains a unique number that identifies it and the machines that will operate during that production order which include its ID and the tasks that will be performed. Each of the tasks has an ID and the quantity of units that will be assigned to that task.

Finally, there is the output of the production process which corresponds to the data model presented below.

```
outputModel = {
    "machines": [
        {
            "id": 1,
            "tasks": [
                {
                    "id": 1,
                    "po": 1,
                    "output": {
                        "time": 10,
                        "consumption": {
                            "electric": 10,
                            "gas": 10,
                            "water": 10,
                            "air": 10
                        },
                        "pollution": {
                            "CO2": 10,
                            "CO": 10,
                            "NOx": 10,
                            "SOx": 10
                        },
                        "waste": [{
                            "id": 1,
                            "quantity": 10,
                        },
                        ]
                    }
                }
            ]
        }
    ]
}
```

The output data model is quite more complex since it includes several results that come from production.

It contains all the machines that were used during the production, the tasks performed by them, the production order to which they were assigned, and the output obtained from that task. The output contains the time that the machine took to operate, the consumption of resources, the pollution that was generated, and the created waste.

5 Discussion

Throughout the manuscript, it is possible to observe some strong factors that indicate that a solution of this nature has a high potential regarding the dissemination of the Industry 4.0 vision. Also, the capability of modeling an industrial business through its simulation comes as an important aspect that can revolutionize the whole industry. One of the main points that is highlighted in this project is the fact that this project can bring the possibility of creating highly efficient industrial environments before implementing them which can lead to the reduction of cost drifts and unwanted system behaviors.

It is possible to consider this project as a very complete one due to its characteristics. Its modularity allows it to represent different industrial sectors, and also the way that it is built makes it possible to observe how an Industry 4.0 factory works on a small scale. There is no better way to understand the vision of Industry 4.0 than observing it and being able to make conclusions through data.

As a way to provide a better understanding of how this project can be relevant to the industry a SWOT analysis will be presented below.

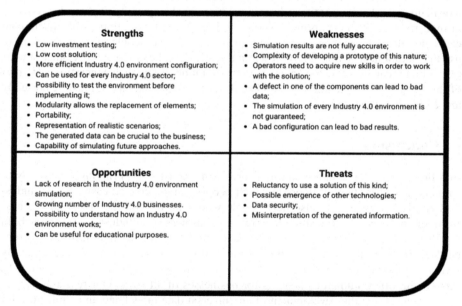

Fig. 3. SWOT Analysis of the solution

In Fig. 3 it is possible to see the SWOT analysis that has been made, being now important to get more into detail.

This project consists of a prototype that has the main purpose of simulating Industry 4.0 environments and creating realistic scenarios. Due to its nature, it is a low-cost and modular solution that allows the modeling of industrial businesses from different sectors. One of its main characteristics consists of data generation, which can be crucial for the business. However, being this a case of simulation, it is crucial to have in mind that the obtained data is most likely to not correspond entirely to reality. Also, the fact that it consists of a simulation leads to the possibility of simulating future approaches, which means that it is possible to simulate environments that do not exist in the present.

It is yet important to establish a correlation between the SCADA system presented in the background section and the system that is being proposed. Due to the similarities between them, it is possible to state that the data collection can be done through a SCADA framework having the prototype all the required elements to do so.

The literature review made it possible to conclude that there is very little research regarding the topic that is being approached, which constitutes an opportunity for the success of this project. Also, the growing Industry 4.0 businesses requires that a bigger number of employees understand its vision which can be done using this prototype since it can be used for educational purposes.

Being this a simulation, the obtained results might not be completely accurate. Besides this factor, if the configuration is not well done, there is a high risk of the generated data being harmful to the business planning and misleading its users. Due to the number of elements that the prototype contains, it is possible to state that developing such a solution can be a complex process and, therefore, it is probable that workers find it difficult to work with it at first. There is an unimaginable quantity of possible scenarios of Industry 4.0 environments and, therefore it is quite hard if not impossible to simulate every possible environment. Like every technology, some people may be reluctant to use this solution, which might represent a threat. Also, the emergence of other similar technologies can decrease the adhesion to this solution. Being data generation a big part of this project, it is essential to guarantee the security of data and, it must be correctly and carefully interpreted.

6 Conclusion

In a broad way, this solution can fill a breach in Industry 4.0 bringing a new way to simulate industrial factory floors in which people can understand easily the 4th industrial revolution vision and also help people who want to build an industrial business from scratch or want to transition their existing business to an Industry 4.0 approach. In conclusion, the development of a modular IoT simulation system for industry is a significant step towards improving the efficiency and effectiveness of industrial operations. By leveraging the power of modularity, the universal model, and simulated environments, this system offers numerous benefits for businesses of all sizes. Our research has led to two key results: the development of an universal data model and an architecture for a modular IoT simulation system as a case study. The universal data model provides a standardized framework for simulating IoT systems, allowing for seamless integration of different components and technologies.

The architecture, designed as a case study for a manufacturing plant, demonstrates the feasibility and effectiveness of the proposed approach. The universal data model offers several advantages, including improved interoperability, reduced complexity, and increased scalability. By providing a common language and framework for IoT data, the model enables seamless integration of different systems and technologies, reducing the need for custom integrations and improving the overall efficiency of the system. The architecture, as a case study for a manufacturing plant, demonstrates the practical application of the proposed approach. The architecture includes a set of modular components, each with a specific function, such as data acquisition, data processing, and visualization. The components are designed to be easily integrated and reconfigured, allowing for flexible and adaptive system configuration. The simulated nature of the system allows for testing and validation of IoT systems in a controlled and risk-free environment. This reduces the potential for costly mistakes and downtime, allowing businesses to iteratively improve and refine their systems before deploying them in live environments.

In summary, the proposed modular IoT simulation system for industry offers a powerful tool for businesses looking to harness the potential of IoT technology. By providing a modular, universal, and simulated environment, this system can help businesses to streamline their operations, reduce costs, and improve their overall competitiveness in the marketplace. As the IoT continues to evolve and play an increasingly important role in industrial operations, the importance of this system will only continue to grow.

Acknowledgements. The authors acknowledge the integrated project be@t – Textile Bioeconomy, that has received funding from the Environmental Fund through Component 12 – Promotion of Sustainable Bioeconomy (Investment TC-C12-i01 – Sustainable Bioeconomy No. 02/C12-i01/202), of European funds allocated to Portugal by the Recovery and Resilience Plan (RRP), within the scope of the European Union (EU) Recovery and Resilience Mechanism, framed in the Next Generation EU, for the period 2021–2026.

References

1. Ghobakhloo, M.: Industry 4.0, digitization, and opportunities for sustainability. J. Clean. Prod. **252**, 119869 (2020). https://doi.org/10.1016/j.jclepro.2019.119869
2. Turkyilmaz, A., Dikhanbayeva, D., Suleiman, Z., Shaikholla, S., Shehab, E.: Industry 4.0: challenges and opportunities for Kazakhstan SMEs. Procedia CIRP **96**, 213–218 (2021). https://doi.org/10.1016/j.procir.2021.01.077
3. Lasi, H., Fettke, P., Kemper, H.G., Feld, T., Hoffmann, M.: Industry 4.0. Bus. Inf. Syst. Eng. **6**(4), 239–242 (2014). https://doi.org/10.1007/s12599-014-0334-4
4. Nayyar, A., Kumar, A. (eds.): A Roadmap to Industry 4.0: Smart Production, Sharp Business and Sustainable Development. Springer International Publishing, Cham (2020). https://doi.org/10.1007/978-3-030-14544-6
5. Zhong, R.Y., Xu, X., Klotz, E., Newman, S.T.: Intelligent manufacturing in the context of industry 4.0: a review. Engineering **3**(5), 616–630 (2017). https://doi.org/10.1016/J.ENG.2017.05.015
6. M. Hermann, T. Pentek, and B. Otto, "Design Principles for Industrie 4.0 Scenarios," in *2016 49th Hawaii International Conference on System Sciences (HICSS)*, IEEE, Jan. 2016, pp. 3928–3937. doi: https://doi.org/10.1109/HICSS.2016.488
7. Atzori, L., Iera, A., Morabito, G.: The Internet of Things: a survey. Comput. Netw. **54**(15), 2787–2805 (2010). https://doi.org/10.1016/j.comnet.2010.05.010
8. Lee, I., Lee, K.: The Internet of Things (IoT): applications, investments, and challenges for enterprises. Bus. Horiz. **58**(4), 431–440 (2015). https://doi.org/10.1016/j.bushor.2015.03.008
9. Li, S., Da Xu, L., Zhao, S.: The internet of things: a survey. Inf. Syst. Front. **17**(2), 243–259 (2015). https://doi.org/10.1007/s10796-014-9492-7

10. Lin, J., Yu, W., Zhang, N., Yang, X., Zhang, H., Zhao, W.: A survey on internet of things: architecture, enabling technologies, security and privacy, and applications. IEEE Internet Things J. **4**(5), 1125–1142 (2017). https://doi.org/10.1109/JIOT.2017.2683200

11. Burg, A., Chattopadhyay, A., Lam, K.-Y.: Wireless communication and security issues for cyber-physical systems and the internet-of-things. Proc. IEEE **106**(1), 38–60 (2018). https://doi.org/10.1109/JPROC.2017.2780172

12. Ochoa, S.F., Fortino, G., Di Fatta, G.: Cyber-physical systems, internet of things and big data. Futur. Gener. Comput. Syst. **75**, 82–84 (2017). https://doi.org/10.1016/j.future.2017.05.040

13. Sigov, A., Ratkin, L., Ivanov, L.A., Da Xu, L.: Emerging enabling technologies for industry 4.0 and beyond. Inf. Syst. Front. (2022). https://doi.org/10.1007/s10796-021-10213-w

14. Bai, C., Dallasega, P., Orzes, G., Sarkis, J.: Industry 4.0 technologies assessment: a sustainability perspective. Int. J. Prod. Econ. **229**, 107776 (2020). https://doi.org/10.1016/j.ijpe.2020.107776

15. Gubbi, J., Buyya, R., Marusic, S., Palaniswami, M.: Internet of Things (IoT): a vision, architectural elements, and future directions. Futur. Gener. Comput. Syst. **29**(7), 1645–1660 (2013). https://doi.org/10.1016/j.future.2013.01.010

16. Al-Fuqaha, A., Guizani, M., Mohammadi, M., Aledhari, M., Ayyash, M.: Internet of things: a survey on enabling technologies, protocols, and applications. IEEE Commun. Surv. Tutorials **17**(4), 2347–2376 (2015). https://doi.org/10.1109/COMST.2015.2444095

17. Othman, M.M., El-Mousa, A.: Internet of things & cloud computing internet of things as a service approach. In: 2020 11th International Conference on Information and Communication Systems (ICICS), pp. 318–323. IEEE (2020). https://doi.org/10.1109/ICICS49469.2020.239503

18. Shi, W., Cao, J., Zhang, Q., Li, Y., Xu, L.: Edge computing: vision and challenges. IEEE Internet Things J. **3**(5), 637–646 (2016). https://doi.org/10.1109/JIOT.2016.2579198

19. Bonomi, F., Milito, R., Zhu, J., Addepalli, S.: Fog computing and its role in the internet of things. In: Proceedings of the First Edition of the MCC Workshop on Mobile Cloud Computing, pp. 13–16. ACM New York, NY, USA (2012). https://doi.org/10.1145/2342509.2342513

20. Dastjerdi, A.V., Buyya, R.: Fog computing: helping the internet of things realize its potential. Comput. (Long Beach Calif) **49**(8), 112–116 (2016). https://doi.org/10.1109/MC.2016.245

21. Pliatsios, D., Sarigiannidis, P., Lagkas, T., Sarigiannidis, A.G.: A survey on scada systems: secure protocols, incidents, threats and tactics. IEEE Commun. Surv. Tutorials **22**(3), 1942–1976 (2020). https://doi.org/10.1109/COMST.2020.2987688

22. Yadav, G., Paul, K.: Architecture and security of SCADA systems: a review. Int. J. Crit. Infrastruct. Prot. **34**, 100433 (2021). https://doi.org/10.1016/j.ijcip.2021.100433

23. Six steps to approaching a case study. https://www.monash.edu/learnhq/excel-at-writing/annotated-assessment-samples/business-and-economics/buseco-writing-case-studies/six-steps-to-approaching-a-case-study. Accessed 17 Jul 2023

3D Printing Using Natural Fibers – An Emerging Technology in Sustainable Manufacturing: A Review

Cristina Oliveira(✉) ⓘ, Denise Carvalho ⓘ, Isabel Moura ⓘ, Bernardo Ribeiro,
and Flávio Ferreira ⓘ

CITEVE (Technology Centre for Textile and Clothing of Portugal), Rua Fernando Mesquita, n°
2785, 4760-034 Vila Nova de Famalicão, Portugal
cmoliveira@citeve.pt

Abstract. The advent of 3D printing has revolutionized the manufacturing industry, granting access to previously unattainable components that traditional methods couldn't achieve. However, most of the existing literature primarily focuses
on synthetic materials for these purposes. Significant applications of 3D printing span various fields such as aerospace, defense, biomedical, healthcare, food,
automotive, architecture, construction, energy, and fashion industries.

Despite some research exploring the potential of natural fibers in 3D printing,
there is still a significant gap in scientific and technical knowledge concerning
the materials required for producing natural-based composite structures using this
technology. Extensive research is necessary to comprehend the distinct properties
of natural and matrix fibers/filaments, their interactions, and the resulting final
properties.

Utilizing 3D printing technology with natural fibers emerges as a promising approach for sustainable manufacturing due to the unique characteristics of
the materials involved and the potential to align with environmental benefits and
sustainable practices. We find ourselves in an era of exciting technological innovations, driving transformative change. Economic paradigms are shifting, and novel
technologies are reshaping product and factor markets, significantly impacting
businesses and the workforce.

Keywords: Additive manufacturing · 3D printing · Biocomposites ·
Natural-fiber

1 Introduction

During the last few years, additive manufacturing (AM) has undergone extensive investigation as a valuable technology that enables the development of components, including
tools and end-use production parts, with intricate and complex geometries. Owing its
potential in the design of new advanced materials and structures, this technological
advancement is transforming industries, by the transition from analogic to digital processes, with potential applications in several areas, including, engineering, imaging,
communications, and architecture [1].

T. Guarda et al. (Eds.): ARTIIS 2023, CCIS 1937, pp. 343–356, 2024.
https://doi.org/10.1007/978-3-031-48930-3_26

AM, commonly known as three-dimensional (3D) printing, is based on a layer-by-layer principle, enabling the rapid production of complex multi-scale composite structures. Thermoplastics and their composites are commonly used in 3D printing processes such as material extrusion (ME) and laser powder bed fusion (LPBF) [2, 3]. By using 3D printing, components that were previously unattainable through traditional manufacturing methods can be created, and three-dimensional pieces find extensive industrial applications in activities like design, prototyping, and production of low-volume end-use parts [4]. This additive manufacturing methodology has experienced significant growth in the market due to its efficiency, versatility, and consistency, making it an appealing choice for numerous large-scale industrial manufacturers. Notably, 3D printing expedites product prototyping, development, customization, and functional integration, resulting in faster production and reduced overall costs, especially for tooling during the initial stages of the product lifecycle [5].

There are several materials that 3D printing can manipulate since a wide range of new polymers have been developed, along with processes, printing machines, and methodologies, varying from a simple extrusion, material jetting, or fine powders melted with lasers [6]. That is leading to more competitive designs, new use of materials, and improved innovation globally.

There are several types of 3D printing technologies: 1. Stereolithography (SLA): This method employs a UV laser to solidify photopolymer resin layer by layer [7]; 2. Digital light processing (DLP): Similar to SLA, DLP also uses photopolymer resin and UV light for layer-wise solidification; 3. Selective laser sintering (SLS): Uses a laser as a power and heat source to sinter powdered material, binding it together to create a solid structure [8]; 4. Direct ink writing (DIW): Is a 3D printing technique, where the materials are deposited in a layer-wise method, by the continuous rising of the print head, aiming to develop a 3D structure [9] and; 5. Fused deposition modeling (FDM): Is one of the most used 3D printing technology for melt extrusion [10]. Herein, a special kind of 3D printing material – thermoplastic filament – is melted, followed by extrusion through a nozzle with controlled temperature and deposited layer-by-layer. It is important to point out that the term FDM usually attends as an equivalent to Fused Filament Fabrication (FFF) [11].

Among the aforementioned 3D printing techniques, FFF is one of the most common and flexible technology through material extrusion with potential application in polymers and composite materials. It allows prototyping components with excellent mechanical performance by controlling printing parameters and slicing [12]. It provides several benefits, like low cost in a short timeframe, reduced waste production, customization of microstructures and their properties, and is able to develop complex assemblies [13].

The gaps between advanced materials and innovative structures can be filled by the use of 3D printing technologies with continuous fiber reinforced polymer composites (CFRPCs), however, some challenges remain. The limited availability of suitable materials, the need for optimizing numerous printing parameters, and the underwhelming mechanical properties of printed components. Among these, the latter, i.e., the subpar mechanical properties, stands out as a significant obstacle in fully utilizing these technologies for load-bearing purposes [2, 3]. CFRPCs are lightweight and boast high specific strength and modulus compared to metals and alloys. As such, CFRPCs have widespread use in automotive and aerospace applications [2]. Nevertheless, advanced composites have a higher cost of raw materials, fabrication processes, and recycling. As a result, thermosetting composites tend to have higher production costs compared to conventional metallic materials. However, they offer several advantageous properties such as high creep resistance, ease of processing, and full recyclability. These characteristics make them ideal for next-gen green composites, and they are currently widely used. Thermoplastic composite forming, such as injection molding and tape placement, relies on the use of a mold, thus difficulting the design and fabrication of complex composite structures [2].

Thermoplastic polymers reinforced with natural fibers such as wood, flax, and hemp offer a promising array of specific mechanical properties, alongside a reduced environmental impact. These biocomposites find frequent use in various manufacturing processes like extrusion, injection molding, thermoforming, film stacking, and vacuum bag molding [3]. Driven by environmental and economic concerns, the exploration of natural fiber-reinforced composites has gained increasing research attention for approximately two decades. It's important to note that this timeframe is relatively brief in comparison to the extensive research conducted on synthetic composites like those reinforced with glass or carbon fibers [13]. The adoption of natural fibers offers notable advantages due to their ready availability, cost-effectiveness, environmentally friendly nature, and biodegradability. Opting for natural fibers instead of synthetic ones for 3D printing filament production can substantially decrease the emissions linked to the manufacture of synthetic fibers, thereby contributing to the mitigation of ongoing pollution concerns [14].

Natural fiber composite materials are created by incorporating natural fibers as reinforcing agents and other agents like compatibilizers and flexibilizers into a polymer matrix. These materials boast low density, high specific strength and modulus, reduced weight, and superior affinity and biodegradability when compared to glass fiber and other synthetic fiber-reinforced composites. As a result, they have gained significance in driving the advancement of green and sustainable economies. However, combining natural fibers as reinforcements with thermoplastics necessitates the careful selection of processing conditions to enhance the performance of the composites while considering the inherent characteristics of both materials [15].

The main objective of this document was to review advances in 3D printing using natural fibers as an emerging technology for sustainable manufacturing. For this, an introduction was made explaining what 3D printing consists of, its importance, and the materials used for it. This process, especially when applied to polymeric composites reinforced with continuous fibers, addresses certain gaps and brings forth additional benefits in the realm of sustainable manufacturing. Later, throughout this document, topics such as the differences between chopped and continuous fibers, the existing natural fibers as well as the properties for use in 3D printing, the most sustainable polymeric filaments for use in 3D printing, and the applications of this type of manufacture using natural fibers. Finally, the future trends in 3D printing of natural fiber-based biocomposites.

The utilization of 3D printing technology with natural fibers represents a promising and emerging approach to sustainable manufacturing. This stems from the distinctive qualities of the materials utilized and the potential to realize concepts that align with environmental benefits and sustainable practices.

2 Chopped vs Continuous Fibers

In 3D printing, there are two main ways to use fibers: continuous fiber and chopped fiber. The choice between these two types of fibers plays a crucial role in determining the suitability of a filament for a specific 3D printing component. The main difference between chopped and continuous fibers is the dimensions and the composites developed. With chopped fibers do not give a suitable increase in strength, it is just possible to improve the stiffness, surface quality, and wear resistance [16–18]. Even though few studies reported the processing of natural fibers by using 3D printing technology, great efforts have been made aiming to develop sustainable components resulting from new materials composites based on natural fibers with improved properties [19].

Since natural fibers are anisotropic and dependent on chemical composition, the selection with an appropriate length is critical to ensure improved composite properties. Both dimensions of the fibers, length, and diameter, have functional significance and affect the mechanical performance of the printed parts in distinct ways. Continuous fibers, when placed in the right direction, can provide the necessary reinforcement for composite manufacturing, as they are well oriented in a consistent manner, contributing to the strength and stiffness of the composite. It is also important to point out that continuous fiber has a minimal layup curve radius, and the fiber's diameter is responsible for the minimum width of a reinforced element [20].

Regarding chopped fibers, generally, they are dispersed in the polymer matrix without any orientation, being responsible for the minor overlap among fibers, and therefore, no fibers cross the adjacent layers [16]. Printed parts with chopped fiber-filled filaments often show even lower mechanical properties than unfilled ones. Indeed, studies have consistently shown that the use of continuous fibers offers improved composite strength compared to chopped fibers. Thus, choosing the former due to the larger specific surface area contact, is an advantage for the overall structural strength of 3D printing filaments applications.

Other studies reported that twisted yarns of natural jute fibers and continuous carbon fiber (CCF) were used as reinforcement in a PLA matrix to prepare a material used in 3D printing technology. The results indicated that tensile strength increased significantly for both cases, namely using twisted yarns of natural jute fibers (435% versus 134%)and was also significantly stronger than fiber-reinforced PLA using chopped carbon fibers [21].

A. Le Duigou et al. [3] studied the mechanical performance of a novel high-performance 3D printed biocomposite based on a continuous flax yarn embedded in a PLA matrix. The results reveal that cFF/PLA printed composites properties remained lower than similar flax/PLA thermocompressed composites. Also, C. Gauss et al. [22], reported the use of cellulose as reinforcement in biocomposites and recent related advances in 3D printing technologies. The authors found out that the versatility of cellulose as a renewable feedstock combined with the freedom of design provided by additive manufacturing is a perfect match for the development of sustainable solutions for advanced applications. Additionally, M. N. Ahmad *et al.* [23] reviewed the natural fiber-based filaments for 3D printing. It discusses the fabrication process and the characterization of wire filament that is fabricated from thermoplastic material mixed with natural fiber. They achieve that natural fiber-reinforced thermoplastics are less harmful to the environment when compared with thermoplastic materials that release hazardous gases. Research carried out by A. Le Duigou *et al.* [13] report studies related to natural fiber biocomposites manufactured by 3D printing (FFF) and 4D printing with mechanical and actuation features respectively, where they found out that the most exciting challenge in the field of the 3D/4D printing of natural fiber biocomposites is probably to overcome the current material design habits by developing real multidisciplinary work involving eco-design, biomimicry, mechanics, materials sciences, technology, and other disciplines.

Our primary objective is to thoroughly explore and harness the potential of using continuous filaments based on natural fibers in conjunction with 3D printing technology. Through comprehensive research and development, we aim to evaluate the effectiveness of this approach in various applications. By focusing on continuous natural fiber filaments, we seek to unlock new possibilities for sustainable and eco-friendly manufacturing processes, enhancing the mechanical properties and overall performance of 3D printed components. Through this endeavor, we strive to contribute to the advancement of sustainable manufacturing practices and the realization of environmentally responsible solutions for diverse industries [24].

3 3D Printing with Natural Fibers

3D Printing technology has been adopted by a growing number of industries as a plan to provide critical components of a certain object that are unavailable and that can match and be combined as needed, aiming to reduce the cost associated with the maintenance and storing parts.

In the last years, 3D printing technology has been widely used as an additive manufacturing process as a prototyping method. Nowadays, the challenge is to use 3D printing technology to design and fabricate final components with applications in several areas. Thus, the modeling and design before printing the final product is critical, to evaluate the complex structure before the 3D printing process. The component design requires the determination of design objectives, as appropriate scaling from the real size of the component, to ensure geometric tolerances and to be adequate for its application. Besides that, it is also imperative to establish several design considerations, such as component size, thermal and physical stresses on the component, environmental conditions of the component, durability, and reactivity of the used materials, and to evaluate the economic impact of the materials and the inherent difficulty level during the manufacture [25].

Currently, 3D printing applied to the final components is unlimited and allows to use of different materials. Besides that, several manufacturers have started using 3D printing technology for the customization and manufacture of their end-use parts owing the several advantages, such as single-demand production, mass customization, spare parts management, enhanced and personalized healthcare demand production, complex design flexibility, and lightweight components [26].

Nowadays, the challenge is to develop and explore 3D printing continuous filaments based on natural fibers, with inherent anisotropic properties, (wood, hemp, bamboo, cotton, etc.) in combination with biopolymers, in order to create high-performance and sustainable new composites materials, to enhance the overall performance of 3D printed components. Thus, appropriate techniques and methodologies to use continuous filaments based on natural fiber as a reinforcement in 3D printing technology is an emerging field.

In the literature, there are several papers reporting 3D printing using continuous filaments based on synthetic fibers (e.g., carbon fiber, Kevlar, glass fiber, etc.). Therefore, there are a few studies reporting the use of continuous natural fibers combined with 3D printing technology. Table 1 presents a summary of these same studies.

3D printing of continuous filament based on continuous natural fibers provides several opportunities to develop high-performance and high-quality new composite materials since it is possible to manufacture more sustainable and cost-effective components, with the required design reducing the waste of material [27].

Tao *et al.* [28], described some research reporting the use of continuous natural fibers. Short natural fibers (sNFs) and continuous natural fibers (cNFs) such as jute, flax, ramie, and pineapple leaf have been conjugated with different polymer matrices by 3D printing. The studies carried out reveal that the reinforced thermoplastic matrices suffer changes in mechanical performance, which varies as a function of the length of the fiber, the used natural fiber, and the 3D printing by fused filament fabrication (FFF), i.e., based on the stage where fiber is embedded in the thermoplastic polymer – nozzle impregnation that occurs during printing or prepreg filament that occurs before printing.

In viewing the expansion of 3D printing technology of continuous natural fibers (cNF) composites and increasing the application of 3D printing of cNF composites in industry, some considerations should be taken into account, namely a more depth research concerning the natural fibers for developing cNF reinforcements for 3D printing, fibers pre-treatment methods need to be investigated detailed, to take more advantage of the geometric freedom of 3D printing and to increase the volume fiber ratio is critical for improving cNF FFF printing performance [28].

Considering Table 1, as well as all the information mentioned above, the following sections focus more objectively on existing natural fibers and their properties, the most sustainable polymeric filaments for use in 3D printing, 3D printing technologies used for the development of continuous fibers, and new applications using 3D printing with natural fibers.

3.1 Natural Fibers for 3D Printing

Natural fibers are widely available and have been used to develop new materials composites by using 3D printing technology. Nonetheless, they require additional processing during assembly to improve the performance of the 3D printed parts and to achieve a specific design criteria.

The properties of 3D printed composite materials are influenced by several factors, including the nature of the used fibers, their stiffness, strength, and ability to bond with the polymer matrix. In an ideal scenario, the resulting composite material microstructure should be uniform, with well-dispersed fibers with a high aspect ratio (length/diameter).

Table 1. Summary of some studies that have reported the use of continuous natural fibers combined with 3D printing technology.

Authors and Year	Study Approach	Conclusions	Ref
A. Le Duigou et al. 2019	Evaluation of the mechanical performance of a novel high-performance 3D printed biocomposite based on a continuous flax yarn embedded in a PLA matrix. **Fig. 1.** (a) Microstructure of a continuous flax fibre/PLA (cFF/PLA) filaments, (b) SEM microphotograph of cross section of untested cFF/PLA samples, (c) cFF/PLA transversally printed (90°) and (d) cFF/PLA longitudinally printed (0°). Details of panel d showing (e) loops overlap and (f) regular loops. Reproduced from [3].	The transverse properties of continuous natural fiber-filled (cFF) composites using PLA as the matrix material was found to be weaker than comparable flax/PLA thermocompressed composites. To address this limitation, future research should focus on enhancing the quality of the flax fiber yarn and its filaments, with particular emphasis on using untwisted ribbons.	[3]
A. Le Duigou et. al. 2020	Exhaustive and comprehensive literature review of natural fiber biocomposites manufactured by 3D printing (FFF) and 4D printing with mechanical and actuation features respectively. **Fig. 2.** (a) Fractured continuous unidirectional jute fibers/PLA sample printed with in-nozzle impregnation. (b) Fractured continuous unidirectional flax fibre/PLA sample printed with pre-impregnated filaments. (c) SEM micrography cross section of Flax/PLA composite microstructure. Reproduced from [13].	The most exciting challenge in the field of the 3D/4D printing of natural fiber biocomposites is breaking away from conventional material design practices. This can be achieved through true multidisciplinary collaboration involving eco-design, biomimicry, mechanics, materials sciences, technology, and other relevant disciplines.	[13]
C. Gauss et. al. 2021	Review describing the use of cellulose as reinforcement in biocomposites and recent related advances in 3D printing technologies, including 4D (responsive/smart) printing and current/future applications. **Fig. 3.** Images of (a) 3D printing of all-cellulose honeycomb structure; (b) The freeze-dried cellulose honeycomb standing on top of dandelion showing its light-weight. Reproduced from [22].	The combination of cellulose as a versatile renewable feedstock and the design freedom offered by additive manufacturing creates an ideal synergy for developing sustainable solutions for advanced applications.	[22]
X. Tian et al. 2022	Review about the development, application, and future perspective for 3D printing of CFRPCs. **Fig. 4.** (a)(b) 3D printing process of the continuous carbon fiber reinforced composite; (c) Schematic representation of the 3D printing process for continuous fiber reinforced thermoplastic composites (CFRTPCs); (d) 3D-printed CFRTPCs and dumbbell-shaped JFRTP tensile test specimens, as well as cross-section of specimen. Reproduced from [2].	The future of green composites lies in the innovative use of recyclable and green raw materials, combined with advanced 3D printing processes. Overcoming the challenges involved requires a concerted effort from researchers across multiple disciplines, aiming to achieve a harmonious integration of materials, processes, and designs for sustainable industrial applications.	[2]
M. N. Ahmad et. al. 2023	Review about the natural fiber-based filaments for 3D printing. It discusses the fabrication process and the characterization of wire filament that is fabricated from thermoplastic material mixed with natural fiber. **Fig. 5.** Process of making the natural fiber filament for FDM and printed sample. Reproduced from [23].	Natural fiber-reinforced thermoplastics offer environmental advantages over traditional thermoplastic materials that release hazardous gases. However, further research on natural fiber-filled polymers is needed to fully realize their potential. To minimize the environmental impact, the focus should be on using industrial waste to produce biobased thermoplastic composites.	[23]

Maximizing the interfacial surface is crucial for efficient load transfer, requiring the reduction of defects or porosity in the matrix and interfacial area [13].

Choosing the appropriate natural fibers based on the desired part specifications (e.g., stiffness, toughness) is the initial step in developing high-performance 3D printing materials. The transfer of stress at the interface is also crucial, and the composite properties depend on factors such as fiber length, diameter, tensile properties, and interfacial shear strength. The surface properties of natural fibers, controlling the interfacial shear strength, are more complex than synthetic counterparts like glass or carbon fibers. Effective cleaning methods, such as water treatment, have been shown to remove low-weight pectin and improve adhesion with the PolyLactic Acid (PLA) matrix. Chemical treatments are also commonly proposed for fiber surface modification [13].

Although natural fibers reinforce the materials, their inclusion can impact the printing process as their polysaccharide components are sensitive to temperature and moisture. High temperatures (above 150 °C) and prolonged exposure times (beyond a few minutes) can significantly affect the mechanical properties of natural fibers. The manufacturing temperature further influences natural fibers' properties, surface quality, and the resulting fiber/matrix interface. For example, a 14-h drying at 105 °C reduces the interfacial bond strength of flax fiber with PLA by 20% due to embrittlement of internal interfaces, surface wettability changes caused by low molecular weight component migration, and surface molecule reorientation [13].

3.2 Sustainable Polymeric Filaments for 3D Printing

Polymeric filaments, particularly thermoplastics, are widely used in composite material applications for 3D printing. Among the most common filaments is polypropylene (PP), known for its chemical resistance, flexibility, and versatility, making it suitable for various applications. Polylactic acid (PLA), a biodegradable filament derived from corn and other biomaterials, is also popular. Nylon (PA6) is another frequently used filament, appreciated for its durability, flexibility, and resistance to chemicals, impact, and abrasion. Acrylonitrile butadiene styrene (ABS) filament stands out for its high impact resistance at low temperatures and the ability to create lightweight parts. ABS is often found in FFF 3D printing, and its popularity extends to vat polymerization methods [29–31]. It possesses chemical and thermal resistance, good rigidity, and high impact resistance, making it a common choice for 3D printing alongside PLA [32].

Additionally, other polymers like polyetherimide (PEI) and polyether ether ketone (PEEK) find applications in 3D printing but require specific conditions for proper usage. Traditional thermoplastic polymers like PETG are favored for their low melting temperature and cost-effectiveness [33]. PETG is particularly suitable for mechanical parts, printers, and protective components due to its flexibility, strength, and ease of printing. Moreover, flexible polymers like thermoplastic elastomers (TPE) and thermoplastic polyurethane (TPU) are used in 3D printing. These materials, similar to rubber in properties, find applications in automotive components, household appliances, and more [34].

To enhance the mechanical performance of printed components, fibers are employed as reinforcing materials. During the printing process, they are combined with the polymeric matrix, resulting in a composite with improved mechanical behavior, overcoming potential limitations and promoting wider adoption of this technology. Apart from the mentioned properties, it is essential to consider additional characteristics of the filaments, including recyclability and biodegradability, which signify their environmentally friendly nature. Several of the previously mentioned thermoplastic polymers, along with other options, possess such eco-friendly attributes, making them even more favorable for widespread adoption.

Materials such as PET, PLA, tire-TPE, and TPU can be recycled. Materials such as PLA, Nylon 11 (PA11), ABS, and PETG are biobased and biodegradable materials. This type of material should be the most adopted due to its sustainability [35].

3.3   3D Printing Technologies with Continuous Fibers

3D printing technologies for the development of continuous fibers are designated according to the used methodology for direct fiber integration, i.e., the way how the matrix and fiber are joined into the print nozzle and deposited. Accordingly, different approaches are proposed:

- In-situ impregnation;
- Co-extrusion with towpreg;
- Towpreg extrusion;
- In-situ consolidation;
- Inline Impregnation.

3D printing of continuous fiber-reinforced thermoplastics based on FDM technology was also investigated [36]. In this study, a thermoplastic filament of PLA was used as a polymeric matrix, and continuous carbon fibers or twisted yarns of natural jute fibers were used as reinforcements. Herein, both materials were fed independently into the printer machine. The process lies in the impregnation of the reinforced fibers with the polymeric filament within the nozzle of the printer previously heated, closely before printing. The results showed that using this methodology continuous fiber reinforcement enhanced the mechanical performance, namely the tensile strength of the composites in comparison with common 3D printing processes.

Even though the existing studies related to 3D printing of composites using continuous fiber filaments evidenced good results, their development based on 3D printing has been customized as a function of the needs, in order to develop printed composites with improved properties.

3.4   New 3D Printing Applications Using Natural Fibers

3D printing with natural fibers is an emerging field and several studies were being conducted to explore the prospects and challenges associated with 3D printing applications. Moreover, the use of natural fibers aligns with sustainability goals, as they are renewable resources and can reduce the environmental impact associated with traditional plastic-based 3D printing materials. Natural fibers have been used in 3D printing for rapid prototyping of various products. This approach allows designers and engineers to create sustainable prototypes to test form, fit, and function before proceeding with large-scale

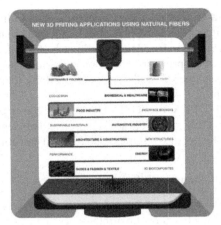

Fig. 6. Schematic figure of 3D printing applications in the market across several industries.

production. Nevertheless, to date, there are no applications in the market using natural fibers (Fig. 6).

Contrarily, synthetic fibers offer unique properties and advantages that make them suitable for specific 3D printing applications in the market across several industries. Some common applications include aerospace and defense, biomedical and healthcare, food industry, architecture and construction, energy, and automotive industry. Another industry that makes extensive use of this type of manufacturing is the fashion industry which creates innovative and unique clothing and accessories. Printing 3D designs onto fabric eliminates the need for glue and opens new possibilities for customized and personalized fashion items. Another industry that uses 3D printing is the footwear industry where designers can easily prototype and iterate shoe designs, create intricate lattice structures and designs, personalize shoe designs, enables cost-effective production with limited edition, use eco-friendly and recycled materials, and create midsoles with customized cushioning and support features. The textile industry also uses 3D printing so that the designers and manufacturers to create custom-fit clothing, develop prototypes before going into full-scale production, reducing textile waste by allowing manufacturers to produce only the required amount of material without excess scraps.

In summary, 3D printing has revolutionized various industries, offering new opportunities for customization, efficiency, and sustainability in manufacturing and design processes. As technology advances, the potential applications of 3D printing continue to expand, impacting diverse sectors worldwide [2, 4, 15, 29] being the challenge, 3D printing with natural fibers, however, it is crucial to improve some aspects, such as the need for specialized equipment and the optimization of printing parameters to achieve the desired material properties and print quality. Nonetheless, ongoing research and development in this field are expected to overcome these obstacles and lead to further innovative applications.

4 Conclusions and Future Trends in 3D Printing of Natural Fiber-based Biocomposites

The development of new materials using natural fibers as an alternative to conventional ones is of critical importance due to the numerous advantages they offer in terms of sustainability, biodegradability, renewability, resource abundance, and low cost [15]. These natural fibers can be combined with polymeric matrices to create enhanced natural fiber reinforced composites, making them ideal materials for a sustainable and circular economy.

Several studies have explored 3D printing with natural fibers to produce continuous fiber-reinforced biocomposite materials. However, there are challenges that need to be addressed to fully harness the potential of continuous filament-based natural fiber composites [2, 3, 13, 22, 23]:

Proper Material Selection: The characteristics of natural fibers can vary based on their source and origin, making it essential to carefully choose the right materials for specific applications;

Controlling Morphology and Thermal Properties: The morphology and thermal properties of the fibers need to be controlled to ensure the filament is printable and results in good printing quality;

Optimize Printing Parameters: Adjusting printing parameters, such as build orientation, fill percentage and layer width, can improve the mechanical performance of the printed parts;

Investigate Materials and Processes: In-depth research and standardization of materials and processes are crucial to ensure the industry can adopt these biocomposites successfully;

Structural Investigation: More investigation is required to study properties like mechanical performance, interface adhesion, and thermal properties to enhance the printing ratio and fabricate 3D printed materials with controlled structural features;

Customization and Design Flexibility: Developing sustainable biocomposites for industrial applications requires interdisciplinary research, covering materials science, processes, equipment, structural design, biomimicry, and final performance.

Further research on natural fiber to develop continuous filament for 3D printing is needed to create new advanced composite materials with improved mechanical performance and biodegradability. The use of industrial waste to produce these materials can lead to more sustainable supply chains and reduced environmental impact. Education initiatives, including research programs, workshops, and accessible design tools and software, are crucial to exploring the potential of 3D printing technology with natural fibers. Responsible implementation is necessary to maximize its positive social impact while addressing challenges such as job displacement and waste management.

Ultimately, 3D printing technology has the potential to reshape the manufacturing industry positively, offering numerous benefits to society. However, it requires careful consideration and responsible practices to ensure a sustainable and eco-friendly future.

Acknowledgements. The authors acknowledge the financial support from integrated project be@t – Textile Bioeconomy (TC-C12-i01, Sustainable Bioeconomy No. 02/C12-i01/202), promoted by the Recovery and Resilience Plan (RRP), Next Generation EU, for the period 2021–2026.

References

1. Mahamood, R.M., Akinlabi, S.A., Shatalov, M., Murashkin, E.V., Akinlabi, E.T.: Additive manufacturing/3d printing technology: a review. Ann. Dunarea de Jos Univ. Galati Fascicle XII Welding Equipment Technol. **30**, 51–58 (2019). https://doi.org/10.35219/awet.2019.07
2. Tian, X., et al.: 3D printing of continuous fiber reinforced polymer composites: development, application, and prospective. Chinese J. Mech. Eng.: Additive Manuf. Front. **1**(1), 100016 (2022). https://doi.org/10.1016/j.cjmeam.2022.100016
3. Le Duigou, A., Barbé, A., Guillou, E., Castro, M.: 3D printing of continuous flax fibre reinforced biocomposites for structural applications. Mater. Des. **180**, 107884 (2019). https://doi.org/10.1016/j.matdes.2019.107884
4. Praveena, B.A., Lokesh, N., Buradi, A., Santhosh, N., Praveena, B.L., Vignesh, R.: A comprehensive review of emerging additive manufacturing (3D printing technology): methods, materials, applications, challenges, trends and future potential. Mater. Today: Proc. **52**, 1309–1313 (2022). https://doi.org/10.1016/j.matpr.2021.11.059
5. Coniglio, N., Sivarupan, T., El Mansori, M.: Investigation of process parameter effect on anisotropic properties of 3D printed sand molds. Int. J. Adv. Manuf. Technol. **94**(5–8), 2175–2185 (2018). https://doi.org/10.1007/s00170-017-0861-5
6. Cat McClintock: Why Is Additive Manufacturing Important?. PTC (Digital Transforms Physical, 24 Sep 2019. https://www.ptc.com/en/blogs/cad/why-additive-manufacturing-important. Accessed 20 Jul 2023
7. Huang, J., Qin, Q., Wang, J.: A review of stereolithography: processes and systems. Processes **8**(9), 1138 (2020). https://doi.org/10.3390/pr8091138
8. Lekurwale, S., Karanwad, T., Banerjee, S.: Selective laser sintering (SLS) of 3D printlets using a 3D printer comprised of IR/red-diode laser. Ann. 3D Printed Med. **6**, 100054 (2022). https://doi.org/10.1016/j.stlm.2022.100054
9. Direct Ink Writing. Empa – Materials Science and Technology. https://www.empa.ch/web/coating-competence-center/direct-ink-writing. Accessed 20 Jul 2023
10. Reddy Dumpa, N., Bandari, S., Repka, M.A.: Novel gastroretentive floating pulsatile drug delivery system produced via hot-melt extrusion and fused deposition modeling 3D printing. Pharmaceutics **12**(1), 52 (2020). https://doi.org/10.3390/pharmaceutics12010052
11. FFF vs FDM: Difference and Best Printers. Top 3D Media – Digital manufacturing news and research, 27 Aug 2020. https://top3dshop.com/blog/fff-vs-fdm-difference-and-best-printers. Accessed 20 Jul 2023
12. Kabir, S.M.F., Mathur, K., Seyam, A.-F.M.: A critical review on 3D printed continuous fiber-reinforced composites: history, mechanism, materials and properties. Compos. Struct. **232**, 111476 (2020). https://doi.org/10.1016/j.compstruct.2019.111476
13. Le Duigou, A., Correa, D., Ueda, M., Matsuzaki, R., Castro, M.: A review of 3D and 4D printing of natural fibre biocomposites. Mater. Des. **194**, 108911 (2020). https://doi.org/10.1016/j.matdes.2020.108911
14. Ahmed, W., Alnajjar, F., Zaneldin, E., Al-Marzouqi, A.H., Gochoo, M., Khalid, S.: Implementing FDM 3D printing strategies using natural fibers to produce biomass composite. materials **13**(18), 4065 (2020). https://doi.org/10.3390/ma13184065

15. Bi, X., Huang, R.: 3D printing of natural fiber and composites: a state-of-the-art review. Mater. Des. **222**, 111065 (2022). https://doi.org/10.1016/j.matdes.2022.111065

16. Kuncevich, L.: 3D printing carbon fiber: chopped vs continuous fiber reinforcement. aniwaa, 10 May 2022. https://www.aniwaa.com/insight/am-materials/3d-printing-carbon-fiber-chopped-vs-continuous-fiber-reinforcement/. Accessed 27 Jul 2023

17. Caminero, M.A., Chacón, J.M., García-Moreno, I., Reverte, J.M.: Interlaminar bonding performance of 3D printed continuous fibre reinforced thermoplastic composites using fused deposition modelling. Polym. Test. **68**, 415–423 (2018). https://doi.org/10.1016/j.polymertesting.2018.04.038

18. Liu, G., Xiong, Y., Zhou, L.: Additive manufacturing of continuous fiber reinforced polymer composites: design opportunities and novel applications. Compos. Commun. **27**, 100907 (2021). https://doi.org/10.1016/j.coco.2021.100907

19. Nazir, M.H., Al-Marzouqi, A.H., Ahmed, W., Zaneldin, E.: The potential of adopting natural fibers reinforcements for fused deposition modeling: characterization and implications. Heliyon **9**(4), e15023 (2023). https://doi.org/10.1016/j.heliyon.2023.e15023

20. Naumov, A.: Continuous fiber 3D printing: 6 tips from Anisoprint. aniwaa, 26 Oct 2019. https://www.aniwaa.com/insight/am-materials/continuous-fiber-3d-printing-tips/. Accessed 27 Jul 2023

21. Tekinalp, H.L., et al.: Highly oriented carbon fiber–polymer composites via additive manufacturing. Compos. Sci. Technol. **105**, 144–150 (2014). https://doi.org/10.1016/j.compscitech.2014.10.009

22. Gauss, C., Pickering, K.L., Muthe, L.P.: The use of cellulose in bio-derived formulations for 3D/4D printing: a review. Compos. Part C: Open Access **4**, 100113 (2021). https://doi.org/10.1016/j.jcomc.2021.100113

23. Ahmad, M.N., Ishak, M.R., Mohammad Taha, M., Mustapha, F., Leman, Z.: A review of natural fiber-based filaments for 3D printing: filament fabrication and characterization. Materials **16**(11), 4052 (2023). https://doi.org/10.3390/ma16114052

24. O'Neal, B.: Natural Fiber Biocomposites in 3D & 4D Printing: A Review. 3dprint.com. 8 Dec 2020. https://3dprint.com/272129/natural-fiber-biocomposites-3d-4d-printing-review/. Accessed 27 Jul 2023

25. Sathish, T., Vijayakumar, M.D., Ayyangar, A.K.: Design and fabrication of industrial components using 3D printing. Mater. Today: Proc. **5**(6), 14489–14498 (2018). https://doi.org/10.1016/j.matpr.2018.03.036

26. 3D printed end-use parts transforming manufacturing. Imaginarium. 1 Apr 2023. https://imaginarium.io/3d-printed-end-use-parts/. Accessed 27 Jul 2023

27. Davey, R.: Researchers Present a Review of 3D Printing with Natural Fibers. AZOMaterials. 02 Aug 2022. https://www.azom.com/news.aspx?newsID=59807. Accessed 27 Jul 2023

28. Tao, Y., Li, P., Zhang, J., Wang, S., Shi, S.Q., Kong, F.: A review of fused filament fabrication of continuous natural fiber reinforced thermoplastic composites: techniques and materials. Polym. Compos. (2023). https://doi.org/10.1002/pc.27477

29. Iftekar, S.F., Aabid, A., Amir, A., Baig, M.: Advancements and limitations in 3D printing materials and technologies: a critical review. Polymers (Basel) **15**(11), 2519 (2023). https://doi.org/10.3390/polym15112519

30. 3D Printing with Polypropylene. Leapfrog – 3D Printers. https://www.lpfrg.com/guides/3d-printing-polypropylene/. Accessed 20 Jul 2023

31. "Nylon 3D Printing – The Ultimate Guide," All3DP (2023). https://all3dp.com/2/nylon-3d-printing-how-to-get-nylon-3d-printed/. Accessed 20 Jul 2023

32. Carlota, V.: All You Need to Know About ABS for 3D Printing. 3D natives – your source for 3D printing (2023). https://www.3dnatives.com/en/abs-3d-printing-060620194/#!. Accessed 20 Jul 2023

33. Vidakis, N., Petousis, M., David, C.N., Sagris, D., Mountakis, N., Karapidakis, E.: Mechanical performance over energy expenditure in MEX 3D printing of polycarbonate: a multiparametric optimization with the aid of robust experimental design. J. Manuf. Mater. Process. 7(1), 38 (2023). https://doi.org/10.3390/jmmp7010038

34. León-Calero, M., Reyburn Valés, S.C., Marcos-Fernández, Á., Rodríguez-Hernandez, J.: 3D printing of thermoplastic elastomers: role of the chemical composition and printing parameters in the production of parts with controlled energy absorption and damping capacity. Polymers 13(20), 3551 (2021). https://doi.org/10.3390/polym13203551

35. Melina. bluhm, Ultimate guide to sustainable 3D printing materials: Pathing the way for a circular economy. Replique, 26 Apr 2022. https://replique.io/2022/04/26/guide-to-sustainable-3d-printing-materials/. Accessed 27 Jul 2023

36. Matsuzaki, R., et al.: Three-dimensional printing of continuous-fiber composites by in-nozzle impregnation. Sci. Rep. 6(1), 23058 (2016). https://doi.org/10.1038/srep23058

aWaRe: Aiming for Water and Waste Reduction, Reuse and Recycling

Margarida Fernandes[2]($\boxtimes$) (iD), Augusta Silva[2]($\boxtimes$) (iD), Carla Silva[2]($\boxtimes$) (iD), Pedro Silva[1], Ricardo Silva[1], Mário Silva[1], Filipe Rodrigues[2], Beatriz França[2], Helena Vilaça[2], Rosa Silva[2], José Morgado[2], and Pedro Magalhães[1]($\boxtimes$)

[1] TINTEX - TEXTILES, S.A, V. N de Cerveira, Portugal
pedro.magalhaes@tintextextiles.com
[2] Technological Center for the Textile and Clothing Industry, CITEVE, V. N. Famalicão, Portugal
{mfernandes,asilva,cjsilva}@citeve.pt

Abstract. In the context of circular economy, the aWaRe project pretended to develop innovative textile solutions using own recycled fibers that were bio-finished with recycled water from TINTEX dyehouse Wastewater Treatment Plant (WWTP). The project focused on two R&D approaches, the treatment of water to a degree that allowed its reincorporation on wet processes conducted at TINTEX, as well as the development of knitted fabrics based on the reuse and recycling of production and stock excesses of the company.

The recycling and upcycling of cellulose-based knitted fabrics was performed by mechanical processes through defibrillation, followed by spinning, achieving yarns with a Ne 24 containing an amount of 40% of recycled fibres. Those yarns were knitted, and the resulting knitted fabrics were bio-finished by natural dyeing using only recycled water or used to create a specific colour pallet, thought the planed blend of recycled knitted fabrics without further dyeing. The low colour difference ($\Delta E < 1$) results from the dyeing, when comparing with samples dyed with fresh water demonstrated that the use of recycled water in natural dyeing process had no impact on the resulting colour. The wastewater treatment was accomplished through ultrafiltration and reverse osmosis, enabling for a water quality that allowed a total incorporation of this wastewater at production level.

The solutions explored in aWaRe represents an innovative approach compared to the solutions available in the market: significant advancements in the recycling processes for textile substrates and wastewaters were made, enabling the production of new recycled natural fibres with the required technical characteristics to produce thin yarns and the efficient reuse of wastewater in a closed-loop system.

Keywords: Sustainability · Upcycling fabrics · Closed loop recycling wastewater · Circular economy · Water and waste reduction

1 Introduction

In Europe, the Textile Industry represents an important contribution to the EU economy holding a solid position in the global market. In Europe, Portugal is one of the main producers of textiles and garments [1]. According to the European Commission, the

© The Author(s), under exclusive license to Springer Nature Switzerland AG 2024
T. Guarda et al. (Eds.): ARTIIS 2023, CCIS 1937, pp. 357–367, 2024.
https://doi.org/10.1007/978-3-031-48930-3_27

textiles production almost doubled between 2000 and 2015, and it is expected to increase by 63% by 2030. Consequently, the negative impacts also have growth, making the Textile Industry responsible for the fourth highest impact on the environment and climate change [2]. In 2023, the European Environmental Agency published a report highlighting these impacts:[3].

- **Overconsumption of natural resources**: in 2015 it was estimated that the global textile and clothing industry used 79 billion cubic meters of water;
- **Water pollution**: it is estimated that the dyeing and finishing products are responsible for about 20% of global clean water pollution;
- **Greenhouse gas emissions**: 10% of global carbon emissions are attributed to the fashion industry. This represents more than international flights and maritime shipping combined.
- **Textile waste in landfills and low recycling rates**: The textiles exported from the EU has tripled over the past two decades from slightly over 550,000 tonnes in 2000 to almost 1.7 million tonnes in 2019. In 2017, it was estimated that less than 1% of all textiles worldwide were recycled into new products, according to the Ellen MacArthur Foundation.

Taking in account this scenario, over the last years, and more recently boosted by European Green Deal and EU strategy for sustainable and circular textiles, Textile Industry, including the Portuguese companies have gone through a significant transformation to implement sustainable technologies and environmentally friendly process throughout all the entire textile value chain. However, Textile Industry stills works based on the traditional concepts of linear economy [4–6]. This type of economy is exhaustive and intensive both financially and environmentally, creating also, consequently, negative impacts at a societal level. With its low rates of use and low levels of recycling, the current wasteful, linear system is the root cause of this massive and ever-expanding pressure on resources [7, 8]. In the last years several initiatives for textile recycling (both pre- and post- consumer textile waste) have emerged. However, circular models that include the recycling of the wastes resulting from the companies different production flows, in an integrated approach focused on the company itself, are missing.

Regarding textile wastewater treatment, the conventional methods are usually based on physical-chemical methods such as such as chlorination, coagulation-flocculation, adsorption, biological methods and the advanced oxidation processes of ozonation, and Fenton treatments [9, 10]. Beside these methods, the membranes technologies are also mentioned as one of the most effective methods for textile wastewater treatment and reuse. Those include reverse osmosis, nanofiltration, ultrafiltration and microfiltration [11, 12]. In literature there are only a few publications regarding the treatment of textile wastewater and its reuse in a closed-loop approach.

TINTEX is a pioneer Portuguese company that has adopted an innovative strategy in their production process, for example by shifting from the traditional dyeing process that uses dyes and chemicals from fossil sources towards bio-based dyeing and finishing processes using dyes from natural sources, including wastes. Taking in consideration TINTEX context as a dyeing company aligned with the principles of circular economy and sustainability, the aWaRe project, Aiming for Water and Waste Reduction, Reuse and Recycling was developed. To assist the R&D activities, CITEVE was selected as a partner.

The main objective of aWaRe was to investigate the conditions for the treatment of water to a degree that allows its reincorporation on dyeing and finishing processes, as well as the development of upcycling fabrics based on the reuse and recycling of production and dead stocks of knitted fabrics. These fabrics, composed of either cotton or lyocell (cellulose-based), were recycled by mechanical processes which eliminates the need of chemical recycling and thus the potential use of harmful chemicals. Using the recycled fibres, yarns with a Ne 24, with 40% of recycled material on its composition were produced. Furthermore, in aWaRe, the optimization of wastewater treatment or the recycling of wastewater allowed the total incorporation of this water at production level for the bio-finishing of recycled knitted fabrics. Thanks to this innovative approach, the sustainability and circularity objectives for reducing water consumption and enabling effective recycling systems, were successfully implemented at industrial level by TINTEX.

According to the previous exposed, aWaRe project is perfectly aligned with European Commission roadmaps such as EU strategy for sustainable and circular textiles and Green Deal since it aims to enable TINTEX to use their own knitted fabrics considered as stock and production excess to produce new recycled yarns and coloured knitted fabrics taking advantage of the original colour of recycled fibers (without further dyeing). Moreover, it also pretended the treatment and re-use of wastewater in order to be re-introduced in the company production processes, namely in natural dyeing of the recycled knitted fabrics.

2   Materials and Methods

2.1   Mechanical Recycling of Textiles

The first step consisted in the selection of TINTEX cellulosic fabrics considered as stock excess and their sorting according to colour (coloured and white), composition and structure. Then, the fabrics went thought the mechanical recycling process itself, which included 4 main steps: cutting, defibrillation, carding, spinning, and knitting (see Fig. 1. Pilot-scale mechanical recycling line).

Cutting and defibrillation   Spinning   Knitting

Fig. 1. Pilot-scale mechanical recycling line.

The first step was the physical cut of the fabrics. Two passages in the cutting machine were need and different cut dimensions were defined according to the fabric structure (see Table 1).

Table 1. Cutting parameters applied according to the fabrics structure.

Cutting parameters	Type of fabrics		
	White Jersey	Marine Rib	Lilac fleece
Dimension of the first cut (mm)	35	15	35
Dimension of the second cut (mm)	25	25	25

Following, in the defibrillation of fabrics a single passage in the five rotating cylinders was performed, according to the parameters detailed in Table 2. In this step the procedure was the same for all fabrics.

Table 2. Defibrillation parameters.

Controlled parameters	1st cylinder	2nd cylinder	3rd cylinder	4th cylinder	5th cylinder
Rotation speed (rpm)	1650	1800	2000	2150	2300
Feeding speed (m/min)	1.15	0.81	0.99	1.29	1.50

Throughout the defibrillation stage, the fiber mantle was mainly composed of short fibers, thread remnants, and occasionally, textile substrate residues. For that, it was necessary to separate fibers, remove neps and potential residues, homogenize the fiber blend, and provide them with some alignment. This was accomplished by carding. Also, at this stage, the blending of these recycled fibers with virgin cotton fibers was manually performed, in the ratio of 40/60% respectively, into a final weight of 0.5 kg. In the end it was obtained the carded web. Then, the carded webs followed to lamination that provides stretching to the web, aligning and orienting the fibers within it to achieve uniform density in the resulting web. For the first pass in the laminator, the two carded webs produced were split in half to achieve a 4-fold. The first laminated web was produced in four identical sections with lengths ranging from 11 to 13 m to undergo a second pass, also with a 4-fold. The theoretical stretching was defined to 2.76 m m^{-1}, which is the minimum configuration possible on the equipment. Regarding the twist, a Z twist (to the right) was defined to produce the mesh. The final step in yarn production was the spinning. The stretch applied was 45 m m^{-1} (meters of yarn per meter of roving), and a twist of 700 turns of the yarn around its own axis per meter of yarn.

2.2 Wastewater Treatment

To implement a closed-loop system for recycling water at TINTEX, a pilot unit in WWTP was installed. That includes two membrane systems: an ultrafiltration stage followed by reverse osmosis. This facility also incorporates two containers for chemicals storage and automatic dosing (one for each treatment stages) and two ultrafiltered water intermediate

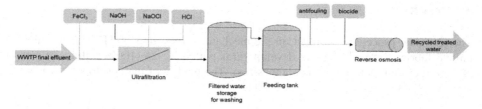

Fig. 2. Scheme of the pilot unit for wastewater treatment and recycling.

tanks: one for storing the washing water and another for feeding the reverse osmosis system (see Fig. 2).

Several characterization tests were performed during the optimization of the pilot unit. The target water quality parameters were pH, Temperature, Turbidity, Total suspended solids (TSS), Chemical Oxygen Demand (COD), Total Nitrogen, Total Phosphorus, Manganese, Copper, Total Alkalinity, Chlorides, Sulfates, Nitrates, Total Iron, Silica, Conductivity and Total Hardness.

2.3 Natural Dyeing and Bio-finishing

After the wastewater treatment, the resulting recycled water was used to study the suitability of using this water for the incorporation in the company wet processes, especially in the dyeing process.

For this purpose, different colours were selected, and by incorporating different percentages of recycled water into the dye bath, samples of fabric were dyed at laboratory scale using synthetic dyes. The selected colours were optical white, two dark colours (marine and black), and a light colour (dusty pink). Those represent colours in which the utilization of recycled water could have more impact in achieving the company quality standards. The conventional dyeing procedure for reactive dyeing was followed.

In the natural dyeing process, the recycled fabrics were dyed following the patented process of Tintex – ColorauTM, to enable a bio-finishing process. The colouration with chestnut and thyme, which are considered representativity for TINTEX, was selected. For that, an infusion of 20 g/L of chestnut and thyme was prepared using recycled water at 50, 75% and 100% (only recycled water), fresh captured water and water from WWTP (without treatment). The prepared solutions were kept in 100 °C during 15 min and then were filtered. For the dyeing process, a ratio of textile material to infusion of 1:100 was selected. This procedure was conducted at 60 °C (gradient of 2 °C/min) for 60 min.

The validation strategy consisted in comparing the colour differences (CIELAB colour space) of the fabrics dyed with different percentages of the recycled water. A control using fresh captured water was also included.

2.4 Yarns and Fabrics Characterization

The tests for tensile strength and elongation at break of the produced recycled yarns were conducted according to ISO 2062:2009.

The colour difference analysis and grey scale was performed in a Datacolor Benchtop Spectrophotometer with the CIE standard illuminant D65.

3 Results

The technical procedures applied on the mechanical recycling of TINTEX cellulosic knitted fabrics were adequate to develop yarns with a Ne 24 (100% cellulosic) using 40% of recycled material on its composition. The quality of the developed yarns was also evaluated by resistance tests (see Table 3).

Table 3. Yarns resistance evaluation.

Resistance test	Yarns produced named by the fabric that originated them			
	White Jersey yarn	Marine Rib yarn	Lilac fleece yarn	Virgin cotton yarn
Breaking strength (cN)	210	160	160	410
Tenacity (RKM)	5.8	4.6	4.4	11.0
Elongation (%)	8.0	8.4	5.8	6.9

The results demonstrate that, as expected, the recycled yarns exhibited tensile strength and tenacity values approximately 50 to 60% lower compared to yarns made with virgin material. However, for recycled yarns, the obtained toughness values were considered satisfactory. The elongation percentage was higher in two of the recycled yarns when compared to the virgin yarn, namely the White Jersey yarn with 1.1% higher elongation and the Marine Rib yarn with 1.5% higher elongation. The Lilac fleece yarn presented the lowest elongation, with a value 1.1% lower than the reference thread. In theory, there is a trade-off between the strength properties of the yarns, such that an increase in toughness leads to a reduction in the elongation percentage. Therefore, as expected the raw cotton yarns presented the best strength properties, since it was made from fibers that have not undergone any treatment and have their characteristics unchanged.

Besides the white fabrics suitable for the dyeing process, a colour pallet of recycled knitted fabrics without further dyeing was created (see Fig. 3).

Fig. 3. Colour pallet of 100% cellulosic recycled knitted fabrics without dyeing.

Regarding wastewater treatment from TINTEX WWTP, to access the treatment efficiency of the installed pilot, firstly it was necessary to characterize the water at the inlet (Table 4).

Table 4. Wastewater characterization at the inlet of the ultrafiltration station.

Analysed parameter	Unit	Reference	Average value	Minimum value	Maximum value
pH	Sorensen	-	7.84	7.53	8.47
Temperature	°C	-	23.10	13.50	28.20
Turbidity*	NTU	< 0	11.30	5.00	20.10
TSS	mg/l	-	32.00	18.00	42.00
COD	mg/l O_2	<100	57.90	47.20	70.80
Total Nitrogen	mg/l N	-	5.35	4.70	6.60
Total Phosphorus	mg/l P	-	4.87	3.74	6.69
Manganese	mg/l Mn	-	0.95	0.50	1.40
Copper	mg/l Cu	-	0.70	0.37	1.02
Total Alkalinity	mg/L CaCO3	-	782	728	824
Chlorides	mg/l Cl	-	2.124	1.621	3.990
Sulfates	mg/l SO_4	-	629	445	833
Nitrates	mg/l N-NO_3	-	2.21	0.95	3.54

The implementation of the pilot unit based on the membrane systems (ultrafiltration followed by reverse osmosis) ensured an effective treatment of the wastewater, enabling a water with a suitable quality, as presented in Table 5.

The results show that, except for the case of manganese, the quality parameters are lower than the reference values for water recycling. Additionally, it was also verified that the treated water quality is very similar to the TINTEX input water (data not shown). The case of manganese can be explained by a lower sensitivity of the analytical method used for low concentrations of this parameter.

For the validation of the recycled water re-introduction in finishing processes at TINTEX, the dyeing tests were performed firstly at laboratory level, using non-recycled knitted fabrics. The results are presented as colour difference (ΔE) of the textile samples dyed with different percentages of recycled wastewater (Table 6).

The results of the colour difference demonstrated that, at laboratory scale, the recycled water had no impact on the resulting colour of the knitted fabrics, as all the tests yielded ΔE values considered acceptable for a dyeing process ($\Delta E < 1$).

Taking in consideration these results, in the following trials the dyeing process was performed in recycled knitted fabrics following the natural dyeing procedure using the

Table 5. Water quality parameters after the treatment.

Analysed parameter	Unit	Reference	Average value	Minimum value	Maximum value
pH	Sorensen	–	5.54	5.17	5.89
Temperature	°C	–	22.9	14.0	28.0
Turbidity*	NTU	<1	0.23	0.12	0.45
TSS*	mg/l	–	3.1	2.5	4.0
COD*	mg/l O_2	–	35.4	31.1	39.8
Total Nitrogen	mg/l N	–	0.61	0.51	0.73
Total Phosphorus	mg/l P	–	0	0	0
Manganese	mg/l Mn	0,20	0.47	0.20	0.90
Total, Copper	mg/l Cu	0,20	0.04	0.03	0.06
Total Alkalinity	mg/L CaCO3	–	16.92	7.55	26.20
Chlorides	mg/l Cl	300	19.2	13.0	22.6
Sulfates	mg/l SO_4	200	0	0	0
Nitrates	mg/l $N-NO_3$	10	0.31	0.16	0.41
Silica	mg/l Si	–	1.94	1.60	2.80
Conductivity	μS/cm	900	87.1	82.1	96.8
Total Hardness	mg/L $CaCO_3$	–	1.02	0.82	1.16

* Analysed on Ultrafiltration Outlet / Reverse Osmosis Inlet

Table 6. Colour difference of the non-recycled textile samples dyed with different percentages of recycled water.

Colour Difference (ΔE)	Percentages of recycled water					
	5%	10%	20%	50%	75%	100%
Optical white	0.16	0.14	0.29	0.29	0.31	0.18
Dusty Pink	0.78	0.74	0.71	0.71	0.7	0.47
Marine	0.79	0.38	0.34	0.46	0.5	0.34
Black	0.78	0.84	0.56	0.71	0.49	0.87

higher percentages of recycled water (50%, 75% and 100%). In Table 7 a visual analysis is presented, together with ΔE values and the greyscale level of the recycled textile samples. The sample dyed with fresh captured water was selected as control.

Table 7. Recycled knitted samples finished by the natural dyeing process with water from different sources.

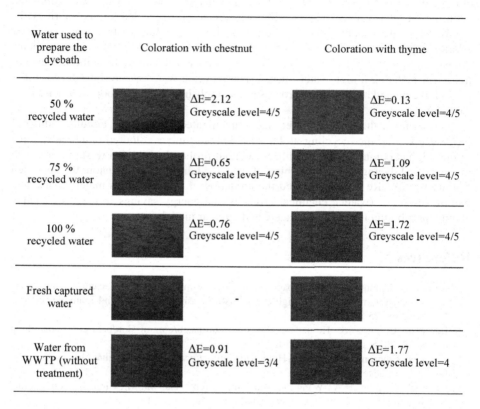

Water used to prepare the dyebath	Coloration with chestnut		Coloration with thyme	
50 % recycled water		ΔE=2.12 Greyscale level=4/5		ΔE=0.13 Greyscale level=4/5
75 % recycled water		ΔE=0.65 Greyscale level=4/5		ΔE=1.09 Greyscale level=4/5
100 % recycled water		ΔE=0.76 Greyscale level=4/5		ΔE=1.72 Greyscale level=4/5
Fresh captured water		-		-
Water from WWTP (without treatment)		ΔE=0.91 Greyscale level=3/4		ΔE=1.77 Greyscale level=4

For the coloration with chestnut, when using 50% of recycled water, a higher colour difference was attained, that could be explained by the visual irregularities seen in the textile structure.

Nevertheless, analysing the results globally, we can conclude that the incorporation of the recycled treated water, by membrane technologies (ultrafiltration followed by reverse osmosis), in the natural and conventional dyeing processes did not compromise the company quality standards, proving the feasibility of using this recycled water in the company wet finishing textile processes at an industrial level, with significant savings in water consumption.

4 Conclusions

The aWare project accomplished innovative developments regarding both textile and wastewater recycling and reuse in TINTEX industrial production. One of the results was the development of recycled yarns with a Ne 24 (100% cellulosic) with 40% of recycled material from TINTEX knitted fabrics considered as stock excess for the company. With the recycled yarns, a colour pallet was created for recycled knitted fabric without dyeing with a suitable performance and quality. In parallel, another achievement of aWaRe project was the implementation of a pilot unit, at industrial scale, based on membranes technologies (ultrafiltration and reverse osmosis) able to perform the wastewater treatment reaching a high water quality. The recycled water was re-introduced in the natural dyeing and bio-finishing processes accomplishing a closed-loop water circuit at TINTEX.

Furthermore, the aWaRe project has implemented a genuinely circular industrial process, covering the recycling of TINTEX knitted fabrics coloured taking advantage of the original colour of recycled fibers (without further dyeing) and wastewater re-use in the natural dyeing and bio-finishing of recycled fabrics. In conclusion, the approach followed in aWaRe project allowed the reduction of virgin textiles materials use and natural resources (water), chemical products and energy savings in the textile value chain, contributing to more sustainable and circular models.

References

1. European Commission Homepage. https://single-market-economy.ec.europa.eu/sectors/textiles-ecosystem/fashion-and-high-end-industries/fashion-and-high-end-industries-eu_en. Last accessed 25 Jul 2023
2. European Commission Homepage. https://ec.europa.eu/commission/presscorner/detail/en/qanda_22_2015. Last accessed 25 Jul 2023
3. European Environmental Agency Homepage. https://www.eea.europa.eu/en/topics/in-depth/textiles. Last accessed 25 Jul 2023
4. Chen, X., Memon, H.A., Wang, Y., Marriam, I., Tebyetekerwa, M.: Circular economy and sustainability of the clothing and textile industry. Mater. Circ. Econ. 3, 1–9 (2021)
5. Furferi, R., Volpe, Y., Mantellassi, F.: Circular economy guidelines for the textile industry. Sustainability 14, 11111 (2022)
6. Koszewska, M.: Circular economy — challenges for the textile and clothing industry. Autex Res. J. 18(4), 337–347 (2018)
7. European Parliament. https://www.europarl.europa.eu/RegData/etudes/BRIE/2022/729405/EPRS_BRI(2022)729405_EN.pdf. Last accessed 25 Jul 2023
8. Salmi, A., Kaipia, R.: Implementing circular business models in the textile and clothing industry. J. Cleaner Product. 378, 134492 (2022)
9. Lafi, R., Gzara, L., Lajimi, R.H., Hafiance, A.: Treatment of textile wastewater by a hybrid ultrafiltration/electrodialysis process. Chem. Eng. Process. 132, 105–113 (2018)
10. Al-Tohamy, R., et al.: A critical review on the treatment of dye-containing wastewater: ecotoxicological and health concerns of textile dyes and possible remediation approaches for environmental safety. Ecotoxicol. Env. Saf. 231, 113160 (2022)

11. Marszałek, J., Żyłła, R.: Recovery of water from textile dyeing using membrane filtration processes. Processes **9**(10), 1833 (2021). https://doi.org/10.3390/pr9101833
12. Azanaw, A., Birlie, B., Teshome, B., Jemberie, M.: Textile effluent treatment methods and eco-friendly resolution of textile wastewater. Case Stud. Chem. Env. Eng. **6**, 100230 (2022). https://doi.org/10.1016/j.cscee.2022.100230

STVgoDigital: A Digital Product Passport Solution

Miguel Sá[1], Catarina Guise[1(✉)], Filipa Costa[1], Paula Rodrigues[1], João Oliveira[1],
Ana Barros[2], Ricardo Silva[2], Toni Alves[3], Manuel Santos[3],
António Miguel Rosado da Cruz[4,5], Marcelo Alves[6], and Carla Joana Silva[1]

[1] CITEVE, Rua Fernando Mesquita 2785, 4760-034 Vila Nova de Famalicão, Portugal
{cguise,cjsilva}@citeve.pt

[2] CeNTI, Rua Fernando Mesquita 2785, 4760-034 Vila Nova de Famalicão, Portugal

[3] Centro de Computação Gráfica, Campus de Azurém, Edifício 14, 4800-058 Guimarães,
Portugal

[4] Instituto Politécnico de Viana Do Castelo, Praça General Barbosa 44, 4900-348 Viana Do
Castelo, Portugal

[5] ALGORITMI Research Lab, Escola de Engenharia – Universidade do Minho, Campus de
Azurém, 4800-058 Guimarães, Portugal

[6] INFOS – Informática E Serviços S.A, Rua Veloso Salgado 971 1011, 4450-801 Leça da
Palmeira, Portugal

Abstract. The Textile & Clothing sector is a significant global industrial sector with substantial environmental and social impacts, particularly in developing countries. Addressing sustainability challenges and promoting transparency and traceability within the industry's value chain have become critical objectives. To this end, the European Commission has introduced the Digital Product Passport strategy, aiming to minimize the industry's carbon and environmental footprint by providing consumers with transparent information. In this context, the STVgoDigital project – PPS1, developed in Portugal, focuses on implementing traceability for textile and clothing products, presenting a possible solution for the Digital Product Passport. The project's goal is to enhance transparency and accountability in the textile industry, empowering consumers to make more conscious and informed choices. By combining traceability and the Digital Product Passport, the textile sector seeks to reduce its environmental impact and promote sustainable practices both within the European Union and globally. This work highlights the results of the STVgoDigital project – PPS1, showcasing the potential for transforming the textile industry towards a more sustainable and responsible future.

Keywords: Textile and Clothing Value Chain · Environmental and Social Indicators · Environmental and Social Impact Score · Digital Product Passport

1 Introduction

The Textile & Clothing (T&C) sector holds significant position within the European manufacturing industry. As per Euratex's data in 2021, this industry comprised approximately 143,000 companies, providing employment to a substantial workforce of 1.3

T. Guarda et al. (Eds.): ARTIIS 2023, CCIS 1937, pp. 368–376, 2024.
https://doi.org/10.1007/978-3-031-48930-3_28

million individuals. Furthermore, it generated an impressive turnover of €147 billion, with 56% of the revenue coming from textiles and man-made fibers, and the remaining 44% from clothing. The T&C sector's importance is evident in its substantial contribution to the European Union (EU) production landscape. Key players in industry, including Italy, Germany, France, Spain, and Portugal, collectively account for a significant three-quarters share in this sector [1].

Over the recent years, Portugal has earned widespread global recognition and a distinguished reputation in the T&C sector, thanks to its exceptional values of quality, innovation, creativity, resilience, and responsiveness. According to the data from the Textile and Clothing Association of Portugal (ATP) in 2021, the T&C sector in Portugal experienced significantly growth in 2021, accounting for 8% of the country's overall manufacturing industry turnover. This solidifies its position as a major contributor to Portugal's economic landscape. Moreover, Portugal's T&C sector secured 5% of the EU T&C turnover, underscoring its competitiveness and relevance on the European stage. Regarding employment, the T&C sector plays a vital role in the Portuguese manufacturing sector, representing 19% of the total employment. On the EU level, Portugal's contribution to the T&C sector's employment impact was also noteworthy, accounting for nearly 10% of the overall EU T&C employment [2].

In 2020, textile consumption per person in the EU led to significant environmental impacts, requiring 400 m^2 of land, 9 m^3 of water and 391 kg of raw materials. Global textile fibre production has nearly doubled from 58 million tonnes in 2000 to 109 million tonnes in 2020, with a projected growth to 145 million tonnes by 2030 [3]. Among various consumption categories, textiles rank fourth in terms of environmental and climate change impact in Europe, following food, housing, and mobility [4].

To address this issue, the European Commission is actively working to improve the sustainability of textiles. The new strategy involves implementing ecodesign requirements for textiles, promoting durability, repairability, reusability and recyclability. It also includes the introduction of a Digital Product Passport (DPP) to provide clear information about a product's environmental performance. Additionally, the Comission urges companies to take responsibility and minimize their carbon and environmental footprints in the textile industry [3].

The European Commission is working on establishing sustainability principles and other appropriate ways to regulate multiple aspects of product life cycles to improve product durability, reusability, upgradability, and reparability, as well as addressing the presence of hazardous chemicals in products and increasing their energy and resource efficiency, as part of its Circular Economy Action Plan [4]. The Action Plan mentions "mobilising the potential of digitalisation of product information, including solutions such as digital passports, tagging, and watermarks [5]. The Wuppertal Institute has released a wide definition of Digital Product Passport (DPP) defining it as a data collection that summarizes a product's components, materials, and chemical compounds, as well as information on reparability, spare parts, and proper disposal instructions. The data contained in the DPP is collected from all phases of the product life cycle and can be utilized to optimise design, production, usage, and disposal.

The EU DPP is a mandatory electronic record that is set to be fully required by 2030, established under the EU Green Deal legislation. The primary objective is to provide clear, structured, and accessible information regarding the environmental sustainability characteristics of products, specially aiming to enhance transparency within the textile industry. According to the Fashion Revolution annual report on transparency in the fashion industry, the current state of transparency in the sector is quite limited. Out of the 200 brands included in the study, not a single brand achieved transparency levels above 70%. In fact, most brands (90%) fell below a transparency level of 50% [6].

Various solutions have been developed in response to the requirement for a DPP, with CIRPASS project offering a comprehensive overview of DPP-related initiatives [7]. Building on these efforts and recognizing the significance of the transparency and traceability in T&C value chain, the STVgoDigital DPP was created as part of the broader STVgoDigital project [8]. The main objective is to provide an innovative and comprehensive solution for the clothing and home textile sectors, ensuring transparency, traceability, and circularity. The work presented in this research paper reflects the key outcomes of the PPS1 ("Sustainable & Circular Textile ID 4.0"), one of the components within the project "STVgoDIGITAL: Digitization of the Textile and Clothing Value Chain" (https://stvgodigital.pt). This larger mobilizing project aims to engage various stakeholders, including companies in the T&C sector and other related industries, to drive the digital transition and embrace the principals of Industry 4.0, with particular focus on information and communication technologies.

In this context, the DPP is a tool that can be used to promote transparency and responsibility in the production of products, allowing consumers to get detailed information about what they are buying and how it was produced. At the same time, companies that wish to demonstrate their commitment to sustainability and social responsibility can also use it as a valuable tool.

2 Research Methodology

This section describes the research methodology used to perform the case studies. To dive further into the detailed intricacies of a given occurrence, a case study technique was adopted, allowing to analyze the particularities of the DPP within a real-case scenario. Using this methodology, we were able to have a complete knowledge of the products and processes involved in the production of the developed demonstrators, enabling to collect and analyze the generated data, and making conclusions.

This section presents de demonstrators and DPP solutions developed, which includes an explanation of the indicators used to calculate the sustainability index of a textile product, considering both environmental and social aspects. The development process focused on two distinct research and development lines, one for clothing and another for home textiles. These lines were carefully tailored to provide to the specific needs and unique characteristics of each sector.

2.1 Environmental, Circular, Economic, and Social Indicators

To conduct a comprehensive quantitative analysis of the total environmental, economic, and social impact of the textile articles, the solution tracked every batch throughout its value chain. This tracking process allowed to obtain a global Sustainability Index, which is a score ranging from A to F (being A the highest), distributed as follows:

- A: greater than 85%;
- B: between 75% and 85%;
- C: between 65% and 75%;
- D: between 55% and 65%;
- E: between 45% and 55%;
- F: lower than 45%.

The Sustainability Index provides consumers with valuable information about the overall impact of the desired product. By making this information accessible, consumers become more aware of sustainability issues and are encouraged to adopt more conscious and environmentally beneficial purchasing habits. This initiative aims to empower consumers, enabling them to make informed and conscious choices when buying textile products.

The Sustainability Index comprises two distinct scores: the Environmental and Circular Score (ECS), and the Economic and Social Score (ESS). Together, these scores enabled the calculation of the total Sustainability Index, providing a comprehensive assessment of a product's performance in terms of environmental, economic and social sustainability. The ECS score focus on environmental and circular aspects of the traced product batches throughout the value chain. It is derived from data values of various indicators collected at different stages of production, being collected every time a new batch is created. On the other hand, the ESS score addresses the economic and social aspects of the companies involved in the industrial activities to generate the specific product. Unlike the ECS score, the ESS score pertains to a specific company and requires annual updates. It is important to highlight that the data used to calculate these scores are collected from various stakeholders throughout the T&C value chain. The ECS score is specific to each product/batch, and the relevant data is provided whenever a batch is produced. In contrast, the ESS score relates to a particular company and must be updated on an annual basis.

Since the ECS indicator score is specific to the product/batch being produced, entails collecting data from a wide range of activities within the textile value chain. This includes both logistics activities, such as transportation, and productive activities like spinning, weaving, dyeing, finishing, and manufacturing. For logistics activities, the environmental footprint is estimated based on factors like means of transport used (e.g., airplane, train, container ship, etc.), the distance travelled, and environmental data obtained from established Life Cycle Assessment (LCA) databases. These databases consider the estimated consumption associated with each type of transport. Similarly, productive activities are assessed based on various factors, including the consumption of water, energy and chemicals, the generation of liquid effluents and solid waste, and the estimated durability of the product, as determined by quality control tests. Once all the relevant data is collected, each variable is appropriately normalized and combined into a structured data model. This data model is designed to create effective indicators that allow for thorough analysis of the environmental impact of each activity within the textile value chain.

The ESS indicator score is derived from economic and social parameters related to the companies engaged in the value chain. These parameters include factors such as the number of employees, their salaries, salaries differences, age distribution, types of employment contracts, work schedules, and training opportunities. Additionally, the

ESS score considers the company's economic situation, certifications it holds, and any social initiatives it undertakes. Similar to the process for the ECS indicator score, the data collected for the ESS score is also normalized and combined using a predetermined model scale. This enables the calculation of the ESS indicator score. Together, the ECS and ESS scores form a comprehensive method for evaluating the environmental and social sustainability of textile products. By calculating the total Sustainability Index using these indicator scores, it becomes possible to determine the overall sustainability performance of a textile product. This approach allows stakeholders to identify areas for improvement within the textile value chain, fostering more sustainable practices and promoting positive social and environmental impacts in the industry.

2.2 Proposed Solution for Traceability in the T&C Value Chain

The proposed solution offers comprehensive traceability throughout the entire T&C value chain, using various innovative components. This includes NFC tags, invisible QR codes induced by UV light or temperature, and invisible yarns. The elements allow for discreet and reliable tracking of textile articles and products.

The traceability features enable the monitoring of environmental and social indicators presented earlier as they are traversal to the T&C value chain. To achieve this, the solution´s architecture comprises several interacting components. Enterprise Resource Planning (ERP) applications used by value chain partners, integration portals, and third-party applications (e.g., IoT agents, mobile apps) integrate with the traceability back-end services through an integration layer API. When a user interacts with front-end applications (view layer), a sequence of actions occurs:

1. Authentication and authorization processes ensure that the user has appropriate access to the platform and identifies the type of operations they can perform within the system;
2. Data insertion operations are queued and handled sequentially by the business layer, which calls the methods of smart contract's/chaincodes to insert traceability data onto the blockchain;
3. Data query operations are directly sent to the business layer, which in turn calls the chaincode's methods to retrieve traceability data from the blockchain;
4. A request to the blockchain is made through the Fablo Representational State Transfer (REST) API to execute a transaction in the chaincode;
5. The chaincode, installed on non-ordered peers and channels, directly interacts with the CouchDB key-value-based database. This database holds the world state, representing the latest and most up-to-date view of the blockchain network's ledger;
6. If the transaction consensus passes, the ledger and the world state database are updated, in case of invoke/put transactions. Query/get transactions, on the other hand, do not require consensus approval.

3   Results

The STVgoDigital R&D project's software artifacts underwent validation tests using two case studies: one focused on clothing with a partitioned supply chain and the other on home textiles with a vertical supply chain. The evaluation of the system's flexibility involved studying the environmental performance of two items with different colours. These case studies were carried out as part of a pilot project involving Portuguese textile producers and covered all activities related to textile product production in the Portuguese textile cluster.

3.1 Case Study 1: A Home Textile Product (Towel)

The first case study focused on a vertical supply chain for a home textile product, in which all production activities were carried out within a single company. The level of detail for analysis was at the batch level, enabling comprehensive processing and examination of collections of textile products. To compute the Environmental and Circular Score (ECS), and the Economic and Social Score (ESS) indicators, data collection began at the spinning activity. The company only needed to specify the raw materials used and their origins. Data was gathered from various production stages, including spinning, weaving, dyeing, finishing, and manufacturing. Additionally, the company identified the customer to whom each batch was sent, completing the data collection process and incorporating the consumption of logistical activities into the textile product's performance assessment.

The collected data was then aggregated in a clear and understandable manner, enabling consumers to make more informed and responsible purchasing decisions. The case study's analysis encompassed the product's composition, colour, environmental score, production journey, ECS and ESS indicators, consumption dimensions, as well as maintenance and care instructions. To facilitate consumer understanding and decision-making, a customer app was provided, featuring detailed screens for each aspect of the product (see Fig. 1).

Fig. 1. Consumer application depicting traceability and other product information, for the Home Textile value chain – Light colour towel. (https://texjourney.com/)

Furthermore, the case study also included a pilot to compare the performance of a dark-coloured towel with a light-coloured towel, evaluating their respective environmental impacts or other relevant aspects.

3.2 Case Study 2: A Garment (T-shirt)

The second case study focused on a clothing product with a partitioned supply chain. The process began with the spinning company providing raw materials information and environmental performance data. Subsequently, the batch was transferred to the knitting company, and this pattern continued for the subsequent stages of knitting, dyeing, finishing, and manufacturing. At each step, the respective company specified the customer to whom the batch was sent and entered data related to the consumption of logistical activities, contributing to the assessment of the textile product's overall performance (see Fig. 2).

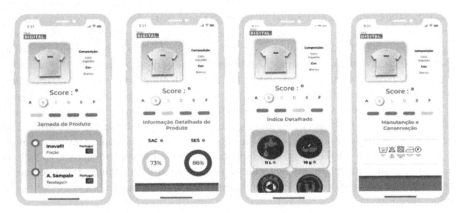

Fig. 2. Consumer application depicting traceability and other product information, for the Clothing value chain – White Colour T-shirt. (https://texjourney.com/)

The system developed for aggregating and presenting traceability and sustainability information in the textile ecosystem proved effective for both vertical and partitioned supply chains. It significantly improved consumer awareness of sustainable textile products and their environmental, circular, social and economic impact.

As expected, the dark coloured products showed a lower sustainability score and higher environmental impact compared to the light coulored variants (see Table 1).

Overall, the case study demonstrated the system's capability to provide valuable insights to consumers and encourage more conscious and environmentally responsible choices in the textile industry. One noteworthy feature was the implementation of smart tags, which allowed consumers to access maintenance and care instructions digitally, potentially replacing traditional physical tags.

Table 1. Comparative analysis between the light coloured and dark coloured products

	Light Colour Towel	Dark Colour Towel	White Colour T-shirt	Black Colour T-shirt
Score	C (69%)	C (67%)	B (77%)	C (67%)
ECS	60%	58%	72%	59%
ESS	90%	90%	85%	85%
Water Consumption	19 L	22 L	11 L	33 L
Chemical Consumption	146 g	203 g	10 g	183 g
Carbon Footprint	0,44 kg CO_2	0,55 kg CO_2	1,08 kg CO_2	1,35 kg CO_2
Recovered Waste	95%	95%	88%	88%

4   Conclusions and Future Work

The STVgoDigital project, particularly PPS1, focused on implementing traceability and storing environmental and social scores for textile and clothing products. This was achieved through the use of Hyperledger Fabric blockchain technology, which decentralises the collected information. The blockchain stores product codes, while a relational database holds related data.

The platform was designed to collect comprehensive environmental and social scores for products at various stages of value chain, incorporating indicators from various technological levels. It seamlessly integrates with ERP system and IoT (Internet of Things) devices and there is a web portal available for manual data collection.

Two case studies were conducted in collaboration with Portuguese textile manufacturing companies to demonstrate the platform's effectiveness. The platform's data collection process encompassed environmental, circular, economic, and social indicators related to the textile supply chain. It then utilised this information to calculate a sustainability index, ensuring complete traceability and transparency from the spinning mill to the final product.

The two tests case scenarios have identified certain limitations, which present opportunities for future work. These limitations and potential areas of improvement include:

1. The tests were conducted exclusively with Portuguese manufacturing companies. Future work could involve expanding the collaboration to include international business partners and actively involving brand managers. This broader participation would enhance the platform's applicability and ensure its effectiveness in diverse global contexts;
2. While the system was tested with linear supply chains, there is a plan to extend its capabilities to handle lot-dividing scenarios, non-linear lot traceability, and circular supply chains involving sorting and recycling companies. Addressing these complex supply chain structures will allow the platform to accommodate a wider range of industries and supply chain configurations;

3. Consumer awareness and understanding of sustainable practices are crucial for the platform's success. Future efforts could focus on increasing consumer green literacy, educating them about the significance of environmental and social scores, and encouraging responsible consumption. Utilising gamification strategies within the consumer app can make the learning process engaging and rewarding, thereby promoting environmentally conscious choices.

In terms of technical improvements, some of these limitations are being addressed in be@t project (https://bioeconomy-at-textiles.com). It will aim to assess the platform's performance when dealing with an increased number of activities on a product batch. This includes evaluating how the system handles a higher volume of transactions and traceability attributes. To optimise performance, the preference is to use querying the ledger to batch tracing.

Addressing these areas of future work will contribute to the platform's robustness, scalability, and effectiveness in promoting sustainability and transparency within the textile industry.

Acknowledgment. This work has been developed in the context of Project "STVgoDigital: Digitalização da Cadeia de Valor do Setor Têxtil e Vestuário" – PPS1 (reference POCI-01-0247-FEDER-046086), funded by European Regional Development Fund (ERDF) through Operational Programme for Competitiveness and Internationalization (POCI) and is being continued with the support of the integrated project be@t – Textile Bioeconomy (TC-C12-i01, Sustainable Bioeconomy No. 02/C12-i01/202), promoted by the Recovery and Resilience Plan (RRP), Next Generation EU, for the period 2021–2026.

References

1. EURATEX Homepage, Facts key figures 2022 of the European textile and clothing industry. https://euratex.eu/wpcontent/uploads/EURATEX_FactsKey_Figures_2022rev-1.pdf. Last accessed 10 July 2023
2. ATP – Textile and Clothing Association of Portugal Homepage. www.atp.pt. Last accessed 14 Jul 2023
3. European Parliament Homepage, The impact of textile production and waste on the environment (infographics). https://www.europarl.europa.eu/news/en/headlines/society/20201208STO93327/the-impact-of-textile-production-and-waste-on-the-environment-infographics. Last accessed 13 Jul 2023
4. https://environment.ec.europa.eu/strategy/circular-economy-action-plan_en
5. https://eur-lex.europa.eu/resource.html?uri=cellar:9903b325-6388-11ea-b735-01aa75ed71a1.0017.02/DOC_1&format=PDF
6. Götz, T., Adisorn, T., Tholen, L.: Developing a Framework for Traceability Implementation in the Textile Supply Chain. Wuppertal Report (2021). https://doi.org/10.48506/opus-7694
7. European Commission. Extended Producer Responsibility for textiles (2023)
8. Fashion Revolution Homepage, Fashion transparency index 2022 edition. https://issuu.com/fashionrevolution/docs/fti_2022. Last accessed 14 Jul 2023
9. CIRPASS Homepage. https://cirpassproject.eu/project-results/. Last accessed 14 Jul 2023
10. STVgoDigital Homepage. www.stvgodigital.pt. Last accessed 14 Jul 2023

Automatic EPS Calculation Guided Genetic Algorithm and Incremental PCA Based DBSCAN of Extracted Acoustic Features for Anomalous Sound Detection

Xiao Tan$^{(\boxtimes)}$ ⓘ and Siu Ming Yiu ⓘ

Department of Computer Science, University of Hong Kong, Pokfulam Road, Hong Kong, China
`xtan@cs.hku.hk, smyiu@hku.hk`

Abstract. This paper focuses on automatic detection of anomalies in audio files. We introduce an automated unsupervised algorithm which integrates AEC-guided Genetic Algorithm and Incremental PCA and DBSCAN to detect the anomaly sound after extracting acoustic features of the normal environments. Technically, Automatic EPS Calculation algorithm (AEC) based Genetic Algorithm optimizes the automatic clustering algorithm's configuration for Incremental Principal Components Analysis (IPCA) and Density Based Spatial Clustering Algorithm with Noise (DBSCAN) to reduce the number of effective components, which is calculated by guided GA, to a manageable count. The DBSCAN uses the output of the PCA and is able to generate predictions with relatively high accuracy. Besides, because of the challenges when selecting the optimized configuration of the IPCA and DBSCAN especially in complex sounds' scenarios, this paper also introduces a self-adaptive architecture trying to select an optimized set of parameters based on different test environments. Experiments show that our results are better than the existing methods with less computing costs and more stability. The algorithm is generic and can be applied to detect anomalies in machines so as to give an early warning to maintenance people to avoid serious accidents or disasters.

Keywords: Automatic Anomalous Sound Detection (ASD) · Unsupervised Algorithm · Acoustic Features · Spectrum-Temporal Factors Analysis · Machine learning · Enhanced Incremental PCA · SVD · SKL · DBSCAN

1 Introduction

1.1 Introduction of Anomalous Sound Detection

Industrial Internet of Things (IoT) is to connect internet to the physical world via computer-based system and ubiquitous smart devices, to improve the efficiency and accuracy. In manufacture, the operations and the process are controlled and monitored by smart sensors to detect the anomalous behaviors of the machines, to remotely control the input and output of each step in the process, and to integrate the physical productions to the inter-connected networks.

© The Author(s), under exclusive license to Springer Nature Switzerland AG 2024
T. Guarda et al. (Eds.): ARTIIS 2023, CCIS 1937, pp. 377–388, 2024.
https://doi.org/10.1007/978-3-031-48930-3_29

Anomalous Sound Detection (ASD) is one type of smart data-driven technologies at the edge of IoT. It is to use scientific methodology to identify whether the sound emitted from the operational machines is normal or anomalous, and send the detected warnings to the operators to avoid the breakdowns earlier. For example, the modern textile industry–uses a wide range of machines, especially those massive heavy-duty industrial machines, e.g.: woolen mill machines, thread winding machines, bleaching/dyeing machines, and scutching machines etc. The costs of detecting the defects of those running machines and fixing them in time are high, not only due to the expensive repair charges but also the cost of the down time. Acoustic monitoring sensor, as a major type of Predictive Maintenance Technologies, is capable to detect the changes of the machine's condition by the sounds of the running machine before the breakdown really happens.

However, ASD is becoming an increasingly challenging task in the last decades with the wide recognition of its importance in the industry 4.0. The major challenges in the practice include:

Imbalanced Training Dataset. In practical applications, anomaly events are much rarer than a long time-series of normal data [1]. Such an imbalance between exhaustive continuous normal data and anomalous data in the training process significantly compromises the performance of popular ASD machine learning algorithms.

Stability of High Performance. To keep the stability of high accuracy of detection and prediction performance is another issue in real practice. Most deep learning algorithms, e.g.: Convolutional Generative Adversarial Network (GAN), can achieve high accuracy after sufficient training. However, the stability of the overall predictive performance is still a concern [2].

Hard-Coded Architecture. Differences of background environments when collecting the sounds and of types of sounds require different parameters settings in the algorithm. Manual selection of the parameters to reset the algorithm to adapt to the environment and specific type of sound impacts the efficiency and accuracy of ASD.

Noise. On most occasions, the real environments to collect the sound data are mixed up with multiple types of sound. Environmental noise is a traditional issue in the audio study [3].

1.2 Methodology Overview

The proposed new algorithm includes two layers. The first layer is to adopt PCA to reduce the dimensions of the dataset converted from the audio files to numbers. The second layer is to use the dimensions-reduced dataset from PCA and apply the DBSCAN to train and predict the datasets.

Because of the complexity of the features extraction of large volume and high dimensional raw data of machines' sounds, we build up the portfolio of acoustic features based on the original sounds data, and then deploy the two-layered machine learning algorithm to extract the features and detect the anomalous sound based on the portfolio of acoustic features. The details of the methodology are described in the next three sections.

Imbalanced Dataset. DBSCAN, as an arbitrary center-based clustering approach, utilizes the density reach ability and the density connection ability to find the optimized center and the radius of each non-overlap clusters when training the unlabeled input data, and detect the anomalous points that are out of the boundary of any existing clusters of the training.

Such architecture of DBSCAN is capable to ignore the normality of input dataset, and thus unbalance is not an issue to impact the performance of clustering in nature.

Stability of High Performance. Because of the different methods for regulatory and optimization process with deep learning algorithms, e.g.: convolutional autoencoder and generative adversarial network (GAN) etc., the IPCA based DSBCAN adopts the linear optimized calculation of the density and radius, and thus is capable to achieve the high stability once it finds all clusters properly after training.

Guided Genetic Algorithm and Optimized Algorithm Architecture. Instead of hard coding the parameters in the architecture of the algorithms, the proposed IPCA based DBSCAN adopts Automatic EPS Calculation and Genetic Algorithm to set its optimized architecture for different types of audio data collected in different environments. Automatic EPS Calculation (AEC) algorithm is used to estimate the EPS and MinPts from the random training datasets as the input for Genetic Algorithm [4]. Such Guided Genetic algorithm is able to auto select the optimized three parameters: number of components of IPCA, EPS and MinPts in the random training datasets, and those calculated optimized parameters after AEC based guided Genetic Algorithm are deployed for validation and prediction. This design reduces computing time as well as keeps accuracy when dealing with large datasets. And, on some level, it helps to improve the self-adaptability of the algorithm and achieve optimized performance with different types of audio data. The details of the AEC based Guided Genetic Algorithm will be described in the section later.

Noise Awareness and Tolerance. The architecture of DBSCAN implements the noise accommodation to identify and remove the background noise from the sound data. The noise awareness is included in the algorithm to add a Gaussian white noise into the original input audio datasets:

$$\tilde{x} = x + \varepsilon$$

where $\varepsilon \sim N\ (-1,1)$ * noise significancy factor. And the output is decoded as $f_{dbscan}\left(f_{ipca}(\tilde{x})\right)$.

Requirement of Lower Computing Capability and Less Computing Cost. With the dimension-reduction technology of enhanced IPCA, the new algorithm requires less computing capability of GPU as well as keeps the high computation performance. Besides, such algorithm is based on the analysis of the extracted acoustic features instead of the audio signals. That could help to reduce the dimensions of the audio data to the numbers of the acoustic characteristics. The details of the algorithm will be introduced in Sect. 2.

2 Automatic EPS Calculation Guided Genetic Algorithm and Enhanced Incremental Principal Component Analysis Based Density-Based Spatial Clustering of Applications with Noise

2.1 Extraction of Acoustic Features

Acoustic features are used to represent and recognize a typical computational sound event or scenario to differentiate with others. The input, as of the discrete time-series audio data of machine's sounds collected from the plant site, is analogue-digital converted, framed and partly labelled in the pre-processing stage, and then is calculated and output as acoustic features by the preset rules. Those digitalized presentations, or acoustic characteristics, are capable of identifying the physical properties of the input audio data, for example, the signal energy, the toneless, the temporal shape and the spectral shape etc.

During the past decades, many different types of audio signal features have been proposed for sound recognition or description. Generally, the audio features can be categorized as either time domain or frequency domain. And in time domain, based on the different computation scopes, we can distinguish between the time extend-validity of the global descriptors which are computed for the whole signal, and the instantaneous descriptors which are computed for each time frame. Time frame is a short segmentation of the signal with a regular duration. In this paper, the duration for the time frame is 20 ms. As the proposed study focuses on the signal analysis of time frames, we adopt the instantaneous features as the acoustic characteristics for machine learning [6]. G. Peeters summarized a set of audio descriptors in 2004 [7], including the temporal shape, temporal feature, energy features, spectral shape features, and perceptual features. This paper adopts Peeters' classification as the main method to extract acoustic features to identify anomalous sound. The descriptors for further machine learning processing include:

Temporal Shape. Features (global or instantaneous) computed from the waveform or the signal energy (envelop). Attack time, temporal increase/decrease and effective duration are the features of this category.

Frequency [8]. Frequency is one of the basic features when describing or recognizing the audio signals. Different with time-domain which is to calculate the distance of two domain samples, frequency is to calculate the period vibration of two frequency band index bins. Short Time Fourier Transform (STFT) based analysis is applied for the linear frequency calculation on the continuous audio signals.

Amplitude. Amplitude is a describer to represent the waveform shape with limited information. Similar to the processing steps of Frequency, in this paper, the amplitude is calculated based on the continuous signals after STFT and is converted to db-scaled from logarithm scaled.

Temporal Features
Auto-correlation Coefficients [7]. The cross-correlation of a signal, as the inverse Fourier Transform of the spectrum energy distribution of the signal, represents the signal spectral

distribution in the time domain. This describer is proven by Brown in 1998 to be a valid description for classification. The formula is:

$$x_{corr}(k) = \frac{1}{x(0)^2} \sum_{n=0}^{N-k-1} x(n) \cdot x(n+k)$$

Each coefficient is in the range of $[-1,1]$. The faster the coefficients decrease with increasing lag, the whiter the signal can be.

Zero-Crossing Rate [8]. The zero-crossing rate is a low-level feature to describe the number of changes of signal values when crossing the zero axis. The concept assumes that the arithmetic mean of the audio signals is zero. The higher the zero-crossing rate the more high-frequency content is, and the less periodic the audio signals are assumed to be.

Spectral Shape Features

Onset Envelope. Onset is the percept related to the time a sound takes to start. Onset envelope is computed as a spectral flux onset strength envelope, and such spectral flux measures the amount of changes of the spectral shapes by the average difference between consecutive STFT frames. Onset strength at time t is determined by:

$$mean_f \max\left(0, S[f, t] - ref[f, t - lag]\right)$$

where ref is S after local max filtering along the frequency axis.

By default, if a time series y is provided, S will be the log-power Mel spectrogram. Onset is correlated with the logarithm of the attack time [5].

Spectral Centroid [8]. The spectral centroid represents the Centre of Gravity (COG) of spectral energy. It is calculated as the frequency-weighted sum of the spectrum normalized by its unweighted sum:

$$v_{SC}(n) = \frac{\sum_{k=0}^{\frac{k}{2}-1} k \cdot |X(k,n)|^2}{\sum_{k=0}^{\frac{k}{2}-1} |X(k,n)|^2}$$

Spectral Roll-Off [8]. The spectral roll-off measures the bandwidth of the analyzed block n of audio samples. The spectral roll-off point is the frequency which the accumulated magnitudes of the STFT $X(k, n)$ reach K of the overall sum of magnitudes:

$$v_{SR}(n) = i \left| \sum_{k=0}^{i} |X(k,n)| \right. = K \cdot \sum_{k=0}^{\frac{K}{2}-1} |X(k,n)|$$

With common value for K being 0.85 (85%). The value range of the spectral roll-off is $[0, K/2 - 1]$.

Mel Frequency Cepstral Coefficients (MFCC) [8]. MFCC is defined as the compact description of the shape of the spectral envelop of an audio signal. It is calculated by the logarithm of the spectrum after Discrete Cosine Transform (DCT) or Fourier Transform (e.g.: FFT). Since MFCC is introduced in 1980, it is proven to be a valid measurement of audio signal classification to contain principal information. In our approach, the number of coefficients is 20.

Other Features' Categories

Intensity. Intensity is a physical and measurable entity, which is related to the human perception of the magnitude of audio signal. In this category, most features are instantaneous features, such as Root Mean Square and Root Mean Square Energy.

- Root Mean Squared Energy. The RMS energy is calculated from the audio samples or from a spectrogram without STFT processing. The advantage of RMSE is the faster calculation speed because it doesn't require STFT processing. And it outputs the RMS of each frame. In this paper, we only calculate RMSE directly based on the audio signals.

Derived Features.

- Tempogram [9]. As a describer of the speed or pace of a given piece, Tempogram is usually measured by beats per minute (bpm). It is derived from the local autocorrelation of the onset strength envelope. For time $t \in Z$ and time lag $l \in [0, N]$, W is for window function: $Z \to \mathbb{R}$ centered at $t = 0$ with support $[-N: N]$, $N \in \mathbb{N}$.

2.2   Automatic EPS Calculation (AEC) – Guided Genetic Algorithm

Genetic algorithm (GA), as one type of global stochastic search algorithms, like evolutionary algorithms, particle swarm optimization and other bio-based search methods, is applied for election of wrapper features [9]. Although the capability of global searching, the exponentially increased computation cost of each candidate parameter restricts the efficiency of the GA. Therefore, the constraint of local optimization is added to resolve this issue.

Automatic EPS Calculation (AEC) of randomly selected training datasets are used to set up the baseline of the initial range of estimated values of the candidate parameters. And such wrapper parameters to be calculated in Guided Genetic Algorithm include number of components for IPCA, EPS and MinPts for DBSCAN. Automatic EPS Calculation (AEC) algorithm is to estimate the EPS and MinPts based on the density of the randomly selected training datasets and the distances between the points in the density region. In the proposed AEC algorithm, the densities are calculated by the Gaussian Kernel after the training dataset is scaled by MinMax. Similarly, the distances are calculated by KD-Tree query after MinMax scaled training dataset. The set of the estimated EPS and the estimated MinPts are the minimum values in all clusters. And the range of the estimated number of components is set between 2 to 10.

The locally optimized three parameters are input as the baseline to set up the range of values of the candidate parameters. The predicted value, the actual value, the difference between the predicted and the actual values, the Mean Squared Error (MSE), the candidate number of components, the candidate EPS and the candidate MinPts, as seven genes, construct the chromosome. The fitness process is to set the reward value to 1 if the MSE is less than the target value of 0.4. And only the rewarded chromosomes would construct the population for crossover and mutation to generate the new generation of populations with the preset crossover probability and specific mutation power [10].

2.3   Enhanced Incremental Principal Component Analysis

In 1901, Pearson introduced an unsupervised algorithm of Principal Component Analysis (PCA), which is to calculate the subspace of largest variance in a dataset. Oja developed neural network implementation of one-dimensional PCA implemented by Hebb learning in 1982. And Sanger further expanded the one-dimensional PCA to hierarchical, multidimensional PCA in 1989 [11].

In 2000, with the introduction of the Sequential Karhunen-Loeve (SKL) algorithm of Levy and Lindenbaum, the enhanced incremental algorithm is developed to resolve the defect of the existing PCA [12]. The computational advantages of SKL algorithm are that with learning rate it continuously updates the original eigenspace and mean, and keeps constant space and time complexity in n, therefore the space complexity as well as the computational requirements is reduced to $O(d(k + m))$ and $O(dm^2)$ respectively. The disadvantage is that it does not calculate the varying sample mean of the training data with the new data in. To resolve the issue, the enhanced incremental PCA is improved by adding the additional vector to the new training data for the correction of the time-varying mean.

In this paper, the input parameter of the enhanced IPCA, the count of components, is selected by Genetic Algorithm based on the most optimized historic results of different machine types, which will be introduced in detail in Sect. 2.4.

2.4   Density-Based Spatial Clustering of Applications with Noise

DBSCAN was proposed by Martin Ester, Hans-Peter Kriegel, Jorg Sander and Xiaowei Xu in 1996. As a density-based clustering algorithm, DBSCAN separates the clusters by low-density regions [13]. DBSCAN is capable of identifying the global anomalies by defining the dense and the arbitrary shapes globally, and therefore fails to identify the local anomalies. There are two main advantages of DBSCAN over other unsupervised ML algorithms. The first one is that DBSCAN doesn't require to define how many clusters to be calculated as an input parameter. It can define clusters of arbitrary shape by itself. Secondly DBSCAN can handle the noise point. With these two advantages, DBSCAN performs well when training and predicting the large volume and unbalanced datasets.

In DBSCAN, for any arbitrary object p belonging to the dataset D, as shown in Fig. 1, the algorithm will retrieve all objects density reachable from p by ε and MinPts values [12]. There are three scenarios for any object p: it is the core object of a cluster, if there are enough other objects q within the distance from $p \leq \varepsilon$ and with the count of $q \geq MinPts$ in dataset D; it is the border object if there is no enough q to be density-connected to p; it is the noise object if it doesn't belong to any cluster. The algorithm will continue the processing to locate all the objects into clusters or noise groups.

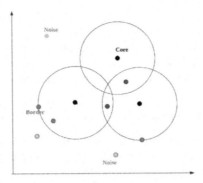

Fig. 1. Three scenarios of DBSCAN: Core, Border and Noise Points

In the hybrid algorithm proposed in this study, the Automatic EPS Calculation (AEC) is adopted to estimate the EPS based on the average distance between the points of the training dataset, and the MinPts based on the kernel density of the training dataset which are the extracted acoustic features of the audio files. And the assumption of the experiment is that the frames of the normal and anormal files have significantly different characteristics in density so that they can be differentiated easily by the hybrid algorithm with reduced dimensions.

3 Experiments

3.1 Dataset and Preprocessing

In this paper, we used the audio data of stepper motors in a plant in Suzhou City China. The original audio data consists of the long time-series normal and rare anomalous sounds of the sample stepper monitors. Each recording is a single-channel 2-sec length audio mixed of both a machine's operating sound and environmental noise. The rate is as standard as 44,100.

Unlabeled data of both train and test datasets are adopted for experiments purpose to test the unsupervised machine learning algorithm for 50 times. The training datasets are mixed up with 190 files randomly selected in the total 228 normal audio files and 20 files from the 120 anormal data files, and the test datasets consist of another randomly-selected 20 anomalous audio data files. 10 acoustic features, e.g., frequency, amplitude etc., from the audio files are extracted as the components for clustering.

3.2 Benchmark System and Result

In this paper, Deep Convolutional Neural Network (DCGAN) is adopted as the bench-mark for the experiment purpose. DCGAN as one type of deep learning algorithms, is a deep convolutional neural net architecture composed of a pair of adversarial models called the generator and the discriminator [14, 15]. The generator creates a noise array or matrix as the fake data to be input to the discriminator. The discriminator segments the real and the fake data distribution, with some policies.

Table 1 shows the results of the benchmark experiments. The benchmark algorithm of DCGAN achieves an accuracy of 0.7. However, the average running computation time of DCGAN is 90 min with 2 Graphics Processing Units (GPU). The computation cost is relatively high compared with those machine learning algorithms.

Table 1. Performance Evaluation of DCGAN

AUC	PAUC	F1 Score	MSE	Spearman Rank Correlation Coefficient	Average Running Time
0.77	0.69	0.59	0.48	0.47	90 min

3.3 Results and Analysis

Table 2 shows the summary of the test results. From Table 2, the performance of AEC Guided GA and IPCA+DBSCAN is acceptable with the average fitness of 0.843, and average MSE of 0.16. And the average running time is less than 0.5 min for total data size of 202,860,000 (training dataset: 185,220,000, test dataset: 17,640,000).

Table 2. Performance Evaluation of AEC Guided GA and IPCA Based DBSCAN

Number of Test Cases	AUC	PAUC	MSE	Hamming Distance	Average Running Time
50	0.84	0.58	0.16	0.16	0.5 min

Figure 2 shows a sample of the prediction performance of the normal audio data changing to anomalous audio data. The normal class is set as "0" and the anomalous class is set as "1". The red line is the predicted clustering class, and the blue line is the actual class. The results show that the AEC Guided GA and IPCA based DBSCAN predict the turning point accurately, and the measurement of AUC is 0.95.

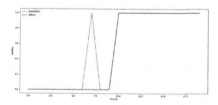

Fig. 2. ROC Curve of IPCA Based DBSCAN Algorithms

Table 3 describes the comparisons of AUC, NMI, and F1 score etc. among 6 unsupervised and semi-supervised algorithms: Kmeans++, one-class SVM, agglomerative clustering, DCGAN, DCNN-Autoencoder, and AEC-Guided GA and IPCA+DBSCAN.

These experiments' results show that both the AEC-Guided Genetic Algorithm and IPCA based DBSCAN of extracted acoustic features and the DCNN-Autoencoder of audio data achieve the highest accuracy with the average AUC of 0.843 and 0.8188 respectively. However, for the stability measures, the AEC-Guided GA and IPCA based DBSCAN of extracted acoustic features shows highest stability among all six semi-supervised or unsupervised algorithms, with its lowest Hamming Loss of 0.16 and highest Spearman Rank Correlation Coefficient of 0.72.

Table 3. Performance Summary of Unsupervised and Semi-Supervised ML Algorithms

Machine Learning	AUC	F1 Score	MSE	Hamming Distance	Spearman Rank Correlation Coefficient
Kmeans++	0.54	0.54	0.47	0.47	0.071
One-class SVM	0.73	0.73	0.27	0.27	0.55
Aggregate Clustering	0.58	0.58	0.42	0.42	0.13
DCGAN	0.77	0.6	0.41	0.41	0.47
DCNN Autoencoder	0.82	0.5	0.42	0.5	0.55
AEC Guided GA and IPCA+DBSCAN	0.84	0.84	0.16	0.16	0.72

Figure 3 shows the ROC curves of those six algorithms. The chart shows that AEC-Guided GA and IPCA based DBSCAN of extracted acoustic features reaches the highest AUC of 0.95, while DCNN-AE and DCGAN gets the lower AUC of 0.84 and 0.719864. The performances of Agglomerative Cluster and Kmeans++ gets the lowest accuracy measured by lowest AUC value as of 0.65 and 0.60 respectively.

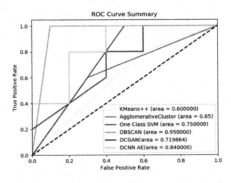

Fig. 3. ROC Curve of Six Unsupervised and Semi-supervised Algorithms

3.4   Noise Tolerance Test

Another series of experiments are conducted for the maximum noise tolerance of the proposed algorithm. The experiments results show that the performance of the algorithm gets lower when the SNR is more than 13.0103 (SNR $= 10 * \log_{10}(1/0.05)$), in which 0.05 is the noise significant factor. This is because that the DBSCAN is allergic to detect and filter the noise outliers instead of the continuous noise pattern added in the clean audio sample. This is the disadvantage observed when it is applied for lab experiments.

3.5   Comparison Between Hardcoded and Parameterized Architectures

To compare the hard-coded architecture and the parameterized architecture, 50 tests with randomly selected training and test audio data were conducted. It is observed that the parameterized architecture takes less execution time and achieves high accuracy. In this experiment, the hardcoded architecture is set as the Eps to be 0.07 and the count of the MinPts to be 2. From the experiments' results shown in Table 4, it is shown that although AUC of hardcoded architecture is 0.82, the stability indicators, including Jaccard Score and Spearman Rank Correlation Coefficient are significantly lower than those of parameterized architecture. Therefore, the performance of hardcoded architecture is not so satisfying compared with parameterized architecture.

Table 4. Performance Comparison Between Hardcoded and Parameterized Architectures

Machine Learning	AUC	PAUC	F1 Score	MSE	Jaccard Score
Hard-coded Architecture	0.82	0.57	0.82	0.18	0.72
Automatic EPS Calculation	0.84	0.58	0.84	0.16	0.76

4   Conclusions and Future Work

The hybrid algorithm to integrate AEC-Guided Genetic Algorithm and IPCA with DBSCAN for Anomaly Sound Detection seems to be a promising direction for ASD when handling different environments issues and different types of audio files. It is noted that when detecting the rare events in multiple scenes (including silence and background sounds), the proposed unsupervised algorithm did not perform as well as the machines' sounds. This is possibly due to the quality of the collected sound because we used the high-quality equipment to collect the machines' sounds in the specific plant site. We expect to improve the noise tolerance of the algorithm for those environments of mix-up sounds, and this will be a future direction.

Acknowledgement. This paper is sponsored by "Research and Development of Blockchain Analysis for Virtual Asset Analytic Project, Department of Computer Science, University of Hong Kong".

References

1. Grueneberg, K., et al.: IoT data management system for rapid development of machine learning models. In: IEEE International Conference on Cognitive Computing (ICCC) (2019)
2. Kuncheva, L.I.: A stability index for feature selection. In: Artificial Intelligence and Applications (2007)
3. Uematsu, H., Koizumi, Y., Saito, S., Nakagawa, A., Harada, N.: Anomaly detection technique in sound to detect faulty equipment. NTT Tech. Rev. **15**(8), 28–34 (2017)
4. Gorawski, M., Malczok, R.: AEC algorithm: a heuristic approach to calculating density-based clustering Eps parameter. In: Yakhno, T., Neuhold, E.J. (eds.) ADVIS 2006. LNCS, vol. 4243, pp. 90–99. Springer, Heidelberg (2006). https://doi.org/10.1007/11890393_10
5. Heittola, T., Çakır, E., Virtanen, T.M.: The machine learning approach for analysis of sound scenes and events. In: Virtanen, T., Plumbley, M., Ellis, D. (eds.) Computational Analysis of Sound Scenes and Events. Springer, Cham (2018). https://doi-org.eproxy.lib.hku.hk/10.1007/978-3-319-63450-0_2
6. Peeters, G.: A large set of audio features for sound description (similarity and classification) in the CUIDADO project. CUIDADO 1st Project Rep. **54**, 1–25 (2004)
7. Lerch, A.: An Introduction to Audio Content Analysis: Applications in Signal Processing and Music Informatics, (Chapter 2.2.3). Wiley-IEEE Press (2012)
8. Zhou, J., Hua, Z., Kurth, F.: A correlation guided genetic
9. Grosche, P., Müller, M., Kurth, F.: Cyclic tempogram—a mid-level tempo representation for music signals. In: 2010 IEEE International Conference on Acoustics, Speech and Signal Processing. IEEE (2010)
10. Tan, X.: Libor prediction using genetic algorithm and genetic algorithm integrated with recurrent neural network. In: 2019 Global Conference for Advancement in Technology (GCAT). IEEE (2019)
11. Kambhatla, N., Leen, T.K.: Dimension reduction by local principal component analysis. Neural Comput. **9**(7), 1493–1516 (1997)
12. Avraham, L., Lindenbaum, M.: Sequential Karhunen-Loeve basis extraction and its application to images. In: Proceedings 1998 International Conference on Image Processing. ICIP98 (Cat. No. 98CB36269), vol. 2. IEEE (1998)
13. Ester, M., et al.: A density-based algorithm for discovering clusters in large spatial databases with noise. In: KDD, vol. 96, no. 34 (1996)
14. Lee, Y.O., Jo, J., Hwang, J.: Application of deep neural network and generative adversarial network to industrial maintenance: a case study of induction motor fault detection. In: 2017 IEEE International Conference on Big Data (BIGDATA) (2017)
15. Kopčan, J., Škvarek, O., Klimo, M.: Anomaly detection using Autoencoders and Deep Convolution Generative Adversarial Networks. In: 14th International Scientific Conference on Sustainable, Modern and Safe Transport (2021)

International Workshop on Electronic and Telecommunications (IWET 2023)

Comparative Analysis Between LTE RSRP Measurements and Propagation Models in Open Area Over 2800 m.a.s.l in Riobamba-Ecuador

Anthony Gualli[✉][ID], Lessly Borja[ID], Anderson Yanqui[ID], and Alexis Leon[ID]

Escuela Superior Politécnica de Chimborazo University, Panamericana Sur km 1 1/2, Riobamba, Ecuador
anthony.gualli@espoch.edu.ec
https://historicoweb.espoch.edu.ec/

Abstract. In this work, three measurement campaigns have been carried out under similar environmental conditions for a comparative analysis of the received power intensity (RSRP using the Network Cell Info Lite application) in band 4 (2140 Mhz) of Claro (Mobile Telecom Service) LTE at different points in open areas of the Faculty of Medicine at ESPOCH, with five propagation models (Log-Distance, Extended Hata or COST-231, SUI, Walfish - Bertoni and Erceg). The best fitting model for the received power range (-60 dBm to -100 dBm) in the Medicine cell is Walfish - Bertoni.

Keywords: LTE · power · propagation · model · mobile

1 Introduction

Mobile communications use radio technologies to transmit information over the air. The first mobile network was 2G, which was limited to Internet browsing. The 3G network had much higher speeds than 2G. The 4G network enabled high-quality video streaming and the latest evolution in 5G mobile networks will provide higher speeds and new services such as augmented and virtual reality, autonomous driving, the internet of things (IoT), etc. [1,2].

Nowadays, the increase in Internet use and the proliferation of wireless data networks are forcing operators to implement new technologies such as LTE (Long Term Evolution), which is a standard for high speed, low latency, packet optimised wireless data communications with flexible bandwidth (1.4 MHz–20 MHz). Its architecture is called Evolved Packet System (EPS), which consists of: user equipment, access network (base stations) and backbone network (access control to the cellular network) [3].

In mobile communications, a propagation model is a mathematical expression that aims to predict the variation of the received power of the electromagnetic signal as a function of frequency, distance and other factors [4].

Supported by GIEM-ESPOCH.

The most commonly used propagation models are: the Okumura-Hata model for signals in the VHF and UHF frequency range in urban environments, the Cost 231 model for signals in suburban and rural environments, considering scattering losses, and the Stanford University (SUI) model with corrections for frequencies above 1900 MHz in three different terrain types: urban, suburban and rural [5–7].

The importance of obtaining accurate RSRP (reference received signal power) measurements in mobile systems, using specialised equipment such as the Narda SRM-3006, or free/paid software from the mobile device, lies in obtaining a reliable model in the selected environment from a comparative analysis between the real measurements with the predictions of evaluated models. Thus, the quality of the signal in the environment can be determined, facilitating the analysis of future communications network planning or any type of telecommunications project.

For these reasons, in this paper, RSRP power measurements were performed at 436 points in the open spaces of the Faculty of Medicine with respect to the nearest base radio (BS) working in Claro LTE band 4 (2140 MHz) using the software "Network Cell Info Lite" which provides detailed information about the mobile network and signal quality [8]. Taking into account the gain of high-end mobile phones (2dB) and performing at least three measurement campaigns in the same environmental conditions in order to predict the best-fit propagation model (Walfish - Bertoni and COST-231) in the selected environment.

2   Theoretical Framework

2.1   Log-Distance Propagation Model

This is one of the most classical models for outdoor environments. This model is based on the idea that the signal strength decreases with distance travelled, but in a non-linear way, i.e. the propagation loss increases with the logarithm (of base 10) of the distance [9].

The attenuation equation is expressed in (1).

$$P_r(dB) = P_r(d_o) + 10 n log(\frac{d}{d_o}) \tag{1}$$

where:

- Pr (dB) = is the power loss in dB at distance d.
- Pr (do) = is the power loss in dB at reference distance do.
- n = is the attenuation exponent to be adjusted for each environment and frequency.
- d = is the distance at which the power loss is to be estimated.

The values of the loss exponent (n) given in Table 1. [10] are for reference only. Care must be taken to estimate the value of n, for the given environment.

Table 1. Loss exponent (n) values for reference only

Environment	Path loss Exponent (n)
Free Space	2
Urban area cellular radio	2.7–3.5
Shadowed urban cellular radio	3–5
Inside a building-line of sight	1.6–1.8
Obstructed in building	4–6
Obstructed in factory	2–3

2.2 Extended Hata or COST-231 Propagation Model

The European Co-operative for Scientific and Technical Research (EUROCOST) established the COST-231 working committee to develop an extended version of the Hata model. [11] COST-231 proposed the following formula (2) to predict the path loss in dB.

$$
\begin{aligned}
P_L = 46,3 + 33,9log(f) - 13,82log(h_b) \\
- a(h_r) + [44,9 - 6,55log(h_b)]log(d) + C_M
\end{aligned}
\tag{2}
$$

where f is the operating frequency in MHz, d is the distance between transmitter and receiver, hb and hr are the correction factors for BS height and receiver height respectively and CM is the correction factor with a value of zero for suburban and rural environments, while with a value of 3 for urban areas.

This model makes use of the correction factor a(hr) from the Hata model, which is a function of the size of the coverage area. For large cities it is given by equations (3) and (4):

$$
a(h_R) = 8,29log(1.54 * h_R)^2 - 1.1 \quad f <= 300\,MHz
\tag{3}
$$

$$
a(h_R) = 3,2log(1.54 * h_R)^2 - 4,97 \quad f >= 300\,MHz
\tag{4}
$$

For medium and small cities it is given by (5):

$$
a(h_r) = 1,1log(f) - 0,7h_r - [1,58(f) - 0,8]
\tag{5}
$$

Model constraints:

- f = 1500 MHz to 2000 MHz
- hb = 30 m to 200 m
- hr = 1 m to 10 m
- d = 1 km to 20 km

2.3 SUI Propagation Model

The Stanford University Interim (SUI) model was developed by the IEEE 802.16 group and Stanford University for the purpose of developing a WiMAX (data transmission at frequencies from 2.5 to 5.8 GHz) channel model for suburban environments. At frequencies around 2000 MHz, the height of the transmitting antenna should be between 10 and 80 m, while the height of the mobile antenna should be between 2 and 3 m. For other frequencies and for receiving antenna heights between 2 m and 10 m, correction terms should be included.

In addition, this model proposes three terrain categories. Terrain A is mountainous with medium to high levels of vegetation, which corresponds to high loss conditions. Terrain B represents an area with moderate path loss, a suburban environment and terrain C has the lowest path loss describing a rural or flat area. [12]

The basic path loss equation with correction factors is presented in (6).

$$PL = A + 10\gamma * log(\frac{d}{d_0}) + X_f + X_h + s \quad for \quad d > d_0 \tag{6}$$

$$A = 20log(\frac{4\pi d_0}{\lambda}) \tag{7}$$

$$\gamma = a - b * h_b + \frac{c}{h_b} \tag{8}$$

where PL is in dB, γ the loss exponent, X_f is the correction factor for frequency, X_h is the correction factor for receiver antenna height and do is the reference distance ($d_o = 100$). The constants a, b and c are given by the terrain type in Table 2. [12]

Table 2. Numerical Values for the SUI Model Parameters

Model Parameter	Terrain A	Terrain B	Terrain C
a	4,6	4,0	3,6
b	0,0075	0,0065	0,005
c	12,6	17,1	20

Correction factors:

$$X_f = 6log(\frac{f}{2000}) \tag{9}$$

$$X_h = -10,8log(\frac{h_r}{2000}) \quad for \quad Terrain \ A, B \tag{10}$$

$$X_h = -20log(\frac{h_r}{2000}) \quad for \quad Terrain \ C \tag{11}$$

$$s = 0,65log(f)^2 - 1,3log(f) + \alpha \tag{12}$$

Here $\alpha = 5.2$ dB for rural and suburban environments (Terrain A and B) and 6.6 dB for urban environment (Terrain C).

2.4   Walfish - Bertoni Propagation Model

This model was proposed by Joram Walfisch and Henri Bertoni, it considers the impact of roofs and building height by using diffraction to predict the average signal strength at street level. [13]

The frequency range in which this model is applicable is 300 Mhz to 3 Ghz, with transmitter-receiver separation from 200 to 5000 m and the base station antenna above rooftops. The loss equation expressed in (13).

$$L_p = 89,5 + A + 21log(f) + 38log(d) - 18log(H) - 18log(1 - \frac{d^2}{17H}) \quad (13)$$

$$A = 5log[(\frac{b}{2})^2 + (h_b - h_r)^2] - 9log(b) + 20log[\arctan(\frac{2(h_b - h_r)}{b})] \quad (14)$$

where:

- A = loss factor for nearby buildings
- d = distance to the BS
- hb = height of the BS
- H = average value between hb and building height
- hr = receiver height
- b = distance between buildings and must be less than their heights (H).

2.5   Erceg Propagation Model

Erceg proposed a model derived from a vast amount of data at 1.9 GHz, which makes it a preferred model for PCS and higher frequencies. [14]

The model was in particular adopted in the 802.16 study group and is popular with WiMAX suppliers for 2.5 GHz products, and even 3.5 GHz fixed WiMAX. The path loss is described in (15).

$$L = L_0 + 10\gamma log(\frac{d}{d_0}) + s \quad for \quad d > d_0 \quad (15)$$

where:

$$L_0 = 20log(\frac{4\pi d_0}{\lambda}) \quad (16)$$

$$d_0 = 100\,m \quad (17)$$

$$\gamma = (a - b * h_b + \frac{c}{h_b}) + x\sigma_\gamma \quad (18)$$

$$s = y\sigma \quad (19)$$

$$\sigma = \mu_\sigma + z\sigma_\sigma \quad (20)$$

$$x, y, z = Gaussian\ random\ variables\ N(0, 1) \quad (21)$$

The parameter values are presented in Table 3. [14] for the different terrain categories.

Table 3. Parameter values in different terrain categories.

Parameter	Terrain Category		
	A	B	C
a	4,6	4	3,6
b	0,0075	0,0065	0,0050
c	12,6	17,1	20
σ_γ	0,57	0,75	0,59
μ_σ	10,6	9,6	8,2
σ_σ	2,3	3	1,6

- A = Hilly / moderate to heavy tree density
- B = Hilly / light tree density or flat / moderate to heavy tree density
- C = Flat / light tree density

Model constraints:

- f = 800 to 3700 MHz
- hb = 10 to 80 m
- hr = around 2 m
- d = 0.1 to 8 km

3   Methodology

In order to obtain the desired results, a flow chart was designed detailing the steps to be followed Fig. 1.

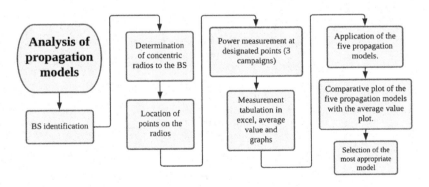

Fig. 1. Comparative analysis flowchart.

The "Network Cell Info Lite" application was initially used, from a high-end mobile phone with a Claro chip, to obtain the base station with the best transmitter signal quality in the green areas of the Faculty of Medicine where the present study is to be carried out.

Figure 2 shows the automatic connection, from outside the Medicine building, of the mobile phone via the app with the best base station (BS), located on Avenida Canónigo Ramos and Nicolás Delgado. At a height of 15 m (above a house) and working in Claro-LTE band 4 at a frequency of 2140 MHz. In summary, the location and height of the BS is shown in Table 4.

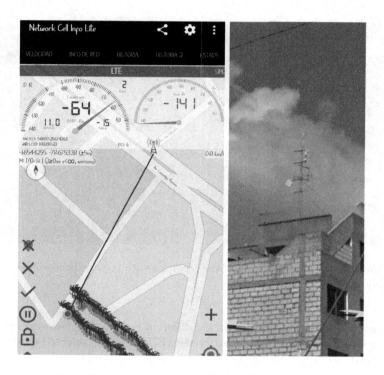

Fig. 2. BS of the Faculty of Medicine.

Table 4. BS Information

Base Station	Latitude	Length	Height (m.a.s.l)	Height (hb)
BS	139'08.46"S	7840'28.51"O	2820	15

Once the BS was identified, Google Earth Pro was used to plot concentric radios to it, passing through the (1 × 1)m gridded area of the Faculty of Medicine cell. This gives a total of 36 radios between distances of 236.51 m to 369.49 m.

Subsequently, the points to be measured (with green placemarks) obtained at the intersections of the concentric radios with the red vertical lines separated every 5 m in the gridded area of the Faculty of Medicine were placed, giving a total of 436 points, as shown in Fig. 3.

Fig. 3. Concentric radios of the BS of the Medicine with their respective points. (Color figure online)

To predict the received powers in the different models, it is necessary to obtain the equivalent isotropically radiated power (EIRP) in the selected environment, for which equation (22) of the ITU-525 recommendation is used. [15]

$$e = \frac{\sqrt{30 * EIRP}}{d} \tag{22}$$

$$EIRP = \frac{(d * e)^2}{30} \tag{23}$$

Figure 4 shows the Narda SRM-3006 (ESPOCH) equipment used to obtain the value of the effective electric field strength (e) [15] at the closest point of Medicine with respect to the BS (at 500 m). For this purpose, the Narda is set to Claro LTE bandwidth 4 (10 MHz) and the centre frequency is set to 2140 Mhz corresponding to the operating frequency of the selected BS. Giving a value of e = 1 V for the Medicine cell.

Substituting the known data into equation (23) gives an approximate EIRP of 46 dBm for the Medicine cell.

Fig. 4. Narda SRM-3006 Device

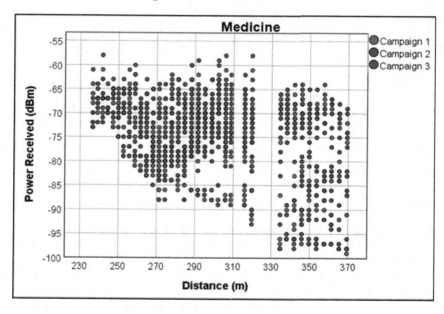

Fig. 5. Medicine Faculty Power-Distance Graph

Figure 5. was made using SPSS software and shows the RSRP powers measured at each distance of the 436 points (between 3 and 9 points for each distance) of the Faculty of Medicine, in each point three different campaigns of received signal strength measurement were executed with a duration of three minutes each of the campaigns as mentioned in the article "Comparative analysis of propagation models in mobile telephony in the 1900 MHz band (LTE) through electric field measurements in the city of Ambato". [16] These campaigns were performed in the Medicine cell during three different sunny days (selected outdoor environment) and from 14:00 pm to 16:00 pm, which allowed to obtain similar power values in the mentioned campaigns.

The real measurements for the comparative analysis are the average RSRP powers of the three campaigns conducted, whose values range from −60 dBm to −100 dBm at the Faculty of Medicine as shown in Fig. 6.

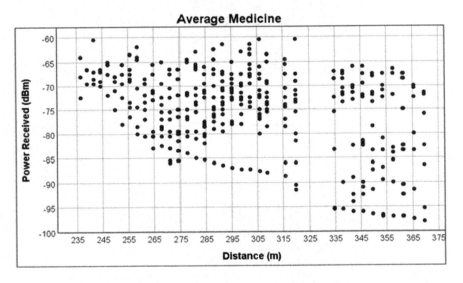

Fig. 6. Average power in the Faculty of Medicine

To find the propagation model that best fits the actual RSRP power measurements, a single point per distance is selected from Fig. 5 with its respective RSRP (in the range of −68 dBm to −76 dBm) for a total of 36 points.

In addition, with the 36 selected points (one for each distance), the basic losses of the COST 231, SUI, Walfish-Bertoni and Erceg models must be calculated using the equations established in the theoretical framework. The parameters and values that were considered to find the RSRP predictions of the Log-Distance model and to find the losses of the 4 models mentioned above are given below.

3.1   Log-Distance Model

Initially, the value of n must be found by calculating the absolute errors between the 36 real RSRP measurements with the first measured power $[P_r(d_o) = -68dBm]$. Then, the logarithmic values of each distance $(10 * log(d/d_o))$ are calculated taking as known distance the first radius $(d_o = 236.51)$, in order to obtain the total sum of the a values $(2 * 10 * log(d/d_o)^2)$ and the total sum of the b values $4(2 * 10 * log(d/d_o) * error)$, which are substituted in equation (24).

$$n = \frac{b}{a} \tag{24}$$

$$n = \frac{387,557}{88,0559} = 4,4013 \tag{25}$$

Since $n > 2$, it is possible to substitute the found values of $n * 10 * log(d/d_o)$ and $P_r(d_o) = -68dBm$ into equation (1) to find the 36 RSRP predictions of this model in the open areas of Medicine.

3.2   Extended Hata or Cost 231 Model

For this model, the value of $a(h_r)$ for a small city is calculated by substituting the frequency of 2140 MHz and the height of the mobile (1.5 m) in equation (5). Knowing the value of $a(h_r)$, the basic losses of the model can be calculated using equation (2) where the C_M factor is zero (suburban areas).

3.3   SUI Model

The first step is to classify the 36 points selected from each radius according to the terrain category to which each one belongs. Obtaining that the first 24 points are terrain C and the remaining 12 are terrain B. The correction factors are found by means of equations (9), (10), (11) and (12) according to the type of terrain and the values of a, b and c are shown in Table 2, both for terrain B and C, and are substituted in equation (8). In addition, the basic losses of the Free-Space model are calculated with equation (7). With all the above data, the losses of the model can be calculated with equation (6).

3.4   Walfish-Bertoni Model

In the Medicine cell, an analysis scenario where the average distance between buildings is 75.33 m is chosen to substitute into equation (14) to obtain the value of A used in equation (13) for the basic losses of this model.

3.5   Erceg Model

For this model we apply the values in Table 3. for a category C terrain present in the Medicine cell (little vegetation) and give Gaussian random values of x = 0.2, y = 0.4 and z = 0.6; necessary to find the values to substitute in equation (15) for the basic losses of this model.

Finally, to find the 36 RSRP predictions of the cost model 231, SUI, Walfish-Bertoni and Erceg, the basic losses of each model mentioned above are substituted into the general received power formula given by (26):

$$P_r(dBm) = EIRP + G_r - L_{pm} \qquad (26)$$

where:

- EIRP = equivalent isotropically radiated power (46 dBm)
- Mobile phone gain (2 dB)
- L_{pm} Propagation losses of each model

4   Results

In this section, the results of the power predictions calculated from the proposed propagation models are analysed in relation to the real measured values of power received at the 436 points with the "Network Cell Info" app in the outdoor areas of the Faculty of Medicine.

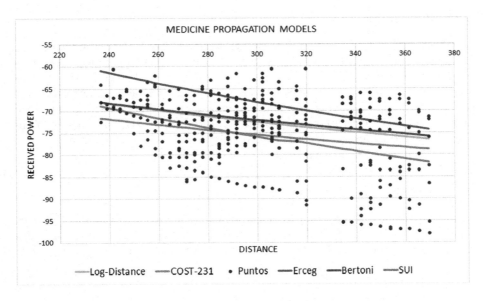

Fig. 7. Comparative graph of the propagation models

As shown in Fig. 7, the received powers decrease with increasing distance, with the exception of specific points where environmental conditions (higher sunshine and winds) or environmental obstacles (buildings, cars, trees, groups of people, etc.) cause higher or lower propagation losses.

In addition, it was observed that at the points where there is no direct line of sight between the radio base and the mobile phone, the received signal is of fair quality (-90 dBm to -100 dBm) due to the attenuation of the signal by the presence of the buildings of the Faculty of Medicine and large trees; while at the points where there is a direct line of sight, the signal is of good quality (-60 dBm to -80 dBm).

To find the propagation model that best fits the 436 real RSRP measurements, the total sum of the 36 root mean square errors (MSE) of each model is calculated using equation (27).

$$MSE = \frac{1}{M} * \sum_{i=1}^{M}[(P_r(real) - P_r(estimated)]^2 \qquad (27)$$

The results of the total mean square error of each model are shown in Table 5. It can be seen that the model with the lowest ERS is the Log-Distance model, which coincides with the results of the article "Comparison of radio propagation models in five LTE coveragecells in Riobamba" obtained in five outdoor environments in the south of Riobamba [17] similar to the environment of the Faculty of Medicine, where it is stated that most of the measurements made in that study fit the Log-Distance model with variation factor (Log-Normal) before and after adjusting the models.

Table 5. Mean Square Error of each Model

Model	Mean Square Error
Log-Distance Model	2,33698
COST-231 Model	6,65415
SUI Model	11,72926
Walfish-Bertoni Model	2,59443
Erceg Model	36,49632

However, this study has a larger number of real measurements which makes it more accurate and therefore seeks to choose the model with the lowest total mean square error, except for the basic model (Log-Distance). That is, the Walfish-Bertoni model with a mean square error of 2.59443 is chosen as the best fit for the 436 RSRP measurements as can be seen in Fig. 7.

5 Conclusions

– Propagation models are essential tools for predicting and understanding how waves propagate in various environments. However, it is important to take into account limitations, validate the models experimentally and consider knowledge of the environment to obtain accurate and reliable results.

- There are several propagation models used in the field of wireless communications to predict attenuation and received power in different types of environments such as urban, suburban and rural. The Log-Distance, SUI, Erceg and EURO-COST are used for this comparative analysis. Each model has its own conditions depending on factors such as frequency and antenna height.

- To obtain the received powers of each model, the specialised Narda SRM-3006 (ESPOCH) equipment is used to obtain the EIRP of the Faculty of Medicine more accurately from the total effective electric field strength at a point close to the base radio, giving a value of 46 dBm in this cell.

- Mean square error (MSE) is a commonly used metric to assess the accuracy of propagation models in various fields, such as wireless communications and wave propagation.

- The Walfish-Bertoni model, with a mean square error of 2.59443, is determined to be the best fit for the 398 RSRP measurements obtained with Network Cell Info. The received power values range from −67 dBm to −76 dBm.

References

1. Pallo, J.P., Carrera, E.P.: Study of mobile communications systems using fourth generation LTE technology for the city of Ambato. Technical University of Ambato, Electronic and Industrial Engineering. Electronic Engineering and Communications, Ecuador (2009). https://repositorio.uta.edu.ec/jspui/handle/123456789/291
2. Mixideal blog, "1G, 2G, 3G, 4G and 5G mobile networks: What are their differences", Technology section (2020). https://www.mixideal.com/blog/tecnologia/redes-moviles-1g-2g-3g-4g-y-5g-cuales-son-sus-diferencias
3. Ramón Agustí Comes and Francisco Bernardo Álvarez, "LTE: New trends in mobile communications", Chapter 1, pp. 46–60, Publisher: Vodafone Spain Foundation (2010)
4. Francisco Javier Garcia Rueda, "Models of propagation for 4G and 5G mobile communications", Higher Technical School of Engineering and Communication Systems (2016). https://oa.upm.es/44152/1/TFG_FRANCISCO_JAVIER_GARCIA_RUEDA.pdf
5. Hata, M.: Empirical formula for propagation loss in land mobile radio services. IEEE Trans. Vehicular Technology, VT-29, pp. 317–325 (1980)
6. COST 231 Final report, Digital Mobile Radio, "COST 231 View on the Evolution Towards 3rd Generation Systems", Commission of the European Communities and COST Telecommunications, Brussels (1999)
7. Erceg, V., et al.: Channel models for fixed wirelessapplications. Technical report, IEEE 802.16 Broadband Wireless AccessWorking Group (2001)
8. Uptodown, "Network Cell Info Lite" (2023). https://network-cell-info-lite.uptodown.com/android
9. Torres, J.M., Mangones, Á., Macea, M.R., Pérez, N.A., Rujano, L.M.: Modelo para la Estimación de las Pérdidas de Propagación en Redes WLAN Operando en 2,4 GHz y 5,8 GHz, para Ambientes Interiores de Edificios Comerciales", University, Science and Technology, vol. 20, no. 78, pp. 43–44 (2016). http://ve.scielo.org/pdf/uct/v20n78/art04.pdf

10. Martínez, O.: Flat and Spherical Earth of Wave Propagation, pp. 17–20, Escuela Superior Politénica de Chimborazo, Faculty of Informatics and Electronics, Riobamba (2021)
11. COST Action 231, "Digital mobile radio towards future generation systems, final report," Technical report, European Communities, EUR 8957 (1999)
12. Erceg, V., et al.: An empirically based path loss model for wireless channels in suburban environments. IEEE J. Select. Areas Commun. **17**, 1205–1211 (1999)
13. Walfisch, J., Bertoni, H.: A theoretical model of UHF propagation in urban environments. IEEE Trans. Antennas Propagat. AP-36, 1788–1796 (1988)
14. Erceg, V., Fortune, S.J., Ling, J., Rustako, A.J., Valenzuela, R.: Comparison of computer-based propagation tool prediction with experimental data collected in urban microcelluar environments. IEEE J. Select. Areas Commun. **15**, 677–684 (1997)
15. UTI, "Recommendation ITU-R P.525-Calculation of attenuation in free space" (2019). https://www.itu.int/dms_pubrec/itu-r/rec/p/R-REC-P.525-4-201908-I!! PDF-S.pdf
16. (PDF) Análisis comparativo de modelos de propagación en la telefonía móvil en la banda de 1900 MHz (LTE) a través de mediciones de campo eléctrico en la ciudad de Ambato. https://www.researchgate.net/publication/370068693_Analisis_comparativo_de_modelos_de_propagacion_en_la_telefonia_movil_en_la_banda_de_1900_MHz_LTE_a_traves_de_mediciones_de_campo_electrico_en_la_ciudad_de_Ambato
17. Bayas, C., Escobar, M., Infante, A., Proaño, A.: Comparison of radio propagation models in five LTE coverage cells in Riobamba. Escuela Superior Politécnica de Chimborazo, Faculty of Informatics and Electronics, Riobamba (2022). https://www.researchgate.net/publication/365877247_Comparison_of_radio_propagation_models_in_five_LTE_coverage_cells_in_Riobamba

Method Hand-Driven Used for Features Extraction in OCT B-Scan Images Processed

Fabricio Tipantocta[1]([✉]) [iD], Oscar Gómez[2] [iD], Javier Cajas[1] [iD],
German Castellanos[3] [iD], and Carlos Rivera[1] [iD]

[1] Instituto Superior Universitario Sucre, Teodoro Gómez de la Torre, S14 - 72 Quito, Ecuador
ftipantocta@tecnologicosucre.edu.ec
[2] Universidad Estatal Península de Santa Elena, la Libertad, Ecuador
[3] Universidad Nacional de Colombia, Manizales km 9, la Nubia, Colombia

Abstract. AMD macular degeneration and glaucoma stand out among the different types of pathologies that exist due to vision loss. The objective of this work is to use a dataset of images of patients with AMD pathology, which were semantically segmented, and to be able to perform the extraction of characteristics of the RNFL layer of the image with artificial vision and statistical methods, to carry out an experimental predictor 168 semantically segmented photos of patients with AMD were used. Through artificial vision, the fibers of the retina, known as RNFL, were highlighted. The Hand-Driven method was applied, which extracts an image's one-dimensional and two-dimensional characteristics; the Information was stored in a matrix, and discriminatory variables were formed. An experiment with a multilayer perceptron was proposed using the matrix of discriminating variables as input. Two outputs were classified; this experiment achieved a 93.94% effectiveness, and the feature extraction's utility was verified. It was concluded that the Hand-Driven method is robust with great functionality.

Keywords: Hand-Driven · Distribution · Artificial Vision · Multilayer Perceptron · AMD · Glaucoma

1 Introduction

Different pathologies occur in the loss of vision in the eyes of people. [1, 2] Among these pathologies appears AMD or glaucoma. Age-related macular degeneration [3], or AMD, is a retina degeneration that causes visual impairment or irreversible blindness. The study [4] mentions that this type of lesion can be used as a biological marker, considering that for people aged 45 to 85 years, this type of degeneration is more frequent, and it is 8.69% worldwide [2]. Existing cases of late-stage AMD in people aged 75 and older are increasing dramatically to 7.1%. Due to the aging of the population, by 2040, it is estimated that 288 million people will be affected by AMD [2].

Glaucoma [5] is another disease that is generated in the retina of the eye. This disease is characterized by the loss of cells that carry information from the eyes to the brain; most forms of glaucoma do not have a specific cause to define this type of disease in such a way that glaucoma produces a loss of field vision in people [6].

T. Guarda et al. (Eds.): ARTIIS 2023, CCIS 1937, pp. 406–416, 2024.
https://doi.org/10.1007/978-3-031-48930-3_31

Clinical trials [1] have shown the value of reducing intraocular pressure in patients with ocular problems, hypertension, or primary open-angle glaucoma, so the patient's decision to treat this disease depends on the progressive risk of treatment.

The study analyzed by [4, 6] evaluates the changes in the thickness of the RNFL, as well as the volumes of each retina; they examined the left and right eye, there being a significant difference between the right eye compared to the left, for this reason, they focused on the right eye. Right to detect signs of neurodegenerative processes.

These types of diseases, such as Glaucoma and AMD, have a social impact that affects 10 million blind people worldwide, according to. [7] In Ecuador, more than 200,000 people have a visual impairment, of which 51,500 are registered. According to the National Council of Persons with Disabilities, 50% belong to patients aged 30 to 65 years or older; this also coincides with an increase in the incidence of glaucoma after 40 years.

In collaboration, there are works such as [4, 6, 8, 9] that have dedicated their career to helping detect these diseases and creating frameworks that allow the creation of predictive classification systems. Such is the work that uses the thickness of a layer of the retina. A predictive system can be carried out to classify using images whether or not a person will have a pathology such as Glaucoma.

The objective of this work is to use a dataset of images of patients with AMD pathology, which were semantically segmented, and to be able to perform the extraction of characteristics of the RNFL layer of the image with artificial vision [10] and statistical methods to carry out an experimental predictor.

2 Method

This section presents the oct B-scan images [11] dataset used and the proposed method for extracting features from them.

2.1 Dataset AROI

The dataset used is an open retinal oct image collection in collaboration with Sestre Milosrdnice University Hospital Center (Zagreb, Croatia); an ophthalmologist collected images from patients 60 years of age or older with AMD diagnoses [2]. This dataset contains 1136 images of different patients, which are separated between 168 raw images and 168 images processed with semantic segmentation, which can be seen in (see Fig. 1).

For the present work, both the images without processing and the semantically segmented images have been used. Next, we present how the characteristics of the figures are extracted.

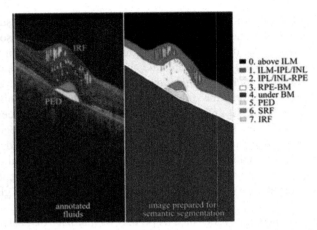

Fig. 1. Dataset with raw and processed oct scan images with semantic segmentation in png format.

2.2 Segmented Image Processing

The work of [4] shows the method called "hand-driven" this method indicates how to extract features from an oct image in 2D, taking parameters that can be extracted from an image by means of artificial vision and statistics, and This paper shows in detail how to remove them.

For our study, a comparison will be made with the work of [4], which takes as a reference a dataset that contains segmented images of RNFL, of the retina, and the real oct image; this work determines in the eyes of a patient if he is healthy or has glaucoma. Based on the thickness of the RNFL layer.

There are different layers in the anatomy of the retina [1], such as ILM: internal limiting membrane, RNFL: retinal nerve fiber layer, GCL-IPL: ganglion cell layer-internal plexiform layer, IRL: internal retinal layer, INL: nuclear layer internal, OPL: external plexiform layer, ONL: external nuclear layer, ELM – external limiting membrane, PR – photoreceptor layer, RPE – retinal pigment epithelium, (see Fig. 2).

Fig. 2. Retinal layer anatomy [1].

For our work, the Ilm and RNFL membranes were taken into account to form a single layer called RNFL since the dataset images are segmented with the mentioned layers, and the others that form the retina also have the AMD pathology. For the present project, a comparison is made with the work of [4], which takes characteristics of thickness in the RNFL of each of the sampled OCT images.

To determine the thickness in our RNFL image, the red channel is chosen and binarized, and the width of each column j of the image is taken, measuring the difference between the I maximum and minimum value, thus forming a vector Ti = {t1, t2, ..., tj}, where each tj ϵ T contains the RNFL thickness of each image.

(see Fig. 3) shows the real image with oct scan, the segmented image, the binarized image of the retina and the image of the rnfl layer.

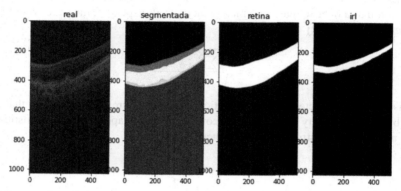

Fig. 3. Images from left to right: Real Image, Segmented Image, Binzarized Retinal Image, Binarized RNFL Image.

According to [6], one-dimensional feature extraction will be applied to the Ti vector, while two-dimensional feature extraction will be applied to the real image obtained from the OCT scan, forming a feature matrix with approximately 23 parameters (Fig. 4).

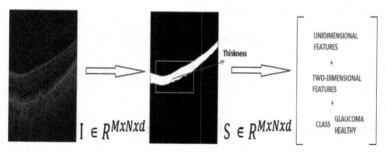

Fig. 4. Extraction of one-dimensional and two-dimensional features together in a matrix (MxN).

2.3 Extraction of One-Dimensional Features

Central tendency measurement characteristics: according to [12], central tendency measurements are statistical measurements that aim to summarize a set of values in a single value. They represent a center around which the data set is located. The most commonly used measures of central tendency are: mean and median.

$$\bar{y} = \frac{\sum_{i=0}^{n} y_i}{n} \tag{1}$$

$$\tilde{y} = y\frac{n+1}{2} \tag{2}$$

Characteristics based on measures of dispersion: measures of dispersion provide information on the variation of the variable. They try to summarize in a single value the dispersion that a data set has. The most widely used dispersion measure would be the standard deviation. [12]

$$s = \sqrt{\frac{\sum_{i=1}^{N} x_i - \bar{x}}{N-1}} \tag{3}$$

Distribution characteristics: in statistics, shape measures are indicators that allow describing a probability distribution according to the shape it has; in statistics, two shape measures are distinguished: Skewness and Kurtosis.

$$g1 = \frac{m_3}{m_2^{3/2}} \tag{4}$$

Where,

$$m_i = \frac{1}{N} \sum_{n=1}^{N} (x[n] - \bar{x})^i \tag{5}$$

Other characteristics: among the discriminatory characteristics, the maximum and minimum values of the Ti matrix are used.

$$Max\,(Ti = \{t1, t2, \ldots, tj\}) \tag{6}$$

$$Min\,(Ti = \{t1, t2, \ldots, tj\}) \tag{7}$$

2.4   Extraction of Two-Dimensional Features (Texture)

GLCM concurrency matrix: According to [13], the co-occurrence matrix describes the frequency of a gray level that appears in a specific spatial relationship with another gray value, with this method characteristics such as: "contrast", "dissimilarity", "homogeneity", "ASM", "energy" and "correlation", within the area of a given window (Fig. 5).

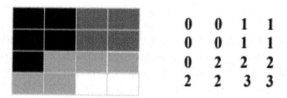

0	0	1	1
0	0	1	1
0	2	2	2
2	2	3	3

Fig. 5. Test image with dimension 4x4 pixels and 4 levels of gray (0, 1, 2 and 3).

LBP local binary patterns: labels the pixels of an image by thresholding the neighborhood of each pixel and considers the result as a binary number; histograms are compared and normalized, obtaining ten texture features.

$$N_i = \frac{H_i}{\sum_{j=0}^{n-1} H_j} \tag{8}$$

The AROI dataset contains images of patients older than 60 years who have the nAMD pathology. In the case of this work, and because there is no dataset with images that suffer from glaucoma pathology, an average of all the thicknesses of glaucoma has been performed. The images and has been separated into two particular cases: Glaucoma and Healthy; Although it is not a real case, this methodology can be applied since it has been tested in some works such as [4, 6]. For this reason, a vector has been created with the classes "0 for Glaucoma" and "1 for Healthy", leaving a matrix of dimension characteristics (168.23) as:

$$Caract_{unidimensionales} + Caract_{bidimensionales} + Clase \tag{9}$$

Of all the extracted characteristics, not all of them are discriminatory. The following section discusses how to select the discriminatory parameters.

3   Selection of Attributes

To find out if the parameters of the characteristics matrix are discriminatory, it is first analyzed whether the data follow a normal distribution with mean 0 and standard deviation 1, N(0.1); for this, the "Kolmogorov-Smirnov" test is used. See ec.10. For the test, a confidence statistic of 0.01 is taken and discriminates between h_norm$_j$ columns, thus knowing two categories, those that follow and those that do not, a distribution with mean 0 and deviation 1.

$$D = sup_{1 < i < n} \left| \widehat{F_n} - F_0(X_i) \right| \tag{10}$$

As a second, the distributions are analyzed with the tests of: "Mann-Whitney U" and "Student's t"; the first delivers the p_values that do not follow a normal distribution and the second for those that do, respectively. Comparing the p_value with the confidence statistic of 0.01, it is determined if the discriminative hypothesis is one if it is and 0 if it is not.

When obtaining the discriminatory characteristics, it is saved in a new matrix that will contain only the elements with the uncorrelated variables and will serve as analysis to make predictions with images of the same category.

3.1 Prediction

As the project focused on taking the characteristics of an image with pathologies different from the work [4], which focuses on the classification of three Glaucoma categories as Healthy, Early, and Advanced, an experiment has been carried out analyzing the RNFL of our data set and has been classified into two possible categories: Healthy and Glaucoma, taking into account the mean of the sampled data, and placing the categories higher than the mean as Healthy and lower as Glaucoma. With this, 20% of the sampled data is separated as a test set and 80% as a training set with discriminatory variables.

Lastly, and thanks to the Sklearn library, an MLP multilayer perceptron is taken for the predictive analysis of the training sample, taking into account the number of discriminatory variables (Fig. 6).

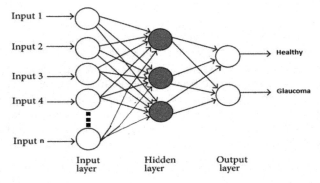

Fig. 6. Multi-Layer Perceptron, for the prediction of the Glaucoma or Healthy class

The following section shows the results of the feature extraction and the classification experiment of the sampled images.

4 Result

4.1 Extraction and Selection of Attributes

With the "hand-driven" method, a matrix of 23 characteristics of a total of 168 images was obtained, having a matrix of dimension M^{168x23} and analyzing the types of correlated variables in the selection of attributes, each of them is shown according to their class in the figure below (Fig. 7).

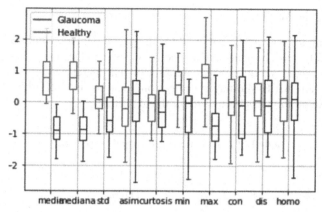

Fig. 7. Matrix of characteristics represented according to their correlation by means of box and whisker figures.

Clearly shown in the figure, the variables that are closer together are correlated variables, and the further they are, they are not. When the matrix was passed through the distribution analysis with mean 0 and standard deviation 1 with the Kolmogorov test, the study was carried out with the "Mann-Whitney U" and "Student's t" tests, thus discriminating only the correlated variables. Delivering as a result of a matrix $M^{168 \times 5}$, with five discriminatory characteristics which were: 'mean,' 'median,' 'std,' 'min,' and 'max.' The correlation matrix of the discriminatory variables can be seen in the Fig. 8.

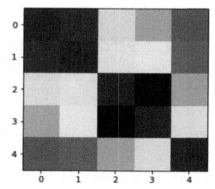

Fig. 8. Correlation matrix of the variables: 'mean', 'median', 'std', 'min', 'max', discriminatory variables of the characteristics matrix.

The discriminatory variables have a reliability of 0.01; it should be mentioned that none of the two-dimensional or texture characteristics were selected in this experiment; the reason that the work [4] differs from ours is that they work with images extracted from the SPECTRALIS machine. This allows obtaining the original OCT B-SCAN images, while in our work, the original OCT images are lowered in resolution and in PNG format; for this reason, the texture variables are not shown as discriminatory variables.

4.2   Training the Model

After extracting the characteristics of all the images of patients with the "hand-driven" method, two categories have been classified: Glaucoma and Healthy; therefore, we have the input and output variables to create an artificial neural network, the model. The chosen one is an "MLP Multilayer Perceptron" that has the ScikitLearn library. The following configuration has been used for the algorithm:

Table 1.   Configuration of the multilayer perceptron

Configuration	MLP
hidden_layer_sizes	[100,32]
Solver	Adam
max_iter	1000
batch_size	Auto
learning_rate	Adaptive
alpha	0.001
Random State	42

Training the multilayer perceptron with the training matrix gives us:

Table 2.   MLP configuration

Results	MLP
Accuracy	0.9394 ± 0.0429
Mín error	0.0183

4.3   Model Evaluation

With the perceptron model at 93.94% accuracy, the model is evaluated with the test matrix, which contains 42 samples, and the following results are obtained:

Taking into account that it is only an experiment, good results have been obtained with the classification in the multilayer perceptron; with this, it is demonstrated that it is a robust system (Fig. 9) and (Tables 1, 2, 3).

Table 3. Model evaluation

Results	MLP
Sensibility	1
Precision	0.8889
F1 - Score	0.9412
Accuracy	0.9459
AUC	0.9524

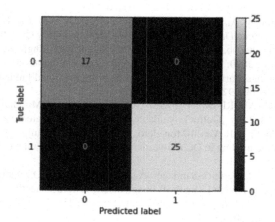

Fig. 9. Confusion matrix of the prediction evaluating the test.

5 Conclusions

The "hand-driven" methodology for the type of image dataset used was a good feature extraction method; all the one-dimensional and two-dimensional discriminative features were used, which were stored in a single matrix, collecting all the rich information of the image.

At the time of discriminating, the Kolmogorov method was used to make a normal distribution of the data, and the student and Mann-Whitney tests allowed selecting of the characteristics that are used to carry out the classification, thus having five main ones for the experiment.

With the characteristics well discriminated and using the multilayer perceptron of 100 y 32 neurons, an Accuracy of 93.94% was obtained, taking into account that there are no prediction errors in the confusion matrix.

References

1. Jung, S., et al.: Retinal neurodegeneration in patients with end-stage renal disease assessed by spectral-domain optical coherence tomography. Sci. Rep. **10**(1), 1–11 (2020). https://doi.org/10.1038/s41598-020-61308-4

2. Melinščak, M., Radmilović, M., Vatavuk, Z., Lončarić, S.: Annotated retinal optical coherence tomography images (AROI) database for joint retinal layer and fluid segmentation. Automatika **62**(3), 375–385 (2021). https://doi.org/10.1080/00051144.2021.1973298

3. Grassmann, F., Ach, T., Brandl, C., Heid, I.M., Weber, B.H.F.: What does genetics tell us about age-related macular degeneration? Annu. Rev. Vis. Sci. **1**(1), 73–96 (2015). https://doi.org/10.1146/annurev-vision-082114-035609

4. García, G., del Amor, R., Colomer, A., Verdú-Monedero, R., Morales-Sánchez, J., Naranjo, V.: Circumpapillary OCT-FOCUSED HYBRID LEARNING FOR GLAUCOMA GRADING USING TAILORED PROTOTYPICAL NEURAL NETWORKS. Artif. Intell. Med. **118**, 102132 (2021). https://doi.org/10.1016/j.artmed.2021.102132

5. Weinreb, R.N., Tee Khaw, P.: Primary open-angle glaucoma. Lancet **363**(9422), 1711–1720 (2004). https://doi.org/10.1016/S0140-6736(04)16257-0

6. García, G., Colomer, A., Naranjo, V.: Analysis of Hand-Crafted and Automatic-Learned Features for Glaucoma Detection Through Raw Circumpapillary OCT Images. In: Analide, C., Novais, P., Camacho, D., Yin, H. (eds.) Intelligent Data Engineering and Automated Learning – IDEAL 2020: 21st International Conference, Guimaraes, Portugal, November 4–6, 2020, Proceedings, Part II, pp. 156–164. Springer International Publishing, Cham (2020). https://doi.org/10.1007/978-3-030-62365-4_15

7. SOCIEDAD ECUATORIANA DE GLAUCOMA, "Semana Mundial del Glaucoma en Ecuador," pp. 1–8, 2018, [Online]. Available: www.sociedadecuatorianadeglaucoma.com.ec

8. G. García, A. Colomer, R. Verdú-Monedero, J. Dolz, and V. Naranjo, "A self-training framework for glaucoma grading in OCT B-scans," 2021, [Online]. Available: http://arxiv.org/abs/2111.11771

9. García-Floriano, A., Ferreira-Santiago, Á., Camacho-Nieto, O., Yáñez-Márquez, C.: A machine learning approach to medical image classification: Detecting age-related macular degeneration in fundus images. Comput. Electr. Eng. **75**, 218–229 (2019). https://doi.org/10.1016/j.compeleceng.2017.11.008

10. Payá, E.: Diseño y desarrollo de un sistema automático de segmentación de glándulas histológicas para identificar el cáncer de próstata en una etapa inicial. Universitat Politécnica de Valencia, 2018. [Online]. Available: https://riunet.upv.es/bitstream/handle/10251/129307/Payá Bosch - Diseño y desarrollo de un sistema automático de segmentación de glándulas histológicas para identificar el cáncer de próstata en una etapa inicial.pdf?sequence=1&isAllowed=y

11. Rocholz, R.M et al.: "SPECTRALIS Optical Coherence Tomography Angiography (OCTA): Principles and Clinical Applications," Heidelbg. Eng. Acad., no. September, 2018, [Online]. Available: https://www.heidelbergengineering.com/media/e-learning/Totara/Dateien/pdf-tutorials/210111-001_SPECTRALIS OCTA - Principles and Clinical Applications_EN.pdf

12. Quevedo, F.: Medidas de tendencia central y dispersión. Medwave **11**(03),(2011). https://doi.org/10.5867/medwave.2011.03.4934

13. Presutti, M.: "La matriz de co-ocurrencia en la clasificación multiespectral: tutorial para la enseñanza de medidas texturales en cursos de grado universitario," 4a Jorn. Educ. em Sensoriamento Remoto no Âmbito do Mercosul, p. 9 (2004)

Empowering Low-Power Wide-Area Networks: Unlocking the Potential of Sigfox in Local Transmission

Manuel Montaño Blacio$^{(\boxtimes)}$![ORCID], Vladimir García Santos ![ORCID],
Daniel Jaramillo Chamba ![ORCID], Washington Torres Guin ![ORCID],
and Luis Chuquimarca Jiménez ![ORCID]

Facultad de Sistemas y Telecomunicaciones, Universidad Estatal Península de Santa Elena,
Santa Elena, Ecuador
mmontano@upse.edu.ec

Abstract. Low-Power Wide Area Networks (LPWAN) have revolutionized long-range communication with low energy consumption, enabling various applications across industries. Sigfox, as a prominent LPWAN technology, operates on a proprietary network infrastructure with base stations deployed worldwide. These base stations receive signals from Sigfox-enabled devices and transmit the data to the cloud platform called the Sigfox backend. This article proposes an innovative architecture that enables local transmission using the Sigfox network. The architecture integrates an ESP32 device to facilitate connectivity with the ThingSpeak cloud platform. The main objective is to demonstrate the feasibility of using Sigfox, even in regions where its infrastructure is not fully deployed yet. The study focuses on transmitting temperature and humidity data to evaluate the network performance. An assessment of the network coverage range based on the Okumura-Hata model is also presented. This analysis provides information on the potential reach of the Sigfox network. The findings of the study highlight that this novel architecture offers a viable solution for various environments, especially in agricultural sectors where it has been implemented.

Keywords: LPWAN · Sigfox · Agriculture · Local Transmission · Ufox

1 Introduction

To improve agricultural performance with fewer resources and labor efforts, substantial innovations have been made throughout human history. Low-Power Wide Area Networks (LPWAN) have emerged as an innovative technology that enables long-range communication with minimal energy consumption. These networks have unlocked new possibilities in all industries, enhancing applications such as smart agriculture [1], asset tracking, and environmental monitoring, among others. Currently, there has been a significant increase in the popularity of LPWAN in the IoT market. This is due to its wireless communication features, which include reduced costs, efficient power consumption, and wide coverage. These technologies offer an affordable and effective solution for

T. Guarda et al. (Eds.): ARTIIS 2023, CCIS 1937, pp. 417–429, 2024.
https://doi.org/10.1007/978-3-031-48930-3_32

IoT device connectivity. With LPWAN, it is possible to establish a robust and reliable network that spans large geographical areas, which is especially beneficial in rural environments or areas where traditional connectivity may be limited. Additionally, the low power required by LPWAN-enabled devices allows them to operate for extended periods without frequent battery changes, resulting in increased efficiency and lower maintenance [2].

In the literature, several comparative studies, and surveys [3–6] can be found that focus on the deployment of LPWAN technologies in IoT applications. Among the most recognized and widely used LPWAN technologies are Sigfox, LoRaWAN, and Narrow-Band IoT (NB-IoT). As a result, these types of networks have been extensively adopted in various application areas. These areas include air quality monitoring [7], smart health tracking [8], botanical park monitoring [9], and environmental monitoring [10]. These applications demonstrate how LPWAN technologies are significantly contributing to the optimization and improvement of different aspects in various sectors.

In the field of LPWAN technologies applied in agriculture, various studies and research have been conducted, yielding significant results. An example of this is the study [11], which proposes an irrigation system based on the combination of LoRa and Sigfox technologies. The proposal has proven to be effective in optimizing water usage in crops. Another interesting approach is presented in the study [12], where the utilization of a combination of EnOcean and Sigfox technologies is proposed for real-time data collection in the agricultural sector.

In [13], a system based on NB-IoT has been proposed for the implementation of wireless sensor networks in potato crops. This solution has facilitated the collection and real-time analysis of data, contributing to improved crop performance and efficiency. [14] and [15] highlight the use of NB-IoT-based technologies. These studies have allowed for the evaluation of NB-IoT network coverage and efficiency in rural areas and greenhouses. In a specific study [16], the implementation of a real-time soil health monitoring system using LoRaWAN technology is proposed. This system has proven to be effective in measuring and analyzing relevant soil parameters such as temperature, humidity, electrical conductivity, carbon dioxide (CO_2) levels, and geolocation data, providing valuable information for agricultural management. In summary, the contributions made in these studies have demonstrated the potential of LPWAN technologies in agriculture by offering efficient and precise solutions for monitoring and controlling agricultural variables. These technologies are revolutionizing the way agriculture is conducted, enabling smarter and more sustainable management of agricultural resources.

Within the LPWAN technologies, this research focuses on Sigfox, which has gained prominence due to its efficient and reliable communication capabilities. This technology operates on a proprietary network infrastructure, consisting of a global network of strategically located base stations worldwide. These base stations act as gateways, receiving signals from Sigfox-enabled devices and sending the data to the Sigfox backend, a cloud platform that processes and stores the information. Thanks to this infrastructure, long-range connectivity and data transmission are achieved with minimal energy consumption.

However, despite the advantages of Sigfox, there are regions where its infrastructure is not yet fully implemented, limiting the availability and coverage of the network. To address this limitation, this research proposes an innovative architecture that combines the capabilities of Sigfox and Wi-Fi to achieve efficient data transmission. The main objective is to demonstrate the feasibility of using Sigfox even in regions where its infrastructure is not extensively developed. The study focuses on the transmission of temperature and humidity data, which are essential variables in agricultural applications, and analyzes the coverage range of the network using the Okumura-Hata model. The results demonstrate the viability of the proposed architecture as a solution for diverse environments, especially in the agricultural sector, where the accuracy of environmental data is crucial for optimizing crop production, conserving resources, and improving overall efficiency.

2 Methodology

In this section, the methodology used in [17] is applied, which includes reviewing previous research and carrying out the design and implementation stages of the proposal. The components used are also described, along with how they relate to the objective of the study, which is to propose a Sigfox network architecture for local transmission.

2.1 Proposed Architecture

A proposed architecture (see Fig. 1) is presented for local data transmission through the Sigfox network, using the Ufox hardware. This hardware enables leveraging the Wisol module to send and receive Sigfox packets over the network. The architecture consists of three Ufox modules, whose main function is to transmit Sigfox packets with a maximum size of 12 bytes. These packets are received by TinyFox, which is configured to listen and receive Sigfox packets. Additionally, the TinyFox is connected to an ESP32, responsible for establishing a Wi-Fi connection with the access point to access the Internet. This way, the temperature and humidity data sent by the Ufox modules can be sent to the ThingSpeak cloud.

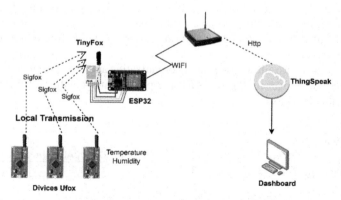

Fig. 1. Proposed Architecture for Local Sigfox Transmission.

This innovative architecture clearly demonstrates the feasibility and efficiency of creating a robust Sigfox infrastructure for local data packet transmission. The combination of advanced hardware and software, along with careful module configuration and design, ensures reliable and fast transmission of information, opening new possibilities in the field of Internet of Things (IoT) applications.

Here are the important hardware features of the used hardware. The Ufox [18] is a SIGFOX communication DevKit board designed for LPWAN IoT projects with Sigfox wireless connectivity. This board features an ATMEGA 32U4 microcontroller compatible with Arduino Leonardo and Arduino Promicro, making it easy to program using the Arduino IDE. The Ufox includes an SFM10R4 (Sigfox RC4) wireless communication module with a power output of + 22.4 dBm, ensuring reliable data transmission. Additionally, it has a 3 dBi helical antenna and the option to connect an external antenna through a U.FL connector.

The TinyFox is a device designed for low-power IoT communications. With its WISSOL SFM10R4 modem, it allows establishing connections to the Sigfox network in the RC4 region. The device is controlled using AT commands, which facilitates its configuration and operation. It has a simple and robust design and comes equipped with a built-in helical antenna. Additionally, it offers the possibility to connect external antennas through a U.FL to SMA connector. The device is compatible with uplink and downlink, enabling data transmission and reception. Communication with the ESP32 is done through the UART Serial RX-TX port at a baud rate of 9600, with voltage levels ranging from 2.5V to 4.2V (typical operation at 3.3V).

2.2 Frame Structure

The packet frame structure is illustrated in Fig. 2, where it is clearly shown that its maximum size is 12 bytes. The first 4 bytes are used to transmit temperature data, which is stored in a float variable. The next 4 bytes are used to transmit humidity. Byte 8 is reserved for future use, such as checking the battery status of the Ufox module. Byte 9 is of vital importance as it stores the local identifier or ID of the device. This ID allows for the identification of the transmitting module and prevents confusion when capturing data with the TinyFox. Bits 10 and 11 are left free for possible additional applications. Figure 2 also presents an example that demonstrates the conversion of data into a hexadecimal format and how the frame is constructed before being sent through the Sigfox network.

This frame structure allows for efficient organization and transmission of temperature and humidity data, ensuring the integrity and proper interpretation of the information captured by the TinyFox.

Byte Position	0	1	2	3	4	5	6	7	8	9	10	11
Variables	Temperature				Humidity				NA	NA	ID_LOCAL	NA	NA	NA	NA
Datatype	Float 32				Float 32						uint 8				
example	18.67				89.38						1				
Hex	0x41955C28				0x42B2C28F						0x01				

Fig. 2. Structure of the local Sigfox network frame.

2.3 Visualization

The ThingSpeak platform plays a fundamental role in visualizing and monitoring data from the Ufox devices in the local network. The integration between Ufox and ThingSpeak allows for easy and convenient access to the collected data, such as temperature, humidity, and other relevant parameters, which can be utilized in future applications.

ThingSpeak offers an intuitive interface that allows configuring customized graphs, tables, and widgets to visually present the data in an appealing manner. In addition to visualization, the platform provides analysis tools and custom notifications, enabling detailed tracking of the recorded measurements.

This integration provides real-time insights into the status of Ufox devices and their performance in the local network. Moreover, ThingSpeak offers data export options and an API that facilitates integration with other external systems and applications.

The ESP32, through its WiFi connection, uses the HTTP application protocol to send the collected data to the ThingSpeak platform. This protocol ensures a secure and efficient transfer of information from the ESP32 to the ThingSpeak server. Using HTTP, the ESP32 establishes a connection with the server and sends the data through HTTP POST requests. These data include the information collected by the Ufox devices in the local network, such as temperature and humidity. The ESP32 is responsible for packaging the data in the appropriate format, following the specifications of the ThingSpeak API, and transmitting them to the server using the HTTP protocol. There, the data is processed and stored in the platform.

Once the data is received by ThingSpeak, the platform interprets and organizes it for further visualization and analysis. The data sent via HTTP can be associated with specific fields in the ThingSpeak interface, enabling the creation of custom graphs, tables, and widgets to display the information in a visually appealing manner.

2.4 Okumura-Hata Propagation Model

To accurately demonstrate the signal attenuation effect due to air propagation, the Okumura-Hata propagation model is employed, which is widely recognized and used today. This model is valid over a wide range of frequencies, from 150 MHz to 1500 MHz [19], which falls within the frequencies used in the local Sigfox transmission network, specifically the Uplink frequency of 920.8 MHz and Downlink frequency of 922.3 MHz.

The Okumura-Hata propagation model allows for the simulation of different types of environments, including rural, suburban, and urban settings. Each of these environments has distinct characteristics that influence signal propagation. By using this model, realistic and accurate results can be obtained regarding how the signal behaves in each of these scenarios. The Okumura-Hata model takes into account various factors that affect signal propagation, such as the distance between the transmitter and receiver, the frequency used, the height of the antennas, and the presence of obstacles. These elements influence signal attenuation and quality. Below, we present the mathematical equations for evaluating the Sigfox network. The equation for loss in an urban environment is as follows (1).

$$L_u = 69.55 + 26.16 \, log_{10} f - 13.82 \, log_{10} h_B - C_H + \left[44.9 - 6.55 \, log_{10} h_B \right] log_{10} d$$

$$(1)$$

where:

- **f:** The frequency of the signal in MHz.
- h_B: The height of the receiving antenna.
- h_M: The height of the transmitting antenna.
- C_H: The height correction factor of the receiving antenna, which varies depending on the type of environment.
- **d:** The distance between the transmitter and the receiver in kilometers.

In this formulation, the mentioned parameters play an important role in predicting and analyzing signal propagation. The frequency (f) determines the wavelength of the signal and its propagation behavior. The heights of the receiving antenna (h_B) and transmitting antenna (h_M) influence the signal path and its effective range. The height correction factor of the receiving antenna (C_H) takes into account the environment characteristics to adjust signal propagation based on the height of the receiving antenna. Lastly, the distance (d) between the transmitter and receiver is a key factor that directly affects signal attenuation and quality.

For urban environments with small cities, Ch takes the value given in Eq. (2).

$$C_H = 0.8 + (1.1\,log_{10}f - 0.7)h_M - 1.56\,log_{10}f \tag{2}$$

The attenuation equations in suburban and rural areas are influenced by the corresponding equation for the urban environment (L_u). In the specific case of a suburban environment, Eq. (3) applies.

$$L_{SU} = L_U - 2\left(log_{10}\frac{f}{28}\right)^2 - 54 \tag{3}$$

L_{SU}: Loss index in suburban environments. And finally, for rural areas, Eq. (4) applies.

$$L_o = L_U - 4.78(log_{10}f)^2 + 18.33\,log_{10}f - 40.94 \tag{4}$$

L_o: Loss index in rural environments.

3   Result

The scenario in which the local network proposal is evaluated is in the city of Loja. Initially, an evaluation is carried out using the Okumura-Hata model to estimate signal losses in the environment. Once the theoretical evaluation is completed, practical tests are conducted with the implementation of the system. These tests are performed to verify the range of the transmitters and the efficiency of the received packets (PDR). Line-of-sight configurations are used, meaning that the transmitting and receiving devices have unobstructed direct vision between them. During the tests, data is collected, and results are analyzed to assess the transmission quality, packet delivery capability, and system stability under real conditions. This allows for obtaining accurate information about the performance and effectiveness of the implemented local network in Loja.

It is important to highlight that conducting tests in a line-of-sight environment provides an initial evaluation, but other factors of the real environment are also taken into account, such as the presence of obstacles (buildings, trees, etc.) that affect the network performance.

3.1 Okumura-Hata Model

Data for model evaluation:

- Transmit Power: 22 dBm
- Initial Distance: 0 m
- Maximum Distance: 25 km
- Distance Increment: 50 m
- Packet Size: 12 bytes
- Receiver Sensitivity: −130 dBm
- Frequency in MHz: 920.8
- Transmitter Effective Height in meters: 25
- Receiver Height in meters: 1.5
- Propagation Model: Okumura-Hata
- Simulation Environments: Rural, Suburban, and Urban.

The following are the results of the Okumura-Hata model (see Fig. 3). In a rural environment, the proposed system demonstrates a maximum range of 20 km. This means that the Ufox devices in the local network will be able to effectively transmit data within a wide range in rural areas. With a transmission power of 22 dBm and a receiver sensitivity of −130 dBm, reliable and stable communication is expected in this environment, enabling data collection and monitoring in rural areas.

In a suburban environment, the system has a maximum range of 5 km. As a more densely populated environment is introduced, the presence of buildings and other obstacles can affect the coverage of the local network. However, with a transmission power of 22 dBm and a receiver sensitivity of −130 dBm, it is expected that the Ufox devices maintain reliable communication within that range in suburban areas, enabling data monitoring in residential and suburban environments.

In an urban environment, the maximum range of the system is further reduced, reaching 2.5 km. Densely populated urban areas have more obstacles and sources of interference, which limits the coverage of the local network. However, with a transmission power of 22 dBm and a receiver sensitivity of −130 dBm, it is expected that the Ufox devices maintain reliable communication within that range in urban environments, enabling data collection in urban areas with a high concentration of devices and users.

These results indicate how the range and efficiency of communication vary in different environments. Each environment presents unique challenges in terms of coverage and signal quality, and it is important to consider these limitations when implementing and evaluating the local network in rural, suburban, and urban settings.

3.2 Implemented Architecture

The results obtained from the tests conducted in a controlled environment with the implemented architecture demonstrate the influence of distance and obstacles on the

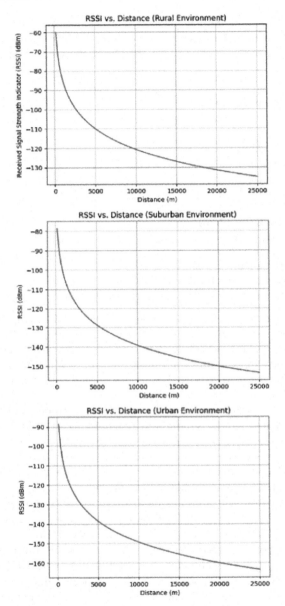

Fig. 3. Okumura-Hata Model Results

degradation of the network signal. In particular, it is observed that in urban environments, where the density of buildings and obstacles is high, the signal degrades more rapidly compared to rural and suburban environments. This is due to the greater amount of interference and blockage present in urban areas.

To visualize the signal strength in different locations, a heat map was used in Fig. 4. In this map, the color red indicates a strong signal intensity, which represents a 100% delivery of transmitted packets. As the transmitter moves away from the receiver and encounters obstacles such as buildings or other elements, the colors yellow and blue depict a decrease in signal intensity and a possible packet loss.

It is important to note that line of sight between the transmitter and the receiver has a significant impact on the signal range. In situations where there is a clear and unobstructed line of sight, a maximum range of up to 8 km (tested) is observed, as shown in Fig. 4. However, in the absence of line of sight, the signal has a more limited range, highlighting the importance of considering the environmental conditions when planning the placement of Ufox devices to ensure optimal communication.

These results highlight the importance of evaluating the performance of the local network in different environments and considering the influence of distance and obstacles on signal degradation. Furthermore, they provide valuable information for optimizing the placement of devices and ensuring adequate coverage in urban, suburban, and rural areas.

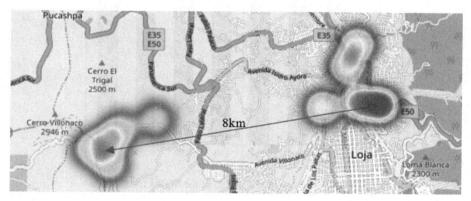

Fig. 4. Coverage Heatmap of the Sigfox Local Network.

3.3 Packet Delivery Ratio (PDR)

In the evaluation of the efficiency of the local network, the metric known as Packet Delivery Ratio (PDR) is used, which is calculated using Eq. 5. This metric provides information about the proportion of successfully received packets in relation to the total number of packets sent.

$$PDR = \frac{\sum number\ of\ packets\ received}{\sum number\ of\ packages\ sent} \tag{5}$$

The tests are conducted in controlled scenarios with clear line of sight between the transmitter and the receiver. Different distances are evaluated, starting from 1000 m up to 7000 m, with a transmission rate of 10 packets per minute. The results show that at a distance of 1000 m, the network efficiency reaches 100%, indicating that all sent packets are received correctly. At distances of 2000 m, the efficiency slightly decreases to 80%, which can be attributed to the presence of obstacles in the environment that affect the signal quality. This demonstrates the adaptability of the local network and its suitability for low-power, long-range (LPWAN) applications.

In summary, the results obtained from the tests indicate that the implemented local network is efficient and reliable for data transmission over long distances. The packet delivery rate demonstrates its ability to overcome obstacles and ensure effective communication in line-of-sight environments (see Fig. 5). These findings support the feasibility of the local network for applications that require extensive coverage and reliable communication in controlled environments.

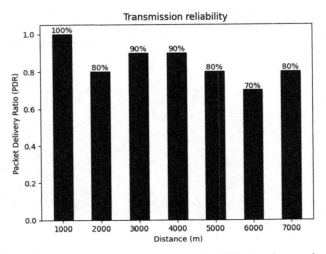

Fig. 5. Packet Delivery Ratio (PDR) of the Sigfox local network.

3.4 Data Visualization

The ThingSpeak platform plays a fundamental role in visualizing the data generated by the local network. As mentioned earlier, through the integration between Ufox and ThingSpeak, simple and effective monitoring of parameters such as temperature and ambient humidity is achieved. This visualization capability allows for a concrete demonstration of the operation of the local Sigfox architecture and its ability to send data to the cloud.

In the context of smart agriculture, the ability to monitor and record temperature and ambient humidity data is of vital importance. With the help of ESP32, the local network is capable of collecting and sending test data related to the crop environment. This data can be used to monitor and control plant growth, enabling farmers to make informed decisions and improve the productivity of their crops.

The local Sigfox architecture provides a reliable and efficient solution for agricultural monitoring. By sending data to the cloud through the ThingSpeak platform, farmers can access real-time information about the environmental conditions of their crops. This allows them to track temperature and humidity variations in a detailed and precise manner, facilitating decision-making processes. For example, it enables them to optimize irrigation, control diseases, and maximize crop yield.

The synergistic convergence of Sigfox's local architecture, the potential of ESP32, and the versatility of the ThingSpeak platform blend into a comprehensive and highly effective solution for monitoring and representing data in agricultural environments (see Fig. 6 and Fig. 7). The ability to transmit data to the cloud and access it remotely provides farmers with the opportunity to implement intelligent agricultural strategies, enhance efficiency and productivity, and make informed decisions supported by up-to-date and reliable information. In Fig. 6, the visualization of ambient temperature is facilitated, where each red dot represents a data point captured by the IoT platform, displaying temperature values along with the corresponding date and time of recording. On the other hand, Fig. 7 displays humidity levels expressed in percentages, which eloquently confirms the effectiveness of the established communication.

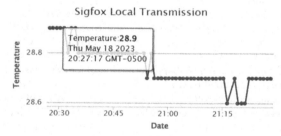

Fig. 6. Visualization of temperature monitoring.

Fig. 7. Visualization of humidity monitoring.

4   Conclusions

This study demonstrates the feasibility of using Sigfox technology in regions where its infrastructure is not fully implemented, through an innovative architecture. The integration of the ESP32 device enables local transmission of the Sigfox network to be visualized on the ThingSpeak platform. The main focus is on the transmission of temperature and humidity data, crucial aspects in sectors such as agriculture. Additionally, a performance evaluation of the network is conducted using the Okumura-Hata model to determine the coverage range.

The results obtained highlight that this architecture offers a viable and efficient solution in various environments. The ability to transmit data locally and utilize the ThingSpeak platform for monitoring and data analysis provides a valuable solution, especially in the agricultural field. These findings support the utility and feasibility of LPWAN networks, such as Sigfox, in different contexts, and pave the way for future applications and improvements in this area.

References

1. Montaño-Blacio, Manuel, et al.: Diseño y despliegue de un sistema de monitoreo basado en IoT para cultivos hidropónicos. Ingenius **30**, 9–18 (2023). https://doi.org/10.17163/ings.n30.2023.01
2. Qadir, Q.M., Rashid, T.A., Al-Salihi, N.K., Ismael, B., Kist, A.A., Zhang, Z.: Low power wide area networks: a survey of enabling technologies, applications and interoperability needs. IEEE Access **6**, 77454–77473 (2018). https://doi.org/10.1109/ACCESS.2018.2883151
3. Montaño, M, et al.: IoT management analysis using SDN: Survey. In: International Conference on Applied Technologies. Springer International Publishing, Cham (2020). https://doi.org/10.1007/978-3-030-71503-8_45
4. Ayoub, W., et al.: Internet of mobile things: Overview of lorawan, dash7, and nb-iot in lpwans standards and supported mobility. IEEE Commun. Surv. Tutorials **21**(2), 1561–1581 (2018)
5. Qadir, Q.M., et al.: Low power wide area networks: A survey of enabling technologies, applications and interoperability needs. IEEE Access **6**, 77454–77473 (2018)
6. Raza, U., Parag, K., Sooriyabandara, M.: Low power wide area networks: an overview. IEEE Commun. Surv. Tutor. **19**(2), 855–873 (2017)
7. Zheng, K., et al.: Design and implementation of LPWA-based air quality monitoring system. IEEE Access **4**, 3238–3245 (2016)
8. Popli, S., Jha, R.K., Jain, S.: A survey on energy efficient narrowband internet of things (NBIoT): architecture, application and challenges. IEEE Access **7**, 16739–16776 (2018)
9. Klaina, H., et al.: Implementation of an interactive environment with multilevel wireless links for distributed botanical garden in university campus. IEEE Access **8**, 132382–132396 (2020)
10. Tong, J., et al.: Surrogate model-based energy-efficient scheduling for LPWA-based environmental monitoring systems. IEEE Access **6**, 59940–59948 (2018)
11. Fernández-Ahumada, L.M., et al.: Proposal for the design of monitoring and operating irrigation networks based on IoT, cloud computing and free hardware technologies. Sensors **19**(10), 2318 (2019)
12. Dai, J., Sugano, M.: Low-cost sensor network for collecting real-time data for agriculture by combining energy harvesting and LPWA technology. In: 2019 IEEE Global Humanitarian Technology Conference (GHTC). IEEE (2019)
13. Castellanos, G., et al.: System assessment of WUSN using NB-IoT UAV-aided networks in potato crops. IEEE Access **8**, 56823–56836 (2020)
14. Valecce, G., et al.: NB-IoT for smart agriculture: Experiments from the field. In: 2020 7th International Conference on Control, Decision and Information Technologies (CoDIT), vol. 1. IEEE (2020)

15. Zhang, F., et al.: Smart greenhouse management system based on NB-IoT and smartphone. In: 2020 17th International Joint Conference on Computer Science and Software Engineering (JCSSE). IEEE (2020)
16. Ramson, S.R.J., et al.: A self-powered, real-time, LoRaWAN IoT-based soil health monitoring system. IEEE Internet of Things J. **8**(11), 9278–9293 (2021)
17. Blacio, M.A.Montaño, et al.: UISRAEL, 284 páginas; 21, 0 x 29, 7 cm. Libro digital-PDF, p. 101 (2021)
18. Teca. Ufox devkit Sigfox RC4 GitHub (2022), https://github.com/TECA-IOT/Ufox
19. Munera Sánchez, A.: Modelado y evaluación de la tecnología Sigfox para NS3". Diss. Universitat Politècnica de València (2018)

Innovation in Educational Technology
(JIUTE 2023)

Towards New Acoustic Narratives on University Campuses: Potential as Non-formal Educational Tools

Alberto Quintana-Gallardo$^{(\boxtimes)}$, Fernando A. Mendiguchia, and Ignacio Guillén-Guillamón

Center for Physics Technologies (CTFAMA), Universitat Politècnica de València, 46022 Valencia, Spain
alquigal@upv.es

Abstract. University campuses are social communities with their own traditions, customs, and even culture. Those traditions' history and evolution dramatically influence how students learn, professors teach, and other university employees interact. However, this influence is not apparent and, therefore, often neglected. Most university students do not know their university's history, which worsens their ability to fully take advantage of the possibilities university life offers them.

This study analyzes how to use new technologies and narratives to convey that information to students and university personnel. In this case, the Polytechnic University of Valencia Campus de Vera has been studied through a series of sound essays distributed online as podcasts. The sound essays reflect on the university's history, the architectural environment's influence on social interactions and non-formal learning, the soundscape of the campus and its relationship with university users, and the limits of the university itself and the speculative future.

The approach comprises three distinct stages. The initial stage involves conducting a literature review of UPV's history and examining architectural projects and published books related to the university. This step is essential for contextualizing the study. The second phase entails capturing campus soundscapes through ambisonics microphones, conducting sound walks with binaural microphones, and conducting interviews with professors, students, and other staff members. The final stage involves editing the audio recordings using a Digital Audio Workstation (DAW).

After the study, it can be concluded that using new means of communication can foster the interest of the university community in knowing and understanding the history of their university and the role they play in it. That ultimately can create students that are more aware of their own context.

Keywords: Sound Essays · Non-formal Training · Podcasts · Soundscapes

1 Introduction

University campuses are unique places that can host thousands of people daily. Over time, these places generate their own culture and traditions, which are influenced by the history of the university, the natural and architectural environment, the university degrees taught, and the societal context. Being aware of this history and culture can have an enormous impact on the way students learn. If they know the campus better, they can take full advantage of the opportunities it brings and even avoid the dangers. Moreover, it can increase their proactivity and engagement in the classes they take and the university curriculum. How can universities and educational institutions awaken students' interest in knowing their university better?

The rapidly changing technology industry forces educators and education centers to rethink how they train their students [1]. The newer generations absorb content in new ways. Their attention span is shorter, and the attractors they need to be engaged have also changed. For that reason, how educators convey information to students needs to be reimagined [2].

It is not always the content that needs to be adapted but how it is conveyed. Marshall McLuhan, a prominent Canadian philosopher and media theorist of the 20th century, introduced the concept of "the medium is the message." The meaning of this sentence is that the medium through which a message is conveyed changes how that message is perceived and understood [3]. That means that the medium, rather than the content itself, is the primary driver of social and cultural change. McLuhan argues that the intrinsic characteristics of a medium shape how information is received, processed, and interpreted by individuals and society. A medium can be described as a tool used to transmit information.

The medium has evolved over the years along with technology, from inscriptions engraved in stone to papyrus and paper to modern-day communication systems and digital media. Each medium has unique properties like speed, interactivity, and sensory nature. McLuhan also coined the idea of the message as extension, which means that every medium extends a different human capability or function. For example, the printed medium extends our ability to process written information, while television extends our visual and auditory senses. McLuhan states these extensions profoundly affect how people interact with each other and the world around them. It even influences perception and social dynamics, as different mediums have the potential to create distinct perceptual environments and social structures. The characteristics of a medium can foster or attenuate things like individuality, critical thinking, social cohesion, and so on. It also shifts communication patterns that can lead to reshaping social structures. The immediacy of communication in the digital era has brought profound changes that we are only starting to understand [3]. While many can argue that McLuhan's theories undervalue the importance of content and context, it is undeniable that every new medium brings new perspectives and social changes. Therefore, taking advantage of the mediums we have at our disposal is critical to engaging the audiences, especially young people [4].

"The medium is the message" can also be applied to education. The choice of medium in educational settings significantly influences the learning experience and outcomes. In conventional education, the medium primarily consists of textbooks, lectures, and physical classrooms. However, over the last decades, the medium of education has expanded because of digital technology, online platforms, and multimedia resources. The characteristics of each one of those educational mediums, such as interactivity, accessibility, and personalization, shape how information is conveyed and received by learners. This affects not only the delivery of content but also the engagement, participation, and interaction among students and educators. Understanding the influence of the medium on education is crucial for designing effective learning environments that enhance the educational experience. Whether through podcasts, online courses, virtual reality simulations, or collaborative platforms, the choice of medium in education transforms teaching and learning practices and creates new challenges and opportunities.

One way in which these new mediums can be used in education is as non-formal training tools. They can generate more interest in the content and increase engagement. Non-formal training is a way of learning that does not follow the traditional formal education system, which means it does not follow the standard curricula. Non-formal training can take place both in academic and non-academic settings. Often, non-formal training aims to foster specific skills and practical competencies for adult learners. However, it can also be used to complement formal learning. Several traits characterize non-formal training. One of them is flexibility, mainly regarding content, methodology, and timing. This kind of training can be tailored to the needs of the learners [2]. The second one is the informal structure. While some forms of non-formal training include issuing certificates for the participants, it is not a requirement, and it does usually not imply a strict curriculum and assessment process. Another important trait is the audience. More often than not, these kinds of training courses are designed for specific target groups. That helps in addressing their particular requirements or needs. The last one of these characteristics is its relationship with lifelong learning by offering continuous learning opportunities to people of all ages and abilities [2].

Educational podcasts can be a valuable tool for finding new ways of engaging students. Educational podcasts can be considered a form of non-formal training. Podcasts are the transformation of radio to the new digital era, a digital medium that allows for disseminating educational content in audio. There are podcasts of almost any genre imaginable; they often feature discussions, interviews, lectures, or presentations on various topics. Some are designed purely for entertainment; others provide listeners with valuable information, insights, and learning opportunities.

Educational podcasts share some of the traits that define non-formal training. They have an informal structure. Their episodic format covering different topics or themes allows the learners to choose whether to listen only to the ones that interest them or follow a chronological order. Also, accessibility helps people of all ages listen to them at any time, regardless of age or background, in their preferred schedules. Educational podcasts can also be characterized by their targeted content. While an educational podcast does not provide hands-on experience, it offers a valuable learning resource. Podcasts can be supplementary tools for acquiring knowledge, exploring new ideas, and staying informed on various subjects.

Over the last decade, there has been a tremendous increase in the number of educational podcasts [5]. However, there are examples of educational podcasts that date back to the early 2000s. Science Friday is one of the most famous examples. In 2005, being a well-recognized radio show, Science Friday started uploading their episodes online Grammar Girl's Quick and Dirty Tips for Better Writing was probably one of the first educational podcasts to be released strictly as a podcast. Mignon Fogarty, also known as Grammar Girl, started updating episodes regularly on improving people's grammar in

2006 [6]. A year later, in 2007, the History of Rome podcast was released. This podcast, created by Mike Duncan, was a comprehensive narration of the most notable events during the Roman Empire [7]. Another educational podcast from those years is Writing Excuses. Released in 2008 by a group of writers, Dan Wells, Brandon Sanderson, and Howard Tayler, this podcast provided a loosely structured guide to science fiction and fantasy writing [8].

The podcasting scene in Spain has been growing fast over the last few years, especially in 2020 [9]. Crims, El Gran Apagón, and Todopoderosos are only examples of the many well-known podcasts currently in the Spanish context [10].

Some companies have also started promoting non-conventional or even experimental podcasts. That is the case of Podium Podcasts, one of the country's better-known podcast producers [11, 12]. As the popularity of podcasts grew, many artists and content creators started defying the idea of what a podcast should be. Many tried to go beyond the conventional structures of podcasts by adding transdisciplinary elements and mixing different genres. Those elements include sound art, science, narrative fiction, or poetry.

One of the most notable examples of this current is the Spanish writer, artist, and all-around creator Jorge Carrión. Jorge Carrión released back in 2020 a podcast called *Solaris: ensayos sonoros*, which can be translated into Solaris: sound essays. This concept of sound essays, first introduced by the producer of the show María Jesús Espinosa de los Monteros, brings a new genre to the Podcast industry[13]. Despite not being self-described as sound essays, there have been other shows that could be categorized like that. That is the case of the new Jorge Carrión Podcast called Ecos, which builds on the idea of Solaris and adds a different take [14]. The transgressive podcast Tácticas de Choque is also worth mentioning, whose format also resembles the de idea of sound essays [15].

The main objective is to build on the idea of *Solaris: ensayos sonoros* by Jorge Carrión and produce sound essays in a podcast form to provide knowledge on the context of the UPV to the university community, including students, educators, and any other kind of employee. The project seeks to help the university community understand the origins of the university, the current situation and reflect on how it might change in the future. With that, it is expected to foster engagement between the people and the university.

2 Materials and Methodology

Approaching the narration of a place forces us to think about its intrinsic characteristics. The methodology for producing these sound essays is to create a transdisciplinary perspective to narrate the university campus as a character. Many books, series, and art pieces have had their own take on this. The HBO's award-winning series The Wire approached explaining the context of the city of Baltimore through the perspectives of people from different backgrounds and professions. This way of approaching the narration of a place follows the concept of "Total Novel," coined by the Nobel Prize winner Mario Vargas Llosa. That concept refers to those narrations that convey a location and a context to their fullest, reaching all perspectives and levels of society [16]. Some experimental writers have explored those narrations over the last few years. That is the case Ensayo y (error) Benidorm. This book explores the historical context of Benidorm through a series of transdisciplinary texts that include poetry, short stories, essays, short movie scripts, and testimonies [17].

This study aims to build on those works and apply these theories to the educational context. The methodology can be divided into two distinct parts. The first one is a study of the history and context of the university. That allows for the accuracy of the content. The second part is the design of a narrative structure, the recordings, and the edition of the content into episodes.

2.1 The Polytechnic University of Valencia

The Polytechnic University of Valencia (UPV) is the biggest polytechnic university in Spain. The UPV started its activity in 1968 during the latter days of the Franco regime. This university was built in a context in which the need for qualified professionals was higher than the rate at which those professionals could be trained at the learning centers in the country. One year before, three other universities with a similar purpose were planned at the same time: the Autonomous Universities of Madrid, Barcelona, and Bilbao [18].

The UPV, initially named, Instituto Politécnico Superior, was established in what was at the time cultivation fields in the northern part of the city. The first building can be seen marked in red on the lower left corner of Fig. 1. This building designed by Carlos Prat Cambronera y Joaquín Hernández Martínez hosted at the time the four degrees the Institute offered, Agricultural Engineering, Industrial Engineering, Civil Engineering and Architecture [19]. The building was singular and in accordance with the time in which is was designed. Although it is in use to this day, it was initially planned to be used temporarily until a more permanent building was built. It is a building organized with a three meters' modular grid. Conceived as a single-story building with over dimensioned spaces for circulation and branches representing the classrooms for the different university degrees. The most notable trait are the three interior courtyards diagonally placed to provide visuals. The over dimensioned corridors respond to a trend in Europe at the time that wanted to emphasize the importance of informal training, the learning that takes place outside the classroom when the students talk to each other and share experiences. At the time, those spaces for social interaction were considered as important as the classrooms themselves.

In 1971, the institute was officially named Universidad Politècnica de Valencia. A new set of buildings was constructed following the design of the architectural firm L35 Arquitectos. The project followed what at the time was an innovative architectural trend called Mat-building. Mat buildings are large-scale, high density structures organized in a modulated grid [19]. It was designed as a functional system to fulfill the needs of the architectural competition, as it needed to host the four degrees. It was carried out as a departmental spatial organization, which was the trend at the time in all Europe, which contrasted with the American way of organizing campuses, in which each building represents a different school. The building was configured as a grid in which the departments were located. That way, the students could configure their own curriculum by moving along the departments. The section was configured in three levels. The parking and the labs where located in the ground floor. The first floor was the place the classrooms were located. The offices were located in the second floor. In this case, the buildings were organized around an agora with an east-west axis that represents power, in the west side the office of the dean, representing the governmental power, and on the east side the central library, which represents the power of knowledge [20].

Since those days, the university kept growing and adding new facilities. The year 2002, the concrete platform was removed and the cars were banned in most spaces of the campus. Those decisions completely transformed the overall landscape of the campus. Removing the platform isolated the buildings and the different university degrees, which made the original concept of Mat-building more diffuse [20]. On the other hand, those decisions included adding more gardens and fostering the integration of nature inside de campus, including several species of birds, which dominate in many of its areas the acoustic environment.

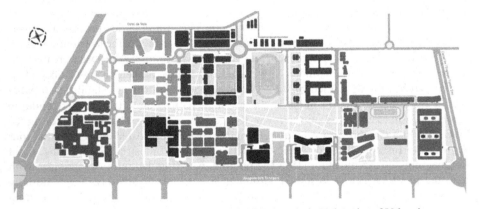

Fig. 1. Map of the Campus de Vera of the Polytechnic University of Valencia

2.2 Acoustic Environment

The audio format has been chosen as the most suitable way to conduct the project. Understanding how environment and sound have been studied in the past is crucial to create new acoustic narratives. The relationship between acoustics and its environment was revolutionized in the 1960s with a pioneering initiative called the World Soundscape Project. This project, led by the Canadian composer Murray Schafer, pioneered the concepts of soundscape and sound walk.

Soundscapes refer to the acoustic environment of the surroundings of a particular location. They encompass all the sounds that shape the auditory perception of a specific place or space. This term goes beyond noise or music. It emphasizes the totality of sounds and their interaction with the surrounding environment.

Soundwalks, on the other hand, are experiential journeys that involve the listener moving, intentionally or unintentionally, through the location. They focus specifically on exploring and engaging with the soundscape of a particular location. Sound walks can be guided or self-guided, where participants actively listen to sounds around them, aiming to deepen their sensory perception and understanding of the acoustic environment.

Soundscapes and sound walks aim to heighten awareness of the acoustic environment and its influence on our perception, emotions, and well-being. By actively engaging with the sounds around us, we can better understand a place's cultural, social, and ecological context. Soundscapes and sound walks offer a unique way of immersing the listeners in their surroundings. Soundscapes and sound walks emphasize sound's significance in shaping our world experiences. These concepts inspire artists, researchers, and enthusiasts alike to explore the rich range of sounds surrounding us and uncover their hidden stories.

The work is articulated using sound walks, soundscapes, and narrative tools to convey the campus story. Besides that, the work also encompasses using audio-recorded interviews and narrative fiction. The audio pieces will be used in the following way:

- Sound walks: carried out following the techniques proposed by R. Murray Schafer. These walks will be carried out by tracing a route during which a binaural recording will be made, giving the listener the sensation of walking through the sound.
- Soundscapes: will be carried out through field recordings of the places relevant to each episode using ambisonics or binaural microphones, depending on the circumstances. The recording will be done following the guidelines of the international standard ISO/TS 12913-2:2018.
- Interviews: We will seek to involve the university community through interviews with people related to the subject matter of each chapter.
- Narrations: they can be done the same way as the interviews or utilizing a condenser microphone connected to a sound card and processed with a digital audio station. The members will write the fictional narratives of the project, the students of the UPV Narrative Classroom, and other people from the university community who wish to participate.

The impulsive responses of the chosen places will be obtained for the recreation of sound spaces. Through the impulse response, it is possible to recreate and simulate sounds in rooms or areas different from those in which they took place employing a convolution. This is achieved by considering each listening point as a linear system invariant in time. The different pieces will be mixed and edited, grouped in chapters by thematic proximity using DAW (Digital Audio Workstation) software, such as Ableton, Audacity, or Adobe Audition. The work will be uploaded to different digital platforms and distributed free of charge. The main equipment used can be seen in Table 1.

Due to the dialogical nature of the sound essays, this creation process does not follow a traditional preproduction, production, postproduction process. On the contrary, it follows a recursive process. The different interviews, which are traditionally part of the production phase, change the script, and even lead, which is part of the preproduction. The process starts with the writing of a draft script and planning of the interviews, after conducting each interview the script is updated and changed by the statements of the interviewee. After finishing the interviews, the script is finalized and the postproduction process begins.

Table 1. Equipment employed to capture the acoustic environment.

	Function	Model
Ambisonics microphone	Record the soundscapes at different locations	Zoom VRH-8
Binaural dummy head	Capture the audio of the sound walks	3DIO Free Space Binaural
Dynamic microphone	Record the interviews	Shure SM58 or similar
Audio recorder	Recorder with microphone inputs	Zoom H8 portable recorder
Digital Audio Workstation (DAW)	Edit the audio files	Audacity V3

3 Results

After the preliminary study, a interdisciplinary podcast structure has been developed to create an holistic picture of the place. The chosen structure resembles the idea of a dialog, in which the narrator gives the word to other participants to share, oppose and interchange ideas on the topic. The structure can be seen in Table 2.

Table 2. Structure of the episodes

Section	Content
Intro	Opening of the Podcast explaining the overarching idea of the sound essays and the project
Hook	An explanation on the content of the episode that arises a question that the dialogue tries to answer
Narrator opening monologue	The narrator starts the dialogue with a on opening statement on the topic. This part will include facts, data and open questions to be answered along the episode
Interviews and speeches	After the narrator, several interviews will be concatenated and mixed with soundscapes
Narrated soundwalks	Soundwalks will be recorded in chosen routes inside the campus. The soundwalk will include a narration describing some parts of the path
Narrative fiction	Pieces of narrative fiction on the topic of the episode written and narrated by local writers. The objective is to approach the topic not only from facts but also from the collective imagination
Conclusion	The narrator gives a closing monologue encompassing the most important takes from each intervention

The planned distribution by chapters also follows the idea to create broad picture of what the campus is:

- Chapter 1. Seeds and limits: An exploration of the origin of the university and its boundaries. A quest to understand where the university begins and the city ends, where the university ends, and l'horta begins. Does the university fence protect the university from the outside or the outside of the university? The chapter will feature interviews with some of the people who were there in the early years of the university; sound walks through the entrances and boundaries. This episode seeks engage the historical context of the university. Understanding the context will allow for students, educators and other university personnel to understand the origin of many of current university customs and procedures.
- Chapter 2. The sound of numbers What does the UPV sound like? A reflection on the acoustics of campus spaces and the tension between natural and technological sounds that inhabit the university. The sound walks through the areas of the university will be mixed with interviews with experts in architectural acoustics, environmental specialists, and researchers in telecommunications, computer science, and other experts in digital signals. The objective of this chapter is to contribute to a closer relationship between the people at the university and their surroundings, helping them understand both the building environment and the nature present on the campus.
- Chapter 3. Neverland: Generational tensions at the UPV. The university lives in continuous generational renewal, with an eternally young and changing student body that contrasts with the life of the workers. This chapter will deal with the generational tensions in the university and how its protagonists live it. This chapter aims to bridge the gap between the different generations that coexist in the university. Alleviating the generational tension is key to improve the relationship between students and educators. Understanding each other's background can improve the learning environment and their mental health.
- Chapter 4. The end of the Polytechnic: This chapter seeks to imagine the future of the university and its possible end. When will the UPV end? There may come a day when universities are no longer necessary; perhaps it will end when it is no longer needed when technology kills technology itself. Futures in speculative fiction. The purpose of this chapter is to foster critical thinking on what the purpose universities have and what is the overall purpose of pursuing a university degree. Reflecting on this can help in finding new ways of learning and teaching, as well as to create a more aware university community.

4 Discussion and Conclusion

One of the intentions of this study was to highlight the need to rethink how education is conducted and the importance of generating engagement. Engagement is essential not only for students but also for educators. That was one of the primary reasons to dedicate a chapter to the generational gap in the university. It is necessary to reduce that gap or at least find ways to reach a common understanding. Through new tools, it is possible to motivate both groups of people. Thanks to the tools necessary to produce this kind of educational content being more accessible than ever before, it is possible to develop initiatives such as this one with relatively like funding. One crucial factor that makes podcasts and sound-based content suitable for non-formal educational projects is that it allows learners to multitask. While online educational platforms such as Coursera, EdX, or Khan Academy are incredible resources, they require complete attention. Podcasts, however, allow the listeners to engage while performing other activities. That can be a solution for people with time constraints and also removes barriers for them to start engaging.

After this study, the following conclusions can be drawn:

- Experimental podcasts can be a viable tool for generating engagement in the university community.
- Using an audio form to create new narratives can be powerful due to the sensory predominance of our sight.
- These kinds of projects can be a complement to formal education and a source of inspiration for both students and educators alike.

Acknowledgements. The authors want to thank the Office of Cultural Action of the Polytechnic University for cofinancing the project Dialécticas Politécnicas under the PC_ACTS 2022 call.

AQG gratefully acknowledges receiving funding from the Spanish Ministry of Universities and the Polytechnic University of Valencia under the 'Plan de Recuperación Transformación y Resiliencia' (investment funding from the European Union Next Generation EU) under the Margarita Salas postdoctoral fellowship.

References

1. Bruggeman, B., Tondeur, J., Struyven, K., Pynoo, B., Garone, A., Vanslambrouck, S.: Experts speaking: crucial teacher attributes for implementing blended learning in higher education. Internet High. Educ. **48**, 100772 (2021). https://doi.org/10.1016/J.IHEDUC.2020.100772
2. Shala, A., Grajcevci, A.: Formal and non-formal education in the new era. Action Res. Educ. **7**, 119–130 (2016)
3. McLuhan, M.: Understanding Media: The Extensions of Man. McGraw-Hill (1964)
4. Bond, M., Bedenlier, S.: Facilitating student engagement through educational technology: towards a conceptual framework. J. Interact. Media Educ. **2019**, 1–14 (2019). https://doi.org/10.5334/jime.528
5. Riddell, J., Robins, L., Brown, A., Sherbino, J., Lin, M., Ilgen, J.S.: Independent and Interwoven: a qualitative exploration of residents' experiences with educational podcasts. Acad. Med. **95**, 89–96 (2020). https://doi.org/10.1097/ACM.0000000000002984
6. Grammar Girl - Quick and Dirty Tips. https://www.quickanddirtytips.com/grammar-girl/. Accessed 02 Jun 2023
7. The History of Rome: Archives. https://thehistoryofrome.typepad.com/the_history_of_rome/archives.html. Accessed 02 Jun 2023
8. Season 01 | Writing Excuses. https://writingexcuses.com/category/season-01/page/4/. Accessed 02 Jun 2023
9. López Villafranca, P.: Estudio de casos de la ficción sonora en la radio pública, RNE, y en la plataforma de podcast del Grupo Prisa en España. Anu. electrónico Estud. en Comun. Soc. "Disertaciones" **12**, 65 (2019). https://doi.org/10.12804/revistas.urosario.edu.co/disertaciones/a.6547

10. Forbes 50 Best in Podcasting: los mejores podcast de España, https://forbes.es/mejores-pod cast/. Accessed 04 June 2023
11. Podium Podcast | Lo mejor está por escuchar. https://www.podiumpodcast.com/. Accessed 04 Jun 2023
12. Legorburu, J.M., Edo, C., García González, A.: Reportaje sonoro y podcasting, el despertar de un género durmiente en España. El caso de Podium Podcast. Estud. sobre el Mensaje Periodístico **27**, 519–529 (2021). https://doi.org/10.5209/esmp.71204
13. Solaris – Podium Podcast. https://www.podiumpodcast.com/podcasts/solaris-podium-os/. Accessed 05 Jun 2023
14. ECOS – Podium Podcast. https://www.podiumpodcast.com/podcasts/ecos-podium-os/. Accessed 04 Jun 2023
15. Tácticas de Choque - Un podcast contra casi todo y contra casi todos. https://tacticasdech oque.com/. Accessed 04 Jun 2023
16. Novoa Castillo, P.F.: Desmontaje del artificio de la "Novela total" en "Conversación en la catedral" de Mario Vargas Llosa. Tonos Digit. Rev. Estud. filológicos **38**, 61 (2020). ISSN-e 1577-6921
17. Multiple authors: Ensayo y (error) Benidorm | Editorial Barrett. https://editorialbarrett.org/ tienda/ensayo/ensayo-y-error-benidorm/. Accessed 05 Jun 2023
18. Castellanos Gómez, R., Domingo Calabuig, D.: 1969: Las Universidades Españolas a Concurso. Bases, Resultados Y Polémicas. Proy. Progreso, Arquit. **7**, 104–121 (2012). https:// doi.org/10.12795/ppa.2012.i7.07
19. Domingo Calabuig, D., Castellanos Gómez, R., Ábalos Ramos, A.: The strategies of mat-building. Archit. Rev. **1398**, 83–91 (2013)
20. Gómez, R.C., Calabuig, D.D.: Project and system: Instituto Politécnico Superior de Valencia. arq Archit. Res. Q. **20**, 357–369 (2016). https://doi.org/10.1017/S1359135517000045

Language as a Moderating Factor in Cyber-Safety Awareness Among School Learners in South Africa: Systematic Literature Review (SLR)

Amukelani Lisa Nkuna and Elmarie Kritzinger[(✉)]

School of Computing Science, Engineering and Technology College, University of South Africa (UNISA), PO Box 392, Pretoria 003, South Africa
48242411@mylife.unisa.ac.za, Kritze@unisa.ac.za

Abstract. The internet has become an integral part of everyone's daily activities, both professionally and socially. Cyberattacks and risks have increased due to internet usage. Schoolchildren are targeted since they lack awareness about cyberattacks or internet safety. It is important to educate learners on how to stay safe while using internet platforms. This article identified socio-demographic and operational factors affecting cyber-safety awareness in South African schools. This study examined how teachers implement the school's language policy and use language in instruction. Language is the main factor affecting school cyber-safety knowledge Methodologically, the PRISMA guideline for Systematic literature review (SLR) search was used. SLR is a comprehensive method of examining literature that identifies, evaluates, and synthesises all relevant research. SLRs outperform narrative or scoping reviews and are the gold standard for knowledge synthesis. The keywords were searched using standardized search strategies from 6 databases which includes Elsevier, Scopus, ScienceDirect, IEEE Xplore, ACM, Springer, and Web of Science. From the databases, 118 articles published between 2014 to 2023 were retrieved and 47 articles were included for this study. The findings reveal that schools apply language policies differently depending on their preferences. This study also shows gaps in knowledge of cyber-safety and language learning and instruction's mediating role, suggesting further research in several areas. It is evident that language does play a significant role in raising cyber-safety awareness in South Africa.

Keywords: Cyber-safety awareness · language · factors

1 Introduction

Due to rising internet use, communities, especially schools, must address cyber-safety [3, 11, 35]. Five-year-olds use the internet [5, 41]. Because they are uninformed of cyber dangers and internet use, schoolchildren are vulnerable to cyberattacks [20]. Cyber-safety awareness is crucial to educate and empower internet users and for the government to have adequate measures to boost school learners' knowledge and ability to act securely online [16].

T. Guarda et al. (Eds.): ARTIIS 2023, CCIS 1937, pp. 444–456, 2024.
https://doi.org/10.1007/978-3-031-48930-3_34

Kritzinger [19] suggests age-appropriate cyber-safety materials and advanced school curricula to raise awareness. Weng et al. [45] note that in South Africa, teachers and parents lack information, resources, safety awareness, and knowledge to prevent security threats to learners and communities. Farhangpour et al. [10] found that rural areas lack educational resources, and that English is not the first additional language in South Africa's provinces, so its use in the classroom is questionable. Most learners and teachers speak their native languages, therefore there are little opportunities to practise and improve English in the classroom [10]. South African children's cyber-safety systematic reviews have been published [10, 13, 18, 27, 33]. These cyber-safety articles focused on a specific sector. Maluleke [27] contributes to this literature by concentrating on teachers' use of Language of Learning and Teaching (LoLT) to promote cyber-safety awareness among South African basic education schoolchildren. Teaching internet survival skills is now as vital as reading and writing [27].

South Africa (SA) is multicultural. Language diversity and multilingualism make SA diverse. This diversity of multiple official languages make communication difficult [37]. Language and language policies affect how teachers educate and how learners communicate. Kritzinger [18] examined if language affects cyber-safety awareness. The results showed that many learners and teachers prefer cyber-safety awareness or ICT instruction in their native language [18]. Thus, the South African government must consider language while establishing cyber-safety awareness in schools [18].

This article examines SA schools' cyber-safety awareness deliverables and teachers' views on indigenous South African languages utilised for learning and teaching. The study also examines school language rules and the challenges of promoting cyber-safety in diverse languages. This article is organised as follows: Sect. 2 provides the methodology of the study. Section 3 outlines the results and discussion through the 4-dimensional layers developed in this study and Sect. 4 concludes the paper.

2 Methodology

In this study, a Systematic Literature Review (SLR) was adapted to search through the identified literature. SLR is a rigorous and exhaustive approach to reviewing literature that seeks to identify, evaluate, and synthesize all research evidence pertinent to a specific research question. SLR have been useful in recognising the potential and problems associated with putting cybersecurity awareness efforts in place in communities and schools in South Africa. The search was limited to studies published between 2014 to 2023, from different databases which includes Elsevier, Scopus, ScienceDirect, IEEE Xplore, ACM, Springer, and Web of science. The selected search period was chosen based on the currency in the selected articles, content, and scope. During the screening stage of 118 identified articles, title and abstract were examined to exclude irrelevant articles. Reviewing the full text for research eligibility, further articles which did not contribute to the research objective (i.e., "cyber- safety awareness education in schools, teaching and learning, language policies") were excluded. Hence 47 articles were included in the literature review.

The research source type includes journals, articles, and conference papers. The review was retrieved using the specific query as depicted in Table 1.

Table 1. The Search Keywords.

Search Keywords
(Cyber* OR internet OR online OR web) AND (learner* OR child* OR pupil OR student OR adolescent OR teen*) AND (systematic literature* OR review OR systematic* OR meta-analysis) AND (risk OR danger OR safety OR threat OR harm)
(Awareness OR training OR guideline OR tool) AND (demographic*) AND (policy OR rules OR protocol) AND (Recommendation* OR framework* OR standard*)
(Language in education* OR language* OR school Act* ICT instruction* learning & teaching OR policies*)
(South Africa OR SA* South African Provinces) AND (School OR university OR college) (Education OR implement* OR learn* OR class* OR lesson* OR teach*)

The keywords query and combinations were used for the successful search in the literature.

2.1 Preferred Reporting Items for Systematic Reviews and Meta-Analyses (PRISMA)

The researchers conducted the literature search following the PRISMA steps of identification, screening, and inclusion of the articles. The PRISMA standards have been widely accepted and used in SLRs by the scientific community to ensure that there is an accurate review process, which increase the study's validity, according to the authors. The study used PRISMA to ensure a comprehensive, open, and objective review. As depicted in Fig. 1, the PRISMA shows the number of records identified, how many records were included and excluded.

2.2 Research Inclusion and Exclusion Criteria

Inclusion Criteria: The study included records that were: (i) written in English; (ii) Search keywords appear in the title, abstract, or article keywords; (iii) Studies published in journals during the period 2014–2023; (iv) Studies that focused on school leaners, teachers, young people, other role-players and relevant to cyber- safety awareness education or schools. **Exclusion Criteria:** (i) Studies published in languages other than English; (ii) Studies that do not address the research questions or sufficiently identify the subject; (iii) Duplicate research articles.

This paper has 3 research questions and are answered in the result section:

1. What is the importance of factors in promoting cyber-safety awareness in schools?
2. What are the tools/methods that teachers can use to promote cyber-safety awareness in schools?
3. Does language and language policies have an impact on cyber-safety awareness education system?

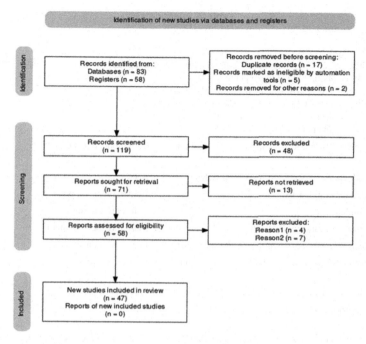

Fig. 1. 2020 PRISMA flowchart indicating research strategy protocol.

3 Results and Discussion

Whilst it is crucial to know the factors influencing cyber-safety, it is also important to consider how schools can implement the resources, knowledge, frameworks, educational methods to strengthen the current state of cyber-safety. Literature identified all possible factors that influence cyber-safety awareness. Table 2 depicts the literature matrix of factors influencing cyber-safety awareness.

Table 2. Literature Matrix of Factors Influencing Cyber-Safety Awareness.

No.	Authors	Factors
1	Scholtz, Kritzinger, and Botha, 2019; Siddiqui et al., 2020	Age
2	Abdullahi et al., 2021	Gender
3	Kortjan and von Solms, 2014; Fatokun et al., 2019	Educational Level

(continued)

Table 2. (*continued*)

No.	Authors	Factors
4	Kritzinger, 2017; Rahman et al., 2020; Nkosi, 2020; Dlamini, 2020; Alhazmi et al., 2021; DiPietro et al., 2018; Kim et al., 2015; Maluleke, 2019; Kretzer, 2018; Li et al., 2019; Li et al., 2018; Sharafaldin et al., 2020; Soudani, 2019; Walter, 2020; Ragin et al., 2021	Language
5	Vazquez, 2019; Glober, Van Vuuren & Zaaiman, 2019	Geographical location
6	Makhitha & Ngobeni, 2021; Aghaei & Kian, 2021	Race
7	Kayastha et al., 2018	Employment status
8	Abdullahi et al., 2021	Religious affiliation
9	Mittal & Ilavarasan, 2019	Marital & parental status
10	Kayastha et al., 2018; Mittal & Ilavarasan, 2019	Financial status
11	López-Meneses et al., 2020; Solano & Peinado, 2017	Socioeconomics
12	Kritzinger, 2020; Smith et al., 2014	Knowledge
13	Livingstone & Helsper, 2020; Makhitha & Ngobeni, 2021	Ethnicity
14	Farhangpour et al., 2019; Hendrix et al., 2016; Kritzinger, 2017; Mabitle & Kritzinger, 2020	Educational tools & methods: Video games, brochures, e-Learning
15	Asfoor & Rahim, 2018; Hashim & Mahamad, 2017	Computer literacy status
16	Mabitle & Kritzinger, 2020; Walaza et al., 2014	Awareness
17	Crawford, 2019; Gcaza & von Solms, 2017	Educational frameworks
18	Department of Communications (RSA), 2010; Dlamini et al., 2011; Kritzinger & Solms, 2012	Policies & procedures
19	Gcaza et al., 2019 Govender & Skea, 2015; Mabitle & Kritzinger, 2020	Resources
20	Huda et al., 2017; Kritzinger, 2016; Livingstone et al., 2015; Mabitle & Kritzinger, 2021	Learners' differences
21	Aghaei & Kian, 2021; Skea, 2015; Makhitha &Ngobeni, 2021	Internet experiences
22	Eddie et al., 2016	Context
23	Fatokun et al., 2019; Cox et al., 2004; Smith et al., 2019; Al-shanfari et al., 2020	Motivation Self-efficacy, response efficacy, perceived level of Severity
24	Ong'ong'a, 2021; Kritzinger, 2016	Skills

The study's findings classified 24 socio-demographic and operational impacting factors through a systematic literature review. Following the process of determining these factors, language is recognized as a factor that indicates a gap in promoting awareness in South African schools. According to the literature, minimal study has been conducted on how language affects cyber-safety knowledge in schools. Thus, the research findings below are structured according to the proposed research questions.

3.1 The Importance of Factors in Promoting Cyber-Safety Awareness in Schools

According to the literature review, there are numerous factors that can contribute to promoting cyber-safety awareness in schools. As technology becomes more ingrained in our lives, cyber- safety is becoming more important. Promoting cyber-safety knowledge in schools can assist reduce cyber risks and to prevent learners from unconsciously engaging in prohibited online behaviours such as piracy or sharing improper content [22]. Promoting cyber-safety awareness in schools requires a holistic strategy that entails education, policies and procedures technology, social influence, parental involvement, continuous training, and support. Therefore, schools must be aware of these factors and tailor their cyber-safety education programs to address the unique needs and challenges of their learners.

The Process of Identifying Factors for Cyber-Safety Awareness

Identifying factors for cyber-safety awareness through a literature review entails evaluating relevant academic research and publications acquire information on how various factors may influence individual's awareness and comprehension of cyber-safety practices. In this study the process involves 4 steps as depicted in Fig. 2 below.

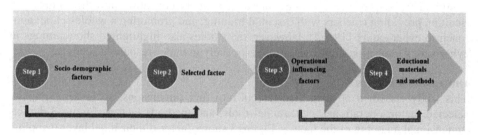

Fig. 2. Steps for identifying factors for cyber-safety awareness.

Step 1: In this step, defining the research scope, literature search, inclusion & exclusion, data extraction, data synthesis & analysis, interpretation & discussion were considered to successfully execute the search of factors that positively influence cyber-safety awareness in schools. The step examined socio-demographic factors of interest such as age, gender, language, race, educational level marital status, financial, employment, socioeconomics, religion affiliation and geographical location.

The review revealed that these factors play an imperative role in promoting cyber-safety awareness in schools. For instance, [13, 17] study demonstrated that younger learners in SA exhibited lower levels of cyber-safety knowledge than their elders. The age-related inequality in awareness can be linked to younger learner's lack of experience and developmental stage. Therefore, learners tend to be more vulnerable due to the knowledge and skills to navigate online platforms safety. After identifying all these, this study selected language as the factor of choice to further investigate how language impact raising of cyber-safety awareness in schools. Language was also chosen since SA has 12 official languages, which can influence how learners are being taught in schools considering that most learners speak different languages. Thus, step 2 was introduced.

Step 2: Language as the moderating factor in awareness among South African schools. Language barriers can make it difficult for learners to obtain cyber-safety knowledge and academic materials, especially when the materials are mostly provided in a language which learners may not be proficient in [17].

Step 3: Operational influencing factors were searched through the literature following the similar processes used in step 1. In this step, factors are identified to represent the broader social and cultural settings in which learners and teachers operate. According to the literature, there is insufficient cyber knowledge, a lack of policies and procedures, and an educational framework that serves as methods to promote cyber-safety awareness in schools. Thus, it is important for this step to highlight all necessary factors to advance understanding, promote consciousness, and affect behavioural change in schools. For schools to implement effective strategies about cyber awareness it is important to understand the educational tools and methods to enhance the state of awareness in schools. Therefore, step 4 was considered.

Step 4: This step focuses primarily on the educational materials and delivery strategies. The school environment must provide learners with adequate training and tools to guarantee safe internet technology use. For instance, video games, pamphlets, and academic material have improved school cyber-safety knowledge [5, 12, 21] The review identified the importance of integrating cyber- safety education into the formal curriculum, providing teachers with essential training, and promoting a whole-school approach to cyber-safety [19, 25]. However, the studies also highlighted shortcomings in cyber-safety education implementation, especially in under-resourced schools.

Dimensional Layers

This study classified all identified factors into four dimensions: socio-demographic, selected factor, operational, educational tools, and methods factors. Figure 3 depicts dimensional mapping of the factors. Figure 3 shows factor-dimensional layer mapping.

The study then mapped the socio-demographic factors with other factors that influence cyber-safety, this is vital for developing effective strategies and interventions to improve cyber- safety. Mapping socio-demographic factors with other variables that influence cyber-safety awareness is essential for generating personalized interventions, detecting risk factors, integrating cultural considerations, bridging digital gaps, and developing successful regulations. Teachers may increase cyber-safety awareness and empower learners to navigate the online world safely by considering the characteristics and demands of different communities. In addition, mapping these factors assists in identifying groups that may be more vulnerable or encounter unique issues in terms of online safety. Understanding these disparities enables interventions to be created that specifically meet the needs and issues of various communities, resulting in tailored awareness and education. Mapping factors and dimensional layers help improve how school role players (principals, teachers, School Governing Body (SGB)) engage with school communities (parents or guidance) to implement and promote knowledge of school language rules and procedures. This method improves curriculum planning for safe, responsible,

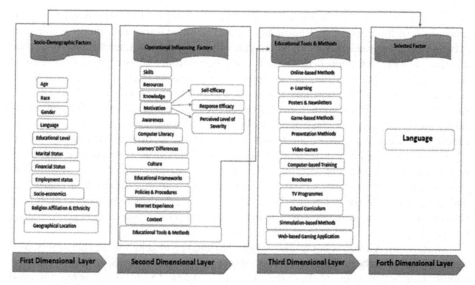

Fig. 3. Dimensional layers with factors that influence cyber-safety awareness.

and ethical online activity. Language policies will be used to evaluate educational deliverables. Finally, the method will help create complete policies that reflect teachers' and learners' teaching and learning practices, technology, and tactics.

First Dimensional Layer: Socio-Demographic Factors - The literature revealed that socio-demographic factors affect school learners, instructors, and parents' cyber-safety awareness [21]. Scholtz et al. [34] found that early cyber-safety education in South African schools is crucial. The school atmosphere lacks cyber-safety understanding that may improve both genders' internet safety. According to Fatokum et al. [10], rural ICT adoption is hampered by lack of awareness, lack of skills, high internet costs, security concerns, and social pressure. Cyber safety issues increase with poorer education. Thus, schools must educate cyber-safety knowledge to safeguard learners from cyber-attacks and cyber-bullying. This layer examines how socio-demographic factors affect cyber safety knowledge among South African kids, teachers, and parents. Early exposure to and teaching in cyber-safety can help learners grasp internet safety, according to the researchers. Studies [11, 34] underline the importance of cyber-safety education in curriculum. Scholtz et al. [34] believe schoolchildren should understand cyberthreats and protect themselves against cybercrime. The study by Fatokun et al. [12] emphasized that knowledge and expertise also help rural ICT adoption. Schools can improve cyber-safety knowledge and encourage safer access to the internet by identifying and addressing the difficulties and requirements for learners based on their socio- demographic backgrounds. Using inclusive and culturally sensitive approaches will guarantee that all students have the knowledge and abilities to properly navigate the digital environment.

Second-Dimensional Layer: Operational Factors -
This study found barriers to introducing ICT and cyber-safety awareness into the school

system and classrooms for teaching and learning. Kritzinger [18] lists role-player igno-rance, lack of finances for ICT equipment, policies/procedures, and teacher training as cyber-safety awareness factors. In recent generations, these characteristics have become transparent and strengthened ICT use in education and the classroom. ICT in schools has made learners and instructors targets of cyber-attacks and cybercriminals [7]. South African schools will use teaching resources and practises to improve ICT and cyber-safety awareness. This section discusses the challenges of incorporating ICT and cyber-safety into South African classrooms. Role-player ignorance, a lack of ICT equipment funding, regulations and procedures, and teacher training all hinder cyber-safety knowl-edge. However, the current generation has increased school ICT acceptance and open-ness, offering cyber-safety solutions. Kritzinger's research supports this assumption, emphasising the importance of stakeholder knowledge and investment in infrastructure and training to effectively adopt ICT and cyber-safety practises in schools [18]. ICT in schools makes them more vulnerable to cyberattacks, necessitating strong cyber-security measures.

Thus, South African schools' second-dimensional layer is ICT and cyber-safety edu-cation. To lessen cyberthreats and crimes, educators, learners, parents, and administrators should have better access to these technologies. Studies [15, 37] demonstrate the need for effective training and education programmes to improve cyber-safety awareness and resilience in different scenarios. Siponen et al. [37] believe training and awareness cam-paigns can improve company security culture and reduce employee cyber-risk behaviour. Kim et al. [15] also stress the need for education in cyber-security.

3.2   The Tools/Methods that Teachers Can Use to Promote Cyber-Safety Awareness in Schools

Research question 2 was answered through third the dimensional layer: educational tools and methods. According to the literature reviews, there are many delivery methods for raising cyber-safety awareness and improving the educational systems [2, 3, 19, 25, 47]. Gamification helps teachers teach cyber security. Yardi et al. [46] found that quizzes and games increased student engagement and cyber security knowledge retention. Davis et al. [8] found that gamification increased student engagement in South African cyber security training curricula. Cybersecurity awareness can be taught through simulation. DiPietro et al. [9] and Alhazmi et al. [4] showed that cyber security simulations improve cyber threat awareness and reaction. Virtual worlds, role-playing games, and incident response simulations are examples. According to Seyal et al. [36] and Rahman et al. [32], teachers promote cyber security awareness by using case studies. These case studies assist learn-ers grasp real-world circumstances and cyber security risks. Case studies help learners grasp cyber risk prevention and mitigation. Furthermore, interactive presentations and examples help kids comprehend cyber security. According to Li and Markettos [24] and Bocij et al. [6], interactive presentations and demonstrations promote learning and student engagement. These presentations may show hacks in real time or teach digital device security. To add on, teamwork and collaborative framework can also help pupils comprehend cyber security. Peer mentoring, team-based exercises, and group projects improve cyber security knowledge and abilities, according to Ragin et al. [31] and Wal-ters [44] Learners can work together, share ideas, and learn from each other throughout these activities. The literature defines how schools may enhance cyber-safety awareness through educational materials, tools, and processes. Video games, pamphlets, and academic material have improved school cyber-safety knowledge [11, 25, 47]. Vanderhaven et al. [42] used a serious game to study the teacher's role and influence in the classroom, while Kumar et al. [22] used storytelling and games to teach cyber-safety. This study used a dimensional approach to employ factors and educational approaches or training tools. Teachers can use this method to improve language instruction and follow school language policies.

3.3 Language and Language Policies Have an Impact on Cyber-Safety Awareness Education System

Research question 3 of this study was answered through a fourth dimensional layer which is the selected factor of the study. Language and language policies have a considerable impact on the development of cyber awareness education systems. The language used to give cyber-safety awareness instruction is crucial to its success. Language affects people's understanding of cyber-safety ideas and protocols. According to research, using the learners' native language or a language in which they are fluent improves understanding and engagement with the content [15, 30]. [31] a study by the Journal of Cybersecurity Education, Research, and Practice indicated that employing learners' native languages in cybersecurity education improved comprehension and memory of the concepts. The delivery of cyber-safety instruction in languages that are widely spoken and understood by the target audience must be given priority in educational programs to address this. Li's [23] research suggests that language may affect how individuals understand cyber security or cyber-safety practises and behaviours in a global context, as many languages lack exact terminology, making it difficult to express cyber security principles. Sharafaldin et al. [39] and Soudani [40] underline the importance of linguistic variety in cyber security awareness education initiatives in Europe and the Middle East. These studies suggest that a common language helps communicate cyber security information and recommended practises across disparate groups [40]. Cyber-safety materials, rules, and policies should be translated and localized into multiple languages to ensure greater accessibility. According to research, translation and localization are critical in reaching out to varied linguistic populations. According to [24], translating instructional resources into many languages guarantees that people from different languages can benefit from the knowledge and acquire a greater understanding of online safety behaviors. This strategy overcomes the language barrier and ensures that critical cyber-security information reaches a larger audience [24]. South Africa's heterogeneous and multilingual population makes cyber-safety awareness marketing challenging. Nkabinde and Chauke [29] found linguistic barriers in cyber-safety and cyber security awareness programmes in South Africa. Kretzer [17] examined South African classroom language from teachers and learners in Limpopo Province, South Africa. The finding shows that teachers employ multiple languages to teach concepts and start sentences in English and switch to Sepedi [17]. The province's mother tongue is African Sepedi. Code-switching uses two languages to assist learners understand concepts presented in the classroom [10, 27]. Teachers said language swapping helps learners grasp classroom concepts. The school language policy prohibits code-switching in most South African classes. The report underlines the importance of language diversity in cyber security awareness courses given the nation's many languages. The study found that South African languages had different cyber security vocabulary, making it difficult to understand and communicate cyber security and cyber-safety principles. Community leaders and activists who speak the local language and language-specific training materials should be used to reach more people.

It is crucial to note that language policies in South Africa may differ between schools and provinces. The South African government has issued guidelines and frameworks to help schools adopt language policies, but implementation varies depending on local context and resources [4, 9, 44].

4 Conclusion

Language plays an important role in moderating cyber-safety awareness among school learners in South Africa. The research evaluation shows that language helps South Africans understand cyber- safety. South Africa has 12 official languages, including English, therefore language diversity must be considered while promoting cyber-safety. Thus, it's crucial to emphasise internet safety's benefits rather than its threats. The socio-demographic and operational factors suggest that schools should prioritise cyber-safety awareness to educate learners and staff about the risks of using the internet and social media. This study also shows that cyber-safety's mediation role in language learning and instruction may be understudied, suggesting various areas for further investigation. Safety-oriented leadership behaviour has been studied more in recent years, mostly in the USA. To improve learning, teachers should be aware of their learners' linguistic preferences and needs.

References

1. Abawajy, J.: User preference of cyber security awareness delivery methods: search point for Cranfield University. Behav. Inf. Technol. **33**(3), 237–348 (2014)
2. Abdullahi, A., Muhamad, M., Hajar, S., Zogaan, W.A.: Cybersecurity Awareness of University Learners in Nigeria: Analysis. Appr. Turk. J. Comput. Math. Educ. Res. Article **12**(12), 3739–3752 (2021)
3. Alotaib, F.: Evaluation and enhancement of public cyber security awareness. University of Plymouth, England (2019). http://hdl.handle.net/10026.1/14209
4. Alhazmi, W., Bell, M.P., Reilly, R., Matthews, L.: Cyber security simulation game: a pilot study. J. Educ. Learn. **10**(2), 147–157 (2021)
5. Bada, M., Von Solms, B., Agrafiotis, I.: Reviewing national cybersecurity awareness in africa: an empirical study. Think Mind (2018), 78–83 (2018)
6. Bocij, P., McFarlane-Morris, T., Deaville, J.: Enhancing cyber security education through real world examples. J. Inf. Syst. Educ. **32**(1), 11–18 (2021)
7. Cox, M., Abbott, C., Webb, M., Blakeley, B., Beauchamp, T., Rhodes, V.: ICT and attainment: a review of research literature. ICT Schools Res. Eval. **17**(1), 1–58 (2004)
8. Davis, C.L., Whitney, L.E., Bhattacharyya, R.: Gamifying cyber security education: a South African perspective. J. Inf. Syst. Educ. **32**(1), 19–29 (2021)
9. DiPietro, A.M., Sciarini, L., Wadell, C.: Online cyber security simulations for teaching technology risk management. J. Inf. Syst. Educ. **29**(2), 115–126 (2018)

10. Dhlamini, S.: Language of Teaching and Learning (LoLT) as a barrier to learning Mathematics: impact on mathematics learners in higher education, vol. 1, no. 2, pp. 1–9 (2020). https://iie space.iie.ac.za/bitstream/handle/11622/580/SemakelengDhlaminiReseearch

11. Fatokun, F.B., Hamid, S., Norman, A., Fatokun, J.O.: The impact of age, gender, and educational level on the cybersecurity behaviors of tertiary institution learners: an empirical investigation on Malaysian Universities. In: Journal of Physics: Conference Series, vol. 1339, no. 1 (2019). https://doi.org/10.1088/1742-6596/1339/1/012098

12. Fatokun, F.J., Oni, A.: Factors influencing adoption of ICT in rural Nigeria: evidence from South-west, Nigeria. Heliyon 6(12), e05767 (2020)

13. Jobi, T., Kritzinger, E.: Online awareness among sepedi school. In: International Conference on Education (IICE-2014), Dublin, Ireland (2014)

14. Kim, H., Lee, J., Moon, T.: Assessing the effectiveness of a security awareness training program for university learners: a randomized controlled study. Comput. Educ. **163**, 104093 (2021)

15. Kim, D.J., Kim, J., Suh, E.: Understanding cyber-security behavior: a theory of planned behavior approach. Comput. Secur. **48**, 82–913 (2015). http://www.harzing.com/pop.htm

16. Kortjan, N., Solms, R.V.: A conceptual framework for cyber-security awareness and education in SA. South Afr. Comput. J. **52**(52), 29–41 (2014). https://doi.org/10.18489/sacj.v52i0.201

17. Kretzer, M.: South African teachers switch languages in class: why policy should follow. Academic Rigour Journalistic Flair (2018). http://geb.unigiessen.de/geb/volltexte/2018/13505/pdf/KretzerMichael_2018_01_22.pdf

18. Kritzinger, E.: Online safety in South Africa-a cause for growing concern. In: 2014 Information Security for South Africa- Proceedings of the ISSA 2014 Conference (2014). https://doi.org/10.1109/ISSA.2014.6950502

19. Kritzinger, E.: Short-term initiatives for enhancing cyber-safety within South African schools. South Afr. Comput. J. **28**(1), 1–17 (2016)

20. Kritzinger, E.: Cultivating a cyber-safety culture among school learners in South Africa. Africa Educ. Rev. **14**(1), 22–41 (2017)

21. Kumar, P.C., Chetty, M., Clegg, T.L., Vitak, J.: Privacy and security considerations for digital technology use in elementary schools. In: Conference on Human Factors in Computing Systems-Proceedings (2019). https://doi.org/10.1145/3290605.3300537

22. Kumar, P., Vitak, J., Chetty, M., Clegg, T.L.: Co-designing online privacy- related games and stories with children (2018). https://doi.org/10.1145/3202185.3202735

23. Li, Q., Orellana-Rodriguez, C.L., Nezamuddin, N.: The impact of cyber security faculty's mindset and attitude on learners' choice of a cyber security career: a review. J. Cybersecur. Educ. Res. Pract. **1**(1), 57–80 (2019)

24. Li, Y.E., Markettos, A.T.: Interactive cyber security presentations. J. Teach. Inf. Secur. **3**(1), 17–27 (2018)

25. Mabitle, K., Kritzinger, E.: Predicting school teachers' intention and behaviour of promoting cyber-safety awareness. Int. J. Inf. Educ. Technol. **11**(3), 119–125 (2021). https://doi.org/10.18178/ijiet.2021.11.3.1499

26. Madhav, R., Mekuria, F., Mtsweni, J.: Cyber security awareness training for South African organisations. In: Proceedings of the 11th International Conference on Information and Communication Technologies and Development (ICTD 2019), pp. 1–5. ACM (2019)

27. Maluleke, M.J.: Using code-switching as an empowerment strategy in teaching mathematics to learners with limited proficiency in English in South African schools. South Afr. J. Educ. **39**(3), 1–9 (2019)

28. Moher, D., et al.: Preferred reporting items for systematic reviews and meta- analyses: the PRISMA statement (reprinted from annals of internal medicine). Phys. Ther. **89**(9), 873–880 (2009)

29. Nkabinde, E., Chauke, A.: A closer look at the linguistic barriers in creating an awareness of cyber security: a case study of South African businesses. In: Cyber Security and Emerging Technologies, pp. 85–95. Springer, Heidelberg (2021)
30. Nkosi, Z.P.: Teachers' views and experiences on learning isizulu as a second language at a South African (2020). https://doi.org/10.1177/0021909619868742
31. Ragin, A.A., Jr., Gandy, T., Smith, M.A.: Cyber security skills transfer: evidence- based insights from learners' perspectives. J. Strat. Inf. Syst. **30**(2), 101692 (2021)
32. Rahman, S., Ghazi, S.R., Hussein, R.M.: Case studies for cyber security education: a systematic literature review. Inf. Comput. Secur. (2021)
33. Saglam, R.B., Miller, V., Franqueira, V.N.L.: A systematic literature review on cyber security education for children. IEEE Trans. Educ. **66**, 274–286 (2023). https://doi.org/10.1109/te.2022.3231019
34. Scholtz, D., Kritzinger, E., Botha, A.: Underpinning knowledge and skills for educators to enhance cyber-safety awareness in South African schools. Innov. Technol. Learn. **11937**, 278–290 (2019)
35. Senthilkumar, K., Easwaramoorthy, S.: A Survey on Cyber Security awareness among college learners in Tamil Nadu. IOP Conf. Ser. Mater. Sci. Eng. **263**(4), 78–91 (2017)
36. Seyal, A.H., Samuel, R., Jain, V.: Impact of case studies for cyber security education. J. Inf. Syst. Educ. **30**(2), 89–97 (2019)
37. Siponen, M., Mahmood, M.A., Pahnila, S.: Employees' adherence to information security policies: an empirical study. Comput. Secur. **74**, 289–304 (2018)
38. Siddiqui, Z., Zeeshan, N.: A survey on cybersecurity challenges and awareness for children of all ages. In: Proceeding 2020 International Conference on Computing, Electronics and Communications Engineering, ICCECE 2020, pp. 131–136 (2020). https://doi.org/10.1109/iCCECE49321.2020.9231229
39. Sharafaldin, I., Habibi Lashkari, A., Ghorbani, A.A., Debbabi, M.: Cyber security awareness in the Middle East and North Africa region: a survey study. J. Cybersecur. **6**(1), 1–18 (2020)
40. Soudani, S.: Towards cyber security education and training in the Middle East and North Africa region. In: Advances in Cyber Security, pp. 53–63. Springer, Heidelberg (2019)
41. South African Department of Basic Education. Information guide for 17th annual NTA 2016. DBE, Pretoria (2017)
42. Vanderhoven, E., Willems, B., Van Hove, S., All, A., Schellens, T. Wait, and see? studying the teacher's role during in-class educational gaming. In: European Conference on Games Based Learning, pp. 540–547 (2015)
43. Von Solms, S., von Solms, R.: Towards cyber safety education in primary schools in Africa. In: Proceedings of the Eighth International Symposium on Human Aspects of Information Security & Assurance, HAISA 2014, pp. 185–197 (2014)
44. Walters, R.: Developing information security principles within higher education courses. J. Inf. Technol. Educ. Innov. Pract. **19**, 111–123 (2020)
45. Weng, C., Otanga, S., Weng, A., Cox, J.: Effects of interactivity in E-textbooks on 7th graders science learning and cognitive load. Comput. Educ. **120**(2), 172–184 (2018)
46. Yardi, A., Sarkisian, G., Khalil, B., Chen, Y.: Gamification as a means to improve cyber security education. Educ. Inf. Technol. **24**(3), 1741–1764 (2019)
47. Zwilling, M., Galit, K., Dušan, L., Wiechetek, L., Cetin, F., Hamdullah, N.B.: Cyber security awareness, knowledge, and behavior: a comparative study. J. Comput. Inf. Syst. **62**, 82–97 (2020). https://doi.org/10.1080/08874417.2020.1712269

Data Analysis for Performance Improvement of University Students Using IoT

Manuel Ayala-Chauvin[1]([envelope]) [ID], Patricio Lara-Álvarez[2] [ID], and Ricardo Castro[2] [ID]

[1] Centro de Investigación en Ciencias Humanas y Educación—CICHE, Universidad Indoamérica, Ambato 180103, Ecuador
mayala5@indoamerica.edu.ec, patolara@uti.edu.ec
[2] SISAu Research Group, Facultad de Ingeniería, Industria y Producción, Universidad Indoamérica, Ambato 180103, Ecuador

Abstract. Using Internet of Things (IoT) devices and data analysis techniques can potentially transform how universities approach improving student achievement. In this sense, the project is based on implementing a remotely operated pneumatic bank applying IoT for university education. With this technology, it is possible to obtain information about the factors that impact student achievement and design targeted interventions to help students improve their performance. The control system with low-cost technology was developed with Raspberry Pi, AnyDesk, and Canvas LMS for the remote connection. The experiment was carried out with two groups of 7 people, and it was identified that there are correlations of 0.87 and 0.62 between the performance of the students and the time they dedicate to studying and the hours they spend on the platform; this suggests a positive correlation between these variables. Therefore, as students spend more time studying and spending more hours on the platform, they are more likely to achieve better academic results. On the other hand, the study time of the group of students who used the bank remotely increased by 32% compared to those who used the bank in person; therefore, we can infer that with the implementation of the IoT, the use of the system is encouraged. Finally, based on the insights gained from the analysis, targeted interventions can be designed to help students improve their academic performance.

Keywords: Pneumatic · University Teaching · IoT · Remote learning

1 Introduction

Data analysis is an extremely powerful tool that allows us to examine, clean, transform, and interpret large amounts of information, with the aim of obtaining valuable insights for more efficient decision-making [1]. Accompanied by visualizations such as tables and graphs, this process becomes a potent instrument for understanding patterns and trends. In our specific case, we have applied data analysis to enhance the real-time performance of university students by utilizing the Internet of Things (IoT).

The accelerated technological advance of processes, techniques, and work methods built since the 1970s has generated challenges for researchers. At the same time has

T. Guarda et al. (Eds.): ARTIIS 2023, CCIS 1937, pp. 457–468, 2024.
https://doi.org/10.1007/978-3-031-48930-3_35

allowed the development of numerous systems, products, and services that make life easier for humans [2]. Likewise, it has contributed to the communities in general, to the industrial sector with the continuous improvement of the means of production, and much more in the educational environment with the development of didactic and intuitive systems [3].

The growth of new IoT technologies has generated innovative learning methods in colleges and universities, and they are being applied more frequently in educational institutions. This improves the teaching and learning process and allows for a more personalized education based on the results [4].

Face-to-face education has had to rapidly evolve and adapt to the digital age due to different natural and human phenomena [5]. Therefore, the Internet of Things (IoT) application has become required to connect real physical space with digital one [6].

The Internet of Things is an emerging trend fast becoming an integral part of our lives. This technology offers endless new opportunities to access, collect and share information. So, it fosters and builds human beings with critical, creative, and ethical thinking [7].

An investigation carried out in Bandung, Indonesia, showed the creation of a graphical interface for the remote use of a laboratory and allows its manipulation through a remote-controlled computer. This study concludes that it is necessary to obtain a good quality operating system and an interface that allows students to access remote laboratories without any limitations [8].

In the study conducted by [9], a framework is presented that includes guidelines for the use of technologies in the classroom. The results obtained conclude that students who used this IoT-based framework achieved better academic performance compared to those who did not use it. This suggests that incorporating IoT in education could be an effective strategy to enhance university students' performance.

In the same context, the study by [10] demonstrates the positive impact of IoT interaction in higher education through smart laboratories. This innovative integration allows students to conduct real-time experiments and receive immediate feedback. As a result, a significant improvement in academic performance, a better understanding of concepts, and a notable increase in motivation to learn are observed.

However, the modernization of virtual education has been affected by the lack of economic, logistical, and digital cultural resources. The government and educational institutions are budgeting for platforms and technology that meet this demand in education. This will allow students to better understand how mechanical systems interact with technology [11].

Several researchers have shown the many IoT applications. For example, systems that allow remote laboratory practices with microcontrollers, machine vision, and automation through a mechanical structure and software can be designed.[12] designed and implemented a didactic training module that allows students to improve their automation skills, thus preparing them to solve industrial problems in real life.

Also, [13] proposes the inclusion of the IoT to modernize teaching methods with a university approach, creating a harmonious environment for autonomous teaching and learning. This research proposes a low-cost system to manipulate a pneumatic test bench in real-time.

An article published by [14] automated a hydraulic process through the internet with a low-cost microcomputer (Raspberry Pi) without using expensive computer equipment as required by the case. On the other hand, he proposed [15] an electro-pneumatic laboratory prototype to support the teaching of industry 4.0 and virtual remote laboratories, mainly using a platform of a web browser and a PLC.

On the other hand, [16] mentions that the education sector was severely affected in the areas where it is required to manipulate physical variables. To overcome this, remote and virtual laboratories are implemented. So that students can carry out their practices in a real laboratory and manipulate them remotely through the Internet. This research proposes to recreate the real conditions of the environment through applied technology.

In this sense, the use of IoT in higher education can provide valuable data for the analysis of student performance. However, some ways IoT can calculate and improve student performance have not been presented.

Collecting data on student behavior, such as class attendance, activity participation, time spent studying, and test and homework results, can determine if there are correlations between attendance and test results. In addition, areas for improvement in student achievement are identified. If the data shows that many students have difficulty with a particular topic, steps can be taken to improve the teaching of that topic. Therefore, this information can be used to personalize student learning by providing additional resources or assigning them additional tasks to help improve their understanding.

Mentioned that we hypothesize that students can improve their performance and work autonomously by interacting with a remote pneumatic bench that simulates an industrial process. Pneumatics is a widely used technology in the industry for process automation, and students of mechanical, electrical, electronic, and mechatronic engineering must have a solid understanding of the concepts and applications of pneumatics; this understanding can be enhanced with the implementation of remote systems applying the Internet of Things IoT.

This IoT pneumatic bank will consist of a set of pneumatic elements, a control system, and sensors connected to the Internet. Students can control the bank through a web application and see the data collected by the sensors in real-time. This will allow them to experiment with different configurations and understand how changes to the system affect their behavior. In addition, students can access the pneumatics bank from anywhere with an Internet connection, allowing them to work and learn remotely.

This system is designed to promote remote education. It aims to provide a modern and practical educational tool for teaching pneumatics in university education, allowing the analysis of student performance. Additionally, implementing an IoT platform will allow students to gain experience in emerging technologies in the engineering field, giving them an advantage in the job market.

The rest of the document is as follows: Sect. 2 will present the method, Sect. 3 will describe the results, and Sect. 4 will present the results and conclusions of the study.

2 Method

For the development of this prototype, concurrent engineering was applied to improve the design quality, manufacturing costs, maintenance, and time in the development cycle [17].

2.1 System Design

The proposed bank control system allows the operation of 3 single-acting cylinders, and we have chosen the Python programming language. The execution of the opcode is done using an interface connected to VNC Viewer. The system architecture is designed according to the block diagram in Fig. 1. The system's results are stored in a database for later analysis.

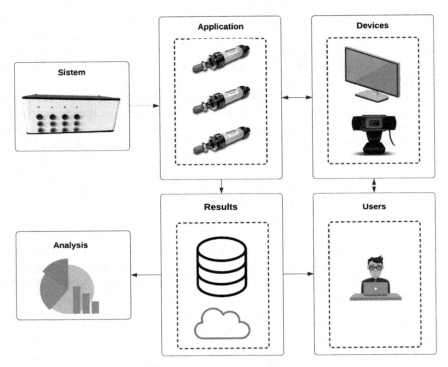

Fig. 1. System control structure.

Solenoid valves that are easily available in the local market were used. Through a website with an administrator and user account, it will be possible to enter the system to carry out the respective pneumatic practices. In addition, the System has a camera to monitor actions in real-time.

2.2 Hardware

The IoT-controlled automatic control bench for university teaching (Fig. 2) consists of the following:

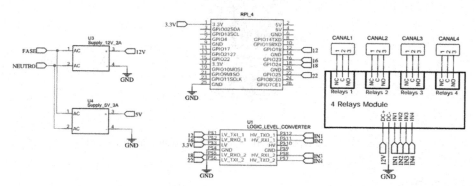

Fig. 2. System architecture.

Raspberry Pi 4. The Raspberry Pi 4 module supports various programming languages such as Python, C ++, Perl, and Ruby. It uses several types of processors; it is a mini-computer that performs basic tasks such as browsing the Internet and sending emails and is compatible with open-source operating systems and applications. It has Bluetooth 5.0 and Wi-Fi 802.11 ac, USB DE 500mA, 2 GB RAM, and support for a 4k monitor. This oversees communicating once the relays are activated and the operation process between the pneumatic control banks.

Logic Level Converter. A device used to convert logic levels from 3vcc to 5vcc or vice versa, it was used since the signal supplied by the Raspberry Pi4 is 3.3vcc, and the relay module works with 5vcc.

Module Relay. This device is a switch to control high voltage loads up to 250V/10A with a small signal. It is compatible with Arduino, Raspberry, ESP8266, Teensy, and Pic. Easily handle loads such as motors, lights, solenoids, and solenoid valves. It activates the NO output when receiving a logical 0 (0V) and deactivates it when receiving a logical 1 (5V).

12vdc and 5vdc supply. Also known as a power supply, they transform alternating current into direct current and supply power to electronic devices connected in the circuit.

Figure 3 shows the prototype assembly that consists of an ESP8266 microcontroller and Raspberry Pi 4 microprocessor + Ethernet/WiFi and communicates through the MQTT protocol. It has a rectangular area of 40 m2, a height of 40 cm, and a width of 15 cm.

Power supply

Ways GPIO

Module Rele

Fig. 3. IoT prototype assembly with ESP8266 and raspberry Pi4.

2.3 Software

The communication interface is the media and protocols for bidirectional data transfer between the computer and the controller card. Through WiFi technology as a means of communication, the operation code is executed in the pneumatic control bench. Through the MQTT protocol, the SSL/TLS protocol can be integrated, allowing computer systems to communicate with each other on the Internet in a secure manner. In addition, the system can be run in two ways from the web or by installing the App.

2.4 Operations

The system's operation is effortless to manipulate; once the VNC Viewer application is installed, the student can check the system's interface, where he can make the desired programming code and check the operation process of the tire bank in real time. The remote connection will be made through AnyDesk, and the records are made through the Canvas LMS of the University. Figure 4 shows the control box and the webcam that allows real-time viewing of the bank's operation.

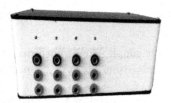

Fig. 4. Control box and webcam for real-time monitoring.

This type of bench is used in tests and trials of valves, cylinders, actuators, and other pneumatic components to determine their capacity and efficiency under different conditions. The operation of the remote pneumatic bench involves the following steps:

Connect the Compressed Air Source. The Remote Pneumatic Bench requires a source of compressed air to function. Therefore, the laboratory operator, who connects the compressed air source to the remote pneumatic bench, performs the first task. The air pressure supplied to the source will depend on the system requirements.

Connect the Pneumatic Components. Once the compressed air source is connected, the operator connects the pneumatic components to be tested. Depending on the planned practice, these components may include valves, cylinders, actuators, and other devices.

Set the Pressure and Flow. The next task is to set the pressure and airflow in the pneumatic circuit, which can be accomplished by using pressure regulators and flow control valves.

Start Remote Testing. Once the pressure and flow conditions have been established, remote testing on the pneumatic components can be started. The tests may involve the simulation of different load and pressure conditions to determine the capacity and efficiency of the components.

Evaluate the Results. After testing, the results must be evaluated to determine if the pneumatic components meet the system requirements. If they do not, modifications or adjustments to the design may be necessary.

Shut Down the System. Finally, the system must be shut down and the compressed air source disconnected.

2.5 Analysis of Data

The analysis of student performance was carried out with the Canvas LMS system that collects data on student performance, such as the time they spend studying, the hours they spend on the platform, the queries made, etc. The Python programming language was used to analyze these data and obtain useful information about student performance. The process is shown below:

Collect Data. Data were collected from 14 students, and data were collected from IoT devices. This was done by connecting to the Canvas LMS system and storing the data.

Prepare the Data. Data cleaning and preparation for analysis were performed. This includes removing duplicate or irrelevant data, removing outliers, and normalizing the data.

Analysis of Data. To analyze data, the Pandas and NumPy libraries of Python were used to carry out the analysis. Pandas to generate descriptive statistics on time students spend studying and NumPy to generate the matrices.

Data Visualization. To visualize the results, the Python Matplotlib and Seaborn libraries were used. This allows you to visualize patterns and trends in the data more clearly and understandably.

Performance Reports. Finally, the data analysis and visualization results were used to generate reports on student performance. These reports can be helpful for faculty and university administrators to assess student performance and make data-based decisions to improve the teaching and learning process.

3   Results

Undoubtedly, the implementation of IoT in the teaching process is a vital tool to improve students' performance and achievement. However, there arises a threat of excessive dependence on technology, which could diminish students' ability to solve problems analytically and critically without constant reliance on these tools.

While the data presented below show an improvement in students' performance, there is also the possibility of a technology dependency. This raises a question of how to find an appropriate balance between the benefits of using technology without compromising students' analytical skills. To address this issue, it is recommended to use technology as a complementary tool rather than a substitute for problem-solving and critical reasoning. This ensures that students develop their analytical abilities and become capable of facing challenges thoughtfully and independently.

This section presents the results of the analysis of student performance. The correlation between the student's performance with the time they dedicate to study and the hours they spend on the platform were analyzed.

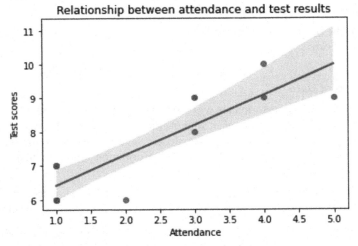

Fig. 5. Relationship between attendance and test results.

Figure 5 shows a correlation of 0.87 between student performance and attendance; this suggests a robust and positive correlation between these variables. This means that as students spend more time attending tutorials and spending more hours on the platform, they are more likely to achieve better academic results.

Figure 6 shows a correlation of 0.62 between student performance and the time they spend studying, suggesting a moderately strong and positive correlation between these two variables. This means that, in general, students who spend more time studying tend to have better academic results.

Figure 7 shows the study time of the students who used the bank in person—having an average of 6.0 h and an average grade of 6.4.

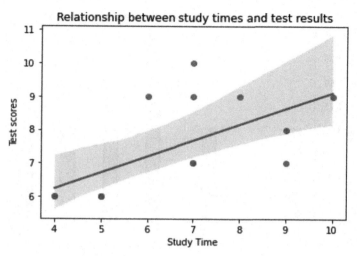

Fig. 6. Relationship between study times and test results.

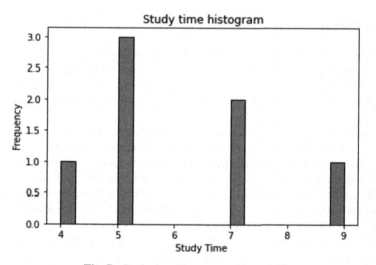

Fig. 7. Study time histogram without IoT.

Figure 8 shows the study time of the students who used the bank remotely. The average remote use of the platform is 7.2 h per month and an average grade of 8.5, representing an increase of 20% and 32%, respectively. As mentioned, it can be inferred that using IoT technologies allows students to access additional learning resources and unavailable tools. This can include learning progress tracking devices, online learning materials, and other digital resources that can improve performance and motivate students to study more.

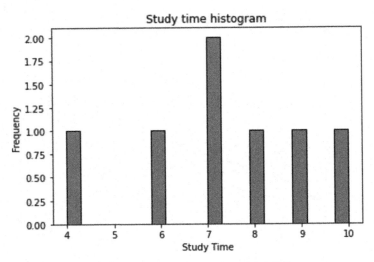

Fig. 8. Study time histogram with IoT.

4 Conclusion

A correlation of 0.87 and 0.62 was obtained between student performance, the time they spend studying, and the hours they spend on the platform; this suggests a positive correlation between these variables. This means that as students spend more time studying and spending more hours on the platform, they are more likely to achieve better academic results.

This correlation can be an essential signal for educational institutions and teachers. It indicates that the time students spend on the platform and their dedication to studying are significant factors that can directly affect their performance. However, it is essential to consider that correlation does not necessarily imply causation; we cannot conclude that the time students spend studying and on the platform is the only cause of their good academic performance. There may be other influencing factors, so further analysis is needed to determine the causal relationship between these variables.

Finally, the average use of the platform is 7.2 h per month, and the average grade is 8.5; therefore, there is an increase of 20% and 32%, respectively. Consequently, it can be inferred that IoT technologies have allowed students to study more efficiently and possibly increased their interest in developing internships. However, it is also important to note that excessive use of IoT technologies can distract students and reduce effective study time.

Acknowledgment. We thank Unversidad Indoamérica for the resources provided to this research under the project No. 295.244.2022, entitled "Big Data y su impacto en la sociedad, educación e industria.

References

1. Ayala-Chauvin, M., Avilés-Castillo, F., Buele, J.: Exploring the landscape of data analysis: a review of its application and impact in Ecuador. Computers **12**, 146 (2023). https://doi.org/10.3390/computers12070146
2. Nižetić, S., Šolić, P., López-de-Ipiña González-de-Artaza, D., Patrono, L.: Internet of things (IoT): opportunities, issues and challenges towards a smart and sustainable future. J. Clean Prod. **274** (2020). https://doi.org/10.1016/j.jclepro.2020.122877
3. Torres, O.D.B., Encinas, K.L.P.: Integración de las TIC en la enseñanza de la historia en educación media superior. Rev. Boletín Redipe, **8**(1), 106–113 (2019). https://doi.org/10.36260/rbr.v8i1.677
4. Francisti, J., Balogh, Z., Reichel, J., Magdin, M., Koprda, Š, Molnár, G.: Application experiences using IoT devices in education. Appl. Sci. (Switzerland) **10**(20), 1–14 (2020). https://doi.org/10.3390/app10207286
5. Palacios, A., Loor, J., Macías, O., Macías, K.: Incidencia de la tecnología en el entorno educativo del Ecuador frente a la pandemia del covid-19. In: Incidencia de la Tecnología en el Entorno Educativo del Ecuador Frente a la Pandemia del Covid-19, vol. 5, no. 10, pp. 754–773 (2020). https://doi.org/10.23857/pc.v5i10.1850
6. Chen, D.: Application of IoT-oriented online education platform in English teaching. Math. Probl. Eng., **2022** (2022). https://doi.org/10.1155/2022/9606706
7. Pascagaza, E.F., Estrada, L.C.C.: Modernización de la educación virtual y su incidencia en el contexto de las Tecnologías de la Información y la Comunicación (TIC). In: Academia y Virtualidad, vol. 13, no. 2, pp. 103–116, 2020, doi: https://doi.org/10.18359/ravi.4724
8. Pratama, L.A., Kustija, J.: Design of graphical user interface (GUI) on IoT-based remote laboratory for programmable logic controller (PLC) practicum and pneumatic simulation. In: IOP Conference Series: Materials Science and Engineering, vol. 830, no. 4 (2020). https://doi.org/10.1088/1757-899X/830/4/042053
9. Verma, P., Sood, S.K.: Internet of Things-based student performance evaluation framework. Behav. Inf. Technol. **37**(2), 102–119 (2018). https://doi.org/10.1080/0144929X.2017.1407824
10. Asad, M.M., Naz, A., Shaikh, A., Alrizq, M., Akram, M., Alghamdi, A.: Investigating the impact of IoT-based smart laboratories on students' academic performance in higher education. Univers Access Inf. Soc.2022). https://doi.org/10.1007/s10209-022-00944-1
11. Kazakova, E.I.: Digital transformation of pedagogical education. Yaroslavl Pedagogical Bullet. **112**(1), 8–14 (2020). https://doi.org/10.20323/1813-145x-2020-1-112-8-14
12. Bustamante, M., Moreno, G., Pelaez, A., Madrigal, C.: Design and implementation of an automation didactic module focused to machine vision and programmable logic control. In: 2014 3rd International Congress of Engineering Mechatronics and Automation, CIIMA 2014 - Conference Proceedings, no. 2007 (2014). https://doi.org/10.1109/CIIMA.2014.6983451
13. Cai, J.Y., Zhang, P.P., Tan, X.: A novel physical education environment plat-form using Internet of Things and multimedia technology. Int. J. Electr. Eng. Educ. (2019).https://doi.org/10.1177/0020720919879390
14. Lopez, F., Torres, F.J., Ramirez, V.A., Nunez, D.A., Corona, R., Lopez, A.R.: Raspberry pi for implementation of web technology in an automation process. In: 2019 IEEE International Autumn Meeting on Power, Electronics and Computing, ROPEC 2019, no. Ropec, pp. 2–7 (2019). https://doi.org/10.1109/ROPEC48299.2019.9057040
15. Francisco, M.B.R.M., Mendes, M.J.G.C., Calado, J.M.F.: An electro-pneumatic prototype to support the teaching of industry 4.0 concepts. In: Proceedings of the 2019 5th Experiment at International Conference, exp.at 2019, pp. 428–433 (2019). https://doi.org/10.1109/EXPAT.2019.8876524

16. Vargas, J., Cuero, J., Torres, C.: Laboratorios remotos e IOT una opor-tunidad para la formación en ciencias e ingeniería en tiempos del COVID-19: caso de estu-dio en ingeniería de control. Espacios **41**(42), 188–198 (2020). https://doi.org/10.48082/espacios-a20v41n42p16
17. Torres, E., Sanz, V., Guerrero, C., Juárez, D.: Ingeniería concurrente aplicada al modelo de diseño de producto. In: 3C Tecnología, vol. 3, no. 2, pp. 87–99 (2014). http://ojs.3ciencias.com/index.php/3c-tecnologia/article/view/180

Smart Tourism and Information Systems (SMARTTIS 2023)

The Impact of Smart Tourism on Tourist Experiences

Camila Lourenço Lima[1], Paula Odete Fernandes[2] (ID), Jorge Oliveira[3],
and Isabel Maria Lopes[2,4(✉)] (ID)

[1] Instituto Politécnico de Bragança, Campus de Santa Apolónia, 5300-253 Bragança, Portugal
[2] UNIAG, Instituto Politécnico de Bragança, Campus de Santa Apolónia,
5300-253 Bragança, Portugal
{pof,isalopes}@ipb.pt
[3] Universidade Nova de Lisboa – Faculdade de Ciência e Tecnologia, Lisbon, Portugal
jmr.oliveira@campus.fct.unl.pt
[4] Algoritmi, Universidade do Minho, Largo do Paço, 4704-553 Braga, Portugal

Abstract. The tourism industry has witnessed significant growth and transformation in recent years, becoming one of the most dynamic sectors globally. With the increasing number of tourist arrivals, the integration of cutting-edge technologies, including Computer Reservations Systems (CRSs), Global Distribution Systems (GDSs), the Internet, and various contemporary smart technologies, has not only enhanced the convenience and efficiency of travel but has also revolutionized consumer behavior and expectations. Modern travelers demand personalized and tailored experiences that cater to their individual preferences and interests. Understanding the technological effect of so-called smart tourism on the tourist experience is crucial for companies and tourist destinations to remain competitive in the rapidly evolving scenario. This article aims to provide a comprehensive review of the influence of smart tourism technologies on the tourist experience. By synthesizing the latest research, examining industry practices, and analyzing tourist behaviors through surveys, we explore the ways in which technology has reshaped the tourism experience.

Keywords: Tourism · Smart tourism technologies · Costumer' journey

1 Introduction

Tourism has experienced remarkable growth in recent years, emerging as one of the most dynamic and rapidly evolving industries worldwide. According to the World Tourism Organization (UNWTO), international tourist arrivals reached 1.5 billion in 2019, marking a 4% increase compared to the previous year [1]. This surge in global travel has been fueled by various factors, including rising disposable incomes, improved transportation networks, and the proliferation of digital technologies.

In our modern society, technological innovations have become an integral part of our daily lives, transforming the way we communicate, work, and interact with our environment. From smartphones to artificial intelligence, these advancements have reshaped

T. Guarda et al. (Eds.): ARTIIS 2023, CCIS 1937, pp. 471–484, 2024.
https://doi.org/10.1007/978-3-031-48930-3_36

industries across the board, and the tourism sector is no exception [2]. The integration of cutting-edge technologies has had a profound impact on every aspect of the travel experience, from trip planning and booking to on-site exploration and post-trip engagement.

The convergence of Information Technology (IT) and tourism has been ongoing since the 1970s, leading to a transformative impact on tourism products and services. Over the years, tourism has evolved into a sophisticated ecosystem that incorporates various technological advancements, including "Computer Reservations Systems (CRSs) in the 1970s, Global Distribution Systems (GDSs) in the late 1980s, the Internet in the late 1990s" [3], and smart technologies in the 2010s.

The integration of technology in the tourism industry has not only enhanced the convenience and efficiency of travel but also transformed consumer behavior and expectations. Travelers now demand personalized, tailored experiences that cater to their individual preferences and interests [4]. As a result, tourism businesses and destinations must adapt and embrace innovative technologies to remain competitive in the ever-evolving landscape.

This article aims to provide a comprehensive review of the impact of the smart tourism in the tourist's experience. By examining the latest research, industry practices and using surveys to analyze tourist behaviors, we will explore the ways in which technology has reshaped the tourism experience.

2 Smart Tourism

Smart Destinations are a particular category of smart cities. It applies the principles of smart cities to urban or rural areas and includes the needs of both locals and visitors [5]. Numerous intelligent tourism endeavors in Europe originated from smart city initiatives, consequently resulting in the emergence of smart tourism destinations in the European tourism industry [5, 6].

The concept of smart tourism encompasses various smart components and layers that are supported by information and communication technologies (ICTs) [7]. The first layer is the smart information layer, which focuses on gathering data. The second is the smart exchange layer, which enables connectivity between different components. Finally, the third layer is the smart processing layer, which handles tasks such as data analysis, visualization, integration, and intelligent utilization [8]. The smart tourism must be able to meet the requirements of "short-term economic needs and long-term sustainable development" [9]. According to the World Tourism Organization, smart tourism has characteristics such as "clean, green, ethical, quality, among others" [10].

Several studies, such as Huang et al. 2017; Lee et al. 2018; No and Kim 2015, suggested a conceptualization of Smart Tourism Technologies (STTs) "attributes that include four key elements, i.e. accessibility, informativeness, interactivity, and personalization. A fifth attribute, security, was put forward" [11].

Accessibility pertains to how easily individuals can obtain and utilize information from various STTs at tourism destinations. High levels of accessibility enhance the ease of use, enabling tourists to access more information and improve their overall travel experience and satisfaction with the destination (Huang et al. 2017; Tussyadiah and Fesenmaier 2007, 2009) [12, 13]. In recent studies, Jeong, M. and Shin, H. demonstrated that accessibility was not a main factor for tourists to maximize the memorability of their experience [14], only six percent of those interviewed considered accessibility as relevant. This might be due to the present technological setup of smart tourism destinations, specifically because the cities chosen for this research were all advanced smart cities located in the United States and had ample bandwidth capacity.

Informativeness refers to the qualitative effect and sense of reliability of the indications given by STTs about the various choices and places to visit. Studies show that there is a significant correlation between "informativeness and tourists' perceptions of the destination" [15]. In a study on social media, Chung and Koo (2015) found that "the reliability of information is a determining factor of the value of social media in information seeking by tourists" [16].

The interactivity of STTs refers to the reciprocal communication among stakeholders. User participation enables these technologies to provide more applicable and relevant information, which facilitates the efficient search for travel information.

Personalization involves offering customized services that meet tourists' specific needs, maximizing their travel experience and satisfaction with smart tourism destinations. Research shows that personalized services positively influence satisfaction by reducing the time spent on information search [17, 18].

Security pertains to the level of privacy maintained for confidential data during different transactions [19]. Within tourism destinations, the adoption of STTs is influenced by how tourists perceive the protection of their privacy and personal information [20]. If tourists perceive a potential endangerment to the security of their personal information, they will refrain from completing the transaction due to apprehensions regarding privacy and safety [21–23].

Intelligent tourist destinations provide smarter technologies (i.e., artificial intelligence, cloud computing, IoTs, and mobile communication) to collect and distribute information about the place without the tourist being there and offer efficient tourism resources [24].

Many cities already have smart tourism as such technologies can be an integral part of their overall satisfaction with the destination and their revisit intention, examples of smart tourism technologies (STT's) include cloud computing, "ubiquitous computing, Internet of Things (IoT) and connectivity through Wi-Fi, near field communication (NFC), and radio-frequency identification (RFID), sensors, smartphones, beacons, virtual reality (VR), augmented reality (AR), mobile apps, integrated payment methods, smart cards, and social networks sites, etc." [25] (Fig. 1).

Barcelona, for example, offers travelers interactive bus shelters that not only provide information about tourist attractions and bus schedules, but also have USB ports for charging mobile devices. Additionally, the city provides bicycles throughout the city, which can be located via a smartphone app, promoting eco-friendly transportation (http://smartcity.bcn.cat/en/bicing.html). In Hamburg, Germany, an important project is the "Tourismus Suite", which is a mobile app designed to offer tourists real-time information, this app covers a wide range of topics including tourist attractions, events, transportation, dining options, and lodging, and also enables users to customize their

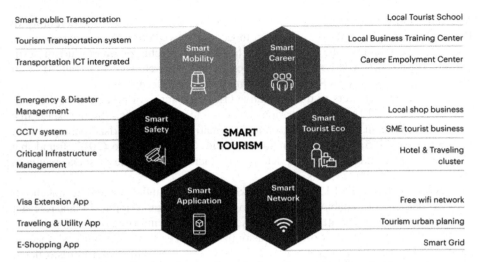

Smart public Transportation

Tourism Transportation system

Transportation ICT intergrated

Emergency & Disaster Managerment

CCTV system

Critical Infrastructure Management

Visa Extension App

Traveling & Utility App

E-Shopping App

Local Tourist School

Local Business Training Center

Career Empolyment Center

Local shop business

SME tourist business

Hotel & Traveling cluster

Free wifi network

Tourism urban planing

Smart Grid

Fig. 1. The application of technology platforms in smart tourism development

itineraries and receive alerts about any special deals or promotions. Mexico has implemented an interesting program involving virtual and augmented reality (AR) technologies to enhance the tourism experience, such technologies allows travelers to explore the country's top attractions, for example Mayan ruins and museums, creating immersive experiences from the comfort of their own homes (https://www.visitmexico.com/vr/).

Given the importance of creating an optimal tourist experience and the growing demand for information technology, hospitality and tourism establishments in smart tourism destinations are increasingly collaborating with visitors to provide STTs that can enhance and personalize travel experiences [26]. This trend is aimed at making the travel experience more meaningful and dynamic for tourists.

3   Stages of a Smart Tourism

Smart Tourism Technologies serve as technological platforms utilized by tourists throughout every stage of their decision-making process and customer journey [27, 28]. Those technologies have brought about a significant transformation in how tourists strategize, engage with, and reminisce about their trips through the provision of real-time updates and individualized suggestions. These innovative technologies enhance the convenience and pleasure of travel for tourists, offering them a more seamless and delightful experience.

The 'customer journey' framework highlights the significant role played by the visitor/customer. It suggests that the customer's experience is constructed over a prolonged period, beginning before the actual experience and continuing after it, encompassing both pre- and post-purchase stages. As a result, the 'customer journey' can be divided into three distinct steps: These three steps are: a planning phase prior to the trip, where you prospect what will be done; an active tourism experience during the trip itself; and, finally, a reflective phase after the trip, in which one considers the lived experience. [29–31].

3.1 Prospective Phase (Pre-visit)

Before the trip, smart technologies can assist tourists with planning their itineraries, booking travel and accommodations, and exploring their destination [32].

It is worth mentioning that when tourists are in the process of searching, comparing, and planning their trip, they heavily rely on reviews that come from real experiences and recommendations shared by their fellow travelers and social media influencers. This demonstrates the significant level of trust they put in these sources while making their travel-related choices [33, 34]. This is primarily due to the inherent risks associated with purchasing tourism products. A growing number of tourists are now leveraging the collective knowledge shared by fellow travelers on digital platforms, relying on user-generated content (UGC) to gather insights that inform their decision-making process [35]. Such knowledge, sourced from real experiences shared by other tourists on social media, proves invaluable in mitigating decision-making risks [36].

Additionally, there is a group of tourists who actively use advanced technologies to search for and obtain relevant information about tourist attractions. They do this proactively to improve your understanding of these attractions and ensure a rewarding and meaningful visit that enriches your overall travel experience [34, 37].

3.2 Active Phase (On Site)

During the trip, smart technologies can enhance the tourist experience by providing real-time information and personalized recommendations. The interaction between humans and computers serves as a clear manifestation of tourists' utilization of smart technologies in tourism endeavors.

Examples of these technologies include Wearable devices that can monitor a tourist's health and activity levels, while location-based services can provide targeted advertising and promotional offers, augmented reality applications can also offer interactive experiences, such as virtual tours and games. These technologies have the potential to enhance and assist tourists in problem-solving, making their visits and journeys more flexible [38, 39]. Additionally, they enable tourists to promptly share their feedback and comments on their experiences in real-time.

3.3 Reflective Phase (Post-visit)

After the trip, smart technologies can help tourists preserve their memories and share their experiences with others [40]. Social media is just one example that facilitates the exchange of individual experiences with others via user-generated content (UGC), including comments, images, videos, among others from any device [41], the tourists also use these platforms to portray, reconstruct, and revisit their trips [42]. This process forms a comprehensive chain of opinions that can influence their peers and potential visitors. Wu and Yan's study [43] revealed that documenting and publishing post-trip experiences aids tourists in reinforcing and constructing their own tourism experiences, while also influencing the decision-making behavior of potential tourists.

4 Methodology

The main purpose of this study is to understand the impact of smart tourism in tourists' experience. To achieve this objective, a quantitative research approach was employed, utilizing an online survey technique.

The research instrument, a questionnaire, was divided into four sections:

(i) About the Tourist, in this section, questions were designed to gather information about the respondents' profiles, such as nationality, age, gender, marital status, educational background, and monthly income;

(ii) Travel, this sequence of questions aims to comprehend the characteristics of the respondents' trips, i.e. Frequency, presence of companions, primary purpose of travel, and which continents are usually visited;

(iii) The penultimate section is related to the usage of Smart Tourism technologies, where multiple-choice questions were posed to the interviewee, asking them to indicate which Smart Tourism technologies they use during their travel journeys; and

(iv) Feedback, finally, there were questions regarding the tourists' opinions about these technologies, including their usefulness, ease of use, fulfillment of expectations, contribution to a positive travel experience, and influence on their decision to visit or revisit any tourist destinations.

5 Results

In total, 53 questionnaires were collected from travelers aged 18 years or older and they were conducted for two weeks. In Table 1 below, a summary of the profile of respondents is presented.

The second part of the research tracks the travel profile of the interviewee. Thus, Table 2 below presents a summary of the respondents' travel profile.

Despite the interviewees being from different continents, the majority travels within the European continent. This can be attributed to various reasons, such as the higher cost of airfare for returning to their home countries, prompting them to stay longer in Europe and explore the region. Additionally, travel between European Union countries tends to be more affordable due to lower expenses for tickets, accommodations, currency similarity, and other factors, thus facilitating such trips.

Table 1. Sample profile (n = 53)

Characteristics	Frequency (n)	Percentage (%)
Gender		
Male	36	67,9%
Female	17	32,1%
Age group		
18 to 24	45	84,9%
25 to 34	5	9,4%
35 to 44	1	1,9%
45 to 54	1	1,9%
55 to 64	1	1,9%
65 or more	0	0%
Educational level		
High school	3	5,6%
Undergraduate student	48	90,6%
Postgraduate student	2	3,8%
Marital status		
Single	49	92,5%
Married	4	7,5%
Divorced	0	0%
Widowed	0	0%
Monthly income		
Under 740€	44	83%
740 to 1000€	5	9,4%
1001 to 1500€	2	3,8%
1501 to 3000€	1	1%
More than 3000€	1	1%
Nationality		
Portuguese	20	38%
Brazilian	23	43%
Angolan	2	4%
Cape Verdean	6	11%
Mozambican	1	2%
Santomean	1	2%

Table 2. Travel profile (n = 53)

Questions	Frequency (n)	Percentage (%)
How often do you travel?		
Once a year	23	43,5%
Twice a year	14	26,4%
Three times a year	4	7,5%
Four or more times a year	11	20,8%
Usually travels:		
Alone	14	26,4%
Accompanied	39	73,6%
On tour	0	0%
What is the main reason for these trips?		
Vacation	34	64,2%
Visit family or friends	16	30,2%
Work	3	5,7%
What is the main continent to be visited?		
Europe	37	69,8%
Ásia	1	1,9%
Oceania	0	0%
África	3	5,7%
South America	11	20,8%
Central America	0	0%
North America	1	1,9%

The third part of the research entails the analysis of whether the respondents employ technologies throughout their journey and, furthermore, which specific technologies they utilize (Table 3).

Using the simple average system (Frequency/Technologies), the smart tourism technologies were utilized an average of 25 times in Prospective phase, 17 times in Active phase, and 16 times in Reflexive phase, indicating a greater usage in the pre-visit.

The final section pertains to the personal opinions of the interviewees regarding the use of these technologies during travels (Table 4).

Despite the most commonly used technologies being in the pre-visit phase, the interviewees found the use of technologies on-site to be more useful, particularly emphasizing the use of online maps. Such technology was utilized by approximately 94% of the respondents.

In general, the STTs received positive feedback in terms of usefulness, expectations, and accessibility, aligning with the previously mentioned first key element of Smart Tourism Technologies.

Table 3. Use of STTs (n = 53)

Questions	Frequency (n)	Percentage (%)
Is the availability of technologies important in tourist destinations?		
Yes	51	96,2%
No	2	3,8%
If yes, what technologies do you most use before a trip?		
Social media or travel blogs	32	60,4%
Hosting sites	41	77,4%
Ticket search sites	35	66%
Google maps	46	86,8%
Weather forecast	36	67,9%
City guide apps	19	35,8%
Sites for advance purchase of attraction tickets	18	34%
Itinerary planning apps	19	36,4%
Augmented reality	4	7,5%
Virtual reality	2	3,8%
What technologies do you use most while traveling?		
Google maps	50	94,3%
Weather forecast	39	73,6%
Mobile payment	31	58,5%
Parking apps	5	9,4%
Touchscreens	13	24,5%
Appliance charging stations	13	24,5%
Traffic redirection apps	10	18,9%
Dynamic kiosks	4	7,5%
QRcode	16	30,2%
Translate	17	32,1%
Augmented reality	2	3,8%
Virtual reality	1	1,9%
What technologies do you use most after a trip?		
Baggage tracking system	10	19%
Feedback system	16	29,8%
Photo sharing apps	42	78,7%
Virtual reality	7	13%
Travel diary apps	6	11%

Table 4. Travelers' Feedback

Questions	Frequency (n)	Percentage (%)
Do you find the use of Smart Tourism technologies more useful:		
Before the trip	12	22,6%
While travelling	18	34%
After the trip	1	1,9%
All the previous options	22	41,5%
On a scale of 1 (a little) to 5 (a lot), how useful did you find the use of STTs?		
1	0	0%
2	0	0%
3	4	7,5%
4	14	26,4%
5	35	66%
On a scale of 1 (a little) to 5 (a lot), did the technologies used during the trip meet your expectations?		
1	0	0%
2	2	3,8%
3	7	13,2%
4	25	47,2%
5	19	35,8%
On a scale of 1 (a little) to 5 (a lot), did you have any difficulty using these technologies during your trip?		
1	19	35,8%
2	10	18,9%
3	6	11,3%
4	12	22,6%
5	6	11,3%
On a scale of 1 (a little) to 5 (a lot), do you believe that STTs contribute to a better travel experience?		
1	0	0%
2	2	3,8%
3	2	3,8%
4	14	26,4%
5	35	66%
Did you feel safer using technology while traveling?		

(continued)

Table 4. (*continued*)

Questions	Frequency (n)	Percentage (%)
Yes	52	98,1%
No	1	1,9%
Would you recommend to other tourists the use of technology while traveling?		
Yes	52	98,1%
No	1	1,9%
Does the availability of tourism technologies influence you to go and/or return to a tourist destination?		
Yes	43	81,1%
No	10	18,9%

In terms of experience, considering only scales 4 and 5, 92.4% of the interviewees believe that STTs contribute to a better travel experience. Furthermore, 98.1% felt safer utilizing these technologies, and the same percentage would recommend their use. Additionally, 81.1% affirmed that these technologies influence their decision to visit or revisit a tourist destination. These figures highlight the importance of Smart Tourism Technologies for both the tourists' experience and the economic aspects of the tourist destinations themselves. These technologies play a significant role in attracting and retaining customers, as they inspire tourists to visit, recommend, and return to these destinations.

6   Conclusions

The main objective of the study was to investigate the influence of smart tourism technologies on tourists' experiences. This research capitalized on existing literature by conceptualizing the dimensions of Smart Tourism Technologies (STTs) and the three phases of the "consumer journey," and developed a comprehensive model of the impact of these technologies on tourist satisfaction and how it influences tourists' consumption behavior after the completion of the visit experience.

The research revealed that the utilization of smart technologies in diverse tourism aspects can have a positive impact on the overall visit experience throughout all three phases. These technologies effectively enhance the attractiveness and memorability of the trip [44]. As observed, there is a positive relationship between satisfaction and intention to revisit.

The development of smart tourism is already underway. It is a natural progression resulting from the widespread use of technology in the tourism industry. However, the organized and widespread coordination, sharing, and utilization of tourist data to create value are still in their early stages. Smart tourism initiatives worldwide aim to establish sustainable smart tourism ecosystems [45]. However, due to the complexity of the sector, it is challenging to go beyond specific innovations related to platforms, technologies, or services. Nevertheless, the push for technology-driven smart tourism is significant, and it is expected that the tourism industry will play a pioneering role in adopting these intelligent technologies.

As this study is limited, we can identify the number of respondents to the judgment, thus, we propose as future work the application of teaching in a larger universe.

Acknowledgements. The authors are grateful to the UNIAG, R&D unit funded by the FCT—Portuguese Foundation for the Development of Science and Technology, Ministry of Science, Technology and Higher Education. "Project Code Reference: UIDB/04752/2020 e UIDP/04752/2020".

References

1. World Tourism Organization (UNWTO). International tourism growth continues to outpace the global economy. https://www.unwto.org/international-tourism-growth-continues-to-out pace-the-economy
2. Zhang, L., Yang, J.: Smart tourism. In: Jafari, J., Xiao, H. (eds.) Encyclopedia of Tourism, pp. 862–863. Springer, New York; Wien (2026)
3. Buhalis, D., Law, R.: Progress in information technology and tourism management: 20 years on and 10 years after the Internet—the state of eTourism research. Tour. Manage. **29**(4), 609–623 (2008)
4. Sigala, M.: Smart tourism ecosystems: towards a comprehensive research agenda. J. Destin. Mark. Manag. **12**, 9–11 (2019)
5. Gretzel, U., Sigala, M., Xiang, Z., Koo, C.: Smart Tourism: Foundations and Developments. Springer, University of St. Gallen (2015)
6. Lamsfus, C., Martín, D., Alzua-Sorzabal, A., Torres-Manzanera, E.: Smart tourism destinations: an extended conception of smart cities focusing on human mobility. In: Tussyadiah, I., Inversini, A. (eds.) Information and Communication Technologies in Tourism 2015, pp. 363–375. Springer, Heidelberg (2015)
7. Hunter, W.C., Chung, N., Gretzel, U., Koo, C.: Constructivist research in smart tourism. Asia Pacific J. Inf. Syst. **25**(1), 105–120 (2015)
8. Tu, Q., Liu, A.: Framework of smart tourism research and related progress in China. In: International Conference on Management and Engineering (CME 2014), pp. 140–146. DEStech Publications (2014)
9. Muthuraman, S., Al Haziazi, M.: Smart tourism destination - new exploration towards sustainable development in Sultanate of Oman. In: 5th International Conference on Information Management (ICIM 2019), pp. 332–335. Cambridge (2019)
10. World Tourism Organization (UNWTO). Report of the First Meeting of the NWTO Tourism Resilience Committee. UNWTO, Madrid (2009)
11. Huang, C.D., Goo, J., Nam, K., Yoo, C.W.: Smart tourism technologies in travel planning: the role of exploration and exploitation. Inf. Manag. **54**, 757–770 (2017)
12. Huang, C., Derrick, J.G., Kichan, N., Chul, W.: Smart tourism technologies in travel planning: the role of exploration and exploitation. Inf. Manag. **54**(6), 757–770 (2017)
13. Tussyadiah, I.P., Fesenmaier, D.R.: Interpreting tourist experiences from first-person stories: a foundation for mobile guides. In: ECIS 2007 Proceedings, pp. 2259–2270 (2007)
14. Jeoung, M., Shin, H.: Tourists' experiences with smart tourism technology at smart destinations and their behavior intentions. J. Travel Res. **59**(8), 1464–1477 (2019)
15. Kim, W.G., Chang. L., Stephen J.H.: Effects of an online virtual community on customer loyalty and travel product purchases. Tourism Manag. **25**(3): 343–55 (2004)

16. Namho, C., Koo, C.: The use of social media in travel information search. Telemat. Inform. **32**(2), 215–229 (2015)
17. Schaupp, L.C., Bélanger, F.: A conjoint analysis of online consumer satisfaction. J. Electron. Commer. Res. **6**(2), 95 (2005)
18. Dwayne, B., Coelho, P.S., Vilares, M.J.: Service personalization and loyalty. J. Serv. Mark. **20**(6), 391–403 (2006)
19. Park, Y.A., Gretzel, U.: Success factors for destination marketing web sites: a qualitative meta-analysis. J. Travel Res. **46**, 46–63 (2017)
20. No, E., Kim, J.K.: Comparing the attributes of online tourism information sources. Comput. Hum. Behav. **50**, 564–575 (2015)
21. Kim, W.G., Lee, C., Hiemstra, S.J.: Effects of an online virtual community on customer loyalty and travel product purchases. Tour. Manag. **25**, 343–355 (2004)
22. Jeong, M., Shin, H.H.: Tourists' experiences with smart tourism technology at smart destinations and their behavior intentions. J. Travel Res. **59**, 1464–1477 (2019)
23. Lee, H., Lee, J., Chung, N., Koo, C.: Tourists' happiness: are there smart tourism technology effects? Asia Pac. J. Tour. Res. **23**, 486–501 (2018)
24. Buhalis, D., Amaranggana, A.: Smart tourism destinations. In: Xiang, Z., Tussyadiah, I. (eds.) Information and Communication Technologies in Tourism 2014, pp. 553–364. Springer, Cham (2013)
25. Hanna, L., Lee, J., Chung, N., Koo, C.: Tourists' happiness: are there smart tourism technology effects? Asia Pacific J. Tour. Res. **23**(5), 486–501 (2018)
26. Piera, B., Micera, R.: The experience co-creation in smart tourism destinations: a multiple case analysis of European destinations. Inf. Technol. Tour. **16**(3), 285–315 (2016)
27. Khan, S.M., Woo, M., Nam, K., Chathoth, K.P.: Smart city and smart tourism: a case of Dubai. Sustainability **9**, 2279 (2017)
28. Neuhofer, B.: Smart technologies for personalized experiences: a case study in the hospitality domain. Electron. Mark. **25**, 243–254 (2015)
29. Voss, C., Zomerdijk, L.: Innovation in experiential services—an empirical view. In: DTI, (ed.) Innovation in Services, pp. 97–134. DTI, London (2007)
30. Ingram, C., Caruana, R., McCabe, S.: Participative inquiry for tourist experience. Ann. Tour. Res. **65**, 13–24 (2017)
31. Dunn, M., Davis, S.M.: Building brands from the inside. Mark. Manag. **12**, 32–37 (2003)
32. Boes, K., Buhalis, D., Inversini, A.: Smart tourism destinations: ecosystems for tourism destination competitiveness. Int. J. Tour. Cities **2**, 108–124 (2016)
33. Alletto, S., et al.: An indoor location-aware system for an IoT-based smart museum. IEEE Internet Things **3**, 244–253 (2015)
34. Zhang, L.X.: A Study on the Use Behavior of Tourism App by Tourists. Master's Thesis, Anhui University, Hefei (2016)
35. Litvin, S.W., Goldsmith, R.E., Pan, B.: Electronic word-of-mouth inhospitality and tourism management. Tour. Manag. **29**, 458–468 (2008)
36. Choi, S., Lehto, C., Morrison, A.M., Jang, S.: Structure of travel planning processes and information use patterns. J. Travel Res. **51**, 26–40 (2012)
37. Chianese, A., Marulli, F., Moscato, V., Piccialli, F.: SmARTweet: a location-based smart application for exhibits and museums. In: Proceedings of the 2013 International Conference on Signal-Image Technology and Internet-Based Systems, Kyoto, 2–5 December 2013, pp. 408–415 (2013)
38. Buonincontri, P., Micera, R.: The experience co-creation in smart tourism destinations: a multiple case analysis of European destinations. Inf. Technol. Tour. **16**, 285–315 (2016)
39. Neuhofer, B., Buhalis, D., Ladkin, A.: Conceptualising technology enhanced destination experiences. J. Destin. Mark. Manag. **1**, 36–46 (2012)

40. Borcic, J., Komsic, J., Markovic, S.: Mobile technologies and applications towards smart tourism—state of the art. Tour. Rev. **74**, 82–103 (2019)

41. Xiang, Z., Gretzel, U.: Role of social media in online travel information search. Tour. Manag. **31**(2), 179–188 (2010)

42. Tussyadiah, I., Fesenmaier, D.R.: Mediating tourist experiences: access to places via shared videos. Ann. Tour. Res. **36**, 24–40 (2009)

43. Wu, Y., Yan, X.: Post tourism experience behavior of tourists from the perspective of performance science: Mining the information of online travel notes. J. Tour. Res. **8**, 1–6 (2016)

44. Neuhofer, B., Buhalis, D., Ladkin, A.: A typology of technology-enhanced tourism experiences. Int. J. Tour. Res. **16**(4), 340–350 (2014)

45. Gretzel, U., Sigala, M., Xiang, Z.: Smart tourism: foundations and developments. Electron Markets **25**, 179–188 (2015)

Impact of Technology Revolution on Economic Development Over the Past Decade

Maria I. B. Ribeiro[1,2] (ID), Márcia C. R. Rogão[3] (ID), Isabel M. Lopes[4,5] (ID),
and António J. G. Fernandes[1,2(✉)] (ID)

[1] Centro de Investigação de Montanha (CIMO), Instituto Politécnico de Bragança, Campus Santa Apolónia, 5300-253 Bragança, Portugal
{xilote,toze}@ipb.pt

[2] Laboratório associado para a Sustentabilidade e Tecnologia em Regiões de Montanha (SusTEC), Instituto Politécnico de Bragança, Campus de Santa Apolónia, 5300-253 Bragança, Portugal

[3] Instituto Politécnico de Bragança, Campus Santa Apolónia, 5300-253 Bragança, Portugal
mrogao@ipb.pt

[4] Unidade de Pesquisa Aplicada em Gestão – Instituto Politécnico de Bragança, Bragança, Portugal
isalopes@ipb.pt

[5] Centro ALGORITMI da Universidade do Minho, Braga, Portugal

Abstract. In the past decade, the exponential development of ICT has generated a fast economic development. So, in order to better understand this phenomenon, a systematic literature review based on the Scopus database was carried out. The majority of the studies was developed in Europe and was secondary (82.4%) and qualitative (64.7%) research. Regarding the microeconomic level, the evidences are: greater efficiency of businesses and companies, improved productivity; reduction of transaction costs; improved profit/economic performance of businesses; creation of closer ties between companies and customers, suppliers and partners/collaborators; changes in the functioning of markets that become more dynamic, challenging and competitive; new ways of production organization, changes in the structure of demand and supply for goods and services; and, the emergence of new products. With regard to the macroeconomic level, the results show that ICT and emerging technologies have positive impacts on innovation, employment, economic and financial development, the human development index, social development, with greater civic participation of citizens in Society, greater social well-being, improvement of living conditions especially in the poorest rural areas, better quality of life, reduction of poverty, although there is also the risk of exclusion of significant parts of Society if not adhered to technologies. There are also researches that highlight the role of ICT in sustainable development (economic, social and environmental). It should be noted that existing studies confirm that the impacts are greater on economic growth when compared to economic development and the human development index.

Keywords: Technology · Economic development · Digital revolution · Digital Economy

T. Guarda et al. (Eds.): ARTIIS 2023, CCIS 1937, pp. 485–501, 2024.
https://doi.org/10.1007/978-3-031-48930-3_37

1 Introduction

In recent decades, digitization, information and communication technologies have boosted the access to knowledge, promoting creativity, cultural and economic development and the emergence of a global world at fast speed [1]. This is why the theme of the ongoing transition of societies and economies towards different organizational paradigms, in which digital technologies are deeply rooted, is at the center of current debates [2].

Nowadays, a new technological wave is emerging driven by the advancement of nanotechnology, genetics, 3D printing, biotechnology, artificial intelligence (AI) and robotics [3, 4]. In this context, it is an important and valuable opportunity to boost and leverage the social and economic growth and development of all countries [3]. Emerging technologies represent the new industrial revolution direction capable to promote economic and social sustainable development [5]. The technology industry, in addition to registering rapid growth, directly creates millions of jobs and it is an important innovation and development facilitator [6]. Technology has often been the main driver of social revolutions and paradigm shifts [7].

The literature provides robust support establishing a positive association of ICT infrastructure with economic growth [8]. The mass introduction of AI technologies can have a significant economic impact on organizations and institutions, as long as investments are made and work practices are changed [9], in the various sectors of activity, namely, finance, health, industry, commerce, suppliers, logistics and public services. Furthermore, for example, AI has a strong influence on achieving the sustainable development goals, namely, reducing poverty, improving the safety and reliability of transport infrastructure, facilitating both economic growth and economic development in emerging economies [10]. AI enables poverty reduction as it facilitates the collection of data on poverty through map making, revolutionizes agricultural education and the financial sector through financial inclusion, and helps previously excluded individuals to participate in conventional economics [10].

Among the new technologies, blockchain has laid the foundations for a revolution not only in the financial field, but also in the healthcare, energy, industry, tourism and supply chain sectors [11].

Using panel data, a study that involved 59 countries was developed. Of these, 19 were considered developed countries, 22 emerging countries and 19 were developing countries [12]. The results of this study confirmed the existence of a positive correlation of investment in ICT with countries economic growth. Furthermore, the results proved that developed countries had a higher return on investment in ICT when compared to developing or emerging countries [12]. A study showed a positive and significant impact of mobile phone and Internet penetration on Gross Domestic Product (GDP) per capita in 40 countries in sub-Saharan Africa [13].

Other studies show the existence of a mutual causal association between ICT and growth and development [8, 14, 15]. Other studies describe economic growth led by telecommunications/ICT [13, 14].

Empirical results have shown that there are short and long-term causal effects between ICT infrastructure and economic growth in Asian countries from 2001 to 2012, as well as between ICT infrastructure and financial development [8]. Causal associations that can be explained by the fact that ICT allow the creation of closer ties between companies and their customers, suppliers and partners/collaborators [8]. On the other hand, ICT also reduce geographic barriers, helping to create new knowledge and to disseminate and transform information faster through more efficient processes, both between companies and between sectors [16].

Other studies reveal the association between ICT and business productivity. For example, a study concluded that business productivity was directly associated to the growth of gross national production. However, it was indirectly associated to quality of life [17].

Taking into account the past decade, this research aims to analyze the impact of the technology revolution on economic development. In this context, this article proposes the analysis of 17 articles published in the last decade (from 2012 to 2022). After the background, the following section presents the methodology, followed by the results and discussion. Finally, the conclusions close the work.

2 Methodology

To achieve the referred objective, a systematic literature review was carried out, allowing the screening of the Scopus database in order to collect and analyze the data. In fact, this database is used to standardize research because it encompasses the main international journals [11].

To collect the data in a replicable and reliable way [18], guaranteeing its reliability, transparency and scientific integrity [19], some criteria were defined based on the Preferred Reporting Items for Systematic reviews and Meta-Analyses (PRISMA) statement [20].

The Scopus database was screened on May 29, 2023, using the terms "Impact", "Technology", "Emerging", "Revolution", "Economic" and "Development". As shown in Fig. 1, eighty-eight publications were found. Of these, thirty-seven publications were excluded because they were not of the "Article" type, namely, Book (n = 3), Book chapter (n = 15), Conference paper (n = 15), Review (n = 3) and Editorial (n = 1). In addition, only articles in English or Spanish language were included (n = 48) from the last decade (n = 38).

After reading the publications' full-text, 17 articles were considered for the present systematic revision of the literature. Subsequently, general data was collected and presented in Table 1 (authors, publication date, continent and country where the research took place, study type and methodology). Articles' aims and results are presented in Table 2.

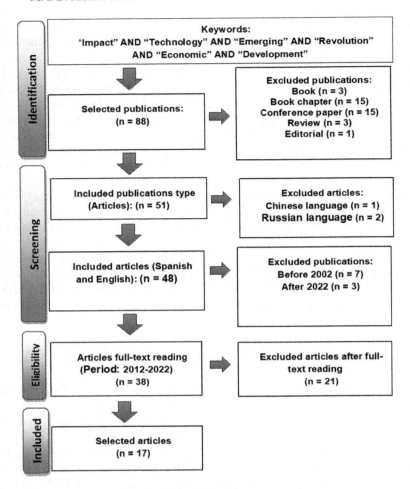

Fig. 1. Systematic review process.

3   Results and Discussion

As shown in Fig. 2, in the period under analysis (2012–2022), 17 articles were published, which obtained a total of 950 citations. 2019 and 2020 stand out as the years that recorded the highest number of articles published (5 in each year). On the other hand, 2021 stands out for being the year with the highest number of recorded citations (74.2% of all citations in the period). An article stood out with the highest number of citations (625 in total citations in the period) [9].

Table 1 presents all the seventeen included articles in this systematic review of the literature by descending order of publication date. As mentioned before, the table also contains information about authorship, publication date, continent and country where the research was developed, study type and methodology. Of the selected studies, three did not have an associated continent or country because they were documentary research

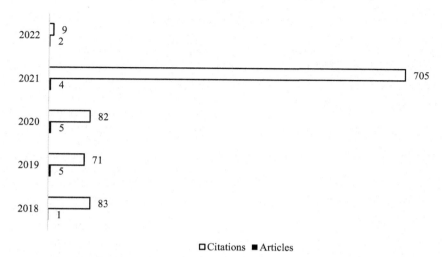

Fig. 2. Citations and articles published during the period under analysis.

or systematic reviews of the literature. One article involved countries on the American continent, namely, Argentina, Brazil, Peru, Chile, Mexico, Colombia and Uruguay [21]. Another article was developed in countries from Asia, Europe and America, namely, Brazil, Russia, India, Indonesia, Mexico, Turkey and China [22]. One article included republics of the Russian Federation from the Asian and European continents [23]. Asia was also the object of studies carried out in Thailand [24], India [25] and China [26]. On the European continent, in addition to those already mentioned, 5 studies were carried out, in Hungary [27], United Kingdom [9], Romania [6], Spain [28] and Italy [2]. Finally, on the African continent, three studies were developed involving sub-Saharan African countries. In the three studies, South Africa was the object of study [3, 10, 29].

Of the seventeen articles considered for analysis, only five are of a quantitative nature [22, 25–27, 29], one is of a mixed nature, that is, qualitative and quantitative [24] and the rest are of a qualitative nature [2, 3, 6, 9–11, 21, 23, 28, 30, 31].

Of the quantitative studies, two are cross-sectional and involved the collection of primary data [26, 27], three are longitudinal and were based on the collection of secondary data [22, 25, 29]. All quantitative studies applied multivariate statistics.

In qualitative studies, authors resort to systematic review [11, 30], document analysis [2, 21, 23, 31], content analysis [10] and focus group [9] and case studies [2, 6, 28].

The impact of emerging technologies on the economy is global as it affects all sectors of activity (Table 2). While some studies [21, 23, 25, 27] focus more on the effects at the microeconomic level, a study [27] focuses on improving the results or economic performance of businesses, other study [21] considers that emerging digital technologies can improve the functioning of agricultural markets at a very low cost for the farmer and improve: (1) productivity, (2) the functioning of agricultural supply chains, (3) traceability, (4) the connection between producers and end customers in the face of climate change and environmental stress. Still in this context, in a systematic literature review, the authors argue that companies that wish to develop and maintain

Table 1. Articles' general data.

Authorship (date) [Ref.]	Continent: country	Study type	Methodology
1. Máté et al. (2022) [27]	Europe: Hungary	Primary, quantitative, cross-sectional	2020–2021; Activity sector and number of companies involved: meat processing and canned goods (97), bakery and pasta (60), fruit and vegetable processing and fish conservation and production of vegetable and animal oil (46) Partial least squares model and analysis of principal components
2. Nitlarp & Kiattisin (2022) [24]	Asia: Thailand	Secondary, qualitative, quantitative	255 articles Confirmatory factor analysis and structural equation modeling
3. Mhlanga (2021) [10]	Africa: South Africa	Secondary, qualitative	Content analysis
4. Gu et al. (2021) [22]	Asia, Europe, America: China, India, Brazil, Mexico, Russia, Indonesia, Turkey	Secondary, quantitative, longitudinal (1990–2017)	Econometric techniques
5. Dwivedi et al. (2021) [9]	Europe: United Kingston	Secondary, qualitative	Focus group
6. Mosteanu & Faccia (2021) [31]	Not applicable	Secondary, qualitative	Documentary research SWOT Analysis
7. Das, Kundu, & Bhattacharya (2020) [25]	Asia: India	Secondary, quantitative, longitudinal	Sources: Global Competitive Index Global Entrepreneurship Monitor Report, 2012–2016 Factor analysis and regression analysis

(*continued*)

Table 1. (*continued*)

Authorship (date) [Ref.]	Continent: country	Study type	Methodology
8. Varriale et al. (2020) [11]	Not applicable	Secondary, qualitative	Systematic literature review Data: 37 documents; Scopus database (2008–2020)
9. Clemente Rincón (2020) [21]	America: Argentina, Brazil, Peru, Chile, Mexico Uruguay, Colombia	Secondary, qualitative	Documentary research
10. Dzhulii et al. (2020) [30]	Not applicable	Secondary, qualitative	Systematic research
11. David, & Grobler (2020) [29]	Africa: sub-Saharan African countries	Secondary, quantitative, longitudinal	Sample: 46 African countries analyzed from 2000 to 2016 Main component analysis and Partial correlation analysis
12. Razvan (2019) [6]	Europe: Romania	Secondary, qualitative	Cases studies
13. Ayentimi & Burgess (2019) [3]	Africa: sub-Saharan countries	Secondary, qualitative	Documentary research
14. Xiao-Bo et al. (2019) [26]	Asia: China	Primary, quantitative	Sample: 159 executives from Zhejiang Province Regression analysis
15. Salimyanova et al. (2019) [23]	Europe and Asia: Russia	Secondary, qualitative	Audits and interviews with executives from medium-sized enterprises operating in Russia in the industrial production and information technology sectors
16. Falcón-Pérez, & Fuentes-Perdomo (2019) [28]	Europe: Spain	Secondary, qualitative	Case study
17. Bertola & Teunissen (2018) [2]	Europe: Italy	Secondary, qualitative	Case study

a competitive advantage or enter new markets cannot avoid adopting new technologies [32]. Finally, ICT have important impacts on transaction costs [23].

The main concern of a study [25] was the sustainability of small and medium-sized companies in a dynamic and challenging technological environment. According to the authors, institutional capabilities, such as availability of cutting-edge technologies, technology absorption at the firm level, foreign direct investment and technology transfer, number of individuals using the Internet and number of broadband Internet subscriptions fixed assets, have a strong impact on the sustainability of a business.

Some studies have a more global vision and more ambitious objectives on the revolutionary effects of technologies [10, 22, 24, 29]. For example, the author of a study [10] argues that AI can help to achieve the sustainable development goals, highlighting the reduction of poverty through the revolution of important sectors such as energy, education, agriculture and finance, with special impact in emerging economies. Also, other authors [31] highlight the benefits of adopting emerging technologies, for example, Fin-Tech and Blockchain, among others, with a high impact on financial development and innovation [6, 7, 26, 30]. Other authors, in addition to demonstrating that the existence of several challenges, opportunities and benefits in various domains, namely, business and management, government and the public sector, they warn of the risks associated with the non-implementation of emerging technologies, namely, exclusion of important sectors of society [22].

Two studies analyzed the impact of emerging technologies on sustainability [2, 11]. One of these studies [11] identified sustainable factors generated by the use of blockchain in supply chains and the other [2] clearly showed that digital transformation, properly conducted, can transform the fashion industry into a more sustainable and truly customer-oriented business.

A study analyzed the performance of telecommunications services, economic growth, economic development, and the impact of telecommunications on economic growth and economic development in 46 countries in sub-Saharan Africa, from 2000 to 2016 [29]. The results confirm that the most sophisticated countries in terms of mobile telecommunications development in Africa, namely, Libya, Gabon and South Africa, were the ones that recorded the highest Human Development Index (HDI), the highest economic growth, as well as the highest economic development. South Africa, despite being the African country that recorded the highest economic growth (highest average real GDP in the period under review), as a result of the greater penetration of mobile telecommunications, recorded moderate economic development and HDI. Similar results were obtained by Gabon. Libya was the country with the best HDI. Overall, ICT has a positive impact on economic growth and development in Africa, although the positive impact is greater on economic growth compared to economic development. In this context, the authors warn of the need for more investment, since the penetration of fixed lines and Internet access telecommunications is low in most African countries. In line with this results, a study developed in Romania concluded that technologies have a positive impact on economic growth. However, the impact is less positive on people's life quality, as a result of excessive abuse and less democratic access to the information [6]. On the other hand, other authors [3] also guarantee that, in Africa, emerging technologies are crucial and can make all the difference, especially when implemented in rural areas,

Table 2. Articles' aims and results.

Ref.	Aims	Results
[27]	Analyze the impact of sustainable technology implementation on business profit/economic performance	Food production companies whose managers think in a viable and sustainable way tend to be more profitable. On the other hand, ecological factors substantially affect profit, while social and economic factors have less impact. Ecological and economic factors strengthened the positive impact of the social dimension on corporate profits
[24]	Develop a conceptual model that illustrates and analyzes the association between digital transformations and sustainable development in the energy sector	Digital technology and green products are key enablers of "Industry 4.0" in the energy sector. This impact factor will benefit organizations that are adhering to the digital transformation, considered the basis for sustainable development
[10]	Investigate the influence of AI in achieving the Sustainable Development Goals with a direct focus on poverty reduction in emerging economies	AI enables poverty reduction through improved data collection related to poverty through poverty maps, revolutionizing agricultural education and the financial sector through financial inclusion. AI also significantly assists education and the financial sector, enabling previously excluded individuals to participate in the conventional economy
[22]	Examine the impact of technological innovation and natural resources on financial development	Natural resources, technological innovation, income, human capital and investment in R&D are important variables that affect long-term financial development. In addition, human capital strengthens financial development, especially if it is led by technological innovation
[9]	Carry out a realistic assessment of the impact, challenges and potential arising from the rapid emergence of AI in various domains, namely, government, public sector, business and management, technology and science	The trajectory towards the increase of applications that make use of AI has the potential to change many aspects of human life and impact society as a whole. The way forward is unclear and the potential roadmap is undefined. There are numerous benefits that can result from AI implementation. However, there are also significant risks that sectors of society could be excluded from the technology implementation

(*continued*)

Table 2. (*continued*)

Ref.	Aims	Results
[31]	Highlight the exposure of the financial sector to technologies (FinTech) that drive exponential development in different scientific areas, namely, geometry (fractal), physics (quantum) and databases (blockchain)	Availability of information and the increasing interconnection of cross-applications for different fields of science determine the rapid succession of revolutions identified as major changes in the economic paradigm. The growing computational capacity and the development of increasingly powerful predictive software lead to a competitive, extremely dynamic and challenging system
[25]	Explore the impact of the volatility of technological environments on the sustainability of Small and Medium Enterprises in developing countries with emerging economies	Both institutional capacities (availability of cutting-edge technologies, technology absorption at the company level, foreign direct investment and technology transfer, number of individuals using the Internet and number of fixed broadband Internet subscriptions) and external capabilities (international Internet bandwidth) become significant when time is taken as a selection variable. The significance of the "time" variable indicates the dynamism of current technological environments. Furthermore, institutional capabilities have a strong impact on the sustainability of a business, compared to external capabilities and the high level of technological volatility
[11]	Analyze the impact of the adoption of blockchain in supply chains based on the three dimensions of sustainability (environmental, economic and social) and to summarize the current state of the art	Blockchain improves profits by ensuring a reduction in transaction times and costs. In addition, it increases the reputation and image of companies by giving visibility to the practices used in supply chains. In this context, it produces enormous positive sustainable economic, social and environmental impacts. The adoption of this technology would allow an increase in transparency towards their partners and customers. Likewise, it would ensure complete and certified monitoring of various activities such as waste management, carbon consumption management, product monitoring and sales forecasting

(*continued*)

Table 2. (*continued*)

Ref.	Aims	Results
[21]	Understand the challenges made possible by digital and mobile technologies, with an impact on value chains, their real and financial functioning and the design of products in the agri-food sector	Success of emerging technological innovations with greater potential for agriculture in Latin America and the Caribbean will depend, to a large extent, on the functioning, evolution and maturity of the innovation systems that leverage the opportunities offered by each country
[30]	Substantiate the impact of Industry 4.0 on strategic company management	The main trends that change technological, innovative and economic development in the context of the 4th industrial revolution are: (1) the development of digital technologies, the unification of the real and virtual worlds; (2) the return of branches of companies and companies that were relocated by technological leaders to other countries due to cheap labor, again to developed countries as a result of the development and advantages of digitalization; (3) the possibility of creating joint innovations, new ways of organizing production; change in the structure of supply and demand, the emergence of new products and services
[29]	Examine ICT performance, economic growth and development in Africa	Mobile telecommunication is growing faster than other telecommunication indicators. ICT penetration has positive impacts on economic growth and development in Africa. Though, the positive impact is higher in economic growth than economic development. Since the penetration of fixed line and Internet access telecommunication are lowing most of the African countries, more investment is needed in fixed line and Internet access telecommunication. This will boost subscription of fixed line and Internet access telecommunication in order to reduce cost of electronic communication and promote the digital economy in Africa

(*continued*)

Table 2. (*continued*)

Ref.	Aims	Results
[6]	Outline some future developments of the contemporary economy within the new digital transformation and development of internet companies in emerging markets; and identify pros and cons, opportunities and threats brought by the expansion of the Internet and ICT	The growth rate of Internet penetration has a positive economic impact and a less positive impact on the population through manipulation and abusive intervention in the decision-making process or even through overcoming democratic barriers through the excessive involvement of public institutions. In addition, the new wave resulting from the analysis of large volumes of data and the dynamics of AI has made it possible to gather, combine, analyze and store large volumes of data indefinitely. Consequently, in recent years, a dominant business model has emerged for most web services based on tracking people online and collecting data about their character, health, relationships, thoughts and opinions, in order to generate revenue. With digital advertising
[3]	Understand and highlight constraints and opportunities to leverage the benefits of the 4th industrial revolution (4IR) in sub-Saharan Africa	4IR offers great potential for sub-Saharan Africa. There are areas of potential transformation that are relevant, namely, energy generation and storage (sun, wind, battery technology, which could mean the self-sufficiency of rural areas in energy); water purification and recycling through solar and wind energy can also ensure safe and affordable water supplies

(*continued*)

Table 2. (*continued*)

Ref.	Aims	Results
[26]	Explore the factors that drive business model innovation and analyze and identify influencing factors in a competitive and uncertain external environment of technological revolution brought by the development of emerging technologies such as big data, cloud computing and AI	(1) perceived technological uncertainty has a negative effect on business model design novelty; (2) perceived market uncertainty has a negative effect on business model design novelty; (3) managers' business ties have a positive moderating effect on the association between perceived technological uncertainty and business model design novelty; (4) managers' business ties have a positive moderating effect on the association between perceived market uncertainty and business model design novelty; (5) managers' ties have no moderating effect on the association between perceived technical uncertainty and business model design novelty; (6) managers' ties have a positive moderating effect on the association between perceived market uncertainty and business model design novelty
[23]	Assess the impact of elements of the digital economy on modern socio-economic processes	Information technology, which is part of the digital economy, has an impact on transaction costs. However, modern society and markets are not always ready to accept and use information technologies. In addition, the strengthening influence of external factors (mainly socio-political), have a destructive impact on development, industry and companies

(*continued*)

Table 2. (*continued*)

Ref.	Aims	Results
[28]	Analyze how cooperatives can be a suitable means to improve social well-being in vulnerable neighborhoods, taking into account that the use of new technologies can attract many people to actively participate in the design of urban regeneration projects	Cooperative initiatives produce cohesive urban neighborhoods and are associated with participatory planning and collective action approaches. On the other hand, the urban rehabilitation cooperative and the use of digital technologies contribute to improve the quality of life and social well-being of citizens under the principles of democratic participation of all citizens, providing greater transparency to the process and to the published information, allowing cooperative members to supervise the information stored on the network
[2]	Provide insights into the current state of the art and main trends of the 4IR identifying its impacts on the fashion industry	Digital transformation, properly conducted, can transform the fashion industry into a more sustainable and truly customer-oriented business. However, the authors highlight the criticism and slowness of ICT adoption by established traditional brands and companies

for the generation and storage of energy, purification and recycling of water using solar energy and safe and accessible water supply, greatly improving the populations' life quality.

A study carried out in Spain in problematic neighborhoods concluded, on the use of a digital platform, that ICT can be a valuable tool for development since ICT provide the improvement of the social well-being in vulnerable neighborhoods, enticing people to actively participate in the design of urban regeneration projects [28].

In summary, and as a study [33] defends, the internet and ICT and, nowadays, emerging technologies, namely those with the capacity to create and revolutionize, are gradually occupying an important and dominant position in the various sectors of economic activity and to become a strategic factor in economic development.

4   Conclusion

A bibliographic search was carried out on May 29, 2023 that included all English and Spanish language articles published in the Scopus database between 2012 and 2022 in order to investigate the impact of technologies on the economic growth and development.

The analysis of the seventeen selected articles allows classifying the impacts of ICT at microeconomic and macroeconomic levels. Regarding the microeconomic level, the evidences presented are: greater efficiency of businesses and companies; improved productivity; reduction of transaction costs; improvement of profit/economic performance of businesses; creation of closer ties between companies and customers, suppliers and partners/collaborators; changes in the functioning of markets that become more dynamic, challenging and competitive; new ways of organizing production; changing the structure of demand and supply for goods and services; and the emergence of new products. At the macroeconomic level, the results show that ICT and emerging technologies have positive impacts on innovation, employment, economic growth, economic development, financial development, the Human Development Index, social development, with greater civic participation of citizens in Society, greater social well-being, improvement of living conditions (especially in the poorest rural areas), better quality of life, reduction of poverty, although there is also the risk of exclusion of significant parts of Society if they do not adhere to technologies. There are also researches that highlight the role of ICT and technologies in sustainable development (economic, social and environmental). It should be noted that existing studies confirm that the impacts are greater on economic growth when compared to economic development and the human development index.

This research has some limitations. On the one hand, it is supported only by articles from the Scopus database. In fact, despite being considered the most comprehensive bibliometric database in terms of peer-reviewed international publications, there are other equally important databases that were excluded. On the other hand, a filter was used to limit the search period from 2012 to 2022 and to select only documents of the "article" type, written in English or Spanish language, omitting literature prior to 2012 and after 2022, as well as documents written in other languages. However, the rigorous and reproducible procedures lead us to believe that the information contained in the excluded publications does not substantially add or change the conclusions drawn in this research.

Taking into account that the analyzed studies are predominantly qualitative, and only two quantitative studies were developed on the European continent, for future research it is suggested to develop a study, in Portugal, following the same methodology applied in an empirical research cited in the present systematic literature review [29]. On the other hand, and given that studies on the impact of emerging technologies on sustainable development are scarce, in the near future, it will be intended to develop a study in this line of research.

Acknowledgments. The authors are grateful to the Foundation for Science and Technology (FCT, Portugal) for financial support through national funds FCT/MCTES (PIDDAC) to CIMO (UIDB/00690/2020 and UIDP/00690/2020) and SusTEC (LA/P/0007/2020).

References

1. Aguaded, I., Civila, S., Vizcaíno-Verdú, A.: Paradigm changes and new challenges for media education: Review and science mapping (2000–2021). Profesion. Inform. **31**(6), e310606 (2022)
2. Bertola, P., Teunissen, J.: Fashion 4.0. innovating fashion industry through digital transformation. Res. J. Textile Apparel **22**(4), 352–369 (2018)
3. Ayentimi, D.T., Burgess, J.: Is the fourth industrial revolution relevant to sub-Sahara Africa? Technol. Anal. Strateg. Manag. **31**(6), 641–652 (2019)

4. Albert, M.J.: The dangers of decoupling: earth system crisis and the 'fourth industrial revolution.' Glob. Pol. **11**(2), 245–254 (2020)
5. Kluczowe, S.: Assessing the criticality of minerals used in emerging technologies in China. Gospodarka Surowcami Mineralnymi/Mineral Resour. Manag. **36**(2), 5–20 (2020)
6. Razvan, S.: Several contemporary economy features, consequences of internet expansion and ICT innovations in the world. Stud. Bus. Econ. **14**(3), 175–181 (2019)
7. Grinin, L., Grinin, A.: The Cybernetic Revolution and the Future of Technologies. In: Korotayev, A.V., LePoire, D.J. (eds.) The 21st Century Singularity and Global Futures. WEGF, pp. 377–396. Springer, Cham (2020). https://doi.org/10.1007/978-3-030-33730-8_17
8. Pradhan, R.P., Arvin, M.B., Norman, N.R.: Technology in Society The dynamics of information and communications technologies infrastructure, economic growth, and financial development: evidence from Asian countries. Technol. Soc. **42**, 135–149 (2015)
9. Dwivedi, Y.K., Hughes, L., Ismagilova, E., Walton, P., Williams, M.D.: Artificial Intelligence (AI): multidisciplinary perspectives on emerging challenges, opportunities, and agenda for research, practice and policy. Int. J. Inf. Manag. **57**, 101994 (2021)
10. Mhlanga, D.: Artificial intelligence in the industry 4.0, and its impact on poverty, innovation, infrastructure development, and the sustainable development goals: lessons from emerging economies? Sustainability (Switzerland) **13**(11), 5788 (2021)
11. Varriale, V., Cammarano, A., Michelino, F., Caputo, M.: The unknown potential of blockchain for sustainable supply chains. Sustainability (Switzerland) **12**(22), 9400 (2020)
12. Niebel, T.: ICT and economic growth–comparing developing, emerging and developed countries. World Dev. **104**, 197–211 (2018)
13. Haftu, G.G.: Information communications technology and economic growth in Sub-Saharan Africa: a panel data approach. Telecommun. Policy **43**(1), 88–13 (2019)
14. Bahar, S.B.: ICT diffusion, R&D intensity, and economic growth: a dynamic panel data approach. J. Knowl. Econ. **9**, 636–648 (2018)
15. David, O.O.: Powering economic growth and development in Africa: telecommunication operations. Appl. Econ. **51**(33), 3583–3607 (2019)
16. Kretschmer, T.: Information and communication technologies and productivity growth: a survey of the literature. OECD Digital Economy Papers 195 (2012)
17. Palvia, P., Baqir, N., Nemati, H.: ICT for socio-economic development: a citizens' perspective. Inf. Manag. ICT Manag. **55**(2), 160–176 (2018)
18. Xiao, Y., Watson, M.: Guidance on conducting a systematic literature review. J. Plan. Educ. Res. **39**(1), 93–112 (2019)
19. Tranfield, D., Denyer, D., Smart, P.: Towards a methodology for developing evidence informed management knowledge by means of systematic review. Braz. J. Manag. **14**(3), 207–222 (2003)
20. Moher, D., Liberati, A., Tetzlaff, J., Altman, D.G.: The PRISMA group: preferred reporting items for systematic reviews and meta-analyses: the PRISMA statement. PLoS Med. **6**(7), e1000097 (2009)
21. Clemente Rincón, L.A.: The new challenges of the agri-food sector: fintech 3.0, AgTech and FoodTech. Agroalimentaria **26**(51), 323–351 (2020)
22. Gu, J., Gouliamos, K., Lobonţ, O.-R., Nicoleta-Claudia, M.: Is the fourth industrial revolution transforming the relationship between financial development and its determinants in emerging economies? Technol. Forecast. Soc. Chang. **165**, 120563 (2021)
23. Salimyanova, I.G., Novikov, A.A., Novikova, E.V., Rudenko, L.G., Allalyev, R.M.: Economy digitalization: information impact on market entities. J. Environ. Treat. Techniq. **7**(4), 654–658 (2019)
24. Nitlarp, T., Kiattisin, S.: The impact factors of Industry 4.0 on ESG in the energy sector. Sustainability (Switzerland) **14**(15), 9198 (2022)

25. Das, S., Kundu, A., Bhattacharya, A.: Technology adaptation and survival of SMEs: a longitudinal study of developing countries. Technol. Innov. Manag. Rev. **10**(6), 64–72 (2020)
26. Xiao-Bo, W., Qi, X.H., An, D.Z., Ming, X.Y.: The impact of perceived environmental uncertainty on the business model innovation: moderating effect of managerial ties. J. Indust. Eng. Eng. Manag. **33**(4), 216–225 (2019)
27. Máté, D., et al.: The impacts of sustainable industrial revolution (IR) on the profitability of Hungarian food companies. Front. Sustain. Food Syst. **6**, 1034010 (2022)
28. Falcón-Pérez, C.E., Fuentes-Perdomo, J.: Improving social well-being through platform cooperativism. CIRIEC-España Rev. Econ. Publ. Soc. Cooperat. **95**, 161–190 (2019)
29. David, O.O., Grobler, W.: Information and communication technology penetration level as an impetus for economic growth and development in Africa. Econ. Res. **33**(1), 1394–1418 (2020)
30. Dzhulii, L., Mironova, N., Stankevych, I., Paunov, M., Syvak, O.: Strategic company management in the conditions of Industry 4.0. Acad. Strateg. Manag. J. **19**(5), 1–9 (2020)
31. Mosteanu, N.R., Faccia, A.: Fintech frontiers in quantum computing, fractals, and blockchain distributed ledger: paradigm shifts and open innovation. J. Open Innov. Technol. Market Complex. **7**(1), 19 (2021)
32. Becheikh, N., Landry, R., Amara, N.: Lessons from innovation empirical studies in the manufacturing sector: a systematic review of the literature from 1993–2003. Technovation **26**(5/6), 644–664 (2006)
33. Yan, S., Shi, L., Wang, L.: Influence of the urban built environment on physical and mental health of the elderly under the background of big data. Comput. Intell. Neurosci. **2022**, 4266723 (2022)

From Information and Communication Technology to the Smart Tourism Experience: Value Co-creation

Pedro Vaz Serra[1,2](✉) , Cláudia Seabra[1,2] , and Ana Caldeira[1,2]

[1] University of Coimbra, Coimbra, Portugal
pedrovazserra@hotmail.com

[2] CEGOT - Geography and Spatial Planning Research Centre, Coimbra, Portugal

Abstract. Tourism contemplates dynamics that are socially, culturally, and economically relevant and that imply mobility, for personal or professional purposes, to destinations outside their usual environment [1]. The intensity and impact of information and communication technologies (ICT) on tourism make the smart concept also applicable to it [2]. The smart tourism experience, driven by aggregated information, the spread of connectivity, and permanent synchronisation [3], tends to be efficient and significant [4]. In this framework, tourists as an interested part, play a decisive role, given that they not only consume, but also create and improve data, which represent the structure of the experience, and, through their digital footprint, access to information and/or add value through mobile devices and tools [5–7]. Given the relevance and timeliness of the topics under analysis—aware of contemporary technological evolution and the impact it contemplates on science and tourist activity—, a conceptual approach is proposed that allows highlighting, through the literature review, the process, unavoidable interaction between technology and the tourism experience [6]. We highlight essential repercussions on the levels of services and destinations, organisations and business models, resources, and instruments, given a more versatile structure and different concepts regarding added value [4], with the consequent innovative impact in terms of services competitiveness, strategic vision, management and marketing models [12], highlighting its usefulness in co-creating positively differentiating tourism experiences for stakeholders, namely tourists, as well as accommodation and destinations.

Keywords: Information and Communication Technologies · Smart Tourism Experience · Value Co-Creation

1 Introduction

Contemporary technological infrastructures create connectivity and interaction modalities, inside and outside travel, therefore impacting the way we understand tourism activity, in general, and the travel process [8].

More advanced mobile technology, as well as social networks, communication, and location tools, mediate and improve tourist experiences through an environment that is reinforced in emotional, aesthetic, informative, recreational, and social terms, generating greater creativity and spontaneity [9, 10].

This evolution leads to the emergence of new behavioural variables when traveling, new conceptions of product and service design, as well as new research and monitoring platforms that lead to new levels in the management of tourist activity [11, 12].

Given the speed with which this exchange of information takes place, particularly via the internet, consumers can organize themselves into groups that often represent a network of advisors, an information network, which makes it possible to learn about the experiences of other people, becoming independent, or constituting itself, beyond corporate information [13, 14].

Information and Communication Technology (ICT), supported by smart technology, including sensors, big data, Internet of Things (IoT), Radio Frequency Identification (RFID), and Near Field Communication (NFC) plays a key role [14–16].

With the Internet and Web 2.0. transformations have emerged with a wide impact on the interaction between consumers and companies, through previously unknown paths, including social networks as platforms that generate new ways of acting along the value chain [11, 15].

The growing demand for co-created experiences [17], more participatory and interactive [15] is significant for tourism, given that, in the face of growing competition, the recognition of its relevance for visitors means that accommodations and destinations also create opportunities for attractive and memorable experiences [9, 18].

Technology has a decisive role, as far as (i) it helps tourist and hotel agents to practice dynamic management of information; (ii) enhances the satisfaction of consumer needs, related to the search for up-to-date and instantaneous information; (iii) provides competitive advantages by assisting in decision-making processes [12, 15].

We find in the literature that ICT, significantly changed the access and consumption of tourism products, providing new needs, expectations, and opportunities in accessing data and, thus, a better understanding of the travel behaviour [2, 8, 14].

A conceptual approach is proposed - addressing the topics technology and services, technology in tourism, the smart tourism experience, and co-creation of value, before the final considerations-, where, highlighting the interaction between ICT and the smart tourism experience, we defend the value co-creation, contributing to the outline of current scenarios and future perspectives, with an impact on the level of management of accommodation and destinations, as well as in the decision-making processes of tourists, covering research areas of great relevance to tourism.

2 Technology and Services

Contemporary technological evolution has an inevitable and relevant impact on service provider companies, on linking strategies with consumers, with their needs and expectations [19, 20].

In the literature, the main technological advances with the capacity to impact the company-customer relationship are identified as the 5th-generation mobile network (5G), Artificial Intelligence (AI), Augmented Reality (AR), and Virtual Reality (VR), RFID, smartphones, and applications (Apps) [15].

Multiple online social platforms have become privileged places for tourists to share information related to their travels, changing the way experiences are shared [21].

Thus, smart technology interferes with tourists' opinions and perceptions and influences their behavioural variables, covering five key elements: information, accessibility, interactivity, personalisation, and safety [4, 13, 14].

2.1 Enabling Technologies

Enabling technologies, i.e., those that have the potential to generate a disruptive change, contribute to innovations capable of applying technological advances in the domain of the relationship between companies and customers, with important impacts at the micro and macro levels [15], with service systems and the underlying service experience arising from the integration of innovation resources that have evolved because of technological advances [19].

In a little more detail, let´s look at each of these main technological advances.

5G technology is a wireless telecommunications system capable of influencing the speed with which data transfer occurs, namely through digital networks and mobile devices, enabling a smart environment, through connectivity and the appeal to IoT [22].

The impact of 5G technology on more innovative services is translated into the provision of faster data to consumers, as well as more connections supported by IoT, generating a greater appetite for services framed by greater automation of urban net and personal devices [22], offering tourists more convenient conditions to contact anyone, at any time and in any place, also aiming sharing of experiences [21].

AI corresponds to a technology capable of realizing an occurrence that, if carried out by a human, would imply intelligence, identifying itself with the ability to learn [23], feel, but also reasoning and action, as well as detection, deliberation, and development of the necessary actions that allow obtaining elements, or attributes, considered to be more predictive [24], contributing to the products and experiences design that consider the consumers' needs and expectations, based on the treatment of big data [25].

Currently, AI occupies an important space in decision support, susceptible of being applied to business environments, including sales, marketing, and customer service [26], leveraging more integrated consumer resources [15].

RFID technology uses local storage in microchips, activated with NFC, which detects, stores, and transmits environmental data [27], and is already widely used, by incorporating, for example, mobility and security-related solutions, bank cards, passports, suitcases, hotel keys, among others, being particularly useful in conjunction with global positioning systems (GPS) as it allows tracking movements and time, facilitating a variety of services based on location [28].

Smartphones and other mobile devices today have micro-computing capacity, being used by approximately 40% of the world's population, even with some discrepancies between continents and geographic zones, becoming the configuration that prevails to access the internet [29]. Increasingly sophisticated technology incorporates new valences and support the most intense and wide AR and VR adoption, in a 5G environment, with faster content, enhancing telepresence in real-time [26] and allowing tourists to experience interactive environments supported by their mobile devices [30].

Therefore, more consumers use their smart devices, aware of the context, with a proactive and/or reactive attitude toward the information they obtain, that is, personalizing experiences or in response to an unforeseen event, respectively, assuming the role of a digital concierge [15].

Apps are applications that make smartphones usable and interact with all the resources, with the potential to optimize the experience, relating, for example, points of interest of a destination, maps, personal travel guides, transport services, converters of languages and currencies, as well as specific hotel services, having significantly increased its use and utility by smartphone users [31].

Thus, these enabling technologies led to several innovations in the context of services, reflecting multiple dimensions associated with a model that values co-creation [19, 32], being strategically important, due to its implications, the smart environments, the cybersecurity, and the gamification [33, 34].

Smart contexts adopt technological solutions that include sensors, telecommunications, IoT and Apps, with a view to providing resources with efficiency and sustainability criteria and, at the same time, new insights into complex data operations for companies and other stakeholders [35].

In this context, the IoT corresponds to a technologically disruptive and ubiquitous model, connecting all people and all places, leading to innovation that enhances new tools and services [34], such as those provided by hotels where, increasingly, smart environments in guest rooms allow better management of needs and expectations and, in this way, the emergence of service innovations, through co-creation and the delivery of personalised experiences, identified with the moment, and prices [17].

In summary, technologies do not translate the critical factor, corresponding, yes, to the route solution to the customer [19], in line with what [20], for whom value is uniquely and phenomenologically determined by itself.

3 Technology in Tourism Activity

Let us see the technologies that have been gaining an important expression in tourism activity, with immense potential in terms of the customer-company relationship: VR, AR, Location-Based Services (LBS), and autonomous devices [15].

VR corresponds to a set of technological bases that allow the total immersion of the user in an artificial scenario, leading to the alteration of their sensorial perception through the experience supported by screens, haptic interface systems, i.e., with force feedback in the user's hand, and exoskeletons, i.e., that work in harmony with the user's body, inducing in the human mind the interpretation of external signals, as embodied experiences in a virtual environment [36].

VR challenges the notion of travel, in the sense of real activity in the place, proposing the use of imagination, where the body can assume multiple contextual configurations, anywhere [37]. Applied in service design, it leads to rigorous prototypes, which are especially useful in hotel marketing, such as, for example, virtual walks, the anticipation of arrival, teleportation experiences, and time travel, among other uses [38].

In turn, AR uses devices such as smartphones, or glasses, among others, issuing informational data regarding the user's context, activated through the recording of images and location technology, superimposed on information that enhances the appeal to the senses, processed at expressive speeds, making real-time experiences viable, leading to new forms of communication, with frequent applications in museums, for example [15].

About LBS, they call for the integration of contextual data from sensors and autonomous agents, generating an offer based on mobile technology, such as equipment that allows the detection and/or measurement of physical characteristics and data recording, with RFID, susceptible to be sent to consumers' mobile devices, when close to certain points of sale [15].

Finally, autonomous devices, the result of technological disruption manifested at the macro and micro levels, i.e., structural, and operational, respectively, comprise embedded technologies such as virtual operators, robotization, drones, and autonomous vehicles, among others [15].

This disruptive technology already has an operational impact, for example, catering, with the adoption of robots to serve or even, in some cases, to prepare food or plating it, in a fast-food and fast-casual environment [15, 15].

4 The Smart Tourism Experience

Smart tourism, the result of combining ICT with the tourist experience, is also a social phenomenon, whose co-creation dynamics stem from the psychological effects of which the tourist is the bearer, as far as it translates a contribution with physical and/or mental dimensions that allow interaction with other actors in the experiential scenario [14, 39].

The smart tourism experience is technologically mediated [15], driven by aggregated information, the spread of connectivity, and permanent synchronisation [3], tends to be efficient and significant [4].

In this framework, tourists as an interested part, play a decisive role, given that they not only consume, but also create and improve data, which represent the structure of the experience, and, through their digital footprint, access to information and/or add value through mobile devices and tools [6, 7].

The meaning resulting from the smart tourism experience is identified with the objective of the various actors, connected, and results from obtaining distinctive and remarkable experiences with sustainability criteria, guided by the digital channels of the main business variables and the versatility of the organisation [40, 41].

A significant part of smart tourism, therefore, depends on tourists who voluntarily provide data in exchange for a perception of context that improves their tourist experiences—their digital footprints being significant—resulting in high costs in the management and sharing of data, which need to be institutionalized, which is not simple in a fragmented tourist activity, where micro-enterprises are the majority, many of which are already lagging about to digital developments, which is why knowledge/technology transfer and training are critical [15, 42].

In this way, the technological platform that surrounds it is decisive, given that the experience is optimised through the Wi-Fi/mobile devices connection with big data, framed in an environment of smart technology, which will lead to enriched consultations and guidelines, contextualized and value-generating [12, 14, 42].

However, the adoption of a certain technology, by itself, does not correspond to an intelligent accommodation or destination, requiring a multifaceted structure of intelligence, which is, thus, capable of generating value for stakeholders, increasing competitiveness, and allowing the sustainability [43, 44].

Companies will have to compete for the attention of smart tourists, yet their willingness to co-create and obtain meaningful experiences may mean that they are motivated to process information [6, 7, 42].

The resulting interactions put the subjectivity of tourists and guests face to face, leading to a shared environment, where emotional, evaluative, optional factors, ideas, and ideals coexist [45], and the resulting connection is rich in references, interpretations, affections, and feelings [39].

Thus, the recognition of a participatory posture stands out, with the inevitable connection, in the co-created experiences, considering that there are several dimensions - emotional, cognitive, physical, and social - involved in the experiences, which can be close and intense [7, 39].

Although, in the literature, the relevance of the positively differentiating experience and, therefore, able to generate value is consecrated, it is verified that the analysis of the cognitive and functional effects, such as knowledge or skills, on users in smart technology contexts and subject to intensive use and processing of information is less expressive [42, 46].

By generating value—resource integration methods bring benefits (i) to the environment; (ii) reinforcing the relationships between the various actors, promoting the well-being; and (iii) better, more innovative services that provide a more competitive economy [8, 17]—, co-creation enhances sustainability, translated into more alternatives that enhance economic, social, and environmental differentiation, with the involvement of stakeholders, among them and in the first place, tourists [21].

Another prominent issue, in addition to security, is related to privacy associated with the intense use of technological resources, namely those based on location which, although of great utility for users, makes them more exposed, even though the concept of privacy in tourism is something atypical, since the relationship with providers is short-term, which conditions an effective environment of trust, which is sometimes undervalued [6, 16, 47, 48].

5   The Value Co-creation

The relevance of co-creation in tourism activity stems mainly from three circumstances: (i) technological evolution, which generated processes in companies, prone to consumer participation [7]; (ii) empowerment of customers, who want to actively control what they consume [49]; and (iii) companies' perception that consumers can be a relevant and useful co-producer in the creation, communication, and delivery of products and services [13].

In the literature, we find a growing number of authors who have studied co-created tourism experiences—which implies a perspective of collaboration between the various actors, from the outset providers and consumers, who, together, create value, [13, 17, 20,

39, 46], and which, given current trends, proves to be strategic, requiring special attention in terms of management and marketing, namely accommodation and destinations [39].

The analysis is carried out from a double perspective (see Table 1), theoretical and applied, varying the objective of the approaches according to the specifications, but always in the sense of (i) clarifying contemporary changes in the value chain; (ii) investigate the global experience at the destination; and (iii) to explore innovative marketing approaches [39, 50].

It is therefore desirable to increase interactions between operators and customers, being expected to obtain better operational results (i) if they are more capable of adopting ICT; (ii) if they have the resources to strategically align different objectives; and (iii) if they demonstrate the ability to establish partnerships that generate co-created value [43, 61].

Thus, the co-creation process is facilitated through ICT, which promotes the exchange and interaction between different partners to create better value propositions for customers, to enhance their contribution to the design, production, and consumption of experiences, praising the involvement of tourists in activities that meet their needs and expectations and deserve their attention [68], with the environment, the natural one, being described as a space where staging can generate in tourists an involvement with on-site experiences [9].

Companies and consumers are increasingly collaborating, praising co-creation the role of the consumer, placed in a privileged position, being recognised the decisive function that has in the origin of the process underlying the experience and corresponding increase of value [20, 46, 69].

From the assumptions of the Service-Dominant Logic, the co-creation of value is generated *with* the consumer and not *for* him, it contemplates two essential assumptions, (i) the client's contribution to the creative process of the experience; and (ii) it is the customer who creates and determines value, by consuming and using value [20].

In the tourism market and due to the impact of ICT, consumers interact with other users, namely digitally [14], with the value co-creation as a collective, collaborative, and dynamic process (see Table 2), which came to replace the exchange process, not only with a company but also with entire groups of professionals, service providers, other consumers, and other interested parties [17].

In this context, it is essential to have a forum for dialogue between the consumer and the company, as well as the regulation underlying participation in this forum, to guarantee an orderly and effective interaction [15, 41].

The co-creation environment must necessarily include ICT so that the consumer's involvement with service innovations is maximized, as well as the promotion of innovative ways for experiences and value proactively co-created by tourists, considering the various stages of the trip [71], constituting ICT an unavoidable source of competitive advantage [14].

The multiple forms that ICT can adopt frame co-created experiences, generating a system of interactions that, about consumers, (i) provides them with greater control; (ii) establishes the relationship with providers; (iii) encourages the active creation of experiences, and, as shared environment, they allow tourists to assume various roles,

Table 1. Co-creation in the tourist experience: Definitions and dimensions

Reference	Definition	Dimension
[51]	The customer and the company create value together	The tourist is an active participant at the experience design and production levels; interaction with the value chain; subjectivity
[52]	Tourists as co-producers of experiences, actively engaged by interacting with other contextually important actors such as operators, staff, resident community and other tourists	Active construction; interactions with the environment, organizations, employees, residents, and other visitors; psychological dimension
[53]	Active tourists, as actors available to put their knowledge and skills in interaction with other actors, aiming at value creation	Active participation; emotional, physical, and mental connectivity; social and environmental interactions; reflexivity
[54, 55]	The tourist participates in the value creation process, contributing with resources to obtain the experience	The involvement and participation of the tourist in the experience creation; customer, product, and company interactions before, during, and after the trip
[56, 57]	The company appears as a link for value creation, but the consumer is the only creator of value	Social interaction, intersubjectivity, the tourist as a bearer of psychological phases, symbols and meanings, skills and body postures during activities, practices, and experiences
[58]	The great meaning for tourists of the experiences they create	The tourist as an active participant, physically, mentally, and emotionally connected; interaction with other actors and with the experiential context
[59]	Stakeholders actively and reciprocally committed to permanent connections of references and guidelines, in multiple aspects of the organization-consumer relationship about how they can develop and optimise the experience by actively contributing	Active guest involvement before, during, and after the experience building; socialisation; subjectivity
[60, 61]	Consumers adapt their experiences through personalization, according to their needs, in interaction with providers and technologically mediated	Differentiating experience resulting from personalisation

(continued)

Table 1. (*continued*)

Reference	Definition	Dimension
[60, 62–65]	Co-creation implies active participation throughout the experiential process	Smartphones, tablets, and digital cameras can improve participation, interaction, and involvement in the tourist experience
[66, 67]	Consumers co-create their experiences as they engage through personalised settings and options	Greater involvement enhances a memorable experience

Source: [39, 50]—adapted.

Table 2. ICT-enabled co-creation: Examples

Reference	Result
[71]	Typology of experience of nine fields, driven by technological intensity and co-creation
[72]	The degree of co-creation of hotel guests is a function of the perception of value through co-creation and future behavioural variables in a hotel where technologically mediated co-creation is possible
[73]	The contribution to experiences and the connection between tourists and providers are linked to co-created experiences. Co-created experiences, satisfaction, expenses, and happiness are positively related. There is no relationship between shared experiences among tourists and co-created experiences
[74]	Smartphone apps in pre-travel, on-site, and post-travel contexts
[75]	Sharing experiences by tourists on social networks
[76]	Smartphones promote a feeling of union and independence during family holidays, are mediators and enhance the memory of experiences
[77]	Co-created value leads to greater pre-availability to support higher prices for the hotel room, resulting from involvement in the context of online booking
[78]	Robotics in a hotel context
[79]	Use of gamified technology during the trip
[80]	Technology-based souvenir design
[81]	Use of Virtual Reality application in cultural heritage sites
[82][83]	Participation of tourists in online platforms
[84]	Interactive technologies in museums

Source: [39, 50]—adapted

namely in terms of design, communication, and facilitation of experiences, enhancing a wide spectrum of value [4, 7, 14, 64].

It should be noted, however, that interaction between humans should not be replaced by technology—first because it needs the voluntary adherence of consumers, as well as their data so that it can be framed and optimised [14]—but complement it, enriching the tourist experience [50].

6 Concluding Remarks

Technology emerges as a relevant instrument in the operationalisation, structuring, and strategic vision of organisations [2, 15], constituting a relevant centrality factor for products, and more innovative management models [7, 26, 38].

Effectively, the internet generates a connection platform between people and companies around the world, with social networks in a web 2.0 environment representing one of the most technologically important scenarios that have occurred in the recent past, offering a vast number of instruments that enable a more interactive and participatory consumers´ attitude, by contributing, sharing, and creating content, opinions, and experiences, with organisations and each other [7, 15, 44].

The proliferation of technologies with social interaction has had a disruptive impact, given the vast field of action that allows important value additions in the creation of services, experiences, and value [14, 20], with an evident role played in the empowerment and co-creation of and by the consumer [7, 12].

Smart tourism resources and connections depend on voluntarily contributed by consumers, it seems important to have new investigations that focus on health risks and the resulting psychological effects, considering the intense use, which allows assessing its availability for the cooperation, creation, and usufruct, and the importance of the use value generated by them [4, 5, 42].

Issues related to privacy and trust – as well as technological illiteracy, which occurs in consumers, but also in tour operators and intermediaries – also reveal some complexity and require investment, monitoring, and commitment [42, 85].

Although it is not exempt from constraints, latent and explicit, smart tourism enshrines a stimulating context, underlying actors, including residents and tourists, holders of resources and connections; to areas that are more inviting, safe, and tend to be competitive and sustainable; experiences differentiated by personalisation; conditions conducive to creative and innovative services and businesses, with more flexibility and adopting new ways of creating value [14, 17, 84–86].

The smart tourism system is characterized by the services scalability and is based on the trust and openness of the actors, so the creation of markets and distinctive experiences stems from products conceived and framed dynamically by providers and consumers [17, 70, 87].

This approach makes several significant contributions to the tourism literature, by extolling how smart environments can exert a transforming action in terms of structures, processes and practices, with the consequent innovative impact in terms of services competitiveness, strategic vision, management and marketing models all stakeholders [12], highlighting its usefulness in co-creating positively differentiating tourism experiences for stakeholders, namely tourists, as well as accommodation and destinations.

Acknowledgments. This research was supported by the Geography and Spatial Planning Research Centre (CEGOT), financed by Portuguese funds through the Foundation for Science and Technology (FCT) under reference UI/DB/04084/2020 and, also by FCT, financed by Portuguese and European funds, under the reference UI/BD/154288/2022.

References

1. UNWTO: UNWTO Tourism Definitions (2019)
2. Gretzel, U.: Tourism and Social Media. In The Sage Handbook of Tourism Management, pp. 415–432. SAGE Publications, Thousand Oaks (2018)
3. Neuhofer, B., Buhalis, D., Ladkin, A.: Smart technologies for personalized experiences: a case study in the hospitality domain. Electron. Mark. **25**(3), 243–254 (2015)
4. Lee, T.-H., Jan, F.-H.: Development and validation of the smart tourism experience scale. Sustainability **14**(24), 16421 (2022)
5. Gretzel, U., Sigala, M., Xiang, Z., Koo, C.: Smart tourism: foundations and developments. Electron. Mark. **25**(3), 179–188 (2015)
6. Jeong, M., Shin, H.H.: Tourists' experiences with smart tourism technology at smart destinations and their behavior intentions. J. Travel Res. **59**(8), 1464–1477 (2020)
7. Neuhofer, B.: Innovation through Co-creation: Towards an Understanding of Technology-Facilitated Co-Creation Processes in Tourism (2016)
8. Xiang, Z., Du, Q., Ma, Y., Fan, W.: A comparative analysis of major online review platforms: implications for social media analytics in hospitality and tourism. Tour. Manag. **58** (2017)
9. Elshaer, I.A., Fayyad, S., Ammar, S., Abdulaziz, T.A., Mahmoud, S.W.: Adaptive reuse of heritage houses and hotel conative loyalty: digital technology as a moderator and memorable tourism and hospitality experience as a mediator. Sustainability **14**(6), 3580 (2022)
10. Henkens, B., Verleye, K., Larivière, B., Perks, H.: Pathways to service system smartness for firms. J. Serv. Res. 10946705221132584 (2022)
11. Arnaboldi, M., Diaz Lema, M.L.: Shaping cultural participation through social media. Financ. Account. Manag. **38**(2), 299–321 (2022)
12. Buhalis, D.: Technology in tourism-from information communication technologies to eTourism and smart tourism towards ambient intelligence tourism: a perspective article. Tour. Rev. **75**(1), 267–272 (2019)
13. Polese, F., Botti, A., Grimaldi, M., Monda, A., Vesci, M.: Social innovation in smart tourism ecosystems: how technology and institutions shape sustainable value co-creation. Sustainability **10**, 140 (2018)
14. Zhang, Y., Sotiriadis, M., Shen, S.: Investigating the impact of smart tourism technologies on tourists' experiences. Sustainability **14**(5), 3048 (2022)
15. Buhalis, D., Harwood, T., Bogicevic, V., Viglia, G., Beldona, S., Hofacker, C.: Technological disruptions in services: lessons from tourism and hospitality. J. Serv. Manag. **30**(4), 484–506 (2019)
16. Sklyar, V., Kharchenko, V.: Application of the Booking.com Analytics Software Tools in Reliable Processing of Big Data in Hotels Management (2019)
17. Bhuiyan, K.H., et al.: Smart tourism ecosystem: a new dimension toward sustainable value co-creation. Sustainability **14**(22), 15043 (2022)
18. Del Chiappa, G., Buonincontri, P., Errichiello, L., Micera, R. (eds.): Tourism, Hospitality and Culture 4.0. McGraw-Hill, New York (2022)
19. Helkkula, A., Kowalkowski, C., Tronvoll, B.: Archetypes of service innovation: implications for value cocreation. J. Serv. Res. **21**(3), 284–301 (2018)

20. Vargo, S., Koskela-Huotari, K., Vink, J.: Service-Dominant Logic: Foundations and Applications, pp. 3–23 (2020)
21. Wang, Y., Gao, S., Xu, W., Wang, Z.: Nanogenerators with superwetting surfaces for harvesting water/liquid energy. Adv. Func. Mater. **30**(26), 1908252 (2020)
22. Palattella, M.R., et al.: Internet of things in the 5G era: enablers, architecture, and business models. IEEE J. Sel. Areas Commun. **34**(3), 510–527 (2016)
23. McCarthy, J., Minsky, M.L., Rochester, N., Shannon, C.E.: A proposal for the Dartmouth summer research project on artificial intelligence, August 31, 1955. AI Mag. **27**(4), 12 (2006)
24. Sterne, J.: Artificial Intelligence for Marketing: Practical Applications/Jim Sterne, 1st edn. Wiley, Hoboken (2017)
25. Gretzel, U., Zheng, Z.: Tourism in the age of artificial intelligence. J. Tour **35**, 1–3 (2020)
26. Wirtz, J., et al.: Brave new world: service robots in the frontline. J. Serv. Manag. **29**(5), 907–931 (2018)
27. Lee, S., Jung, K.: A meta-analysis of determinants of RFID adoption around the world: organization, technology, and public policy. Asia Pac. J. Innov. Entrepreneurship **10**(1), 67–90 (2016)
28. Oghazi, P., Fakhrai Rad, F., Karlsson, S., Haftor, D.: RFID and ERP systems in supply chain management. Eur. J. Manag. Bus. Econ. **27**(2), 171–182 (2018)
29. Rodríguez Sánchez, I., Williams, A., García-Andreu, H.: Customer resistance to tourism innovations: entrepreneurs' understanding and management strategies. J. Travel Res. (2019)
30. Tussyadiah, I.P., Wang, D., Jung, T.H., tom Dieck, M.C.: Virtual reality, presence, and attitude change: empirical evidence from tourism. Tour. Manag. **66**, 140–154 (2018)
31. Xia, M., Zhang, Y., Zhang, C.: A TAM-based approach to explore the effect of online experience on destination image: a smartphone user's perspective. J. Destin. Mark. Manag. **8**, 259–270 (2018)
32. Yu, E., Sangiorgi, D.: Service design as an approach to implement the value cocreation perspective in new service development. J. Serv. Res. **21**(1), 40–58 (2018)
33. Bellovin, S.M., Dutta, P.K., Reitinger, N.: Privacy and Synthetic Datasets (2018)
34. Lu, Y., Xu, L.D.: Internet of things (iot) cybersecurity research: a review of current research topics. IEEE Internet Things J. **6**(2), 2103–2115 (2019)
35. Salguero, A., Espinilla, M.: Ontology-based feature generation to improve accuracy of activity recognition in smart environments. Comput. Electr. Eng. **68** (2018)
36. Kang, H.: Impact of VR on impulsive desire for a destination. J. Hosp. Tour. Manag. **42**, 244–255 (2020)
37. Godovykh, M., Baker, C., Fyall, A.: VR in tourism: a new call for virtual tourism experience amid and after the COVID-19 pandemic. Tour. Hospital. **3**(1), 265–275 (2022)
38. Velychko, D.: How technology is disrupting the restaurant industry. PaySpace Mag. (2021)
39. Campos, A.C., Mendes, J., do Valle, P.O., Scott, N.: Co-creation of tourist experiences: a literature review. Curr. Issues Tour. **21**(4), 369–400 (2018)
40. Buhalis, D., Amaranggana, A.: Smart tourism destinations enhancing tourism experience through personalisation of services. In: Tussyadiah, I.., Inversini, A.. (eds.) Information and Communication Technologies in Tourism 2015, pp. 377–389. Springer, Cham (2015). https://doi.org/10.1007/978-3-319-14343-9_28
41. Yu, Y., Wang, H.: Study on the construction of smart tourism ecosystem and polycentric governance mechanism. Smart Tour. **3**(1), 9 (2022)
42. Gretzel, U., Reino, S., Kopera, S., Koo, C.: Smart tourism challenges. J. Tour. **16**, 41–47 (2015)
43. Boes, K., Buhalis, D., Inversini, A.: Smart tourism destinations: ecosystems for tourism destination competitiveness. Int. J. Tour. Cities **2**(2), 108–124 (2016)
44. Vecchio, P.D., Mele, G., Ndou, V., Secundo, G.: Creating value from social big data: implications for smart tourism destinations. Inf. Process. Manag. **54**(5), 847–860 (2018)

45. Bochner, A.P., Cissna, K.N., Garko, M.G.: Optional metaphors for studying interaction. In: Studying Interpersonal Interaction, pp. 16–34. Guilford Press, New York (1991)
46. Silva, R.: Co-creation of tourism experiences and the use of social media (ICTS) as key tools for innovation an value creation in the tourism industry (2019)
47. Hassan, M.A., Ali, S., Imad, M., Bibi, S.: New advancements in cybersecurity: a comprehensive survey. In: Ouaissa, M., Boulouard, Z., Ouaissa, M., I. Khan, U., Kaosar, M. (eds.) Big Data Analytics and Computational Intelligence for Cybersecurity. Studies in Big Data, vol. 111, pp. 3–17. Springer, Cham (2022). https://doi.org/10.1007/978-3-031-05752-6_1
48. Imad, M., Abul Hassan, M., Hussain Bangash, S., Naimullah: A comparative analysis of intrusion detection in IoT network using machine learning. In: Ouaissa, M., Boulouard, Z., Ouaissa, M., Khan, I.U., Kaosar, M. (eds.) Big Data Analytics and Computational Intelligence for Cybersecurity. Studies in Big Data, vol. 111, pp. 149–163. Springer, Cham (2022). https://doi.org/10.1007/978-3-031-05752-6_10
49. Piller, F.T., Gülpen, C.: Beyond the offer: co-creation in tourism: when your guest becomes your partner, value emerges. In: Egger, R., Gula, I., Walcher, D. (eds.) Open Tourism. TV, pp. 413–421. Springer, Heidelberg (2016). https://doi.org/10.1007/978-3-642-54089-9_33
50. Carvalho, M., Kastenholz, E., Carneiro, M.J.: Co-creative tourism experiences – a conceptual framework and its application to food & wine tourism. Tour. Recreat. Res. 1–25 (2021)
51. Cabiddu, F., Lui, T.-W., Piccoli, G.: Managing value co-creation in the tourism industry. Ann. Tour. Res. 42, 86–107 (2013)
52. Lugosi, P., Walls, A.: Researching destination experiences: themes, perspectives and challenges. J. Destin. Mark. Manag. 2, 51–58 (2013)
53. Mathisen, L.: Staging natural environments: a performance perspective. In: Advances in Hospitality and Leisure, vol. 9, pp. 163–183. Emerald Group Publishing Limited, Bingley (2013)
54. Prebensen, N., Vittersø, J., Dahl, T.: Value co-creation significance of tourist resources. Ann. Tour. Res. 42, 240–261 (2013)
55. Prebensen, N., Woo, E., Uysal, M.: Experience value: antecedents and consequences. Curr. Issue Tour. 17, 910–928 (2013)
56. Rihova, I., Buhalis, D., Moital, M., Gouthro, M.-B.: Social layers of customer-to-customer value co-creation. J. Serv. Manag. 24, 553–566 (2013)
57. Rihova, I., Buhalis, D., Moital, M., Gouthro, M.-B.: Conceptualising customer-to-customer value co-creation in tourism. Int. J. Tour. Res. 17, 356–363 (2014)
58. Bertella, G.: The co-creation of animal-based tourism experience. Tour. Recreat. Res. 39(1), 115–125 (2014)
59. Lugosi, P.: Mobilising identity and culture in experience co-creation and venue operation. Tour. Manag. 40, 165–179 (2014)
60. Minkiewicz, J., Evans, J., Bridson, K.: How do consumers co-create their experiences? An exploration in the heritage sector. J. Mark. Manag. 30(1–2), 30–59 (2014)
61. Sugathan, P., Ranjan, K.R.: Co-creating the tourism experience. J. Bus. Res. 100, 207–217 (2019)
62. Chathoth, P.K., Ungson, G.R., Harrington, R.J., Chan, E.S.W.: Co-creation and higher order customer engagement in hospitality and tourism services: a critical review. Int. J. Contemp. Hosp. Manag. 28(2), 222–245 (2016)
63. Buhalis, D., Sinarta, Y.: Real-time co-creation and nowness service: LESSONS from tourism and hospitality. J. Travel Tour. Mark. 36(5), 563–582 (2019)
64. Kirova, V.: Value co-creation and value co-destruction through interactive technology in tourism: the case of 'La Cité du Vin' wine museum, Bordeaux, France. Curr. Issues Tour. 24(5), 637–650 (2021)
65. Ponsignon, F., Derbaix, M.: The impact of interactive technologies on the social experience: an empirical study in a cultural tourism context. Tourism Manag. Perspect. 35, 100723 (2020)

66. Erdogan Tarakçi, I., Uysal, B., Ulusinan Çubukçu, E.: The investigation of the consumers' tourism preferences in the Covid-19 pandemic. Int. J. Health Manag. Tour. (2021)
67. Zatori, A., Smith, M., Puczko, L.: Experience-involvement, memorability and authenticity: the service provider's effect on tourist experience. Tour. Manag. **67**, 111–126 (2018)
68. Dimanche, F., Andrades, L.: Co-creation of experience value: a tourist behaviour approach, pp. 95–112 (2014)
69. Prebensen, N.K., Xie, J.: Efficacy of co-creation and mastering on perceived value and satisfaction in tourists' consumption. Tour. Manag. **60**(C), 166–176 (2017)
70. Vaz Serra, P., Seabra, C., Caldeira, A.: Smart tourism ecosystem perspective on the tourism experience: a conceptual approach. EAI Endors. Trans. Smart Cities **6**(4), e3–e3 (2022)
71. Neuhofer, B., Buhalis, D., Ladkin, A.: Technology as a catalyst of change: enablers and barriers of the tourist experience and their consequences. In: Tussyadiah, I., Inversini, A. (eds.) Information and Communication Technologies in Tourism 2015, pp. 789–802. Springer, Cham (2015). https://doi.org/10.1007/978-3-319-14343-9_57
72. Morosan, C., De Franco, A.: Investigating American iPhone Users' Intentions to Use NFC Mobile Payments in Hotels, pp. 427–440 (2016)
73. Buonincontri, P., Morvillo, A., Okumus, F., Van Niekerk, M.: Managing the experience co-creation process in tourism destinations: empirical findings from Naples. Tour. Manag. **62**, 264–277 (2017)
74. Sarmah, B., Kamboj, S., Rahman, Z.: Co-creation in hotel service innovation using smart phone apps: an empirical study. Int. J. Contemp. Hosp. Manag. **29**, 2647–2667 (2017)
75. Wang, L., Alasuutari, P.: Co-construction of the tourist experience in social networking sites: two forms of authenticity intertwined. Tour. Stud. **17**(4), 388–405 (2017)
76. Yu, X., Anaya, G.J., Miao, L., Lehto, X., Wong, I.A.: The impact of smartphones on the family vacation experience. J. Travel Res. **57**(5), 579–596 (2018)
77. Tu, Y., Neuhofer, B., Viglia, G.: When co-creation pays: stimulating engagement to increase revenues. Int. J. Contemp. Hosp. Manag. **30**, 00 (2018)
78. Tung, V., Au, N.: Exploring customer experiences with robotics in hospitality. Int. J. Contemp. Hosp. Manag. **30** (2018)
79. Aebli, A.: Tourists' motives for gamified technology use. Ann. Tour. Res. **78**, 102753 (2019)
80. Anastasiadou, C., Vettese, S.: "From souvenirs to 3D printed souvenirs". Exploring the capabilities of additive manufacturing technologies in (re)-framing tourist souvenirs. Tour. Manag. **71**, 428–442 (2019)
81. Briciu, A., Briciu, V.-A., Kavoura, A.: Evaluating how 'smart' Bra?ov, Romania can be virtually via a mobile application for cultural tourism. Sustainability **12**(13), 5324 (2020)
82. Lam, J.M.S., Ismail, H., Lee, S.: From desktop to destination: user-generated content platforms, co-created online experiences, destination image and satisfaction. J. Destin. Mark. Manag. **18**, 100490 (2020)
83. Shin, H., Perdue, R.R., Pandelaere, M.: Managing customer reviews for value co-creation: an empowerment theory perspective. J. Travel Res. **59**(5), 792–810 (2020)
84. Phi, G., Dredge, D.: Critical issues in tourism co-creation. Tour. Recreat. Res. **44**, 281–283 (2019)
85. Cheng, Y., et al.: Visitor satisfaction and behavioral intentions in nature-based tourism during the COVID-19 pandemic: a case study from Zhangjiajie National Forest Park, China. Int. J. Geoherit. Parks **10**(1), 143–159 (2022)
86. Liu, Y., Henseler, J., Liu, Y.: What makes tourists adopt smart hospitality? Digit. Bus. **2**(2), 1–10 (2022)
87. McCurdy, A., Peoples, C., Moore, A., Zoualfaghari, M.: Waste management in smart cities: a survey on public perception and the implications for service level agreements. EAI Endors. Trans. Smart Cities 170007 (2021)

Author Index

T. Guarda et al. (Eds.): ARTIIS 2023, CCIS 1937, pp. 517–521, 2024.
https://doi.org/10.1007/978-3-031-48930-3

Printed in the United States
by Baker & Taylor Publisher Services